PENGUIN BOOKS

SEX

Harry Maurer is the author of *Not Working: An Oral History of the Unemployed, Strange Ground: Americans in Vietnam, 1945–1975*, and, with Kurt Mirow, *Webs of Power: International Cartels and the World Economy.* He lives in New York City with his wife and two children.

Sex

Real People Talk about What They Really Do

HARRY MAURER

PENGUIN BOOKS

PENGUIN BOOKS
Published by the Penguin Group
Penguin Books USA Inc., 375 Hudson Street, New York, New York 10014, U.S.A.
Penguin Books Ltd, 27 Wrights Lane, London W8 5TZ, England
Penguin Books Australia Ltd, Ringwood, Victoria, Australia
Penguin Books Canada Ltd, 10 Alcorn Avenue, Toronto, Ontario, Canada M4V 3B2
Penguin Books (N.Z.) Ltd, 182–190 Wairau Road, Auckland 10, New Zealand

Penguin Books Ltd, Registered Offices: Harmondsworth, Middlesex, England

First published in the United States of America as *Sex: An Oral History* by Viking
Penguin, a division of Penguin Books USA Inc., 1994
Published in Penguin Books 1995

1 3 5 7 9 10 8 6 4 2

The names and identifying details of each individual
whose story is told in this book have been changed.

Portions of this book first appeared in *Playboy.*

THE LIBRARY OF CONGRESS HAS CATALOGUED THE HARDCOVER AS FOLLOWS:
Maurer, Harry.
Sex: an oral history/Harry Maurer.
p. cm.
ISBN 0-670-84564-7 (hc.)
ISBN 0 14 01.7145 2 (pbk.)
1. Sex customs—United States—Case studies. 2. Oral history. I. Title.
HQ18.U5M365 1994
306.7´0973—dc20 93-27432

Printed in the United States of America
Set in Bembo
Designed by Katy Riegel

For Heather,
comme toujours—

and for Jonah and Luke

CONTENTS

A NOTE TO READERS

To protect the privacy of the people interviewed for this book, I have changed descriptive details in the introduction to each interview, and in many cases I have changed such details in the interviews themselves. All names have been changed, those of the interviewees and of anyone they mention. The interviewees' professions, their parents' professions, their locations of work and residence, where they grew up, and sometimes their ages have been changed, as have any other details that might indicate a speaker's true identity. I have, however, endeavored to keep the altered details similar in spirit to the true ones. Street sweepers have not been turned into lawyers.

I should also acknowledge that the grouping of the interviews into chapters has an element of arbitrariness. Many of the interviews touch on more than one theme and thus might belong in more than one chapter. For example, some interviews in Chapter 3, on long-term relationships, might also have been placed in Chapter 9, on turning points in people's sex lives, or in Chapter 10, on sexual fulfillment. The final groupings were made, in part, because I felt the interviews in each chapter commented on each other in interesting ways.

SEX
Real People Talk about What They Really Do

INTRODUCTION

THIS BOOK WAS BORN in my bedroom. I am forty-four, married, with two young children. I have known my wife for ten years, and we have been married for six. We live in New York City, have friends of various sexual persuasions, and consider ourselves open-minded. Yet we noticed, some years ago, that when it came to talking with each other about sex, an awkward silence prevailed. It was most acute around the physical details: who did what to whom, how it felt, how it might be different. But we could barely talk about other questions, either: when to make love, how often, what we wanted out of it, what fantasies we had, what it all meant.

In thinking about our sex talk, I realized something else: that simply saying certain words did funny things to my mouth. I could name most body parts—*hand, knee, armpit*—without any discomfort, but to speak the name of almost any part linked with sex—*penis, anus, vagina, clitoris, nipple*—brought a subtle but definite tension to my lips. The more specifically sexual the word, the more tension, with a kind of middle ground occupied by words like *thigh, mouth, tongue.* Slang was no different: *cock, pussy, ass, tits,* all the words were charged, not with pleasure but with anxiety, even though I had been saying them for nearly three decades.

I also began to notice how other people talk about sex. Nearly ev-

1

eryone loves to gossip or brag—who's sleeping with whom, who just had a hot night. Many people have some idea of what their friends' sex lives are like—how often they have sex, with how many partners, whether or not it's enjoyable. But I realized that I had almost no idea of what my friends actually do in bed. What do they like? What do they avoid? What do they think about? What do they feel? I asked other people if they knew what their friends did, and with few exceptions the answer was no.

Perhaps that's how it should be; perhaps reticence about sex enhances its excitement by protecting its mystery, and perhaps there are simply things we shouldn't know about each other. But I am convinced that many people's reluctance to speak openly with even close friends is linked to their unease in speaking with lovers, and to their resulting silences in bed.

Thus was hatched the idea for this book, a book of ordinary Americans talking in an extraordinary way about sex. The fifty-two speakers range in age from twelve to sixty-nine, and in income level from wealthy to working-class. They live in cities and towns in different regions of the country. They are straight, gay, lesbian, and bisexual, straitlaced and far-out. They describe sex in minute detail—what works for them, what doesn't. But they also talk about the emotions suffusing sex; about its meanings, acknowledged and only suspected; about the joys of monogamy and of promiscuity; about intimacy and distance; about honesty and lying.

There is plenty of good sex in this book—and bad, too. There is sweet, warm, lyrical sex, and raunchy, tough, ugly sex. The book is not designed as an instruction manual, though I hope readers will have questions answered, doubts eased, and imaginations piqued. It is, rather, a series of dispatches from the realm of the senses, dispatches that spring from one simple question: What is sex like for you?

The reasons men and women give for not talking about sex mostly boil down to one fear. They are afraid of being judged.

I am as fearful of judgment as anyone. Not long after I had the idea for this book, I had a dream in which I explained it to my father, who had been dead seven years. I expected him to react with scornful disapproval. Instead, he was pleased, even enthusiastic. I woke up the next morning elated, just as if I had received permission.

I'm not sure how my father would have responded in real life, but what intrigued me about the dream was how I had called him into play. Why? I had not had such a dream before starting any of my previous books. Part of the answer became obvious as I broached the subject with friends. Sex, some clearly felt, was not serious. In fact, it was vaguely silly. Didn't everyone talk about sex too much already? I felt nervous admitting that I was preoccupied enough with sex to write a book about it, and I recognized this feeling as a variety of an old one. Since well before puberty, I have performed an intricate dance that both conceals and reveals my sexual persona. We all dance that dance: with our speech, our eyes, our clothes, our posture, our movements, we send signals minutely calibrated to convey the right mix of interest and disinterest. (Anthropologists have a term for a certain come-hither stare: "the copulatory gaze.") We know that to express too much interest is to risk censure and rejection.

Even greater than anxiety over the sexual impulse itself is the fear of anything outside the realm of "normal." Again and again, people I interviewed would confess to some fantasy or practice and then ask, "Do you think I'm normal?" or "Is that really strange?" I soon remarked that those who were most afraid of being judged were often the quickest to judge others. I came to call it the Rule of the Weird: What I do is okay (though some things make me nervous), whereas what you do is bizarre if not downright disgusting. The fact is, however, that in sex there is no such thing as normal. We are all unique, and therefore all abnormal. Every child experiences myriad events that leave him or her with sexual wiring as different from everyone else's as his or her fingerprints. In the words of the late Robert Stoller, a psychiatrist who wrote on gender and sexual behavior, "All erotic behavior is aberrant." So my tastes are neither more nor less weird than yours, as long as they involve consenting adults.

The same reasoning can be applied to sexual orientation. Whatever the causes of homosexuality—both science and common sense suggest a mixture of genetic and environmental influences—one would search in vain for a "typical" homosexual. Stoller again:

"When talking about those people with conscious homosexual erotic preferences, it is better to talk of the homosexualities rather than of homosexuality. Beyond that, there are as many different homosexualities as there are heterosexualities," and "as many heterosexualities as there are heterosexuals." Gore Vidal even argues that "the dumb neologisms, homo-sexual and hetero-sexual, are adjectives that describe acts but never people."

In short, nothing about sex can be arranged into neat categories with moral values attached. It is much more accurate to picture sexual activities or proclivities as continua with nearly infinite gradations. In terms of sex among consenting adults (although when "adulthood" begins is open to debate), one end of the continuum would be absolute chastity in thought and deed, and the other end would be, perhaps, the most compulsive and dehumanizing perversions. Located somewhere in between would be loving sex between long-term partners, promiscuity, sex in public bathrooms, singles-bar pickups, sex for money, S/M, bondage, countless varieties of fetishism, orgies, phone sex, and so on. In terms of orientation, the continuum might begin with someone purely heterosexual in thought and deed and proceed to someone purely homosexual, with the midpoint occupied by someone equally drawn to men and women. Very few people occupy the extremes of these continua; the rest fall along the line, with their own peculiar styles and targets of arousal. Gender, of course, is another continuum, with everyone possessing a more or less muddled mix of "masculine" and "feminine" qualities. Even sex assignment itself, the division of all people into physical males and females, is dubious, as a recent *New York Times* article by Anne Fausto-Sterling points out. As many as 4% of live births are children whose sex organs are hermaphroditic or ambiguous—chromosomal males with female genitalia, or the reverse. Most of these children are assigned to one sex at birth and are often surgically "corrected," but Fausto-Sterling argues that instead they should be left to find their own paths, and that the number of recognized sexes should expand from two to at least five.

One further goal of this book, then, is to bring readers up against their sexual prejudices, just as doing the interviews brought me up against mine. In listening to tales of erotic enemas, cross-dressing, bloody whippings, multiple personalities, golden showers, three- somes, swinging parties, leather masks, and the like, I was forced not only to suspend my judgment while the tape was running—since my interviewees were exquisitely alert to any hint of shock or disapprov- al—but also to revise my own notions about what is "sick" and what is "healthy." I began to picture myself on a raft floating down a wide river of stories, at the mouth of which lay a vast, amoral, sexual sea.

A landmark on the trip was my talk with Lloyd Rappaport, the swinger in Chapter 5. He tells of a long-standing ménage à trois in- cluding himself, his wife, and a much younger protégée, Helen, with whom he played sex games involving dominance and submission. Af- ter a night during which he "gave" Helen to an elderly man who coldly used her for his pleasure, Lloyd pondered "the beyondness of it all, the atmosphere of beyond good and evil." But was it be- yond good and evil? Many will disagree with Lloyd, and of course we have not heard Helen's side. I would simply suggest that before judging Lloyd or anyone else in these pages, readers proceed with caution.

The people in this book almost all came to me through word of mouth. When I started, it seemed that everyone I knew had the per- fect person for me: "Oh, she's a real sex fiend, she *loves* to talk about it." These first subjects passed me on to others—fiends and nonfiends—who in turn passed me on. As time went by, I began to look for specific types, people of a certain age or situation or procliv- ity. I took out two ads in newspapers, one looking for people having extramarital affairs, and one for people over sixty. The average inter- view lasted five hours; some lasted two, some ten. Usually I saw people more than once.

Many people, of course, declined to be interviewed. Several can- didates made dates with me and then called back to say that their spouses or lovers had vetoed the idea. One Ohio college student tear- fully told me that her fiancé, a marine, would not countenance such a thing; they had just finished fighting about it, and he was standing over her shoulder while she made the call. Other people showed up for the interview but had clearly decided in advance not to reveal anything dicey, while still others revealed themselves and later had misgivings. Those interviews are among the sixty-some I recorded but did not use.

The speakers who appear in the book, then, by no means make up a representative sample of Americans, either demographically or sexually. These are people I was able to meet, who were willing to be interviewed, and who spoke more or less openly. I have no idea whether they are more sexually "free" than those who declined or were more guarded, or even whether sex looms larger in their thoughts. It may be that they are simply more exhibitionistic. A number are the "sex fiends" I mentioned above, who devote remarkable amounts of time and creative energy to the pursuit of pleasure. But most people in the book have sex lives that course in narrower channels, either happily or miserably.

Are they telling the truth? Memory is notoriously malleable, even concerning quite recent events, and it is probably even more unreliable when it comes to sex, an area of experience, as psychoanalyst Louise Kaplan writes, "governed almost entirely by fantasy." And since the interviewees' fear of judgment was palpable, their stories no doubt were shaped, consciously or unconsciously, by the desire to portray themselves favorably. To guard against wholesale invention, the interviewer relies on intuition, and on techniques such as going over a story more than once, or looking for a certain kind of quirky detail that can attest to a tale's truth. But a problem even greater than boasting or embellishment is point of view: These are accounts of sex in the eye of the beholder, and it is common for two people to make love and have quite different experiences. On the few occasions when I interviewed both halves of a couple, I was impressed by how similar their perceptions proved to be. But one incident cut the other way: After I spoke with a man who had just ended a passionate year-long affair, he showed the finished version of the interview to his ex-lover. The account seemed to her so false—not so much in the sexual detail, but in the emotional tone—that she broke off her friendship with him in outrage, and he called me to "repudiate" and withdraw the interview.

• • •

If the people interviewed here are not a perfect sample, and the accuracy of their reports is unknowable, what can we learn from them? Each of the interviews turns on an issue, or issues, common to everyone who has sex—issues such as power, aging, communication, intimacy, perversion, change, risk versus safety, lust versus love, and the shifting foundations of masculinity and femininity.

What first struck me was that women seemed more eager to be interviewed than men—straight men, that is, since gay men were perhaps the most eager. Many women relished the idea of spending hours minutely examining sex, something few of them had ever done. Men, on the other hand, often recoiled at the thought—and even when they consented, they seemed less comfortable describing the nitty-gritty. I had expected the opposite—that women would be nervous talking about sex in private with a man they didn't know. Now it seems obvious that I should not have been surprised. Gender roles and behavior have changed since the so-called second wave of feminism gathered force in the mid-sixties, but men have changed less than women. As a rule, they are still less inward-looking, less open to emotion, and more self-protective. Many fewer men than women confessed to the bafflement and insecurity that afflict nearly everyone at times in sex.

The interview situation itself, I believe, contributed to men's uneasiness. For a man to talk candidly with another man about sex immediately rouses competitive instincts, and, even worse, the problem of attraction. It is difficult to discuss sex openly for hours without becoming aroused at some point. In my interviews with straight women, such arousal was, so to speak, permissible for both sides, and it contributed to the fun of the talk. But homoerotic feelings remain a great horror for most straight men. I suspect that, whether conscious or not, the fear of mutual turn-on kept some conversations from catching fire.

Something else that has not changed much is the double standard. The word *slut* came up again and again in talks with women, having apparently lost little of its power—even over young women, who should have benefited most from new attitudes. Women are still afraid of being "sluts" if they take a man home from a party, or if they act too wild once they get there, whereas only one man in this book—Billy Hasser, an Illinois farmboy—expresses the worry that his playboy reputation might make it hard to find a "nice girl" to marry. And he adds that he would never marry, or even date in public, the kind of girl he usually "boinks."

As for the gender divide in terms of sexual practice, some convergence seems to be taking place. In *Re-making Love: The Feminization of Sex,* Barbara Ehrenreich and her co-authors note that the sexual revolution was really a *women's* sexual revolution: "It is not only that women came to have more sex, and with a greater variety of partners, but they were having it on their own terms, and enjoying it as enthusiastically as men are said to." These interviews tend to bear that out. True, men are still more likely to be the initiators and the directors in bed. True, many women still encounter self-centered lovers, like the one Rachel Monroe, in Chapter 4, calls the Rabbit: "It still enrages me: Through our whole relationship the motion of sex was fast and hard, and it couldn't be any other way. It was like he had absolutely no control over his body, and every encounter was a quickie. And he couldn't take instruction or guidance, he felt that was an insult." No man will admit to such behavior, though thirty-year-old James Atkins comes close: "When I'm in a relationship, I get complaints all the time, because I'm like, No foreplay for me, let's get down to it. If I'm with somebody that I've never been with, I'll be soft and tender and everything, but after a while it's like, Forget the foreplay, baby, let's do it." Other men report that they often don't know whether their partners have an orgasm. But comparing accounts from different generations offers grounds for hope. Almost all the speakers over sixty remember long years, entire marriages, in which sex was lonely and stunted. Some baby-boomers do, too. But young men and, more important, women—since women used to suffer in silence the wham-bam syndrome—seem well aware that such sex should not be tolerated. One twenty-three-year-old, fresh out of college but with forty lovers already in her past, looked at me in astonishment when I asked if she had much experience with men like the Rabbit. "I don't think I've ever slept with anyone like that," she said, "and if I had, I certainly wouldn't do it twice."

Women in their twenties and thirties also seem remarkably open to lesbianism; I was surprised by how many of them had made love with other women, or expected to. Some did so out of anger at men and a conviction that relations with women, both sexual and emotional, would be happier; some simply wanted to experiment; and some, like Rachel Monroe and Jackie Dunhill, are actively bisexual. On many campuses, I was told, it is virtually de rigueur for politically aware females to go through a "dyke phase." Needless to say, very few straight men described homosexual encounters after adolescence, and I only heard one report of college men trying out gay sex to be hip. In that realm, as in others, I expect men will follow women, but slowly.

Another great divide in these interviews separates people who link their best sex to intimacy and those who favor some degree of distance. For most of us, the ideal encounter lies somewhere between the zipless fuck and ecstatic union with a soulmate whose every secret we share. But in some form, the paradoxes of intimacy and passion plague nearly everyone I spoke to. How can I stay hot for my spouse? How do I handle lust for the new? And what is that about, anyway? Why do I pant for this tight-lipped, leather-jacketed type, while this sweet guy who talks about his feelings leaves me cold? Even the experts are split. Sex researcher C. A. Tripp, in his classic *The Homosexual Matrix,* states that "sexual attraction clearly thrives on a degree of tension and distance between the partners. . . . Conspicuous by its absence is the love-story dream: the ongoing, sexually vivid, delicately intimate monogamous tie. It exists—like mermaids, perpetual motion, and heaven itself—in the human imagination." But psychoanalyst Muriel Dimen argues that the reason for sexual ennui may be too little intimacy, not too much: "This boredom is born of the fright we feel when we reach the end of the routine pathways to intimacy, and the unknown looms before us. In thus confronting the problem of creation and of the new, we become anxious and then, to calm ourselves, bored."

The question of eros and intimacy has long been seen as a field of fire in the war between the sexes: Women want loving closeness, while men want hot, fantasy-laden sex. There is some truth in this cliché. But a deeper truth, to judge from my interviews, is that both

sexes want both, especially since the sexual revolution. What's interesting is how they go about getting what they want—or giving it up.
The speakers in this book pursue a plethora of strategies. Some of the
marrieds (or quasi-marrieds, including gays and lesbians) opt for the
relative simplicity of monogamy and focus on the joys of connubial
sex. Joe Hoffman, forty-five and on his second marriage, remarks that
"Barbara and I have talked about me being on the road so much
these days, it would be easy to have affairs. But I can't handle that
emotionally. I'm old enough to know I don't want that kind of doubt
and grief." The other classic approach is the double life, either as an
escape from stalemate at home or as a means to radically different
sex. One example of the latter is the case of Hugh Sullivan, who
makes love with his wife frequently but also carries on a dramatic
S/M affair with a man. Some people, like Jon Benjamin, use masturbation to contain unruly impulses; when his cross-dressing and
transgender fantasies caused tensions in the marital bedroom, he
confined them to solo sessions where he imagines being fucked as a
woman. Other people jettison monogamy or the pretense of it and
work at various kinds of "open" relationships.

But few people I interviewed feel they have "solved" the problem
of familiarity versus newness, intimacy versus distance. If they opt for
one, they miss the other; and trying for both is a high-wire act. As a
group, the monogamous marrieds in this book seem the most content; several of them say that sex with their spouses is never boring
because it is never the same twice. But even they often express wist-
fulness for unruly passions. The more restless folk remain troubled.
Robert Rauh, a "married" gay man with a taste for anonymous encounters, takes a night off each week so he and his lover Dan can enjoy sex with others. He talks about the difficulty of turning Dan into
a stranger: "How do you do that? How do you lose the person? I
can't make him not be Dan, but I think if I could figure that out, it
would be the first step toward having a great sex life together." Sally
Laughlin and her boyfriend Greg "think alike, I can commune with
him"—but their sex is so-so. Meanwhile, an old lover is perfectly
wrong for her but touching him "renders me speechless. . . . It isn't
fair that I have this with someone I can't get along with."

• • •

A few weeks after our talk, I heard that Sally had split up with Greg and was happily seducing a teenager. That illustrates what I came to call the Snapshot Factor—the accident that these interviews took place at a certain hour on a certain day in the subjects' lives, and might have been quite different a month earlier or later. Indeed, Hank Castleman, who appears in Chapter 3, told me when he showed up for the interview, "God, I'm glad we're talking tonight and not two days ago. Colleen and I had a huge fight about sex. I would have told you how horrible things were." As it was, even recalling the fight, he painted their erotic life in warm colors.

Sometimes the interview itself—or just the prospect of it—altered the snapshot. "When did you last have sex?" I would ask, and would be told, "Well, last night, actually. I didn't want to tell you we hadn't made love in three weeks." Or people would say, "Ever since you called, we've been talking about sex a lot. It's funny, it made a difference." But the difference more often came after the interview. In meditating out loud about sex, people were surprised by what they said, or by the feelings that surfaced as they said it. Two men were enough taken aback by their own bitterness that they realized they had to talk to their partners. In one case the result was explosive, since his confession revealed his infatuation with another woman. Both men reported, however, that once the shock subsided, the relationships improved.

These interviews, then, capture the speakers at one moment in their sexual history—and the key point is that *it is a history,* not a constant. Before starting this book, I unconsciously tended to imagine other people's sexuality as fixed. In fact, sex for most of us is always in flux. It changes, most obviously, as we gain knowledge of it, beginning when we are young children. It changes as we gain or lose confidence in ourselves. It changes with our status in life. It changes from relationship to relationship, and with luck, it changes within every relationship. The theme that runs through all these interviews is that of discovery, of possibility, of territory won painfully or playfully.

Sex is one of the best windows on the self, and we all choose, every day, how far to open the curtains.

The explorations recounted here range from the minute to the stunning—from Jim Hollister's awkward attempts to learn how to touch his wife so she could "unlock the door," to Archie Hunter's discovery that for him, the pinnacle of rapture could be reached by kneeling naked in a bathtub in a sex club and having men urinate on him. There are accounts of couples anxiously (or angrily) negotiating to harmonize clashing sexual styles, of people embracing the pleasures found in pain, of women first sensing the power sex could unleash, of men battling sexual addiction. As disparate as they are, these speakers are all in motion.

Some of them make sex, if not their life's work, then something approaching it. They train themselves, as Andy Bevilaqua says in Chapter 7, "to go to the limits, to push it." A fantasy, to them, is a challenge. Bevilaqua talks about drawing out his "dark side" and that of his partners, both on the phone and in bed. Other players have similar terms: Lloyd Rappaport refers to "DTs," or "dirty things"; Archie Hunter favors "sloppy sex"; Matt Sherrill calls it "electric sex"; Judith Rothstein and Sandra Marquez like the word "animal." They all mean roughly the same thing: sex that brings to life the urgent whisperings of the libido.

Of course, sex can take many shapes when you "push it." Married, monogamous partners may push it to ever-deeper knowledge of each other. Eastern sex rituals, notably the Tantric tradition, can push it to ecstatic spiritual insight. Or pushing it may mean acting out a scenario that dramatizes one or more of the terrors underlying sex, terrors rooted in early childhood: of regression, aggression, breakdown of gender identity, engulfment or violation by the other. According to Freud and most psychologists since, we all harbor unconscious desires to mutilate and destroy, as well as desires to passively surrender. We all fear the loss of self that fusion might bring. We all dread our shameful, humiliating wishes to be the other gender. So a sex game may take the form of S/M, B&D, cross-dressing, role-playing; it may be angry, sad, funny, or all three: but it always touches on these terrors. Everyday sex, what the S/Mers term "vanilla sex," calls them up too, though they are played out more subtly, with the lovers either conscious of them or not. In "kinky" sex they are simply highlighted.

Nowhere were these highlights more clear for me than in San Francisco, where I interviewed several members of the "sex radical community." This scene—it is too anarchic to be called a movement—grew out of gay life and New Age thinking, and rests on three main poles: spirituality, S/M, and pansexualism, a breaching of the walls of sexual orientation. It is hardly unique to the Bay Area, but has achieved greater mass there than anywhere else. Central to its ethos is the word *queer,* which for sex radicals does not mean "gay male" but rather anyone whose sexuality is not "straight"—that is, conventionally heterosexual. Lori Eschilman, the lesbian in Chapter 10 who "tops" both women and gay men, proudly calls herself queer. James W., who has sex with men and women, as a bottom and a top, and in several different personas, may be the epitome of queer.

In talking with people like Lori and James, I found my notions of sex itself expanding. Is it sex to wear a dog collar under your turtleneck all day as a reminder of your slave role? Is it sex to pierce your torso with a dozen stainless steel pins, hang metal bells from them, and dance naked around a bonfire? Is it sex to sit in the lotus position and stare into your lover's eyes? The answer, obviously, is that sex has no fixed boundaries. Yet many of us stick to our familiar backyards and have little idea what lies across the road, let alone on other continents. This was brought home to me in my favorite moment from hundreds of hours of interviewing. I was talking to Claudia, a Boston call girl (Chapter 6). She said that to prevent herself from having orgasms with clients, she sometimes steers her sexual energy away from her genitals to other parts of her body—her hands, her feet. "Really?" I asked. "How do you do that?" There was a pause as she looked at me. Then she said, "Do you know *anything* about sex?"

• • •

Like gender, sexuality is political. It is organized into systems of power, which reward and encourage some individuals and activities, while punishing and suppressing others.

    —Gayle Rubin, "Thinking Sex," in *Pleasure and Danger*

It is a curious time to be writing about sex. We are living in the age of AIDS—and AIDS, whatever else it signifies, has become above all a metaphor for punishment. Nothing new here, as Susan Sontag notes in *AIDS and Its Metaphors:* "Considering illness as a punishment is the oldest idea of what causes illness," dating back no doubt to prehistory. Sexually transmitted illnesses in particular lend themselves to fantasies of retribution, but so do other epidemics. Sontag quotes a *New York Times* writer from April 12, 1866: "Cholera is especially the punishment of neglect of sanitary laws; it is the curse of the dirty, the intemperate, and the degraded." Sound familiar?

Conspiracy theorists could do wonders with the coincidence that AIDS appeared early in Ronald Reagan's presidency, at the flood tide of conservative backlash against the changes of the sixties and seventies, and proceeded to devastate the most "intemperate" and "degraded" erotic minority, gay men. AIDS, perhaps, was not necessary to right-wingers and fundamentalists, who were already loudly condemning promiscuity and were being echoed by the media. But AIDS was perfect. Unlike herpes, it was apparently always fatal, so it terrified everybody. And it first struck the shock troops of the sexual revolution. Sontag writes that in the seventies, "many male homosexuals reconstituted themselves as something like an ethnic group, one whose distinctive folkloric custom was sexual voracity, and the institutions of urban homosexual life became a sexual delivery system of unprecedented speed, efficiency, and volume." She goes on to link the "fashionable libertinism" of the seventies with consumer culture, where "appetite is *supposed* to be immoderate. The ideology of capitalism makes us all into connoisseurs of liberty—of the indefinite expansion of possibility." No one championed the expansion of sexual possibility more than gay men, who openly flouted one of America's most fearsome taboos, thus calling into question the very nature of masculinity, and who made a virtual ideology of the notion, "If you can imagine it, do it."

This is not to deny that the sexual revolution led to all manner of excess. Excess is what revolution is about. But while revolutions, by definition, turn behavior and institutions upside down overnight, attitudes change slowly. Once the upheavals are over, the advances made, the victories won, people tend to wake, as out of a trance, and

shake their heads wonderingly and ruefully at the excesses committed along the way. Then comes the counterrevolution, or at least the
reaction. So it has been with sex. Given the sexual mores we drank in
with our mothers' milk, there is no way most Americans could have
seen AIDS as anything but divine retribution on a nation of bad boys
and girls. We were not ready for revolution. It was—it is—
intoxicating, confusing, disturbing, and at times destructive. On
some level, many of us wondered if we deserved to be punished.

So the age of AIDS naturally became an age of limits. Excess of
any sort—sex, drugs, drinking, cigarettes, unhealthy food—became
suspect. This is partly salutary, of course. AIDS is real, and safe sex
is necessary. The speakers in this book make it clear that behavior has
changed, though not as much as it needs to for maximum safety. People still take risks, even gay men, who presumably are playing the
worst odds. But as one single woman told me, "If I'm out to dinner
with a guy, and I could go either way, in the old days I would have
said, 'Why not?' and slept with him. Now I figure it's too much
worry, so I go home and watch my VCR."

An age of limits, however, is not a full-fledged counterrevolution.
Recently the media have been signaling a sexual revival. Some of it
comes in the form of voyeurism, the theory being that since people
are doing it less, they like to watch it more—in movies, ads, art, TV
programs, lap-dancing bars, Madonna's book. But the real thing may
be coming back, too. To the alarm of the authorities, sex clubs are
proliferating in cities. A *New York* magazine cover story on "Sex in
the Nineties" proclaims, "There's more of it going on—gay and
straight, safe and unsafe—than you'd think." The authors of *The Janus Report,* a survey of sexual attitudes and practices published in
1993, trumpet a "Second Sexual Revolution," stating that "although
the changes in how Americans interact sexually have been dramatic,
overall sexual activity has not diminished in mainstream America; in
fact, we found in our study that, in the past several years, overall sexual activity has increased." And not just any activity, but kinky activity: "Many experts predicted the demise of American sex in the wake
of the panic generated by AIDS. We found, instead, a continuous and
increasing variety of marginal sex."

So the New Right's efforts to stuff the Dionysian genie back in the bottle have failed—thus far. One sex educator confidently told me that "Sex is going to be the issue of the nineties." True, he said this at a time when the issue of gays in the military was front-page news every day; but even if he overstates the case, sex will certainly be a key testing ground. The abortion battle continues, and the abortion battle is in no small part about women's sexual freedom and men's desire to keep them in their place. Fundamentalists are organizing intensively in states and towns across the country, often using homophobia as their central theme; they have been joined by one school of feminists in a holy alliance to suppress pornography. In New York City, schools chancellor Joseph Fernandez was ousted after he backed a plan to distribute condoms in high schools and tried to institute a curriculum that contained a tiny, innocuous section suggesting gays are regular folks. School libraries continue to ban books with any hint of controversial sexuality.

The struggles rage—but the speakers in this book prove the impossibility of returning to the stifling sexual atmosphere of only thirty years ago. If the sex radicals are a vanguard—California, of course, has a long record of pioneering in sexual matters—we may be edging toward an America in which homosexuality no longer horrifies; in which monogamy is no longer the moral standard; in which bisexuality is less of an aberration; in which people who are predominantly gay, lesbian, or "het" feel free to make pleasure together. In short, an America where "queer" is no longer queer. Such an America is not around the corner. These radicals may be as far off track as the socialists of the thirties and sixties who foresaw imminent overthrow of the ruling class. But perhaps not.

Why should "normal" Americans care about the visions of a band of sexual freaks? Because we are all queer—and to some degree, we are all hiding. A psychiatrist friend of mine who read an early draft of this book said he was struck by how alone many speakers seem with their sexuality and their stories. If these interviews reveal anything, it is the toll exacted by that solitude. But they also reveal the bravery and ingenuity of ordinary people determined to push past barriers, to reject the shame and silence their parents handed down. The six men and women in the final chapter have little in common in terms of what they do in bed. But they have all learned to speak, sexually, with voices and bodies. Maybe the most touching is Eli Gregory, the Protestant minister whose wife of forty years is the only lover he has ever had. He sadly regrets the time when sex was merely a release for him and a duty for her. Now, after a painful process of teaching each other, "Often when she has an orgasm she will burst into tears. What a joy—I love her. She'll sigh and gasp and the tears will come. Then she'll let me know when it's enough and it's beginning to hurt a little bit or something, and she'll take me in her arms and thank me, and we're just there together with the awareness of our pleasure. It's full, we've come to the ultimate of why we've done what we've done."

It took Eli decades to reach "the ultimate," to move past his own conviction that sex should come naturally—without effort, without study, without compromise. But he is a seeker, as are most of the people in this book. Somewhere along the line, he learned two crucial lessons: that sex, like anything else, must change or die; and that the change is up to us.

1

AWAKENINGS

A MOS HARTIGAN, twelve years old, speaks first—
and the subject, naturally, is masturbation. More precisely, the
ridicule attached to masturbation. The boys in his school rag each
other mercilessly about it, and even though Amos is wise to the
teasing—"I think most of the people who make these jokes are the
people who actually do it on a regular basis"—he has already learned
some essential lessons about sex: It's embarrassing. You can't tell the
truth about it. You may be punished for it. (He carefully hid his few
girlie magazines until he figured his parents were closing in, at which
point he sold them.) He finds all this vaguely humorous, and the forbidden naturally carries a charge. But sex, for him, remains an
enigma wrapped in anxiety, to be puzzled out alone.

Four other speakers in this chapter have recently crossed the sexual threshhold. They range in age from sixteen to twenty, and their
stories, too, are striking accounts of the pain that accompanies pleasure. Discovering sex is rarely easy, as anyone who remembers adolescence knows. The lessons Amos is learning are followed by others
more harsh: People may lie and manipulate to get laid. They may
make you an object while doing it. They may betray you afterward.
Or you may do all of the above to them. The intoxication of skin

touching skin, the pure urgency of the urge, are fogged by fear and confusion.

Virginity is of little concern—except for how to lose it. And the fear of pregnancy has largely been displaced by the fear of disease. These teens are very much aware of AIDS, but they also display the classic "It can't happen to me" syndrome. Shannon Stansell, eighteen, should know better; her first boyfriend gave her herpes and blithely denied he had it. But she still says, "Once I start fooling around, it's hard for me to stop. . . . Plus with AIDS, I can't go around having sex with everyone. Well, I don't really think about AIDS, I just threw that in there." Patrick Jordan, twenty, laughs as he tells how he furtively crosses himself before an episode of unsafe sex. "That's kind of a stupid way of trying to protect yourself, and I'm not really a religious character, but sometimes you got to give it up to the Lord, man." And sixteen-year-old Andy Cassavetes describes two different worlds: New Orleans, where he started high school, and Stinson Beach, California, where he recently moved. For Southern teens, he reports, casual sex is the rule and AIDS is distant thunder. But to his Marin County crowd, unsafe sex is the ultimate in uncool.

Gender roles are split, of course, but perhaps not as sharply as one might expect. Shannon worries about being a slut and stresses that "sex changes everything," but she is perfectly capable of picking up a pretty boy in a bar and going home with him. She is struggling—as teenage girls still do more than boys—with the distinction between sex for sex's sake and sex as a means to building a relationship. As a result, she often feels used. But even Patrick, who can be predatory in classic male fashion, laments, "It's weird, it's a bad feeling, not being able to have no conversation afterward. It's like the relationship is just physical, which is not cool at all." The clearest expression of how much things have *not* changed comes from twelve-year-old Amos. He can't figure out how sex "starts," yet on one thing he's perfectly clear: "It's all because of the boy. The boy makes stuff happen."

The sixth speaker here is sixty-eight years old. A few months before our talk, she moved out from her husband of forty-eight years, not least because sex with him had always been an ordeal. She first learned to have orgasms in her late forties, when she took a lover. Now she is reveling in sex—with the help of personal ads. She has a handful of occasional boyfriends, each quirkier than the last, but she seems fond of them all. After decades of troubled sleep, she, too, has awakened.

AMOS HARTIGAN

He is twelve years old, a sixth-grader. His father is a corporate manager, his mother a social worker. They live on a leafy street in a Chicago suburb. He has not yet kissed a girl.

• • •

In my school, if someone's in the bathroom a little longer than normal, and they come out, and there are two people waiting, the first one says, "Your fly's open," and the other one says, "Oh, I wonder why." If there's a teacher around and they can't say the joke, there's a little symbol [makes masturbating motion with his hand] and a little noise that goes with it. Or if you say something in the wrong way—like we had this little workshop on spending time alone. The director gave us a sheet, and it said, "Out of an hour, how much time would you spend with yourself and how much time would you spend with a friend?" One person had an unusual amount of time with himself, and everyone made jokes about, "Oh, what's he doing in the bathroom with the Vaseline?" I guess he hadn't been at school long enough to know the normal terms, so he said, "No, no, I just play with myself," and everyone started laughing. It's what we talk about most of the time, though I don't think I've ever heard any of the girls laugh at these jokes. They consider it one of the stupid things boys do.

There was another kid—I think it's been four years since he graduated from my school. Everybody used to talk about how he was always in the bathroom fifteen minutes during lunchtime, and finally one time he left the door unlocked and Kevin walked in and saw him and said [screaming]: "Aaaahhhh!" Everyone has their own version

of the story, even people who weren't here when it happened. It's
been passed down for three or four years.

I think most of the people who make these jokes are the people
who actually do it on a regular basis. They can't talk about it with
anyone, so they make jokes about it. Saying "He does it" is a way of
releasing their little bottled-up secret. I don't know why it's so not
okay to do it. It's kind of taboo. I think someone somewhere might
have gotten the idea that only gay people masturbate. It's not okay
even to talk about it. You can get pushed into a wall for saying that
about someone, even if it isn't true. And no one would ever admit it.
If you did, no one would need to make jokes about anyone else, because there would be a real case. People would laugh and say, "You
stupid fag." Even though most people realize it's something people
do at this point in their lives, and it's not like you're some kind of
weird person because you do that.

Do you do it?

Occasionally. Not every day. It's not like a big thing for me.
Maybe once a week.

Do you ejaculate?

No, but there are other parts of puberty—like I'm getting hair in
certain places.

I used to have some porno magazines, but I sold them. I thought
my parents were getting close to finding out. I go backpacking a lot,
so I had them in a pouch in my backpack, and I kept that in a little
pile at the bottom of my closet. But I thought my parents had sort of
figured out that I read these magazines, and they were going to start
looking to see where I was hiding them. It seemed more and more often they would walk by whenever I was looking at the stuff. Sometimes I would lean up against the door of the bathroom. Sometimes
on weekends late at night, I could be watching "Saturday Night
Live" and turn down the volume on the commercials, and since my
parents were probably watching "Saturday Night Live" upstairs, they
wouldn't come down, and if they did I'd hear them coming. But there
was one time when my dad came down and locked the back door
twice. That was when I realized they were catching on. So I sold the
magazines.

I remember when I was nine, just barely getting into this stuff, I found a Victoria's Secret catalogue, and my mom found me looking through it. She was pretty mild about it, she knew I was only nine and I obviously hadn't realized what this was all about, but she did notice I was becoming interested. She knew I didn't know I'd done anything wrong, so she just told me she didn't like me reading that.

Why didn't she want you looking at it?

For the same reason I found it interesting. It was women dressed the way they aren't normally dressed.

That was pretty much the end of that, until I got these magazines from my friend. He lives a few blocks away, and he has this *Playboy* subscription at his sister's apartment. He knows what day it comes every month, he has it marked on his calendar with some little code, like "Report due for school." He goes over there before she gets home and gets it out of her mailbox. A friend of his has a whole operation to get an even wilder magazine, *Hustler;* I've only seen one of those a couple of times. Normally the ones you see are *Playboy* and *Penthouse.* I used to go over to my friend's house and look at them, and he said, "I'll sell you one of these for four dollars." So I bought a bunch of them, at one point I had four or five, and the only reason I didn't have any *Hustler*s was because he charged four dollars for *Playboy,* five dollars for *Penthouse,* and twelve dollars for *Hustler,* because each one of those costs seven dollars and you're more likely to get busted by your parents for having one. Dealing with them is a higher risk, so you can charge more.

He has about a hundred of these magazines in his room. I can go over there and look at them because he usually has the house to himself from four to six. I don't think his parents know he has them—he hides them all over the place. He actually has two layers thick under his mattress. And he has a deep enough drawer that he can keep about four layers and right on top of that about a quarter inch of newspaper. Then he's got stacks in his closet with sheets draped over them. I don't think most kids' parents would go searching for this stuff, but when it gets to the point where you're the person who's supplying it to about five percent of your school it becomes not okay. That's the kind of thing your parents could bust you for, being a porn dealer.

I don't think I'd get extremely busted for having magazines, I'm not sure if there would be any kind of punishment. I know my dad is quite aware he did the same thing at my age. But when I first learned about this stuff, it was something you had to hide from your parents. That's just the way everybody does it. Nobody really knows why. One kid I know, he had four magazines, his parents found out and made him spend the evening cutting them up with scissors. Then he had to put them in a big tub of water, swish it all around, and toss it in the garbage can. My mom being a social worker, she may have read some of the reports that only nine percent of teenage psychologists said they thought it would corrupt a thirteen-year-old's mind to have posters with naked women in his room. I can't remember where I got that from, I think it was on TV. And the nine percent who did think it would be detrimental thought it would change kids' sense of what an attractive woman would look like and give them too high hopes. They said the only reason these women are in these magazines is that they're the only women in the world who actually look like that, and any boy who's seen this stuff and decided that's what he's gonna look for in a woman is not going to end up with a girlfriend but is going to end up smoking cigars in a cheap apartment, reading this stuff more.

From my opinion, I have to agree it's part of your sexual growth, and I understand all women aren't going to look like that. But I do know it's a very intricate part of my life, the porno mags and stuff. It's the main thing that happens in my life right now. I haven't even gone on a date. I would say the farthest I've gone is talked with a few girls about dating, but that's pretty much it. I guess maybe half the people my age are dating, and about three percent are actually having sex. I don't know anyone my age who is. The three percent is just my estimate.

I think it's going to be a while before my parents stop thinking of me as a little innocent child, and see that I can have some of the same problems they have and do some of the same things they do. I'm not really that much of a child anymore. I think they know something is happening, they aren't naïve enough to think this isn't a part of my life. I do know some people who would cry if they found out their little baby had been exposed to this corrupt world. But most parents understand that this is the world, and this is the same thing everybody else is exposed to. I really don't think the parents of a twelve-year-old should think they're trying to take care of their little baby.

That's one of the main reasons I'm not quite ready for my first date—I'm not sure how my parents are going to react, and it would be embarrassing if whomever I went on this date with saw that my mom was standing there in the doorway giving me a kiss good-bye and crying. I don't want to let them know about my first date. My plan is to get into the habit of going out in the evening with friends, and then they won't really know until they get the thought, Well, maybe there are girls involved. I think that would be the best way for them to understand. Not letting them know until it's obvious.

My parents are actually kind of loose about sex. They've tried to open the discussion. My mom told me the way her dad tried to inform her—when she was fourteen and her father figured out she had started dating, under her pillow she found a book about how cows make babies. She became a little bit upset but figured her father was only trying to do what he could. I'm not sure if she even bothered to read it, but it helped her relax a bit, knowing that her father knew she was dating. My parents try to make it very easy to talk about anything I might be curious about. I'd say it's working, because if I ever did have a question I think I could talk to them. The only important question I have that I don't think I could get a straight answer to is, How would you react if I told you I'm having my first date?

At school I've had some formal sex ed. In health class, in the beginning of the year, we have a discussion about it. And we watch movies, *The Miracle of Life* and *The Miracle of Birth*. People make lots of jokes about those movies because they show a man and a woman having sex, and they have a close-up of the in-and-out. But you don't learn much about the details of sex in school. It's what most of the boys talk about, telling each other how they do it and who they do it with. What I've found is most girls have experienced this stuff before most boys have. There are only a few boys in my school who I've heard talking about kissing someone with the tongue and I've actually believed them. Some of the boys talk about feeling certain parts of their girlfriends' bodies, but I don't believe most of it.

In conversations I've had with my parents—I'm not sure why, but they've made requests. Not until you're sixteen. I think it might become a possibility for me at the age of fourteen. I don't think I'll be having sex regularly until I'm fifteen or sixteen. It's not something I'm dying to do, because I question what you're supposed to do. I've seen it on the video, the in-and-outing, but how does that start? I'd say that's the main thing that makes most people my age not quite ready to have sex. Trying to figure out or make up how it works or could work. First there's the question of how girls have sex with you, and then there's the question of how to get girls to have sex with you. The first one is one of the most important things I think about now, how it happens. I've seen enough and heard enough to understand how kissing works, but I don't know how to get from that to having sex. I suppose that's the next bridge to cross, how to turn kissing into sexual intercourse. At school it's perfectly all right to talk about it happening, but there's no way of coming out and asking your friends how it happens. It's one of those things that everyone thinks about but no one's able to admit it. You think, Maybe everyone else understands this. Maybe they're going to think less of me. I remember figuring out the definitions for different words, like *hooker*—I had to hear *hooker* three times before I figured out what it meant. It was not okay to ask your friends, you had to squeeze it out of a conversation, because maybe he's not going to be my friend anymore because I don't know about this stuff. So no one is going to come out and ask, How do you get a girl to have sex with you? Or, How do you start having sex?

On some of the late-night TV shows I've seen people making out on the couch, and then it cuts off right where the guy unbuttons the girl's top button, and it begins again in the morning, where they're lying in bed. There's no way to figure out how it starts. I don't think girls know either, but I have the feeling that it doesn't matter what the girl does, it's all because of the boy. The boy makes stuff happen. It's the boy's job to start it, to physically start having sex. I can see on TV that the girl doesn't start unbuttoning the boy's shirt, it's always the boy unbuttoning the girl's shirt. They always go home to the boy's apartment. That just gives me the idea the boy is the person who starts it.

It creates a certain amount of pressure on me. I need to know what I'm doing or else there's going to be the really embarrassing situation of it not working and nobody knows what to do, even though we want to do it.

But what if the girl made the first move?

I've never seen it work that way, and I'd be extremely uncomfortable if it did. In this society, that's just not the way it works.

ANDY CASSAVETES

Dressed in black jeans torn at the knees, a tie-dyed T-shirt and black high-tops, sporting a buzz cut and a gold stud in his left ear, he is the image of hip Marin County teenagerhood. He does drugs, stays out dancing all night, gets in trouble at school. But while the look is tough, he seems rather sweet—making sure I get a cup of herbal tea, asking about my work and family. He has the gangly awkwardness of his sixteen years, though he is not at all shy. He lives with his mother, a nurse-midwife. "She left my father when I was one, and he moved to New Orleans. I was completely independent by the age of thirteen. I went food-shopping with my mom and got everything I needed, did my own dishes and laundry ever since I could reach the washer. Being brought up that way by the single mom, watching money—I've grown up fast, is what I'm getting at.

"I lived here till I was fourteen. Then I decided I wanted to get to know my dad better, so I moved down there for two years. Got kicked out of high school for organizing a political rally during school hours. Wasn't getting along too well with my dad anyway, so I moved back up here." *He has just discovered books after being "a TV kid" all his life, but he has no plans for college.* "I got into construction down there. I'm helping build a house right now, working as a carpenter. If I go to college it'll be under my own power. Maybe at night. I know I can't be a carpenter forever."

Sex has always been an open subject at home. "I've known about it ever since I could talk—where I came from, how it works. My mom made sure I knew it's okay to play with myself, and to have sex, and for men to do it with men. She wouldn't care if I was gay or straight. It's okay for me to have people stay over. I've been very hip about it all my life because of my mom."

• • •

My first sexual experience was in fifth grade. I went pretty close with a sixth-grade girl. That was my first kiss, and we took off from there. Oral stuff—but it wasn't like it is now, it was more petting. I only had her clothes off one time. She was a knockout, great-looking girl. The prize of the sixth grade. To give you an idea—on her high-tops she had her phone number written, nice and big. I've always been attracted to that kind of girl, the kind that doesn't give a shit about morals or the police or anything like that. Drugstore cowgirls.

In sixth and seventh grade it was the Friday-night party, where there was a lot of petting and kissing and fondling. In eighth grade double dates were real big, watch a movie and fondle. That was pretty much it, but I'll tell you, I was constantly thinking about it. I'd be talking to someone and be thinking about it. I used to make references for later that night. I'd see a girl and go, Oh wow, I'm gonna think about her tonight. Like when I masturbate.

The first time I had sex was in the ninth grade, in New Orleans. This ditsy girl—it was her first time, too. We told each other right before, I was like, "I'll just ask you, is this your first time?" "Yeah, first time." "Mine, too." We had been seeing each other for a couple of weeks. It was at my dad's house, I kicked him out that night and made a nice dinner and had wine. I didn't want a back-of-the-car job. It was pretty cool, but I didn't get off. She didn't either. I think we were just happy to get it over with.

We experimented for a while and then broke up a couple of weeks later. She turned out to be the whoever-wants-it-I'm-spreading-'em type. I was her first, and she was off and running.

The next four or five times I was completely shit-faced. They were all different people, stupid situations where you wake up with your pants in the toilet and you're pissing in the hamper and throwing up in the sink. [Laughs.] My fourth time, I woke up in a Holiday Inn with someone and I didn't know who she was or how we got there. Apparently some friends dragged me to a party there, I was completely gee-gongered. Somehow this girl got my clothes off. Those times were traumatic for me, I think. I had a bad conscience afterward, I felt like shit, and I feel like shit now when I think about it. It's not that I did anything to them, because we did it together, but

I feel guilty I let myself do it. I'm not a happier man today because of it, and I didn't so much enjoy it then.

The first good sex I ever had—I met this girl on Saint Patrick's Day. In the South they make everything a party, close the streets down and have live bands. I picked this girl up. I don't like doing that, but I felt inspired. I was standing on the corner with my friends and all of our jaws dropped when she walked by. She was my height, long brown hair, and she was a sizzler, a Southern beauty, full-figured, just amazing. And she was wearing a very slutty outfit, cut-off shorts and a halter. I was the hero of the night because I went right up and made some comment like, "Do those legs go all the way up?" I'm serious, it was that level of idiocy from a drunken individual, but she loved it, she said, "As a matter of fact, they do. My name's"—I can't remember her name, but her nickname was Woody. I got her phone number and my buddies like tackled me, I was the hero.

She was a twenty-year-old college student. I lied to her about my age, I was fifteen then, but I told her I was in high school. I took her out and we had Greek food and went bowling, we had a great time, drinking all night but not heavy drinking. She liked me a lot and we were very attracted to each other so she invited me up to her apartment and made tea and it took off from there. She advanced on me, which I like a lot, when a girl can take control. After she served me the tea she came and sat on my lap facing me, and then she got an ice cube out because I said the tea was too hot. She rubbed the ice cube over my face and then down to my neck, and then undid my shirt from there. Then we were on the sofa. We were going full force, clothes coming off, and I remember we both clicked about a condom, and I looked up at her and she went, "There's a bowl of 'em over there. Right by the ashtray." That really got me going, I was like, Woo-oo!

It was a great night, I probably had three or four orgasms, and she had three or four. It was like a religious experience. We had sex on the sofa first with me on top. That was the only time we used a condom. Then we did it in a hammock with her on top. Then I went to get something in the refrigerator, I was sitting in front of it drinking some juice, and she kind of tackled me and we had sex on the floor. Then later she was making eggs and I started playing with her and we had sex on the kitchen counter. We pretty much went all night, both of us yelling and panting and howling, making a lot of noise. She showed me a whole new world—different positions and different places you could do it in, just a different outlook on it. She showed me that the more imagination you put into it, the more fun you have. That's what I learned out of that night. Also that older women are my thing.

She pretty much had control all evening. She was teaching me, and I was hoping she didn't know she was teaching me, but she must have known because I wasn't taking the lead. I tried to make it look like I knew what was going on. She showed me what a woman's orgasm is about. She had her first one from fucking, and then we did sixty-nine on her bed and we came almost together, that was cool. I could see her motions, and I could check different places inside of her that she liked better, and once I got the idea of how to do it, I was like a million volts of energy. Now I know that girls always have different places, and when you get the right place, like when you're fucking, you go for it. I've gotten good at it, I pride myself on that now. When they get really taken over they go *voom,* they just downshift and floor it.

I got my first real blowjob that night. That was incredible, the kind where you grab the sheets with your butt-crack. Whoo, she was good at it, probably the best I ever had. She was into that deep throat thing—once she had me all the way deep-throat she'd wiggle her jaw or vibrate her mouth or something, and boom! She had me completely in her power at that point. She could take all my money, take my car keys, I wouldn't give a shit. Euphoria, I think they call it. [Laughs.] My first experience with euphoria.

She had all these little tricks, like when she was riding me, she'd get to the top and come forward a little bit, toward me, and then come down again, *voom.* It was amazing and she knew it. That's what makes me think this is her scam, meeting young guys and taking them home. That's cool, I was happy, but afterward I felt a harshness about it, 'cause I never heard from her again. I told her, "You call me," and she never did. I ran into her a few weeks later and she was like, "Hi, how ya doin'?" "Fine." "Good, talk to ya later." I wanted to have a relationship with her but she was intimidating to the point where I didn't call her. I thought, Well, if that's all she wants, fine, I'm not gonna pursue it anymore. The way I look at it now, it's the first night I had wonderful sex. Yet also it was pretty painful. I wanted it to be more than it turned out to be.

From there I learned about nightclubs, things like that. I said, Fuck these high school girls, I'm going after big game. And I did. I'd go out and have one-night stands. It's all a sales pitch, from the minute you walk up to 'em, you're pitching to get 'em in bed. I remember this one girl Danielle, I met her at a nightclub. She was an Asian girl. I bought her a drink and she asked me if I wanted to go for a walk, and then we went back to her place. She drove a Nissan 300ZX, incredible, this was the car of my dreams. That was better than the sex, driving in the car, watching her do the stick shift. The sex was pretty much the ten-minute deal. Work up all this energy and then release it. We didn't have the same personality type, I'm more the wild-thing type and she wanted something else, I don't know what. The rhythm wasn't coming together. It seemed like a lot of work. She wasn't too happy with it. Neither was I, really. It was bad sex. I've had a lot of bad sex.

Then there was my big relationship. Girl named Alice. We saw each other seriously for a couple of months, which is the longest I've ever seen anybody. Another ditsy Southern girl. I met her in a club, too—short skirt and a smile. She had blond hair, big butt, wore Southern blouses, drove a Mustang. My friend called her [in a deep drawl] "a fast bitch in a fast car—has her pants down quicker than you can say, 'Drop her down to fifty.' " She was seventeen, and she'd slept with something like twenty-four guys, which is pretty good for seventeen.

We were both into sex anywhere, anytime. We did it in a couple of pickups. We did it at her grandparents' house. In her swimming pool. In the shower. But sex with her wasn't that great. She wasn't very experimental. Down and dirty, that was her business. It reminded me of being married. She'd bitch at me afterward, "Get your shit off the floor, gimme a beer!" We'd hang out at her house and watch TV all day and every once in a while we'd do it. The same orgasm with the same girl, over and over again. It scared me, I felt like a trapped human being. But I thought I was in love with her. We were into these fantasies of the future, kids, a house, that's all we talked about. I hardly ever used birth control with her, either. She used these inserts sometimes, put them in twenty minutes before and it would be like coated down there, all warm and tingly. One day she called me, "You have to get over here right now." I lived ten minutes away. Got in the car, tearing around the corners, making a U-slide into her driveway—jumping with excitement, one big hormone drive. She was in her robe and I didn't even think about it, had full-fledged sex, came two or three times inside her on like the eighth or tenth day of her cycle. I thought for sure I knocked her up. And in a Catholic family, that baby is coming out, and it's staying with her. I'd be ten pounds bigger and sipping on a Natural Light in Louisiana in air conditioning right now.

Instead I came back here. She gave me a going-away party and I got blood-alcohol poisoning, I drank so much, so we had a weird breakup. I'm kind of confused about it—my whole experience in the South was confusing. I mean, I learned a little bit, but mostly I was confused and kind of scared about doing it right, or being cool. And my dad, I was always on the edge with him, so my way of getting out of there was to go have sex.

Then I come back here and everything I know about sex is wrong. That's the message I'm getting: Welcome to the Bay Area, everything you know is wrong. Out here it's more like a teenager's parents would want to think. Girls are going, "No, no, got to wait a while." Mostly because there's so much shit happening with AIDS and sexually transmitted diseases that it's not even worth it. Down in the South they're so damn ignorant that they don't know what can happen to them. A lot of them get pregnant, and safe sex isn't really practiced. The girls sleep with as many guys as they can, put notches on their beds. I've really changed my attitude since I moved out here. Down there I was gung-ho, my philosophy was, Fuck and suck anything that moves. I could have gotten laid every weekend if I put my mind to it. Out here, the attitude is, You don't go out and look for it. And you can't have one-night stands, they're just too dangerous. Plus they're painful. It's painful to do that to someone, or for them to do that to you. If you do it, you don't talk about it. Down South it was like a trophy on your wall.

I laugh at these guys when I see 'em now, the guys out in groups chasing skirt. I think it's funny 'cause they're hating it so much.

Now I go out dancing, that's very sexual, and I do drugs. In school I put myself with the stoners instead of the sleazy guys, the ones who are into scoping out and flirting and pickups and a lot of sex. My group, we sit around and make each other laugh. We're more into our intellectual sides. I've only had sex with three girls since I moved back. The first time we were all high on mushrooms and I did it just to see what it would be like. Another time I got drunk with this girl who's a friend, and we spent the night, that was a mistake. Then I had a thing with this twenty-seven-year-old girl I met dancing. We went away for a weekend, stayed in a motel on the ocean. That was cool, we had great sex together. She was as wild and crazy as I am, if not ten times more. We fucked for hours. She brought along all this lingerie and modeled it for me. But I told her I was nineteen, and really I was fifteen. I had to lie about everything, and it was awful, I hated it. When I told her, she was pretty hurt, so that's a shitty thing to do to somebody. One way or another, I've had mostly painful experiences so far.

It seems like my sex drive is over for a while. I don't have the urge anymore. I get hit on a lot when I go out, but that's probably because I'm not looking for it. I think New Orleans was my sexual peak, I really do. No matter how early it was, that was it. Maybe I'll have another drive when I'm twenty or thirty, but hopefully it'll be with just one person. I used to dream about having this machine, like a photocopy machine, where I could put in a picture of a girl from a magazine and the real girl would come out the other side. Well, if she walked in that door right now, I'd say, "Nice to meet you. Have I introduced you to Harry? I'm going out, see you later, lock the door when you leave. . . ."

SHANNON STANSELL

She is eighteen, just out of high school. Shoulder-length blond hair, blue eyes, a pretty face, and an outfit that plays up her curves: tight jeans and a tight shirt, unbuttoned to reveal cleavage. Through our talk she fidgets, smokes, and laughs nervously.

She lives in the San Fernando Valley. Her parents divorced when she was six, so she and her older sister divide their time between two households. "My dad is very unaffectionate. My sister gets along with him better, but he looks down on me because I didn't do well in school. My mom and I have a great relationship, very close. She talks to me about her problems. She trusts me a lot. She lets me do whatever I want. Like I have guys over really late at night, and I don't feel weird about it. We drink beers with my mom around, or smoke pot—well, I do that in my room, but she knows and she doesn't say anything. The atmosphere about sex is pretty relaxed. We tell dirty jokes, we watch dirty channels on cable. I think we have a cool family. Definitely not uptight. That's the difference between my mom and my dad. He's very unrelaxed. She's very mellow.

"I don't really talk to her about sex. I was going to ask her yesterday when she lost her virginity, but I got nervous. I never tell her sexual things that happen with me. Except this really bad thing—I have herpes, and I finally had to tell her, because it was getting out of hand. Other than that, she just tells me, 'Shannon, you have to have respect for yourself. You can't just sleep around.' And it's true, you shouldn't be having sex with anyone you don't know really well."

• • •

I had my first kiss in ninth grade. That's kind of late. I was a prude for a long time. My best friend lost her virginity in the eighth grade, so that was weird. It wasn't really weird, she was a slut. Everyone called her a slut because she would always fool around with guys. Penny had sex before she did anything else, before she got fingered or had oral sex or anything. It was a dare. She's just wild. She used to always take off her top at the beach. I was a lot more conservative than her, I wouldn't take off my top. She was crazy like that. I always felt uncomfortable with her about sex because I knew she was much more experienced than me.

In tenth grade I went out with this guy named Monte who I lost my virginity to, and who gave me herpes. He's been in my life forever. He taught me everything. We started going out when I was fifteen, and I lost my virginity last year, when I was seventeen. We kept trying but I couldn't do it. I guess I was too tight or something. We tried forever. I thought there was something wrong with me. I was really shy. But I was *so attracted* to him. He could touch my toe, and I'd be at his— I just wanted him all the time. Also his image, he was real popular, I know that had something to do with it. And he was two years older, he was experienced, he definitely knew what to do. His touch felt so good and I was just so into him. It was gross. He played with my mind for the past three years. I guess I was obsessed. Every time I think about it, I want to kill myself.

Monte's not really cute. He's short. He has really nice skin, no pimples or anything. He dresses really nice. He's charming, he's funny, he has a really good personality. He always made me laugh. He worked near my house and I was walking by one time and he came out, it was the summer, and he was like, "What's up?" We started talking. A few days later he called and asked me to go out. We went out a couple times, and we were at this party. All of a sudden he came over to me. It happened so fast. We started kissing, it was amazing. Stars lit up, it was so good. I felt it everywhere, in my knees. We were just kissing, but that's always how it was with him, total lust. One time he was over at my house and my mom was away. We were in the living room, on the couch. He was licking me everywhere. Sex wasn't an issue yet. For some reason he didn't ask me to have sex, it was still the very beginning. He took off my shirt and he was licking me all over here [indicates breasts] and on my stomach and it was so good. He always knew what he was doing, but it wasn't mechanical, it didn't look like a routine that he did with every girl. I loved his hands. He was really into my body, which I loved. I think that's what makes it good or not, if they're into you, and he was just so into me. Sometimes it was like we wanted each other so much, when we'd see each other we'd rip each other's clothes off.

For a couple of months we just fooled around. Feeling each other—it wasn't like him feeling me up, me feeling him down. It was like being all over each other, touching each other everywhere. He would finger me and stuff—just the whole thing was so good, him touching me, him being on top of me, our nakedness was really good. If you're not comfortable with your body, I don't think you can have good sex, and Monte was definitely comfortable with his body. He would touch me everywhere—not with his mouth, more his hands. We did oral sex, but not much. I don't like giving oral sex. I hardly ever do it unless I really like a guy. And I really liked Monte, but I still didn't do it. He was too big, I just couldn't take it. I could never finish. I'd get tears in my eyes. He'd be like, "That's okay." I don't think he was into doing it to me, either. I think I was the first girl he ever gave oral sex to. I love it, I always wanted him to do it, but he just wasn't into it. And I felt uncomfortable asking him, which sucked. I was comfortable around him, I could be naked, but I couldn't ask him to do things to me.

The first time we tried to have sex, we were at one of his friends' parties. We were fooling around, and I had to go home because I had a curfew. Of course he always started fooling around right before I had to go. He's like, "You always do this." I'm like, "I can't help it. I have a curfew." Then I said, "Come home with me." That was the first time a guy came home with me at night. He said, "What are we going to do there?" I said, "We'll have sex." He was like, "Yeah?" "Yeah." That's how it went, very casual. We went back to my house and started to fool around and we tried it and it didn't work. It hurt so much, I was really not into it after a while. It was so not passionate. He was trying, and I was lying there like a rug. I wanted it to happen, but I was getting so tired of it. I wanted to lose it, though. I was curious as to what the hype was about.

We kept trying to have sex, but it got so monotonous. It would be good to the point where we'd try, and we couldn't do it, and that got annoying. It was so predictable. He would go in a little bit and then it would hurt too much. I was tense. My heart would be beating fast, like when you go to the gynecologist, you get all tensed up but you don't realize it. Your legs just close a little more. We used lotion, but nothing helped. And the relationship was so on and off, it was so unstable. Going to school together wasn't good, it was always weird in school. We didn't really have a talking relationship. Even though we weren't having sex, it was totally sexual. I wasn't in love with him, not at all. We'd break up, and we wouldn't see each other for a really long time, and all this lust would build up. Then I'd see him again and it would be so good. But I'd get hurt because he would never call. I never knew what was up with us. He never told me how he felt. I'd always hear about him with other girls.

Finally he got his own apartment, so one night we're at his house, in his room, and it just worked. Things were good again between us, we were seeing each other. The night before it kind of worked but I don't think I lost it. Then we had sex the next day and there was blood all over the sheet. I couldn't believe it, I'm like, "I'm sorry," but he was cool about it. Then we had sex a lot that night. It didn't hurt at all, I was definitely ready. Maybe it was also that we were at his house and I didn't have to worry about my mom or anything. Except I remember the next time we had sex, I cried, I was crying while we were having sex. I got really upset, I was like, What am I doing back with him?

After that we had sex every time we saw each other, like once or twice a week. We'd have it a lot, a bunch of times every night.

It took a while before I started having orgasms. It didn't bother me, because I didn't know what they were. It was never like I'd build up and couldn't get any further. After we started having sex, I still wasn't sure until one time I was at the peak, and I was so satisfied I didn't need to have sex again. Since then I have them pretty regularly, but only from having sex, not from me being eaten out or anything.

I always asked him to talk to me during sex, but he felt weird about it. I was like, "Can you talk dirty to me?" He did that one time, he said, "Oh, I want to fuck you," but it was out of forcing him to say it. My friends were always telling me how their boyfriends talked to them, or asked them to masturbate and do things like that. I thought,

That's cool. Penny used to tell me these stories—she'd tie up her boy-friend. And I'm like, "Monte's so not like that, and I wish he was. I wish he was really kinky."

We didn't use a condom. We were having sex all the time, and we never used a condom. Then we stopped seeing each other and I slept with this other guy. I regretted it at the time, but I just had to do it so Monte wouldn't be the last person. His name's Kevin. We had sex, and it was so bad. We were hanging out with some friends and they left, and I'm like, "Kevin, just stay." I was so up for this to happen. We started fooling around and we had sex. He didn't want to use a condom, and he's so uncomfortable with his body, which made it really bad. He had to have the sheets over him. He wouldn't let me turn on the lights, he was like, "I'm really skinny." I don't think he was that experienced either. He didn't really touch me—it was like, first base, second base, that kind of thing. It was really boring, seriously, I just lay there. It was probably bad also because I was just doing it to do it.

Then a few days after that I went to a party, and afterward I called Monte at like two A.M. He came over and we had sex. I said, "Do you have a condom?" He's like, "No." I said, "Aren't you nervous, how do you know I haven't been with other guys? How do you know I don't have a disease?" It's so weird, because that's when I got herpes. He was like, "Have you been with other guys?" I said, "Yeah," and told him about Kevin. I guess he cared, but he doesn't like to show his feelings. So we had sex, and then I got this weird feeling, I felt really uncomfortable the next day, and I asked my friend Penny the slut, I said, "Penny, I felt really weird after we had sex," and she said, "It's normal, it's like friction." I said okay but it got really bad, so I went to the gynecologist and he was like, "It's eighty percent that you don't have it." I called back a week later, and I have it. I called Monte up, and I wasn't even mad, I was like, "Monte, you have to get your-self checked." He was a little too cool about it, he's like, "Okay." The next day, he's like, "I don't have it." I was like, "Really? That's not possible, because I used a condom with Kevin." I know Monte gave it to me, but I believed him, I'm so dumb. He still wanted to have sex with me, and I've learned that guys don't want to have sex with you if you have herpes. So the more I think about it, the more it seems like he's been lying this whole time, and he had it, and he knew he had it.

For a while he was still having sex with me, so herpes wasn't that big of a deal. Then he went away to college, and this guy Andrew— we're cool with each other, we were fooling around for about a year, but we're friends. Andrew came over during baby-sitting and we started fooling around. I was really unsure, but I said no. The next day I thought, maybe I will. We talked about it for an hour. The only reason I didn't want to was I was scared I would like him too much. But we did, and it was really nice. I didn't tell him I had herpes because I didn't think I had to unless it was active. We used a condom, too. I wouldn't put anybody at risk now. Then, two days later, he called me up, he's like, "I heard you have herpes." I couldn't believe it. All of a sudden every guy I ever fooled around with started calling me up and saying, "You have what?" It turns out Penny told two people. She says she was concerned that I was having sex with Andrew without telling him. That's so ridiculous, it's so stupid. I was like, "Andrew, I don't have it." We had sex again. He kept asking me, "Shannon, I've been hearing so many rumors about you, and I want to believe you so much." I said, "I don't have it, I swear." Then we had sex again, but I felt so guilty, because I really liked him. So finally I had to tell him, and he was really cool. But he can't have sex with me anymore. He's too scared. Which I guess is understandable.

Anyway, the whole world knows now. I can't tell you how many people know. It's so embarrassing, it's horrible. I used to deny it, but now it's ridiculous.

Then I was having sex with this other guy, Zeke. And I don't even like this kid. I don't know what I was doing. I was just being crazy. I was being very promiscuous, fooling around with a lot of guys. One night I was at this club, and Zeke was there. I had heard about him from my friends, they were like, "Oh, he's really cute." So I was automatically, Wow, he's really cute. He looks like James Dean kind of. He has a girlfriend, but she's a virgin. All of a sudden he started kissing me. We were kissing, and we decided to go back to his house, and we had sex. It was really fast. It was cold, two people fucking. I've never experienced that before, it was so unpersonal. I could have been anybody. I felt really slutty. So the minute we had sex, I left. I find myself doing that a lot. I didn't have any feelings toward it, so I just wanted to leave.

I had sex with him a few more times after that, and almost every time it was just fucking. It's really weird when you're having sex with a guy and he does something—like he holds your hand, something that you'd do with someone you really like, but I hardly know this guy. Fooling around I think is a lot more personal than having sex. Sex can be really mechanical, not even touching each other. Sometimes I look up and I'm looking at his face and I'm thinking, What is going on? What am I doing? Who is this? I look down again and I get—not nervous, just weird, strange.

One time at my house, he came within a minute. Not even a minute, it was like forty seconds. I was really pissed off. I said, "I'm tired, can you go?" I was being rude, but I just didn't like him. He said, "You're throwing me out." I said, "No, I'm just really tired." He was like, "Are you mad?" I was like, "No." But I was just mad in general. The whole time I was with him, I was mad. I think I was mad because everyone knew I had herpes. I was mad at Monte, I was mad about a lot of things. I was bored, too. I was being really bitchy, and I cried all the time. All of a sudden by myself I'd be crying, and I never knew why, but that was probably why.

I was going to break it off and then I was like, Let me try it one more time, maybe it'll be cool. Of course that was the one time it was personal. And of course it was the last time. We hung out, we were just sitting in the mall talking, so we're getting to know each other. Then we were hanging out in his bed watching TV, and I didn't even think we were going to have sex. When we did, it was nice and friendly. A lot of touching, the face and hands and stuff. I was like, Wow, this is good. And of course afterward he said, "I'm just waiting for the day my girlfriend finds out." That made me feel really bad, so I said, "Fine, let's break it off." He said, "Okay, fine." I thought he was going to say, "No, I really like you," or something, but he wasn't like that at all. He said, "It was just an affair." He was really nonchalant. He said, "Don't be mad, we can still be friends." I was kind of laughing. I was upset because he was nonchalant, but I was also put-ting on an act. I said, "I'm just going to see you later, bye." He said, "Don't I get a kiss good-bye?" I said no, and that was it.

Things like that always happen to me. Me and guys are not cool. They always hurt me in some way. Another guy named Alex—I met him in a club, too. I'll never forget it, because it was the best experi-ence in my life. This was in that same promiscuous time. It's weird, because that night before I went out, I was like, God, I feel like hav-ing sex. I was going to call an old friend, but I was like, No, that's stu-pid. So I went out instead and saw this really fly guy. He's so good-looking, he has blondish hair, slicked back, he's a model, he has tattoos, which is really sexy, and he's tanned. He's pretty tall, he's thin, but he has a really nice body, you see his muscles but it isn't like he's a he-man. I was being so aggressive because I wanted him so much. We were kissing, and then we went in his car, and I was like, "Do you have condoms?" Just in case we get there and he doesn't have anything. He was like, "How do you know we're gonna have sex?" I was like, "Come on."

The minute we got to his house, we started kissing and stuff. Our clothes came off really fast. He was pinning me down and eating me out. He didn't want me to do anything to him. He just wanted me to lie there. He was so into me, it was unbelievable. He was kissing and licking me everywhere and eating me out the whole night. He wanted to touch me every second. He was talking dirty to me, and I liked it. We didn't have sex, because he drank too much, and he couldn't get it up. At first I was kind of upset, just to myself. I wasn't mad at him. I really wanted to, but it was kind of good we didn't, because I don't think it would have been so prolonged. Then he was like, "Please sleep over." I tried to but I got uncomfortable. I have to sleep in my own house, I have a thing about it. So I left in the middle of the night. I tried to wake him but he wouldn't, and I couldn't leave a note be-cause it was really dark, so I just left. I've seen him a few times after that, but just like, Hi. I went to explain, I was like, "I'm sorry I left." He was like, "I don't care." Every time I see him, I want something to happen. He knows I'm interested, but I'm going to lay off because I don't want to look stupid. My friends say he probably feels bad be-cause I left so abruptly. I think he knows I slept with Zeke, so maybe he thinks I sleep around. So I'm like, It was just one night, I'll live in the fantasy of that one night.

This guy I'm seeing now, we haven't had sex, but one day he goes, "Physically, I'm so infatuated with you." Isn't that intense? Or he tells me I'm beautiful. I have a big problem with that. My family, like my aunts and everyone, they think of me as the pretty one, and my sister's the smart one. My stepfather once said to me, "Your sister got the brain and you got the looks." I couldn't believe he said that to me, I'll never forget it. That's why I get mad when my friends tell me guys never ask them to have sex right away. A lot of my friends are beautiful. My best friend's beautiful, but she's more innocent-looking. I guess guys consider me really sexy. I remember Kevin once told me I was walking down the street and his friends were like, "That girl's made for sex." I was a virgin at the time! It makes me so uncomfortable that people think of me like that. I wish I could stop it. I'm not like that at all. I'm not made for sex. I don't think about it constantly. I don't have sex all the time with a million different guys.

Sometimes when I'm stoned I get these really intense thoughts about myself being sexy and how I don't mean to. Weird thoughts. I start to really hate myself. I can see through people like crazy when I'm stoned, including myself. I think, Why do I dress the way I dress? I hate it that people look at me that way, so why do I do it? I guess it's just more flattery for me, but I don't really want it.

When I was younger, sex was a really big thing, but as I get older, when my friend tells me she had sex with some guy, I'm like, "Oh, was it good?" I'm not, "You did? Oh my God!" It's not a big deal anymore. Even to me it's not. I wish it was kind of a big deal. It bugs me that it's so easy to have sex. I could go to a club every night and have sex with a different guy. Sometimes I don't have control over—I want to not have sex, but once I start fooling around, it's hard for me to stop. I don't even want to stop, but I know I should. Plus with AIDS, I can't go around having sex with everyone. Well, I don't really think about AIDS, I just threw that in there. It's just that you can't be promiscuous at this time, plus I don't want to be sleeping around. It's a little bit how they feel, like I'm a slut, but more how I'm going to feel the next day. I don't want to feel bad about what I did. I get emotional a lot about sex. If I don't like them and I do it, I find myself just feeling shitty, like I have a pit in my stomach or my heart hurts or something. When I breathe, I feel it in my heart. It's a scared feeling, like I want to be a little girl.

Fooling around is fine. Sex just changes everything. I can't stress it enough. That's what I say to all my virgin friends. Sex changes everything, you really have to like a guy to do it. You have to know it's okay. You can't be unsure. Otherwise you're going to feel so shitty. A lot of guys I've fooled around with are like, "It's not a big deal if we have sex, we're almost doing it anyway. There's no difference." But there is. There's a huge difference. At least for girls. At least for me.

LARRY SCHOENBERG

He lives with his parents in the small Pennsylvania town where he was born. He is the youngest of six children—a lanky college student with short blond hair and a neatly trimmed mustache, wearing blue jeans and a plaid flannel shirt buttoned up close to his neck. His mother and father are conservative and Catholic, and so is he: "I go to church every single Sunday. I can't remember when I missed a mass. One reason I go is to make my parents happy, but I have had a lot of things popping up lately and by going to church I feel better. I feel like there's somebody looking over me, somebody that will help me out.

"I'm one of the few students in my high school class whose parents are still married, so I'm thankful for that. I try not to think about their sex life [giggles], that's kind of gross. They still sleep in the same bed, and as far as I know they're sexually active. I found out about sex in school, not from them. My mom gets embarrassed about it. If we sit down and watch a TV show, she will get shocked at what's being said, and she'll get up and leave the room. My dad is a little more tolerant. There'll be a show on HBO or Cinemax where there's bad language and touchy situations, and I'll walk into the room and he'll be laughing. He'll snap out of it real fast and probably turn the channel. He's not a dirty old man or anything, he would just rather not have me know what he's watching.

"As far as real sexual activity, believe it or not, I'm twenty now, and it just happened a month ago. I'm probably the only person in my graduating class who waited this long to get involved."

• • •

I can remember sexual thoughts as far back as seven years old. I didn't understand the full picture until I was probably nine, but I remember that me and my friends who lived on the street, we'd go out and play doctor. We'd also play school. Everybody would say, "Okay, physical time," and we'd go down in the basement of my friend's house. Her father had porno materials, so we'd take magazines down in the basement and look at them and get naked and investigate each other's parts. I can remember a feeling of excitement.

The magazines weren't graphic, it was men and women together but no physical contact really. It's funny—even to this day when I see these friends, for some reason I feel embarrassed, because I know we did some bizarre things. Like when we went down to the basement for some reason everybody had to pee in this jar. Then we would put on shows and play strange games with everybody naked. We'd fondle each other, but as far as penetration, no. No kissing either, we were just examining each other. I don't think any of us knew too much about sex.

I started masturbating at thirteen. I remember the first time I had an orgasm, I wasn't quite sure what was happening to me, and I had traces of blood. I was really scared, I was going to go to my father and say, "I don't know what's going on, I need to go to the hospital or something," but after that it never happened again. I also remember thinking that if I was to masturbate and have orgasms, I was going to use up all the semen and I wouldn't have any in the future. Part of me said, I'm gonna stop doing this because I do want to have children when I get older. So I sort of limited it. Then eventually I was hearing my friends saying there's always production, so I started on a daily basis. Plus I was still playing games with my friends. We'd get the hose in the backyard and play Truth or Dare, we would ask a question and you would have to answer it honestly, but if you didn't want to, we would take the hose, stick it down your pants, and squirt the hell out of you. The reason we did it was when you stuck the hose down there, you got to sneak a peek.

When I was fourteen, instead of just having the urges, I started to have some deep feelings and know I wanted to get involved with somebody sexually. But I haven't really had the opportunity since then. My friends outgrew the games or they moved, so I was there all by myself, and it was kind of traumatic, losing your friends and also the activity. That's when I started getting into pornography. I wasn't comfortable talking to anyone at school about sex, and I was pretty

much a loner, I didn't do any dating or anything because I was focusing on my goals. I have always had my goals set aside. I've been
working really hard since I was twelve, doing a lot of odd jobs, and
I have always wanted to be a scientist. I know a lot of people I went
to high school with think I'm weird. Instead of going out and causing
trouble on Friday or Saturday night, most of the time I was at home
studying. I sacrificed going to the parties and stuff, but I didn't really
miss it. If I would have had the idle time, I think I would have started
getting in trouble and breaking the image my mother had of me, and
I don't want to do that because I don't want to hurt her.

So things didn't progress, really. I got porno magazines and movies. At first I was stealing them from my brothers, they had a large
amount so they wouldn't miss a magazine here or there. There was
Puritan and *Club* and some no-name things, hard-core. They also had
movies. I would put a blank cassette in the box so it looks like it's still
there, and I would sneak one. As far as buying them, I was under age,
and it's not like I can have them sent to my house, so a year and a half
ago I opened up my own post office box. I have my own TV and
VCR in my room, I've got everything I need up there. I keep it all
very well hidden. If my parents were to find out, they would be
crushed. They know my brothers possess this stuff, but since I'm the
baby of the family, and since I haven't gone out and gotten in
trouble—well, they don't think I'm an angel, but my mom does think
I'm a little bit special, and they would be disappointed that I actually
am getting in trouble at home.

So it was just me and my books and magazines and movies. As far
as other people, for instance, after gym class we'd be in the shower
and I'd see other people and it was enough for my imagination that
I could fantasize. There wasn't any physical contact or touching, but
it was enough for me.

These were boys you were curious about?

Yes.

And the porn was heterosexual or gay?

Heterosexual. But that changed this summer. I'm still questioning
what I really feel. I knew I was attracted to boys way back when I was
seven, but I denied it, and when these games were taking place, I figured since I wasn't pushing anybody to do this and they weren't

pushing me, it was just a game. Deep down inside I knew it was more than that, but I never admitted to a single person I had these feelings, until this October. When I masturbated, my fantasies were mostly about men—strictly about men. When I looked at the porn I by-passed the women and I'd focus on the penises. There were certain parts of the genitals I would focus on—at one time it might be the testicles, or the head, or the hole, or the veins.

In school I had been labeled as being gay when I was—I can re-member all the way back to the sixth grade, people making com-ments. I did a fair bit of lying, I would be sitting in study hall and somebody would say, "Yeah, I went out with this girl this weekend, and we slept together," and just because of all the pressure I'd start saying the same thing. Or I would go to the movies with a female just to set the record straight. I did not have a single male friend all the way through high school. All my friends were female. When I was in eighth grade I did date a girl for about two weeks and it didn't go well at all. And people felt, well, if that failed, there must be some-thing wrong. So my high school years were hell. I was miserable. Peo-ple used to call me a faggot. I think that term was used on more people than just me, it was an in thing to say, but there were people who honestly thought I was a fag. That hurt, it really did, I had to learn to ignore it, and I had to set my mind in a mode where I was saying, I am going to be better off than all these people by working harder. Hopefully I'll succeed in life and pass them up, and even-tually I'm going to turn the tables and say, Look what I've done with my life, while you're stuck in the street, you're uneducated, you're shit. That's what I'm working for. Some people may not think that's a positive motive, but I do. This is something I want badly.

It was just last August that I sent for my first gay movie. I don't know why I held off for so long—to a certain point it was denial, and believe it or not, I was embarrassed ordering it through the mail, even though I would never meet those people from the company in Cali-fornia. Just the thought that on my credit-card bill it would say Lei-sure Time Products, for some reason I was embarrassed by that. But the feelings I had toward males got stronger and stronger, so I de-cided to order the tape. At first I was like, This is disgusting, I had a weird feeling seeing these guys. But the more I saw it, the more interesting it became.

The best thing for me was ending up at State. It wasn't my first choice of college, but I ended up there, and that's where I had my first sexual experience. This past summer, after my freshman year, I was working at the information booth and this guy came by. He has a very high position at State, and he asked me if he could sit down at the desk and write a note for somebody. I said sure. He sat down and we started talking and he asked me what my major was, and I told him, and he said he had majored in math, and eventually he started smiling and being really nice and the next thing I knew he grabbed my crotch. I was like, This person has a pretty good job and he took a big risk. But I was very offended. I pulled away, and he got the hint that I wasn't sure about what was going on. As soon as he left I called my boss and complained about it, I was really mad. My boss was very understanding, she wanted me to know I wasn't wrong for having a negative feeling about it. She said that nobody should force themselves on me, and she urged me to file a complaint. But I didn't want to do that, I don't want to hurt anybody. If they're nice to me I'll be nice back, and if they show me love I'll show love back. But I was confused, this person was being nice, but at the same time he was pushing himself on me. I didn't know what to think about it.

I didn't see this guy for the rest of the summer, and then when the school year started up again I was walking past his office one day and he called me in. He said, "Hey, would you mind having a seat?" He asked me how things were going and I said okay, and he said, "You don't sound too convincing, what's going on?" Eventually he came right out and asked me if I was gay, and I said, "I don't know." He said, "Well, here's my telephone number and my beeper number. If you have any questions, if you want to hang out, or if you need to talk to somebody, feel free to call me." I said sure, thanks, whatever, and I put the thing in my pocket.

I was ready to have somebody who would understand what I'm going through, but I wouldn't have felt comfortable calling up and saying, "It's me." Later that night I was at home and I got a phone call. He said, "I just want you to know that what we were talking about today was in the strictest confidence, and I am here for you." Then he asked me if I wanted to get some ice cream. I said sure. He picked me up and we ended up driving around for about two hours, never did make it to Friendly's. We talked about fantasies and stuff, and he was being very, very detailed, he was telling graphic details about his friends and relationships, describing different techniques they had used, describing their genitals. I thought it was strange, I would be lying if I said I wasn't nervous. So we just drove around and at the end of the night he took me home and we said good-bye. My mom asked me who did I go out with and I said, "Oh, a couple of friends from school."

The next night he called again and asked if I wanted to do something. So we went out, and he wanted to take a walk. We went to the elementary school playground. It was late at night, and it was very cold out, and—I still feel weird talking about this. He asked me to give him a hug. I was like, Fine. Then he tried to start kissing and everything, and it was strange, because it was something new to me. Building it up for twenty years is kind of unusual. I always thought the concept of kissing was disgusting, to have somebody else's tongue and saliva—but it was very comfortable, I really liked it. He was a smoker, I mean you could smell and taste it, but that didn't even bother me. I was falling for him. I felt like he cared for me, which is something I've been seeking. I would like to be told by somebody other than my family that they care about me and they love me. So I thought I was on the right track, this was something that I wanted for a long time, and it was pretty natural.

Then he started going all over me, and the next thing I knew he asked if he could undo my belt. I said, "Sure, that's fine." Keep in mind that this is on the elementary school playground, and it's late and it's cold. October 22, twelve fifteen A.M. So just like that—well, before I get into that, I should mention that when we hugged I was kind of excited, and—you know, certain things were happening, and he could feel it. He was like, "Wow," and he asked me if I was hard, and I was like, "Yeah, I can't deny that." It was pretty obvious. So he went to town with oral sex. Before that he had asked me what my fantasies were, and I said that I thought it would be really neat for me to have my penis touch his penis. I don't know why I said that, it was just something that seemed exciting. So he was working on me, and eventually he stood up and undid his pants, and I went ahead and fulfilled the little fantasy. Then right back down he went. He's shorter than I am, so he was in a squatting position, and he was masturbating, and he ejaculated, boom, his clothes were back on and he said it was time to go. He packed up his goods and pulled his pants up, and he literally said, "Okay, let's go, I'm freezing." He fulfilled his need and he didn't even think about what I wanted. I said, "I didn't have an orgasm," and he was like, "Well it's cold out here, let's go." I guess if I would have forced him he would have stayed out there, but he didn't want to do that. It was over.

I didn't give it a whole lot of thought until later that night. I was extremely happy, I thought it went really well, I was excited, and I couldn't wait until the next day to go back to school. Then I was in the booth and he happened to walk by, and I was giving someone information and I couldn't think about what happened the night before, so I just started laughing. Then we hung out some more, we'd go driving or go out to eat, but it was very fast, I would meet him, we would eat, and then it was over. He was very distant, and eventually he stopped calling. I asked him, "What's going on?" and he said, "I have a lot going on in my life right now, and I can't take on your problems, too." I said, "What problems?" He said, "You're unsure of your sexuality." I said, "No I'm not, if I was unsure I wouldn't have had sex." But he was still kind of distant. This was on a Friday, and I thought about him all weekend long, wondering what I had done wrong. I was thinking, Why do I keep doing this? He doesn't care about me, he isn't going to call me. I was thinking of calling him and the phone rang. It was him. He said, "Let's get together, I have an hour and a half, and we can talk." So I drove to his house and we took another walk and it was daylight and he said, "I was psychoanalyzing you, I'm trying to figure you out." All this crap, he's trying to understand me. Then he said, "Well, I've got a little bit of time, I'd like to mess around, would you?" I was wondering if we would ever do anything again. So we went back to his house and went into his bedroom. Once again he started hugging me and kissing me, and then the same thing, "May I?" I said, "Sure, why not?" So once again he went to town, I was standing up and he was sitting on his bed, and then he started masturbating. He had his clothes on but his pants unzipped. He was masturbating and performing oral sex on me. We had also talked before—another fantasy I had was putting someone else's semen on my penis. So once again he ejaculated and I reached out and got some semen and put some on me and then he got up real fast, went to the bathroom, cleaned up, and I heard him yelling, "I've got to go now, c'mon, hurry up." Once again I didn't get my needs met.

And that was the last time I heard from him. I mean, we see each other in the halls, and he'll say hi in passing, but that's the extent of it. It's really hard to work in the same building together. For a while, I wanted to be with him all the time, but I knew he was busy and I was busy. At one point we said after midterms were over we'd have time to do something. But I never got any calls, and by not hearing from him I thought more about him, and knowing he could just cut me off, I felt really hurt and I couldn't put those feelings aside. I had a female friend who died of cancer in high school, and I hate to say it, but this was more powerful. Now I'm on prescription medicine for depression and it's working, but it was to the point where I would be at work, and just like that I would be in my boss's office and she would be holding me and I would be crying. I couldn't control my emotions, I couldn't eat—I have lost about twelve pounds, and I'm just starting to put it back on. It has been extremely hard. I've been seeing a counselor at school, and I talked to my family doctor, so there's no need to get alarmed, but I had actually thought about committing suicide at one point. I thought it would be an easy way out.

We have this gay and lesbian organization at school, and my boss told me I should speak to someone there, so I talked to the person in charge. When she asked what was going on, I didn't mention this guy's name, but after about three sentences she said, "Let me guess," and she named him right off. I said, "You've got to be kidding," and she said, "I've got somebody who had the exact same experience." And then I was approached by two other guys who had the same thing happen. By me finding that out, it helped a little bit to feel it's not something I did that turned him off. Because I was thinking, What did I do wrong? I wanted to know if I wasn't able to satisfy him for some reason. But he cut me off, he would not talk to me, I would go to his office and he'd shut me out, he'd say, "I'm busy." Meanwhile he was talking about me to another person, a professor who's a homosexual, and this professor talked to someone I worked with, and from there she spread it around everywhere, including the intimate details. This guy had made a comment—I'm going to be very blunt about this, that first time at the elementary school he made a comment about my large penis, he said, "You've got a huge cock." I said, "Oh, really?" Because I hadn't actually seen a mature adult nude, except in locker rooms and stuff. I said, "I thought it was a beanpole." He said, "Beanpole my ass, it's a fencepost." That got around to the people in my office, my boss—I mean, twenty or thirty people heard it. That's what hurts. He told me, "I will always be there for you, everything will be in the strictest confidence," and then he turned around and stabbed me in the back. So I have a big problem now with trust. It would just kill me if my parents ever found out, or anybody in my family.

But the hardest thing overall is losing him. That's the hardest part. And then everybody finding out. It's an unbelievable amount of pressure. The thing I'm having a hard time with is that I'd like to find somebody else to get involved with, but I don't want to jump into it too quickly, and I don't know how to go about it. I don't know how to approach anybody. There's no guarantee on who is and who is not a homosexual. You can't just ask somebody, and there's really no way to tell. I don't want to be alone at this point. I mean, I've got my family, but I would like something else. That would be a nice change, because I've been alone a lot.

As far as my future relationships, I don't want them to be superficial. I don't want them to be completely physical. I want somebody who I can run around with, who's going to be there for me. I want loyalty, I want honesty, I want monogamy. If I were to sum it up in one thing, I guess all I want is a friend. I still think if the right female were to come along, somebody I was physically attracted to and had inner beauty as well, that's something I would consider. I do believe I want to get married and have children, but who knows, that might be just to please other people. I'd like kids because I want somebody to need me. In all of my friendships, these people would survive and be happy without me. It doesn't really matter if I'm around. With a kid, you mold them, you shape them, you give them love, and in return you hope they love you back.

But first I'd like to have another male relationship. Because this relationship has turned me off to a certain extent. I don't know whether I should try again or just give up, because I don't want to get hurt again. But I do want to try again. I'd like to give it at least one more shot to see if it was just this one person that screwed up. My counselor says he's a sick person and he needs help. But I have to admit I have had some negative feelings toward other homosexuals—that they're not monogamous, that they aren't there to help you out in time of need, they just want to satisfy their needs, they're liars and two-faced and I can't trust them. Then I think, Well, what about me? I justify it by saying I don't know what I am, and I must not be gay. But deep down I know that's not true. Deep down I know I have these feelings and I can't cover them up for another twenty years.

PATRICK JORDAN

He is tall, dark, and handsome: a twenty-year-old black youth living in Spanish Harlem. He insists on meeting me at the subway, presumably to guide me safely to his "crib." The crib, which he shares with a roommate, is a mess—rumpled clothes everywhere, old pizza boxes on the coffee table, record jackets strewn on the floor around the stereo. One wall is dominated by a poster of Bob Marley, another by a triptych on velvet of Malcolm X, Martin Luther King, and Nelson Mandela. The music of choice is reggae, in keeping with Patrick's upbringing: He was born in the Bronx, but when he was thirteen his mother took him to Jamaica, her family's homeland, to escape the mean streets. He returned to New York at seventeen, after high school. His ambition is to become a pop music star. For the moment, he is waiting tables in an upscale restaurant. At the beginning of the interview he is so nervous that he can barely catch his breath; then the tales of his family, the islands, and his sexual exploits pour out in a torrent.

His parents separated when he was five. He spent weekends with his father before the move to Jamaica, and summers afterward. "Poppa James" has worked all his life in a midtown garage, and has labored to keep Patrick on the straight and narrow. "I love that man to death. I'm so glad he's my father, you know what I mean? He always told me, 'If you're gonna make some mistakes, don't make my mistakes.' He felt like he threw away his life, had kids too young and whatnot. When he moved out of this apartment, packed up all his stuff, it was really funny. He had boxes, and his clothes, and a little jewelry. He said, 'Come in here.' I was like, 'What's up, man?' He said, 'This is all I have. This is all I have for forty years. These are the only things I have.' Something clicked in my head. It was like, That's not a lot of shit to have."

• • •

When I was fourteen, in Jamaica, my cousin introduced me to this girl Denise. That was the first girl I ever fell in love with. And I mean this girl was bad. She had skin like brown buttercup, and she had a nice figure. Probably her figure wouldn't be all that nice now, but it was like puppy love. Y'know, so the cats was like, "So, Patrick, you ever eat out a girl?" At this time I was just kissing Denise. I was like, "No." They was like, "What? You crazy?" So I started lying. "Yeah, I did it." "What does it taste like?" The big thing was, a girl's poontang smells like fish. I was like, "It taste like salt fish." They was like, "Oh yeah?" I was like, "Yeah, yeah." So at this point, now I'm looked at as a stud. I did the dirty. Which I was still a virgin.

Denise used to come to my house after school. The big song back then was "Into Me." One day I turned the music real low. So I'm taking her bra off back there, which was impossible. I didn't know how to do it. I tried until I got fed up, and I was like, "Can you take that off?" She got a kick out of it. She took it off for me. I think she'd had sex before. She's like, "Have you ever done it before?" I'm like, "Yeah, I know what I'm doin'." So we got down to the nasty. I was moving, I was moving like a jackrabbit, and next thing you know, it was *boom*. And I was tired as shit, like Shheeewww, I did my job. [Laughs.] I did my job, and I felt like a man. I walked her to the bus stop, and I had the pimp lean. The brothers was like, "Patrick, 's up?" I was like, "Uhhhhhhhh." I got her on the bus and went by the basketball court. "You want to play?" I'm like, "No." "Wow, what's up?" "I'm tired." "Wow, what'd you do?" "You know. I got some." They was like, "Oh really?" These cats, I guess they didn't do it yet, so they was like, "What was it like?" I went through it detail by detail. "Well, y'see, the boobies was just about a handful." I started bragging, "Yeah, she was screaming." Which the girl didn't say a word. "Yeah, she was screaming, she started biting me, she pulled my hair out and all that." They were like, "Cool."

So now me and her were having sex. But we really didn't have the place. It was just every time my mom was at work. I'd go pick her up after school. "Come on to my house." [Imitates Jamaican dialect]: "No, no, me no want to go yet, me no want to go yet, got to go home and study." I'd be like, "C'mon, c'mon." I be talkin' like I talk now [imitates deep Barry White voice]: "Come on, baby, don't worry

about it, you can study tonight." But it took a lot of coaxing, "Please,
please." Begging all the time.

I never really got into asking her if she liked the sex. I believe she
did. I don't think she came. Just a lot of moaning and shit, like
"Mmmmmmmmmm," her eyes closed. My eyes were open. [Laughs.]
I still don't ask girls, "Did I satisfy you?" I think that's kind of selfish,
not asking, but then again, if you give your all, like after two or three
times, and she still isn't satisfied, something's wrong. [Laughs.] It's
like God forbid you have to go again, be like a dead turtle layin' on
the sand.

Did you use any birth control?

Hmmm, no. I pulled out. Except that first time, I didn't pull out
at all. I just started moving like a jackrabbit, and *Uhhhhhh.* But then
again, I was a young age, I don't know if the sperm was developed
and all that. I don't think it was ready to get the job done. [Laughs.]
Go through those walls, and the one lone soldier just be like, Uhhh,
found the egg. She used to tell me some stupid stories, man, like what
would happen if she got pregnant. Talkin' about taking a hanger and
puttin' it up there, all that shit. I was like, Ehh, don't tell me about
that. We'll just scrounge up like three hundred dollars, because I
knew about abortion. I asked her if she was on the pill, and she was
like, "No." I was like, "All right, cool." I didn't care anyway, I was
like, Party! I pulled out.

Next thing you know, I came to New York for the summer. And
my best friend jerked me. He stole my woman. I was callin', tryin' to
get what was goin' on. Papa dude got a phone bill for five hundred
dollars and change. Talk about bein' banned from a phone. I felt really bad 'cause I loved this girl and I thought she loved me too. But
it was great while it lasted, I was able to go around the neighborhood
and be like, Yeah, I got my rocks off.

I didn't get it again till I was prob'ly like fifteen, fifteen and a
half. That was cool, 'cause it was like party New York and party the
island, coming back and forth. I remember, my pop had porn movies
here, like Vanessa del Rio. Oh, I found that tape! I saw some shit I
did not think was possible. I was so horny, watching that tape, I was
about to explode. I was like, Oh man, oh man, so I went in the bathroom and tossed a puppet. Wooooo, Vanessa del Rio, boy, even

though I would like to meet her and do the job with her, I would be
scared, because I don't think I could get the job done. [Laughs.] That
would be too much of a hard feat for me. That would be like climb-
ing Mount Everest with no hooks and no rope. This lady be gettin'
the job done with two men, boy, and they don't even do the job right.
You see her have that look like she is not satisfied. Oooo, I never saw
a blowjob before. The different positions. All I thought was you lay
on top of her, and just make boom. And eating out, I was like, Oooo
man, he's eating her out. I saw the girls just bug when they get eat
out. That was fly. I was dead set against eating out a girl, like num-
num [shakes his head]. So later on I tried it for the first time, and I
was like, Ohh, this is so nasty. But after a while, I was like, This is
gross, but it tastes good! So I was getting the job done, boy, and that
girl, she was screaming. I mean, she was wailing. And I was just all in
there, all in the pussy. I was like, *Rrrrooowww,* like a demon. I took
off her panties, *RRROWWWWW,* and then I was in there, back and
forth, back and forth.

When I was seventeen I moved back up here. Moved in with
Poppa James. Working at a jazz club. This girl named Laura. Laura
was twenty-six years old. First older girl I had ever been out with in
my life. Laura, oh boy, Laura was bad. Then too, she was the first
white girl I ever dated. But you know the way I think about her now,
she was a tramp. She was a "ho." She had everything. Her parents
owned the jazz club, they had like a house out in Connecticut and a
condo in mid-Manhattan. And she just wanted a little puppet, someone she could boss around, and be like, "Okay, make me laugh. Oh,
you so cute." It was cool while it lasted. Actually it wasn't cool while
it lasted, because she used me. She used me sexually. Which I didn't
mind at all, but then she would do some stupid shit. Like when her
friends would come into the restaurant, it would be like, "Let me
show you Patrick." That's how she would introduce me.

But sex was great. She turned me on to some shit. She was the
first girl who ever gave me a blowjob. I saw it on tape, but I couldn't
never get any girl to do it. So Laura, she had her own apartment. I'm
in her house, and she undressed me. This was a change, I was like,
Ooooo. I sat down on the couch, and she unbuckled my belt, zipped
down my pants, and started doing the job. It was wild. Then I wanted

to pop, and I was like, "No, stop, stop, stop, stop!" I was trying to pull her up, and she just held there, *boom!* I popped in her mouth, and she was like, Party! I was like, "I'm supposed to have sex with you now, right?" So I had sex with her, and she's like, "Kiss me." I'm like, "Uhhhhhhhh-uh." [Laughs.] No, no, no, no, that does not work, I'm sorry. That shit does not work. She thought it was funny, she spit the shit out. She wiped her mouth with a towel. I still didn't kiss her, but I had sex with her, I did the job. I was Rambo, I stayed hard, came twice. Boom, I came, and the second time, I didn't come as quick, I was moving back and forth, she's like, "I'm tired." I'm like, "Wait, baby, just a little bit more. Hold on a minute now." I came inside her, too, because she's on the pill. Rock solid.

Then she was cuddling, and she wanted to kiss me. I got smart. What I did, I'm like, "You know what? I'm gonna go use the bathroom for a second, okay?" So I used the bathroom, and she freshened up, and she's like, "Why won't you kiss me?" I'm like, "Do you feel like brushing your teeth?" She got a kick out of that, she laughed and brushed her teeth. Came back to bed and crashed. "Aren't you gonna kiss me?" "Did you brush your teeth?" "Yeah." "Okay, cool, let's kiss now." I know it sounds disrespectful that I don't want to kiss them after. It's just like, it's gross. Like, c'mon, God made the sperm to go in the canal and tunnel right up there, but it wasn't meant to be swallowed. If it starts dripping down the mouth, y'know, and then *mmmmm-mmmmm* [kissing noises]—Uh-uh, eewww, I ain't kissing you, baby, shit. You gotta find somebody else to do that shit. That's gross. If you think about it, it really is gross. You can get a kick out of it, if you want to be the domineering man and feel like you have some power, be like, "Yeah, I came in her mouth. Exploded. And she took every last drop." With me, it's like, Naaah, I don't think so. Even after she brushed her teeth and washed out her mouth with Listerine, kissing her was hard. I'm like, So, did you ever have another dude come in your mouth before? I didn't ask her that, but I thought about it.

Another time, something she did, wasn't nothin' big, she held my hands down. Held my hands down when she was kissing me all over. She's like, "Don't touch me." What are you talkin' about? I got a rock-hard dick and you are tellin' me don't touch you? She's kissing me, and she's like, "Don't touch me, don't touch me, the feeling will last a lot longer." I'm like, Oh, shit, now I'm in bed with a demon. So I'm like, "All right, fuck it, I won't touch you." Then she cuffed one arm to the bedpost. I wasn't having that shit, I was like, "Nope, take this shit off now. No, no, no." She's like, "Oh, come on, please please please." "Take this shit off *now.*" She's like, "No, no, I'm not going to take it off." So I was struggling to take it off, and meanwhile she's giving me a blowjob. I dunno, I just feel really fucked up about not having no use of my hands. Being somewhat trapped, I hate that. That sadomasochist shit, no no no. The day I have sex with a sadomasochist and she hits me with a whip, I'm gonna take it from her and hit her back harder. [Laughs.] The shit just does not work, I'm sorry. So I still had the use of one hand, and she was like, "You'll like it." But I was not into it, maybe I watch too many movies, I think she's going to pull an ax from under the bed and chop me up. She's giving me the blowjob, and I'm like, "Yeah, okay, I'm not into this shit, you know that, right?" She's like, "All right, all right." She took the handcuff off me, and I was like, "Cool, now we can get busy." Prob'ly I sound fucked up, like not open-minded, be like, Yeah, I'll try it. But noooo, Fuck that.

After a while I started feeling really fucked up about going out with her, because it looked like I was the token black cat. Her people was lookin' at me like, Oooo, she's going out with this young guy. So Laura and me had some fights, and one day I came in to work, and I guess they couldn't pay the rent on the club, or they were losing money, so they sold out. I didn't have a job. New management, new employees. They was like, "You're out of work." I felt used, like she couldn't even tell me two days or a week ahead of time. I was pissed. So she calls me up, and she's like, "Oh, I'm sorry," and the next thing you know I'm cussing her out, like "Fuck you" and all that. She's like, "Oh well, you can do that, 'cause you're young." That kinda destroyed me, too.

Nowadays, I would love to have a steady relationship, but in New York it's so hard. I find that the girls here won't give you the time of day unless you tell 'em you're doing something that's cool. If I meet a girl, it'll be like, "So what do you do?" "I work in a restaurant." "Oh, really? What a boring life, see ya." Don't you even want to take the time to find out what I'm about, how much I really know? But I guess when the right girl comes along, I'll see her for what she is, and she'll see me for what I am, and we'll make it happen. I date a lot.

Every time I meet a girl, I think about how cool it would be to spend a while with her. Dating seriously, hanging out all the time. That's the first thing that's on my mind, instead of just having sex. Yet and still, I found out that some girls, they use alcohol as an excuse. One glass of wine, "Oh, I'm tipsy, I might do something I'll regret for the rest of my life." Like say you're out drinking with a girl. Alcohol, man, alcohol makes you say shit that you wake up in the morning and you be like, Oh God, I can't believe I said that. Like this girl I went out with two weeks ago, her name is Kathy. We was out drinkin'. She has a friend who lives in Indiana. This friend is bad. I'm dying to have sex with her. I was like, "So what does Charlayne think of me?" Kathy was like, "Oh yeah, I threw some base for you." Like putting a good word in. I was like, "All right, cool." Next thing you know, the conversation got turned around. By this time the bar is closing out, and I'm not just a little drunk, I'm staggering like a motherfucker. I know what I'm doing, but—do you ever have that thing where you know what you're doing and you know it wouldn't be a good idea to do it, but you do it anyway? You keep going ahead, going through the motions. We started talking about sex, like how many people she had sex with, and how she liked it done. She was giggling, I was like, "I can do it better." She was saying she likes doggie-style, and I was like, "Ooo, I can party with you." I said that, and in the back of my mind was a voice [deep voice]: "Patrick, I think you should go home now." Next thing you know, I'm drifting, getting closer, getting ready to kiss her, and I peck her and I'm like, Oh wow, I just blew it. Because she didn't kiss me back. She just stood there. The back of my mind was telling me I shoulda went home and just kept this girl as a friend. Next thing you know, she's like, "Let me give you a better one than that." And she French-kissed me.

So we're walking home. She lives about five blocks from the bar. Walking down the street to her house, it was odd, because I knew what I was gonna do. Okay, I'm gonna have sex with her, and I don't know if I'm gonna call her up the next day, so should I end this right now and go home? I wanted to, but the little head starts thinking for the big head. So I'm like, Okay, chill. The voice was like [deep voice again]: "You shouldn't do this." But damn, she kisses really well. "It's a bad move." Well, I'll go ahead and see what happens. I might like her more than I like Charlayne. After I walked like two blocks, that voice was pretty much shot. [Laughs.] I saw myself shooting myself, like *Boom!* You die! And the devil was like, Party!

It's strange, before I have sex I have these weird thoughts. It's like watching a lava lamp happening in my head. I think about what I'm gonna do first, and how I'm gonna do it. What's the easiest way to get her clothes off? What's she wearing? Okay, a blouse, and jeans— jeans are hard when they're tight. Damn. She got boots on, too. Fuck, boots are bad, boots are really bad. Then I actually see myself going through the actions of having sex. I even have the music all set up. I'm gonna take the blouse off, I'm gonna take the bra off, I'm gonna caress her back and all that, rub her boobies, nibble on some boobie. Go down, prob'ly eat some bush. I was thinking of that, and it got funny to me, so I started laughing, 'cause I was like, If you only knew what I'm thinking, you wouldn't want me in your house. I don't think I'm perverted or nothin', I just think it's odd. I should be thinking, like, I'm gonna have sex with this girl for the first time, I should be really excited that she is willing to give me her love. But I'm like, Okay, what's the subtlest way I can get her to give me a blowjob?

We get there, walk up to the fourth floor. Walking up the stairs is pretty cool because she's in front of me, I'm watching her behind, and I'm like, Yeah! We get up there, we start kissing and necking and all that. I got the blouse and bra off, I managed to do that, but the jeans and boots, that's hard. So she did that herself. We're on her bed, it's not a regular bed, she's got a mattress on the floor. So I'm kissing her and eating her out, right, and she wants to turn the light off. I'm like, "No, don't turn it off." She's like, "Yeah, c'mon, please." I like to see what's going on. I even kiss with my eyes open, I like to see 'em close their eyes and go *Mmmmmmmm* [moaning noises]. So we came to a compromise where we lowered the light down really low. I'm eating her out, and she's pulling my hair and

pulling the sheets on the bed. I'm like, I'm gonna play with her for a
while. She's moaning, and I'm like, "Not now, I'm gonna do the job
with the tongue a little while longer." She's like, "No, no, no," so she
grabs me and pulls me up, turns me over, gets on top of me, and just
starts, *boom!* I was shocked, like, Oh, take me to the motherland,
baby! She's like "Aaaaahhhhh," and I'm screaming this and that, and
now it's almost like rough sex, because she sort of dropped me over,
and I'm like, No, I want it like this, so I turn her over and get on top
of her, and I'm doing the job and the next thing you know, she gets
up and she's like, "From behind, from behind!" I'm like fuckin'
Cowboy Bill. I get a kick out of doggie-style. I'm there and I'm just
swingin' her back and forth, right? She's like with her head down in
the pillow screaming, pulling the pillow, and I'm like, Oooooo. I have
this thing about quoting verses from songs. So I start singing this
song by Steel Pulse [sings]. She's like, "Oh yes oh yes oh yes," and I
pop, and I assume she came, she told me she did.

I put on a condom just before we had sex, when I was eating her
out. Which was pretty hard, I'm eating her out, and I'm stretched
out, I have my hand by the dresser trying to find the condom, knock-
ing some shit over on her dresser. I find the condom, look and see
what I'm doing, I'm sideways fiddling with the condom, I get it open,
and Goddamn, I put it on backward. [Laughs.] I had to stop at one
point to fix it, because I'm like, What's wrong? It won't go on. So I
flip it over and put it on. I have been in situations where I took
chances. Y'know, just saying, Well, I think she's clean. It's a gamble,
like Eddie Murphy says, playing craps with your dick. Like, "C'mon
sevens, c'mon sevens—oh shit, craps! My dick is gone!"

Actually, I took a chance with Kathy the second time. I took off
the condom and we did sixty-nine, and after we came out of that I
went back in and did the job. Then I was like, "Let me put on a condom." So I pulled out and put one on. But still, even if you take it off
for a split second, you can get something, right? So I'm kinda scared
about that. But I think she's clean. Usually, before I have sex, I sneak
in the sign of the cross. I'll move to the side, or while she's getting undressed, I'll be like, Father, Son, and Holy Spirit [furtively crosses
himself]. That's kind of a stupid way of trying to protect yourself, and

I'm not really a religious character, but sometimes you got to give it up to the Lord, man. [Laughs.] You got to talk to him every now and then. The next morning when I left her house, I was like, "Oh God, please don't let me have nothin', please please please." I be serious an' shit, too. People see me walkin' down the street, and I'm prayin', and people watchin' me like, Uh-oh, sick dude walkin' down the street.

The next morning I had to get out of there quick. I told her I had to be someplace at nine o'clock, which I didn't. It's odd, being at someone else's house, because you're pretty much in their control. That's why I like to have girls here, because it's my castle. Being at her house, waking up in the morning, what's gonna happen, she wants to cook me breakfast, but I'm like, "No, it's all right, I'll get a bagel down the road." I left, and I'm like, Phew. Damn. The voice in the back of my head got up, like reincarnated: "Did you enjoy it?" I did. And I told him, too. I was like, Yeah, I had a good time, 'cause I didn't listen to you. Party! [Laughs.] But still, I was like, I should have listened to you, because now I feel fucked up. I don't have many feelings for her. Is that really strange, for a kid my age to think like that?

I called her up three days afterward. I should have called her up the next day. 'Cause if I don't call her the next day, she prob'ly feel like, Oh wow, I did something wrong, here's another dog. They got too many brothers out there doin' it that way. But it's odd, when I call her up, all we talk about is, "Hi, how are you?" "Okay, I'm fine." "Yeah, so what are you doin'?" "Nothin'." "So you goin' out to-night?" "No, I'm stayin' home." "So how's work goin'?" "Oh, it's goin' alright." "Okay, well, I got somethin' on the stove, y'know, I'll give you a call later on in the week, see how you doin'." "Alright." "Okay, bye." Click. It's weird, it's a bad feeling, not being able to have no conversation afterward. It's like the relationship is just phys-ical, which is not cool at all. Even though it's prob'ly good for some people, to boost up their ego or whatever. But ego boosters, they don't happen. It's like doing crack—you're up for one minute, and then you're down, and you're wondering why.

So now I'm focusing on not just having sex, but trying to find somebody that's worth having sex with. That's prob'ly why the phone isn't ringing off the hook, but I guess a lot of brothers go through that. Because I'm getting old, I'll be twenty-one in two months. Got to find somebody to settle down with. I don't want to have kids right now, it's cool hanging out with the brothers and all that, but every man needs love.

EMMA KARSTEN

At sixty-eight, she is on her own for the first time since she was twenty. She is renting a pleasant but characterless furnished apartment in a new complex east of Los Angeles. Retired from a lifetime of work in the city bureaucracy, she has enough income to support herself, her photography hobby, and even some of her husband's bills. She is brassy, warm, humorous, with a big head of curly auburn hair and a "full figure," in the words of her latest personal ad.

"I was born in Wyoming. My parents divorced when I was six, and I've lived in California since the sixth grade. I grew up very poor in the Depression. My mother worked as a maid in a boardinghouse for a dollar a day. She was married five times and had numerous live-in boyfriends. She died of alcoholism and mental illness when she was fifty-nine. I left home at fourteen and went to work as a mother's helper. But I went to high school and married in the eleventh grade to a very illiterate man. That marriage lasted a year. I married my current husband when I was twenty. He was in the army. We both went to college after the war. I got a BA, he got a degree in education. It turned out I couldn't have children, so after eight years we adopted three kids."

* * *

I had a very difficult sexual adjustment in my marriage. My husband was quite shy, he was still a virgin. And I was very shy, too, even though I had been married. I had never practiced birth control other than withdrawal, and I was very antsy about getting pregnant. So we had a terrible sex relationship because I was so anxious. I was too bashful to be fitted for a diaphragm, and it was before the birth control pill. And I never even thought of condoms [laughs], it just never occurred to me. In retrospect, I've said to my husband, "You should have taken me by the elbow and *made* me go to the doctor and get birth control." But he retreated, and he would make noises at parties about "My wife always has a headache," or "My wife undresses in the closet." Well, I did undress in the closet, we had a wonderful apartment with dressing rooms. But I never had a headache. I was uptight about a lot of things, that's true, but he didn't do anything to make it any better. And when he would go out and tell everybody I always had a headache, that just turned me off all the more. I'm sorry for all those years that sex was terrible, it's an awful deprivation. But we both bear the blame. One of us should have walked away. We were in marriage counseling forever, and it never resolved anything.

Finally, when I was forty-seven, I decided I could not go on in the marriage the way it was. I had never had an orgasm. I was very prim and proper. So I asked around and found a support group for pre-orgasmic women that was just forming. There were twelve women, very diverse. The class went on for three or four months. It was a wonderful experience. By the time it was over, I had a lover.

He was an artist, hair down his back, tie-dyed clothes, the whole sixties bit. I met him at a church camp. He was my massage partner. Two minutes into the massage I knew I was lost. I thought, Oh God, this is my Waterloo, I know I'm going to have an affair with this man. The second night at camp, while his wife was in the rest room, he was giving me oral sex in the dark on the porch of our cabin. This man did not waste a second. He was very, very sexual. He was a man who could give me an orgasm just by running his hand down my arm. I had sex with him every Thursday for ten years. I sneaked away at my lunch hour and worked overtime to make it up. He gave me such a wonderful gift—he taught me how to have sex without feeling guilty or terrible or I'm a bad person. I learned to have sex and feel glorious.

After ten years, though, I got tired of his problems. I still see him, he's a good friend, but he turned out to be a mean, grumpy, ornery son of a bitch. I had a few other lovers over the years, and five months ago I left my husband. I don't know where the marriage will go from here. I'm happy living alone. It isn't that my life is so thrilling, although I guess it is compared to most women my age. I'm able to have friends and come and go as I choose and work on my photog-

raphy. I absolutely love it. Although I don't have a lot of sex compared to what my husband imagines. I may have four or five partners
in a week, and then no one for a month. Most of the men I know I
don't see very often. They're busy, they travel. I'm also not pushing.
I guess I'm afraid of intimacy. Very frightened of falling in love again.
I go to a therapist every month. She said, "What do you need me
for?" I said, "I want to know if I'm crazy at my age to be leaving my
marriage." She said, "As far as I'm concerned, I've never heard more
sane reasoning in my life. If all my patients were as sane as you, I'd
be out of business."

The men I've been seeing for the last year and a half, I met most
of them through want ads. I've run an ad maybe four or five times.
The first two ads, I had over ninety men answer. The last one, I had
sixty. I don't meet all the men who call—like of the sixty replies I met
twenty-six of the men. From those twenty-six, I had sex with four.
And I think there's only one I had sex with more than once. I'm looking for single men now. I don't want to be involved with married
men. I want someone who's available weekends. So it ends up most
of the men I see are in their thirties and forties. Very few are over
fifty. Most men over fifty are either married or workaholics or couch
potatoes who have no interest in sex. In order to have a sex partner
who has any juices flowing, you have to go to a younger man. People
think, Well, you're dating a younger man because he's cute, or he can
go all night. That's not it. You date a younger man because he asks
you. They're also a lot less inhibited about sex. But the reality is that
these relationships don't last a long time. I may see a man for three or
four months, maybe six, and there's not a strong emotional compo-
nent. But I never go to bed with men I don't really like. I have met
some super-nice people through want ads.

Just yesterday I had an experience with a man who's a painter and
lives in this grungy little apartment. We have marvelous phone sex
and he's a lovely man, really sweet. Yesterday was the first time I'd
seen him in person, and we had a good time, we tried bondage! I'd
never done that before. Really a trip. He hadn't either, so he was tentative about how it works. One day we were having sex on the phone
and he said, "I'm feeling really dominant, are you feeling submissive?" I said, "If you knew me better, you'd know I'm never submis-

sive." He said, "Well, you have to be submissive if you're gonna get to see me." We teased about that for a while. One day he left a message saying he wanted me to put on panties and bra and nothing else and come over with my coat on and surprise him. I was in a frightful mood that day so I didn't call back. But a few days later I called and left a message that I was feeling lewd and lascivious, and if he was still interested, I was. He called and said, "I'm still interested, can you come over? Just wear your panties and bra and coat and bring your vibrator. All the way over here I want you to be thinking of me and getting wetter and wetter. Then park your car and use your vibrator till you're really, really wet." This man is good. I don't know how long he's been playing this game, but he has this fantastic soothing voice and he's always very graphic and I get really turned on.

I went over there and he had bought a little piece of rope. He made up the sofa bed in front of the TV. He had some porno tapes. He tied me up, and I thought, I am insane to go to a strange man's apartment and let him tie my hands and feet. But he's always been so sweet on the phone, I just knew he'd be a lovely person. And I figured if he takes a meat axe and cleavers me, at least I'll have gone out in a blaze of curiosity.

He tied me spreadeagled on the bed with my panties and bra on. Then he used the vibrator on me until he drove me crazy. He took off my bra and sucked my breasts, which also drives me crazy, my breasts are my sensual area. I couldn't have an orgasm with my panties between me and the vibrator, but I was on the edge so long, and I was pulling on my hands and feet, so I got really tired. I asked him to untie me, and we cuddled and talked. He fixed me a glass of iced tea. Oh, and I gave him oral sex just before he untied me. He didn't have an orgasm, and he was embarrassed because he kept losing his erection. I think he was nervous, he kept saying, "Are you comfortable? Do your wrists hurt? Do your ankles hurt?" So we left it there and I went home. It was very sweet. I think we may do it again and go further.

I've had a lot of sexy experiences as a result of these ads. Another man, we met for coffee and he showed me a Polaroid picture of himself out in the backyard nude with a full erection. He's a tall, athletic man, works out a lot. He has a plumbing supply business in a warehouse. He invited me there once and said he'd do a striptease for me. He turned on the radio and climbed up on the table and did a complete striptease, down to fully nude. Then he made me get on the table and he stroked me and made love to me. We didn't have intercourse but he went down on me and I went down on him. It was very nice, very erotic. In fact, he came by Saturday. He's happily married, he doesn't have much time because he's very busy, so he came by and all he did was unbutton my blouse and play with my breasts and I played with his cock and then we kissed good-bye and he went home. It was lovely, I got a big bang out of that. It's like I'm making up for all my rigid teenage years. Nobody ever unbuttoned my blouse, nobody ever touched my breasts before I got married.

I get together with a doctor periodically. He's in residency, he's thirty-two, an interesting man. Very idealistic. Not great to look at, but a wonderful lover. He answers a lot of ads wherever he goes. He's just a delight. One of his favorite lovers is a lady he met through a want ad who weighs over three hundred pounds. He says she's great in bed. He and I have lots of sex play, I don't know if we've ever had intercourse. Lots of oral sex, and he's not averse to fingers in the anus or going around the world, things like that. Which surprises me in a doctor, I've heard that's a good way to pick up hepatitis. He does it to me, I wouldn't do that. I'll put a finger in, but I won't put my mouth on your anus, I think that's asking for problems. He's very oral, and he's gifted about knowing where to put his tongue. I guess he's got a good GYN background. We go for hours just exploring and licking and touching. He loves my breasts, loves to watch me use my vibrator. No great compulsion to have intercourse. That's one thing I'm noticing, I think sex is changing a lot. People are going a lot more to tactile stuff and a lot less to penetration. And a lot of men, young men even, are not that tied up in having an ejaculation. "Thanks, don't worry about it, it was great the way it was, next time we'll do that." A real rebuttal of the wham-bam-thank-you-ma'am kind of lovemaking. I think it's super.

I have learned not to be shy about my vibrator. A lot of people say, "Oh, you should never show a vibrator to your lover, he'll feel inadequate." I don't see that. It's just another sex toy, and most men get off on watching me have an orgasm with a vibrator. That's fine with me, because I really don't have an orgasm with just a partner. Even oral sex, I rarely have an orgasm. Even though I had that orgasmic training, I guess I wasn't their A-number-one student, although I certainly give them credit for changing my life.

I have sex with a seventy-four-year-old man who I've known a long time. His name is Carl. He was one of two men who gave me my only ménage à trois, for Valentine's two years ago. I think Carl is really bisexual, but he could never acknowledge that. He's very repressed. He likes to look at men's cocks, and I think it's really a sexual interest. He also has an interest in watching animals. There must be a farmer who advertises in some sexual magazine that you can go watch his animals mate, 'cause Carl showed me a roll of pictures he had taken at the farm. I said, "What are these!" He said, "Can't you see?" We used to have sex, but his main interest in me now is that he loves to play with my breasts, because his wife won't allow him to do that. In addition, he likes to look at women's genitals closely. So we get together and he touches me, he looks at me, but he doesn't ever put his cock inside me because he promised his wife he wouldn't have any more sex with other women. He'll put me under the lamp, examine me minutely. He may put his finger in and move my labia around, but he doesn't do more than that except play with my breasts. He thinks I'm the living end because I don't judge what he does. I couldn't care less, he can do anything he chooses, I'd still think he's a nice person.

I have a new ad in the paper right now because I'm sort of running out of men. This is the first ad where I ever admitted to being fat. It's also the first ad that gives my age. I say I'm over fifty. [Giggles.] On the phone I'm very clear about that, I say, "I'm in my fifties, I want you to know that before we have lunch," because I don't want to waste anyone's time. And my ad is one of the few from a woman that doesn't talk about marriage and commitment. Every man mentions that when I ask why he answered. "Well, you're very open, and you don't ask for commitment." I had a man who said to me the other day, and I thought this was really perceptive, he said, "Why in the world would any woman want to have a relationship or commitment with a man she didn't even know? I wouldn't have anything to do with a woman that dumb."

One thing I find hard is—well, women are supposed to peak when they're forty to forty-five years old. I just feel more sexual every year. It's a cruel trick of nature, suddenly you're seventy years old and you feel more sexual than you have your whole life, and there's no availability. Most women are much too shy to advertise. Most women live in a place where there's no place to advertise. I'm in a big city with all these Californians going to the devil. [Laughs.] And I must say, I'm obsessed with sex these days. If I don't talk to five or six men over a weekend—not necessarily to have sex with them, just talking on the phone—I get very depressed. It feels validating to call a man and talk for a bit. Maybe we'll get together, maybe not. Like this last week the doctor came over on Friday night, and we had lovely sex. He spent four or five hours here. He left his underwear, I don't know how he'll explain that to the lady he's living with. Saturday the plumbing supply man came over and we had this great breast play and cock play. Then Sunday I went to this tie-up session. And when I got home I called another man I see and talked to him for an hour. So I had a lot of male contact.

I used to feel so embarrassed about my body, but I don't think anything anymore about taking off my clothes. It's the most wonderful thing in the world, because I've battled my weight since I was about thirty. I never wanted to strip in front of anybody. Now I feel perfectly okay about it, no big deal. This is who I am, and if you don't like me that's too bad. I hear so many women say, "Oh, I can't have sex, I got so fat." What does that have to do with having sex? They think if they put on two pounds their lover will notice. Well, I don't think you do sex a service by pretending it's a time you're showing off your body or your beauty. Sex is just when two spirits meet. It has nothing to do with how you look. It may be a shock the first time you see someone, maybe they're not what you expected, but if they're a beautiful person I never again notice what they look like. Men probably don't think that way, because all the ads say, "I want an attractive woman, slender," blah blah. But I noticed if I answer their ads, they're very grateful because they don't get many replies. Obviously they've intimidated the whole population by asking for these exquisite women. Hardly anybody is *Playboy* pretty. What does that have to do with real life?

I have my bad times, certainly. I feel bad that out of the sixty replies to my last ad, none of them turned into a relationship. I've gone out with young men—not often, but occasionally—who feel like I've sold them a bill of goods in my ad, and they get snotty and walk away. Those things hurt, but I'm not gonna let one rotten person spoil my outlook. I still have five or six long-term men I really like. That's what infuriates my husband. He's had sex with three or four people in his lifetime. He says to me, "I feel so cheated. All these years you didn't want to have sex, you were cold, and I had nothing. Now you're so sexual. I want to know—how did that happen? I can't believe you turned from night to day!" Well, I spent twenty-five years working on this problem. It didn't just happen, it was a lot of hard work. I just feel so happy, I think it's a miracle. He thinks I'm a hooker handing out her calling card, but I don't consider my relationships just flings. I consider them to be human relationships. Men and women are sexual. I feel sorry for all the women I know who don't have any men in their lives, who are much younger and better-looking than I and haven't had a cup of coffee with a man in twenty years. The world is full of people afraid to ask for what they want. I feel like, if you don't ask for it, it won't happen. If it's important, you better look to yourself to provide it, because no one else is gonna do it for you.

2

WILD OATS

T O B E S I N G L E , traditionally, was to inhabit the stage before marriage during which you "got it out of your system"—if
you were a man, that is. Women were not supposed to have anything
in their systems except instincts for motherhood and monogamous
love. That began to change in the 1950s, with the mass movement of
young women into the cities; and Helen Gurley Brown's 1962 best-
seller, *Sex and the Single Girl,* both documented and celebrated the
trend. Now women, too, were allowed their stretch of independence
and sexual browsing before settling down.

But singlehood (revealingly, there is no good noun for it that covers both sexes, *bachelorhood* being the province of men) actually
takes many shapes these days. Besides the youthful years before marriage, people may spend years being single *between* marriages, or
they may stay single for life after a divorce. Or they may never marry.
And though lifelong bachelorhood is still acceptable while "unmar-
ried women" are pitied, that, too, is changing. At least in urban areas,
single motherhood is an increasingly acceptable option, and the
phrase *old maid* has an archaic ring.

The interviews in this chapter can be divided into two groups.
Billy Hasser, Sally Laughlin, and James Atkins, all thirty or under, are
singles in the classic sense: they seem headed for marriage and are

stretching their wings along the way. Matt Sherrill, Judith Rothstein, and Wayne Corvallis, ranging from early to late middle age, seem likely to stay single and seem reasonably content with that.

Otherwise, contentment is not much in evidence here—but then, sowing wild oats, either temporarily or permanently, is not supposed to be about contentment. It is about newness. Nearly all these speakers, faced with the intimacy/distance divide, come down on the side of distance. Only Billy, the farmboy whose one serious girlfriend broke up with him ten months before our talk, laments that his best sex happened when he was in love.

The purest expression in this book of the distance-is-hot position comes, surprisingly, from a woman, Judith: "There's nothing like the excitement of the first night. The newness, the strangeness. Once you know somebody, they're human. But that first time, you're not a human being. You're a faceless fuck. You can make up for it later with emotion and love and tricks and all, but nothing can compare with that first night with a stranger."

Other speakers have different ways of keeping their distance. Wayne, the bachelor swinger, likes intimacy up to a point, and he freely uses the word. He has been seeing the same woman every week for six or seven years—but she is married to someone else. James is a conoisseur of his lovers' sexual tastes, but he always keeps more than one affair going. Sally has her best sex with men who are plainly not marriage material. And Matt, the gay man who describes a phantasmagorical night in the baths, makes an art of "electric sex" with strangers or "fuckbuddies"—a quintessentially gay form of relationship.

Again with the exception of Billy, who seems the most conflicted, all these people know what they like, though they can't always find it. They describe their sex in sharp detail. They also pine, vaguely or poignantly, for what they don't have: security, companionship, love. Distance has its rewards—and its price.

BILLY HASSER

For three generations his family has farmed seven hundred acres in south-ern Illinois. He comes from German Catholic stock, as does nearly every-one he grew up and went to school with. "It was a public school, but it was all Catholics," he says. "They let us out two study halls each week to go to religion class—off the school grounds but right across the street." His parents have been married for forty years; he has six brothers and two sisters. The family is known as one of the most prosperous in the region. He lived on the farm for twenty-three years, before moving away a year ago to "finish up school" at a state college nearby. Now he looks forward vaguely to a job "in sales." We meet in the suburban apartment he shares with two classmates. The walls of his room are plastered with posters fea-turing bikini-clad women advertising various brands of beer.

"Mom and Dad don't show a lot of affection, but they're very caring, you can tell that, and they get along excellent. They hold hands, kiss ev-ery once in a while in front of the kids, but other than that—well, they had to work as a team on a big farm. Mom was probably eight months pregnant and still out milkin', just to give you an example of how hard they had to work. But they're not homebodies, they like to go out. When I was young, they'd go out every Friday and Saturday to polka dances, or out to eat. Or they'd go on two-day trips when the kids got old enough to take care of the farm.

"I had a very happy childhood. I worked a lot, but I like the outdoors. And there's nobody in my family that doesn't get along. Honestly, it's amazing. The way I picture my family is trying to be the perfect family, but underneath we're not. We're not morally perfect, but you keep up the image that you are, that's all that matters. That's what the farm family is like. It's a good life—the community is great, you go into town to pick up food, you see friends every day, they come over and help you farm, you go over and help them farm. It's a pure part of America. It's what America should be."

• • •

I can remember when I was thirteen saying, Jesus Christ, there is no way I'm ever gonna kiss girls. There is no way I'm ever gonna do *anything* with a girl. I thought it was totally wrong, and I was going to be Mr. Straight all through high school, the good little kid that Mom and Dad thought I was. Well, by sixteen I was having sex already. Me and my brothers were all pretty promiscuous, I guess. Every one of us but two was voted the class flirt, including me. Like I graduated with a 1.98 average, and I know why—when I turned fifteen all I was worried about was my social life. I didn't know what I wanted to do. I was bouncing ideas back and forth, kept changing my program. I was in Future Farmers of America for like a million years. Quit that. Then I just fucked off my entire last year 'cause I knew I was going in the National Guard. I had a good time, and I'd do it over again. Being popular and getting along with people is more important than good grades, I think. So there's no regrets.

When I was fourteen, fifteen, my cousin—who didn't even have his license yet—we'd go up to Silverwood, and for some reason, there were ten or eleven Silverwood girls who were hot after us. I swear, I made out with every one of them. Which is strange, to look back— we'd go to parties, and you could just sit on the couch and make out in front of people. I can't even kiss a girl in public now. Then I had my first date with one of those girls. I had just turned sixteen. I brought her back to her house, and I had a great big car, a Monte Carlo, and we were in the front seat, and she more or less asked me to boink her. We were making out, I had my hands down her pants, and I wanted to eat her out. I thought most girls want that, y'know, so I said, "Well, what do you want me to do?" She just nodded her head, she goes, "Yeah." I knew what she wanted. I was like, Jesus Christ, this is my first date, what am I getting myself into? So I said, "No, I don't think so." I just finger-banged her and she gave me a hand job, and that was it. After that, I thought, Boy, did I fuck up. I really should have. To this day I wish I would have.

The first girl I had sex with, I was sixteen—it was funny, there were three girls I would take back and forth to band practice. And depending who was the last girl I dropped off, that was the one I got hold of. They all knew what was going on. This one girl, whose name was Mary, she would be the last one I dropped off nearly all the time 'cause she was hot, really good-looking. There was this road called Robinson Road, we'd always go park there. And we would do freakin' everything, she didn't care, we'd do everything but fuck. It would be like her pants down to her knees, my pants down to my knees. Shirt unbuttoned, and the bra off. That was it—taking clothes off, you didn't cross that line. Then in August they had the big festival in Xavier, that's my hometown, where everybody goes and gets drunk. I saw Mary and I said, "Meet me at the car at twelve o'clock." We drove out to Robinson Road, and we were gettin' it on, and I just wanted to experiment a little bit. I thought, Okay, I'll put it in once, no big deal, it's not really sex. Well, you know, it just didn't stop at puttin' it in once. We had sex, it was her first time and my first time. No birth control, I pulled it out, which wasn't really that successful. And we didn't have sex again until a year and a half later. I didn't even want to speak to her for a while. I felt damn guilty 'cause I used her, I really did. It was like I crossed that line. Also I was lookin' at her as a big disappointment in my life, I was like, Dammit, I did it. I was gonna wait till I got married.

Just to go on with that Mary story, we ended up going out later for like two years. We just broke up ten months ago. I thought I wanted to marry this girl. But back in those days I had a chance to go out with so many girls, I didn't want to date just one person. I mean, by the time I was twenty years old I had not boinked, but had made out with probably seventy-five different girls. That's not braggin', just statin' the facts. In my whole life I've had sex with maybe twelve, and three of them were since Mary and I broke up, those are probably—what's the term?—revenge fucks. Revenge for her breakin' up with me. Didn't make me feel any better, though. She's engaged now. Bitch! [Laughs darkly.]

I could kick myself in the ass, too, for what I did in high school. I dated so many nice girls. Two, three dates and that was it. So many nice girls—I mean, I'd just love to be married to one of them, but they're married to somebody else now, all because I didn't want to date anybody back then. I've only dated two serious girls in my whole life, and they fucked me over, both of 'em, so maybe God's punishing me for all the fuckin' around I did.

The first one was Linda. I went out with her for nine months. I was a senior, she was a junior. We never even slept together, that's what was really amazing. I really cared about her, and she was a virgin. I had in my plans to marry her, but she was too young and I was too young. I didn't push sex very hard, and we did everything, I mean *everything* but. We got out of the parking stage, we either went back to her house or mine. Downstairs we have a huge fixed-up basement—it's funny, I get on people if they treat that couch bad. I'm like, "It's a family heirloom, you don't know how many girls have been fucked on that couch by seven brothers." But Linda and I didn't cross that line. Then after I graduated, I went away to basic training, and when I came back I found out she had slept with like eight guys.

After that I'd be with girls—it got to the point, like if I had sex with a girl I wouldn't speak to her again. Which is terrible, but that's how it was. I wasn't ashamed, but I felt guilty, I guess, I put the blame on me. Plus I was afraid they'd be pissed at me, so if I didn't acknowledge 'em, I wouldn't have to acknowledge the fact that we had sex. I tell you what, it was pretty much the old thing, the wham-bam-thank-you-ma'am type. I didn't care about 'em at all. The next morning you wake up and you remember, and you have mixed feelings, like, Boy, that was all right. But then: God damn, another couple of months worrying about whether she got pregnant. Early on it was morals, but later it turned into, I'm gonna fuck up my life here real soon.

All this while Mary was going out with another guy, but there came a time about two years ago that she had just broken up, and I eased my way in there. She was the first girl I ever made love to—that's a big difference to me, having sex and making love. You've got the animalistic, and then you've got Mary. After the second time we had sex, that's when we said we loved each other, and from then on it was great every time. She was in college, so I'd go spend the night with her, or she'd come home—it was just great, we could have sex for hours. And it was mature sex, we weren't taking advantage of each other. I didn't care about myself at all. I didn't care if I got off, just so she did. Or after we both had one, I was like, I want to give you another one. But probably the biggest thing was that I didn't feel guilty, 'cause I knew I loved her. I didn't have to justify anything, it was just natural. After a year I didn't even worry about getting her pregnant, I was like, if it ever happens we'll get married.

She was great in bed, she probably knew more than what I did, which was amazing. She was in control, she knew what she wanted. Like different positions, and she knew how to give herself an orgasm. Being on top—we would start out and she would be on the bottom, and we'd have sex until I came. Then we'd just roll over and we'd have sex until she came. That was the only way she could. She had like a G-spot, I swear she did. Once she'd go on top she would find her spot, and she'd go to town, God. She was just amazing, she was so involved, she was so into herself. You know that scene in *Basic Instinct,* when the killer was on top? It was exactly like that. Except the killing part. She never did kill me, though she'd probably like to. I'll never have an experience like that again. Well, maybe, but I doubt it.

One night we had sex like thirteen times, I couldn't believe it. She probably had like eight orgasms. Three bottles of wine, a hotel room. . . . We took a vacation, we went down to an amusement park. Spent the weekend away from everybody, roommates, family—phew, it was total abandonment. She was like the sweetest little girl you'd ever meet, she was beautiful, petite, came from a good family, and she seemed so innocent outside, but you got her in bed and she was just an animal. Very, very passionate. I guess that's every guy's thing, a girl that acts like an angel through the day and behaves like a slut at night. When they're a slut by day and a slut in bed, that's nothing, they're a dime a dozen.

Then, I don't know, there were a lot of problems. At first I was totally in control, but gradually she got in control, and all of a sudden I was so involved that she had complete control. She had me. Whatever she wanted to do, she could do. She said I wasn't assertive enough. Like she'd say, "Billy, where do you want to go tonight?" And I'd say, "I don't care, wherever you want." And then she got so fucking independent—she went to Mexico for a semester abroad, I was going to propose to her when she got back, and she met another guy there. I was calling her and saying, "Look, if your feelings aren't the same, I just want to know." She's like, "No, Billy, I just don't know what I want." Then she comes back and tries to be with this other guy at the same time. And ten months later they get engaged.

Now I date girls but my mind is still with Mary. I love her and I can't even think about dating anybody serious. Like this past year I boinked these three sleazeballs back home. The first one, she was only eighteen, nineteen, she had a really bad rep, but she was as cute as could be, and I thought maybe she was just gettin' a rep. So I took her out twice to give her a little bit of respect, I treated her like a queen, I thought maybe that would snap her out of it. I took her out to eat and I didn't touch her. Well, I tell you what, this girl didn't want that. She wanted to be treated horrible. One night I took her home, I'm sittin' on her couch, and she's like, "I'm gonna go change clothes, I'll be back." She comes out in just a T-shirt, and she grabs my hand and says, "Come back here." I'm like, "No," because her bedroom was right opposite her mom and dad's. She's like, "Well, we can hear my dad snoring, and my mom's always awake, but she doesn't care." I figured, what the hell. But she was horrible in bed, probably the worst. I actually tried to make love to her. I tried to show her—not that I loved her, but I wanted to act like I did. She didn't want any part of that. She wanted to be boinked and that was it. I tried to take it slow, not just get on her like a rabbit, ask her what she wanted, and man, she didn't want any of that slow stuff, she was like, "Fuck me hard." She wanted me to hold her arms down, stuff like that. I'm not mean when I have sex with somebody, and that did not turn me on at all. I'm surprised she never suggested tying me up, I'm serious. Other than that, it was like nothing. She'd lie down, I'd lay on top of her and it was just boinking. I'd be done, we'd put our clothes on, and she was happy with that.

The next girl—my brother had a graduation party at our house, a big party. I was home for the weekend. I said, "Ethan, are there any women out there for me?" He said, "I don't know, they're pretty young." I was kind of kidding around anyhow. I went out to the keg, and Ethan comes up and goes, "Billy, just stay here, Erika may want ya." I'm like, Okay. Erika comes up, she's a senior in high school, she puts her arm around me, and I look at her and say, "Are you horny?"

She goes, "Yeah, a little." I ended up taking her in the hayloft, it was funny, she gave me a blowjob up there. I was fingerbanging her, nothing big, but we were up there for an hour, and when we got down everybody was gone. I had to take her home, which I was not very happy about, and on the way she's like, "Billy, I'm still horny." I'm like, "Well, I kind of am too." So we parked and she gave me a blowjob like forever, man, and she was not very good, really rough. I think I ate her out, too. It's sad, I'll tell you, because I got gonorrhea from her. I never in my wildest dreams imagined I'd get VD. I didn't even boink her, but she gave me a blowjob, and I guess the gonorrhea can stay in your mouth. She didn't want me to boink her, maybe she knew she had gonorrhea, who knows. She certainly wasn't a virgin. She was a slut, she had a rep, I knew that for a fact. And of course she didn't have an orgasm. Of all the girls I had, I can think of only two that ever had an orgasm. Maybe I didn't do it long enough. With her I stopped because I wanted to, you can only eat a girl out for so long, right? Girls are fuckin' weird, I don't even know why they want to have sex. Some girls have sex all the time, and you know damn well they don't have an orgasm, there's no way. They probably don't even know what one is. I don't understand that. Why do they have sex in the first place?

This girl I had about two weeks ago—I kind of like this girl, I might take her out. I went out with one of my friends and these three sisters. Veronica is the youngest, she's twenty. She asked me to take her home, and the bar was only two miles from my house, and I had to get some gas. So we got home and I said, "Do you want to come in for a while?" We go down to the basement, she's sitting on the couch, and I turn the TV on. I was just gonna lay my head in her lap to watch TV, seriously, that's all I was gonna do, but she starts making out with me. I was thinking, What the hell. So I lay down with her. She got down my pants first and gave me a hand job. Then I got down her pants and started fingerbanging her. I was actually only gonna eat her out, and when I pulled her pants down she told me she wanted to get her panties off. That's a key, if they want their panties off. So we started having sex, and I stopped myself and said, "Do you want me to wear a rubber?" She goes, "Well, it's a little late, isn't it?" I said, "No, I'll get one." So I went and got one and we finished having sex. She didn't have an orgasm. This sounds bad, it sounds like I'm bad in bed or something. But that was it. She wanted to leave and I was like, "Stay here and lay with me for a while." So she did, and I said, "This is the best part of having sex." She goes, "You know what, this is kind of scary, but I agree."

I didn't feel bad about that one afterwards, 'cause she kind of instigated everything. I mean, she apparently wanted it. Not that all the girls I was with didn't, but she wasn't naïve, that's the big thing. She knew. Whereas the girls who never had sex before, I felt like I took advantage of them. Anyway, I kind of like Veronica, she's cute, though she's got a bad rep, too, which I'm sure she deserves, and you can't take a girl out that's got a bad rep. If you take her out on a date, and you're seen out in public, then everybody knows you were with this girl, and everybody looks down on you. I'll only date a girl if there's a possibility of me getting married to her, and I definitely ain't gonna marry a girl that's got a bad rep. I couldn't trust her, for one thing.

Course, I have a bad rep too, God. Even my brothers—I tried to live up to my older brothers' reputation as ladies' men, which I guess I did. We still call each other up and tell stories, but I should shut my mouth. 'Cause they call me a real slut. They think I'm scum. They call me "sleazeball," and they figure if I'm with a girl I boinked her. I'm like, "No, I didn't boink her," and they're like, "We know better than that." That pisses me off, I've got this rep I can't get rid of. Whatever happened to me going out with Mary for two years and I never cheated on her?

I wish—I wish—if my life was planned the way I wanted it to be, I would have gotten married at eighteen. I wanted to get started with my life, know what I mean? I'm twenty-four years old, I'm not dating anybody, I just wasted—well, not wasted, but I just spent two years of my life in a relationship and now I'm out on my own. I feel like I should be grown up by now. I have a cousin my age, he owns a big farm, a big house, I'm sure it's paid for, he's married, got a kid on the way, and where am I? I don't know why I can't find a nice girl. I'm really questioning that. Where the fuck are they? Back home they're all taken. And down here—nobody knows I've got a rep around here, but it's hard for me to meet girls. We don't have any background. It's not like with girls back home, you know their sisters or their brothers or where they're from. How do you approach a girl down here? I'm not shy, but what do you fuckin' say?

Sometimes I think sex plays too large a part in my mind. If I could take a pill to get rid of it, I probably would. I just want to find a girl I can get married to and have sex whenever I want and it's legal. That's not the only reason I want to get married, but that's part of it. After a while I'm sure it's gonna get old, but it'd be neat if sex didn't carry that much weight. Because it interferes with everything.

Like with that last girl, Veronica—I guess if I didn't have sex with her I'd feel a hell of a lot better about taking her out. Then there's nothing hanging over your head, it's just, You and me are friends, and we didn't do anything wrong. All the wholesome feelings you're supposed to have in a relationship—friendship and trust and caring, the whole bit. With Veronica, it's already climaxed in one night. Nothing to look forward to. I done experienced the greatest thing with her, except maybe better sex. Even afterward—funny, we were talking and I said, "I'm really sorry I was so bad in bed." 'Cause I came fairly quick, not like *bam* but she hadn't orgasmed. She goes, "Don't even talk about it." I'm like, "What?" She goes, "I'm embarrassed, I barely even know you." And I thought, You're fuckin' right—you barely know me, and you just had sex with me. Boy, you should have thought of that about ten minutes ago.

SALLY LAUGHLIN

She is twenty-four, about to start graduate school in social work, sharing an apartment in Washington, D.C. She was raised nearby in an upper-middle-class suburb, her father a partner in a big law firm, her mother a housewife until the kids were grown and now a computer expert at a brokerage firm. "I grew up pretty normal, except I don't think I had a very happy childhood. My mother was depressed most of the time. She has always been the martyr type. When I was thirteen I was convinced she was going to divorce Dad any day, because she obviously hated him. It was a rude awakening for me to realize, Wait a minute, she's going to stay with him. When I was about fifteen she happened to tell me that she and my father had gone two years once having no sex. They weren't very affectionate—a cursory peck maybe once a day, either hello or good-bye.

"I had all kinds of information about the logistics of sex, from my mom. I always knew what was involved in making a baby. I knew about my period long before it was going to come. I feel like I was prepared for all that." But two events in her adolescence marred her sex life for years. Her sister got pregnant at sixteen and had an abortion, much to the horror of her parents. "She swore to them she had been using a diaphragm. I found out at twenty-one that no, she hadn't put the diaphragm in. I was furious with her. I was like, 'Angie, do you know how scared I have been about contraception because of you?' I was convinced you would get pregnant the minute you had sex." The other, more serious, trauma was sexual abuse at the hands of a foster brother who came to live with the family when Sally was thirteen. "He was eighteen, and he hated me. I don't remember exactly when it started, maybe three months after he moved in. Basically what he would do was, if I were studying on my bed, he'd come in and get on top of me, and hold my hands back, and say, 'Try to move your hands, Sally, try to move your hands.' All clothes on, he never undressed me. Then he would hump me until he ejaculated into his pants. For a while I didn't realize what he was doing. I would tell my par-

ents about it, but my father didn't have much of a response, and my mother's was to talk to my brother and try to get him not to do it. After two years they said to him, 'If you ever touch her again, you're out of the house.' That's how it finally got okay."

• • •

In high school I liked kissing a lot, but I didn't really want to do anything else. I didn't mind boys groping around my shirt and I didn't mind kissing, so that's what I did. By my junior year I made up my mind that I needed to learn how to perform oral sex, figuring, bright as I was, if I did that they weren't going to bother me too much. High school boys are easily pleased. So I did a very interesting thing. I have this best friend Dennis. We had dated and kissed some, nothing else, but there was some sexual energy. When I was a junior and he was a sophomore, sometime when my parents were away I invited him over. I got him kind of drunk, and I was like, "I'm going to perform oral sex on you to figure out what to do. You teach me." I still can't believe I got him to go along with it. He didn't come, but I totally learned. What he told me was, don't ignore the balls. Touch them, lick them, suck them. People love that. I was like, okay, cool. And he told me basically to let myself go. Lick, don't bite. He told me each person was going to have a particularly sensitive spot on their penis, so listen for the big response and go for that. And don't suck. The point is not to suck. I thought you sort of nurse on the thing until it comes, and you get what you were sucking for. He knocked that thought out of my head pretty quickly, and it was good he did.

The next boy I did it with—I swear, I was like, Let me see if I've learned this right. Well, for the next year and a half he would follow me around like a puppy. "You're the most incredible person I have known in my life, you're the smartest thing in the world, you're the most beautiful." I'm like, "Yeah, yeah."

Then I went off to college. I was very afraid I was no longer going to be able to say no to sex. I finally had sex in my sophomore year, and I slept with a couple of other guys in college, but the sex never felt very good. After college I moved back to D.C. and met one of my old boyfriends, the first guy I kissed, in seventh grade. He and I promptly fell in love for two months. He was the first man I ever had an orgasm with. I masturbated in front of him. First I made him do it in front of me. He was like, "Well, okay." He did, and then I did. I was very embarrassed. But I wanted to have orgasms with a man, and I felt like I ought to, and after all I was in love with this man, and so in my script he had to be the first person I had an orgasm with. After that we used to work it out so I could masturbate while we had sex. It was decent sex, it was fun and good, but it only lasted two months.

Then I met another guy, Alvin. He was completely different—he was black, from a welfare background, had been in jail, had pulled himself up by his bootstraps. He was street-smart and no-nonsense, and very sexual. I remember one night we went out dancing, and we had sex three times before we went out and four times after. And he's like thirty-two, it wasn't like he was eighteen or something. One night I stripped for him, to music. He was the first person who used to fantasize out loud to me about what it looked like, what we were doing. He'd say things like, "You're so hot, you're gorgeous, you're so sexy," while we were having sex. That was fun. Alvin was the beginning of me realizing that not only could I have sex, but I could probably have really good sex. I think I'm a very—a fairly sexual person, and Alvin was when I thought, Yeah, I've got a lot of energy in this area that has been cut off.

Back then I was living in a big apartment with a lot of roommates. After I broke up with Alvin I had a few one-night stands, and then, in August of that year, one of my roommates had a friend over named Mikey. About seven or eight of us sat around having a big talk about what's good for each of us sexually. All the women were dying to have sex with Mikey after this talk. There was a self-assurance about him that dared us all, we were like, All right, put your cards on the table if you think you're this great. He talked about liking to try a lot of positions, and liking to work it out so the woman could masturbate, because that's a good thing for women to do. We all perked up our ears to that. There was one woman who definitely wanted to sleep with him, and I was like, No, I'll sleep with him. You won't. And I did. It was a lot of fun. I went down on him, and he was like, "Wow, I haven't had good head in a while. That was real good." I'm like, Cool, my trick works. [Laughs.]

Mikey and I ended up going out for a year. He was interesting, he was Italian, working-class background, had this shaggy hair cut short in front and long in the back, which where I grew up, it would be like, That's disgusting. He was the same about me, like, Oh my God, she wears her hair long and stringy, and she wears these dresses that aren't dressy, and she never wears tight jeans and midriff tops and she doesn't foof her hair out. We had this cultural barrier. But he was cute, and he was good in bed. Sex was it, that was what we had. After we slept together a couple more times, I broached the subject of a relationship. We decided, yeah, we'll go out and be a couple. But from the beginning it was great sexually and not working any other way.

Mikey and I would fantasize, fantasize, fantasize. If we didn't have much time but we wanted to be sexual, okay, we'd both masturbate, and we'd help each other out, like, "What do you want to hear about? Want to hear about us having sex in the park? Okay, I'm in the park. . . ." And we'd just get each other off. We'd talk about doing it in public, or me going down on him in restaurants. My favorite thing to do while masturbating was to go down on him, and he'd tell me a fantasy. Usually I'd be on my back, because I prefer masturbating lying on my back, with my head turned to the side and him in my mouth. He wasn't really fucking my mouth, it was more like it felt good on my tongue and my lips. In that situation the point was for me to get off, so whatever I wanted to do to his penis was cool. Sometimes, if we were really in a hurry, I'd stimulate a breast with one hand, masturbate with the other, suck him, listen to him talk . . . [Laughs.] How to have sex in sixty seconds. Then usually what I'd do is kiss him or suck on his balls while he masturbated, and he'd get off.

As far as Mikey is concerned, there should be a shrine to me somewhere about how I give head. He was like, "God, I'll have this etched in my memory." We had one game—this was one of those things where I'd go, Don't even think about it, Sally, if it turns you on it's okay. We'd pretend he was my uncle and I was his little niece, like thirteen, fourteen. And my gift, like, "Uncle has a present for you"—i.e., he's going to come on you. Or in you. This was the prize, the wonderful thing that's going to happen—he's going to come in my mouth. Ahhhh. Or he'd come to babysit, and we'd play this real fun game. I'd sit on his lap and find—"What's this thing? Can I play with that? You let me last time." He'd be like, "Well, I'm not sure if we should do that." I'd be like, "Please, I really liked it. Didn't I do a good job last time? Wasn't it fun?" I'd pout if he wasn't going to let me, because it was the best toy, and it does that really fun thing after you play with it for a while. He used to love it when I would lick him while I looked at him, so I would do that as the niece: "Am I doing it right?"

Oh, it felt great, I really got into that role. It felt like all this energy I had that was so new, and somehow endless. Which I think is how my sexuality felt to me at fourteen. When I was in the fantasy, I felt, Yeah, I have this wonderful person to share it with, he lets me do anything, he does lots of fun things to me, he loves me, he's my uncle. [Laughs.] And I'm his special little girl. It's about being able to go as far as I want, and never finding myself saying, "Shouldn't we do this from the chandelier?" and someone going, "You've got to be kidding. You think of fucking from the chandelier? That's disgusting!" Like my current boyfriend, Greg—I think I'm more sexual than Greg. It's like he wants to make love and I want to fuck. [Laughs.] The people who I've had the greatest sex with are Alvin and Mikey, who were both so sexual, and were willing—like, anywhere I wanted to go, they would go. And they took me places and it was fine.

There was one problem with Mikey—he didn't perform oral sex on me as much as I wanted. I did it all the time for him because he loved it so. I found out at the end that it's not something he likes to do all that much. I was like, "Jesus, Mikey, you could have just told me, then it would have been a little easier." It wasn't until toward the end that I started counting it up. He did it maybe three or four times. One of which was incredible. We'd broken up for a while and he invited me to go to a New Year's Eve party in New York. I flew up, wearing this teeny dress and spike heels. We went to this party, and the whole night, being around one another but not being able to have sex, and he was so into me, he would stroke me and touch me and hold me. Then we went—it was a warm New Year's Eve, and we went to the roof of this place. There was a view of the Twin Towers. I went down on him, with him leaning against a wall and me kneeling. Which he told me looked wonderful, and I'm sure it did in this outfit. I took his penis out of his pants—I used to do that a fair bit, in odd places. I'd tease him, I'd be like, "No, it's mine. It's not yours. I get to touch it anytime I want." So I'm kneeling in my dress and spike heels, and after he came I didn't even expect him to go down on me, because that's not usually what he did. I thought maybe we'd have sex. But we're on this roof, and other people are coming up there off and on. Then he started lifting up my dress, and I said something like, "No way, Mikey, you're going down on me?" He was like, "Yeah." I stood up, he was kneeling, and this dress is so small and tight—you just squinch it up a bit and it stays there. He pulled down my stockings, I'm not sure if I was wearing underwear—that's another thing I would do with him. The feeling of it—oh, when he would go down on me, he would go down on me well. I remember the feeling of my fingers in his hair, my back against the wall, and there was this heater blowing, this exhaust thing, so it was warm enough, and staring at the World Trade Center. . . . And he was very good at switching from one thing to another just when the first thing was getting a little too much. The best oral sex for me is a lot of stimulation in different ways, and then when I'm close to coming, just having my clit sucked on a little bit, and then I come. He did that. God, it was good, I haven't done anything like that in a while.

You could play this tape for Greg—it's funny, because it wouldn't even work. It's so strange how with some people the emotional stuff is important and with some people it isn't. Greg could never do that to me, that way of going wild on my body. Mikey would forget I was there, and I liked that, 'cause I'd forget he was there, too. He was never concerned with, How is Sally taking this? How does she feel about me? Does she feel I'm objectifying her? Mikey never thought about that stuff. It was like, My God, you're so hot. And just pawing me all over and kissing me and devouring. Being overcome with what he wanted to do to me, and just doing it.

Fucking was great with Mikey, I loved it. Fucking with Mikey—first, it was interesting because he always wore a condom. Early on I was like, "No, come on, don't you stop doing this eventually?" Then I found out it was absolutely no. He was going to use condoms the whole time I was with him even if we were monogamous. He was like, "Look, I'm going to be out there in the world for years and years. I've gotten used to wearing condoms, and it's really hard to go back and forth. Once you get used to doing it without, you don't want to start wearing them again. So I'm just gonna stick with it." I couldn't believe it, but after a while I actually liked the break, when he'd get up—because the condoms were always by his bureau. He'd hand me the condom and I was supposed to open it. I always liked the moment when he put it on. He was very good with condoms, he put a little bit of KY Jelly on the inside and a little bit on the outside. I guess it improved how much it would move around on him. And it was great to have KY on the outside, because that's one of my biggest problems with condoms, I tend to get sorer quicker.

So there would be this moment—he gets up, we put the condom on, this moment of anticipation. This point when I knew he was going to come back and start fucking me. He was incredible about teasing me, even before getting the condom on. I mean, there is no way—if I'd been him, we would have been fucking, but he was able to not go ahead. I'd be yelling at him and clawing. He'd go put the condom on, and sometimes I'd say, "Tease me more when you get back." I'd arch my body in such a way that he'd have to go in, and he'd be like, "No, no," and I'd be like, "God damn it, stop it!" I loved every minute of it.

When we'd start fucking we'd usually drop whatever fantasy we were in. Maybe if we were doing uncle and niece, I'd say, "What else can you do with this nice toy?" He'd be like, "Well, there is this special place I can put it. It feels really good." "Oh, does it?" Then we'd start having sex and we'd lose the fantasy because you get to where it becomes speechless. We'd start out having sex in a pretty traditional way, him on top, and from there we'd go through four or five different positions each time we had sex. Like spoons, or me on top, or him on top of me with us stomach-down. Sometimes the exact reverse, with me on top of him looking up at the ceiling. That's a fun position, I like that one, maybe because I usually masturbate lying on my back, so it's like, Oh, this is much nicer than the bed under me.

I'd almost always have a few orgasms, but only once in my life have I been what I think is technically multiorgasmic. From that book *Our Bodies, Ourselves,* I realized I'd been using the term wrong.

Multiorgasmic isn't when you have one orgasm, pause, and then another. It's just orgasming continuously. You stop when you can't breathe, you're dehydrated, you're exhausted. Well, I was dating two guys at the same time, and it was the most sexually frenzied time in my life. One day, it was in the summer, I masturbated until I was multiorgasmic and I was drenched in sweat. It's never happened since, and I don't know whether it could happen with a man, but it's the wildest feeling of this continuous orgasm. No matter what I touched, anywhere, any movement around my genitals, I was coming and coming and coming. Wow—it was like finding out you have a Ferrari when you thought you had a Honda. But I've only done it once. I don't think I can really try to do it. It's not about stimulating myself enough, it's more like the four winds align, and the moon is in the right spot.

Greg, my boyfriend now—he's the only man I've ever come with just from fucking. Three different times, when I was on top of him. Otherwise I always touch myself. I don't get it at all, because sex with us isn't that great. And it's not the best orgasm. To be honest, I think he just has this prominent pelvis bone or something. Well, maybe I do feel comfortable with Greg in a way I never did with Mikey. When it happens, there's a feeling of, Oh wow, I finally did it. I started to cry the first time. We were fucking, and I was on top, and I was like, "Oh my God, Greg, I think I'm going to be able to come. This is incredible, I've never done this before." And I did. It's neat to come that way. I'm less in control if it, I don't even expect to come.

Otherwise our sex has always been rotten. [Laughs.] In fact, we haven't had sex in a month. Which is like, Aw, why? We have a hell of a lot more in common than Mikey and I did. It's been more emotional than any other sex I've had, and there was one time when it was emotionally and physically great, so I think, See, it can be really good, better than anything I've had before. But sex with Greg and me is not very sexy. It's very loving. Which drives me crazy. It always feels as if he wants something from me when we have sex, and I feel turned off by that. I mean, what does he want? I'm not exactly sure. We often have troubles in the relationship, but Mikey and I could have troubles up the wazoo, and we'd be like, It's time to fuck? Okay, time to fuck! Greg and I are much more real with each other than

Mikey and I ever were, so it's hard to ignore what's going on and just do the sex.

It's really bad—often what happens is we'll start kissing, and I just turn off, I'll be like, I can't do this. Now we aren't even trying, because it's hellish. The way he kisses me drives me crazy. It's this tentative, "Mother-may-I" kiss. I'm like, God! Fucking kiss me if you want to kiss me, and if you don't, for some reason. . . . It's like he's asking for permission, or do I love him? And once the kissing is off to a bad start, it's hard to go on from there. When I try to tell him about it, it's hard because he doesn't quite get what I mean. He's also never been able to suck or touch my breasts in a way that excites me. I like my nipples sucked, touched, bitten a little bit. He gets in the general area, but he doesn't actually make a lot of contact with the nipple. He doesn't use his tongue hard enough, doesn't graze over the nipple enough. I've tried to explain, and I'm sure he's trying, so I start to think, God, maybe that wasn't it. That's what I thought the other men were doing, but maybe not.

Sometimes fucking has been really good with us, but it's more emotional than physically wonderful. Around when we first started being sexual and we were having problems, I said, "I feel like you want something from me when we're sexual, what is that?" He said, "I think you've had sex with people who just wanted to have sex with you. They didn't want to love you and express their love through doing this." That was a very intense moment. I just looked at him and said, "Is that what you want to do?" He said yes. I went, "Ooo." We had sex after that, and it was great. It felt full of future. It meant something other than just, for the next twenty minutes I will feel good. I thought, This is solved. We've figured it out, it's going to be emotional sex. This is wonderful. But somehow it wasn't. It was a breakthrough for that night, but not for the rest of the relationship. That was the height of it. When it works now it's this mellow thing, fairly loving, gentle. It's never frenzied, I'm never submissive, never his niece. The only time it flows is when it has this high emotional content, and it's hard to sustain that. When there's less emotional content, there's no physical turn-on to fill the space.

I think about my old boyfriend Matthew, who just moved to D.C. I used to see him once every six months or so, and we'd always have

sex, even if we didn't think we were going to. Like one time he was
visiting me, and we were walking around the Lincoln Monument,
and we were in that I-wonder-if-we're-gonna-fool-around stage of the
day. We sat down and he asked me if I would scratch his back. I was
scratching his back, and it got so intense, and I started stroking his
back and his chest. I'm rendered speechless doing that kind of thing
with Matthew. With most people it can be good, but it doesn't render
me speechless. That's ten minutes into fooling around with Matthew,
and we stay in that area for hours, where I lose track of where I am
and where he is, not even knowing who's making what sounds.

The thing about Matthew is I've known him for ten years. Talk
about safe, he's so safe. And fun. We laugh a lot having sex. There's
no performance involved. Matthew is just Matthew. He turns me on
because he's Matthew. But we could never have a relationship. I'm in-
trospective, I talk all the time. Matthew is like, "What? What are you
talking about?" So it would never work. About two months ago we
went out one night. We weren't sexual because I'm dating Greg. The
next morning I masturbated and I was crying, I kept saying over and
over again, "I want to know why, I want to know why, I want to know
why." I do, I want to know why Matthew does that to me and Greg
doesn't. It isn't fair that I have this with someone I can't get along
with. It's great energy, but I'm also like, Can't we turn it off? Won't
it go away if we want it to? It seems to be no, it won't. Yet there's
Greg, we think alike and I can commune with him, and the sex thing
just isn't there. With him, it's, Let's try Technique Number 212. I
wish I knew why.

JAMES ATKINS

"I grew up in a small town—a small, close-knit little town, and that is exactly the same way my family is. My mom and dad's relationship is very good. My dad loves my mom to death, he would do anything for her. They get along great, but that's because of my dad. He keeps the peace when she gets hotheaded and moody. It's just how the blood is on her side of the family. To tell you the honest truth, it is a different type of blood, and I've got some of it. It's a very sexy family, too. That's what I'm saying about the blood. Sex is a major topic, the notches you put on your belt, and that has rubbed off on me."

By his count, which he keeps on his computer at work, he has forty-six notches, a respectable number for a bachelor of thirty. It is easy to imagine him notching many more, since the word hunk *certainly applies—he is about six feet two inches tall, trim, with ebony skin, a stylish flattop haircut, powerful legs, big biceps, and big hands. He has just come from the gym and is wearing a Central High Tornadoes T-shirt, red sweatpants, and running shoes. Basketball was his ticket to college, and though he didn't make the pros, he graduated and now has a low-level management job in a city near his hometown. The twang in his speech, and the mounted six-point buck on his living-room wall, hearken back to his country-boy roots; he still goes home often to hunt, or just hang out.*

He lost his virginity in sixth grade, and by high school his pattern was established: he had a main squeeze and someone on the side. *"I was dating Martha, but there was this little girl called Penny Shaw—it got to the point that I was strokin' Penny on my lunch hour, and this went all the way through my senior year. We would go out on the football field and do the do. Finally Martha caught on, and we broke up my senior year for a little bit of time."* From that point on, his account of his sex life is fairly dizzying.

• • •

My freshman year in college was pretty well dull, because it was a big adjustment for me, going from the country to the big city. I would come home just about every weekend. Then my sophomore year I started dating but I was still seeing Martha. My junior year is when a lot of the sexual activity started to happen. I was getting big on campus thanks to basketball. I started to play some in my sophomore year, but I was a starter my junior year, and college was wild, wild. It got to the point where there might be three different girls in one day. I mean this wasn't an everyday occurrence, but let's say a couple of weekends out of the month, Martha would come up. We would go at it all weekend. But then as soon as she would leave, I would be with somebody in the afternoon and maybe with somebody else that evening. I would say three people has been the most in one day for me, but that probably didn't happen more than five, six, seven times, no more than that.

Right around when I graduated, like my last week in school, I met this girl named Ellen. Me and Ellen started having sexual relations, getting very, very tight. But all at the same time I was still seeing Martha and these other girls, Laura and Sharon and—that might have been it. Then I came home one weekend and there was this older lady, she'd been after me for a while. She's a hillbillyish type woman, I have no idea why I did it. She was married but she would always follow me around, waiting for me to talk to her, so one night I go out to a bar and when I leave, she follows me out. We're drivin' in our cars, like on a back road, and I stopped out there and went back and talked to her, and we started kissy-kissy, and I ended up having sex with her right there inside her car.

So every weekend I was goin' home, me and this older woman was gettin' together, but obviously she was havin' sex with other people too, because she gave me the crabs—at least I think it was her— and I turned around and gave the crabs to Ellen, I gave them to Laura, I gave them to Martha, but if I gave them to Sharon she never said anything, so that kind of tells me she was probably having sex herself with somebody else. Anyway, that was a major fiasco—I mean major—but somehow I lied out of it, and me and Ellen stayed together through it all.

Then she graduated and went back home to her mother's, so I didn't get to see her very much. And at work I met this girl Angela. I am still with Angela to this day, she lives in Chicago right now, but probably Angela will be the one I end up marrying. It started off that we were friends. Then it ended up where we went on a date and it was like automatically we had sex, like two animals. It was good, good sex, real good. As a matter of fact, at that time Angela was by far the best sexual experience I had ever had. It got to the point where I had this little cubicle at work, and me and Angela was havin' sex inside my cubicle. I'd make her take off her panties and have her sit there in her little chair and give me flashes. Or I'd stand up and she'd suck my dick in my cubicle, I'm standin' up lookin' around and she's sittin' down in a chair. Or every single lunch hour we'd go to this little park, or in the middle of the day she'd come and say, "Oh, I've got this major craving"—she was just as bad as I was—so we would leave work, go to the end of the parking lot, have sex in her car, and then come back into work like nothing happened. Actually it got kind of bad, because people started talking about it.

Angela and me got so heated that everything else was pushed to the wayside, it was basically just Ellen and Angela. One day, this was while Ellen was living at home with her mother, she makes a little surprise visit. Me and Angela were sittin' on the couch, just about ready for intercourse, I remember plain as day, and Ellen pecked on the door. I couldn't answer the door because Angela didn't have any clothes on, so Angela runs to the bathroom and she just never came out for God knows, ten, fifteen minutes, and then Ellen sees her come out and goes all spastic so we break up. But I continue to see Angela. Me and Ellen stayed apart for three or four months, and then she came back to me. Why, I have no idea. This continues on and on and on. Every now and then I'm seeing Laura, too, whenever Ellen worked the swing shift, and I'm more or less abusing Angela, just poppin' in and strokin' and leavin'. And this is when it all starts comin' back in my face. Ellen went on a vacation to Jamaica, and she cheated, she slept with a Jamaican, and that just totally, totally crushed me. I couldn't handle it whatsoever. Even with me knowin' that I've been doin' this my entire life. That's when I started respectin' women. Because I was totally crushed. That's what really made me realize I had no respect for women, but now I do, even though I'm still doing whatever I'm doing.

I started seeing only Angela because I was so crushed. Angela was there for me to cry upon, so she helped me through it, but after she helped me through it I started to get to where I could go out again. I was out with some friends and started up with this Mexican girl, Consuela. This was all a part of it comin' back on me. Me and Consuela, we were kickin' it real good, because she was a pretty girl and she let me do whatever I wanted. I mean she masturbated for me, she did anal sex, she shaved her pussy without any hesitation, where I had begged and pleaded with Laura and Angela and Ellen to do that. She definitely liked oral sex, probably the most out of all of 'em, like when she was on her period, she would have me get over on top of her, I would be leanin' on the bedboard, and I would literally fuck her mouth. To me that was great, 'cause that way I didn't have to worry about fucking her, 'cause she was on the rag, and I don't do that.

Time goes on and I'm gettin' all into it, and then Consuela comes up sick and goes to the hospital. When I call I find out that she's engaged to be married, and her fiancé grabs the phone from her. So that was crush number two. Another reality check. She fooled the master, that's why I sit back and laugh at it now, even my friends, they're like, "Aah, she got you good, buddy. You thought you was Mr. Joe Stud, but she gotcha." Which is all good, I'm thankful all this happened. Because I would be totally out of control.

After Consuela I fell back on poor old Angela again. She has always been there for me. Then I decided to move down here, get away from all that. So I moved—oh, I'm forgetting something in there. This girl named Daisy. I met Daisy at a bar. She's real natural, pretty, no makeup, long blond hair, good-lookin' but kind of plain because she dressed like a student, funky clothes. I knew she could never be my girlfriend, because I guess I'm into looks if she's gonna be my girl. She's kind of like Annie Oakley, the earthy type, she doesn't dress properly, at least not to my taste, but I respect her because she's her own person. And the chemistry—I mean, I knew from the very first time I met her, I could tell from the vibes we were both puttin' off.

That night we went home to my apartment. We kissed for a while, there was touchy-feely, and she unbuttoned her blouse. She was real proud of her breasts, she loved her breasts, and she did have a nice set. I was kissing and sucking on her titties, but she has morals, she wouldn't let anything happen. So we did that till like five o'clock in the morning. Then I walked her to her car—and this was kind of forceful, 'cause I got her pinned up against the car, and she had this little skirt on, and I slipped my hand up underneath there real quick, under her panties, and she was just soppin', soppin' wet. That's her natural state. I mean, she's so wet that she would have big spots in the bed just from herself. Also while I had her outside I pulled my dick out, I do remember that, she was like, "Huhh." [Takes in sharp breath.] That's how she was, her eyes would get real big and she'd get all excited.

The next time, she called me late, like after ten o'clock. She came over and I was already in bed, so I put on a pair of shorts to go downstairs and open the door. Then I laid back in bed, I took off my shorts in front of her, but I had my underwear on. She was all hyped, she had just broke up with her boyfriend. We were talking, kissing, and I was trying to be real persuasive, and I got her down to her underwear. I remember she was sitting across my lap, and it got kind of heated, so she started performing oral sex on me. That's her way of trying to protect herself from actually having sex. I knew if I let her keep on I would come, so I didn't let it happen. Then we got going and that's the first time we had sex. She stayed that night till six or seven o'clock in the morning. When I first went inside of her she had an orgasm, and that's what totally blew her mind, because she had never had that happen to her before. I mean the excitement level was to that height.

The thing was, she was just as sexual a person as I am, if not more. Not the type who's gonna go out and sleep with every Tom, Dick, and Harry, but the type that if you're with her she's gonna stroke you half to death. Which is fine with me, that's right down my alley. It was like me and her were made for each other. I don't care how many times I would come, or how many times she would come, each time the intensity level was there. For me the excitement level depends on how hard I get. The harder I get the better it's gonna feel for them, because sometimes I might get a hard-on but the head of my dick is not really hard. I never had that problem with her. It would be swollen hard to where I could go through that concrete there. And still she was never gettin' enough. She was the closest thing to a nymphomaniac I ever was with. That's why I probably only seen her like twice a week. If it was up to her, she'd probably see me twice a day, but I kept it to twice a week. I mean, I'd go to work exhausted the next day, all red-eyed and barely makin' it through without fallin' asleep. It was so good that in the heat of the passion I thought I was deeply in love. Then as soon as it stopped, no, not even close. All those lovin'-type feelings would end.

She is probably the most sensuous girl I have ever been with. She's got nice thighs, firm but real soft, her skin's real soft, she's got a real nice stomach, not super-toned but not flabby either. I like a soft little pouch right there. And her titties are just—they're small but they're perfectly shaped. And her body is so sensitive—see, I get off by watching how the woman gets pleased, and we were together so much that I knew just how to touch her body. My clue, if I get in good with a girl and I get her to masturbate, I sit there and watch exactly how she touches herself, and it sticks right up here. [Points to his head.] Then I just imitate her. Not only that, it was good communication, 'cause she told me—for example, the first time I performed oral sex on her, she's so sensitive that you can't actually touch the clit. You got to lick around it, 'cause if you touch the clit it would like take her breath away, it was too powerful for her. And sucking on her titties, no, that was too much for her, you had to lick around them. But as time went on, her body started to change, to where it hardened up a little bit. Like by the end I could suck on her clit, where before I couldn't.

What blew her mind, she had been engaged, she lived with this guy for years, but she didn't know it could be so good. Like vaginal orgasms—she never had anything like that before. I mean, she had it through the clit, because she masturbated quite a bit, but not through the vagina. Where with me, she was the type that would orgasm like this [snaps his fingers rhythmically]. We're goin' along and she's poppin' it off, boom, boom, boom, one right after another. I would get a rhythm but I'd change it up, and each change would create an orgasm for her. I'd get the rhythm real good—boom, there goes one, then stop, two minutes later get the rhythm, hit her real hard, boom, she's gone.

We didn't do anything wild, just normal. It took us months before we even did doggie-style, because it was so good the regular way. It was funny, it got kind of routine, straight down and dirty ninety percent of the time. There would always be some type of oral sex first of all, but to me that's not really foreplay. I mean, a lot of women, they want you to be kissy and all that stuff before they perform oral sex. To them, that's still straight to the point. But with Daisy there was no kissy. She would go for me first, but I wouldn't let her suck my dick because I knew she had that power over me where she could send me off to the moon within seconds. So I would usually go at her first, oral sex, that would make her pop it off just one time. Then as soon as it popped off I would get in her. She liked being on top 'cause she could really work her clit against my stomach, so we would always start up on the couch, and she would sit on my lap. She would start [snaps fingers]. She told me that after that first one she would never stop, to where she constantly had her eyeballs rollin' in the back of her head. So she would pop off however many times, and then it was my turn, and I would either lay her down on the couch or we would go to the bedroom. I liked it missionary 'cause she would open up more, I could go deeper, and I could feel her much better, I could feel every single inch of her body—oh, yeah.

Even after I moved down here, I would meet her halfway in a hotel and we would go at it. Plus all along we would have phone sex, too. Even while I was at work we'd have phone sex. If I'm not busy at work, I think about sex a hundred percent of the time. I have to stay busy in order not to sit there having a hard dick all day. I stay in contact with a lot of my old girlfriends, so I'll call them up and we'll talk about sex, recallin' some times, or like, "Wouldn't you like for my dick to be in you right now?" I know all the people in my office love to listen—either that or they think I'm a freak.

But see, this is one of the reasons I moved, to get rid of all my past up there. I knew if I stayed there, I would keep doin' the same thing. Down here, I was thinkin' either I was gonna find a black woman that I could get along with, or this was gonna be my chance with Angela. So I'm tryin' to be good. And for the first six or seven months I didn't have any type of sexual relations here. Then one night I went over to this bar and there was this little girl and her friend. I seen she could dance pretty well. She could see I was watchin' her, so she motioned to me and I started dancin' with her. She was half tipsy, a young girl, only twenty-one, but she was married and had two kids. We're dancin', and then I go upstairs to go to the bathroom. You get there through a little hallway. She pulls me back in there where it's all dark and just starts slobberin' all over me. That's all I need, 'cause I unbutton her top and she doesn't have on a bra and I start suckin' on her titties, and it gets all heated, so we go outside and do the do right there in her car.

That didn't lead to anything, 'cause she was married, and after a while Angela moved down this way and I decided to let her move in with me. Biggest mistake. She didn't have a job, she didn't have money, and things got totally out of control to where we started fightin', actually fistfightin'. She is the only woman out of all these that has made me mad enough to where I could do bodily harm, which is ridiculous, because I'm not that type of person. So we're not gettin' along and I kick her out and she moves back to Chicago. Now I'm back seein' her, drivin' back and forth every weekend, but I'm also seein' some little twenty-three-year-old student, a white girl I met in a club.

Sex with Angela—we're very inventive, there's not a whole lot that doesn't go, I mean, dildos, vibrators, or readin' books to one another, masturbatin' beside one another, telling about fantasies, or maybe she won't wear underwear, and if we're in a public place she'll give me a puss flash. Now, Angela isn't a comer, so she likes it hard and fast. She likes being pounded, that's good sex for her. But she has never come from actual fucking. Strictly from her own hand, never from me. What I'll do is flip her over and lay her on her side, I'm comin' in from this side here, and she's workin' her button. Or I'm over on top of her where I'm holding myself up with my arms and she's down there doin' it. I have only masturbated her once where she has come, one time when we were drivin' in my truck. Even from oral sex she's never done it. That kind of bothers me about her, but then again it's total excitement to sit there and watch her play with her pussy, so I'm like, well, I can sacrifice that. It's a mental block, I wish she could go see a psychiatrist or some sexual-type person about it. I know it's a mental block because I imitate her movements to the T, and I'll come close but it just won't happen except for that one time, and that had to be a fluke. I'll perform oral sex on her for an hour, or I'll just sit there and rub it, even with a vibrator, and she's enjoyin' it to the fullest, 'cause we'll be on the telephone and that's all she talks about, "Oh, God, I wish you were here to eat my pussy." She loves it, but no coming.

Angela is not an extremely wet person, which I hate—and this is where the foreplay thing comes in. When I'm in a relationship, I get complaints all the time, because I'm like, No foreplay for me, let's get down to it. If I'm with somebody that I've never been with, I'll be soft and tender and everything, but after a while it's like, Forget the foreplay, baby, let's do it. Like she might say, "Touch me, kiss me, instead of just divin' into my pussy." Or she might put my hand on her titty, or somewhere else. There's a little tone of resentment, anger, whatever you want to call it. Frustration. Now, that totally turns me off. I think the reason why is because I'm a spoiled brat, just from the fact that I've had my way so long with so many people, to where if somebody tries to tell me something it turns me off. Let's say we're lying in bed, no kissing goes on whatsoever, I'll spit on my hand and rub her and then crawl on top. She's like, "No, if you play with it a little while, it'll get wet." That'll start an argument, I'm like, "Oh, forget that." The selfishness and the spoiled brat come out. That's when I'll just spit on my hand again and go ahead and do it. She'll lay there like nothin's happenin', I'll bust a nut and roll over and fall asleep.

It's kind of fucked up, I might meet some Joe Blow off the street and treat her more tender than I would Angela, and I've been with Angela for years. It's probably some mental disorder in my head—I like to suck 'em in and then have control over 'em, tryin' to get 'em under my power. I know how most women are, and by me tryin' to play Mr. Tender, I know that night I'm gonna get into their pants.

When I'm bein' all touchy-feely and kissy-kissy, I know it's gonna get
me to my end purpose at least nine times out of ten. But these days
I'm softenin' up, there's more foreplay on my part with Angela. I'm
tryin' to change in thataway, yes I am. And it feels good, provided
we're not arguing. If we're gettin' along well, I'll put an effort forward. Maybe just more patience, a little more control before I actually go to it. Maybe it has to do with my age, growing up, starting to
realize things. Like in order for me to work in a relationship I am
gonna have to start giving in.

Right now, me and Angela are trying to build a relationship. And
except for this little girl Suzie—well, I'm weaning off that. More or
less tryin' to tell her to stay away from me. Sometimes I wonder if I
have a problem, like if I should seek some type of counseling. I don't
think so, I guess I'm just a high-strung sexual person. But I feel guilty
that I can't ever say no, that I'm constantly out there schemin'. This
might sound funny, but I am not that aggressive of a person, I'm really not. I would hate to see me if I was an aggressive person.

See, I don't have to have emotional ties to have good sex. Not at
all. I could meet some joker off the street tonight and have good sex,
and she might think I'm totally in love with her after the first time,
and after that it's like, Nah, hit the road. That's why a lot of people
say I'm coldhearted. But ever since I was hurt, since that Ellen deal,
when she slept with that guy in Jamaica, that warped me in the love
stage. I'll never again get to where a woman can hurt me like that,
never. If Angela did that—well, she better never. I would hurt her,
physically hurt her, if she fucked somebody else. I would be that upset. I know I'm wrong in thinkin' thataway, I know it don't make any
sense, but it's just the way I am. I know it's a double standard. And
by me being this way, it makes me very untrusting of other people,
'cause I know they can be scheming just like I'm scheming. I think
women hide so many skeletons. They do things you'll never know, I
mean they sleep with people—women are very sneaky. I honestly believe women are more sneaky than men. I believe that a woman gets
away with a lot more than a man does. How many married women
have I been with, and their husband has no clue?

So I would be very upset with Angela, just from her being with
somebody else. It's part egotistical, that she would have to go to

somebody else to be satisfied, but it's the emotional side too. I couldn't put up with that. If I found out she did it, she'd hit the road. Yet she's been with me for years, she knows what I've done. She's even caught me in situations.

Course, she tells me every day now, if she finds out about anything, she's gone. Without a doubt. If it happens again—Bye-bye.

JUDITH ROTHSTEIN

At fifty-seven, she figures she has slept with more than a thousand men, and she didn't really begin until her thirties. She is the daughter of Orthodox Jewish immigrants from Czechoslovakia. She grew up in poverty on the Lower East Side of Manhattan, in a culture that "does not value girls at all. I was the fourth child, but my mother's feeling was that I was the fifth wheel. Often she couldn't remember my name. That colors my entire attitude toward life—having to survive being rejected." The household was crowded, uproarious, and sexually repressive—but not asexual. "My mother claims that until my father was eighty and got sick, they were still having sex. She was a warm, earthy person, so I would assume she was the aggressor. My father was extremely reserved. In my whole life he never kissed me. But I was madly in love with him. I always blamed my mother for all my problems. Only in recent years and after a lot of therapy have I come to accept that all my strengths are my mother's, and I'm very much like her. Whereas I idolized my father because he was so distant."

She married at eighteen to escape her family, and soon found herself trapped with two children in a marriage that was disastrous sexually and in every other way. In eight years she never had an orgasm. "After I got divorced, I started an affair with a married man at my job. With him I had my first orgasm. To this day, I have had many, many love affairs and sex affairs, but no one has represented love and sex combined the way that first affair did."

Now retired from her job as a social worker and subsisting in part on disability pay from a job-related accident, she lives in an airy apartment on the East Side. Photos around the apartment show her as a buxom, blond beauty; today her thick hair is graying, the years have rounded her figure, and she recently recovered from a life-threatening illness. She mostly dates younger men, some of whom she meets through an organization called Anachron. Once a year, she puts an ad in its newsletter, and her new ad just came out. It reads: "FEISTY FIRM FIT FREETHINK-

*ING 55er FINDS FABULOUS 40ish FINE FOR FOND FONDLING
FRIENDSHIP, NOT FLABBY FLACCID FLATULENT FATUOUS
FRANTIC FRENETIC FOOL. FINI."*

• • •

I would say I'm attracted to the strong, silent type. When men
have come on to me strong—and I have had many, many proposals of
marriage—I'm always turned off. The only men I'm attracted to are
the ones where there's a challenge. If I can take someone like my father, who was a bachelor until his forties, someone who shows absolutely no interest in me, and if I can get that man to love me, well,
that's an accomplishment.

The best example is this bachelor I went out with for ten years. I
met him in '68, '69. Singles dances were popular then. I went to
one—I remember like it was yesterday. I saw this very handsome guy.
I engaged him in conversation, and we talked for an hour or so. Then
he said, "I think I'm going to wander around," and I said, "Wait a
minute, you've taken up all this time, you're not going to take my
phone number?" He said all right. He didn't offer to take me home.
If he had, I would have gone to bed with him. This was the sixties,
don't forget. I had discovered orgasm, I found out I had a clit. The
sexual revolution and the antiwar movement were going on. I didn't
have my kids living with me. I was finding out that I liked sex. Even
for an unattractive woman, there's no problem getting somebody to
go to bed with, and I was a very attractive woman.

But I thought, This guy must not be interested, if he didn't offer
to take me home. Then he called on Tuesday and made a date for Saturday. Turned out he was nine years older than me—I was thirty-four,
he was forty-three. He was a Jewish bachelor. Not only that, but he
still lived with his mother. This was getting better, as far as I was concerned. [Laughs.] The challenge was getting better and better. First
date: We went to dinner. Nothing seemed to trigger a conversation. I
thought, This is the most boring date. Handsome as he is I'm just not
interested. I can't sit through this Silent Sam treatment. But we came
home, and we were sitting and kissing and necking on my couch.

Very shortly I said, "Let's go in the bedroom." And that developed into a ten-year relationship. We saw each other every other weekend. It was the best sex I ever had, and I have had sex with a lot of people. I found out that not only could I have an orgasm, I could have twenty-six orgasms. And he would not stop until I had all twenty-six. He was a craftsman. For him, this was a work of art he took pride in. He knew how to control his own orgasm. He would only have one to my twenty-six. He could maintain the erection for all that time. It wasn't that it went down and it went up. He maintained an erection for two, two and a half hours. And he did everything to me except go down on me. He would not do that. He was very bright, sarcastic—and very cold. In those ten years he never once said, "I love you," or "I like you," or "You turn me on." He would not talk at all.

Still, I thought this was like heaven. I mean, to find out you can have twenty-six orgasms! And I didn't feel like I owed him anything, that was the beauty of it. He didn't give the feeling like, C'mon, have those twenty-six orgasms so I can come. That's what most men do, not even with twenty-six, but with one. Most men's attitude, even if they do know how to play you, is: Hurry up so I can do my thing. His was: This is giving me great pleasure to give you pleasure. And to see if we can break our record of twenty-six. [Laughs]. And there is no hurry. I know I'm gonna come. I have no doubt that I'm gonna come. When I come, that's it for the day, so let's do whatever we can to prolong this.

One of the great things about sex with him is that we both saw it as a game. We could talk during sex. We could say, "That was number three, that was number four [Laughs.]." It was wonderful. The only thing is that I did get emotionally involved. I did want him to say, "I love you." I would have liked him to say, "I'll come during the week," or "I'll come every week," or "Let's get married." But he kept it rigidly to this every other week. And the understanding was that we would both go out with other people. I had this idea that either he was gonna turn fifty, or his mother was gonna die, and one of those things would have this effect on him, and he would fall into my arms. Well, his mother died. And he turned fifty. And he decided to move to California.

In the meantime, for all those years with him, I was dating. Probably in the whole thirty years of my being single, I've had at least one thousand guys. That sounds like a lot. But if you think about it, just in the ten years I was dating that bachelor—let's say I met three guys a week. A singles dance, or a bar, or out to dinner, or a protest march or something. In one year, say fifty weeks, that's one hundred fifty people a year. Over ten years, that's fifteen hundred. It probably wasn't that many, but what I'm trying to say is that one hundred fifty a year is not a large amount. To me, three dates a week—what was I doing on the other four nights? I was feeling lonely! Really! I don't consider three dates a week a lot of dating. And I always had sex on the first date. Either you turned me on, and I had sex the first night, or you didn't turn me on, and I was never going to have sex with you. I've had several long love affairs; those were people to me. The rest were just numbers.

People were always telling me, "Give this guy a chance." These men would propose marriage to me, men who were successful, doctors and lawyers and businessmen, but I wasn't physically attracted to them, and there was no way I was gonna spend my life with somebody that I didn't enjoy sex with, not after my marriage. Even though it meant I stayed a social worker in the slums, and I hated it. And I couldn't get custody of my kids. There was no way I could hook up with somebody I didn't find attractive. Sex was too important. My women friends and I used to do this Sunday-morning quarterbacking—every single Sunday morning, talk about our Saturday-night dates. Could he get an erection or couldn't he? How long did he last? What did he do to you? We rated the guys. Some women didn't care if they didn't have an orgasm, or if the guy couldn't maintain an erection. I have friends who are fifty who I think are still virgins. I had other friends who were virgins till they were thirty. To whom sex was just a necessary evil or a means to an end. They all thought I was crazy, because I had an attitude about sex like men did. Which was: It's great, and you don't have to say "I love you." If I saw someone I liked, I'd walk over to him and say, "Hi, I think you're handsome, do you want to fuck?" He didn't have to be the right age, the right religion. He wasn't gonna be my husband. I already had this boyfriend I really liked. This was just bed. My ideal was that if I met somebody who was better than my bachelor friend, I would have gone with him.

But nothing like that ever happened. So that's how it became ten years. I never found anyone that satisfied me the way he did.

On some other level, I think I also always hoped these men would find my fucking so exceptional that they would want to love me and take care of me and nurture all my other needs, which I definitely had. I'm not saying I didn't have emotional problems and I wasn't very needy. I think a lot of the time I would have been happier to not have sex, if I could have crawled up on his knee and been babied and held. But since you can't do that—you can't say to a stranger, "I'm really feeling very low, can I climb on your knee?" But you can say, "I want to fuck." So out of the sex, I got my emotional needs fulfilled for the moment. I was being held, I was being complimented, I was being wined and dined. I was also getting an orgasm. Then afterward—I used to have a foyer that was twice the length of this one, and as I walked down the foyer with them after the first night, I'd be saying, "When am I gonna see you again?" Or I'd call and say, "That was so wonderful, when are we getting together?" I'd be still on this high, and if I had a good orgasm I tended to romanticize it. This was going to be the start of something big. Whereas to him, it was just a fuck. And he'd say, "I don't know," or "I'll call you," or "Leave me alone." Sometimes there would be a second or third date. Some relationships lasted three weeks, six weeks, but very few.

Also, most men disappointed me. I have to say that as a result of having been promiscuous, I lost a lot of respect for the male race. [Laughs.] I was amazed to find out how many men could not maintain an erection. Or could not hold it long enough for me to have the orgasm. I would say, "Look, I know I'm capable of having the orgasm. I'm capable of having twenty-six. If you don't satisfy me, it's your problem, not mine." For some of them, it was the first time a woman had ever said that. Some of them had been married, and their wives divorced them, and they still didn't know why.

Well, you can imagine this didn't sit too well. I had men literally get up in the middle of the night, hurry up and put their pants on, and run out the door and bang on the elevator button. [Laughs.] It takes a long time for that elevator to come, and I'd be telling them what I thought of them. It was traumatic for an awful lot of men. I can tell you, of the thousand guys, probably nine hundred ninety of them have been lousy in bed. They don't know how to satisfy a woman. They don't know what a woman is capable of. They're selfish. They think only of their own orgasm. I really hope your book gets this across. It might be a revelation to the world to find out how unsatisfied women are. The men act like they're the ones who always want sex, and the woman always has a headache. Well, she has a headache because it's a headache to bother getting all excited, and the guy leaves you high and dry. It's easier to just say, Forget the whole thing, I won't bother having sex.

So what is it I like about men, since I see their frailties? There's something about them being sexual, about them having penises. Even when I know they can't use them, when they're stupid little boys. Something about them being men overrides the disappointment. I have to say, I have contempt for humanity in general. I think I'm smarter than most people. I think I'm more sincere, more generous, more passionate. I do wish I could find my counterpart. And I can't. Not as a friend, not as a lover. That's my frustration, that's what the loneliness is. I've come to the realization that I probably won't, and I've come to accept my own company as preferable to being with people who frustrate me or bore me. But given that I don't have a high opinion of people in general, I prefer men's company. They matter more to me. I have had an awful lot of women friends, but I'm not interested in women, I never have been. Whereas at least a man can fuck me. There's always that frisson, that sexual tension, even if he's someone I'm never going to bed with. I relate it to this thing about my father. If I had to live in a world of just men, I'd be happier. I like them for their maleness. I like their voices. I like the hair on their arms. I just like men. That's a big turn-on for them, because a lot of women don't. I mean, I'd like to be a man. But if I can't be a man, I want to be one of the boys. I tell dirty jokes. I have this need to be in control, a sense of power, which is a male prerogative. And I want to get laid.

A lot of my sex felt hostile. Part of it was this competition, this sense that I wanted to be the man, and I wanted to have his cock. I almost always felt, If I had your cock, I would know how to use it a lot better than you do. If I had your cock, I would be president of the United States. I would be God. I would be fucking every woman in the place, and I would do a better job of fucking than you. If I had your cock and my brains, there would be no conquering me. I felt most men were wasting this great opportunity God had bequeathed upon them, just being men. Because men had the right to have sex without guilt, without being called whores, without worrying about pregnancy. Men were the aggressors. They were the ones on top. They determined how long it lasted. Men have all these prerogatives, and they don't even know what to do with them.

See, I think to be a good fuck, for a man, is not to have an emotional involvement. What makes a good fuck is not what makes a good husband. It's his ability to distance himself from you. To make it a purely mechanical act, like running a race. Being a good human being and a good lover are antithetical. That's why I've always found the first night is the best. Once you know somebody, they're human. But that first time, you're not a human being. You're a faceless fuck. You can make up for it later with emotion and love and tricks and all, but nothing can compare with that first night with a stranger. That's one of the reasons I was willing to have a thousand first nights! [Laughs.]

I like tender and gentle, but not in sex. I want someone to bring me flowers, I want someone to care about my problems, but not in the sex act. I feel the sex act isn't tender and caring, even between tender, caring people. If it's good, it's not tender and caring. So there was hostility even in the forcefulness of my response. I didn't lay there like a dead lox, as the expression goes. I took control. I might say, "I really want you to thrust hard into me." I didn't want it to be loving, caressing. I wanted it to seem like I was being assaulted. People often used to say that my screaming—and that's another thing: I scream so loudly that I've had people put pillows over my face—I've had people be afraid the police were gonna be called. Or they think I'm faking it. Well, I'm not. I speak loudly anyway, but if I'm having what to me is successful sex, I'm screaming to the point where my throat gets hoarse. You can hear me a block away. Some men find that hostile. They feel my wanting to scream, to thrust so hard, is all hostile. I've had men say, "Kiss me." Kiss you? That's not what I'm into at the moment! I don't want to kiss you at all! I want to fuck! The affection is before, or after, but not during the act itself. The act itself is two animals clawing at each other, thrusting their bodies as hard as can be, until they elicit this scream from each other. Where is there affection and love in that?

I talk a lot during sex. I wish more men would do that. I would like a man to think aloud. Not to censor himself. I can give you a list of what I like to hear, though I seldom hear it. "I really love fucking you. I love your big tits. I love your juicy cunt." My ten-year boyfriend talked like that. Most men say nothing, or they grunt. Or if you say, "Say something," they think you want to hear "I love you," which is not what I'm looking for. I say things like, "I love how you feel. I love feeling you fuck me. I love your big hard cock. I love the way you smell." Or I tell them what to do. It's a constant stream of talking. I'm either breathing hard, screaming in ecstasy, or telling them what I'm feeling.

It's also important for a man to tell me he's coming. I don't even know sometimes. They don't breathe harder. They try to keep it all in. You don't know in any way that they're coming. Whereas the act of a man coming turns me on. If he lets me know, usually I can come just by virtue of having made him come, 'cause it's such a turn-on to see someone so excited.

One thing I can't stand is when they put all their weight on your chest. Those are usually the worst lovers. They enter you, they put all their weight on your chest, and in a few minutes they've come. And you haven't felt any movement. Most of all you feel like all the air went out of you. A good partner never has his chest on your chest. He's on his knees, and he's doing this movement, back and forth, back and forth. It's the back-and-forth rather than the in-and-out. When he's on his knees doing it back and forth, it permits the woman to move as well. To lift your hips so you get the angle right. Most men seem to forget that a woman's clitoris is in the front. It's not inside her vagina. You could be pounding away at her vagina, and she's not going to feel anything. What she needs to feel is some friction against her clitoris. So by being on his knees, leaning over her, with his hands on either side, she can tilt herself up so it's hitting her in the right place. That's the best position.

I will say one position I don't like—well, I don't mind it as part of the menu. I don't mind having somebody come into me from behind, because it's just another position. But I had one guy who preferred coming like that. I don't like the guy to come like that, because it's a way of making me not me. It's too impersonal. And when he comes, he can't fall into my arms. See, I never want you to forget that I'm me. If the guy is facing me at the moment when he comes, he's remembering that I'm me, and hopefully he'll be feeling as grateful to me for the pleasure I just gave him as I feel. So I always prefer that the man come in my arms facing me. Preferably with him on top. For psychological reasons, I really prefer being fucked from on top, with hard thrusting, so that I feel taken possession of. That I'm almost raped: Take *that* and *that* and *that*. That's why I say I don't consider the act itself loving. Being female, with the man on top, and he has this penis, I like the sense that for a few moments I've been completely overpowered.

I think good sex also means that not only can I have a fantasy but I can tell you about it. And you not only will not be turned off by it, you'll be turned on by it. Let's say we've gotten to the point where we're undressed, you're on your knees, and you're going down on me. I'm well aware it's you. Yet on another level my fantasy takes over. My fantasy might be that while you're doing that, I transport myself back to being sixteen. My father has come to the door, and he sees you doing this to me. Or maybe not my father, maybe an old boyfriend, it doesn't matter, I can change it. The point is, for me, bringing in another person to be a voyeur is a big turn-on. Generally that person is a male. Or a hundred men. I could be a stripper, or the star of an orgy. But always I'm the center of attention, which I have a strong need for in real life. So I'd have this fantasy, something to do with this other man watching you do that and getting very excited and either jerking himself off or wanting to come right after you and me. Then I might come as you're going down on me, and the guy in the fantasy comes, and now I'm back with you again.

Now we go on to some other facet of our lovemaking. At some point we're going to rest a little. While we're resting I might say, You know, that last orgasm, I had this really great fantasy, and I could tell it to you. For some guys that would be a turn-on. For some it would be neutral. And some guys would be terrified to think I was having a fantasy about another man while they're with me. They think it's a

real put-down of them, or they're afraid of their own fantasy life, I'm
not sure why, but they really think I'm a crazy lady. They might in fact
get up and leave. So talking about what makes for a good lover, I
think it's someone who wants to hear it. Even better is someone who
tells you his.

In the era when I grew up, sex was forbidden. So in the fantasies,
the forbidden part, and my flaunting sex, and being caught at it, are
all part of the turn-on. I'm so sexually driven that in spite of the risks,
my father walking in, I'm swept away by the force of my need. That's
what I'm looking for. The reason I'm calling up this fantasy while
you're playing with me is to give me this freedom. And what's going
to give it to me? The sense that at this moment, nothing matters but
fucking. Nothing. The fantasy's function is to get me in touch with
what is really happening, which is that I am this fucking machine. In
fact, I've used that expression, and men have used it for me. That I
become a fucking machine. And it's a big turn-on to men. Of course,
I've had men say to me in anger, or when they're throwing me out
or leaving, "You're nothing but an animal." As a terrible put-down.
When I thought that's what the purpose was! Or I've had them say,
"You want me to be an animal. I'm not an animal, I'm a professor!"
Or "I'm sensitive!" When all I wanted was for you to be an animal!

For the most part, aside from sex, I have a lot of difficulty relaxing. I am always observing, always thinking, always planning. I don't
know how to relax. My need is total escape. And the only way I can
get that total escape is to have this wonderful orgasm. And the only
way I can have that orgasm is if I feel you know what you are doing.
I don't have to be alert to tell you, Do this, do that. And you're not
going to come too soon, so I can give myself up to this sexual experience of feeling you are going to fuck me right. And you are going to
take me into this other dimension. And for those thirty seconds, I am
going to be out of myself. I am at such a level—it's not just the
screaming and the coming, but I have gone into some kind of wonderful white space. This total nirvana escape.

The big orgasm might be the first one, or it might be the last. I
don't try to save it. Absolutely not. I don't trust men enough. Even
with men who I know are good at waiting, I want to make sure I have
mine. So if I can have the big one right away, I'd just as soon have it

right away. I want to be able to reach a point where, okay, anything after this is gravy. If the man comes, he comes. If he loses it, he loses it. At least I have done all this coming. And when I reach that white space, that's the kind of sex I will be a slave for. I literally have said [panting heavily]: "I will be your slave, will you do that again?" I don't care if you're married, I don't care if you're 3,000 miles away, I don't care if you want me to pay you, I would be your slave for that. I will put up with your nonsense of not seeing me more than once in two weeks. I will put up with your telling me about other people you fuck. I will put up with making all the meals and paying for all the dates. I will do anything if you will come back and give me this great orgasm again. I will be your slave.

In general, I have a lot less sex now than I used to. Part of it's because of AIDS. I mean, I still do have sex, I just try to be careful with whom. By that I mean he's middle-class, not a drug user, not bisexual, that kind of thing. And I insist he uses a condom. But whereas at one point I would have said to myself, What the hell, let's have sex even though I'm never gonna see him again, the tendency began to be, What the hell, let's not bother. Why take the risk, I'm never gonna see him again. Plus, a lot of other things have happened. Having gone through menopause a year ago, having been sick, having faced death, it changes your perspective. As an example, I'll tell you about my most recent younger man. An older younger man—he was forty-one. He was the first one who came into my life after I decided I wasn't even going to be bothered with sex. I really enjoyed the sex. He said he was going to school three nights a week and playing the piano three nights a week, so mostly we were seeing each other on Sunday. Then after a few weeks, he said he was free on Tuesday, not on Sunday. I said, "What are you doing on Sunday?" He said, "Well, I was busy, um, er . . ." I said, "Are you seeing another woman?" He said, "Yeah." I said, "I don't want to be part of a harem," and I hung up and that was the end of it.

But I realized that at another time in my life—see, I think it was hormonal as well as emotional. I had a very strong sex drive, and a lot of it was hormonal. I menstruated until I was fifty-five. If I didn't have sex, I got depressed. But having gone into menopause, and whatever psychological thing is going on about death, I can say, "I don't want to be part of a harem." Two years ago, and anytime prior to that for twenty years, I wouldn't have wanted to be part of a harem. But at least I'd be getting laid on Tuesday, if not Sunday. Something is better than nothing. That was my pragmatism. I wouldn't have told the guy off. I think, in retrospect, I would have been better off if I had. I might have gotten one of these guys who was dating other people. Maybe he would have said, "You're so important to me that if it's you or the others, I'll take you." I never did it. I wasn't willing to risk it. It was too important just to get laid. What I felt with this guy was, It's reassuring to find out I'm still sexually arousable. Because of having sex with him once a week, I was in a state of arousal the rest of the week. And by cutting it off, I was able to go back into my quiescence. I was able to say, Fine. I don't feel anything. I don't need it. I don't want it. It's not important enough anymore.

WAYNE CORVALLIS

He is reluctant to give his age but looks to be around fifty—tall, lanky, with frizzy dark hair surrounding a bald spot. He lives in Los Angeles but was raised in rural Oklahoma. Inherited oil properties, which he still manages, help to support him comfortably. We talk in his living room, in an apartment on a high floor of a handsome old building. Behind his big reclining chair are floor-to-ceiling bookcases, with many books on psychological subjects; over the couch where I sit is a painting of a young, voluptuous nude. Psychotherapy and sex: these are the twin poles of his life.

"I grew up in a little town, about eight hundred people. My father was in business. He died when I was thirteen, and that changed my life more than anything. I gave up on sports and extracurricular activities and worked at a gas station we had. I took on adult responsibilities. That suited my mother, she was strong on the work ethic. Plus, she was afraid I might have a normal sexual adolescence. I can remember a friend of mine and I sitting in the car one time talking about a classmate, a girl who had gotten pregnant. I always thought she was such a nice girl, and the fact that she got pregnant, I couldn't believe how a nice girl could do such a thing. That was my attitude about sex."

He did his first necking as a junior in college and lost his virginity on his wedding night. He was twenty-eight, a Baptist minister, and his wife was twenty. During the marriage she had several affairs, and he began to long for more experience. They tried swapping mates with other couples a few times, but finally divorced. Along the way he had discovered therapy, returned to school as a graduate student, and moved to LA. "I started to try to date. I had trouble even getting phone numbers. When I finally got going, I had a very big moral problem. Very big. I can remember in one seminar there were two women that I'd been to bed with. I felt very guilty about that. This was a horrible thing, and I was a horrible person. I was really breaking the traces."

• • •

One woman I ran into, we were making love, and she told me she'd been to a swing club. She said she'd go with me. I had been looking for someone who had gone there. Now I had found one, and I was scared to death. The night before, I tell you, I was crawling the walls. My desire clashing with my prohibition. This was really bad, this was the worst, to go to a place like this. So we went over to the house where this club was. We ran into another couple and split up, I went with the woman, and she went with the guy. The woman and I—we had our clothes off—we went into the big swing room. Now, I'd never seen people make love before. God, I was just blown out of my mind. I was completely impotent. I couldn't do anything with this woman. I said, "Hey, you go find someone else, I can't do you any good." And she said, "No, no, I know how it is the first time, I'll stick with you." So she stayed, and we lay there and I just watched. [Laughs.]

I dated that woman a few times, and I didn't have any trouble with potency when I was with her alone. Then I started going regularly to the club. By this time I'd slept with quite a few women. These were my therapy years, and many of us in therapy training were living out our sexuality. Some of the women therapists were fooling around also. [He opens a file cabinet, takes out a thick file folder, and shows me the pages.] This is a list of the women, going back to before my wife and I separated. I kept track of the first one hundred sixty or so. I put down their response and my response, and whether I thought their development was mainly oral, anal, phallic, or genital.

I have been a very driven person. Driven to work, driven to play, driven to sex. At the height of my swinging, I'd go swinging every weekend. I'd either have a party here, or go to a party, or go to a club. And then I'd see two or three women during the week. I had to have an orgasm—probably from the time I started masturbating, I needed an orgasm every day for the tension release. Now the tension isn't so high, I've moved from needing one every night to every two or three days. And I always was seeing more than one woman at a time. When I'd get to bed with one, I'd work very hard to find another. I used to have a rule that whenever possible, I'd never be with the same woman twice in a row. I'd see them as long as the sex lasted, from several times to a few months to years. I was so afraid of—I was very vulnerable to being taken over by a woman. If you fall in love, you surrender yourself. That's threatening. It feels wonderful when it's going good, and terrible when it doesn't, when you're so dependent. So I would spread myself out.

I've probably had more swingers' parties here over the years than anybody in the area. I tried very hard to have nice, nice people. By "nice" I mean people who were friendly, who were reasonably attractive. They didn't have to be beautiful, but not unattractive. Not too pushy or aggressive. There are very nice people in swinging, cutting across the socioeconomic groups, with a lot of ministers, teachers, social workers, psychologists, therapists—people-oriented professions.

What happens at a party—you just go with a turn-on. It starts with the eyes. I don't usually approach a woman if I don't have some eye contact that signifies some interest. That greatly increases your possibilities. A lot of people have the idea that swinger parties are big orgies, where everybody jumps on everybody else. It isn't that way. People are selective, like they are anyplace else. They go with who they want. So if the interest continues from eye contact to talking, and to desire, there's touching. You just go with it. I very often follow women's cues on this. As a rule, if a woman wants her hand held, she'll start moving her hands around to where you can touch one. She'll lay it on the table or someplace where you can get at it. Once in a while, a woman will take the initiative and touch your hand or your arm, but more often she'll just make herself available. So you go from talking to touching, and at a swinging party you can go from the touching to bed. Or you can start kissing and caressing in the living room, and sometimes I've made love right in the middle of the floor here, with people all around, when I was in a really hot turn-on with somebody. That tended to be more my early years in swinging. Now I prefer more privacy at parties. I have these two big beds, and then I have three or four smaller mattresses I move around. I put one down at the base of the big bed in the bedroom. That's my favorite place. It's a bit out of the way, a cabinet is on one side, so I have a little bit of privacy. [Laughs.] That way I can get more into meshing, melding, fusing with a woman, without distractions.

When the parties were at my place I had more anxiety because I felt a responsibility. I'd take everybody's name down when they came. Check it against my list. Introduce them around. Rarely did I ever start making love before others did, because I wanted to help people feel comfortable. The other part of the anxiety would be the moral conflict. Everybody who's breaking the rules feels anxiety, and the people who come to parties come because those rules were so heavy, so strong and repressive. Particularly the women. I've spent a lot of time at parties helping women break down the barriers. Some think they're not going to do anything, but there's a little part of them that wants to, and if there's group permission, and you can draw them out, they will get into it and have a good time. Lots of times here on the couch I'd be sitting next to a woman, somebody new, and talking to her. How does she feel about this? At the same time I'd have my arm around her and be holding her hand if possible, caressing her. My therapy background helped me, of course. I can pick up on people's conflicts, what's bothering them. What I found as a rule, it's best to get a woman going as much as possible in this room. To get her really hot, to caress her breasts and her pussy, and a lot of kissing. Get her hot enough that she's ready to go to the bedroom. If you try too soon, she's not ready. A lot of women go with the feeling, when the feeling gets strong enough. They go with their heads, their indoctrination, until the turn-on gets strong enough to overwhelm the prohibitions.

I remember one girl, a twenty-eight-year-old from Ohio. She'd never been to a party like this. She sat there in a chair. The guy she was with was busy. She just came so he could get in, basically. I went over and sat by her, and I started asking her how she felt about it. She said she hadn't had that much sex in her life. As I was talking to her, I gradually put my arm around her and touched her a little on the shoulder. And as I got her to talk out her mixed feelings, I would touch her a little more. She wasn't pulling away. I said at one point, "Well, have you ever seen people make love? Maybe you'd just like to look at them. That's what I did when I first went to a swing club." She says, "Well, okay." We were sitting right there, and we went into that east bedroom. She watched for a while. At the same time I had my arm around her. Then I started unbuttoning the blouse of her dress. And she just said, "Oh," and let me keep going. [Laughs.] I took her dress off and started kissing her, caressing her. Got her bra and panties off. Then we lay down there in my favorite place at the end of the bed. A nice young body. I get my finger into their pussy fairly soon, so the juices are flowing. I don't know, I may have licked her first. I don't think so. I think I just came into her. I know it was a long time I was inside her, forty-five minutes or something like that. Just slow, steady intercourse, kissing her all the time. I don't know whether I came or not. I'm not as apt to come at parties, so I'm not sure.

I have developed an ability to be interested in a lot of women. I didn't used to be this way, I was real picky, which was really a way to eliminate most women. You say this one is too small, this one's too large, this one's white, or black. And you think that's the real reason, but it isn't. The real reason is that your authorities said sex and women are bad. As I worked through that in therapy, I found I was attracted to more and more women. So at a party, I would often like to make love with all the women there. Even large women. That took me a little time. I can remember one woman—she was sitting right there, on a footstool at a big party. I had been at a party at her house, she was married, and I had a chance to get together with her, and I didn't want to because she was pretty good-size. But she was nice, she had a nice personality. She came to the party here with her husband, they came late, and I had been making love. She was sitting there, I hadn't seen her, so I came over and kissed her hello. And it was such a soft, warm, passionate kiss, we just kept on kissing. And we went right from the footstool into the bedroom, and I had some of the best sex I have ever had with anybody, because it was such a strong turn-on.

Kissing is very important. I've always liked kissing, but now I really have trouble making love with a woman that I can't kiss. It's too impersonal. With a lot of kissing, you get the oral connection at the same time you have the genital connection, so it's like a circle. I feel much more attuned to the woman. I'm basically a head person, but the kissing gets me out of my head and more into my body. It over-whelms my thoughts. I love lapping up the softness, the soft lips and tongue. It's also very emotional. I've found that when women are afraid of intimacy, they're afraid of kissing. They'll go a lot quicker to sex, which to them is less personal. You do it, you have the orgasm, it's over, and you're not hooked. In general I think women are more emotional than men, but there are women who are afraid of emotion. And maybe you find that more among some swinging women. In the general population, women want you to kiss them first: they have to feel emotional, and then it works down to the genitals. But the women who come to swinging for the fun of it, and for a variety of men, they sometimes don't want to get too involved. I made this mis-take lots of times. If you start kissing her, and she's afraid of emotion, she won't respond. But that same woman, if you start stroking her body, her breasts, work down her legs, her clitoris, she'll let you do it. She'll move into the sexual, and when she gets hot enough she breaks down and she's more apt to allow the kissing.

So I love the kissing, but mostly I'm intercourse-oriented. That's what I'm really interested in. There's nothing in the whole world that feels better than being inside a woman. Many of our nerve endings are down in the penis. A woman has a large number of nerve endings in her vaginal lips. It's like she's massaging my penis, and I'm massag-ing the inside of her vagina. I like massage on all parts of the body, but that's the ultimate. To me, it's—it's a feeding. This is the way we nurture and feed and satisfy each other. They say that babies die if they don't get enough stroking, caressing, touching. It's the same thing, being inside a woman, where it's the softest, the warmest. We come out of a womb, and then spend the rest of our lives trying to get back in. Intercourse is like going back home.

Women at these parties usually have their own birth control. They're on the pill, or they have a diaphragm or a cervical cap or something. As a rule, they don't depend on a condom. I don't have to worry about birth control because I've had a vasectomy. I usually tell them that at some point. You usually talk about AIDS, and now I carry the card that shows when I had my last negative test. I usually get one every year. Back when this AIDS scare started, we all got scared. The first time I went for an AIDS test in '86, after being so active, boy, I was really scared, let me tell you. It was negative, and they've been negative ever since.

At parties, I'd put condoms out all over the place. And it would vary—sometimes I'd find half a dozen of them on the floor here and there, and sometimes there wouldn't be many used. The idea that everybody uses condoms in swinging is not my experience. Everybody makes individual choices on these things, and a lot goes into it—if you've been with a person before, if it's somebody new, how well you do with condoms. I don't do well with condoms, because I'm into intercourse so much. For me it's the intimacy of it, the touching, and condoms decrease that sensitivity. I'll use them when necessary, but it's not my preference.

We have all wondered why nobody has ever gotten AIDS, of all the people we have known in swinging. I'm not as active in it now, but I still hear from people, and I think if anybody got it, it would go around pretty fast. We think it may be because swingers are so much into heterosexual sex. I didn't even know a gay guy until a couple of years ago. No gay guys are interested in swinging, and even guys who are bisexual aren't that interested. Swingers want somebody who turns on strong for sex, they don't want any horsing around, turning on and off. Bisexual guys tend to be more ambivalent about women, and women in swinging want guys who aren't ambivalent. They want guys who are hot into sex like they are. Also, there's little interest in drugs, and there isn't much AIDS among middle- or upper-income heterosexuals. There is some, and how much it has grown, nobody knows. They don't want to break down those statistics because they want to have as much money as possible for AIDS research, so they want to have as many heterosexuals scared as possible.

We're also very careful with our people. We've been very selective in picking nice, high-quality people. I've got another folder here that's a list of everybody who's come to every one of my parties. Twice we've had outbreaks of gonorrhea. That's one reason I keep track of everybody who comes, so if anything happens you can call the people who have been with that person. Still, everybody is fearful, so they've cut down. They've cut down on the numbers of people they see. They see people in smaller groups. After the big scare in '86, '87, it really fell off. But by the time I gave my last big party, in '89, nobody had gotten AIDS and people were getting less scared, so we had sixty-some at that party. In '90 I had smaller parties of a half dozen couples or so. I've kind of lost interest in big parties. In these last couple of years I've thought of more involvement with women. Part of it is that a good friend of mine moved away, so I've been lonely. Swinging is fun, it's exciting, and I did it for a long time for the thrill and the friendships. It's like a big family.

These days I see a woman named Ellen about every week. There's another woman I used to swing with, I see her off and on, every few weeks. Then there are two couples I see every month or so. With Ellen—I've known her for over ten years. She and her husband came to a party here. They told me they had an open marriage, so I started seeing her. I saw her for two or three years every week. She'd come in from the suburbs. Then I felt I was getting too fused, so I said we'd better just be friends for a while. We did that for a few years, then we started up again when I felt less vulnerable, and we developed a won-derful lover–friendship.

She's still married, and I'm friends with them both. She usually comes in Thursday night and goes back the next morning. Her hus-band has also been seeing another woman for about ten years. They used to go to swinging parties, but with the AIDS thing, this is mainly all they do now. Ellen is very affectionate, very soft, warm. Very much a vaginal woman. She doesn't prefer clitoral stimulation. She'll do it if someone wants to, but she prefers intercourse. She and I never do anything oral. Usually I don't even stroke her pussy at all. I'll get hard, and she'll just come on top of me. It used to be I'd come on top of her a lot more, but now I prefer her on me. She does, too, she can move more. We can move more together. And she has multiple or-gasms. She just comes and comes and comes. She's a gusher. Warm lubricant gushes out of her several times during a lovemaking session. With a gusher, supposedly your penis hits the G-spot and it makes a discharge of this light lubricating fluid. But it isn't just a physical thing. Back when we weren't as involved, didn't see each other as reg-ularly, she wouldn't gush so much. It's because we weren't as close. It happens when the intimacy is there.

Ellen loves to kiss all the time. At first I couldn't handle that, it scared me too much. Now I can get just as passionate as she does, and when she leaves I'm not still fused to her. So when we're making love, usually she's on top and we're kissing at the same time. The other thing with her—she's got a direct connection from her nipples to her vagina. When we're not kissing, very often I'll start sucking a nipple. What she likes is a little nibbling on it, a little pressure, a little pain, even. That goes right to her vagina. It makes her vagina more passive. When we're kissing in intercourse, there's more equal movement, but when I'm sucking on her nipple, it overcomes her. She can't move as much, or she doesn't want to. It's like she surrenders more and wants to take it in. A lot of times, that's the way I'll come. She's on top, and I'll be nibbling on her nipple, and she's really satiated and surrendered, and I can thrust as much and as hard as I want, and she just absorbs it.

One thing I often think about when I'm with a woman, I try to imagine what they're feeling. If I had a vagina and a man was putting his penis in, what it would feel like. Before the AIDS thing it wasn't too uncommon to have anal intercourse with women. And occasionally a woman would put her finger up your anus while you were in intercourse. The feeling I had when women would do that was a kind of surrender. It's like the anus is the control mechanism, and this was breaking down the controls, and I was passive. I wonder if that's the way it is with them, if that's what happens when a penis goes in their vagina. They lose control and submit to this intrusion.

I tried the sandwich thing a few times, right here on this floor. I remember one woman wanted a man in each hole. I got on the bottom and got in her vagina, and another guy climbed on top and got in her anus. That was fun as a fantasy, to do it a few times. But a lot of fantasies, I've found, you do them a few times and then you don't care about them anymore. There are other fantasies that you may like a lot longer and keep doing, but for me a lot of fantasies didn't last too long.

I still think it's important to play them out, though. It reminds me of this little book Freud wrote about Leonardo da Vinci. Da Vinci said you should withhold your feelings, your passions, until you thoroughly investigate a subject, or a work of art, and then let them flow. Freud said this is unhealthy. The strongest feelings are often immediate. If you hold them back, you lose that passion, that feeling of turn-on, and you become an investigator instead of a lover. That's what I've noticed many times. If you go with the turn-on right off, it's not clouded by a lot of investigation of what this person is like. The slate's clean. You don't have anything to hinder you, and you just go with the pure, raw turn-on, sexual affection, warmth, fusion, whatever. It's very powerful. That was Freud's point, you miss out on these passionate experiences if you can't go with the feelings. The women I run into outside of swinging so often can't go with the feelings. They say, "I have to get to know you." That can be very nice also, but I know when I'm attracted to a woman, and I'm often ready to go right then.

That's what's so interesting about getting a bunch of people together in a place that's set up for swinging. They get permission, and boy, see what they do. They go to it. [Laughs.] See, I think everybody is at their best when they have freedom. Because a feeling is real. A feeling is as real as a chair or a rug or the wall. If you have a feeling, if you have sexual desire for someone, you can either live it out and get it satisfied, or you can repress it and push it down, where it festers and you don't get rid of it. I think an ideal culture is one where feelings are respected and you don't go by rules and regulations. You go by where people are at. That includes unconscious feelings, too. The job is to get your feelings to the surface so you know what they are. In some ways the ideal situation is what we have in LA, where a lot of people are in therapy trying to bring up their underlying feelings, which are usually patterns imposed on them by their parents. They didn't choose them, and may not even be aware of them. If you can get them out in the open, you can begin to have some choices. Mother said sex is bad. Well, it feels pretty good to me!

MATT SHERRILL

He grew up on a farm in New York State. His father is a doctor, his mother a housewife. He has two brothers. "I had a conventional childhood and youth. A completely functional family. All this business that fucks so many people up didn't happen to me. My parents aren't very sexy people, but they're very committed and devoted and sweet to each other. They're also very churchy, but not doctrinaire. The Methodist church. If you pushed them, they would be secular humanists like most people. They believe in the Sermon on the Mount, love and goodness, be sweet to your fellow man, nothing supernatural.

"They made it easy for me on the gay issue. I never had sex of any sort till I was twenty-two. Then, after college, I would sometimes bring boyfriends home. I was discreet about having sex in my parents' house with young men, but I wasn't particularly secretive about it. I fell in love with a boy who was in graduate school at Berkeley, so I decided to go there, too, to be with him. The weekend I told my parents the plan, I came home late Saturday night, at twelve or one, and there was a light on. My parents go to bed at ten. Mother was in the library with her dressing gown on. She said, 'I want to talk to you about your relationship with Alan.' I was on edge. She said, 'You're going away for quite a long time, at a time in your life when things can happen very fast. So you have to know certain things about us. First of all, we support you to the hilt in whatever you do and how you choose your friends and how you live your life. The only thing is, we want you to be open with us. You have to understand that we accept you absolutely.' She wanted to know if I 'wanted to talk to somebody.' I said, 'I think if there was a possibility for reversing the situation, there would be something to talk about. Or if I was conflicted or unhappy about it. But since neither of those seems to be relevant, I don't know what we'd talk about.' So the key to this, in terms of mental health, was their attitude. It was a great gift to have that laid in my lap. In my en-

*tire life, I have never met a gay person who had anything like this kind of
intelligent love and understanding just handed to them."*

*Now he is forty-five, a stockbroker, living in an immaculate apart-
ment in Greenwich Village—big Persian rugs, classical music on the radio. He is slim, with short blond hair, dressed in jeans and a workshirt.
Among the photos on the walls are several of him as an extremely handsome young man. He makes no attempt to hide his orientation from colleagues or anyone else.*

• • •

The kind of sex that excites me is almost completely anonymous,
what I call electric sex. My friend Calvin, who's dead now, made that
up. You see somebody, and fifteen seconds later you're all over them.
The encounter may not last more than ten or fifteen minutes. It may
or may not culminate in coming home and going to bed together. I do
have four or five people in the city—most of them live within walking
distance—who are sex buddies. This as opposed to electric sex in
commercial establishments. These people call up, or I call up, at midnight, and say, "Do you want company?" They come over and we
have sex, drink a beer, and they're gone in one and a half hours. In
New York, gay people don't stay over, not if they live nearby. It's so
much more satisfactory to just sweep them out. Then you can put on
your nice comfy flannel pj's and get in bed and put on your glasses
and read. Of course, certain people, you're just dying for them to
want to stay, if you're very drawn to them in a romantic way. It's wonderful, but it doesn't happen to me very often.

Actually, I view sex as a sport. To me, it's the most consuming
possible sport. It's putting all of oneself on the line, mostly in terms
of just meat, pure physical attractiveness. It's the lure of the unknown, the feeling that anything is possible. Sex has great power, it
has the power of great, great exaltation, and not often, but once in a
while, you do catch up with someone and connect in a way that
makes you feel wonderful. I suppose there lingers at the back of one's
mind that it's part of the search for the ideal, perfect lover, the be-all

and end-all. I don't think such a thing exists, really. And I think it's unrealistic in any human relationship to put such great demands on any one person. But of course all our literature and our movies do fill us with that expectation. All of conventional society believes that. It's hard to buck the tide completely. But I believe it less and less. When one is twenty-six, all the people who have this idea and who seem likely candidates are also twenty-six. However, now that one's forty-five, there's a twenty-year age gap between me and the likely candidates, because it's mostly in their twenties that people have ideas like that. Then they get knocked down by the roughness of the world. A lot of my older friends have settled down, but they're with people I wouldn't be caught dead with, frankly.

Plus, I'm not very good at love affairs. I'm too sexually voracious. There are people who I think are wonderful, and I'm absolutely smitten by them. Then I find after not many times in the sack—five, six—that I'm thinking about someone else when I'm having sex with what is supposed to be number one. And I think, What's the point? There's an organization called Sex Addicts Anonymous, and I went to a meeting once out of pure curiosity. It was so corny and hokey. People were actually unhappy. And I'm not unhappy. I recognize that I am addicted to instant sex. Lots of it. Lots of electric sex. At an age when most men, straight or gay, are precluded from it, because they're not as attractive as they were at twenty-two, I seem to keep up.

As far as I know, I'm HIV-negative. Since 1979 I've been part of a study that tests my blood every four months. I told them not to tell me if I test positive, but to tell me if my T-cell count goes down sharply. So far it hasn't, so everything seems to be fine. I was very nervous about AIDS for most of the early eighties until they discovered that the only real good way to get it was by being the receptor in intercourse—something which I've never been able to master. I remember having a discussion about sex with an Englishwoman friend in '86. She asked, "What do you like to do? Don't you like to get fucked up the ass?" "No," I said, "I can't stand it. I just never managed the trick of how to expand the stinker enough. I never had it done to me." But did I like fucking people up the ass? Well, no. It seemed rather messy. You always had shit on your dick when you pulled out. So she said, "What do you like to do, then? Do you like sucking people's dicks?" I said, "Nah." She said, "Do you like it when other people suck your dick?" I said, "What I really like to do is hug and kiss people while I jack off. I like to have my tits played with. My tits are really far more sensitive than my dick." She said, "Darling, that's not sex, that's foreplay."

I didn't realize then that this was going to save my life. There have probably been just a half dozen people that I really got into fucking, where it slid in real easy. Because of my squeamishness, that always seemed to be a little pushing the envelope, fucking in the ass. It seemed to be unwise. I just thought that's not what the ass was made for. In the meantime, it's turned out to have saved my life, this funny view which my friends always considered eccentric. It still does seem to me that . . . well, nature made shit very, very smelly for a good reason, to keep us away from it, you know?

The places I have sex—there are various bookstores. There's Christopher Street Bookstore, where you go in and pay ten bucks and it's a vast labyrinth of little booths upstairs and downstairs and any time of day or night, particularly night from about eleven to three, there's fifty to eighty men in there, all having sex. There are various movie houses where this goes on, such as the Adonis on Broadway and Forty-third. Then there are various sex clubs. Over here in the meatpacking district there's the Cellblock. There's another on the corner of Fourteenth and Ninth called Jay's. And then there's the East Side Sauna, one of the last gay baths left in the city. I went there last night. Had some dinner and went there around eleven, stayed there until two, three in the morning, and had a richly rewarding time. [Laughs.] Came home and slept rather well, thank you. Now, this place gets a rather more—how shall I say?—not more sedate, but more respectable crowd, than these late-night bars downtown. A, because of the neighborhood, and B, because it's very clean, well-lit, well-administered. But amazing business it does. They charge you nine bucks to get in, thirteen bucks for a room, for four hours, and the place is packed. I mean, they have hundreds of rooms, and all the little halls and corridors are swarming with people running around who there weren't enough rooms for, who've got their clothes in a locker someplace.

You go in, come to the counter and pay, and they take your wallet and watch and keys and lock it up there, and then they give you a key. There are all these lockers, and a whole warren of upstairs and downstairs and little passageways, semi-lit, and you find your room and let yourself in, and the room is physically about twice as big as that sofa, and it's got a pretty narrow single bed and a little light and a little table and a hanger and a door and that's it. A lockable door. So you take off your coat and tie and jacket and hang 'em up, and then, well, you can go to sleep if you want, or you can leave the door open and see if anyone comes in to visit, or you can lock up the house and go visiting. There's a steam room and a sauna room, and a big shower. There's a big lounge with carpeted tiers with pillows and stuff, and a screen where they show dirty movies, and vending machines so people are having Cokes and coffee and potato chips and bumming cigarettes off each other. But see, nobody has anything on but a towel, a white towel wrapped around their waist, usually folded in half lengthwise so it doesn't dangle down to their knees. There's absolutely no guesswork about anyone's physique or health or skin or anything else.

And there's people of all kinds, people in their seventies, people in their teens. Mostly white, but ten to fifteen percent black. And what people do in these sex clubs is a great deal of endless shopping. I get the impression, and I know this is true for me, that the selection and the conquest is far more exciting than the consummation. The amount of time spent in what someone called S&M, which means "stand and model," checking out who's there, what they look like, what they act like, little visual cues, following people over here, following people over there, all this delicate minuet of courtship, takes an awful lot of time, and part of it is that people are naturally fearful of rejection, so before they take some irretractable step, such as initiating conversation, they want signs to make sure their advances are going to be welcome. Also, there is a great pecking order, from the most desirable person to the least desirable person. A lot of S&M is to determine where you stand in the pecking order. Naturally, people want to fuck up rather than fuck down. [Laughs.] So everyone's paying attention to the people above them on the beauty ladder and trying to ignore everyone below them, and sidestep them, avoid them.

There are relatively few people who are mouth-wateringly attractive, whereas there are a lot of fat old guys who follow you around begging, which is painful. Especially as I believe you can't be rude to people, you can't slap them, they all pay their money, and we're all gonna be in that situation someday, so I always feel like one has a duty to be friendly and not to treat even repulsive people like they're less than human. There's horrible ways and gentler ways to move away from people. But you see a lot of awful behavior. People say, "Get your hands off me, you creep." It makes your skin crawl.

So last night I started wandering around. There's people in their rooms with the doors open, in all kinds of poses, some with the lights on, some with the lights off. Some lie on their stomachs the whole time, indicating that they want to stay on their stomachs and be fucked. Some have brought elaborate equipment in little duffel bags, such as dildos. If someone's lying on his stomach, feet toward the door let's say, with just the light on the table and a big dildo standing beside the lamp, you can figure out what he wants, especially if there's a great big tub of Vaseline. Some people have on various sorts of outfits, fantasy gear, such as a harness or a mask or a bathing suit, whatever that means.

You're wandering around, and immediately people start coming up to you and brushing past you in the corridor, or groping you and saying, "Do you want to come down to my room?" "Thanks, no."

I've always felt like I was skinny and not very strong. I suppose by way of compensation, I'm fascinated by people who are strong and muscled and well made. Strapping people. This goes back to when I was a kid, so I don't think I'm a victim of the New York gym mentality. My focus is on the body, the physique. Genitalia have always been pretty uninteresting to me. Whereas a lot of gay men are riveted by big dicks. And when I had my first gay sex ever, with a bartender in his seedy apartment in Paris, he said, *"Relèves-toi, t'as la plus grande bitte que j'ai jamais vu."* Cheer up, you've got the biggest dick I've ever seen. And everybody else I've ever had sex with who spoke up said the same thing. At first, I thought this was blather. But then I realized I am quite unusual. Probably that's why I'm not that interested in dicks, not feeling deficient in the dick department. But if I go looking to round up somebody to sleep with, I always go to a place like the baths where everybody is naked, or where there's some back room where people are unzipped. Because at the age of forty-five, it's not like being twenty-three, when you walk into a gay bar and all heads swivel and people come over and say, "Hi, my name's Bill, you're a new face in town, can I buy you a beer?" All of a sudden, at about the age of thirty-five, you become invisible.

So in the baths, I just hang the towel around my neck instead of wearing it around my waist. And my dick is usually semi-hard. The effect of anyone paying attention to me immediately perks it up. And I usually have to flash people before I get any expression of interest. So cruel is the world.

Last night, I saw this very nice-looking kid whose name turned out to be Daniel. He was not American. He said, "Come to my room." I said, "No, you come to mine." So he came down. I would say he was about twenty-five. I suppose he stayed in my room for ten or fifteen minutes. But a very strange thing—he didn't want to kiss. And sex without kissing for me is not sex, it's just playing around. Kissing is a necessity. In fact, I have a rule called the "kissing rule." You may wonder if it's dangerous in New York bringing people home for sex. You hear terrible stories of people who get murdered or rolled. I've never had—touch wood—a funny experience. That's because of my rule: Never bring anyone home whom I haven't kissed before. I find you can't lie if you're giving someone a really deep, passionate kiss. You can't disguise how you feel about him. The people who are interested in robbing you or doing something violent, they don't give you that kind of kiss. So I think it's a life-saving rule. I always recommend it to young homos.

With this kid, it was little dry kisses on the lips, mainly heading me off and turning me away. He was big on the tits, he wanted to play with my tits, and for me to play with his. I think he was South American in some way. Black hair, swarthy skin, very good muscular physique. We started out by standing, and eventually we were both kneeling on the bed facing each other, and then I was lying on my back and he was sitting on my chest, and then the other way around. While he was sitting on me he was playing with my chest, and I had a big pot of Vaseline, I was playing with his balls and rubbing Vaseline on his sphincter [makes squishy sound], just playing with his ass, which he seemed to quite like. I found it rather unsatisfying because he wouldn't do certain things I wanted him to. I wanted him to suck my dick and kiss. It's not like I said, "Would you please suck my dick?" and he said, "No, I will not." I did what the monkeys call "present," I sort of pushed his head in that direction and he went in another direction. But he was hot to trot, he wanted to continue, and I had a problem on my hands, because I hadn't been there very long or been exploring. And I feel like if someone won't kiss me, they're keeping me at some sort of remove. I was eager to ditch him and get on to other things. So I stood up, picked up my towel, and said, "I think we need to take a walk, you and I, get some air." He said, "Oh, no, come on," and started to put his hands on me again, and I said, "No, no, let's go." He said, "Well, come visit me later," and I said all right. Then I shooed him out.

Walked around some more. Then I got very excited, because I saw this *very* good-looking person, black hair all wet, dark, sort of Italian, a lean, wiry kid of between twenty-one and twenty-four. Small, maybe five-six, five-seven, and sexy. God, he was a good-looking kid. Strong and lithe and boyish. A wonderful shape to his torso, not a bodybuilder shape, but a beautiful, graceful, athletic body. With olive skin, and he'd been out in the sun too. He was by far the best-looking person in the place, from my point of view.

I was very aware of this boy, I watched where he went, and all of a sudden I realized that, bless his heart, he was returning my attention. I was following him in a covert sort of way, and he'd just pause in little places and look at me, give me little smiles. Then he stopped and waited for me, so it became impossible to follow him anymore. I said, "Why don't you come downstairs to my room?" He said, "Okay." He came in, took charge of the door and closed it and then just turned to me, wrapped his arms around me, pressed the whole length of his body against me and gave me this deep, deep penetrating embrace and kiss that went on for a long, long, time. It was just wonderful. [Long pause.] And, um, then, I don't know, he seemed to have this physical instinct to know what to do. He was very touchy and cuddly and close and intimate, put his hands in all the right places. There are a few people who just seem to be made for sex, who are so affectionate and warm and giving and strong and cuddly and gorgeous and lean and—they can sense that you like to have your tits played with or have your dick played with or have your dick sucked or your ass played with, and he didn't leave anything untouched or ignored, he was immediately there doing it all. I said to myself, Oh, this kid's fantastic, I'll just have to bring him home and install him forever. I often have this fantasy if someone is gorgeous enough, and it's a fun fantasy, but it never happens, of course.

He stayed for maybe forty minutes. I remember one moment with particular ecstasy. He did something that was unusual. He gave me a good rim-job. I find it so exciting to have someone eat my ass, mainly because it seems like, Okay, anything's possible now, this kid's really into it, there's no limits anymore, we're rolling for takeoff. On the face of it, it would seem to be repulsive, but if somebody is so into sex and into me that he's willing to do that, it's a great gift. Most people are too fastidious. For example, I would never do it to anybody. [Laughs uproariously.] It's a form of hypocrisy, I suppose. I'm just too squeamish. It doesn't seem like good judgment to me. [Laughs.] But he did it, for a couple of minutes. And the point is, the thought of his doing it is more exciting than the actuality, as with so many things in sex. The thought of it and the willingness and the wanting to, that's what's neat.

This boy's name was Chris. I always think it's polite to ask. Anyway, at some stage we were both kneeling on the bed and he was playing with himself and I was nibbling at his chest, and all of a sudden he exploded and shot a load all over the sheets and made a puddle. I wished he hadn't, I was enjoying it so much, it really was something special. So I, without wanting to put him on the spot, I wondered if he would sit there and start a conversation and ask me my name and where I was from and say, "Gosh, you're so handsome," and so on. But I'm sorry to tell you, alas, he did not. He bounced up, grabbed his towel, and said, "That was great, thanks, I'll be off." Of course my heart is breaking, and I thought, Well, when you're hot, you're hot, and when you're not, you're not. So that was that.

There's a protocol about coming. In certain heavy situations, such as at someone's house, there's an expectation that things will be reciprocal. If I have already come, it's polite—but it can get to be rather a duty to nurse someone along, sometimes for fifteen minutes on end while they pump away. In a place like this, there's less duty to do so, because there are hundreds of men wandering around with hard-ons not fifteen feet from where you are. And even though I was enjoying this kid immensely, I didn't necessarily want to have an orgasm with him, because that puts an end to the play for the whole evening. Though that was not the issue, the issue for me was, Is this kid going to show any human friendliness and ask me for my telephone number? So that was last night's little heartache. [Laughs.]

Then I wandered around some more. Took a shower. Talked with an old friend. By this time I'd been at the baths maybe two and a half hours. The amount of time I spent wandering around as opposed to actually doing it was a ratio of maybe five to one. Same with every-body else. There was a black guy who looked like a college athlete. Wonderful athletic body, sort of tall, and a fine-looking face. I was transfixed by this guy, who of course was unaware of my existence the whole evening. I kept seeing him, going here, going there, but nothing ever came of it. Then there was this man, I suppose in his thirties, a big guy, standing in his room. I paused at the door and he was looking me up and down, and as I looked at him, he started play-ing with his dick, indicating interest. He looked all right, so I went in and closed the door. All of a sudden the atmosphere changed, and what he wanted was a great dominance-and-submission scene, with him the dominant one. I closed the door and he said [mimics low voice], "Get on your knees and suck my dick." So I just left. [Laughs.] I smiled and said, "You're pretty quick on the uptake, aren't you?" Not that I was opposed in the last resort to sucking his dick, but I thought he was giving himself airs to start so fast, so corny and blatant and old-fashioned, straight out of a claptrap porno novel. I almost laughed in his face.

Eventually I thought it may be time to go home. Then I happened by Daniel's room, and there he was. He had the light on and he smiled. I hadn't told him earlier that I had broken it off because he wouldn't kiss me—I don't believe in pointing out people's faults to them—but I think he'd figured it out. When I stopped by again he was a little more eager to kiss me. Still not satisfactorily, still not in the way of the dark young Italian, who just swallowed you. But I had a most unusual orgasm. I was sitting on his bed sideways, my back to the wall, and he was kind of sitting on my knees, playing with my dick. He had a smooth sculpted body with big shoulders and arms and pecs. All of a sudden I was transfixed by his body, and I was feeling all around his lat muscles, and he had marvelous intercostal muscles, and a washboard stomach. He liked to have his tits played with and sucked and nibbled, so we were doing all that, and I was getting quite turned on, especially since he told me all kinds of things that were heartwarming, "Oh, I've been thinking about you all evening," so I felt gratified. I had on two big cock-rings around my dick and balls, and a leather strap around my scrotum, and all of a sudden— you know how sometimes before you have an orgasm, there's a little bit of pre-come juice that comes out of your dick? Well, I could tell I was close to coming, and instead of a few drops of pre-come juice, quite a bit of come, a whole drool of it was running down my dick. I thought, Oh, God, I had *ejaculatio praecox* without the sensation. But I could tell by playing with my dick that I was still hot, and the come provided all this lubricant, so I jacked off a little more and came again. First time in my life—sort of like a double-yolk egg.

You know, most of my friends my age don't behave like I do at all. They gave up this kind of behavior ten years ago because it wasn't rewarding. If there are no goodies up that alley, they don't go up that alley anymore. Well, there are still goodies up that alley for me, lots of them. I'm slim, my hair hasn't turned white. A lot of people, in order to avoid being cast on the waste heap, spend time pumping up and building up their bodies, trying to be attractive that way. So I'm just as happy to have a useful endowment. One time when I was at the Chelsea Gym with an Italian friend of mine who I often had sex with, we were standing in line for the pec-deck machine, and he said, "Matt, look at all these people waiting to do the pec-deck. What they really want is a dick like yours, but there's no such thing as a dick machine."

These days, at least fifty percent of my hunt for sex is the affirmation that I can still pull 'em, as my friend the Englishwoman used to say. She had quite a bit of sexual success herself. One time I went to her house and I asked, "Well, how'd you get on with the carpenter today?" And she said, "Pulled 'im." He'd fucked her standing on the basement stairs. So, I don't know, maybe it's not fifty percent, but it seems like the curiosity and the adventure is at least fifty percent, and the actual pleasure of the thing is more than fifty percent, so it adds up to far more than one hundred percent. I'm endlessly curious about people's bodies, what they feel like. I just love touching their torsos and their arms and their chests. It's terribly satisfying to touch firm, hard, young flesh. It makes me feel more fully alive than anything else. But proof that I can pull 'em is a big part of it. Now, this raises the question, What's gonna happen in the future? What's it going to be like when I'm fifty or sixty? The prognosis is fairly grim. But I don't worry about it. I think it'll take care of itself.

3

THE LONG HAUL

THE SIX INTERVIEWS in this chapter examine sex between partners committed to a life together. Of course, this is not the only chapter to contain such interviews; what distinguishes these is the way they zero in on the pleasures and perils of sex with a spouse in diverse styles of relationship.

Hank Castleman, the first speaker, is thirty-eight, married, monogamous, with a young son. He opens with the frank admission that he is drawn to women, like his wife, Colleen, who are sexually more timid than he: "Somebody who's a little tentative or shy, that allows me to take charge, and I feel much better." But this makes for built-in frustration: He wants more sex than she does, and she is rarely as free as he might like. Nevertheless, he and Colleen have discovered a way of making love that seems to please them both, and that somehow is the same but different every time. According to Hank's description, he appears to set the pace and direction of sex. He often fantasizes, the point of the fantasies being that Colleen has become the voraciously sexual woman of his dreams. And when they are at the peak of passion, "I don't believe this, it's wonderful—she has become the woman in the fantasy." He ruminates about the years before marriage, when sex seemed a "voyage of discovery." Now it seems more a "refuge" from the squalls of life. He longs for it to happen more often, but he is clearly a man in love.

Hank's interview touches on many of the themes of married sexual life: Which partner wants more sex? Who seems less constrained? Who runs things in bed? How does the couple work out differences? How do they perfect the acrobatics of intimacy and distance? How do they keep sex fresh? Are they content with a zone of comfort, or does it seem a curse?

The other speakers here naturally have answers different from Hank's. Ted Stewart's wife is so inhibited that for years it was "like I was fucking an inanimate object." But Ted, a "shy guy," is no sexual dervish himself, and he stayed with Mary for other reasons. Slowly, they too have developed a style that works, though they still have great trouble talking about sex. Ted also has "flings"—not long ones, and not often, but the possibility is always on his mind. Is this because sex at home is so circumscribed? Not necessarily. Some studies, including Pepper Schwartz and Philip Blumstein's *American Couples,* suggest that there is no relation between infidelity and quality or quantity of sex at home, or even general satisfaction with the marriage. Schwartz and Blumstein add, however, that adulterers do tend to be less "certain that their [marriages] will last" than are monogamous partners.

Erica Miller, a lesbian "married" for three years, lives in fear of that notorious affliction, "lesbian bed death." Most couples of any orientation lament the waning of lust, and biochemists have even begun to explain why it happens. New lovers are flooded with natural amphetamines that make for dizzy passion, but the body develops a tolerance, so after a few years the high wears off. What replaces the amphetamines are endorphins that promote peace and calm—the "comfort" many of these speakers refer to. Lesbian couples apparently do face the greatest danger of sexless relationships, not for chemical reasons but sociological ones. Still, Erica's passion has not cooled, and for her, intimacy feeds the fire: "I'm so comfortable with Arlene, I trust her so much, and I feel like anything is allowed."

Robert Rauh and Lloyd Rappaport also have marriages where anything is allowed—up to a point. Robert and his lover Dan are both wedded to sex with strangers and have given up on monogamy: "The problem is, I'm not his best sex partner, and he's not my best partner. We know that. What he likes and what I like are so different that we still haven't found the meeting ground." They are working on hotter sex at home, and trying out the type of open relationship often favored by gay men—but they find that taking nights off for fun elsewhere is not so simple.

Lloyd and his wife have been "swingers," on and off, for twenty-five years. When Lloyd recounts their adventures at parties and sex clubs, it is clear that what he searches for is a complex connection with her. "Somebody at a club hurt my feelings a few months ago. He said, 'I can tell you like to watch your wife get fucked.' I didn't get into a discussion but I felt like saying, 'No, I like to *participate* in my wife getting fucked.' "

Fantasy, flings, straight talk, deep trust, group sex: all are tools in the toolbox. Finally, Marge Strothers, fifty-two and on her third marriage, has an attitude toward sex probably common to a great many women. After two poor choices—her first husband slept around, her second beat her up—she now lives with a warm, honest man. Their sex is not spectacular. They have their troubles in bed. But it is loving and pleasurable, and that, for her, is more than enough.

HANK CASTLEMAN

"After years," he says, "you realize that you've become a kind of specialist in having sex with your wife." The statement seems to surprise even him, for he has just finished recounting his hell-raising period, years of heavy drinking, recreational drug use, and aggressive pursuit of "just about any attractive woman I came across." Now he has, in classic fashion, settled down. He is thirty-eight, married five years, the father of a two-year-old boy. His sandy blond hair is receding fast, and he worries about his weight, his gums, his liver. He is a magazine editor who lives on the East Side of Manhattan.

He first met Colleen in a nightclub when she was twenty-seven and he thirty. The next night they went out to another club, where, sitting on the floor, they kissed. "It was probably the best kiss I ever had. I'll never forget it. It was so soft. But not just soft—cooperative. It was totally warm and soft, and she was completely relaxed. She has the best lips of anybody I know. From that point on, I was hooked."

• • •

Her being Catholic has something to do with it. On some deep level, I don't even know why, it's tremendously attractive to me. I'll see these women, and I know the look: open face, white skin, freckles. This Irish Catholic look. It's mostly in the face, it's not necessarily the body I'm attracted to. Other women's bodies can be much more sexy to me, but the attraction I feel for Colleen or women like her is more profound. There's a longing and an excitement and a need that goes beyond the sexual part, and I feel in love. Something about these women makes me feel safe, and that makes me feel excited. And the women I get involved with often have a hesitancy about them in bed. Colleen was that way, she was nervous, a bit passive. I like that. A lot of the women I ran into were more active, but to be honest, that frightens me. Somebody who's a little tentative or shy, that allows me to take charge.

The sex was kind of awkward at first. In fact, what drew me to Colleen was not the sex. Sex was better with other women. It took quite a while for Colleen and me to talk about what would really get us excited. For example, she gets much more turned on if when we're fucking, I rub her clitoris. That's how we do it, how we've done it for years. That's what she likes. She would never have told me that at the beginning. It took months of getting to know each other before she did. Eventually, she told me that was the way she always came. I was shocked. I used to think, Well, if she can't get excited by my fucking her, something must be wrong, she's not really turned on to me if I have to do this. I felt self-conscious about it, and that added to the awkwardness. At the beginning I resisted doing it, but I soon realized that she didn't come if I didn't do it. Part of my pleasure is to get her excited. So I started doing it. When we have sex now, I don't even think about it. It doesn't seem awkward, it's just what we do. I've gotten quite skilled at it. And it sure does make a difference.

I have similar things—like I don't get that excited from a blowjob. It's okay, I usually wouldn't say no, but it's not my big thing. And in a way, there's something upsetting about it. At some point I get anxious. I want to enjoy it, but for some reason it just doesn't work. In sex, I often have a clutter of comparisons with other people in my head, and most guys I know love blowjobs. But I don't. It seems weird to me, so I was reluctant to tell her that. I wasn't that courageous about it. I had all these fears I brought to sex, and they linger on, although less than before.

I also have fantasies a lot during sex. Although I'm attracted to Colleen because she's not active and she makes me feel safe, the fantasies are the opposite. I fantasize about her being the aggressive one. For instance, I have fantasies that we're in a group of people around a dinner table. Maybe her family's dinner table. Her parents are away, and there's a group of several couples. We're playing a card game, strip poker, or a type of elaborate strip poker where anybody who wins gets to have the person who lost do anything they want. And the fantasy is always of Colleen becoming very sexual. All she's interested in is sex. Fucking, sucking, exhibiting herself, that's it. Nothing else. It's mostly a seduction fantasy. She might seduce one of the guys at the table by walking up the stairs and stripping off her clothes as she goes. Then she'll get on her hands and knees on the stairs and want to fuck there. That's enough. It usually doesn't get any more elaborate than that. It's the process of setting it up, watching her become totally sexual. There's this beckoning quality to her in the fantasy, like, Do it to me. I'm often watching. She'll have sex with somebody else, or I'll feel that it's happening, and then she'll want me. Sometimes I have sex with other people in the fantasy, but I'm always very aware of Colleen. What happens is it becomes more and more purely sex. There's a complete breakdown of inhibitions. There's no competition. There's no feeling insecure about my sexuality or the size of my cock. There's no sense of being burdened with responsibility because I'm the main performer. In the fantasy this sex isn't all directed at me, it's part of a group. Or there's another guy who can function just as well, and I can lie back and be excited.

The problem is, when we're actually having sex, she's not this complete sexual person very often. When it happens, it's extraordinary, it's like a whole world. I try to get her to smoke pot from time to time, because it happens more often when she smokes pot. But it makes her nervous, to give up that much control. I remember one time, we had gotten some pot, and she put on a Jon Lucien record, this kind of overdone sexual music. I couldn't believe she even had this record. She went into the back room and came out in this black teddy and started to dance. She had never done this before. Then she took it off and was standing there in the living room naked, with this music going, and completely aroused. I felt like this was the best thing that ever happened to me, and I was in love with her utterly. That's what makes me hang in there, because without a doubt, it was the sexiest thing I've ever been involved with. Years pass [laughs], but there's always a sense it might happen again. You could never figure out what right combination of emotion or chemistry or whatever went to make that moment, but suddenly we were having sex in the living room in a way that was so exciting, and she was so beautiful.

Most of the time, we have a way of having sex that we don't change that much. We try from time to time, maybe change the location or something, but as time goes by we change the location less. So our way of having sex is very familiar. It doesn't seem old, it seems like, Here we are again, this is what we like to do. I used to think that would bother me a lot. In the back of my mind there's a voice, an old tape saying, The same meal every day can't keep you very happy. But you don't interact with a meal. Even the same type of sex, we bring different feelings to it every time.

The "way" is in our bed, rather than in the living room or the kitchen or the bathroom. It usually starts the same way. Like today, Colleen was wearing a pair of underwear and a shirt. I just had some shorts on. We lay in bed. We kissed a lot. One of the things I like is to look at the top of her ass and the way her hip goes down to her stomach and her navel. She's lying on her side. I like to look at her and slowly begin to take her underwear off. I usually don't pull the underwear far enough down to see her pussy at this point. I like to spend a few minutes at that, running my hand over her, kissing her on the belly, and nice long kisses on the mouth. Then over the next few minutes take the rest of her clothes off. Usually move my hand down between her legs to see if she's getting excited. If she isn't I'll back off a bit and take more time. If she is, I'll start to rub her clit.

After that I might eat her out, if that's what she wants. If she tastes really good I don't mind doing that for another fifteen minutes. I like to lie there eating her, rubbing my hands on her stomach or her legs, or reaching up to rub her nipples. I usually try to look up and see her face and see if she's getting very excited. But I also like to turn her over on her stomach, I like to look at her that way. There are points when I want to really be with her, and other points when I like to get some distance. A more active woman would interfere with this process, but she lets me do what I want. I particularly like when she's on her stomach to raise up her hips and stick my fingers in, because I can rub her clit nicely that way. At those times I don't want to see her face. I can get lost in my fantasies, and the sex itself becomes a bit of a fantasy.

Then I might get her on her hands and knees and fuck her that way, reach around and rub her tits and clit. In that position the clit sticks out. That's the way to get her most excited, and it's best for me because I can really feel her clit, it's perfectly formed in my fingers.

But I don't like to come in that position. After a while I shift around and lie on my back and have her get on top of me. That's the beginning of what I find the most exciting, because this is her being active. It fits in with the fantasy. And I like the way it looks. There's a sense of her being an animal on me, not a person. Using me. Her fucking me, or getting herself fucked by me. I'll lean up and kiss her breasts. Like today, I had her wear pearls. She had the pearls down around her nipples and I couldn't stop putting my mouth there, kissing the pearls and her nipples.

But I also like to look at her ass. I like the way she spreads out on me. It works well with another fantasy I touch on from time to time. In this one, I'm on a porch with some people, and she comes up from the beach and opens up her robe, and she's naked, and she walks up to somebody on a lounge chair and gets on top of him and fucks him, just like that. Could be me, could be somebody else, but it's important that it not be just me. That fantasy fits in with her being on top. We'll fuck that way for a while. I'll have to get a condom or something, that always wrecks it for a moment. Then she'll get back on top of me, and it's perfectly comfortable for me at this point to reach underneath. One of the best things when we're really fucking is to rub her clit and move my other hand around and stick my finger up her ass. This feeling of her being between my two hands is the most exciting thing. I feel like I've got complete control of her. I can get her right up to the point and then stop her by rubbing her clit faster or slower, or lighter, or stopping. Early on is when I play with that the most. There's a final point where we're going to come. Then I'll just rub her, I stop thinking about it. It's as if I'm not aware of it anymore, thank God. At the beginning it was a problem, I'd get a cramp in my hand. But now that never happens. By the end, she bends down over me and I'm not looking at her at all. I don't know what I'm doing. Sometimes I lose sense of things, of where my cock is. It's like there's a cloud, this erotic cloud, if she's really wet. So I'm concentrating down, all my attention is on that, on fucking and the sound of her.

Usually we come together. We're pretty good that way. I tend to make more noise than her. Often I begin to laugh. I'll come and I'll start to laugh, I can't help it. Which she used to think was weird. She'd ask me afterward why I was laughing at her, and I'd have to assure her that I was just laughing. She's a very discreet person, in the sense of making noise, even when she's coming. And we don't talk as much during sex as we used to. At the end, I'll start to talk about wanting to fuck her, and at the very end she'll say, "Fuck me, fuck me." That tells me we've passed—what's it called, when you're about to fall into a black hole in space? The "event horizon." You're under the influence of the black hole until you pass the event horizon. At that point it's all over, you're quickly swooped in and sucked into the black hole. So I know we've passed the event horizon when she says, "Fuck me." I've come to find that tremendously sexy, her not talking until we've passed into that zone, and then it suddenly becomes hot in a way it wasn't before. Right at the end she likes me to rub her nipples with the flat of my hand in a circular motion, not violently, just brushing them softly. If she's getting ready to come, that'll put her over the top. I can't do both breasts at the same time, because one hand is at work on her clit. Sometimes she'll do it for herself, she likes to do that. I know she's really excited when her nipples are standing out hard. And her lips get all puffed up and swollen and wet, and her hair is hanging down, and it's like, Holy shit, I don't believe this, she has become the woman in the fantasy.

I never fantasize about other women when I'm with her. I used to, and if I'm jerking off I'll think of other women. But most of the time I fantasize about her. That's a nice thing for a husband to do. [Laughs.] It's true, I think she's sexy. Eight years into a relationship, it's nice to fantasize about your wife. It probably contributes to the sex continuing to be good. When I lived with my old girlfriend I used to fantasize about other women, and it pulled me away from her, it made me want other women more. I feel with Colleen that there's so much more we could have, so many ways that our sexuality could be increased, that it keeps me drawn into her. Even when I get nuts and frustrated and angry at her about the sex not being good enough, there's a certain amount of hope there. We'll get into these arguments when I'm despairing and angry, but I'm trying to rouse her in some way, stir her up, maybe with a threat, because she has a tendency to accept things the way they are, which is like death to me.

We have sex a couple times a week nowadays. I wish it was more.

During the week, I often get home at ten, my son Paul's up until late, we're tired, and we just want to rest. Colleen has to take care of Paul by herself three nights a week, and it's hard for her not to feel angry about it. So we usually have sex on the weekends. And the week starts to seem like one long time in the desert.

If I had done this interview in the middle of this week, it might have sounded completely different. Colleen was angry at me for not being around. I was hyper, I was anxious, I was out of it. But I wanted to have sex anyway. I thought, Maybe it'll help me get my brain back together. So I said, "Let's go to bed," and Colleen didn't say no. We started to fool around, and I realized she wasn't into it. But she wasn't saying anything about it. I said, "Do you want to do this or not?" She said, "Oh, yes." We kept going, and after about ten minutes I finally said, "No you don't, you don't want to do this. This is embarrassing. This is humiliating. I don't want to be with anybody who's just going through the motions, and if you don't want to do it, tell me." She said, "Well, yeah, you're right, I don't want to." I said, "Fine, but it hurts my feelings that you wouldn't tell me that." So it was a bit of a disaster. I would have been disappointed if she said no about the sex, but don't get me riled up and then tell me you didn't want to. Or worse, go through the motions. We're living together eight years, and she's going through the motions?

At times like that I say to myself, Not only is this relationship horrible, but the sex is horrible. Mostly because we don't do it enough. I know two times a week isn't so bad, but in the middle of the week, it's a wasteland. I experience time as having come to an end. [Laughs.] On that weekday night, I'm trapped in a nightmarish zone without any connection to the future or the past. In these moods I'll be so bleak, she'll say, "It's like what happened on the weekend never happened." And to tell the truth, that's how I experience it. I've talked to people who don't have sex for a month. If we were having it once a month I'd go crazy. We'd either be in therapy or broken up. Colleen would be more capable of accepting it, as long as other things were nice and comfortable. But I wouldn't be comfortable—not if we weren't having sex.

When I was younger I used to think I was on a sexual voyage of discovery with all these women. Now I feel like I've come to a stop with this voyage business. Most of my attention isn't on sex, it's on my work, it's on Paul, it's on the demands of living. What sex has become is a refuge. Mostly I see it now as a place where I can have comfort and pleasure at the same time, a way to be with Colleen that's not full of stress, that's tender and close.

ERICA MILLER

"I have this theory," she says, "that a lot of people think being a lesbian is the lack of being a straight person, as opposed to being an extremely sexual person. Like it's a slight twist on spinsterhood." She herself admits to some worries on this score, wondering if she and her lover Arlene are falling victim to what she calls "lesbian bed death." But she is determined not to succumb, "because I'm not going to just have a roommate. Forget it. That happened to my last relationship, and I'm not doing it again."

She is slim, pretty, dark-haired, forty, a free-lance art critic and curator who lives in a Victorian house in Chicago. Her own paintings—small, delicately colored, dreamlike—decorate the walls. She was raised in the suburban Midwest, and her childhood was happy enough, but her parents' marriage wasn't, not least because of sexual tension: Her father was impotent with her mother, who talked to Erica about it from the time she was nine or ten years old. After Erica and her brother left for college, her mother announced that she wanted a divorce, whereupon her father died of a heart attack. Her mother remarried, this time happily. "I know she rediscovered her sexuality after my father died. What a shame it took so long."

Erica discovered hers at a tender age: she remembers masturbating during naptime in nursery school. By the age of six she was teaching her method to friends. "I had a little studio bed with bolsters on it. I took the bolsters down and rode on them. This girl Kathy would come over, and we'd do it together." In retrospect, she realizes that by eight or nine she was sexually focused on girls, and by high school she was madly in love with one friend, though she refused to admit it. She had her first sex with a woman at nineteen, and her first years as a lesbian were conflict-ridden and miserable. She has slept with men on occasion. Now, "I have very few doubts that I'm gay, but I think the early part was as much a retreat from men as it was an attraction to women. If I had it to do over again, I'd be *with men some more. I think I'd still choose to be with women, but part of me would like to make sure this is a complete choice, and it's not a result of being afraid of men."*

• • •

The last time I had sex was the night before last, Monday night. We were lying in bed making jokes about how we had to make love, because I was doing this interview. It hadn't been all that long—maybe a week, which seems to be about how often we're having sex in the last few months. That's a big drop for us. And it takes me longer to get turned on than it used to with Arlene, for sure. So what else is new? It's starting to alarm me a little bit. One thing I was talking to her about is that the longest I've gone in a relationship before lesbian bed death sets in is three and a half years, which is how long we've been together. I don't know what that means. I don't know if people aren't supposed to be monogamous for that long. It's kind of panicking me, and panic makes me stubborn and resistant.

So I was feeling very tired and blocked and tense, and it took a lot of talking for me to get relaxed. It started by her telling me how much she needed me and wanted me. Seducing me. I still felt tense, but then it just turned over. It starts from deep within, and then you totally give it up. Except that in times gone by I would have felt that warm buzz before we even did anything.

We started out with clothes on. I took mine off. She took hers off. We used to make a big deal of taking each other's clothes off. I don't like that a lot. I mostly don't like it because it takes too long. Maybe I'm getting too businesslike, but I don't get turned on by languorous unbuttoning. I'm just trying to get mine off—call me a narcissist. I remember in the beginning we would have dry humps, when we would do it partially clothed, or even fully clothed. I was amazed at how turned on I got through clothes. Now we play with clothes a little. If I'm wearing jeans, she'll pull up really hard on the back of the jeans, which is great. Or she'll do that with my panties. Usually the panties go quickly, but sometimes we do it over them, because that can be a turn-on. We haven't done much dressing-up stuff. We talk about it constantly, but what we do and what we talk about are two different things.

At first on Monday I was on top of her, and after we took our clothes off I wanted to continue that way, but she wanted to get on top of me, so she did. I still wasn't completely relaxed. For many, many months, she could awaken my neck in a way it has never been before. She could kiss my neck, and I'd feel it immediately in my crotch. But when I'm tense, it tickles, so on Monday night I started laughing, and that discouraged her. Sometimes she'll laugh with me, and she did, but I think she felt a sense of failure. I could tell she was upset about it, so I committed myself to trying to relax more. I told her not to stop, and it changed.

Then we kissed a lot. That's always a strong part of our lovemaking, real deep kissing. That's what finally turned me on. And after that, it was quicker than it usually is. We started sex-moving almost from the beginning, moving our hips, all of that. There wasn't as much breast stuff as there usually is. We didn't meander much. She was on top of me, and I was stimulating her, but mostly not inside. We've always had a problem with simultaneity. We often start out touching each other at the same time, and then we get very turned on, but I think we've come together maybe once the whole time we've been together. A lot of it has to do with size. Arlene is taller than me, so if she's on top of me, I find it difficult to get my fingers inside her at the same time she's inside me. But if I'm on top of her she seems to be able to get inside me without too much problem. So what happened on Monday was I withdrew my hand from Arlene and she just finished with me, and that was great. When I say "finished with me," I mean I came. I hate the way that sounds, "She finished with me." Sort of goes with the word *service*.

She usually puts two or three fingers in me, but it varies. Sometimes I don't even know. It partly depends on how wet I am. She usually doesn't massage my clit at the same time. It's nice when she does, but I don't care about it that much. On Monday, I was asking her to be very slow. I did that because lately I've been coming really quickly, and it's been bugging me. I had this instinct that I wanted long, slow stuff. When I told her that, I was picturing her never picking up speed, which she invariably does, because I tell her to with my body.

But I was picturing it just getting deeper and longer and slower, and I would do nothing, it would just come over me. Usually I participate so much—that's what makes it mutual, us fucking instead of her fucking me. Especially toward the end, I get very assertive, I'm grabbing her in with my hips. I can almost feel myself drawing her in with my vaginal muscles. I'm participating so much that I'm partly doing it to myself, because I know it's going to feel great. I don't know if I'd do so much of that with somebody else. I'm so comfortable with Arlene, I trust her so much, that I feel like anything is allowed.

One thing about our lovemaking from the very beginning is I've been real penetration-oriented. More so than with other people. You know why I think it is? All the years I've masturbated—and I started early—it's been so clitoris-oriented, so this is my way of making a major distinction. When Arlene's inside me or I'm inside her, I have no doubt that we're fucking. Our rhythms are the same. We're at the same level of excitement. It's deeper. There's rarely that feeling of one person servicing the other. Penetration feels more adult to me, and that's sexier. It's more suggestive. It brings me in touch with different parts of my body in a way that clitoral stimulation doesn't do until the end, when I'm very excited or having an orgasm. When Arlene is inside me, I get dreamy. I go outside myself. I feel the limits of my body less. I blend into her. It's a fuller, richer kind of making love.

Sometimes when I'm having sex, I daydream. Not sexual fantasies, and they might not have anything to do with her. It's a state like I get in right before falling asleep, or as I'm waking up. I'll flash on an image from my childhood that I'd forgotten about for twenty years. Some moment with a friend, a feeling I had, or something I learned. It just comes back to me. Or sometimes I think about painting or drawing. Sometimes colors, very vivid colors. It's like communing with myself. I love that, and very few other things in life give me access to it. It happens particularly when I'm going down on Arlene, and more with her than ever with other people. I don't know why, but it gets me so relaxed that I free-associate. There's a solitude about it that I rarely get even though I'm alone a lot. A happy solitude, yet I'm with her.

It's funny—I didn't used to like going down on women so much. It felt impersonal. It felt foreign. I wasn't at the face, the center of ex-

pression, so it felt like I was a million miles away and I felt very insecure and distant. Now it not only doesn't feel foreign, but it has this
great coming-home quality. It's exciting, but it's also very comforting.
It's part of how I express myself in the world.

We usually do a fair amount of breast stuff. I fondle her and lick
her and suck her a lot. She likes it when I suck really hard. When I
go down on her, I also squeeze her nipples, and if I time it right I can
see the connection, it's like a pipeline to her vagina. My breasts, on
the other hand—they're my worst area. I don't have super-responsive
breasts. My vagina, my ass, my breasts are my private parts—if I'm
not totally relaxed or turned on, there's a little veil of forbiddenness
about them that makes me tense. I would like it if Arlene were very
slow and gentle with my breasts—not with any other part of my body.
I've been hesitant to ask her that. It's funny, you'd think I'd be hesitant to ask her to bite me hard or something. This is the opposite, I
feel ashamed that they're not as developed as the rest of me. Usually
by the time she gets to my breasts, especially with her mouth, she's really turned on, and it feels too sudden to me. She sucks me too hard.
I love sucking her breasts, but that doesn't mean I'm going to be
turned on if she does it to me.

We use dildos and vibrators some, but I wouldn't say much. I
prefer hands. Dildos aren't as flexible as fingers, they feel a lot more
impersonal. Dildos that vibrate are certainly better than ones that
don't, and we have one. It has all these ball bearings in the middle
that go around each other when you turn on the electricity. It twists
around in a circle, and it has speeds. We got real excited when we
saw it in the store. It was expensive, more than I ever spent on a sex
toy. We thought it would be great, but it isn't. Well, yeah, it is. We
just don't use it all that much. One thing with dildos is I can't just
plunge one in Arlene or have her plunge one in me. I have to be
pretty turned on. And there's easily as much fussing around as a man
putting on a condom. You can't have it sitting in the box with the
batteries in it, 'cause they corrode. So you've got to put the batteries
in. Plus, my orgasms from the dildo have a different quality than the
ones from Arlene's hand. With the dildo, it feels more as though I'm
being filled. I tend to move against it really hard, almost violently. It
can be a very deep come, but the sensation isn't quite as luscious.

Like all this stuff, I'm sure it's psychological. I think we both feel using dildos is cheating. I'm reluctant to have a stronger orgasm with it
than I do with Arlene because it's an object. That's another thing I'd
like to get over. There's no such thing as cheating, I think.

Some people say lesbian sex is not as orgasm-oriented as heterosexual sex or gay-men sex. Well, mine is very, very orgasm-oriented.
When women say they do fondling and foreplay, and it doesn't matter if they come, I don't get it. I'd say ninety-five percent of the time
we make love, we both come. Although there are times when one of
us is tired and just doesn't feel like it, when I can get her excited and
get her to come, and that's totally satisfying to me. But not usually.
And as I've gotten older my orgasms have gotten so much better.
They're deeper. My whole body is part of it. I lose my sense of bearings. The sensation is more powerful. Everything.

When Arlene's inside me, I feel the orgasm starting in my vagina
and going up through my whole body. A vaginal orgasm has more of
a sensation of waves than a clitoral one, a much more swept-away
kind of feeling. I sound like I'm saying it's better, but I don't mean to,
because a clitoral orgasm is this extremely concentrated, intense,
pure sensation. The vaginal one seems more mysterious to me. First
of all, it can come before I think it's going to, or after. And the quality
and intensity are less predictable. In the worst case I can have this
thing that feels like it's imitating an orgasm but isn't one. I think it's
gonna be great, I'm so turned on, I'm getting incredible vaginal sensation, and I sort of override it. I go beyond it. I get too excited, so
that I have one spasm and say, What happened? There's the pace of
my orgasm and the pace of me moving, my hips moving, and they're
not jibing. It's like the orgasm has its own mind. I love that about it,
but it gets strangely off sometimes, and it feels like I missed it. Boy,
do I hate that. There's no question I'm done. Everything about me is
shut down. I've had something that resembles a culmination, but it
wasn't what I know is there.

I usually come twice or more. Arlene probably more. That's another thing that doesn't thrill me: It's hard for me not to feel competitive. She seems to have these evenly strong orgasms—she can come
once, twice, and a third time, and they all seem to be the same

strength. That's not true with me. If I come a second time, it could be better or worse, but not the same.

What's remarkable with Arlene is that no matter how tense I am, she breaks through my stuff because she just feels more sexual than other people I've been with. Sometimes, when we're starting, she gets these charges of turn-on that make her . . . it's hard to describe. Very passionate. Very forceful. These quick passionate things that can bring me out of a stupor. It's so genuine that it's contagious. So this stuff about lesbian sex being tender stroking—when I'm really turned on with Arlene, I feel a lot of violent impulses. Sometimes I bite her hard. In fact, Monday I was doing that. Not hard enough to leave teeth marks, but I was restraining myself. I was biting her moderately but fantasizing about biting hard. Arms, shoulders. Sometimes I'll do that on her breasts and her nipples, too. Arlene likes her nipples squeezed. She's talked about getting nipple clamps. Her big fantasy, and something that she's done before, is she likes to be tied up. We've done it a little bit, but it's been boring. First of all, we need a four-poster bed. And we were never Girl Scouts, so we don't know how to make the right knots. It's too easy to get out of them. It's no good unless you almost feel that panic, like you have no choice.

I had this friend, a straight friend who slept with many men, and she was talking about this one guy she'd been with, and how she was under him once and said she wanted him to make her invisible. She said it in great passion: Make me invisible, crush me, pulverize me. I remember thinking, Whoa, her self-esteem is down the toilet. But now I know what she meant. Sometimes I want Arlene to make me invisible. It's a feeling of, I don't want to be alive right now, take it away. It's like not having any borders to your body. So this is a huge unexplored theme. It's exciting because it's never satisfied, but it's also frustrating, because if I can't imagine exactly what it is I want, how can I get it, or how can we get it together? When I tell her I'm feeling these violent impulses, her response is always, "You can do whatever you want with me. Absolutely no holds barred." Well, that seems like this carte blanche. It stymies me. It makes me feel uncreative, because what can I do? It almost makes me mad, because I can't come up with what it is. Then I feel angry at her, that she's playing a girly game, like: You think of all the risky stuff, and I'll be more than happy to go along with it.

I'm not sure that heavier S/M stuff would resolve it, because it feels like it has to do with annihilation, wanting annihilation. That's heavy stuff—not depressing, if I'm depressed I never feel it. But there is some sex-death relationship, like annihilation is a turn-on. More S/M might escalate the feeling, but I don't think it would satisfy it. I guess I'm afraid of escalating it. What if I decide to try more S/M and that doesn't satisfy it either, it just makes me want more?

We all have a thin layer—I guess it's there to protect us. I don't know if it's manners, civility, but when I'm feeling these longings beyond the longing for orgasm, I don't even know how to describe them to Arlene. I know it has something to do with violence. I don't have particular violent fantasies, like I want to take a knife or a sledgehammer. I love this person. It's more this longing to be demolished, or to demolish. I just want her to wipe me out.

TED STEWART

"I guess I'm just a shy guy," he says, and that seems true enough. He is tall and slim, forty, and handsome, with pepper-and-salt hair, a high forehead, strong jaw and nose, pale blue eyes—a hint of Mel Gibson. But there is something tentative about him. During the interview he speaks slowly, hesitantly, as if he were second-guessing himself, worried about saying or doing the wrong thing.

He grew up mostly in the South. He has an older brother and younger sister. His father was "an old-line Southern WASP," a traveling salesman who was rarely at home. When he was, he would sometimes drink, "have temper tantrums, and get violent. We didn't know what would set him off, but suddenly something would happen and he'd go nuts. He never hit my mother, but he would throw things around. He would hit us, usually without any real reason. If my mother said, 'Dad's coming home from his business trip,' we'd cringe—Uh-oh, I hope he's okay. But in my case I think the major abuse wasn't physical but psychological.

"In my family, sex didn't exist. My father never told me the facts of life. I learned from a book. I think my mother was fairly unsexual. My father told my sister that my mother was like a dead fish in bed, completely unresponsive. That makes sense, in a way. It goes along with her passive personality. And my father probably had affairs. He was extremely good-looking. He didn't tell me any particular stories, but late in his life, he would mention having fun with this woman or that one. He would get turned on by one hundred women a day, and I guess he acted on that a number of times. Being a traveling salesman, he had plenty of opportunities."

Now Ted lives in a West Coast city and works as a free-lance graphic artist, though not as successfully as he would like. A few months before our talk, he married the woman with whom he has lived for nine years. He is, he says, like his father: "loyal to my wife but not faithful."

• • •

My sexual relationship with Mary has never been explosive. It's never been really great. It's gotten better over the years as we've gotten to know each other's ways, but for the first five or six years it was kind of boring. It's more a relationship of compatibility. There's a fondness, a familiarity, a comfort. Last year I was having dinner with the woman who was my first real love. She knows my feelings toward her are still strong, and she challenged me, she said, "Well, you just want to be comfortable." That hit a nerve, because I guess it's true. And it's not just sexual—when I say I didn't have passion for Mary, that goes beyond sexual, it's a passionate feeling of being in love with someone, and I never felt that. I didn't feel an electric spark. For years, I thought, Maybe I should break up with Mary and go back to Jaqueline. Or if not go back to her, try to find someone I felt passionate about. But I know in the past I've been with women who were really great, and I broke up with them for no reason except I wasn't ready for a real relationship. So I just kept thinking about how compatible we were, and I didn't want to give that up.

Temperament has something to do with it. We're both pretty easygoing. We share interests in politics, art, everything. We like to act silly, goof around. There was one girlfriend I had, I felt like if I put my hands on her it was almost like I had to have permission. I don't like to feel self-conscious about that. Being shy, it's hard for me to express myself physically. Mary and I don't have any boundaries about stuff like that. We're always putting our hands all over each other. And not just in affectionate ways, but in ways that might be offensive to some people. I'll grab her and stick my hand right up her crack, or I'll do that in a tickling way. Crazy things. How many times a day do I go up to her and grab her breasts? Or she'll grab me. She's very affectionate, I like that.

It was mainly the sexual side I was dissatisfied with. In the beginning—more than the beginning, at least half the relationship—I felt she was very passive. Which might seem to contradict what I said about her being affectionate, but there's being affectionate and there's being sexual. There wasn't this feeling of getting hot and bothered, where you're moving your bodies and there's rhythm. There were times when I could almost scream, because she would just lie there. I felt like I was using her, like I was fucking an inanimate object. I don't mean that quite literally, but almost. I'd say, "Well, do you want me to go down on you? Do you want this, or that?" She'd say, "Oh, I enjoy it all." I always said, "How could you enjoy it? I don't feel like you've come alive. I don't sense there's something sexual happening to you." I had to accept what she said at face value, but I didn't totally accept it because I know what it's like when a woman is really turned on. Not that everyone has to respond the same way, but I knew Mary was missing out on something.

If I went down on her, an orgasm for her was this little blip. A little tremor, a half-second shake, like if you get the chills you go like that [mimics a shiver]. That was it. No heavy breathing or anything. She wouldn't build up to it. I'd be going down on her, she'd be lying there, and then it would happen. Of course, how do I know ultimately what's an orgasm? It's so completely different for a woman, or if it's not, I don't know. It just didn't seem like enough. I did ask her, when we first started going together, I'd say, "Are you enjoying this? Did you have an orgasm?" So I knew that was supposed to be her orgasm. I say "supposed to" because it was such a subtle thing that I thought, Maybe she's really not having an orgasm and she doesn't know what one is. Now I believe that's her orgasm.

One of the biggest frustrations for me was that I felt ineffectual sexually with her. It didn't make me feel that I was inadequate. I just felt that with her I was ineffectual. Whereas with other women, I had an effect, or we had an effect together.

What's happened over the years is that we've gotten closer in the physical aspects of sex. I think she's getting into it more, but it's been a very gradual thing. She still doesn't have orgasms when we have intercourse. In the nine years we've been together, she's had an orgasm that way just a few times. That was really good, that was what I'd expect, in a sense. I mean, it wasn't like—there are some women who scream when they have orgasms. I've never been with a woman like that [laughs], and I'm not sure I'd want to be. But Mary's was never anything like that. Still, it was a mutual orgasm, a mutual turn-on. There are lots of times now when maybe she won't have an orgasm through intercourse, but there's definitely something going on. She's getting a little bit more vocal. And I guess I am too, making little noises that indicate pleasure, so that someone will know what's good and what's not. Before, she made noises, but they were random or arbitrary. They weren't reactions to specific things I did. It was a general humming or cooing sound.

I don't think there's anything specific we're doing differently now. We just gradually got more adapted to each other's bodies and more sensitive to each other's pleasures. I'll try to get specific. It's funny, you're with someone for nine years, and you'd think sex is the same all the time, but it isn't. Half the times we do it, it feels like a new variation. And I don't mean we try all these different positions. Generally other positions haven't been as good as the standard missionary or the other way around, with her on top. But we don't do it exactly the same way. Sometimes we kiss, sometimes we don't at all. Lots of times I'll go down on her, because it seems to lubricate things as well as turn her on. I know I'm contradicting myself: I say she doesn't get turned on, and now I'm saying I go down to turn her on. I guess, even if the evidence of her being turned on is minuscule, I still feel like I want her to get something out of it. But it also makes it more fun for me, because she's got kind of a tight vagina. I'm not very big, I'm one of those guys with a small penis, but still, sometimes she's just too dry. That's another thing—a lot of women will get wet when you start kissing, or in foreplay, and that makes it easier to have intercourse. That never happens with Mary.

When I go down on her, sometimes I'll take her to the point where she has a few orgasms, a few tremors, and sometimes I won't. She likes it when I go down on her, but when I'm down, frequently she'll reach for my arms and gesture for me to come up. It's like she's eager for me to get inside her. That's nice, because then I know she enjoys intercourse enough for me to switch from that to intercourse. It's kind of nice to know that for some women, intercourse is actually enjoyable.

Then we have intercourse until I come. Usually it's not that long. Sometimes I have quick ejaculations, either I was overstimulated in my thoughts or by her. Other times it'll take quite a while. I hear about people who do it for an hour, and that doesn't happen to me. Maybe the longest, twenty minutes to a half hour.

If she's not having an orgasm from intercourse, what do you think she likes about it?

[Big laugh.] That's the big question. I have no idea. What do women like? It's one of those mysteries. Honestly, I have always been baffled by that. Maybe if I knew more about what it really felt like, I would feel less guilty about having sex with women, or I'd be able to give Mary more pleasure in some way. When I say "guilty"—part of my assumption has been that men get more pleasure out of sex than women. I'm not sure that's true, but it's part of my conditioning. If I were really convinced that women enjoy it, then I'd be more inclined to accept my own sexuality and my own desires. But I don't get very clear responses from her. Generally she'll say, "Oh, it's all good, whatever you do, it's good." That's not very helpful. Sometimes I ask her if she likes me staying inside and not coming out, just staying deep. Or sometimes I'll ask her if it hurts, what I'm doing, because I get mixed signals. Let's say if I'm riding low, or I'm in a particular position, I'll say, "Is this good, do you like this?" And she'll say, "Yeah." Then I'll say, "How about this?" And she'll say, "Yeah." So I don't get good feedback.

But I guess I don't give good feedback, either. One time recently we were lying side by side on our backs and she was playing with my penis. She was rubbing her fingers around it in a circle, not up and down but around it, very gently and slowly. Something about it was driving me crazy in a good way. I was moaning and groaning. She said, "You like this?" Later on I told her that was about the best manipulation of my cock I've ever experienced. But then she couldn't remember how she had done it. She was trying something about a week later, and she said, "Oh, this is what I was doing the other night, isn't it?" I just said "No, not exactly." I guess next time the situation arises I'll have to remind her, because I knew exactly. Somehow she didn't remember that clearly. She was doing some up-and-down thing on the front of the penis, it was totally different. It was good, but different.

Basically I'm happy in my sex life with Mary. We do it about once a week. I'm happy doing it once a week with her. But that doesn't mean I'm happy about—well, I'm frustrated that I'm not able to meet more women and have more affairs. Flings, that is. *Affair* implies something ongoing. I have maybe one fling a year at the very most, but it's always on my mind. I can walk down the street and fall in love every twenty minutes. No, every five minutes. There was someone last night on the subway who smiled at me, and it made me feel so good. I thought, Maybe I should talk to her. But I almost never do. Once in a while something happens, but usually I'm too shy to know what to do. The worst is when I actually do talk to someone, and we go have a drink, and she finds out I'm living with someone and gives me dirty looks. One woman started yelling at me. This woman was all over me, kissing me, I was in her apartment and when she found out I was living with someone, she started calling me all these names. So I stormed out. We were bombed on martinis. I can't remember how she found out, somehow I mentioned it. I don't like to deceive people, but you don't go up to women and say, "Hi, I'm Ted Stewart, I'm married." She was just being puritanical, because a lot of people have affairs, and the fact that someone's married doesn't matter. So obviously for me, the ideal person to meet is someone who doesn't have a hangup about it or someone who's married, too. There's always the risk that you'll fall in love with someone, but if you're married and you have a fling with another married person, there's a balance there.

One of the greatest experiences I ever had was not too long ago with one of my best friends' wives. Oh, God, it was great. These people live in New York. Over the years, I'd occasionally have a job out there, and they would let me stay in their apartment. Their names are Sean and Michiko. She's Japanese-American. I sensed that she was attracted to me, but I wasn't sure. Last year, I went out there again. Sean had just taken a job in Washington, and he was commuting back to New York on the weekends. When I called to set up my trip, Michiko made some reference to spending time with me alone, so I arranged to get there on a Thursday. We went out to dinner. She said something a bit startling. We're sitting there eating, and she said, "Well, I just want you to know one thing. I like to be taken." I had never heard that before, but I knew what she meant. I guess she sensed that I'm kind of low-key, so I might expect the woman to take the initiative. I said to myself, Okay.

We went back to the house, put on some good music, and made martinis, so the ice was out and all the glasses were on this ceramic tile counter. A lot of times people say the best sex is when you don't plan it and it just happens. But this was something completely premeditated. We even adjusted the lighting. We were creating a romantic mood. The music, the martinis, we were dressed up. We were dancing around, and then I lifted her up and put her on the counter. She's pretty small. I took one of the ice cubes and started rubbing it on her wrists, and then up her arms, and then up the other arm, and around her neck. It drove her crazy. We went into the bedroom, found a condom for me, and started fucking. It was great sex. And part of it was—I don't have that much experience with condoms, but that thin little layer can reduce the sensitivity of the penis. What that meant was, I wasn't having an orgasm, but I was completely turned on. We just kept going and going for something like half an hour. She was having orgasms one after the other. I found that to be very satisfying. Most of the women I've slept with don't have orgasms from intercourse. But in this case, I wasn't having one. And it didn't bother me. It was so wonderful to be rocking and rocking and rocking, and feeling that I was giving this woman so much pleasure. I never had an orgasm the whole night.

It was pure lust. There was no question that her relationship with Sean is good, and that mine with Mary is good. There was no risk involved, aside from being found out—no emotional risk. That made it fun. So in my heart I'm not monogamous, even though I'm married and in a pretty stable relationship. I feel perhaps there's a basic biological difference between men and women. A lot of people feel this way, but they may not say it. From what I've observed, women need the stability, because they give birth to children, and if the man is out doing something else, there's an instinct that they have to take care of the kids. So women have a stronger desire for a stable home life with a man to protect them—I'm talking in cavepeople terms, not current reality. Whereas a man, he can be the father of a child and go off and there doesn't seem to be as much responsibility for the child-rearing, in biological terms. Of course these days that's irrelevant, but one's biology doesn't change just because society does. I used to think, Well, it was important to be really open in a relationship and say what you're doing, and talk about these issues of monogamy. I don't believe that anymore. Why challenge women about something they don't want to change? My attitude now is, if I play around, I don't tell her about it. If she plays around, I don't want to know about it. It might seem hypocritical, but I think it's the best for everybody. I guess I wish I lived in Europe, where mistresses and having affairs aren't such a big deal.

But I'm still very reticent about starting anything. Maybe it's because of all the horrible things that women are presented with, guys always coming on to them. I associate it with being dirty, being bad. Even when I wasn't living with someone, I still felt like my interest in a woman was something bad. I guess that's a common affliction in American society, where sex is bad. It's really stupid. Tragic. Probably people think about sex a tremendous part of the time and act on it a fraction of the time. It reminds me of this other girl—she was a girl at the time. I was working on an ad campaign, this was eight or nine years ago. It was for lingerie. I was drawing sketches. She was a young model, and she wasn't at all shy about standing in the studio, taking off her underwear and putting on other underwear. I found myself being turned on by this, because I thought this woman was really attractive. Later on she came back to my studio alone to look at the sketches. We were hanging out, it was twilight, and I wasn't sure whether she just wanted to look at the pictures and leave, or what. I could have taken the risk of rejection, but I didn't. It's almost uncanny that it's so hard to say certain things about sex without sounding moronic. But what goes through my head: Here's a young woman, I'm a young man. Why is it so hard for people to look each other in the eye and say, Shall we or shan't we?

ROBERT RAUH

He came of age—and came out as a gay man—in the early seventies, the dawn of the Big Party. Over the next twenty years he partied with the best, reveling with lovers and strangers in the baths, in the streets, on the phone, in bars, cars, trucks, warehouses, abandoned piers, rest areas, offices, stairwells, theaters, T-rooms—public rest rooms where men have sex—and, yes, bedrooms. Even now, in the plague years, he regards Eros as a calling. At the time we talk, he and the man he calls "the love of my life" have been together for one and a half years. Both wear wedding rings as an emblem of devotion—though not as a pledge of monogamy.

He is an attractive man, tall, big-chested, blondish, bearded, dressed in tight-fitting denim and scuffed cowboy boots. A ponytail and a gentle tenor voice soften the look. He grew up in the Long Island suburbs, one of three children of a doctor and a housewife. "My activist friends would be horrified to hear me say this, but my childhood was the classic model for a gay man: distant father, and a mom who was too close and overbearing. I'd have dinner with my father maybe once a week and once on the weekend. I had almost no contact with him, and the contact I remember was lots of anger. My mother was very attentive day-to-day, but when it came to intimate stuff, giving of herself, something shut off. She was always on me about achievement, that was big in my family, much to my detriment I would say. The overall feeling I have had my whole life is that I am not good enough."

He has not lacked for success, however. He owns a small art gallery that was an instant hit when he founded it in the seventies. Since then its fortunes have waned and waxed again. His lover, Dan, is an accomplished film editor. Their lifestyle is upscale Manhattan: house in the country, dual therapists, active night life. Both are politically active in the gay community. Dan is HIV-positive; Robert is not.

• • •

A quick plane story. I'm at the Marine Air Terminal here in New York, which is a small place. This guy starts cruising me, and he clearly wants me to follow him into the rest room. I'm not into it, this is too public. The plane we're flying on is called an Otter, which is an eighteen-passenger plane, no curtain even between the pilot and the passengers. He goes to get on the plane and I sit next to him. He has a newspaper. We take off, and I look over and see that he's rubbing himself. We get up in the air and as soon as we start to level out, he gets up and goes to the back of the plane. The only two-passenger seat is in the way back. He goes to that seat. I wonder, and I look, and he's looking at me. All the other seats are full. I can't resist. So I get up and go back and sit next to him. I see he has his dick out and a huge erection. I'm like, Oh, my God, this is amazing. I sit down next to him, and for the next half hour the two of us are jerking each other off and feeling each other's balls and playing with each other's assholes. He has a raincoat spread across our laps. We shoot in each other's hands. Fortunately we had Kleenex to clean it up. I couldn't believe it was happening. Right after we come, the pilot comes on the intercom and says, "Is it hot enough for the two of you back there?" It was winter, by the way, so no one else on the plane got it, but he knew what was happening. Then getting off the plane and looking at the pilot, who was very cool, didn't say anything to us, I realize he's gay and totally into it.

That was one of the hottest things I have ever done publicly, because it was so different from making it in a rest room on a 747—I've done that, too—or making it on a bus, which I've done when I was younger. The forbidden quality is number one, but there's also the creativity of it, like a puzzle that you have to figure out. How can I make this happen, how can I piece it together so it's a hot sexual scene and I'm not gonna get caught? My excitement definitely does not come from being in a safe situation, two guys in a bed. For me it's the fear of getting caught, being a bad boy. The baths were never as much a turn-on to me as they were for other people, even though I had some really good sex there and met some really nice guys. I didn't like the idea of paying an admission fee and having this sanctioned sex. It wasn't dirty enough for me.

Through the eighties I went to the clubs a lot, did the rest areas, T-rooms, had various boyfriends, drank a lot, did a lot of coke, stopped doing coke—you know. Then I met Dan in 1990. I met him at GMHC. It wasn't about being totally turned-on for one another, it was something that built up over a while. Finding out who the other one was, that we shared interests, that we had both lost lovers. We worked on a few GMHC projects together. And one day I did get turned on—he had just come back from a trip, and I said, Wow, he looks great. He walked me home from a meeting, we kissed each other good night, and I think we both knew something was up. So we made a date and had dinner and went over to my apartment and made out for four hours but didn't have sex. I felt like I didn't want to. I knew this wasn't a trick, it wasn't a one-shot deal. I wanted something more, so I was scared. I wanted to prepare myself more. I asked him if he could see me on Saturday night, and he looked at me very sheepishly and said, "Well, no, I have this fuckbuddy who I've been seeing Saturday nights for the last couple years." I was like, Oh. So we saw each other Friday night.

The first time we had sex it was very passionate, but it certainly wasn't the best sex I have ever had. I remember at the end feeling inadequate. For one thing, I didn't come. I remember kissing a lot. Dan likes having his nipples played with, he has huge nipples that he uses suction cups on. I remember being amazed by his chest. He goes to the gym all the time, and he has a beautiful chest. I don't remember if we blew each other or what, but I didn't come, whereas he came and fell asleep. I felt confused about that—was he bored? Was he not attracted to me? Or was it just that he got his rocks off and that was that? In reality I think he got his rocks off and he was tired and he went to sleep.

The other thing going on that night—my big issue lately is that I have not been able to fuck guys. When I go to fuck a guy I lose my erection. I can jerk off, I can get blown, I can blow a guy, the whole range, so it is not technically impotence. I get full erections. But something happens to me when I go to penetrate a guy. I can't do it. This goes back about ten years, to when I broke up with a guy named

Billy. We were together six years, and it was the best sex I've ever had with someone I cared about. I fucked him all the time, but ever since then I haven't been able to. The other side of it is that I never felt comfortable getting fucked. A couple of weeks ago I was saying to myself, If I can't fuck a guy, and if I can't get fucked, it has got to make me feel pretty inadequate. Those are two big things that gay men do. Most men don't do both, but they do one or the other. I'm doing neither. It's only in the last year that Dan started helping me get into my ass, like with a butt plug, and I'm starting to understand what guys are feeling and why they like to get fucked. So I think on that first night, I was feeling anxious about not being able to fuck him. Fucking to me is by far the most intimate form of sexual activity. It's the closest you can be to another human being, to penetrate them. I knew it was something I seriously wanted, and being with Dan brought it all up for me.

Plus there was something romantic going on here. That was hanging over the sex. My therapist says one problem with my sexuality is that I have too much invested in it when it's someone I care about, as opposed to my anonymous stuff. I want too much, and I feel like I have to give them something. She says the best sex is selfish, it's all about you. But for me there's this element of wanting to please the other person, like, Did I do a good job? What's he gonna think of me? You don't have any of that stuff if you don't know someone, because if they don't like it, you leave, or you go on to the guy in the next stall. It's much freer.

The other thing is that before we even made out the first time, Dan told me he's HIV-positive. He said, "You need to think about that, is it okay or not?" I had already thought about it. First of all, if you meet someone these days, it's as likely as not they're positive. I had decided that if I liked someone, I was going to take the whole package. But it's not a minor detail.

I remember waking up that first morning thinking, Well, I guess this isn't gonna go anywhere. But that wasn't the case. I talked with him about how I felt, and he was reassuring, and we went out again, and after the second date we were with each other every night. At first we went back and forth, he would come to my house two or three nights a week, and I would go to his house the other nights. Finally it became too much of a hassle, so now pretty much I stay at his apartment. During the first year we were monogamous—and really monogamous, not that we were fucking around and just not telling. I told him I wanted him to be my love slave. That turned him on. But I'd say about eight months in, our sex began to decrease. A few months after that we went on vacation and talked about some arrangement where we'd be allowed to fuck around on the side. I remember we both lit up with joy at the thought. And almost at the same point each of us got so depressed about breaking up our monogamous relationship. It represented failure. We had both been so turned on by this love slave idea and wanting to be monogamous. I had never wanted that before in my life—well, I shouldn't say that, I wanted it with Billy, but I knew early on that he wasn't going to give it to me, so I changed course. Monogamy wasn't something I valued too much, or thought it made any relationship more sincere or deeper. I thought it was ridiculous for gay men to try to be monogamous. But with Dan I wanted this devotion, and he felt the same thing.

The problem is, I'm not his best sex partner, and he's not my best partner. We know that. What he likes and what I like are so different that we still haven't found the meeting ground. This love slave thing—the idea turned me on, but in reality I wasn't able to make it happen. Dan is heavily involved with the leather scene. He loves getting tied up and handcuffed and fucked and all that stuff. I have always flirted with that in fantasies, I find guys in leather extremely hot and sexy, and when I see guys in chaps it does drive me wild. But I don't think I have the same gut reaction to bondage as he does. When I think of people handcuffing their partners, I kind of giggle, and you're not supposed to giggle.

Dan is real tough. He has a temper. So there's an issue of intimidation. For us to have satisfying sex would involve him being tough and me being even more so. Me having to dominate him and fight back and hold him down and restrain that part of his personality. His sex is about anger, about angry men dominating him and him giving them attitude back. It's about humiliation and getting this aggression out. That's what he's looking for, and I don't think I can give it to him. I can pretend to give it to him, but the guys he's doing it with really do give it to him. He likes my bigness, my size, but basically I'm too gentle, and he wants this heavy top number.

On the other hand, when I realized how into this stuff he was, and that it was a chance for me to try some of it out, I did. I did go out and buy ropes and chains and bolts to connect them with. I did get off on how creative you can be. Dan would be wearing his chaps and leather vest with nothing underneath, and his ass and his cock would be exposed, and it would be sexy. He likes tit clamps, he would put them on me, and it was the first time I experienced that. I remember getting somewhat into the bondage and feeling like I was doing a good job at it, too. I was certainly satisfying him, he would say things like, "God, Robert, this is so much better with you than with my fuckbuddy, it means so much more that I care about you and you care about me." Which I needed to hear.

These days, one of our sessions might start with me lying in bed and him going down on me or licking my balls. I love to be licked between my balls and my ass. I'll start playing with his tits or fingering his asshole. It generally ends up where I'm either finger-fucking him and seeing how many fingers I can get in—I haven't fist-fucked him, but I have been pretty close. A lot of times we'll play with dildos. I'll pull a chair up and either make him sit on a dildo and he'll blow me, or I'll sit on a butt plug and be fucking him with a dildo. Mostly he doesn't play with my asshole, which would help this newfound discovery that I have an asshole that feels good when you play with it. It's just not his inclination to play with other guys' asses. It's *his* ass he wants played with. We do some making out, kissing, and a lot of jerking off. We have gotten into scenes where I have tied his hands behind his back and had him sit on the toilet and blow me while I'm standing with one foot on the bathtub and the other on the floor. I'm really spread out, and he's blowing me, and the whole idea of being in the bathroom, the dirtiness of that . . . What would add a whole new dimension is fucking, because what I miss is that closeness when you have your dick in a guy's ass and his legs are up like that and you're making out with him, you're kissing him and fucking him and it's all about connection and feeling each other. Whereas the kind of sex we have is more about me getting him off and him getting me off. A lot of times he'll come first and then I'll go squat over his face and he'll lick my balls and I'll shoot all over his chest. That's hot, but it's different when you're fucking a guy and there's the rhythm of the two of you, and you hold back until the other one's ready to come and you explode and come together.

We still do little top-bottom things. I wear this black underwear that's like a thong, it's really like wearing no underwear, and Dan loves it. So the last couple times we've had sex, I'm wearing my underwear and he'll take it off and put it on his face and smell it. Last week he put it over his head and used it like a mask, he couldn't see me, and I was fucking his face while he was wearing this underwear over his eyes. It was so hot, it was about really dirty stuff, and it felt great. I think if we could get to more of that stuff with each other—but it's like work. Which is okay. I think it's always work to have that with someone you care about. I don't know if we're going to find it even with work, but I think we can find a lot better sex. Like last Saturday, with the underwear, I felt pretty satisfied. I felt like we had hot sex by anybody's standards. If anyone would have photographed it, it would be hot sex. But from Dan's side, I don't know—without the other elements, ropes and clamps and all this stuff, I don't know if it's really hot sex for him.

Anyway, about the time we exchanged rings, we said, Time to try something else. We made some rules. We would take Thursday and Friday nights off, during which time we were allowed to fuck around with whoever we wanted. With certain stipulations: They couldn't be a mutual friend. Nobody from GMHC. And this was going to be about sex. It wasn't going to be about intimacy, about going to dinner or the movies or anything that smacked of having an affair. No staying overnight or having anybody stay overnight. Billy and I used to have a rule where three times was the limit—you could fuck somebody three times, and that was it. Dan and I didn't make that rule, because Dan's sexuality is a lot about fuckbuddies. There were two guys in his life who he had been seeing for years, and who he stopped seeing for me. Guys who have remained strangers to him. Part of the turn-on is that he may not even know their real names. They have to contact him, which is all part of the dominant-submissive thing. Dan is always at their mercy. But they don't know about each other's outside lives. It's just hot sex. So that rule wouldn't work for him. His sexuality is all about developing scenes, week-by-week scenarios. Mine is about strangers, my dick-a-day thing.

The other rules were that you didn't talk about it. You didn't come home on Saturday and say, "Boy, did I have this hot number last night!" You were supposed to be discreet, not leave rubbers on the dresser. And what evolved is that we didn't talk to each other after six or seven in the evening on Thursday night. You were allowed to call the other person, but it was at your own risk. If there was no answer and you ended up feeling bad, it was tough shit. Even if you called at two a.m. and there was no answer, it was tough. So what happened is we didn't speak after six or seven on Thursday. Or now, on Friday. As of last week we're now at one night a week, just Friday.

Why the change?

It's a long story. [Laughs harshly.] And not a pretty picture either. I'm feeling a lot of jealousy, which I wasn't feeling for the first few months. I'm feeling like Dan is getting sexually satisfied, and I'm not. I'm jealous of Dan's other guys and me not being included. I'm also jealous of his sexual development. Dan is someone who spent ten years of therapy unearthing his sexuality, working at getting rid of the garbage and the inhibitions and the shame. He told me one of the turning points for him was having sex with a guy and the guy was almost growling at him, he was under Dan and he said, "Do you want to fucking spit in my face? Go ahead and spit in my face!" So Dan did and he said it was amazing to be able to be that hostile to someone, that into it. Well, I want some of that. I certainly get excited, and I like my anonymous stuff, it gets me off and I have lots of orgasms every week, but Dan's sex is more intimate. Even though they're strangers, it's still about being with someone for three or four hours.

Finally my jealousy got so bad that I said, "Look, we have to talk." He assured me that there was no one else he cared about. I believed him. He said, "I totally adore you." I believed him. He said, "This other sex stuff that I do, these people mean nothing to me, they're not people I want to have dinner with. It's just sex." I said, "I don't know where to go with it, because even knowing that, I still feel jealous. On the other hand, I know that if we try to be monogamous, that's not the answer either." He said, "Would it make you feel more secure if we only took one night off a week?" So that's what we're doing.

Now, on my nights off—if you read the fine print, the rules never said you had to confine your outside sex to Thursday and Friday nights. The rules just said those nights were the free-zone period. I do a lot of T-room stuff in the daytime. That's kosher as long as it's not known what I'm doing and when I'm doing it. But my nights off vary a lot. Two weeks ago, I answered this guy's personal ad. An older guy. I have a thing now for older men. The ad said he was fifty, and he weighed this, and he liked this. . . . I called him up and he sounded hot. We had a very sexy phone conversation. We decided to meet. He lives in a high-rise on the East Side. The whole time I'm going there I'm saying, Please let this be at least passable. In my experience, the few times I've hooked up with people from phone sex—first of all, everyone says they're a hundred fifty-five pounds, blond hair, blue eyes, major chest, gym body, and then you get there, and it's like, Hello, are you the exterminator, or what? As it turned out he was pretty much what he described, and I did get turned on. He showed me the view on his balcony, and there was a porn flick on when I came in, and I decided I was going to put on a show for him. He was wearing shorts and he already had a hard-on. I excused myself and went into the bathroom. I took my pants off, put my boots back on, I had a black T-shirt and black underwear, and I came out like that. Then I just sat back on the bed, put my foot on the chair, and acted like nothing had changed. I was listening to what he was saying, he was trying to pay attention and act like everything is normal here, except I'm spreading my legs in front of him, which turns me on, not only the exhibitionism, but being cool about it.

I was telling him all these great sex stories from my past and getting him hot. His erection went down below his shorts, and *that* was hot. Then he came over, got down on his knees, and started blowing me. I had brought a butt plug and he didn't even know what it was, and I said, "Well, you've got to learn about this." He was blowing me—in fact, he was eating my ass. What can I say, I know I shouldn't have been doing it—not for my sake, but for his. But once you start—he started below my balls, and it was like, Down, down boy! The sensation is so incredible, and he was so good at it. He ate me out for a really long time, and it felt great. I was jerking off. We were doing poppers* and I was drinking beer. Then I got the butt plug out and started fingering his ass. I told him to turn around, I wanted him to bend over and show me his cheeks. He put on his whole show for me, then started fingering it. To me if a guy gets into doing that, putting on a show, doing what you say, spreading his ass—even getting him to do that is exciting. I went to put the butt plug up his ass and it was like a vacuum cleaner sucked it up. I was like, "Are you sure you haven't had stuff up here, like maybe baseball bats?" But I could tell from the way he was responding that he had never had that sensation.

So I had the butt plug up his ass and I put mine up me, and we managed to figure out this position where we had our feet connected up against each other, my left foot was up against his right foot like this, and I used my other foot to hold in his butt plug and he used his to hold in mine, and we started fucking each other with our feet moving the butt plugs, pushing. It was incredible, very much in sync with each other. The poppers helped, but we were pretty creative. I have to take a lot of the credit, because I was the one making all the moves, which is wonderful, I knew I was taking him somewhere he had never been before. And I had never done this thing with the feet. We took one last hit of poppers and he said, "I can't hold it anymore, I've got to shoot it," and he did. Then I made him eat my ass some more and then I shot. Afterward he said, "I think that was the best sex I ever had in my life." Which was like, Wow—on the one hand, it was good, it was real good, but it wasn't the best for me. On the other hand I felt great, because he was so thrilled by this thing up his ass and the whole scene.

Other nights, maybe I'm too tired, or I just don't feel like going out, or last night it was raining—it can be something as practical as that—I stay at my place and do phone sex. I called this line for bisexual men, because I have a lot of fantasies about making it with a straight couple, and the porn I like is straight porn. I said, "Anyone into talking about pussy?" There was this guy on the line who I had phone sex with maybe a month before, a really hot married guy. The

*Capsules of amyl nitrate gas, which delivers a brief, intense high when inhaled.

last time we spoke he supposedly was going to talk to his wife, because they swing together and he brings home guys and has them
fuck her. We talked about his wife, and I asked him was he into dick,
and he told me at his office he regularly blows these two married guys
who stay after hours. That was really hot to me, and I said I'd like to
watch him and his wife, and was he going to talk to her. I'm very verbal, I like words, clinical words. I like *penis* more than *cock*. I like
ejaculate more than *come*. There's a whole list of words that turn me
on: I like the word *vagina,* and I like *anus* and *rectum* more than I like
asshole or *ass*. There's something about the formality of the words
that makes the reality dirtier. So I'm talking to this guy, and I'm saying, "I have this really thick big erection in my hand and I'm thinking
about you masturbating. I wish I could watch your penis going in and
out of your wife's vagina. . . ." I can make it go on and on. Usually I'm
in my bed. Sometimes I do it in my office, sitting on a butt plug in my
chair.

One interesting part of my sexuality is this straight thing. Why am
I turned on by straight porno? Why are my fantasies straight? Why
do I want to watch a guy fuck a woman so much? I had a girlfriend
in college for nine months, but that was twenty years ago, and I have
never actually watched a guy fuck a woman. It doesn't seem like it
should be hard to set up, especially since women come on to me like
crazy. A few weeks ago I took out an ad for a couple that would like
to have a man watch them, but so far no one has answered. I wanted
a low-pressure situation, where I knew that whatever I did was cool,
and if all I wanted to do was stand back and watch, or jerk off . . . My
ideal would be a couple with a bisexual male. One thing I think
would be so hot, I'd love to lick a guy's cock while it's going in and
out of a cunt. Just positioning myself under there and looking up . . .
I've done that with guys while they were fucking an ass, and I would
think most straight guys would really enjoy it if they weren't too
homophobic. I sure know I could make it feel good to them.

So I hope I'll hook up with a couple, and I hope to get into some
leather stuff, and I plan to start going to bars and clubs. I'm thinking
I'll try going home with people more. It's not that I want to get to
know them, but I want to see what it's about when I spend three
hours having sex with them, as opposed to twenty minutes in a

T-room. The experience of going to that older guy's place was very warm. Being in someone's home, being offered something to drink, talking—I may never see him again, but it's an experience I'll remember. It's an experience with some meaning. It was an evening with someone. I want more of that. More closeness. More connection, somehow.

But I still don't feel like my jealousy thing is resolved. I also don't feel like I'm crazy for feeling it. These feelings are why people stay monogamous and put up with the torture of that. I don't want to be just Dan's companion, and he doesn't want that, but to try and keep your sex life going while you're trying to figure out an arrangement that works on the outside is difficult. So when we have sex now, which runs about once a week, I go into it wondering if I'm gonna be okay, if I'm gonna be able to loosen up enough. I always make sure we smoke a joint. What's so hard for me—I don't know if I will ever get this sex stuff with a permanent partner. The idea of making each other strangers, which is what my therapist talks about—you're objects, you're just bodies. Well, I have been into piss scenes many times, but the thought of pissing on my lover and then the next day thinking he's the sweetest guy on earth—they don't go together for me. I can't think about spitting in Dan's face, even if he wanted me to. Which he may—he's never said it to me, but he may. It wouldn't feel real to me. I don't want to spit in his face, I want to kiss him. Do other guys do that with each other and then go to brunch the next day? How do you do that? How do you lose the person? I can't make him a stranger, but I think if I could figure that out, it would be the first step toward having a great sex life together.

MARGE STROTHERS

She lives in a new housing development outside Durham, North Carolina, so large and labyrinthine that she picks me up at a nearby McDonald's for fear I will lose my way. The bed of her pickup is packed with flats of flowers; she runs a small greenhouse that sells plants to garden stores. Her husband is a middle manager at a big tobacco company. She is a tall, big-boned, earthy woman of fifty-two with short bleached-blond hair, dressed in blue jeans, work boots, and a gray hooded sweatshirt. We talk in her tidy living room—baby blue wall-to-wall carpeting, comfy sofa and chairs, photos of kids and grandkids, wall display cases with miniature porcelain figures. At one point her husband phones, and in the course of a flirtatious conversation she genially tells him, "Kiss my ass, fucker."

She was born in a tiny Carolina town, youngest of six daughters in a strict Baptist family. "My mom was always very sick, she died when I was thirteen, so I was mostly raised by my sisters, 'cause my dad sort of went off the deep end. Sex was never discussed. My oldest sister got pregnant before she was married, and this was the cardinal sin, my mom and her didn't talk for a year after the baby was born. Then my next sister got married, she had health problems but she had five kids when she wasn't supposed to have any. I'd overhear mom and dad talking about her husband, how he takes her to bed and gets her in trouble, draggin' her down more and more. I think a lot of my problem with sex was that I was always taught it was dirty, and you only have sex when you're married, and the man's the only one that has any enjoyment. Sex was negative, negative, negative. That was criminal, in a way, when I think about it."

• • •

When I graduated high school I was dating this guy six years older than me, he had been in the service and came home. I was a virgin when we got married, which is totally unheard-of anymore, I assume. And I can't say sex was ever good. First of all, I didn't know anything about it. I was really afraid to make love that first time. I didn't even know about birth control. I got some Norforms, which are not birth control—I don't even think they're on the market anymore. All they are is a cleansing agent. But that first month we were married, I'd figure, Well, we'll probably make love tonight, so if I put these things in early, I won't get pregnant, right? Needless to say, I got pregnant right away, which was not my idea.

And the sex—I thought, Walt's six years older than me, he's been around, he should know. It's not like he was a virgin by any means. We did some heavy pettin' before we got married, but not after. We'd get in bed, and he'd roll over to me and kind of bing me in the back end with his penis so I'd know, Okay, tonight's the night. Then he'd say, "Roll over, Marge," and that's it. I'd turn over on my back. I was always on the bottom, he was on the top. He'd get inside me and come almost instantly. It was like a release valve. There was no love involved. No touching, no feeling, no talking. Usually it hurt like hell 'cause I wasn't wet, except way back in the beginning, when I had those Norforms in me.

One day I had some friends over for one of those stupid decorator parties. Some of the women were talking about orgasms and stuff, and I thought, Say, I want to listen to this, because I'm not sure what they're talkin' about. Well, I come to find out I have had two children and never an orgasm in my life. I didn't know you were supposed to. I never masturbated—still haven't, fifty-two years old. [Laughs.] I was under the impression that all women endure sex and it's just for the male. These gals were sayin', "Boy, I can hardly wait till the next time." I'm thinkin', What the hell are you waitin' for?

After that party, in the back of my mind I kept thinkin', There's got to be more to it than this. I kept waitin' and it never happened, so I felt, Well, maybe if I'm a little aggressive. I tried that and he was very offended. I acted like I was gonna go down on him. He said, "That is gross, don't even do that. That's called oral sex, and we don't do that." Okay. I got some guts up a little later to try something else.

I asked him if he'd touch me. He said, "That's masturbation. We don't do that shit. I'm not gonna jack you off." I said, "Fine, okay," and just backed off.

Well, in between there we had some very sick kids, and I think he felt neglected. I don't know if that's the reason, but he started runnin' around, and I found out about it. It took me a long time, but eventually I caught on and filed for divorce after eight years of marriage. And he was not a good provider afterward. He never saw the kids, didn't want nothin' to do with 'em, didn't pay his child support. So I started workin' different part-time jobs in this little town.

At night I tended bar or waited tables, and I met a guy there once, his name was Tim. He told me, like all guys tell ya, "Yeah, I'm divorced, my family lives in Kentucky, I go home to see them sometimes." Well, he was a good lover. I finally knew what an orgasm was. It's such a shame you're not taught, nobody tells you anything, that this is part of it. I see him now every few years and it puts a smile on my face. Just like, Thank you, that was nice, that was super!

I guess Tim is the only one who has ever been able to totally satisfy me. On the other hand, he did have a drinkin' problem, and most of the time we made love, we'd both been drinkin', so maybe that helped to relax me. But the touching, the feeling—I mean, there wasn't a lot of heavy pettin', it was the exceptional caring. Tim was interested. Tim was talented. He didn't have an orgasm instantly. He could endure and wait for me. And he talked to me during sex, which makes a world of difference. It was like I was up on a pedestal. He wanted whatever made me feel good. I was scared to death to say what made me feel good, but he had enough sense about him to know. To touch, and kiss, and he gave me oral sex for the first time in my life, everything all into one. And me being so open and wantin' to learn, because it had been so many years. It was overwhelming. I was in shock. Here's what these girls were talkin' about, and it was happening to me. Geez, it was great!

That's why I was so devastated when it ended. It was my first good sex that ended. I found out he was still married, and *pfft,* it all went down the drain. But he taught me a lot.

After Tim I dated some guys, no big deal, and then I got real sick and had to have three operations, and I was broke. In between the second and third operations I met this older guy Elroy, he was real nice to me, seemed like a nice human being. So dear old Elroy kept hangin' around, and even though my kids were dead set against it, I married him. He had four children of his own, he had just split up with his wife. I moved with him down to Georgia, where he had a construction business.

Everything was fine at first, and sex was good. Lots of touching and feeling. He didn't talk during sex, though, didn't say anything nice, didn't say he loved me. And when we got down to Georgia all hell broke loose. He started doin' a lot of threatening and beating and stuff. Then he'd be very forgiving the next day. He didn't beat on the kids at that stage, so I'd just let it ride. Nowadays they'd call me a battered woman. Back in those days there was nobody to help you. I tried to swear out a warrant and the sheriff laughed at me. We moved to this old farmhouse, and Elroy started keeping me more and more in a shell. He wouldn't let me leave the house. He might come home anytime during the day to see if I was there, and if I wasn't I got a hell of a beating. He'd get me to do things by holdin' a loaded, cocked gun to my head, with the kids watchin'. And sex was violent. Almost like being raped. He'd take me outside sometimes and just rip my jeans off. He was into—I guess you call it dog-style, but later on I could see it was just his ferocious way of doing things. He would take my head—I can remember one time he took me outside and there was a woodpile and he kept shovin' my face down in it while he was fucking me. I had cuts on my face from the wood. It wasn't pleasant. But that was toward the end of it, so in order to protect my kids I'd do anything. If that's gonna satisfy him and shut him up and he'd go in the house and go to sleep, the rest of us were safe for the night.

Finally I stole enough money from him that I could escape with my kids. It was like something out of the movies. He traced us to one apartment around here but we got away again. I still run into him once in a while, and it's the most scary thing in the world. I have no doubt the man would kill me. I keep a sawed-off shotgun at the greenhouse, and I'd use it if he came after me.

After that fiasco I got a divorce and started working at a chemical company. Taking care of three kids, living in an apartment. And I worked my way up the ladder, that's one thing I can be proud of. After nine years I was head of the import-export department and did a lot of travelin'. I didn't date a lot right away. There was still a lot of hangups from Elroy, it took me a while. I kept thinkin', I'm not the most ugly woman in the world. I got a decent personality. I was a lot thinner then. It's not like I'm some drudge from down under. So why did I pick these weirdos? I have no idea, but it's a pattern. I feel sometimes like I bring out the worst in a man. That's what Elroy would tell me. "You're just a no-good slut, and this is what you get for being a slut," and on and on. You can take that for so long, and then you think, Is it really me? Am I what's doing this? Is it me that made my kids' father run away, made him go look somewhere else? It took me a hell of a long time to realize it wasn't me, they were the abnormal ones. And I was just looking for something normal in my life.

Well, I finally started seeing Kurt, my husband now. For a long time we were just friends. He was married, we worked together. And then one night it suddenly changed. He had a bad day at work, we went out for dinner, and we sat there and we were talking and talking, and all of a sudden it was twelve midnight, and it seemed like the topic changed from talking about business to talking about our lives. It just went from there. People probably thought we were having an affair for two months before he even kissed me. It was like if he kissed me, we were committing adultery. He had never cheated on his wife. He had never been with another woman, period. Then I started trying to seduce him and it took me months before he would go through with it.

Eventually they split up and we got together, and we've been married ten years now. We get along pretty good. He's bullheaded, I'm bullheaded. I'm very domineering, so is he. We do a lot of yelling and screaming and arguing, but that's okay. He's a very brilliant man, very hardworking. Self-centered, arrogant, but he's got a heart of gold. He doesn't know how to communicate, I guess is the word.

My sex with Kurt is not hot and heavy. I can't say we make love a lot, maybe once every two weeks. He's fifty-five, I'm fifty-two, but that has nothing to do with it. He's had a lot of prostate problems. And he's had a vasectomy. He swears up and down that made a difference in his sex life. I said, "Do you think it's psychological?" He goes, "No, I really don't. My body just doesn't react the way it used to." His doctor told him a lot of men have that problem.

It's not like he can't make love. It's just that your frame of mind has so much to do with it. When Kurt comes home from work, he sits in that chair and you can see everything just drain out of him. The man is exhausted 'cause he puts so much of himself into whatever he's doing. But it doesn't bother me. My sex drive isn't near as strong as it used to be. To me, caring, being together, that's a lot more important at this phase of my life.

We have comfortable sex. It's good sex. It's guaranteed sex. It's not wild, crazy sex. He can get a hard-on instantly, all you gotta do is touch him and he's ready. But he comes too quickly, the poor guy, and then he feels terrible. For a while, this one medicine he was on for a prostate infection, we'd get in bed together and start foreplay and he'd come just like that. I wouldn't even touch him there. He went through a lot of frustration, it messed him up mentally. There were days when he said, "I'm just no good, I'm not much of a man." I keep telling him, "Don't worry about it, there's all kinds of things we can do." But as far as discussing sex, we don't do that much. It's not one of his open topics.

We do a lot of foreplay, which does help for me. He knows what to do. Kissing my neck, oral sex, playing around my butt—but don't insert that sucker. [Laughs.] The only thing he doesn't do is talk to me, that's the one thing I really miss. I'd like him to talk about memories: "It's like in the old days," or "It's like the first time we made love." Little things that bring back the days where everything was so special, the feelings and the love and the hell we went through to be together. I don't want him to talk dirty, that doesn't do anything for me. I'm more of a softie-type person.

I can't do much to him. I have a hard time even stroking his chest without him getting ready to come. That ain't a whole lot, right? It's tough on him. When he does oral sex on me, he can't be lying on the bed, he has to be up on his knees so he's not rubbing against the sheet. And I have to make sure I don't touch him—legs, feet, anything. I try to keep my hands on the pillow, and if I'm gonna have an orgasm, that's not the easiest thing to do. Or sometimes he'll turn around and we'll do a sixty-niner. That's nice, he can handle that. But he comes real quick. I can't give him a blowjob without him coming in three minutes. I don't know what the norm is, but I would say that's pretty fast. I can feel he's ready to come as soon as I start.

He tries, he tries so hard, it's almost sad how hard he tries not to come. I can hear him muttering to himself, "No, no, no, no." He doesn't know he's saying it out loud. It's like he's trying to concentrate on something else so he won't come so fast. But I don't talk to him about it. I think if he realized how much I know he's tryin' to prevent it, he'd get embarrassed and withdraw even more. I know he's got a problem, so it's a matter of working with it but not making it obvious that I'm working with it.

When he comes inside me he usually comes right away, but he doesn't stop. And he's well-endowed enough to where it's not instant Minnie Mouse. So a lot of times when we make love, I'll have two orgasms, which is fantastic. One while we're fucking, or maybe beforehand from oral sex, and one afterward. The ones from oral sex aren't as dramatic. It's an orgasm, but it's not the kind where you shudder from your head all the way down, and you feel your body pumping, pumping, pumping. I think it's because the penetration is so much nicer. And then I'll have another one when we're cuddling at the end. I enjoy that one just as much if not more, I honestly do. By that point, my body is ready, where he's totally finished. At least he understands, and it's not snore city in my ear. I lay on my side, and he's behind me, and he has his penis up next to me even though he's out. Just the sensation of it, if he touches me like that, bingo. It's like my body is all tingly just waiting for that one split second, and that's all I need.

I have to say, if something were to happen to Kurt today and he could never make love again, it wouldn't bother me. When he first started having the prostate problems, I know he was scared about cancer, and I told him at the time, "If you have to have surgery, it will not bother me." I can honestly say that, because of the love we feel between each other. If he has a bad day and I put my arms around him, just some special little moment, I get tingly feelings. It's almost like an orgasm, if you can believe that.

In my life I've had the good, the bad, and the ugly. This is fine.

This satisfies me. Kurt doesn't beat me, and that's so nice. God, it's nice. I have orgasms. I have money. I have somebody that loves me. My kids are grown, they've turned out fantastic. I couldn't ask for anything more. [Laughs.] I always used to think I was looking for another Tim, that first guy I had good sex with. Tim was extraordinary. But I don't know if I could handle that fantastic sex all the time. I guess that sounds stupid, but there's gotta be something other than the sex. Like the hugs that give you chills from the top to bottom. I never had a hug like that from Tim. I would feel a sexual urge, but it was like an animal instinct. And at the Tim stage, Marge was a hurt little girl. Marge didn't feel loved. Marge needed to be told she was pretty. Marge hadn't proved what she could do in life. Anybody that would say "I love you," it was like I'd slit myself down the middle and say, Okay, here I am, take every bit of me, sexually, mentally, whatever you want.

So I can't really compare Tim and Kurt—there's so much water over the dam, I'm such a different person. With Tim there wasn't the kind of mental sex that Kurt and I have. Mental sex is when I get the goosebumps from a hug. With Kurt, it's love and sex. The whole thing makes a complete circle. Without that complete circle, it's nothing.

LLOYD RAPPAPORT

There is something elfin about him: he is smallish, slight of build, with a halo of frizzy hair and a smile hinting at worlds of mischief. He has been exploring those worlds on his own since his late teens, and in the company of his second wife, Ruth, since his late twenties. They have what might be called an open marriage: both have had affairs, though hers have been less frequent and less serious, and together they have enjoyed swingers' parties, sex clubs, and ménages (see Chapter 5). "Sex," he says, "is a very large part of my life. At various stages, the whole life has been built around it." But now that he is fifty-five, a writer for movies and TV, a theater director in Boston, and a father of two girls, "sex as the absolute center of my days and my thinking has receded. Sometimes I have a feeling of nostalgia, but that's all right."

His father was a businessman, his mother a housewife. "I once asked my mom's cousin what held my folks together, because they would quarrel an awful lot, and they were about as opposite as a couple could be. The cousin said it was sex, that it was a very raunchy relationship. I never felt that. I always thought of my mom as cool and remote, and my father as being obsessed with making money and building his empire. He was very macho, a rough human being, dropped out of high school. He worked from four in the morning to six at night and he'd often come home like a firecracker. So I had a pretty troubled childhood. In those days it was unusual for a well-brought-up kid to go to a shrink by the age of eleven, but I did."

He met Ruth and had a short affair with her while he was married. Then, as the marriage was ending, he ran into Ruth again. They have now been together twenty-five years. Raising children—and the advent of AIDS—curtailed their swinging in the eighties, but at the time Lloyd and I talk, it is undergoing a resurgence. He recently ended a two-year affair that was "very serious and big, it nearly ruined our marriage." And he and Ruth are going to parties and clubs again.

• • •

We know a couple named Ethan and Meg, a couple we used to swing with or have orgies with four years ago. Good people, very attractive. Last weekend they invited us to this party. We got there late because we'd been to a movie first. Usually there's a ritual of an hour or two of conversation, eating, getting to know people, but when we got there we were just about the only people with our clothes on. We were greeted by a couple wearing towels. It was a small apartment, but there were forty people at least. And just two bedrooms, so you couldn't be private anywhere. You couldn't even have just six people, which is relatively private. But it was very pleasant, very sexual, a steamy atmosphere, women wearing sexy undergarments. Off to the left was a darkened room where people were making love in groups of four and six, with other people standing around observing, touching themselves. I guess you could say there was a great deal of group grope going on, and some hard-core lovemaking—or fucking, because maybe you can't call anything in such an atmosphere lovemaking. It's just dirty sex.

We didn't do anything for a long time. First we wanted to get a drink, and there was food, and then we took off our jackets, and eventually we started shedding clothing, but only after we had a kind of rapport with one or two couples. Some people are more exhibitionist than others, and women at these parties tend to be a lot freer than the men. This is something I've noticed for twenty years. Eighty percent of the women I've met in the world of swinging are bisexual. They may not be bi in their everyday lives, but they are at these parties. The men are almost one hundred percent hetero and a little bit shy of contact with males, apart from a pat on the back or something. But there's all types of behavior. You have a wide population of what you might call traditional wife-swappers, guys who get into swinging just so they can score with someone other than their wives or girlfriends. You even get guys who will pay a prostitute to go to a swing club so they can score with other women. That's a bad scene, because you never know what you can get from a prostitute. But I think most people at swing parties like to be with other people. At least we do.

There's a feeling of connectedness with the couples, rather than just wandering off and trying to score. That's why a party is more desirable than a club, where the sex is more anonymous.

We were there maybe an hour and a half before we started getting it on at all. Then we ran into a couple we had met at a sex club once. Nothing happened at the club, because even though she's a very beautiful woman, I don't respond to her. She didn't want any kissing, and she didn't want any sucking of her pussy. She had stated it from the outset as we were on the mattress, all four of us. It was so cold, there was no way I could get it on with this woman with all these areas of non-entry. We played with each other for a little while, but nothing was happening, so Ruth and I had moved off. Now, a few weeks later we met them again at the party. The guy still wanted to get it on with Ruth, but she did not at all want to get it on with him. She was not attracted to the guy, he's a bit of a pest. He started touching her, so she went into the other room and we eased ourselves away. That's always an issue at these events. How do you politely turn someone down, when everybody's there for the same thing? It becomes even more tricky if you're having oral sex, let's say, and another person comes by and starts sucking her breasts, or a woman comes by and starts playing with you. Most people, once they're hot and in the middle of the sex act, if somebody else joins it's quite allowable. But with Ruth, if somebody joins in, unless she's really far gone in her heat to the point where her eyes are closed and she doesn't know what's happening, it will spoil it. She has to say "Leave me alone," or I'll say, "It's not the right time, go away."

Then we met another couple. They were very attractive, striking, and very adventurous and sexy. It starts the way it does at any social gathering—you make eye contact, you trust the person instinctively. Ruth liked the guy, they started talking. The conversation is the usual thing: Where do you live, do you know people here, what do you do, do you plan to stay the night? Are you married, are you living together? I felt a little out of it, actually, because he introduced Ruth to his lady and I was standing right there and I had to introduce myself, because he wasn't paying too much attention to me. Nor did I feel his partner was paying attention to me. I had this sinking feeling that the three of them wanted to get it on and wanted me to disappear. He was an artist, very handsome, suave, sophisticated, intelligent, and attentive to Ruth. That's the important thing—he didn't take anything for granted, he was attentive. But it was clear he wanted to get to it, and it was clear that his wife wasn't into it at the moment.

So he and I and Ruth went into the bedroom. We took off Ruth's clothes. He was already undressed except for his shorts, and I got undressed, and the two of us started making it with Ruth. Then his wife came back, and it looked like the four of us were gonna get closer. But the TV was on, they were showing some porn movie, and Ruth was getting very hot, and all of a sudden people began discussing whether they should turn the sound up. Then they started telling stories about watching television at clubs, and this porn movie is really great, and the Germans make better ones than the French, and it was so distracting that the sex that was about to happen disappeared. Really, it's ludicrous, you're in the middle of getting it on and conversations can break out all over the place. Two feet from you, it's "Have you seen Susan in the past two weeks?" "Oh, I heard she had a cold. . . ."

So I said to Ruth, "Let's leave the room," because we were getting into the mood to have something happen. But we went into the other rooms and found the same thing, they were so crowded. Then we drifted back to the TV room, and the guy she liked found us there, and we started getting it on. I don't think he fucked her. He did a whole lot of other things with his hands and his mouth, but he didn't fuck her. I fucked her at that point in a very difficult position, it almost broke my back. I was half on the bed and half off, like a bridge with my ass off the bed, and my shoulders and head on it, and my feet on the ground, and her on top of me. If I did that every day I'd develop great stomach muscles. I came pretty quick, I was disappointed that I came so fast, because as soon as I come I'm shot for a while. But I found the whole scene so exciting, other people handling her while I was fucking her, that I didn't have such great control. The guy was fingering her in the ass, and some other guy was playing with her breasts, and there was another woman, quite beautiful, who was watching intently. The whole thing was very hot. After I came Ruth got on the bed, and another guy started sucking her, and pretty soon she was engulfed with attention. I went to get a drink.

Years ago there were more drugs and more drinking. At this party there were three bottles of vodka open, and not one of them was finished at the end. I had three or four drinks. Most people were drinking wine or Coke. There was a little bit of marijuana going around. No cocaine, nobody's gonna bring cocaine when there are forty people. There used to be a lot of poppers, everybody would do poppers, but no more. And all the men wear condoms. There are little ashtrays with condoms all over the place. Some women don't care one way or the other, but most do. And I have never heard of anybody in the world of swing—which is a very gossipy world—who has ever had AIDS.

The scene has changed a lot. There are many fewer clubs. There are still little groups that get together, but there's an aura of caution and health about the whole thing. It used to be dirtier. When we first started swinging, most of the people who would answer ads were blue-collar workers, firemen, plumbers. A fairly rough group who were into domination and a hard, smacking kind of sex life. Big bodies and rough customers. Suddenly you find all sorts of "well-bred folk" into it. Ruth would probably say that they're still a bunch of sleazebags, but I think they're more considerate. I look back on one party years ago—it was a black-and-white party, everybody wore black and white, and there was a lot of S/M, dressing up, whips, the women looked like men, a lot of hermaphroditic types. The kind of party you might say would be a breeding ground for AIDS, but this was before AIDS. And there was a lot of plotting going on, conspiring, groups piling up on an individual. The scene had a raw tone. I remember that evening fondly as one of excess and mystery. I think sex should be dirty, in the sense of forbidden, antiromantic. I associate the word *romantic* with pure and from the spirit. I don't think my sexual urges, which have nothing to do with romance, necessarily make me less romantic. But I like sex when it's cool and detached from romance and purely physical. I like the whole display, getting off by sharing Ruth's pleasure, even when the pleasure doesn't look like pleasure, when it looks like a struggle, when it seems to be callous or controlling. "Open yourself up now, sweetheart. Do it. Now." That's the kind of sex these parties can encourage. But what has happened is you have a bunch of New Agey, pure-spirit types invading

the scene, who want to talk about the deep ethos of their relationships. I see an awful lot of missionary-position fucking, instead of
what you used to see, where four or five individuals would be holding
one down, fucking her or doing all sorts of things to different parts
of her body. That kind of wild scene, what you call a dirty scene.

I guess the crowd is also getting older—thank goodness.
[Laughs.] Because I am.

Anyway, at the party, we had a period of walking around and
watching. We went back into the same room, and the artist guy came
back with his woman. We were all four of us touching and turning
each other on, and then I fucked Ruth again side by side on the bed
while he fucked his lady. The two women were touching each other
as we were fucking, and this woman was really good with Ruth, she
took her hand and was playing with Ruth's clit while I was fucking
her, and they were kissing, very free with each other and getting into
it. That was great, because I felt we were forming a relationship with
this other couple. The whole thing with them was better than it's
been in a long time with anybody we've met. We really hope we'll see
them again for a foursome or a sixsome in a more civilized atmosphere than this huge party.

Then Ruth had a thing with Ethan. He was the only other person
besides me who fucked her that night. We've been with him before,
he's really crazy for Ruth. I participated for a while, Ethan and I took
turns with her, but there wasn't as much for me in it. I was fondling
her, playing with her ass, but I felt like he really wanted to be with her
alone. As far as he was concerned, I was a bit of an intruder, but he
knows us well enough to not show it. So I took a stroll around, filled
my drink, came back.

I can be very possessive with Ruth at these parties. It's hard for
me to wander away, and that's even more true now than in the earlier
days. Maybe I'm becoming more monogamous. I go there to share
the evening with her. I'm not interested in proving myself with a
woman. I don't have to score. I have a very happy sex life with Ruth.
But I want to be part of her scene. It's not really a feeling of jealousy,
though that happens from time to time. I just want to be there and
take pleasure with her. I think I'm a little extreme in this, even
though there are quite a few couples that stick together. I cling more

than most. I don't know if it's something I should be ashamed of and try to let go of. Somebody at a club hurt my feelings a few months ago, he said, "I can tell you like to watch your wife get fucked." I didn't get into a discussion but I felt like saying, "No, I like to *participate* in my wife getting fucked." I can't really take pleasure at one of these things unless I see that she's getting it on. As I see her getting more excited, then I get excited. If I see that she's getting excited in a way that excludes me, then it tends to have the reverse effect—I get excited but impotent. But if she's getting excited and at the same time reaches out to me, that's the optimum.

There has been tension between us about this. Sometimes she'd like to seduce a guy at one of these things, which rarely happens, because she's choosy. She'd like to win the guy on her own. She sometimes feels she has to acquiesce to my extreme need to be around her. She used to really resent that. I think, from her point of view, I used to behave more obnoxiously than I do now. I can step away now, give her room if she wants to operate with her own seductive wiles.

She also used to feel that I wanted to put her on display, that I'm showing off my manipulation of her. That's not the way I would state the case, but she would. That I get off on being in a dominating position, exposing the parts of her sexuality that she would rather have discovered very gradually, or not at all. It's humiliating to her to be exposed, even though deep down she's not ashamed at all. It's just not something she likes broadcast. So there's always some tension—am I gonna expose her? Yet at the same time there's an excitement that she might be exposed.

By the way, I don't think Ruth has ever come at one of these parties. You don't need to come to have a lot of pleasure. Maybe a man depends more on an orgasm to feel satisfied, but Ruth needs a whole lot of oral stimulation to come, and it's got to be done in a particular way. Nobody's gonna be able to do that at a party where there are so many distractions. She'll be getting hotter and hotter and never relax enough to let it happen, but that doesn't mean she isn't having a wonderful time.

I really think she has a healthier connection with this whole scene than I do. Healthier in the sense of less tangled. She doesn't have any vast needs that are connected to me, whereas my pleasure hinges so much on her response to me. If Ruth goes off to another room to be with somebody, even though there might be somebody who wants to be with me, I have no interest. I will want to say to her, and it's not always easy to, "We can get it on if Ruth is by our side. Let's do something to bring her in, then we can have some fun." I need Ruth to be a catalyst. I can't get an erection if she's not. Which makes me feel a bit strange, because the majority of guys have no trouble that way.

In my own bedroom I never have trouble getting an erection, particularly with Ruth. But at these parties, the whole atmosphere—some people take it casually, but it makes me very fluttery in the stomach. I can go through a whole evening at a sex club with my soldier sleeping. I can be very excited in my mind, but there's an inhibition. It does bother me—not the way it might have ten or fifteen years ago, when I would mope about it. But it's certainly in the back of my mind. If I'm at a club, I'm thinking, eighty bucks to get in and I can't even make the thing stand up!

A sex club is different from a party—it's more crowded, more anonymous. There are two private clubs left in Boston. They're both very expensive, and it's a marvelous experience to go because it's so surreal. You see people up in their seventies and kids in their twenties. A whole spectrum of races. Very fat people and beautiful people with movie-star physiques. Very overweight guys with beautiful Polynesian girls. One club is a little less raunchy, a little more middle-class, more gentrified. There's a wider selection of people at the other one. And there's one very large room, where I'm telling you, seventy-five people can be getting it on at once. Upstairs you have all these little private rooms, and there's an area downstairs that has six little private swing rooms with doors you can close. There are shower rooms and lockers to put your clothing. There's a little room with a bar and a disco floor, but they don't sell liquor. There are fruit juices, and usually food, quite a banquet out there drying up and rotting, because people are not that interested in food. There's a swimming pool—more like a hot tub. I'm sure people have had sex in it, but I've mostly seen a lot of groping and kissing. And upstairs there's a narrow passageway with rooms off the sides, and if you get more than twelve people up there you can't help but be squeezed up against strangers. It's like a grope area where people just stand around touching each other. If you open your eyes and there's someone you want to get together with, you just stumble a pace or two backward and there's a room with a mattress on the floor, but that's really an exhibitionist area, there's no way to be private, so if you're gonna get it on you're gonna have an audience, and that audience pretty soon will want to grope in.

Ruth and I have been to the clubs a few times this summer. I guess there are some denizens who go every week and they have little cliques. I have always been envious of that, because Ruth and I never know anybody and that puts us at a disadvantage. A whole night will go by and maybe we'll make contact with one other couple. And often that's just to prevent spending eighty dollars and going home without meeting anyone. By the end of the night we'll settle for whatever comes along, and sometimes it's not that satisfying. It's just that the experience is so extraordinary. Even if we drive home at three thirty in the morning not having scored happily, I would say it was worth it. Of course, no one wants to pay eighty bucks and say it's not worth it, so we say, "Oh, it was worth it because it's such a trip."

The last time we were in there, Ruth and I hadn't been with anybody, and I said, "Geez, we should just get it on with each other, we're not gonna let the whole night go by without something." We were in a room upstairs where people could look in—not that there were so many people looking in. Eventually we were on the mattress fondling each other, just relaxing and touching in a lethargic way, and this guy came in, a bodybuilder, a really fine specimen. He said, "Can I join you?" We said sure. If Ruth didn't want him to be there I would have known, but it was ever so clear that she would not object to this guy. He was clean-looking, strong-looking, he had a good face, he was about twenty-eight, and he was obviously someone who wanted a good time. It was just a shame he didn't have a female with him, then we would have stayed with each other longer. As it was, the whole thing was over in fifteen minutes.

He started going to it pretty quick, and as she started getting more and more excited, I started getting real hard. She was sitting up, I was behind her, he was in front. He was holding her arms back and fingering her and kissing her. She was starting to relax and get into it, and I took her hand for my own pleasure, so she could touch my cock. Then we moved around and I fucked her while she sucked him off, she was lying on her back and he was kneeling over her, and I came and then he went and fucked her. By the time he was finished I was hard again, so she had it again from me. It was straight fucking and touching, there was no conversation, no small talk. What turned me on so much was sensing her being turned on, and also that she was able to be excited by him and still touch me at the same time. Even when he was fucking her, it was like I was fucking her. It's like my girl is being stolen, yet she's still there. So the two men had a very good time, and Ruth had a very good time, except it was kind of abrupt. As soon as he came he got up and said, "By the way, my name is Tommy, what's yours?" And he walked off. We suggested he bring his girlfriend back, but that was it.

I was thinking about him the other night when I was having trouble sleeping. People have said to me, "How can you engage in casual sex?" And it occurred to me that it's not casual at all. It may seem casual, and it certainly can be anonymous. You go into a room, you strip down, and if the dynamics are right it doesn't take a long time for it to happen. You might be getting it on with someone whose name you don't know. But there's a whole lot of giving of your soul or spirit. I want to have this on record, that my attitude toward swinging is anything but casual. Even the word *swinging* sounds casual. But I don't think anything is casual about sex, quite the opposite—it's very intense. I wish I were *more* casual. My heart beats like crazy as I drive up to the door for something new. As many times as I've been to one of these things, there's always an element of the unknown—which could just be the kind of eyes I'm gonna look at for the next couple of hours. Is this person gonna reject me or accept me? To be or not to be loved—even though the word *love* might seem demeaned, I would argue that it's in the room somehow. Love is peculiar: If you go to a shop as a kid, and you just have thirteen cents and the candy bar is fifteen and the guy lets you have it, that's a little bit like, The world loves me today. Or like Mom saying: I know you broke the dish, but you didn't mean it, it's all right, I still love you. This business about how love is awarded, by the shopkeeper, or by a woman in an orgy—even though she's taller than you, let's say, and beautiful, maybe she's gonna look upon you and see who

you are for a minute, and you're gonna get lucky. It's mysterious, marvelous, almost like magic.

My sex with Ruth has never been better. It's incredible how much
we enjoy each other. And as I get older, part of me says, Enough with
making such a huge deal of sex. When I was first aware of that, about
a year ago, I couldn't believe it. But I remember a quote by Elizabeth
Hardwick, a snippet from an essay about how Americans talk about
sex and parade it on the TV to a degree so out of proportion to what
it really is. In most cases it's over in less than an hour. We spend much
more of our time doing other things. When I read that, twelve or thirteen years ago, I smiled and thought, I may come around some day,
but later on for that, Elizabeth. Now, maybe, I'm coming around.

4

MASCULINE/FEMININE

It would be hard to find a time in human history when the ideal of male virility and the ideal of female purity did not prevail. . . . Societies function on the basis of a precise gender differentiation, but there is nothing natural or god-given about all this. Gender roles are learned and are an effort on the part of society to channel and regulate an otherwise errant sexuality.

—Louise Kaplan, *Female Perversions*

L IZA S WAN, who opens this chapter, describes one of her lovers as "very male, very dominant, very lustful." In six words, she has summed up American gender roles as they apply to sexuality.

Are men biologically coded to be the dominant sex? The lustful sex? The nature-nurture controversy on these scores is far from settled, but one of the latest writers to weigh the evidence, anthropologist Helen Fisher, argues in *Anatomy of Love* that some differences may well be innate: men are more mathematical, spatial, and aggressive, and women more verbal, intuitive, and nurturing. As for lust, however, the observable disparity seems purely a relic of the double standard—male virility, female purity—that arose around the time the plow was invented. "With the introduction of the plow—which required much more strength—much of the essential farm labor became men's work," writes Fisher. Men seized power, turning women into child-producing property, and imposing lifelong monogamy on women to ensure paternity.

The five interviews here focus on questions of masculinity and femininity in bed. The first question is the not-so-simple matter of attraction—boys are supposed to be attracted to girls, and vice versa, but almost all of these speakers are attracted to both, and are pondering what that means. Then come the *qualities* usually assigned to one sex or the other: active/passive, lusty/loving, rough/tender, selfish/giving, restless/faithful, closed/open. Here, too, matters turn out to be murky. For one thing, Liza's "male, dominant, lustful" lover is a woman.

Liza, a lesbian who occasionally plays with men in threesomes, says she "identifies with men" but sometimes takes the femme role in sex. Rachel Monroe, one of Liza's lovers, tends to be submissive with both men and women, and she complains that men are often loutish in bed. But listen to her description of getting oral sex from her boyfriend Bruce: "It's a mixture of knowing that he enjoys it but not even caring if he does. I need to feel that sometimes, like I'm completely in control. Like he has no more will." Jon Benjamin and his wife, early in their relationship, played sex games in which he was the "top." But he also loves to put on lingerie, and has a vivid fantasy life in which he is a woman being fucked.

In short, these speakers continually cross the porous border between "masculine" and "feminine." Is Jon any less a man when he puts on tap pants and imagines himself a teenage girl? Is Rachel any less a woman when she aggressively uses a dildo on a girlfriend? It is interesting that the most traditional gender portraits in this chapter come from the two speakers who arguably have the most conflicted sexual identities. Marcia Cotler, the male-to-female transsexual, hated her sex as a man: it was too urgent, too orgasm-oriented. Her sex drive was much stronger when she was loaded with testosterone, she recalls, or maybe it was just different—a drive to mount, to conquer. Now, as a woman, "I want to be close. I want to be sensual. I want to be dominated. I want to be fucked, as opposed to doing the fucking. I want somebody to come on top of me and protect me." And Hugh Sullivan's double life seems clearly a reaction to the abuses his mother inflicted on him for being effeminate. He is married and has "very fulfilling" sex with his wife. But his hot sex happens during trysts with his male lover, whom he dominates, humiliates, and excites by turning him into a woman—complete with high heels, stockings, garter belt, makeup, and perfume. "I'm always amazed he's up for this," Hugh says— "if you'll pardon the pun."

LIZA SWAN

She is thirty-two, a pianist. She just moved into her San Francisco apartment; the furniture is sparse, the books in milk cartons, the living room dominated by a Steinway. Her hair is a mass of brown curls, her figure slim, her lips sensual. She is shy, boyish, a Peter Pan dressed in jeans and a T-shirt. "I was a real tomboy, and I never grew out of that phase. I played with dolls one day in my life. I didn't even date in high school. I was totally into my own stuff—music and sailing and swimming—and I just never had an idea about dating." She had her first sex in college, with a woman. They were lovers for a year and a half. Then she had a relationship with an older man. After that, "I was almost back at square one. It was like, Okay, so now what? But after college I met this woman who was six years older than me. We started spending a lot of time together, talking late into the night. One night she said, 'You know, I'm gay.' I was stunned. It was like a light going on. I thought, Well, of course, shit. How come I didn't realize this before? We started a relationship right then."

Since ending that romance, she has had several shorter ones, numerous crushes, a smattering of one-night stands, and a long-running affair with her friend Rachel, who is primarily straight, and whose interview follows Liza's.

• • •

I finally realized, just a few years ago, that I identify with men as sexual beings. If we have to put roles to everything, I would definitely be more the male. Rachel and I were looking at a magazine, *Marie-Claire* or something, and we noticed that when we were looking at a picture of a guy, she would think of wanting to be with the guy, and I would think of wanting to *be* the guy. It's not that I want to be male, 'cause I don't. But the way I dress and the clothes I'm attracted to in stores are generally male. And the more female-type woman I'm around, the more male I act. I suddenly feel more . . . I don't know how to describe it exactly. Say I'm walking down the street with somebody, and we're going out, I'll do gentleman-type things like hold the door, let them in first. I'll be more dominant. Then if I'm with someone who's a little more male, I can have more of a female side. Like with Jackie, the woman I've been seeing this week. She's a real dyke dyke. Male in her perception of everything. It's nice to have that side for a while. But I'm generally more attracted to the female type.

Jackie and I had an affair for a while, and then I panicked. I backed off because I'm afraid of getting too involved. We still see each other, and I care about her tremendously, and this week we've been sleeping together all week. It's been weird, because I haven't been able to make love to her. It has a lot to do with this straight woman I'm crazy about. I told Jackie that I didn't want to make love to her because I didn't feel it would be fair if I was thinking about somebody else. But it was okay if she was making love to me, because then I don't think about the other person. I also have a problem making love to her because as is the case with a good number of women, and I would venture to say a lot of lesbians, she has become hooked on the vibrator and therefore lost a lot of sensitivity. In fact, she can't have an orgasm without it. For me, it makes making love, like . . . what's the point? It's hard for me to start making love to her and then have her pull out a vibrator to have an orgasm. She wants to try and lose it, but you have to cut it out entirely. It's a strange phenomenon, those things are so powerful, and if you use them too much you can really become addicted.

In terms of sex, Jackie is very male, very dominant, very lustful. There's not a lot of tenderness. Well, she's tender, but she can get very wild in sex, very forceful. She's a big woman, brunette. She dresses like a guy, always in jeans and shirts. Her hair is fairly short, no makeup. If you have any dealings with lesbians at all, you know right away she's a lesbian. She plays the trumpet, hangs out with the guys, talks very crudely sometimes. And she's from Virginia. She grew up very macho. I always get the impression that she wishes she had a penis. I mean, I don't think she wants to be a guy—well, maybe she does. During sex she's on top most of the time. And she's very vocal about her attraction to me. We'll be out shopping, and she'll say, "Oh, I'd love to go to bed with you right now." Or we were in a restaurant, and she says, "I want to fuck you right here and bend you right over the table in front of everybody." I'm shocked that she even thinks that way. [Laughs.] It's really funny, I expect to turn around and see a guy there.

There's very little foreplay with her. No warm-up toward sex. She's like, boom, you're either having sex or you're not. There's no gradual getting into it, touching or kissing. There's no subtlety and no patience. It's just, "We have to take care of this situation right now." We go straight to the bedroom. We start making out on the bed immediately. She'll take my clothes off and not take hers off. That's fun, when she leaves her jeans on. Then she's kissing my breasts or my face or my legs, anyplace she happens to be at the moment. It's like she's in her own space, and I have to let her go.

She heads right for my clit with her mouth. She likes to pick me up and move me around, and she's big enough to do that without my having to help a lot, which is great. She'll flip me over a couple of times. She likes my ass a lot, and I like being on my stomach, so sometimes she'll be fucking me in the ass with her hand and I'll be masturbating myself. Other times she uses her mouth the whole time. I don't like to come too quickly, but sometimes she needs to have me come right away 'cause she gets afraid she's not doing well. I'd just as soon go on for a really long time. Getting to the orgasm is not so important to me. I think it's more important for her, both when she's making love to me and when I'm making love to her. Which I always consider a male kind of thing.

There's a lot of thrashing around with her, she gets almost violent, not hurting, but her motions are violent. Sometimes if she's got her fingers inside me, she'll almost bang, and I have to stop and say, "What are you doing?" I think she forgets what I'm feeling. Even when she's going down on me, it's generally too fast right from the start. I've slowed her down a lot, I'll tell her, "Too fast, take it easy for a while." Part of it is because of the vibrator. A vibrator is fast and hard from the beginning to the end, so I don't think she understands the give and take of how her body goes, and therefore how mine would go. Again, it's like with a guy, 'cause they don't know exactly what I'm feeling, they don't have the same equipment.

Last time she brought her dildos over. She has two of them, a small one and a bigger one. The small one is like a molded plastic penis. The big one has like waves, or ripples. Just your basic dildos, not one of those ones that looks like a dolphin [laughs], or like fingers. I like the small one in my ass sometimes, especially with her, 'cause she really gets off on that and is very vocal about it. "I love to fuck you in the ass," that kind of thing. I don't always like dildos, but this time it was fun. It's a matter of how close you want to feel physically. I don't want to always use them because you can become dependent, you come to expect it when you make love. But they add excitement.

Lately she is getting a little more gentle, rather than working so hard and fast and worrying about how she's doing. This week we actually spent one whole morning in bed, and that was very nice. She's never done that. She always feels like you have to do a certain thing at a certain time of day. And the sex was the best we've ever had, because she took her time. I almost wanted to stop and say, My God, you're doing it so different. I could sense that she was enjoying every minute of what she was doing. She even said afterward, "I really did, I enjoyed every single second of it, and I didn't want to stop." In fact, I came, and she kept going. Usually I have to rest for a little bit, but she kept going with her mouth. It was very slow and very gentle. I had a second orgasm that built, and it was fantastic. I think she was surprised at how relaxed she could be and still have such a great time, not feel like she just had to get there.

I let her run the show more than I do. It's like I'm watching it happen to me. There's an intrigue about that, but sometimes she's so male that when I have to make love to her, I'm not that interested. It's her interest in me that's a turn-on. I mean, I love her and she's terrific, but I never make love to her the same way I do to Rachel or someone else who's more feminine. I have more power with Rachel, which is a turn-on in itself.

I've known Rachel for six years and we've been lovers for two. It's very casual. We're best friends and lovers and family. She's not gay. She calls herself bisexual, but I don't think that's even true, 'cause I'm the only woman she's slept with. Well, that's not technically correct. She's been with occasional women back in college, but never alone, always in threesomes with men. She told me once that she'd be faithful to me, she wouldn't sleep with any other woman. That's very cute. [Laughs.] We've had threesomes with her exes and her currents. It's a nice relationship. Very comforting. Sometimes we don't sleep together for months. Like this summer, she was spending a lot of time with Bruce, her new boyfriend. In the last few months we've made love maybe twice. But even when she's off with somebody else, I know that no matter what, there's a spark between us.

I'm not sure why I'm so attracted to her. A lot of it is just her beauty. She's very graceful. And she brings out something in me—it could be something as basic as confidence. I don't feel so confident being the female in sex, I feel like I'm just taking and not giving anything back. But her body is so intriguing to me, I just can't keep my hands off it. It's just perfect. The size of everything is just right, and the texture is just right. She knows she's very attractive, and she uses that, and I enjoy it. She knows how to talk to somebody with her body. She knows where she is sexually and she knows how to send messages. If we're just sitting in a room, I can tell when she's open to sex and when she's not. Jackie is much more blatant. If she's feeling sexual, she'll put it right in your face. With Rachel, I might just run my hand down her arm. Just a little touch, like a reminder. We don't have to make love right then, but it's a sexual touch.

When I make love to Rachel I don't care about myself at all. It's just how I'm feeling about her body and what I'm doing to her. I don't need to have her make love to me at the same time or immediately after. Also, Rachel responds to every touch, she'll make a sound, a moan, or a movement to show that it's okay, it's a good thing. Even just touching her arm or back, she's very sensitive. Something as simple as nibbling on the quick of her arm or around her ears. It might drive her totally crazy, but she loves being driven crazy. She likes being on that edge for a while, and I like holding her there.

We also like to come in similar ways. She likes it really slow—at least with a woman, I'm sure it's different with a guy. She also likes—I tied her hands behind her back one time, she loved that. I'm not into that myself. I don't mind being held down a little bit, that can be fun, but I don't like being tied up and useless. My favorite way to come is from her mouth, with her fingers inside me moving very slowly in and out. I like it when her tongue is flatter, rather than pointed. In fact, she learned my favorite way one day when I was making love to her. I was licking her, and she said, "My God, you're going in circles!" Because my tongue was moving in circles around her clit, kind of flat. It was a revelation to her. She never realized what I was doing. I said, "Yeah, that's what I happen to like." Now she does it, pretty well I might add. It can be a very diffused kind of feeling. It doesn't have to be the tongue moving directly on my clit. And her fingers don't have to be very far in. The opening is the most sensitive spot of all. I don't need to be filled up. It just has to be gentle. I like it when it's more of a wash of feeling that completely overtakes me, so I don't have to concentrate on one spot at all. It feels like my whole body is coming.

It's interesting—I've been with straight women, and women who have only been with women. And I've found that lesbians are not necessarily the best lovers. They're not always better than a woman who has never slept with a woman before. Rachel was surprised when I told her one time that she was the best lover I ever had. She goes, "You've got to be kidding." I said no. She was so thrilled, she goes, "Oh, I'm better than the lesbians!" [Laughs.]

The first threesome we did was with an ex of hers. It was her idea to go over to his apartment, get him drunk, and have him watch us make love. I said okay. I knew him and liked him a lot. We went over, had some wine, and she just started things with him. It led to a very long night. I felt comfortable because Rachel was sort of a mediator. I was only interested in her, and he was interested in both of us—me because I was new, and Rachel because he was comfortable with her. Basically, I went down on Rachel a lot. And he'd go down on me. I let him go inside me, but I didn't let him come in me. And he wanted Rachel, which was fine. That's the way it has always been when I've done a threesome with a guy. If he's interested in my body, that's great, and it's a turn-on for me, absolutely. But I'm not interested in giving him any pleasure. Not that I don't want him to have any, I just don't want to do it. That's why it was so great that Rachel was there. She could take care of him, give him a blowjob or whatever, and it was fine. Sometimes it was triangular, he'd be eating me, and Rachel would be giving him a blowjob, and I'd be doing something to Rachel. That's the best time I ever had with three in bed.

The other times were with Rachel's boyfriend Scott in LA. We were together for two whole weeks. The first day I got there, I was making love with Rachel and he came home and we were still in bed. He just joined us. It was intense, spending two weeks with two people like that. It led to some intense arguments, too. There were times when he seemed more interested in me than in her, and she got upset with him. And she was pissed at me sometimes because I wouldn't communicate. Like one time, we were making love and as soon as he got inside me, he lost all thought of what I was feeling. It was like a door closed. There was no communication, he was just there for his own pleasure. He was totally fine until he got inside, everything was going great, and all of a sudden—he even admitted it afterward, he said, "I started thinking with the wrong head." He was banging on me, and it was painful for me, and he didn't have any idea. Rachel sensed something was weird and stepped back. He just kept going. She was sitting on another bed, and he wasn't even aware she had moved away. I was getting tired of it, and Rachel was pissed, and I was thinking about what she was feeling, and I finally said, "Stop, there's a problem here." Then she was asking him, "How can you do that? Why does this happen with you?" After that, we didn't have any sex at all for four or five days.

Some lesbians have a violent reaction to sex with men. They can't handle a penis. That doesn't bother me. To me, sex is sex, sharing bodies, and that's fine. But in these threesomes, it's like the guy is a sex toy for me. Whereas when I'm with a woman, I could give a shit about my own pleasure half the time. I get as much pleasure from making love to a woman as I do from being made love to by either sex.

My problem with men isn't just physical—it's emotional, too. I mean, I can be buddies with a guy, but I can't open up. I just don't feel that connection. I think women are superior to men. It's hard to verbalize this, especially to a man. But women have more of an understanding of love and life and relationships. You have to explain to men, you have to be real patient. I have some gay male friends who are very interested in knowing what's going on with me, my emotional and sex life. I'll try to talk to them. But as I'm describing it, I feel like they don't understand. Their whole concept of sex is different from mine. It's like they change their personalities when they get into sex. I think they really do love each other, but they're both promiscuous, and I think sex is just sex to them. It doesn't really matter who it is. They're always looking around at other guys like crazy. I hate that. Jackie has that kind of way of looking at women. It's very male, and it turns me off. She'll get the *Sports Illustrated* swimsuit calendar and put it up and get off on it. I'm like, "Stop that, that's disgusting!"[Laughs.]

She is thirty-one, a dancer living in San Francisco. In manner and appearance she is soft, "feminine," even girlishly innocent at times, and her emotions are close to the surface. "When people first meet me, they often think I'm tentative and vulnerable—more than I really am. I don't show the other side of me much." But the other side shows itself in her bold brown eyes and the playful set of her smile. "It seems to me that you aren't supposed to think so much about sex. Sometimes I feel wrong to be so interested in it. But recently I've come to say, Fuck it. It's a great pleasure, and it feeds the rest of my life.

"My father was unhappy when I was growing up. He had a very good social side, but he was scary in private: very volatile. I learned how to get around him. I could get him to do what I wanted if I acted the right way: very feminine, asking advice, coming from an under position. But I always felt like a butterfly around a vampire. Is everything okay? Am I doing the right thing? I guess that's where I get the idea that there are so many rules and regulations."

She masturbated at an early age and began having intercourse at fifteen. Since then she has mostly slept with men, though she had several experiences with women before Liza. "I think all my life I've been more in love with the idea of a man than with the actual men. The masculine, the presence, more than the individual. I needed some boyfriend all the time. The way I see it now, I needed backbone, strength, power. I always felt I wanted to be protected, to have things done for me. I've learned that I need to do that for myself."

• • •

I don't call myself either straight or bi. I don't think I'm totally bisexual, because I don't think I could have an exclusive relationship with a woman. Sometimes I see women as an artist would, just admiring curves, color, smell, taste. Other times I want to have them. The ones I want to have are the androgynous types, like Liza. Thin, with small breasts. Slightly boyish, or masculine, but not at all butch. With some of those women, I actually try to flirt. But it's odd, nothing ever comes of it. I've never picked up a stranger.

Actually, I don't often have lust for strangers. I have lust for somebody I know is attracted to me. Maybe it's self-protection—I wait till I'm sure of something, and then I feel lust. When I see someone on the street, a man or a woman—it's like the difference between brain desire and body desire. I feel a fascination. My brain gets attracted. My hands get attracted. But not between my legs. There's a feeling of longing, especially for a man, needing to be with him, wanting to find out about him, wanting to touch him. But I don't get turned on. I get drawn to him. I don't always get aroused when I see Liza. I think she's beautiful, but that's looking at her as an artist again. My lust comes in when the person is very, very close, and there's a sexual aura. Then I'm there, completely there, in a second.

I've known Liza for six years. We were just friends. Then two years ago, it finally happened. I was just ready to—I can't say "give in to her," because it was my impetus, too. It was a hot summer day. I was in her apartment and I wanted to take a nap. I asked her if she wanted to lie down with me. We were both lying there on that tiny little bed. I said, "I'm not going to be able to sleep." I was really aroused for the first time with her. I think I had my period or something, so we couldn't do all that much that day, but it was one of the most exciting moments of my life. It was so forbidden, and my whole body was an electric current. She was just touching me, seducing me. It was amazing. It felt like I had never done it before. Plus it was the culmination of years of friendship. And I felt from the first moment, Jesus, this is a skilled lover.

The special thing about Liza is that when she touches me, it feels like she's taking in something. Nourishing herself with something she desperately needs. It feels like your whole body is there for her, giving something to her. Even if you're not doing anything, you're satisfying her by letting her touch you. And the sounds she makes are amazing. Moaning—moaning with an urgency in it. When I come, and she's going down on me, she's moaning almost more than me, she's so turned on. I'm honored to get that sound from her. Not many men moan when they are going down on you.

And Liza says it's so wonderful with me because I guide her, I tell her what I want. She wants to be taught. Also for me, it's the most animalistic with her. There's no more thinking involved. I wish I could find that with a man.

Liza understands that a woman's arousal zones are not only breasts and cunt. She taught me about the crook of the elbow, and the place behind the knee. Licking there. The neck, the ears. She showed me my G-spot. She touches my whole body with her breasts. Touching her breasts, the softness of them, feels forbidden every time. And she never touches my cunt too soon. That's a problem with most men, touching there too soon. And then the way she kisses. It's extraordinary. She feels like she's all there, like whatever her mouth and hands are doing, that's what she wants to be doing for that part of her life.

Sex with a woman, at least with Liza, is very one-sided. With a man, you've got the penis in there and you're holding his body, so it can be a mutual satisfaction. With a woman, you give sex or you receive sex. We tried spreading our legs and putting our cunts together, but it didn't do much, we laughed the whole time. And we don't like doing sixty-nine very much, because it's hard to concentrate enough to have an orgasm. So we get along great, because we enjoy doing one or the other. First she's doing something to me, and then I'm doing something to her. Before Liza, I never allowed myself to lie back and receive pleasure.

Mostly she makes me come with her mouth. She uses a kind of circular motion with her tongue on my clitoris. And she puts her finger inside me—just one. She can do two, but I prefer one. Men think they need more than one for the thickness, but that's not it at all. If you have just one finger in there, you can be much more subtle. I don't need a lot of movement. It's not the friction I'm after. It's more a probing motion, in and out. Or on the surface, just moving it at the opening. Teasing, but forever.

She's great with her hands. I never feel like it's "foreplay." Every action with Liza is an act unto itself. It doesn't need to go anywhere from there. There's no hurry, no impatience in the touch. One time we bought this harness and dildo. She doesn't want a man, but you get to a certain point in lovemaking where you know how good it would feel to have something inside you. And I want that power, something hard to stick in her. We tried it one night with the harness and dildo. It was difficult, because we weren't used to it. The angle was always wrong. And I never knew if I was hurting her, because I didn't know how far it was going in. We laughed a lot that time, too. It wasn't ideal, so it's better to use dildos with our hands. We do that. Not enough, but we do it.

I guess there's a routine how I get her excited. Breasts, neck—just starting up. Recently I really get into teasing. People don't tease enough for me—like threatening something but not doing it for a while. I've been doing that to her, playing around her endlessly but not touching anything of substance. [Laughs.] On her pubic hair, on her bone, on her legs. When I do touch it, finally, there's quite an explosion. Then I move my mouth there. She's usually on her back. She has her legs bent, and she moves her pelvis for a while—not when she's ready to come, but before that. I love to bite her. She likes quite hard biting on her breasts, but sometimes I get carried away and I hurt her on her inner thighs.

I think she's not as experimental as she could be. She has had a lot of tough women, I think, and maybe she doesn't want to be tough with me. But it might be interesting to get a little harder, a little rougher. I'm definitely the more feminine one in general, but I need to dominate at certain points. I sometimes like to feel I can throw someone around, or be thrown around. It has to be in context, and it has to be part of the surge of lust. Sometimes with her I get very controlling or aggressive. I'll very roughly hold down her hands so she can't use them. I'll say, "What do you want? Do you want it harder? I'm not gonna do that yet." Then she has to say, "Yes, yes." She comes faster, she gets aroused more, when I'm talking to her in this smutty, aggressive way. It's a side of me that doesn't come out very often, but when it does, it's exciting. I would love to tie her up.

This reminds me of one night when we were in bed with my boyfriend. We were all a bit drunk. Threesomes can be difficult—someone always seems to feel left out—so we were trying to play this game. I was whispering in his ear what he should do to her. It was like I was touching her, but only through my whispering. I was guiding him because I always thought he was too quick. It was going great. He was doing everything I said, stroking softly, kissing everywhere. Then it got to the point where he was going to put his penis in her. This was my big moment, because I always want a penis with her. Now I was gonna get to fuck her, using him. Just at the last moment he said, "Okay, that's it, don't you think I can handle it from here?" I was so upset, it completely broke my mood. I didn't know what to do. Then he just started raping her, pounding away, just what I didn't want him to do. It was a disaster. I sat on the floor for a minute and watched them. He was fucking her and she was looking at me, like, Help me, what do I do? She was too shy with men to say, "What the fuck are you doing? Get off me! Don't you see Rachel isn't involved anymore?" I started to walk out of the room, and then she called to me. I was mad at her, too, for allowing him to rape her. Finally he stopped. He was totally sarcastic and didn't realize what had happened. He was probably too drunk. He didn't like the game part of it. It could have been exciting, though.

That's fairly typical of the men I've been with all my life until now. Really, until a couple of years ago, I never expected pleasure out of sex. I'd think, Maybe I'm not a good lover. I didn't know there were things I could ask for, things I could do and fantasize about. Sometimes I would get really excited, but I've had sex many times when I never got wet. I just knew *they* wanted it. Even with most of the main boyfriends in my life—like Scott. I called him the Rabbit. It still enrages me: through our whole relationship the motion of sex was fast and hard, and it couldn't be any other way. It was like he had no control over his body, and every encounter was a quickie. And he couldn't take instruction or guidance, he felt that was an insult. Or with Noel, another lover—I'd say "'Slower, go slower, not so hard." Two or three times he stopped completely and lost his erection. Now, it's possible I was saying, "Slower!" with some irritation in my voice, and that's what affected him. But when you say it over and over in a nice way, still in the mood, and it doesn't work, you get frustrated. It seems like they're no longer there as people. Once the penis is in there, it's for them. It's just this movement, frantic and hard, and then they come and fall asleep. Before the penis is in there, it may be okay. But sometimes, what I need is the penis in there and not really moving. Men don't get into that, at least the men I know. They're *all* like rabbits. It's true!

Only recently, I mean very recently, can I feel comfortable taking as long as I want with foreplay. That was always a problem in the back of my mind—I'm taking too long. Also the sheer clumsiness of my lovers. As if they've put novocaine on their hands, tongue, lips. It feels like the fingers are made of soft wood. It feels like they're doing something they know I want, but they aren't really into it. You can tell when somebody loves to do something, or when they're doing it out of duty. If they love it, there's direction, movement, delicacy, like they're touching something precious. I've hardly ever felt that except with Liza. Not even with Bruce, my main boyfriend now. Liza is the only one who touches my body as if it's something so delicious.

If Liza's going down on me, she understands that if I push her head a little bit away, that means there is too much pressure. It's instinctual for me, and she knows it doesn't mean, Stop, I hate you. But Noel—sometimes if I try to push him away, he goes harder. A few weeks ago, I made the mistake of telling Noel that I had gotten into a little spanking. He's tried this before with me but I could never take it. This time, he started spanking me—he was inside me, slightly rolled over, so we were face to face and he was hitting my ass. He is very strong. . . . [Long pause, deep breath.] And in a way it's very exciting. But he has no sense of his own strength. He was hitting me so hard that I was almost yelling, and trying—my hands were pinned somewhere or other, and he—I was saying in all seriousness, "Stop this," and he went harder. Really painful, over and over and over. I was almost crying, and I jumped out of the bed, and—I was so furious. We had a big fight. He tried to pull me into his arms and apologize. In a split second, I had to choose which way I would go. I could cry and say, "It hurts so bad," and fall into his arms and let myself be comforted like a child. But I realized, "Don't be a fool." I got really angry and got dressed. We were yelling at each other. I was saying, "You asshole, don't you know when to stop? How could you possibly think it means go on further when I'm in pain? Why do you go harder? Do you think I'm lying? Do you think I'm saying one thing to be coy and meaning another?" He looked devastated and said he would never do anything on purpose to hurt me, but he thought I was enjoying it. He was trying to read my body, and he thought I liked it. He didn't realize how hard he was hitting me, and so on.

I'm sort of embarrassed to tell you how it ended. After we were arguing and he was completely dressed, he got his coat and was ready to go. By that time he was feeling so sorry and so terrible that he came over and kissed me good-bye and it started all over again. But I wouldn't let him use his hands at all. I pushed them above his head and made him stay like that. Then I began to touch his ass. And he reacted so strongly that I went and got my dildo and pushed it in him. I'd wanted to do that for a long time but it never happened before. It had never happened to him either. He had the most amazing orgasm I'd ever seen. He was on his side, and I was playing with his penis in my mouth and my hand at the same time—it was crazy. It turned out he had always been violent because he wanted violent things done to him and never knew it. But of course, afterward he said, "I don't know what your problem is with fucking in the ass, that didn't hurt at all."

Ugh, this is depressing. Let me tell you about last weekend with Bruce. He lives up in Sonoma, works in a winery there. I got there late at night. I put on this lingerie and we watched porn videos. I really get into videos, even if they're raunchy. I've never seen one where the woman is truly having a good time, or where the routine is altered: he eats her, she gives him a blowjob, and they fuck. It's boring. But I can have incredible orgasms. They're not the kind of orgasms where I'm concentrating on the person with me. It's not loving at all. It's pure sex, pure lust. But that can be fun sometimes. Usually both of us are staring at the screen, fucking madly but with no contact. It's bizarre, like strangers. But this time—it was Bruce's idea, he completely concentrated on me with his mouth. And I looked at the screen. He said, "Lie back and enjoy yourself," and he went down on me.

Bruce loves oral sex, but he doesn't like pubic hair. I don't want to shave mine, I just don't. It feels like too much catering to the man. Sometimes I get nervous that people who watch too many pornos get a certain idea of what women should look like. How exposed, how tied up, how much lingerie, how high the heels. It's like they're trying to imitate the movies, duplicate the doll-like quality of the woman's body. Dressed up, or shaved for easy access.

The key to oral sex for me is to feel the person can go on forever, and that I'm totally free. With Liza, I've been having fantasies that I told her about, that she's my slave and I can tell her she can never stop. I get so excited as soon as I feel that they'll go on forever. And they automatically get more sensitive. Their mouths get more tuned to the pace of satisfying me, which is very light, no pressure. A long buildup. Light for a long time. Right on the clit, or at the vaginal opening. I like the mouth on the clit and the finger in, and sometimes I put my own finger in my ass. When I do that, though, I can feel inadequate, that I need all my holes taken care of, that I need too much stimulation, that I'm not equipped right. That I'm not "correctly" having an orgasm.

So Bruce was going down on me, and it was enjoyable, but I knew I couldn't come. There was a piece of me that was still observing, instead of just feeling. There was a little thread of worry. Bruce's tongue was too sharp and too insistent. So I told him, "Have a flatter tongue, not so pointed and sharp. Softer, flatter." That I learned from Liza. He did it immediately, and it was incredible. There was this movie on, and he was down there, and I didn't have to look at him or think about him, and then it became like—I lose touch with my body. I lose all inhibitions. I stop worrying how long it's gonna take. It's a mixture of knowing that he enjoys it but not even caring if he does. I need to feel that sometimes, like I'm completely in control. Like he has no more will. I can't feel his skin, just his hair. He's not human anymore.

Then I put his finger in me, and somehow he knew not to move it a lot. And I was half watching the video and being in this trance.

Oh, it was a great orgasm.

After I come, I can't do anything. I have to rest a little bit. I'm in another world. Then we turned around and I went down on him. I've only started enjoying that recently. God, I get so turned on to do that now. I remember Scott didn't like blowjobs. He could stand it for about two minutes, but for him to come it had to be violent, so he couldn't do it in my mouth. He'd be more and more frustrated. But Bruce loves getting blowjobs. He wants to stay on the edge for a long time.

I was on all fours. I couldn't see the TV screen. I started at the tip. I like to be teased, so I assume other people do, so I start at the tip. Usually, I like to wet my whole hand with my saliva so I can run it up and down. You have to go by his sounds and his breathing. The penis is like velvet. It's like washed silk. It's like—something you need. It feels so powerful, like you can get something from it. It's mine for a while. I can't wear it, but I can own it, and there's a lot of power in there. Sometimes I find myself groaning, doing it, because I get so turned on.

Then he wanted me to make him come, but I wasn't sure, because I wanted to go on after that. He said it would be okay. So I did.

Then we lay around for a while, watching the video. I started touching myself, and he got hard again. He put on this lambskin condom and we started fucking. He wanted to do it from behind. I was nervous because I never came that way, but I propped myself up with two pillows, watching the movie and touching myself, and it was fantastic. Then he started spanking me. He hits me just right—he gets this little sting, and in between the hitting, he rubs it, soothing where he hit. His spanking isn't frantic, just once in a while, and lightly. I've asked him if he likes to be spanked, but he's noncommittal. I'd like to do it. I fantasize about it. But my fantasies are a little more violent, and I don't know how to use my body as a violent tool. I need something in my hand to make it harder.

So he's spanking me, and I remember half-watching the video. By this time we had changed movies, now it was a futuristic thing where men were learning to be good lovers. This woman was telling this guy how to fuck another woman. Training him. That was exciting. The words that were coming out of her mouth were so vulgar and sexy. Some of the movie seemed dangerous—like, about the fucking, she was saying, "Stick it in her, hurt her with your penis, she wants you to hurt her, watch her face, look at her eyes, she likes it." I wondered about that, spreading the idea that women want men to hurt them that way, but it turns me on, too. Then the guy in the movie was fucking her so fast, they were like two quivering bodies. It blew my mind. Then I came.

Only a few times in my life have I had an orgasm with a man the normal way. I mean, whatever normal is. Without touching myself. Without using my hand while we're making love. The slower and lighter lovemaking starts, the faster I'll have an orgasm. In the beginning I like it really slow, hardly moving. I like to be in control. In the end, when I'm getting near orgasm, I don't want to move at all, and I want them to just do it perfectly. And not to stop. I don't like having an orgasm after they do. I like to be the first one. I can do it afterward even if the penis is a little bit soft, but I don't want to be late. I don't want them to have to wait for me, because they might lose interest after they come.

Sometimes I use fantasies. They might have to do with somebody raping somebody. Me raping somebody. Me having a penis. It's very violent and painful for the other person. One takes place in a jail cell. The inmates are all male. One of them is really enormous and very brutish. There's a guard who is in on it, watching the rape and enjoying his power, that he could stop it but he doesn't. The big guy is raping a small guy. There's a candle or something underneath the small guy's cock. A lit candle. I don't know why, but he's supposed to keep an erection. He's crouched over it on all fours, and in order to get away he would get burned, so he has to stay against the rapist. It's a torture fantasy. I have it in different forms. Sometimes I'm licking a virgin girl until she's excited, or I make her suck my penis, and then I rape her while she screams for me to stop. Disgusting, huh? But I love the feeling of all this power.

It's funny with Bruce. In some ways, he is the best lover I've ever had—the most caring, the most innovative. He's taught me some things—like the hitting, how much I like it. And about bondage turning me on, though I haven't done much with it yet. He tied my hands behind my back one night, which was so exciting. On the other hand, sex with him sometimes feels like it means nothing. When I'm in bed I want to feel that I'm making a dent in somebody's life for that second. That's why it's fun with Liza, because I feel so powerful and so important. With Bruce, sometimes I feel like a whore, like a slut, like

I might as well be paid for it. But I keep trying with him, because there's a lot of excitement, too.

A friend once told me that in certain legends, after a goddess made love she would cleanse herself to become a virgin again, symbolically. With water, with prayer. It's a good idea for a woman if you want to sleep with people and not get hooked in the wrong way. Because a woman is just opened and opened. And I get left open. When I sleep with somebody, I start thinking I have the right to own them and be owned. I get jealous and possessive and I don't think about what I need to do in this world. So after sex with men, I do this closing ritual. I wash myself when I'm alone. I don't think you can do it with the man around, at least I can't. It's mostly a visualization, you can do it with or without water. I visualize myself whole again, or without a hole again. [Laughs.] It's some kind of coming back to myself, closing the barriers.

Usually the more I'm with somebody, the more I become blinded to my original wariness. But I hate that feeling of being blinded by men. I don't want to be needy. I don't want to feel lonely and obsessive. I don't want to depend on anyone in my life, the way that I have. So I need to close myself off after sex, to imagine my cunt closing back up. Sometimes I speak out loud: "Close, close, close." I get back to my inner self, my inner strength, where I don't need a man to fill my empty spaces.

MARCIA COTLER

"I was born Mark Robert Cotler on January 8, 1963," she begins, going straight to the heart of the matter: Once she was a man, now she is a woman. About eighteen months before our talk, at the age of twenty-seven, she had a sex-change operation. Knowing that is a bit eerie at first; I find myself searching her face for masculine features and finding them, glimpsing what she looked like as a man. But were I to pass her on the sidewalk I would never guess. She has shoulder-length blond hair, a shy smile, a soft voice, and a big, soft body dressed in a loose T-shirt and cut-off jean shorts. We talk in an upstairs room of a house she shares with her mother and brother in a working-class suburb on Long Island. In one corner of the room is an electric guitar; on a nearby shelf are pictures of her playing in an all-woman rock 'n' roll band. At one point we adjourn to her bedroom, where she logs onto one of the computer bulletin boards she subscribes to. This one is called the English Palace, and caters to fans of S/M and its variations. Her ease with the computer is well-earned: She works as a programmer for an aerospace company.

Her father made picture frames; her mother, while Mark was growing up, was a housewife. It was an unhappy marriage that finally ended in divorce when Mark was sixteen. "There was a lot of fighting in my house. It used to upset me quite a bit. I had a severe weight problem. I didn't like myself, so I used to eat more. Then there was the gender identity thing. It wasn't as strong back then, but it was there. I used to sit at school and wish I was a girl. I remember when I was four or five, being out in a playground. There were these two girls playing with Barbie dolls. I walked up to them and asked if I could play with them. They looked up at me and started laughing. "Boys don't play with Barbie dolls!" I'm like, "Why not?" They were laughing hysterically. I'll never forget that. Ever since then, I always examined every situation to see how gender applied to it. If it was something feminine, I avoided it like the plague."

But the feeling that something was wrong never left him. By the age

of eleven or twelve he had heard about transsexuals on TV and was fur-
tively reading whatever he could find on the subject in the local library.
When he started masturbating, his fantasies were of being a woman. But
aside from one brief, unpleasant encounter with a man, his sex as a man
was with women—and there was not a lot of that. At nineteen he mar-
ried Kathy, the first woman he ever slept with. They stayed together for
six bumpy years and had two children. After the first child came, "I real-
ized I was getting deeper into the husband-father role. I still wanted a sex
change, but I was very scared. I also thought I was nuts. I started to be-
come a basket case. Finally my mother said, 'What's wrong with you?
Can I help?' I was so miserable that I guess I didn't care anymore. It took
me like three hours to spill my guts out. She suggested going to get some
therapy. I guess we both thought the therapist was going to straighten me
out, but he helped me learn about myself. I realized I felt I was a woman,
but I was in a man's body. And these feelings were never going to go
away."

   Still he hesitated. He told Kathy of his desires, and "she became hys-
terical. I couldn't blame her." Finally, after the birth of a second child,
Kathy left him when he confessed he was secretly taking estrogen. Soon
afterward he decided to go through with the sex change.

· · ·

Having sex with a woman as a man wasn't great, but it was okay.
First of all, socially it was okay, so I didn't have that obstacle to overcome. And physically, I'm turned on by women. Back then there was
also my sex drive, which was very strong. I had testosterone in me
back then, and testosterone increases your sex drive, whether you're
male or female. My testosterone level is nil at this point, so the sex
drive decreases. Or it's much different, maybe that's a better way to
put it. It's not that drive where you want to conquer, you want to
mount, you want to ejaculate. When I was a male, my sex drive could
get so strong and so overwhelming that that's all I thought about. I
hear my women friends now, especially the ones who don't know
anything about my past, they'll sit around and say that men think

with this head [points to crotch] and not that head [points to head]. I sit there and laugh to myself, because it's so true.

As a male, I knew that once I ejaculated, I could relax. But as a female, I want to be close. I want to be sensual. I want to be dominated, as opposed to dominating. I want to be fucked, as opposed to doing the fucking. I want somebody to come on top of me and protect me. When I'm getting screwed, I like it slow and steady. I don't want it to be over. Even once I have an orgasm, I want it to go on. A male orgasm, it peaks really high and then drops way down. That's why a lot of guys, as soon as they come they're exhausted. I know I was, and the experience I've had with men is the same thing. Once they come, they want to roll over and go to sleep. Women say, Oh, men are so insensitive. That's not true, 'cause I can attest to it. I remember what it was like, getting so intense and then all of a sudden dropping off. It drains your system, and you're tired. But as a woman it's not like that. You get wet, you get into it, and you can keep going. It's not such a hard peak. It gets up there much more slowly, and it drops down much slower, too.

These days, if somebody can get me horny enough, I'll say, Great, it'll be nice to come, but it's not like there's nothing else in the world that matters—that was my experience as a male. You know what was funny, though? I hated that feeling. Physically, it felt good to come, but mentally I didn't like it. It felt like my body was taking over, and my head had no control. When I'd get aroused, my body wanted to come so bad that there was no turning back. It would make me do things I didn't want to do. If I was supposed to go out with my friends and I was horny and I was there with my ex, I'd end up saying, Screw everything, I just want to fuck. It used to drive me crazy. After I came, I felt like, I can't believe I gave that up to screw. It's like I was two different people. I even disliked it during sex, because I knew what was going on. Like, Oh, God, here we go again. But we're here, might as well go ahead and do it.

With my ex, I would always prefer if I could screw as quick as I could. Get the orgasm over with. Then I could go back and concentrate on foreplay. Also if my wife wanted to have sex again, we could have intercourse but I could be more sensual about it. I expressed it to her: Let me get it over with the first time, 'cause that way the second time when I get hard I won't have this extreme desire to come. We used to have very slow, rhythmic, very sensual intercourse, and she would enjoy it and so would I. We'd do a lot of kissing and hugging and be a lot more affectionate, as opposed to it being hard sex, straight intercourse.

We almost always had sex with me on top. Which I also hated. It was okay the first time, but once I came and I was in a more relaxed state, I definitely wanted to be on the bottom. Being on top, I could control the situation. I could get it over as fast as I wanted to. Being on the bottom is a little different. I would think about certain things—what I was doing with my hands. What I wanted to touch. How I wanted to make myself feel good, or her feel good. Lovemaking. But a lot of times she wanted to be on the bottom, too, and she wanted me to stay on top. We used to fight over it. That was funny: Once she realized one of the reasons why I liked to be on the bottom, she wouldn't allow it. In her mind I was fulfilling my desire to be a woman, and she didn't want me to have that.

After we split up I went into full mode of taking hormones and doing electrolysis. I arranged a time when I was going to start living full-time as a woman. I started learning how to dress. I used to have a big humongous Jewish nose. I decided there was no way I was ever gonna pass as a woman with that beak. I came to the conclusion, I'm gonna get a nose job, and that will be a good point to go into transition. So I took off a few weeks, got the nose job. I left as Mark Cotler and came back as Marcia Cotler.

For a year I was in transition. That was an awful time. I went through all kinds of nightmares at work, even though the company was very supportive. I looked okay, but I had a hard time passing. There were a lot of things I needed to work on—my look, my walk, my talk, everything. I didn't feel like a man, and I didn't feel like a woman. I felt like a thing. I felt weird in the shower, knowing that I'm legally Marcia, I'm going to work as Marcia, but here I am standing in the shower with boobs and a penis. I couldn't go into a women's room and feel safe and secure. Kathy insisted I wear men's clothes whenever I saw the kids. We were getting into a nasty divorce. There was a lot on my shoulders.

Eight months into transition I decided I wanted to get back into music. I've been playing music since I was twelve. I didn't know how the world was gonna accept a female lead guitar, but I figured what the heck. I started answering some ads in a music paper. One band wanted me to come and try out. It was three guys that had a blues-rock type band. I tried out. They didn't want me. They said, "You do play pretty well for a girl." But one guy named Nicky called me up and asked me out on a date.

You have to keep in mind, I wasn't complete at the time, but I was so flattered. The guy was extremely cute. I figured, I'll just go on a date with him. Before you knew it, we were dating full-time. The first few months were hectic. I met him in December, and I got my final operation in April. Four months, something like that. He told me he was in love with me. But he wasn't real pushy about sex. He told me he would like to make love to me, but I kept on telling him I wasn't ready, because I was going through a divorce and so on. I guess because he was so into me, he was willing to wait. Over the first couple months we didn't do much sexually. Some kissing and holding hands. That felt good. It felt great. A little scary, because I thought, Well, if I go this far, what comes next? I was also scared to get too close, because what if accidentally he happened to rub me in the crotch? A couple of times he did brush across there, but I think at that point I was so atrophied that it didn't matter. From taking hormones, your testes shrink up to almost nothing. Your penis decreases in size, too. So there wasn't much there for him to notice.

After a while he would start to kiss me and do more things, rub me and touch me, see how far I would let him go. I remember he'd say, "God, I'm getting so hot and horny." I'd sit there and say, "Well, you better take a cold shower." He goes, "Aw, you don't want to do nothing." I'm like, "Naah, I really can't." "Well, why can't you?" "Oh, I'm just not ready yet." At one point he was really pushing me. I could tell he wanted to have sex, and I couldn't blame him. So what I did—he was sitting on this convertible chair, a recliner. I could tell he was hot and horny. I pulled his pants down and gave him a blowjob. He was shocked that I was doing it. He definitely didn't push me away, he was more than receptive. Later he confronted me and said, "Why are you willing to do this but you aren't willing to have regular sex?" I said, "Well, it's different." He goes, "Well, how's it different?" I just said, "It is." He didn't push me. He was grateful enough to be getting some kind of sex.

It wasn't my first time giving a blowjob, I had done it once in high school, but it was my first time being comfortable doing it. I was more into it because I knew I was going to be satisfying him. I wanted him to feel good. I cared about him. To say I enjoyed it, like it was the greatest thing on earth? No, I'd rather be eating a hot fudge sundae. But it was okay. After having a penis for twenty-six years, I know exactly what one feels like. I know what makes a penis feel good. I know the different parts. I know exactly how to touch it, and how much pressure. Matter of fact, various times that I've given guys head, I've gotten the same reaction. It's like, "My God, you know exactly how men feel." I'm like, "Hey, well . . ."

Finally I got my operation. April 15, 1991, I was in the hospital in pain. Everybody in the world except my mother and my brother thought I was on a business trip. I finally came back. Lots of pain, a little more pain than I thought I was gonna have. Nicky kept on going, "Why can't I come see you?" It was almost a month I hadn't seen him. Finally I let him come see me. He goes, "What's the matter with you?" I just said, "I threw my back out." He bought it hook, line and sinker. About six weeks after my operation I started feeling pretty good. I said, Well, I guess it's time to get laid. I was scared but I wasn't scared. I was looking forward to it. I had the operation. That little growth was finally gone. I was feeling wonderful. So I went to bed with him. It was a little uncomfortable, because I was still kinda healing down there. But it was weird, it felt so natural. It felt great. I felt like I was on top of the world for the first time in my life, at least sexually. I felt so complete. God, I never screwed so much as in that next week. We just screwed and screwed and screwed. It was really kinda funny. Nicky had a great old time.

The operation itself—generally there's two ways they do a sex-change operation, male to female. One is pretty new. The other has been around for twenty years or better. It's known as the penile inversion technique. That's what I had. What they do is they take the penis, cut it open at the base around where the scrotum is, and literally peel the penis like a banana to get the meat out of it, 'cause all they want left is the skin. Then they make an incision, an opening like a canal up where the vagina should go, and they take the remaining skin from the penis and invert it. So the skin that was the outside part of the penis is now the lining of the vagina. A lot of times what they do is use a piece of the head of the penis as the clitoris. They remove the testicles and use the skin of the scrotum to become the labia. Now, with this technique, if you have a small penis, you're not going to have a very deep vagina. Or else you're going to have to rely on skin grafts. My doctor said to me, "It ain't the biggest in the world, but it'll have to do." He gave me about four and a half, five inches worth of depth. There's times, when I'm with a guy with a big penis, that I can feel it bottoming out, and I wish I was a little bigger, but it's not that bad.

One problem is there isn't much natural lubrication. You know how when you get aroused, you get this pre-ejaculation stuff, this clear liquid that doesn't have any semen in it? Well, the duct that makes that fluid, they leave it inside you. It produces the liquid, and that's the only lubrication you get. But it's generally not enough. So you have to use KY jelly or something like that. Also, with the penile inversion method, you have to do what they call dilation. You have to use a dildo to make sure it stays open and stretched. Otherwise it can close up on you after a while. At first you have to do it quite often, like quite a few times a day. Then once a week. Or if you stay sexually active, you don't have to do it at all.

And Nicky and I were certainly active. One thing I like to do is give a guy head in the shower, and I'll get my hand real soapy and go around his derriere or his anus and start rubbing and massaging. I don't actually go into his anus, but right up through the crack. All soapy and slippery. I tell him to spread his legs and I get him super-hot. It's amazing. I know for a fact that Nicky never had anything like that done to him. He said to me, "A month ago, I never would have dreamed I'd allow somebody to touch my anus that way." I'd say in a very seductive, sexy voice: "It feels good, don't it?"

Now, during the whole time I was going out with Nicky he knew I was going through a lot of things, but he didn't know what. I was starting to feel for this guy, and ever since I went to bed with him he was using the love word more and more. Finally I came to the conclusion that I either gotta break up with him or tell him. 'Cause if he finds out the wrong way, it could be trouble, and I don't want to hurt this guy.

One night we were out to dinner. He said to me, "Look, there's something wrong with you. I wish you would share it with me, because I really care about you. I love you and I don't want to see you hurting." I looked at him and said, "Nicky, I don't want to hurt you, and I don't want to make my problems your problems." He said, "What could possibly be so wrong?" And he started asking me questions. "Did you murder somebody or something like that?" I go, "No, it's nothing like that." "Did you rob a bank?" At one point he asked me if I was a lesbian. I started playing with him: "Well, what if I was?" He goes, "Well, I don't know, I wouldn't care, I guess, just as long as you're not fooling around with anybody while you're dating me." I go, "Well, okay." I kept on avoiding the subject and being vague. So he goes—and he said it sarcastically—"What, were you once a guy?" I kept my composure. I said, "Well, what if I was?" He goes, "Oh, I dunno, I never knew you any other way, it wouldn't matter." I kind of laughed. I was treading water, trying to decide if I should tell him. I finally figured, Yeah, I better, he seems to have a good attitude about it. I looked at him and said, "That's it." He goes, "What?" I go, "I had a sex change." He starts laughing and says, "Yeah, right." I go, "No, seriously." He goes, "C'mon, get outa here." I said, "No, I did." He still didn't believe me, but I kept on talking to him, and he started realizing I was dead serious. For the next hour or so we talked. I told him about all the aspects of my life I had been keeping quiet all that time. At first he grabbed me and hugged me. He said it didn't matter to him, that he still loved me and cared about me. I felt so relieved. But the next day he starts acting funny. The following day I get this letter. He says he cares for me very much, but it's been driving him crazy the past two days and he needs to break up with me. I was very hurt and scared. I was thinking, God, is every relationship going to be like this? Once a freak, always a freak?

But we got past that. We stayed together. A few months after that he moved in here. We lived here together for eight months. Then the relationship started to go sour. I think I latched on to him for some of the wrong reasons. He was a very sweet, gentle, wonderful person. But he wasn't a very stimulating person. And I have to admit, after a while the sex got boring, too. Not that he changed that much—it was more because I changed. The early sex I had with him, I was more excited just because I was having sex as a woman. But I came to realize I wasn't into him sexually. Partly because of his inexperience, and because he was self-centered when it came to sex. He wouldn't take much time to help me get off or to do things to me. Like I'm very much into sensual massage. He was never into that. He'd do five minutes so he could jump my bones and screw. And toward the end of our relationship, I started thinking, Well, maybe I'm not into men after all. I started to look into the lesbian side of myself. I said, Wait a minute—I enjoy sex with men, but yet I had sex with my wife and various other women all these years. So I started wrestling with the idea: Am I a heterosexual female? Am I bisexual? Or am I truly a homosexual female, and what I'm having with men isn't that great? I was very uncomfortable, but I slowly started realizing I must be bisexual.

Then I started meeting a lot of people through these computer bulletin boards. One of my friends is into the S/M scene out here. She goes, "Hey, why don't you get on the bulletin boards at least and check it out? There's all kinds of people on there, not just B&D and S/M." I figured, All right, I'll try it. So I got on the English Palace. I'm not really into the scene, but I've been hanging out with people who are heavily into it. I've done some playing, but I don't know if it's for me.

I met this girl named Melissa on the bulletin board. One day we said, "Hey, let's get together," so we did. Then I went to one of these dinners the English Palace organizes. After dinner, people usually go back to a local hotel. I mean like fifteen or twenty people. Everyone will have a room, and various degrees of sex will be going on. Some people will be having straight sex. Some people will go to sleep. Some people get involved in the wildest B&D scenes where they'll have the whips and chains and leather and restraints. The first dinner I went to, Melissa was there with her master. They asked me if I wanted to come back to the room. I knew she had the hots for me. I figured what the heck, I'll go and see what happens. I guess there were ten people in the room. People were demonstrating different things and joking around, doing odds and ends. Everyone was getting nude, but there wasn't so much wild sex going on. At one point her master, Andre, told everyone to get out of the room. He wanted to play with me. So it was the three of us. We didn't get into any wild S/M stuff. It was straight sex, a lot of oral and sensual stuff and touching. I first made Melissa come. Then at one point she made me come. It felt so wonderful. I was able to relax with her, which surprised me considering it was the first time.

I'll be honest with you, I haven't had many orgasms since my change. One from fingering myself. One from having Melissa eat me out that night. So just two orgasms. They're weird, they feel like orgasms I had as a male, but not nearly as intense. And a lot of times I don't get to the point that I want to come. It's not like before, when if the wind blew I'd wanna come. Now I want to be rubbed and hugged. I love the closeness, but to actually come is not that important. It also takes more concentration. I'm still very sensitive down there even though it's been a year and a half since my surgery. There's a lot of spots that are tender, and some numb spots, dead spots—I guess 'cause of the way the nerve endings heal. The doctors said it can take quite a few years to get the way it's finally going to be.

I remember the first time Nicky came inside me, it was like the confirmation of my completion, that a guy came in me. Then I slept in the wet spot. That wasn't so wonderful. But it's neat, feeling a man pulsate in me. The satisfaction of knowing I can make somebody come. That's what I get out of it. I like being penetrated, I enjoy it, but I don't necessarily go crazy for it, like I'll do anything to get it. It's more the feeling of the man being on top of me, and being screwed. I like to wrap my legs around him and pull him into me. There's not much sensation in my vagina from the penis going in and out—it's more pressure and what I can do to get him to react. I have very strong muscles down there. When somebody goes into me I can squeeze. Any guy that's ever penetrated me, I make him go through the roof when I squeeze. He's like, "How the hell do you do that?" Most women—I don't know if they can't do it, or their muscles aren't very strong there. It's neat for me, I'll be going at it and I'll have my legs wrapped around him and all of a sudden I'll squeeze and feel

him squirm, getting all excited. I've been with five different guys—
wow, I never realized it was that many. Every single one of them, I've
made them moan, "Oh, my God." The classic line. It's neat knowing
I can do that.

So not coming doesn't really bother me. It's more frustrating for
other people who try to get me to come. Well, it's a little frustrating
when I sit there and think, These people are coming, why don't I?
But I'm pretty content with how my sex is, and my relationships. I
like other people to feel good even more so than myself.

JON BENJAMIN

He is thirty-eight, married, with a two-year-old son, and still adjusting to his role as "the man who brings home the bean sprouts—there's no bacon in our house." The role doesn't come easy, since he grew up without male models: his father left when Jon was two, and his mother raised three children alone in a Southern city. They were poor; she suffered from depression. Jon attended a state college, married young, divorced, moved North, and tried various forms of therapy, self-help training (such as est) and New Age spirituality. Now he lives in an apartment over a store in a suburb of Washington, D.C., has been married for three years, and manages a bike shop. Money is tight, since his wife, Sue, stopped working as a massage therapist to devote herself to mothering.

He is a thin man of moderate height with a receding hairline who likes to analyze himself, worrying every side of an issue, wondering aloud if he's being honest. There is a hint of femininity in his movements and features, and he is fascinated by his "feminine side." For years he has been bisexual in fantasy, though largely heterosexual in activity. The bisexuality applies not only to his imagined partners but to himself—that is, he fantasizes having sex with either men or women, as either a man or a woman. Early in their marriage, he and Sue played with the fantasies— but they have now become something of a sensitive subject.

• • •

A lot of this came out right after Sue and I got married. I think I know why—I was in a safe enough place to explore some taboo feelings. With my first wife, a few times I played with putting on her underwear and doing some gay fantasizing. Then when I met Sue and we started dating, we'd do things like tie each other up or do dominant-submissive role-playing. One thing I liked was for her to tie me up and force me to eat her, and slap my face hard if I refused. She'd tie me on my back spreadeagled, hands and feet tied to the bedposts, blindfolded. We also did stuff with her in the submissive role, where I'd tie her up and put vibrators in her ass and vagina and have her suck my cock and I'd stroke her breasts, all at once.

Then we got married and went to Cancún for our honeymoon. There wasn't much to do besides eat, sleep, go to the beach, and have sex, so we played around some more. And right after the honeymoon, like a day or two after, I told her that sometimes when we made love, I fantasized being a fourteen-year-old girl. This is a long-lived fantasy of mine. The girl is pretty, with a petite body, probably five-one, five-two, cute ass, maybe light brown or dark blond pussy hair. Small to medium-size breasts. Medium long hair. Kind of sweet-looking, virginal. A little upturned nose and slightly full lips with a little poutiness. Doelike expression in her eyes. I've even wondered why she's fourteen, but I don't know. That seems to be the right age. Anyway, Sue got into it, like we were two girlfriends sleeping over and she was a couple years older and she was going to show me some things. I happen to be very sensitive around my nipples, so she'd say, "Oh, you have nice little nipples, you're gonna have very pretty breasts." Then she'd massage my crotch like she was massaging a vagina: "Do you like it when I pet you down there?" And she'd show me what to do to pleasure her, how to masturbate her and go down on her. I'd be in awe of her beautiful womanly body.

We played around with that for a few months. Sometimes Sue would play a man, she'd tell me what to do or even make me do something, like lie down and take off my clothes and spread my legs for her. There were times when she'd be on top, and I'd imagine she was a female with a penis. I preferred that to her being a guy, actually. I've seen some pornography on it, they call it chicks with dicks. We did buy a dildo and harness, and we got an underwear set for me, camisole and tap pants, from the Avon catalogue. One time she put the dildo and harness on with some jockey shorts over it, so she had the dildo poking out through my underwear and she was going to fuck me that way. But something happened, it was a little too much for one or both of us.

When I'm fantasizing that way, I get into a relaxed, sweet, gentle, loving kind of mode. I let go of all my business about being in control. Lots of times when I'm being the guy, and I'm on top, I don't relax. I'm thinking about too many things, or I'm trying too hard. Am I doing this right? Where are we going? Is she getting stimulated? Am I getting stimulated? What should I do next? All this effort can make me miss my own orgasm—I'll have one but it'll be just a physical release instead of a visceral, sensual moment. But if she's on top of me, and I'm having my fantasy that it's her penis in my vagina, after she comes once or twice I can feel this heat spreading through my vagina, and when I have my orgasm I really let go into it.

We started this stuff in February, and in July, without telling her, I shaved my body hair. Chest, stomach, legs. Not my pubic hair, most of that I left alone. I trimmed the hair on my scrotum. I remember how hard it was to shave my stomach hair, it was every bit as coarse as a beard. Shaving really helped me get into the fantasy.

I would masturbate a lot—there was always more masturbating than doing it with Sue. One thing I liked to do, I'd put on a pair of Sue's panties and pull them up in G-string fashion, up over my hips so there was just a bit of material in the crack of my ass and a bit in front. I'd tuck my penis and scrotum between my legs, and with the panties over me, it looked very feminine. Very smooth skin and just a little mound where my pubic hair was. It was a real turn-on, I'd look at myself and play with my nipples and imagine someone telling me what a pretty girl I was. Then I'd pull out my penis and masturbate and close my eyes, and I'd be a girl getting screwed by a guy, or maybe by a woman with a penis, or maybe I'd be with another woman having lesbian sex.

Well, around this point Sue got concerned because my fantasy was dominating our love life. She was also annoyed because if I'm off in a fantasy, I'm not really with her. That can be okay for a bit, we call it dessert sex. But if it becomes the main thing, then there's no intimacy. There's someone watching their own movie and someone else obliging them. Another concern of Sue's was that a lot of my fantasizing was beat-off stuff, not sharing-with-her stuff. She wanted to have a sex life with me, she wasn't interested in me having a sex life with my right hand. So we called a moratorium on it.

It's funny, though, she remembers it a little differently. She says that the more she got interested in it, the less interested I got. That may be true. For a while she was very supportive, helping me pick the stuff out from the Avon catalogue. Sometimes I think if we had hung in there with it, she might have gotten to explore something that turned her on. I had this idea that I'm the one who has these free-flowing fantasies, I'm so liberated and open, and Sue is kind of a prude. But maybe I had my own limits. As long as Sue was the police-man, I could go ahead and get wild. If that limit was taken away, it's like, Whoa, wait a minute, I'm not so sure about this. I do remember times when she was on top and she'd know I was into my fantasy that she had the penis and I had the vagina. She'd look at me in a way to say, Go ahead and fantasize, that's okay. And I'd get a little squeam-ish about it, or I'd snap out of it. We'd talk afterward and she'd say, "Was that nice for you?" Meaning, did you enjoy the fantasy? And I'd go, "Yeah, it was nice, but I kind of lost it in the middle." Which would confuse her. Well, which is it, do you want it that way or not?

I still masturbate once or twice a day, and I have lots and lots of fantasies, including gay fantasies when I'm in the mood. I imagine myself being seduced by a man. He's usually bigger and stronger than me, two or three inches taller, twenty or thirty pounds heavier—a muscular kind of heaviness. Not very hairy. Well-built and very self-assured and in command, so he guides me through, takes care of me if I'm feeling scared or I want to back out. One of my favorite stories is I meet this guy through work and he decides I ought to come work for him. He gives me a big raise, I get to use my talents more fully, and I become a close adviser to him. Then we take a business trip to-gether, and that's when he seduces me. We're getting ready for bed, we're in a hotel room with separate twin beds. He's just coming out of the shower, and I'm wearing the robe the hotel supplies. He's naked and toweling himself off and he's just standing there about ten, twelve feet away from me, and he's mostly dry except he's drying his hair, so his head is kind of covered and I notice he's partly erect. When I see him like that, I get really—I just swoon. It's like I'm on autopilot, I walk over there, I drop my robe, I kneel down in front of him, and I start stroking and kissing his penis. As I'm doing that he drops his towel, puts his hand on the back of my neck, and pulls me closer, and that's it. Part of the fantasy is that I know he's not promiscuous at all, he's happily married, we've talked about fooling around and said that we're not into it, so I know it's okay to swallow his semen and have unprotected sex.

Now, while I'm having the fantasy, what I'll do is kneel with my arms resting on a low couch, and I'll use a dildo in my ass, and since I'm in a kneeling position, I'll have it so the base of the dildo is resting against the floor, so I can ride up and down on it and pretend I'm being fucked. That leaves my hands free to play with my nipples and my penis. While I'm doing that I'll say things out loud, softly, I talk to the guy screwing me, like, "I want to suck your cock," or "I want to taste your come in my mouth. Stroke my little titties, let me be your wife, I'll shape my body for you and wear pretty things for you. I'll greet you when you come home on my knees, and I'll suck you and stroke you and you can fuck me, and I'll worship your cock twenty-four hours a day." That's what I'll say, and in the meantime I'll be stroking my nipples with my left hand and stroking my penis with my right hand and I'll come.

I always have mixed feelings about masturbating. No matter what the fantasy, I have mixed feelings. It's definitely my drug of choice. I don't do pot. I don't do other drugs. I don't drink at all. Sue has this book called *Overcoming Overeating,* and I haven't read that much of it because it's too upsetting, but all you have to do is substitute *masturbating* for *overeating,* and it fits. I beat off to calm myself, just to feel okay. It's like my real life has gotten too stressful, and I want to get away for a while. Maybe that's just being human, and maybe it's a weakness, I don't know. Sometimes if I stop in the middle I'll notice that there's some sadness, some old pain that I haven't wanted to think about. And if I can think about it and feel sad, or maybe if Sue is around, if it's at night and she's asleep, and I cuddle up to her so I have someone to hold while I'm sad, the desire to beat off might pass. I also realize I may always beat off, but it seems like some other balance is possible, where there's a little less beating off and a little more intimacy with Sue and Casey, and more energy for my spiritual self and my exercise and my work.

Sue and I don't have a lot of sex these days, but that's okay. There are hugs and kisses and cuddles, and we're relaxed about it. We don't fight. There was a time after Casey was born where I was bitter about our not making love as much as we used to. I came to see I had sex tied up with love. If you love me, you have sex with me. If you're not having sex with me, you can't possibly love me. After a year and a half of that, I started letting go. I saw that our relationship could be okay even if we weren't making love. And I'm trying to be more present when we make love, as opposed to being in my own head. It's like that old joke: "Why didn't you make love last night?" "I couldn't think of anybody." Well, I have to get away from that. Sometimes when we're making love and I'm on the bottom, I go off into the fantasy, but I don't stay there. I get into it for a minute and then go, Nah, and go back to being the guy on the bottom. We don't talk about it. I'm not obvious about it, and she doesn't want to hear about it. It's a kind of an avoided subject.

I could look at it as a sacrifice, but the problem with sacrifice is it's all about losing. Like, Oh, I'm giving something up for someone else, and I don't really want to. Where's the fun in that? I look at it as a matter of priorities. The priority is my family. If something doesn't support my family, it's not a priority. Our lives are so full, there's so much to cope with, it's the wrong time to make a big issue out of dessert sex. With a little kid and no money, we're doing fine if we get to the appetizer—let alone dinner.

Still, one of my fantasies is we're having sex and doing the fantasy thing again. She knows I want to be the female, so she starts playing with my nipples a lot. In real life she's a little hesitant to play with my nipples because she's like, Am I just going to send him off into his female trip? But in this fantasy, out of love and trust she says, "I want you underneath me." I know what she means. She strokes my nipples a lot, goes down on me and gets me hard, and then climbs on top of me and looks me real sweetly in the eye, stroking my face with one hand and holding my throat with the other. That's a very submissive feeling, to have someone's hand on my throat. And she tells me to open for her.

I hope we'll do that again sometime.

HUGH SULLIVAN

He is a self-described "control freak," and after listening to his story, it is not hard to guess why. He was born in 1953, the oldest of four children in a middle-class Irish Catholic family in Kentucky. "It was the classic overprotective-mother, distant-father situation. My mother drank and used pills. My father was absent because he worked all the time. She was very dominating and put him down a lot. And with me, she was extremely demanding, extremely overpowering, and extremely obedience-oriented. When she was drinking and she was with her friends, or even my aunts and uncles, she would say that I was neuter gender, because I liked to play with dolls, and because I was so quiet. I never knew what neuter gender meant, but it would always get a big laugh. I can remember being a little kid, like first grade or before, and her putting red nail polish on my fingernails and sending me out to play with other kids. Just to be in control, to show she could do it to me. I remember my father sitting there watching. You think that as a child you forget these things, and they don't have an impact, but they have a major impact, right up to now.

"I went to an all-boys school, and I was taunted as being effeminate. I used to have a lot of fantasies about boys but never acted on them, because I did then and still do see myself as heterosexual. No sex at all through adolescence because it's a sin, but I had girlfriends as opposed to boyfriends. I went to college and withdrew from everyone. Remained a virgin throughout college. I had opportunities, but my approach was that if I postponed having sex with either a male or a female, then I wouldn't have to decide. I masturbated constantly, like three or four times a day. My fantasies were all about men, and male children being feminized. Lipstick, nail polish, being humiliated. Otherwise, celibacy to the max— which may be the reason I'm still here today, what with AIDS."

He first had sex at the age of twenty-six with a man in a car. For some years afterward, he mostly had anonymous encounters with men, but there was one year-long relationship with a woman. Today he lives in a

large Midwestern city, works as a stockbroker, has been married for six
years, and has two young children. He has also been having a secret affair
with a man for a year and a half. He is a brisk, funny man who seems, in
his inflection and mannerisms, like a gay person not especially concerned
about passing for straight.

• • •

For the first six months I dated Sarah we didn't have sex. Finally
she said to me, "Look, I really can't stand this anymore, it's just too
much tension." So I started trying to have sex with her, and I wasn't
very successful the first couple of times. I was afraid I wasn't going to
satisfy her, that I wasn't going to get it up. At that point it had been
almost two years since I'd had sex with a woman. But one morning I
woke up with a hard-on. She was very turned on by this, so we didn't
waste any time, she grabbed me and pushed me in. Then I really got
into it and she really got into it and ever since, we've never had problems. I remember when we were getting married—I have a lot of gay
friends, and one of them said to me, "This is all very well and good,
I hope you'll be very happy, but you have to understand, at some
point in time you're going to have to fuck this woman. She's going to
expect sex." I told him, "We have sex constantly." That gives you
some understanding of the image I was putting out then.

I would say we were at our sexual peak in the beginning, before
we were married and right after we were married. On our honeymoon we had sex a couple times a day. Now we do it maybe two or
three times a week. It's romantic, sexy, fulfilling, happy for the most
part. Of late, she's been tired. There's a lessening of interest on her
part. She doesn't like to kiss as much as she used to. But it's still very
fulfilling, she's a very sexy person. We had sex last night because I
knew I'd be talking to you today. [Laughs.] She wasn't really into it,
then she got into it, and it was very satisfying. Then at seven-thirty
this morning, I got to work early, there I was jerking off in the men's
room. What does this say about the whole thing? That it wasn't fulfilling? I'm oversexed? I can't get enough?

Sex with Sarah starts out with kissing and fondling and hugging and sometimes tickling and nibbling. Then there's clitoral stimulation. She doesn't like to suck me because she gags a lot. She will to some degree, but I want to prolong it, and she wants me to come, so that's a struggle, it's clear that this is not what I want to do to my wife, make her gag. So once in a while we start with that, and maybe once a month we carry it all the way through. But even then, I'm trying to come faster than I would with somebody who's really devoted to it.

Then she gets wet and I enter her. Usually we fuck in missionary position. That's very married to me. Sometimes she puts her legs up around my neck, or she spreads her legs all the way apart. We've tried it with her on top, but she's a big woman, and she's just too heavy to be on top. We usually come together, or she comes first, and then she comes again when I do. Then I withdraw, and I'm usually flaccid immediately. Sometimes I stimulate her manually afterward as well. Or with the mouth sometimes, even though she's not really into that. She says it frightens her.

Really, whenever we try to do anything that's out of the ordinary, it makes her afraid. Even if she talks a good game and acts like she wants to do it, in practice she finds it frightening. Like she says she wants to be fucked in the ass. But when I want to lick her ass, which is a prerequisite for me, she doesn't want me to. Or playing around with dildos—she says she'd rather have the real thing, which I can understand. But I can't make her see that she can have a real one and a supplemental one. It just doesn't appeal to her. I'd like her to use dildos on me. I see a therapist, and I've talked to him about acting out my hard-core female fantasies, with makeup and costumes and wigs. Having her strap on a dildo to fuck me with. But I can't cross over that line and do that with her. It's too bizarre and revolting for her. She's clumsy with it, or it's just not right. We say, Let's try it again another time, but then she doesn't want to try it again.

I would say our sex starts out romantic and slow and then heats up and gets more athletic, if you will, more rough, more passionate, more involved. But I'm focused more on her than I am on me. It's my understanding that as a male I'm supposed to obtain less than I give. I imagine my penis going in and out of her vagina and rubbing against her clit, and her coming. Am I doing enough of this and enough of that? Am I too fast? How much longer do I have before I come? I'm detached, but there's Operation Central in my head, all these dials and monitor screens are going. I feel that this will be good sex if she's satisfied, but I'll feel shitty afterward if she isn't.

I've thought a lot about how passion works with a man and how it works with a woman. It's been my experience that sex with a woman is much more fulfilling than this get-your-rocks-off-with-a-man type thing. It carries more weight. For two men to get aroused, it's no big deal. But for a man to go through all this work to arouse a woman, if she's not aroused, it's a major production. It's more satisfying when she finally comes, and you want to do it a few more times, because it's so much work to get there. A male-female relationship is more involved and more genuine. It's like an eight-course meal versus fast food. Why do I go toward the fast food? Why do people eat junk food, anyway? Because it's a quick fix, and it's satisfying, and it's there.

Of course, it could be that thinking about women is better because I know I'm doing something that's seen as acceptable. In my little twisted mind, it makes me more mainstream, more normal. Which is something that I'm always aspiring to. So there's satisfaction in knowing that I'm fulfilling what I say I want to do. I'm not just presenting a heterosexual image, or giving lip service, or going through the motions. I love this woman. I'm having sex with her. We have children, and it's a committed relationship. When all is said and done, that's what I see myself as wanting to do. Moving in a heterosexual direction, and getting better and better at it. While at the same time having this side life.

I'd say that sex with Sarah is fulfilling only to a degree. I have to know I have my male lover as well. My therapist says I have a biological attraction to certain men. I can either choose to follow through or not, but it's something I can't deny. When it comes to raw sexual energy, it's about men. I have a different kind of arousal with them. It's more immediate, and there's more attached to it, because it's more forbidden. It's more raunchy or more thrilling or more . . . something. There's more energy there.

And men are always coming on to me. Like my lover—I met him on the street. He had on a baseball cap and a long coat and black cowboy boots, and I thought, This guy is watching me a lot. There was decided cruising, but more on his part. I was in control. That fulfills my ego. There's this whole male power thing—men dominate men in sports, they dominate men in business, they dominate the men they have working for them—so I wanted to get him to cross the street and I wanted to get him to talk to me and I wanted to string him along and see how much power I could have over him. It's my worst side coming out, but it's what I wanted. Finally he crossed the street. Now, as soon as they start to do what I want them to do, I get nervous. So we started talking, and he wanted to know if I could go to lunch. I said, well, no, let's have coffee and talk, because I had an appointment. He said, "Well, I have coffee at my apartment," and I thought, Okay, shit. We went to his apartment and had coffee. He was leaving that night on vacation. I said, "Oh, are you going alone?" He said, "No, I'm going with my girlfriend." I said, "Well, that's interesting." He saw I had a wedding band on, and he says, "So you're married?" I said yeah. He said, "To a man or a woman?" I said, "Guess." He said, "To a man." I said, "No, I'm married to a woman and I have two kids." He said, "Oh, that's real interesting."

Finally he came in for the kill and tried to kiss me. I thought, Well, I'll let him kiss me. It was a little nothing first kiss, and he had bad breath, and I was like, Who needs this shit? He gave me his number and I gave him my office number. He called me and it was clear he was very interested. I thought, I don't get this, what's the attraction? I feel like I'm sliding into middle age, he's late twenties, and he hadn't seen me with my clothes off or anything. Was he just horny that afternoon? Is he really into me, or he just wants one more dick to suck? Every man who gets involved with men questions all this. Is he looking for money? Is he looking for some kind of connection? Is he looking for cachet? Or is he really into me personally? And how does he know, on the basis of a fifteen-minute conversation?

Our second encounter was at his club. I saw the personality go from the man in the Brooks Brothers suit, so straight and rigid in the leather chair, to this crazed maniac boy in his apartment afterward. We went there and he became very aggressive, and he was in my pants, and expressed, shall we say, wonderment and desire. It became clear that he was putty in my hands, and this was something I could really exploit. He wanted to suck me off, but I wasn't going to let anybody suck me without a rubber, so he wanted to go get one, and that's where I drew the line. I was pulling his head between my knees. He was kissing my penis and stroking and licking it, but I wouldn't let him put his mouth on the head. I was in control from the beginning. Plus he saw me as so much more established, because I had a wife and children. He saw that as being very grown-up and mature.

After that we talked a lot on the phone. I wanted to find out if there was anything really psycho about him. I wanted to make sure he wasn't into guns or snakes or drugs or weapons. And I dropped a lot of hints about how I wanted this to work, and he responded. I made it clear that I was going to be in control. I was talking about me shaving his body, him wearing high heels, him wearing makeup, him being in a submissive role. I remember he was laughing and giggling and he said, "I don't think that's going to happen," and I said, "Oh no, you don't understand, I'm in control of this, and this is what we're going to do." He was like, "Yeah, I'd like to see you try it," and he was laughing more. I said, "I'm not kidding around. This is really what's going to happen." Then he said, "Well, I'd really like to try that."

One thing I had seen in his bathroom was an exposed pipe that went along the ceiling. I thought I could tie his hands and hang him from the pipe with his feet just touching the ground, and he would be in front of the mirror. It would be great, we could have a whole scenario. I thought, This is some kind of gift, I hope this pipe will hold him. So when I went to the bathroom I was doing chin-ups on the pipe, and I thought, This is worth a try.

Finally I said to him, "I'll be there on Tuesday at four. I want you to be naked, because we're going to have a lot of fun." He said yeah. I showed up a little after four to make him wait. He was naked. It wasn't difficult to overpower him, although I let him struggle and thrash around a little bit. I got his hands behind his back and I twisted his arm and tied his wrists and said, "We're going to play a new kind of game here." I took my shirt off but I didn't take anything else off. Then I strung him up in the bathroom with his arms over his head. I just said, "Put your hands over your head, it'll be all right, I'm not going to hurt you." It amazes me how you can talk people into shit and they will do it. But now he knew we weren't just fooling around. He was scared. You know how you think someone's kidding, and then you realize this isn't fun and games anymore? Now he has a stranger in his apartment whom he's met twice before, and he's helpless.

I had this bag with me, and I pulled out a straight razor. He got really nervous and tense. I said, "We did talk about this on the phone." I didn't want him to cry, but I wanted him to understand. Of course I had a shaving brush and shaving soap and I went through this elaborate thing of lathering up his whole body. He's fair-skinned, but he's hairy. He was begging me not to shave him. I was saying, "It's not going to hurt, don't worry, you'll look nice and clean like a statue. You're going to be very pretty when I finish with you." He was kicking his feet, and I said, "We're going to have to tie your feet down, because you're not being a good boy." So I tied his feet together. I played around with his ass a bit and soaped it up and soaped all around his cock, which made him very, very hard. But he was sure I was going to shave his whole body. He was pleading and crying and I said, "Be quiet, or we're going to have to put a gag in your mouth."

Under normal circumstances, you can have sex with a man, and then you can have sex with your girlfriend, and she doesn't know you just had sex with a man. But as soon as you show up with a hairless ass or hairless armpits, it's like, what happened? That's what he was nervous about, begging and whining. I took the straight razor and ran the hot water and shaved both his armpits. Then I wiped him with a towel and put talcum powder on because I was trying to be considerate, so it wouldn't burn. I said, "How do you like it?" He was begging me to stop so I said, "Well, let me just shave a little bit of hair on your ass." Of course I went to town and shaved it all off. He couldn't see because the mirror was over the sink. I said, "How do you like it? This feels really good." Then I started massaging his ass, and he came. He went from tears to being really into it.

After that, I said, "I'm going to let you down." His hands were still tied, and his feet. I bent him over the sink and put on a condom and I fucked him very fast and very hard with him looking in the mirror at himself and looking at me and seeing that this is the way it's going to be. He now had my mark on him. Then I came and he came again. We got in the shower. There was more hugging and caressing and he was telling me I'm a really powerful person, all this crap. Then he saw his body in the mirror and he was intimidated again and teary and unhappy. I said, "Don't worry, this is all we're going to do." I put the razor away where he couldn't find it, so there wouldn't be any retaliation-type shit. I said, "If you're not a good boy this is what happens, so you have to behave yourself." Then since I wanted to go for maximum fun and games the first time around, we went into the bedroom. We were both naked. I had a shopping bag with two pairs of high heels in it. I said, "Now we're going to play Cinderella. You try these shoes on and see which ones you like." We had talked about what size he was, but he didn't believe I'd show up with two pairs of high heels. He was crossing over a line into a Wonderland thing.

I had fantasized about this stuff for years. I had read about it in trashy magazines and seen it in porn movies. I used to make my little brother do stuff like this, not shaving his ass and fucking him, but I used to make him put on my mother's high heels. So this guy put on the high heels and he was really into it. He was swinging his hips and walking like a pro. He was hard again, but he has a small penis, so I'm like, Oh, you're hard, ho-hum. Then I said, "Now let's do this other thing with high heels," and I fucked him with the point of the shoe. Which wasn't real pointed, it was round. Then I had some makeup and lipstick and stuff. I held his head between my knees and said, "Now, you're going to be a really good girl." I put makeup on him and took him in the bathroom and showed him in the mirror. I was getting extremely turned on. So I got another condom, and with him looking in the mirror at himself with the makeup, I fucked him again and it was much, much better than the first time. Now that I had done all this, emasculated him, feminized him, made him submissive, brought him to his knees, it was a much better orgasm.

Then I made him kneel down and thank me and tell me he was going to be a good girl, the whole bit. I said, "I have to go now. We're not going out to dinner, we're not going to have candlelit Chinese food and watch two boys fucking on your VCR. I'm leaving." I got on my clothes and he's like, "I'd love to have you stay," and I said, "That's it, I'm going now." That established it: I'm in control, fast and hard, you're the woman, good-bye.

Since then I made him realize that I'm very busy, my time is valuable, and I'm in demand. I can see him for an hour or forty-five minutes, but that's it. I exaggerate the extent of my busyness to make me more precious. He works out of his home, and he apparently doesn't have to work that much because he has money. I usually call early in the morning to set up a time. I make it at three or four in the afternoon, and I leave my office early. And we play out this dominant-submissive thing. He does the makeup, the high heels. He wears stockings and a garter belt that I brought over. He went out and got a bra himself. He looks ridiculous, but he thinks it's great. I call him a girl, because he likes that. When I show up, he's usually naked in his high heels, and aroused, with a lot of makeup and cologne and perfume on. Acting very seductive. We go through this thing where I push him away a lot. Sometimes I play a pure macho role where I refuse to have sex with him. I won't take my clothes off, and I'll smoke a cigar and slap him around a little bit. He's really into it, being this businessman and then making a flip-flop into this love-slave role. I make him shine my shoes while he's naked and submissive. Other than that, I fuck him. I just pull it out, I don't take my pants off, and I won't let him turn around or look at me at all. I do it very fast, very hard. It's for my pleasure. I pinch his nipples till he screams out, and I twist his balls and his dick. Maybe one time out of ten we do it in bed. Usually it's in the bathroom with him standing and bent over. I don't know if he comes. I don't care if he comes.

Now, you're probably going to ask if he's ever fucked me. The answer is yes. I occasionally submit. Maybe once a month or every other month. We'll be talking on the phone, and he says he'd like to be on top tonight, it's his turn. I'm going, "Wait a minute, I tell you, you don't tell me." Then we go through this whole negotiation. We communicate. We should be on a talk show about couples who communicate, that would really go over well. We talk about how long it's been, how he really wants to do it, how he's tired of being fucked. I go, "That's how this game works." I want to hear him beg, which he knows. At a certain point he starts to beg and whine. "Oh please, please, I deserve it. I've been good. I did this for you, I did that for you. I let you fuck me." Then I say, "Well, we'll see if you've been a good girl. If your apartment is clean enough. If you shine my shoes right." Any number of things.

When he fucks me, he's on top and I'm on my back. I'm on the
bed. He does a lot of foreplay, working on me with oil. It's the other
extreme from this domination thing, it's very romantic with soft music and candles. I get very hard, but when he's fucking me it's like,
Let's get on with this. I'm very tight, so I don't get fucked much, but
he's very small. It must be like what women feel all the time—Oh
good, I don't have to do much work, I just have to lie back and he's
going to mount me, and he's going to pump, and I just have to lie
there. Maybe I'll go, "Ooh ooh aah aah." To make it more interesting,
I have used a dildo on him while he's fucking me. Then when we're
finished we reverse roles and I tell him he has a small dick and he
should just be a woman and he shouldn't try to fuck men. He gets off
on that and jerks off while I'm saying that to him. But then I'll tell
him to stop and I'll slap him around.

The other thing we do occasionally is go out in public. How to
humiliate your male lover, lesson number 79: Drive to a Greek diner.
I make him glue on fake fingernails that are very long and painted
pink. He's going, "No, no, I don't want to do this," and I'm going,
"You have to, I'm the boss and I want you to." Then I send him in
and watch through the windows. He's standing there in a suit,
button-down shirt, striped tie, and he's got these pink nails on, and
all these big Greek boys are laughing at him, they think it's a riot.
And I'm outside getting very hard. I'm beyond hard, I'm already
starting to drip. Then I take him home and fuck him. I tell him,
"Those boys are laughing because they're jealous, they want this, too.
That's why they call you 'honey' and 'dear.' " Another thing I like, especially after a hard day when we're both tired, is to take him out to
look at lipsticks. I'm going, "Try this one," and he goes, "No, people
are watching," and I'm going, "I told you to try it on." He tries it on
and wipes it off quickly. Then I make him buy it, or I make him ask
the man behind the counter—we always look for men behind the
counter—what he thinks of it, is it a good color. I'm always amazed
he's up for this, if you'll pardon the pun.

So why do I like making him into a girl? One, so I can justify it,
like I'm with a woman. Number two, my mother called me neuter
gender and put nail polish on me and I'm reliving that, acting it out
and getting revenge, if you will. If you asked me what to do to emas-

culate a man, to get power over him, if you didn't cut off his dick and you didn't take away his money, well, if I could get him to dress up and act like a woman, and be submissive and have sex with me as a woman, that's the ultimate thing I could do to this man, no matter who he is, whether it's Arnold Schwarzenegger or George Bush. I could act this out in sex with a woman, but I've always been brought up to be polite and wholesome and normal with women. So where can I get rid of this pent-up frustration, this rage? I've never had any kind of physical contact with men based on sports or anything acceptable. But I'm doing this to him and getting rid of it, and he likes it. When I'm fucking him, I feel real aggression. I'm pumping into him hard, slamming him into the front of the bed, or the sink. I feel like I want to shove my dick right through until it comes out the front. In many ways it's like rape. Rape is a crime of aggression and virility and physicality. It's not about making love. This is like, We're here for my pleasure. It doesn't have anything to do with you. Whether you come is not an issue. Whereas with my wife it's a big deal.

The flip side of all this is me being submissive to someone more powerful. Occasionally we've tried putting makeup on me. It's very stimulating, but I don't want him to do it. I don't want to reverse roles with him. I want some huge muscle-bound greasy-type guy to feminize me and put me down. In my dreams I would like to be strung up and shaved by some marine drill sergeant with a crew cut who would yell at me and humiliate me and spank me and put lipstick on me. But I don't think that's going to happen. Once again, I'm a control freak, and it would be dangerous, because it's going to be someone I can't overpower, who's bigger than I am. Ultimately I would love to lose control, but it's also the most frightening thing in the world.

Meanwhile, with this man, there's no sign of boredom. I never show up and find him in a T-shirt and jeans saying, "Tonight I'm going to smoke the cigar, and you're going to wear the lipstick." In fact, if I feel that I'm too stressed from work or whatever, my solution is to deny him that week, and then come back and have some kind of major thrashing scene. We do new twists, but it's the same attitude, the same shtick. We're still involved with our women, so we know this is forbidden. It's very hidden and closeted and careful. It's very precious. And to this day I think I make a better heterosexual than I would a full-time gay man. I think I'd be one of those self-hating, bitchy, nasty, miserable gay men. This way, it's like the lesser of two evils. I'm not a miserable straight man. I'm a compromised straight man.

Whenever I get involved or start to have a flirtation with a man, I always feel like I'm the only man in the universe who has these issues. But everyone goes, No, there are so many men who have arranged marriages, or have a happy marriage with a woman but they just have to have sex once a week with a man. They go to a therapist and fuck him on the couch. They go out and fuck in the back of a car. It's accepted and agreed upon. And I'm like, Oh, I'm the one who's naïve about this. The rest of the world operates this way.

5

WHO'S ON TOP?

POWER IN OUR CULTURE is linked to gender. Starkly put, men are supposed to have it, women are not. This chapter, a kind of companion piece to Chapter 4, examines one angle of gender geometry.

In the bedroom, power assumes many guises and meanings. Sexuality itself can be a fount of personal strength: someone who feels entitled to pleasure, or who *learns* to feel entitled, often carries that sense of entitlement into the world. Another kind of power can be exercised by denying sex to a partner. Between lovers, every nuance of sex—what acts are performed, in what order, in what position, in what mood, for how long, to what end—reflects power relations. Lori Eschilman, whose interview appears in Chapter 10, coins the perfect epigraph for this chapter: "I can't imagine a sexual encounter that doesn't involve a transaction of power." Sex in this respect is like most other human intercourse, in which power hierarchies are subtly expressed; but many people don't look at sex in that light.

This chapter contains three interviews in which power exchange is played out consciously, and one in which it seems less conscious. The word *play* is important: In the S/M and D&S worlds, to play— as in, "Do you play?"—means to engage in eroticism involving overt power exchange. We first meet Jackie Dunhill, whose interview ends with her blindfolded and on her knees, surrendering on the dunes to six men, all strangers except for her lover Dennis. She recounts her discovery of S/M and her life as Dennis's sexual slave: "Him giving me orders. Him saying humiliating things to me. . . . Being very rough and pushing me around, calling me a slut, calling me a cunt. Making me crawl around the room on all fours and beg to suck his cock. And hitting, lots of hitting with different kinds of things."

What is the difference between this and rape? Obviously, there is the critical question of consent. Jackie and Dennis are acting out a theater of cruelty spun from their fantasies. Some feminists argue that this is the "consent" of the oppressed, that S/M replicates and reinforces the power imbalance of the patriarchy and the violence it produces. But Jackie points out that in the S/M world, both women and men overwhelmingly prefer to be "bottoms." So we turn to James W., who "plays" as both a top and a bottom but whose bottom experiences are the most profound. For him, S/M and spirituality are inseparable, and his surrender as a "priest-slave" to his "goddess-mistress" is a kind of transcendence.

The two other men in this chapter describe different types of power play. Lloyd Rappaport tells the story of his romance with a much younger woman, his protégée. The older, accomplished, married man and the starry-eyed virgin—a classic recipe for an abusive affair. And Lloyd does seem to be in control, both making the rules and wielding the whip. But as he says, the dynamics of dominance and submission are not what they seem. "The position of lying back and allowing yourself to be tied up or whipped gives you so much power, in a way. That certainly was the case with Helen. When she was in that position, everybody was on to her. She became the star. Whatever thwacks the flesh took were nothing compared to the attention and devotion that came her way."

There is nothing theatrical about Cash Riordan's sex—no blindfolds, no ropes. And in describing how he makes love with his wife, he reveals a knowledge of physiology unmatched in this book. He is a man alert to every tremor and goosebump of his partner's response.

Also unmatched, however, is the extreme split between his activity and her passivity. At least as Cash tells it, he makes love the way he might pilot a plane. To use another S/M term, he "runs the fuck" absolutely—one indicator of power in bed, and sometimes in a relationship.

JACKIE DUNHILL

She is a sexual adventuress, and she started early. "I have lots of memories of sexual activities by the time I was seven or eight. I masturbated at least once a day from then on, and I played sex games with other little boys and girls." Between the ages of ten and twelve, she had "full-blown" lesbian sex with several girlfriends, until she and one friend were caught by the girl's outraged mother. She lost her virginity at sixteen, had numerous lovers through college, and married when she was twenty-two. After some years of life on a small commune in an open marriage, she and her husband split up, and Jackie became exclusively lesbian. She lived for ten years with a woman and had a son by artificial insemination. As that relationship ended, Jackie's interest in men revived, and she now lives with a man, Joey, whom she plans to marry. But her car still sports a bumper sticker reading BISEXUAL PRIDE.

Her most powerful fantasies, beginning in her early teens, have been sadomasochistic. For most of her life she never acted them out, and during her lesbian years, when she was a passionate feminist and gay activist, she tried to repress the fantasies themselves—they were "politically incorrect." By the early 1980s, however, as some groups of lesbians and feminists began to advance a new view of women's sexuality, "I decided it was perfectly fine for me to have S/M fantasies." When she had her first affair with a man after ten years of lesbianism, she was ready to go beyond fantasy.

She is now forty-three—voluptuous, fast-talking, quick to laugh. She is a doctor who practices family medicine in a working-class—but gentrifying—neighborhood of Brooklyn.

• • •

I met Dennis when I was still living with Cynthia. He was a gay man—I didn't know any straight men, and I didn't want to. He became my best male friend. He and Bob and Cynthia and I were friends as couples, but Dennis and I had a friendship independent of that for a couple of years before we ever got to be lovers. Both of us sort of missed straight sex. He gave me an article once from the *Advocate,* where the writer tossed off this line that if a gay man and a lesbian have sex, it's still gay sex. Those were the ways I rationalized it. Cynthia knew, though. She knew it wasn't harmless.

It happened about the sixth or seventh time we slept together. We were fucking, and I was on top of him. He had poppers, and I had never done poppers before. Poppers raise your pain threshold. I was on top and he just started spanking me, while we were fucking. He was spanking me and spanking me. Then he took his cock out of my cunt and put it in my ass, and I loved it. It was the first time I'd ever been fucked in the ass. So I was being hit and fucked in the ass at the same time, that was my first S/M experience. From then on, the two of us, we had a ball. He had played with a few men—that's what they call S/M sex, playing. And he was into being a dominant, a top. That's what he enjoyed. I was into being a bottom.

Hitting and butt-fucking were the two things we started with. Then we got into dominance and submission. Like him giving me orders. Him saying humiliating things to me while we were having sex. Being very rough and pushing me around and giving me orders, calling me a slut, calling me a cunt. Making me crawl around the room on all fours and beg to suck his cock. And hitting, lots of hitting with different kinds of things. Besides his hands, we quickly got into paddles and cat-o'-nine-tails and crops and bamboo canes. And a belt. And blindfolds. Tit clamps. A lot of dress-up scenes. I'd be wearing nothing, maybe a dog collar, and I'd be on all fours, and he'd have leather chaps, and I'd have to put his chaps and his boots on. He'd have nothing on under the chaps. I'd have to lick his boots, kiss his boots, then I'd have to lick all the chaps, shine the chaps and the boots before I could get fucked. I'd beg for it. That kind of thing carried us for a long time. [Laughs.] Then for a while we got into some public stuff. We'd go to the Vault* together and he'd spank me there and we'd go home and fuck. We went to Fire Island, and we'd go to the Meatrack together. That's the dunes between Cherry Grove and the Pines where men go to have sex. We'd find a place where there was a not-too-well-traveled path. I'd have my clothes off, and I'd have to kneel and suck him off on the path. And he'd be cruising men walking by while I was sucking him off. We'd pick men up and do stuff.

Was it a surprise to you that you liked S/M so much?

It wasn't such a surprise. By the time Dennis came along, I had done everything but do it. I'd been reading about S/M, I'd been talking about S/M, Dennis and I had had conversations about it. We gave each other porn to read. It was a small step, in a way. I was ready for a long time, I just had nobody to do it with. Now, how much I liked it, how quickly I liked it, how much pain I could take—all that surprised me. Certainly liking butt-fucking as much as I did. For a long time Dennis and I never cunt-fucked. I only wanted to ass-fuck. So there were specific acts that were a surprise. Like, "Oh, gee, I didn't know I'd like this." Some of it was acting out fantasies that I'd had since I was thirteen, but some of it was totally new stuff that I never thought of. Very early on Dennis and I developed this thing, we'd joke with each other, that we'd never say we didn't like something until we tried it at least twice. The thing about Dennis is that he probably has the healthiest attitude about sex of anyone I've ever met. To him, nothing was bad. Where sex was concerned, he had the brain of a reptile. His main question was, Is it logistically feasible? Meaning, can you get into this kind of position or find a toy that will do this? I mean, butt-fucking, for crying out loud. Dennis was a gay man. He'd fucked a lot of asses. I didn't know until I was taught that your asshole opens up after you're turned on. So that the timing of when you butt-fuck is critical. And that lubricant is essential. There aren't too many people who can butt-fuck without lubricant. But in this culture, lubricant is something you use only if you're inadequate and you can't get your lover turned on enough. People don't even have lubricant around. So there's a certain technique involved in this stuff,

*An S/M club in lower Manhattan.

which Dennis knew something about. If you're going to hit some-body, for example, people get much more into it if you start out gently and build up. If you just whack somebody real hard, it's not nearly as much of a turn-on. You can take much more pain after a gradual buildup.

When I first started doing S/M, I felt like one of those new con-verts, when it's all you can think about. I just walked around with a smile on my face, wanting to tell everybody about it. Occasionally I would have moments of, Oh, my God, this is too weird and strange. But mostly it just became the major topic on my mind. One thing that was helpful was joining the Lesbian Sex Mafia, because among other things, LSM is a real support group. I'd learn from women who had been into it for a while. They'd joke around, "Oh, yeah, when you're first into the scene, you just eat, drink and sleep S/M, that's all you want to do, you don't want to have any other kind of sex. But no, you're not going to be like this for the rest of your life." I'd have mo-ments when I'd think, I've become a sex-starved maniac. I'd have days where I'd be so horny thinking about being with Dennis that I'd cancel the rest of my patients just to go over there and fuck. Really, it's all I wanted to do. It'd been a long time coming. That was part of it, too, the feeling of, My God, I've wanted to do this forever. I've been waiting all my life for this.

Right from the start I thought of S/M as like a sexual LSD expe-rience. Of course, S/M isn't one experience, and I'm not talking about the technique, I'm talking about the emotional and physical and mental experiences. The fact that it's so varied is part of the at-traction. But when I had sex before, just straight vanilla sex, there'd be times when my mind would drift. Or I'd be almost spectatoring, watching myself. When I do S/M, I get totally lost. In fact, there's a kind of comedown experience afterward—I mean, normal sex is like that sometimes, too, any kind of real hot sex, afterward it's like com-ing down. Whoa, where was I? But with S/M sex it's like that from start to finish. I get much more absorbed in it, I stop thinking—or at least I come as close as I ever come to it. I don't have fantasies when I do S/M sex, because I don't ever think enough to have fantasies.

One of the things that happened to me, especially at the begin-ning with Dennis, and this was kind of freaky to me, is that I would feel like I was reliving another sexual experience, usually an early childhood one. Sometimes with my father—who knows if they were real or fantasies. I'd have a strong sense that I was reliving something, and I was totally lost in it. I'd suddenly hear myself saying, "Daddy, Daddy." I was in another place. Those were powerful experiences, and they were scary until I got used to them. I've had other times when I felt like I lost the boundaries of my body. Like the other person and I were patterns, nothing but patterns and colors. I wasn't even closing my eyes, everything was just patterns. So doing S/M, my consciousness gets really altered. It's hard to describe it, but I suppose the essence is being completely lost, abandoned. It feels like dissolving and floating free. Being one hundred percent sensation. No mind.

And early on with Dennis, I discovered that even if we didn't have S/M sex, even if all we were doing was vanilla sex, it somehow became S/M sex. The whole dominance-submission thing colored the rest of sex. Dennis and I even had sex where if you would look at it, it would look like he was the bottom. I would tie him up or string him up and hit him, or fuck his ass. Joey and I do that, too. I fuck him in the ass with a strap-on dildo, but I'm still the bottom. The psychological part is just as important as what you're actually doing. In those kinds of scenes, I'd be doing stuff to Dennis, but he was the top, and I was doing it because I was the sexual slave who was submissive to him and doing anything possible to make him feel pleasure.

I used to worry a lot about what it all meant. Am I sick? How can I be a feminist and still want to be his slave? That was before I found out that the S/M world is full of bottoms. There are many more bottoms than there are tops. And it's no more common among women than men. Almost everybody wants to be a bottom. I have a friend who I met in LSM. She'd never had any kinky fantasies in her life. She became a top, and I said, "How come?" She said, "First of all, I got a lot of dates that way. Then I started to get off on it." That's true of a lot of tops. It's not that they've always had fantasies about hitting somebody. What they got off on was how turned-on they could get somebody by what they did. "Wow, I can do these things, and this person is writhing at my feet and begging for more."

So I don't think it's a male-female thing at all. When I go to the Vault, the single most common thing is men with foot fetishes. I have to brush them away like flies. "Mistress, mistress, can I suck your toes, can I lick your feet, can I lick your shoes?" There's a million male foot fetishists out there. They want to grovel at a woman's foot. They want you to step on them. So humiliation works for a lot of people. Who knows why? I've spent hours thinking about it, and I see it as an imprinting process, like imprinting in animals. A lot of sexual tastes are acquired when you're a child. The closest I can come to it is that in childhood, there's not much distinction between any state of high arousal, whether that state is fear, anger, pain, or sexual excitement. So I think something becomes sexualized about punishment. Fear of parents, fear of adults, being punished, being shamed—they become eroticized. Spanking becomes eroticized, pain becomes eroticized. The flavor of a lot of S/M scenes is like that. The waiting, for example. You wait and you wait and you wait, and then you get hit. It often makes me think about kids being told they're going to get spanked when Daddy gets home. Kids who know they're going to get punished, they're in a state of anxiety and anticipation. That becomes sexual arousal. Then the hitting and humiliation become a release.

In S/M, dominance-submission is more important than the pain. I've done lots and lots of scenes that involve no pain. A lot of bondage scenes don't involve any pain. Just a lot of taking orders, being humiliated. The first time with Dennis, there was pain in being hit, but not in being fucked in the ass. That didn't hurt. Anyway, when you're talking about S/M, and probably any kind of sex, hurt is an awfully subjective term. There's good hurt and there's bad hurt. There's hurt hurt and there's hot hurt.

Another thing: I was in love with Dennis, and he was the first person I did S/M with. That made a difference. It meant there was an erotic charge beyond pure sex. When you're having S/M sex with someone you're in love with, it's much more intimate and much more intense. There were things I did with Dennis that I don't know if I would have done with anybody but a lover. It allowed me to get into kinkier stuff. Like when we started doing things with piss, it wasn't just doing a piss scene, it involved all kinds of notions about totally loving somebody, loving everything from their body. Pretty hot, but also extremely romantic. The other thing, though, is that because I was in love with him, I attributed a lot of the hotness of the sex to the fact that it was Dennis. I have since done S/M scenes with people who were pretty much strangers, and it's been just as hot. So there's a certain illusion that comes about, which made it easier for me to let go and lose control. I felt like I belonged to him, like, I adore this guy, and this is how I'm showing that I adore him. It's like an offering. The evidence that I completely love you is that I'd do anything you want. Anything. There's nothing too humiliating, there's nothing too repulsive, there's nothing too far-out. That became an element of Dennis's relationship with me. How far can I push you? Can I make you do something you really don't want to do? Can I give you an order to do something that you won't do?

And did he ever?

No. [Laughs.] No. No. But he was cautious. When you do S/M, there's a whole thing about people's limits. Everybody's got limits someplace. Over time, your limits tend to expand. But the real fun, or the hottest sex, is in playing around right where your limits are, because that's what's most dangerous. If you can take *x* amount of pain, and then you've reached your limit, the hottest thing to do is play around that area. A fairly common technique of tops is to take people to their limits and just a touch beyond and then stop. That's how limits get expanded, by degrees.

People who do S/M usually pick a "safe word" that the bottom can use. With Joey I use *pink* and *red*. *Pink* means I'm just about as far as I can go, and *red* means it's all over. You use safe words for two reasons. The main one is so that you can yell and scream, "Oh, no, please stop," and not be taken seriously. The other is that it's hard to talk. The state of mind I get into, "red" is about as much as I'm going to be able to say.

Dennis was pretty cautious, he wouldn't go to my limits. That's not true of Joey. The first thing he wants to know is what's my limit, because he's going to go right beyond it. With Dennis, I almost never felt like I'd been hit as much as I could take. I always felt he could have kept going. But there were times when I felt like, Oh, my God,

I can't take any more of this—and I'm not talking about pain, it was really more the altered state, going far out.

The only time I regretted a sex scene with Dennis was one of the first times we went to the Meatrack. It was a wonderful scene, except we had unsafe sex and I was paranoid for six months afterward, getting HIV tests. The Meatrack has been a place for public sex for gay men for years. There's obviously some kind of understanding with the police, because nobody ever gets busted there. This day, it was a Monday afternoon or some unlikely time. Dennis and I expected to get so little action that I don't think we even brought rubbers with us. We were walking through the dunes, on these little paths through low pine trees. They're pine dunes. Nobody goes off the main paths unless they want sex. So we were walking through, and just for the hell of it, Dennis took me to one of the little paths. I was wearing a halter top and shorts, and he ordered me to take off my top so my breasts were exposed. He opened his pants and I started sucking him off. He was standing up, leaning against a tree so he could cruise all the men who walked by. Since I was sucking him off, I couldn't see a whole lot. So I don't know how all this happened, but first one guy came along. He and Dennis started touching each other. They were both standing up, fondling each other's cock. I don't remember if Dennis made me suck this guy's cock, too. Maybe.

Eventually, though, there were five guys there. And I was the bottom for all five of them, so there was a point where I was on my hands and knees, and some guy was fucking me in the ass, somebody else was under me eating me out, somebody else had my tits, and I was sucking somebody off. Nobody spoke a word. I don't know anybody's names. I've had many times since then where I've seen guys from the Pines and I've wondered whether they were part of that scene, but I really don't know, because it all happened quickly and I was in a bottom position.

One guy wanted to kiss me, which was interesting for a gay guy. I was the bottom in the sense that I didn't initiate anything, they could do anything to me that they wanted, but other than sucking off Dennis, all I did was got fucked. And this one guy wanted to kiss me. We changed locale at one point, because we were in the middle of this path, and when the first guys came along, one of them said to Dennis, "Follow me, there's someplace better than this." So there were a couple of words spoken. We all walked, and we found a little space of sand and bushes that was pretty private. Before I was shoved down on my hands and knees again, this guy wanted to kiss me and play with my tits and cunt while we were kissing. He was an older guy. I remember what he looked like, and I remember wondering at the time whether he was bisexual or had been married, because I almost got the feeling that there had been a time in this guy's life when he'd been into kissing women, and it had been a long time ago. It was very sweet. He was very tender. He was a big guy. I can remember feeling like I was melting into his arms and he was holding me up and kissing me and playing with me at the same time.

The problem was that when it was over, when everybody dispersed, Dennis said to me, "Gee, I hope that guy didn't come in you." I said, "What do you mean, you hope he didn't come in me? Wasn't he wearing a rubber?" And Dennis said no. I said, "Dennis, I assumed you were watching out." There was very poor communication between us. I had just assumed that because Dennis could see and I couldn't, he would make sure this guy had a rubber on. But he didn't, and the guy came in my ass. And to have somebody come in your ass on the Meatrack, that's about the most high-risk thing you can do.

That taught me a lot of lessons. One of them is, don't ever count on anybody else to police your safe sex. A lot of the safe-sex education stuff is about negotiating safe sex before you start to do anything. It makes a lot of sense, because when you're in the heat of the moment—I could have stopped it. I could have said, "Wait a minute, I'm going to stop this scene and check." But I wasn't about to stop it. Yes, I thought Dennis was watching, but there was also a part of me that said, Oh, well, I'm sure it'll be okay, somebody else'll take care of it. I didn't want to stop that scene at that moment for all the money in the world. I think that's how a lot of unsafe sex takes place.

I've gone to the Meatrack by myself. I went once and picked up a guy and we fucked. And a couple of times I've gone and done jerk-off scenes. I go to this same kind of place, sort of isolated. I go with a blanket, and I lie on the blanket and take my clothes off. I take lubricant, which I put next to me, and condoms, which I put next to me. And I start masturbating. I've had a couple of scenes where guys come around and touch me and jerk off. Or they watch me but for whatever reason they don't want to come close enough to touch. That's pretty hot. We watch each other and jerk off. Hot.

Sometimes I don't even come when I'm there. I get real turned on and then go home and finish myself. The point is to get real aroused. Coming has changed a lot for me since I started doing S/M. I can have multiple orgasms, but the line between orgasms and what's not an orgasm has gotten very blurry. A lot of S/M is calculated to keep you on a plateau. To take you to a high state of arousal and keep you there as long as possible. Either without orgasm, which is most typical of men, or with orgasms that aren't going to end it. I can have orgasms and keep going. But a lot of the point of S/M is not to have you come. That's why it makes such good safe sex—because the orgasm is the least important thing.

But that guy on the Meatrack sure did come. I had a lot of anger at him for a long time. Maybe he knew he was HIV-negative. I'd like to believe that. But it scared the shit out of me. I had a lot of moments like, My God, I'm going to toss my life away for fifteen minutes of superhot sex? I like sex a lot, but it ain't worth that.

LLOYD RAPPAPORT

He is the Boston screenwriter and theater director who in Chapter 3 described "swinging" with his wife, Ruth. Early in their relationship, they had a longstanding ménage à trois with a young woman.

• • •

The most enduring pattern in my sexuality, from my earliest masturbatory fantasy at age eleven to the present, has been a triangle. The fantasy has me in a room with two women. One of them is dominant and controlling, and the other is passive, submissive, with a tendency toward masochism. The sex play evolves under the directorship of the woman I walk into the room with—my accomplice, the Dark Woman. And it's dedicated to the pleasure, and sometimes pain, of the submissive woman, who wants to be seduced by me, but out of love or being enthralled by me allows the other woman to take the part of me in the sex act. The submissive woman isn't by nature bisexual or lesbian, but it doesn't matter after a while, and it's really the dominant woman who's plotting the script.

For me it's a strange mixture of wanting the dominant woman to do the right thing in turning everybody on, yet on some level I want to imagine I'm in control because I brought all the pieces together. The real sensual part of the control, who's getting who hot, is the dominant woman. I'm getting tremendously turned on by her, as much by her as by the submissive woman, who's my real lover. The other woman is brought into it, I don't even have to know her. I know the submissive one very well. Maybe we've even talked about it beforehand, like, We're gonna find a woman who can do this. But the thing turns around, and by the end of the fantasy, the dominating woman supplants me. While I wanted to have control the whole time, my real pleasure, and my real fear, is that I've lost control. I let it go to the Dark Woman, who has her own agenda in terms of the submissive one, and I end up assisting or just watching. I've always been some kind of border voyeur when it comes to this. I don't get my pleasure from simply watching, I have to play some role, but I'll easily slip into a passive role if things are going well. I'm a little uneasy talking about it, it's a little painful, because there is part of the dynamic where I'm canceled out. Who wants to admit that he likes to see himself canceled out? But it's a scenario that's been acted over and over in my life. I think it was part of the motivation for me to get into swinging in my twenties.

When Ruth and I first got together, I also got involved with another woman, and that scenario was constantly in flow. Unfortunately, Helen has disappeared and made her own life. She married a guy, and the two of them have cut themselves off entirely. In order to be happy they had to totally break off from us, because in a way, they were like our acolytes. Both Helen and Paul had been protégés of mine in the theater. They were both twelve years younger than me, and seven years younger than Ruth, which in those days seemed a significant difference. But it was a lot of fun from 1970 till '80, all those years we carried on. Sometimes the three of us, sometimes Paul and me and Ruth, sometimes Paul and Helen and Ruth. We were like a family. Now we haven't spoken in years, which is a shame.

Helen never lived with us, but she would spend two, three nights of the week. She would take vacations with us, and we'd go on extended weekends together. It was as close to her living with us as possible. Ruth never really wanted a threesome, I think, but we never talked about it at the time. She always took it for granted we were gonna be a married couple with children, even though I never thought in those terms in the early seventies. I just thought I'd go on like that, with Ruth being my main squeeze and everything being just fine. But around the midseventies we decided to get married and have kids, and it became clear to Helen that our little ideal of the threesome or foursome was being broken up by plans for domestic stability. And just about the time our older daughter was born, Helen stepped back and made her own life, and that was the end of that wonderful, delicious period.

When I met Helen she was a virgin. She had no experience. She was nineteen, from a protective family. I think she'd had one bit of a boyfriend, but hardly anything. She was so innocent in that way, but in other ways she wasn't. She was a fairly manipulative young woman even at nineteen—which I didn't give any thought to at the time. Once she started having some sex, she was very, very hot, and eager for it. She was really wet most of the time, and ready. But we didn't immediately jump into bed at all. She asked if she could assist me on various projects at the theater, so she was around all the time. Months went by when we were in each other's company. Step by step, we grew closer. It was never equal, maybe—I was more or less making the rules. I was involved with another woman, and she knew that meant she would be the third party if anything. That was not a problem for her. It seemed to make it more delicious, because not only was it forbidden—she was crossing the line with the older man, the director—but it became clear pretty soon that the only way this thing could get going and be as hot as she wanted was if she could be seductive to the woman as well. Early on she discovered the pleasures of helping me seduce Ruth, so that Ruth would be comfortable having her around. Helen and I could have had a fling on the side, but she wanted more, and the only way more could happen would be if we made Ruth comfortable. In those days, the way to make Ruth comfortable was to turn her on.

In our threesomes, it was Helen as the third party, Ruth as the potential wife, and me as the director, in a sexual sense. I would usually want Helen to act as my accomplice in bringing Ruth to orgasm. Helen and Ruth both enjoyed being submissive, so there was a little conflict over that. Helen preferred the role of being dominated, which is really the role of being concentrated on, to being the accomplice. But she enjoyed being the accomplice for a long time. So Helen and I would possess Ruth and give her pleasure. We'd undress her. We'd practice oral sex until she was very, very, very hungry for it. I would have intercourse with her while Helen was playing with her.

After Ruth was happy, satisfied, which was never easy because her orgasms are not that easy to accomplish, after that we returned to Helen, which was a whole ritual that would include spankings and domination. Sometimes the two of us would spank or dominate Ruth, but Helen seemed to need that more than Ruth. Helen would get off on some serious spanking and whipping. We used to shop for whips. She would even give me whips for my birthday and say I could only use them on her. I wouldn't be surprised if she had outgrown it by now. I wouldn't be surprised if she was something closer to a dominatrix. I could be wrong, but she likes to be in control. Her passivity was like stepping out of this control package for a moment and taking a vacation. It was her play, her fun.

The dynamics of S/M play are interesting. The position of lying back and allowing yourself to be tied up or whipped gives you so much power, in a way. That certainly was the case with Helen. When she was in that position, everybody was on to her. She became the star. Whatever thwacks the flesh took were nothing compared to the attention and devotion that came her way. And that was the position she chose.

We'd have arguments, like anybody else who is close, but there was so much we shared in those days. The sexual part was very powerful. We lived for scenes. Helen and I were like cats, we couldn't walk down the street without seeing potential people to be seduced. Paul entered the scene—he was married at the time, and I told him about Helen, saying this might be exciting. I introduced them one morning and she had no objection at all, we got into it right away. Paul was a serious bodybuilder, so we would surprise Helen with this wonderful hunk once in a while. Nobody whipped her the way Paul did. He would leave marks that would last a long time. We did threesomes, foursomes. When Paul and I would be with Ruth, it was a little simpler, because the two of us would dominate her until she would go crazy from the pleasure of it, and we would take turns fucking or whatever, so we would never get tired. We could relax in between, and Ruth would get a whole lot of jollies out of that. The threesome is a wonderful setup, especially for an aging person who needs to take breaks. I never had any sexual contact with Paul. We

were very close friends, we hugged, but never anything homosexual.
I haven't had any of that since the Boy Scouts.

Helen and I were always looking for something to do that would
be further on the edge. We never scored on the streets, but we did at
parties sometimes. Or we'd look in the papers for S/M couples who
wanted people to come out for fun and games. We'd drive out to
meet some sleazy couple in a bar and go home with them. They'd be
into paddling and golden showers and we would have a time. It was
always funny, something we could talk about weeks later. But there
was always something wrong with it—in those days, no matter what
we did, there was always the feeling that it didn't quite work, that
there was something else that should have happened. One too few
people there, or people without the proper imagination or daring. It
would always fall short of the fantasy. And Ruth hated it, she would
say, "Oh, my God, those people!" She was much more judgmental.
Helen flowed much better, she had much less resistance, and she
didn't judge the people. I mean, both Helen and Ruth were snobs in
a way, but Helen was the greater snob in that they weren't even worthy of her evaluation. Where Ruth would say, "God, these sleazy people," Helen would say, "Well, they're not people, they're just there
for my fun anyway."

Maybe it sounds compulsive, like, Why do it over and over again
if it's not gonna work out? But in a way it did work out, because it
was an extension of our sex in the bedroom, when we were together,
finding each other and loving each other as well as having what we
called DTs, or Dirty Things. That was the way the three of us referred
to sex for a long time, as DTs. We wanna do DTs in the morning.
That didn't imply looking for other couples or parties. It might have
implied that we were gonna get Ruth that morning or evening. Helen
and I had a very happy sex life, just the two of us, but I've always
thought of dirty sex being the best, and sex with Helen became more
satisfying, or "dirty," when Ruth was a part of it. I remember being
struck by a Woody Allen movie with a psychiatrist asking, "Do you
think of sex as dirty?" Woody says, "Is there any other kind?"

We went to some extravagant lengths. I heard through a friend
that there was a politician in Roxbury who really got off on white-

skinned women. Helen had such white skin that it was translucent. So one night we drove up there, to this seedy place. This guy must have been seventy, and Helen couldn't have been more than twenty. She was so incredibly hot that night. Something was going to happen to her, and she didn't know what. I had told her there was a guy she was going to meet, and he was a politician, an older black guy. She hardly said a word, but she certainly wasn't resistant. She asked some question about what was going to happen, and the more I suggested what would happen the more she liked it. We got there, and the guy just wanted her to give him head while he played with her luscious titties. She was all dressed up for the occasion, she wore a green jersey dress I remember, she was so beautiful—she probably still is just as beautiful.

It was very strange. For a while I kind of played with her, too. He was sitting on a couch, and she was kneeling, and I was behind her. Showing him how she liked to have her breasts squeezed. Which was hard, she liked them hurt. But after a while I went into the other room and watched the Celtics game. I could hear them, because he must have been squeezing her pretty hard. There were marks on her breasts the next day. I saw he was going to it, he got pretty hot himself. But I wasn't just gonna sit there the whole time. Nobody was taking clothes off, he just unzipped his pants, and she sucked his dick, and that was it. He might have taken the top of the dress down and slipped the bra off, but I don't think he put his finger in her panties. She was so frustrated, because he wasn't interested in pleasing her in any way. So I went and watched the basketball game.

I was sitting there wondering: Am I cold? What am I doing? This is a moment to evaluate my life. What route led me here, the son of an affluent middle-class family? It seemed like a large moment because it was so extreme, being up in this place, the whole area was so dark and derelict. I felt so detached, and I am not a detached person. There I was, able to concentrate on who was winning the game, and hearing sounds floating in from the next room. I was there and not there—I wasn't there for sex, I wasn't getting my rocks off. And I wasn't getting any money, it wasn't as if I was pimping for her, it was just something to do. That night looms large in my memory, the whole quality of it, and it's gone, it's gone. [Laughs.] All the players are into other things. It's never gonna happen again. And it's just as well, I'm sure. It's bizarre, now that I'm a father—if my little girl, who is now eight, came home with such a story, I'd want to kill the guy. Definitely, without a doubt.

Which guy, the politician or you?

Both, but mainly me. Yet I didn't feel I was a bastard or someone who was abusing Helen. She never led me to feel that. I never felt ashamed of anything I was doing. Even that night I just marveled at it, the mystery of it. I felt it was cold that I should be in there watching a basketball game. But I knew she was measuring this as a larger experience that she wanted. Nobody was pulling her into it. It wasn't even, If you don't do this I'm not gonna love you—which can be a method of very serious control. There was none of that. This was a lark we wanted equally. She was getting more out of it than I was. And we knew we were moving toward an edge more than we had ever done. It felt so strange, that it could be very exciting without me even being in the room. The beyondness of it all, the atmosphere of beyond good and evil—I hate that expression, but I didn't feel as if I was doing anything reprehensible. In my mind, I was taking care of her, wanting the best for her at the end of the day. Yet knowing all the while how society would come down on this if they knew about it. This was breaking every law—racial, age, sex, everything. All the laws of romance went out the window. It felt very free—yet not zip-a-dee do-dah, jumping up and down. It left a strange kind of sober feeling as we were driving home, casting glances at each other—Goodness, what did we do?

We never did it again. We had other strange evenings, but never up there. I don't know why—maybe she didn't do it good. The guy never called back. [Laughs.]

I suppose all the roles sound embarrassingly stereotypical. The young girl follows her mentor into a room, the old pol, he's black, she's humiliated, there's no attempt to give her pleasure. It all sounds classic, except for one important proviso: Helen could not be humiliated. She was an extremely proud woman. Whatever games she allowed herself to play never penetrated that pride. That night she was probably enjoying the play of embarrassment. And my being close by, in the next room, was part of it because we were in love with each other. We weren't just fooling around. There was a tremendous— what had started off as a schoolgirl crush developed into a real love affair. Which was always a bit odd, because she knew that Ruth was there.

I think the problem in discussing all this, the reactions people have to other people's behavior, is that it all tends to simplify. The simplified version is accurate to a point, but it finally betrays the players. The simplified version is that here's this director with a great deal of power in the theater. And the young virginal coed is smitten with this man, who has the power of having been through a lot of stuff she can't even imagine. She'll do anything to get close to him, she'll change his tire, she'll get dirty, she'll carry his books, she'll bring candy-coated apples, whatever it is to get close to this mysterious presence. At the same time, this person directing the play has been revealing himself. Even if she can't put it into words, she knows a great deal. Whereas she's a closed text to him. She's a mystery. She has the edge in that sense. She also has the edge of youth always. So the edge doesn't always go to the person in power, though it may seem like that.

Then a relationship starts, this three-way relationship where theoretically everything was permissible. We'd go to parties, and Helen and I would watch Ruth having sex with some guy, or Helen would. That was the game, that everything was permissible. Truthfully, it was not permissible for Helen or Ruth to lose themselves in someone other than me. If Ruth had fallen in love with some guy and disappeared for a week or two, I'd have lost my mind. That was more permissible for me, to have "affairs." But if I was freer to have outside affairs, maybe that says less about my freedom than it says about my neediness. It's not necessarily the old story, with the man calling all the shots. Everybody was trying to—I don't like the word *manipulate,* but everybody was trying to manipulate the scenario to their own satisfaction.

I often felt as if I was in the world to serve these women. I don't mean sexually serve, but to be available. Helen was just awakening to her sexual powers and potentials. I was the person who was helping to bring it out. And it was coming out in such a rush that it took all sorts of forms, from her discovery that she enjoyed masochism, to having multiple orgasms, to whatever. I was serving that. Ruth was serving her, too, awakening her to the freedoms of bisexuality. When I look back on it now, it seems that Helen was more in charge than any of us. During her playacting of being submissive, she'd say, "I'm the slave in this family." She liked cleaning the house and getting the dinner ready and treating me like a rajah. It was a sophisticated kind of manipulation, which I can't possibly resent, since I was the beneficiary of so much kindness and love. But she was doing what she wanted to do. She has moved on to become a film producer through what she learned by being around us. But I do think she has resentments about what went down in those days, because otherwise she wouldn't be so reluctant to be in touch.

If my daughter got involved in a similar setup, I'd be very worried that the guy was just into it for his jollies. I might say, He doesn't care about you, he just wants your body, he's calling all the shots. But I would not be respecting my daughter if I said that. At the end of the day, I would be disrespecting her, because already at the age of eight she's capable of running the show in many ways. By assuming that she's being victimized, that itself is a victimizing assumption. I'd be canceling out her powers of choice. She has them already, and by the time she's seventeen or so she'll have serious powers if she keeps going the way she's going. Well, Helen had serious power, which she has since shown in her professional life. But the image in those days was very much a slave, a victim. She loved to project that. If I still had those pictures of her, you'd see that look on her face. But consciously or unconsciously, she was working for her pleasure, as people do.

That's why summing it up is dangerous when it comes to sexuality. It's so murky and entangled that the attempts to clarify it are doomed from the start. What makes sex so interesting is that there's a mystery at the heart of it. You can unravel the mystery, go back to childhood and see the infantile patterns, but it doesn't have the texture that sexual response has. I'd like to think I don't understand it at all, and when we try to understand what it all means, who's in the position of power, who was treating who fairly, we always miss it. I guess anatomically, whomever is on the bottom is being taken advantage of. But everybody knows that's bullshit. The person who's on the bottom could be anybody at any moment. Some positions give people more pleasure than other positions, and it could be top, bottom, side, it doesn't matter. In the end, the language leaves us wanting.

JAMES W.

"I'm a man of many parts," he says. "We all are, but it's something I pursue. I work with all kinds of personas—my own, my partner's." By which he means that he recognizes various personalities in himself, some of them shadowy, some of them full-blown characters. "Some of my parts aren't particularly sexual. You've heard of the inner child? I have three little boys in me. They're sensual, like all kids, but not sexual. I have a teenage girl who's sexual, but only with her wife—or her husband—who is my partner, who is herself bisexual and pansexual. There's a prissy faggot in me—different from a homosexual man. There's a leather top and there's a priest-slave. The priest-slave is in a relationship with the Mistress, who's another part of my partner."

He and his lover, M. Cybelle, participate in the sex radical scene. She is a professional dominatrix, he a college teacher, consultant, and writer. He is a big man, forty-nine, sandy-haired, ruddy-skinned, with a strong voice and assertive manner. His East Bay apartment is squeaky-clean and neat, with magazines laid out to overlap perfectly on the table, and several walls lined with books from floor to ceiling.

He grew up in the Midwest, son of a lawyer and a housewife, and knocked around the East Coast before coming to California. He has been bisexual most of his life, having first slept with a woman at fifteen and a man at nineteen. But he calls himself "heteroaffectional."* His loves have been women, and he and Cybelle have shared a "committed, nonmonogamous relationship" for five years. At parties and with other partners, he "plays" in different personalities—but the priest-slave goes the "deepest" and is reserved for Cybelle. "If I had to be a one-sided person, and I could choose the one side, that's who I would be."

---

*He is borrowing here from Mark I. Chester's term, "homoaffectional."

• • •

In my early days in the Bay Area there were a bunch of leather bars. The leather scene was entirely gay male, as far as I was aware. There were bars like the Brig, and the Black and Blue. I was terrified of them. I'd peek into them in the daytime but I'd never go at night. Well, one day I was looking at the local sex newspaper and I got to the D&S ads and something went: Aha! So I took my fear in hand and made an appointment to see a dominatrix. I had no idea of what I was doing. Over the next bunch of years, every now and then I'd go see another professional.

It was usually frustrating because mostly these dominatrixes expected me to have some fetish scenario that they could enact in exchange for the money. I was supposed to want to kiss their boots, or get tied up, or get spanked. Eventually I started saying, "I don't have a scenario. I know most people do because you all keep asking me for it. How about you be you and I'll be me and let's see what happens." The problem, I think, is that most of the professionals I saw weren't into this personally. They were just doing a job.

Eventually I heard about Cybelle and talked to her on the phone. She said, "Tell me what you're interested in, and I'll do some of it—my way." I said, "I don't know, I've been to a dozen pros and I've gotten to point A every time. I want to go beyond point A." She took me beyond point A the first time we met. The difference between Cybelle and the other professionals I had visited is that Cybelle is real. She's in the community. She does D&S in her private life as well as earning a living at it. She really likes to be in charge, and she's really a sadist. She's not going to walk up and down the street looking for people to beat up, but she finds it titillating to cause someone sensation that pushes their limits and makes them generate energy. And she likes to direct the energy, to control the energy flow.

First we talked. Most of the dominatrixes I had visited negotiate in role. The first thing you do is get on your knees. Cybelle does not negotiate in role. You sit in a chair and she sits in a chair. We had a conversation and she got a sense of who I was. Then she collared me. She did a long whipping. She doesn't do as much whipping these days because she had back surgery a couple of years ago, but at that time she was adept with a variety of flagellation instruments. I learned about how endorphins get released, how adrenaline gets released, and how you can change pain into something quite different if you stop thinking of it as pain and you stop holding it in your body. I've done a lot of body work, so it's easy for me to grasp. When most people get hit, they hold it. That creates more pain. But if you get hit and let it through you, *Aaaaahhhh,* then you get a sensation that spreads, and you get a glow. You don't have to define it as pain. The reason my brain needs to say it's pain is to let me know I'm in danger. But I know this isn't going to damage me. I can distinguish between this and catching my hand in the car door.

So she did some whipping. She put clamps on my nipples. And we did a lot of energy exchange. Like if I hurt most people by pinching them, they go, "Argh!" The energy gets dissipated. But instead, you can contain it. I don't mean tighten up and hold it, but channel it. You think of yourself as a clear tube, and envision the sensation passing through you. You become the director of the intensity as it runs through you. You discover *choice* regarding the way you define your own physical and emotional feelings, so you can keep the energy channeling through. What happened for us—the best way I can describe it, she would do something that would call forth an energetic response from me, and I would pass the energy back to her. She'd take it and build on it to call forth a still greater response from me, and I'd pass it back to her again. We did this erotic energy exchange for a long time, and I learned to be multiorgasmic—not ejaculatory, but the full-body orgasm that Wilhelm Reich talks about, which is very much like what some Hindu sects describe as the Kundalini, or life-force energy, rising. I'd feel stirring in the base of my spine, which arguably came from my genitals or my anus, and it would rise up my spine and my head would snap and everything would shudder. I had never felt that before. It's far richer than genital orgasm. That doesn't mean you can't have genital orgasms too, but you can do this over and over, and instead of just being here [points to groin], it's top to bottom, scalp to toe, everything gets tingly and shakes.

The other thing I learned about was genital bondage. I learned about my balls. She was using leather or rubber straps, I forget which. I dislike rubber because it pulls the skin when you take it off, and that's not a sensation I enjoy. You get hold of the neck of the scrotum so the testicles are down there and the penis is up there, and you wrap that. It creates a lot of pressure on the testicles. You can wrap down farther and farther. You can package the testicles into this nice little thing if you want to, or you can separate them with a strap. It's just creating different kinds of pressure. When you take the strap off, everything goes *whoo!* because all the blood returns and everything tingles. Try it for yourself sometime. Just touching your balls is intense because you've got a lot of nerve endings there. The more intensely you touch, the more intensely you respond. And if you stop giving in to fear, stop saying, This is the limit, I can't stand it—if you move that limit, the buildup of tension allows greater release. Much of pleasure is about building tension and releasing it. This is a way to build tension higher, longer, farther, so when the release comes it's that much more profound.

The submission end of it is having your balls in somebody's hands. Especially if your hands are tied someplace. You know how they put rings in bulls' noses? Someone goes behind the bull and holds the balls, and then the bull doesn't move while they drive the ring through the septum. Same game. I'm giving over what I'm taught to identify as male power. I'm a man in a dick-centered universe, and I've got a dick, so if you want to take charge of my manhood then you take that. If somebody has me by the balls and there's this pressure, and I can see my balls in her hands—or if I'm blindfolded, I can feel her hands between my thighs—I can go into a state of feeling owned very easily.

What I want to do is surrender, not submit. I want to be in the place where I *have* given up. I've always felt myself to be very spiritual, though not very religious in terms of organized religions. When I was a teenager I would sit in churches, synagogues, mosques, temples, didn't matter, I wanted to be in a holy space. I've always been concerned with the ability to surrender—in meditation, jumping off cliffs, scuba diving. To not fight against the flow. This is the same. I don't want to be giving stuff up, that's an act of will. I want to be in that *condition*. I want to be in a state of meditation. Pop Christianity plays at the surface of these teachings. You read the Gnostic gospels,

Christ is talking about discovering your own kingdom of God. He's talking about surrendering to your being. We have a culture that's very involved with doing and having, and not very involved with *being*. If you want to *be,* you need to join some monastery. There aren't any monasteries out there that interest me, and I've got a different kind of life. I don't want to get away from the world. But I do like being. Very few writers get to being for me, very few movies, some music, some paintings. I can sit in the ocean and get to being. S/M is a different level of being, and it's erotic as well, which is the icing on the cake.

So I quickly felt at home on my knees with this woman. I quickly felt at home in a collar belonging to this woman. And the priest-slave was born, or maybe I should say recognized. The slave got opened up in the S/M erotic context, which is a great place for identifying personas. And when the slave had a place to put himself, he could start to identify what thoughts and feelings were his. He belongs to Cybelle. He is her slave, her consort, her priest. I see Cybelle not just as a dominatrix but a Goddess avatar, so the slave and the priest are one. The slave wants to serve his Mistress, and the priest wants to serve his Goddess. The priest-slave bottoms only to Cybelle. He has a life apart from her, but he is hers. There's a spiritual part of the leather community where he functions as a priest involved with rituals. And he has what I refer to as a younger brother who is a little less spiritual and much more flat-out submissive, a sexually submissive man who does not belong to Cybelle. His name is Steve. He'll bottom to other women if he can find the right ones.

Once the slave got fleshed out, he got to start living it for a couple of days at a time, or a week. That whole part of my personality got to fulfill itself. In the non-S/M world, I lead a very toppy life. I'm used to directing things. I'm large, I'm loud, I've very sexual, and I'm fairly predatory. When the slave comes out, all that is taken in hand. He's safe for any woman who can read his energy, and that's part of what the San Francisco S/M scene is about, reading energy.

I don't live in that persona much right now because Cybelle has been so ill. As the priest-slave I need a couple days or a week at a time. That's extremely intense, extremely intimate. And for Cybelle it's hard work. It takes a lot of energy to control somebody for that long. If you had to control yourself absolutely for a week, that would be hard with no down time. Now add to that, you have to control somebody else too—when they pee, when they drink, when they eat. We're not talking about spanking somebody, that's fun, but that's not necessarily all there is to being a top. When you're going to be in charge of somebody and be responsible for what you give them and what they give you—it's hard to do that for one night, let alone a week.

When the slave is out for a week, there may be very little activity that's overtly sexual, but it's all erotic. When I'm surrendering that way, it's constantly present in my mind and to my eye. I've made agreements about my behavior which I'm bound to keep. I'm wearing chains, ankle cuffs, wrist cuffs—that's all Cybelle's bailiwick. She decides.

Then you have your day. What does the slave do? One place we've played a lot is where we go every winter solstice. It's up in the country, they've got hot tubs, cabins, it's fairly rustic. No telephones, no computers, nothing to do. You bring your own food in. The cabins are heated with wood stoves. And it's cold. So the slave gets up. Generally has permission to pee, drink water, eat fruit. These are essentials for the body so they're usually granted. The slave turns on water for coffee, starts the fire, gets the house warmed. He's in role—collar, cuffs, genital bondage of some light form. When role is heavy, the slave sleeps in it. When role is light, the slave doesn't.

If the Mistress wants to get up at some particular time, the slave will awaken her with coffee. This doesn't look a lot different from when James and Cybelle are together, James wakes Cybelle up with coffee too. It's attitude. The slave brings the Mistress breakfast and cleans up afterward. The Mistress may or may not get up in a hurry. The slave may go back to bed and read. Or the Mistress may decide she wants to go out to the hot tubs, in which case she will take the collars and chains off and put something on that can go in the hot water. Sheepskin leather cuffs don't do very well in hot water. Plus you don't want to bring your bedroom into other people's living rooms. They may not want to know. So you have something more discreet. A piece of rawhide, maybe. Little wrist things that can be worn in the hot tub, a band of metal nobody is going to notice, but it helps maintain the space.

Or the Mistress may decide she wants to play. That might mean she wants to have her pussy eaten. It might mean she wants to whip the slave. She might want to try out some new equipment. A couple of years ago she wanted to try a head harness. That changes how you experience the world—a tight hunk of leather, not a hood, embracing your head, and a bit in your mouth and a leash on your collar—and on top of that you're supposed to crawl or kneel. Obviously you don't do this without agreeing to it. Theoretically I can always say, Fuck it, I don't want to do this anymore, it's over. But the slave has given his word he won't do that. If he has a problem, he'll bring it up, he'll talk about it, but he's not going to fuck up. There are slaves who are rebels, who want to be forced. I'm not interested in that as a top or a bottom. I'm into submission, surrender, giving it away or having it given to me.

There's sex play whenever she wants it. It may be several times a day. Cybelle is multiorgasmic in a serious way, but she may not feel like it, or she may have her period. The Mistress may decide she wants to suck the slave's dick. Very interesting if the slave is tied up or in chains, and you start sucking his dick, or biting it. Because sucking dick, in the het universe, is supposed to be "Get down there and suck it, baby." When she's sucking it as the top, she's doing it because she wants to. I've had my dick sucked as a top, as a bottom, by men, by women. I've had my dick sucked when I was playing *en femme* and when I was not. Very different experiences. Physically it feels more or less the same, it's wet and soft and pressure, but it's the attitude. It's who I am and who you are. This goes on all the time in sexual relationships, but making it deliberate is part of what makes it a spiritual path. It's a consciousness game, a meditation, being the slave. I am choosing over and over to be this way.

When she's sucking my dick, I am not the penetrator. I am who is being engulfed. I am not in charge of it. I am being taken. And the Mistress always has the option of making it painful. She does like to bite. She does know how to have my balls in her mouth and start to push with the tongue in a way that creates pressure. It's not the nibbling that people find erotic who like having their balls played with. We're into intense sensation that I could call pain, but I'm giving something different to it.

I think she has sucked me to orgasm as the slave, but I don't remember. It's not about that, it's not about genital orgasm. Cybelle likes to see men come. Sometimes she has me masturbate for her. She'll have an orgasm just watching. Sometimes she has a good time bringing me to the brink of orgasm and then not letting me have it, doing that over and over for a period of days. It's very erotic, you can walk around with a hard-on for a week because you're always at the edge. When I'm in role, I already want to please her, but if I'm at the edge of orgasm for days on end, I really, *really* want to please her.

This is one place to make the distinction between sexual and erotic—sexual being genital stimulation with the aim of orgasm. I can be sexual with myself anytime. I can be sexual with a hundred fifty people at a party. But to be erotic—the slave may spend this whole week wearing nothing but collars or chains except for going into public. That's not sexual by itself, but if you're walking around naked and bound at the direction of a dominant sex partner, it can be very erotic. You must be available to her or him, whoever the top is. If the Mistress decides she wants to suck the slave's dick or whip his balls or stuff her hand up his ass, there it is. If she decides she wants to try out this new cane, and the slave's in the middle of cooking dinner, and she says, "Lean over the sink"—that's not sexual specifically, but it keeps the focus on that erotic edge.

Aroused and erect are also not the same thing. At some level I'm probably aroused by talking about it now. A woman can start to lubricate in ten seconds. A man can develop precoital fluid in the same amount of time. That's arousal. As the slave, I'm aroused almost nonstop. Erect comes and goes. When I'm chopping up the chicken and trying to keep the chains out of the way, I'm not erect. But if I haven't come for a day or two or four or five, it takes nothing at all to make me erect. I lie down and the sheet will make me erect. I bend over to pick up a piece of wood, and the pressure makes me erect. If somebody knocks on the door and the Mistress says "Come in," I'm instantly on display, and I'm not likely to get erect but I do get more aroused by the inherent intensity. It's not being humiliated, it's being

humbled. I've got my graduate degrees, all these accomplishments—
"Thank you. On your knees and keep your legs spread—now!" "Yes,
ma'am." It helps remove false pride. The reason I might have an attitude about getting down on my knees is because I think it makes me
less than. But it doesn't. I can do it with real pride, not false pride. It
brings a great grace to the part of the slave, and that grace is imparted
to the Mistress, who can then impart it to the slave.

The slave has never fucked his Mistress—but they do have intercourse. The Mistress takes the slave into her, she encompasses him.
She likes penetration, she likes having the dick in her. But the slave
moves for her pleasure, whereas James is much more likely to move
for his. I've always enjoyed watching my partners get off, male or female. But as a slave I'm not getting her off. *She's* getting her off and
using me to do it. Fucking with a leash on your balls is not the same
as fucking without one, especially when somebody's hand is on that
leash. James and Cybelle fuck like a regular het couple. Usually
Cybelle's on the bottom and they fuck, ordinary vanilla sex. But the
Mistress is much more likely to be on top. The slave may not get to
come. If he does, he comes when she says so. He may not be inside
her. She may use him as a dildo until she's got what she wants, and if
she wants to watch him come, she may watch him masturbate, or she
may not.

As the slave I get into a no-mind state, a Zen state. There's a quality of peace and serenity in giving it up to somebody who is willing
and able to hold it—the mystic "it." It allows me to drop all the de-
fenses and be in the condition of being. Somebody wrote a book pro-
posing that this condition is escaping from the self. That's not my
experience. It's a *transcendence* of myself. I'm fully in touch with me,
with all my parts, and I'm someplace else, too. That's why I say it's a
spiritual path. I don't want to sound as if I think self is bad. This just
opens up another level beyond that. A lot of people do S/M for fun.
I have nothing against that, when I go to parties I do it for fun, too.
But if that's all it was, I could take it or leave it.

The slave used to be out most weekends, and maybe he will again
when Cybelle gets better. It's the entry time that's hard, getting from
James to the slave. If I've been working hard all week, it's going to be
a tussle to pull the slave out on Friday night. It's easier for me to get

into a top mode than a bottom mode. But preparation helps. If Cybelle calls on Wednesday and says, "I want the slave. The Mistress is here, and the Mistress is planning to be here through the weekend," I will start attending to it. I'll do some meditation at an altar for him. I'll dress for him, make sure I'm wearing clothes that are receptive in both the color and the cut, even when I go to the campus. I'll wear some incense that the slave will wear, just as a reminder. When I shower and shave it'll be in the form of ablutions rather than just getting clean. It's hard when I'm driving because that tends to bring out the top real fast, so I have to pay attention. I'll drive in the right lane instead of the left lane. I'll make a point of not going through yellow lights. When I get to Cybelle's, I've already been giving it up in a way. Then if the Mistress says, "Kneel," it's no problem at all.

There was an evening four or five months ago when Steve, my other bottom persona, got the slave's and the Mistress's permission to invite this woman he had been playing with over for drinks. So Cybelle and the Mistress were in this body over here, and the slave and Steve were in this body, which was tricky. The woman who had been topping Steve was there with her partner, who doesn't play. There was a certain amount of tension—pleasant, erotic tension. When they left, I went downstairs to lock the door and I turned back and was partway up the stairs, and no question that the Mistress was in residence in that body, completely in residence, and she hadn't been there for months, and that just brought the slave out completely. I got to the top of the stairs and fell to my knees and wept.

CASH RIORDAN

He was born in 1950 on the West Coast, one of four children in a lower-middle-class family, and he followed the path of many other kids in that era and location: San Francisco for the Summer of Love, a pad in the Haight after high school, and a commune until the midseventies. Then came some aimless, lonely years until he settled down. Along the way he learned carpentry, and he now runs a small contracting business in Oregon. He has shaggy brown hair and basset-hound eyes, and is wearing jeans, running shoes, and a cotton knit shirt that hugs him where he is thickening at the waist. He looks back on his hippie days with nostalgia, because the cares of early middle age seem pressing. Business is only now picking up in the wake of the recession; mortgage payments are high; his wife Lois is troubled; and he has two young daughters to worry about.

"I met Lois in 1981. By that time I had done about everything a straight fellow is gonna do, so I looked at being married as not a sensual adventure at all. I was pretty rudderless, wasting time, and when I met her I decided, hey, she was as good as anybody else and I might as well go ahead and marry her. I was attracted to her and we had good sex in the standard ways, but to be perfectly honest I was committed to being committed more than to her. I had a kind of parent-child relationship with her, but I didn't like that after a while so I spent some time trying to change it. It seemed like we got more comfortable with each other over the years. Then we had the two kids, and they are really the joy of my life. Right now, things with Lois are strained. She has regressed in some ways to where she is very dependent and she's not taking care of herself. She has gotten fat, she's lost her self-confidence. So sex has been pretty rare over the past six months. I'd say we've only done it three or four times. With the kids we hardly get any time to ourselves, and I've been working double shifts, so I'm not around as much as I was. In the last little bit she has really started to sink into a depression, and it's a sad thing to see."

• • •

I always liked sex with Lois. I mean, it's just straight sex, missionary and her on her knees and oral, the standard run of sex that
straight people have. It's not that we don't have a knowledge of other
stuff—Lois and I have read the *Kama Sutra*, and we tried some Tantric yoga when we were first married, because some friends of ours
passed along a book. But it wasn't something that stuck. We're West-
ern folks, we do the comfortable thing.

It goes pretty much the same way every time—when we have
time, that is. One of us expresses interest in having sex. Nowadays,
since the two kids, you have to have some pretty organized signals.
We usually make a date, and then something comes up so we miss the
date, or we end up having hurried sex. The only time we had for extended sex in the past year was when we went to Vegas and had a hotel room for three days.

But the standard routine is, I undress her, and basically I like to
provide pleasure on different parts of her body. Kissing and fondling
and squeezing and touching. Usually I start with loosening up muscles. I've studied some massage, so I can relax her, which is a great
opening step as far as foreplay. The neck and back are the focus of
most people's tensions. Once you relax the outer set of muscles, you
can get at some of the spinal muscles. And I get a feedback feeling
through my fingers. I feel her relaxation, I feel her sensitivity. Her
whole body might arch with a brush of my hand. I do some massage
around the neck, around the ears or the eyes or the temples. I caress
and stroke her hair, and I grab it and pull back her head. The act of
getting into her hair and really working it with my hands—that moves
her head and her neck to the point where she feels real loose and
easy, and when you get that neck and shoulder stuff loose, the fluids
start to flow. She starts to smell unbelievable. When a woman gets
very lubricated she's releasing pheromones, and then your own level
of arousal goes up.

She doesn't have as much ability to relax me. She doesn't have the
knowledge or the hand strength. I mean, everybody can squeeze muscles, but to get at a knotted muscle and relax it takes some ability to

feel back through your fingertips what it is you're trying to do, and some knowledge of physiology. You have to feel the pleasure that you're giving while you're giving it. I don't think she has that ability. She has tried various times, I tried to teach her about it, but she never did pick it up. That's part of the scenario I'm not that fond of. I don't like to be just a perpetrator.

Usually I'm standing by the bed or kneeling between her legs. I need leverage to be able to work muscles. And usually I have a hard-on, so there's two things going on at the same time, the idea that there's a sexual act coming, but we're working on this angle first. Eventually I'll work down between her legs and massage her clitoris. No fingers inside the vagina at this point, but I can make the clitoris erect. I have no idea what a G-spot is, I don't know if that's a reality or not. A few years back I heard that if you reach inside a woman with your thumb and pressure her from the outside of her pubic bone and inside her pubic bone, they like that. But I think it's mostly because you're cradling over the clitoris. So I'll massage the clitoris until she's very heightened sexually. She might roll over at that point and pull her legs up and she'll want to be entered. But if I get into her then, I'll come out pretty soon and start the process over again, because the delay heightens the sensuality. You have to be careful—if you give them straight, direct manipulation of the clitoris for long periods of time, they turn into Jell-O, and they're not as responsive. They get hungry and devoury and then it's too easy, the whole thing's over. It's better to let the thing go on for a while, because for a man, once you start the heavy thrusting, it's gonna be over soon. When you're twenty, all you want to do is get in there and thrust away. Now I take more time.

What I have learned about lovemaking is you have to unlock a person. You have to peel back layers to get at real pleasure. For me, at least, the sex act is a three-stage affair, as far as the woman's levels of excitement. At the end of each stage they're gonna come, but they're gonna come progressively stronger and harder if I do my job properly. The first time you enter a woman, it's the promise made: They're gonna get fucked. So that's cool. But you pull out at that point, see, and you go back to the other things. Which is another promise made, that there'll be more pleasure, other kinds of pleasure than the male pleasure. But first there's the sensitive stage, the fore-play stage, which is a matter of expectation. There's a moment right away when a woman understands that you're not gonna take her and fuck her and throw her aside. There are times when that's fun as well, but it's mostly not fun for her that way. If she understands you're not gonna do that, there's excitement that comes out of that knowledge alone. That's what the opening stage is good for. After some body work and some regular sex, the skin becomes very sensitized. It's a sense organ in and of itself. You can rake your fingernail across it and get it to prickle up into pimples. With enough excitement, that will cause clitoral orgasm. So there's a second level of excitation, another plateau, and more orgasms, and there's another level beyond. That one is really out there. It's a woman in a completely excited state. She is not able to talk, she is not even able to open her eyes most likely. Her world has become so completely focused that it's hard to get her out of there. She is completely abandoned, like when the female pray-ing mantis chews off the head of the male and he's just banging away and that's it, there's nothing else. I enjoy getting a woman to that state. It may have to do with control, but it's also that giving pleasure is fun. With Lois I can't do it all the time, even though she's as good a subject as I ever came across. It's rare even for people who know they can get there. But that's what I'm going for.

So after I pull out that first time, now I want some physical ma-nipulation of myself. I want her hand on my penis. That's what she likes, too. It's almost like, Don't go anywhere, you're staying here for now. It's a good feeling, you're wanted and needed and the promise is being made both ways that there's gonna be more sex. I already made a promise, I entered her, but I'm out again, see, so for her to have ahold of me, it's just the sense that I'm not going further than an arm's length away. And I'll do some more manipulation of her. I find that some parts of her are more responsive than before, and some less. The outsides of her arms may be cooler, but the insides much more sensitive. And certain areas will start to sweat, the upper level of her butt-crack and behind her knees and the balls of her feet. At that point I might go get a towel and wipe her off. I learned to do that early on in my sex life—stop for a moment, go to the bathroom and find a towel, get part of it soaked with really hot water, wring it out, and come back and wash her completely down, the whole body, wash all the sweat off her back, her neck, her legs, and then use the dry part of the towel to rub her down and start up the sex act again. The towel has a different texture, a rough feel, so it resensitizes her. Women always appreciate that, they dig it, I mean they like to get sloppy during the act but there's a point where they like to get cleaned up and go at it again.

Then there's a second period of entry, and I might take her a little more at this point. Turn her over, get her on her stomach with her butt up, and take her a little bit. She may fight at that point, she wants to do her own thing, and that's fine. There's a variety of positions and things to do, so we'll go in and out, changing positions, and all the while there's more arousal. She wants to get to where she's pushing and thrusting on her own and matching your rhythm, so it's a hold-back period as far as I'm concerned. I've got to be careful not to come. I might perform oral sex at this point, 'cause that's when it seems most exciting to her. And one thing I do—I'm in there with my lips and tongue, and it's arousing, but if I want to completely blow her away for a moment, I blow on her clitoris like I was playing a trumpet. I put my lips on her and [puckers his lips and makes a sound like a trumpet]. You have to be careful, if you're too sharp it can be uncomfortable. But if you do it right, she immediately comes, she arches her back and goes boom boom boom, crazy and yelling things. Unfortunately it numbs her, too, so it's quite a while until she calms down again, and you're not going to go on with the sex act for a while. It's not something I do all the time, because I don't like to pull out my full bag of tricks. But it's fun once in a while. Sometimes I get humorous, I'll play a song, like one time I did "The Star-Spangled Banner."

After that we might take a break, but we're also at a pretty aroused state. Then I'll start back in again, meaning I might massage her, or look her in the eyes and talk to her about how she feels, what's going on. And then find out by touch. The breasts sometimes are clammy at this stage, even after toweling off, so they may not want to be rubbed. The skin's texture has changed because of the moisture and the sweat, so rubbing them feels like chafing instead of a nice smooth touch. I notice that, so I don't play with 'em anymore. I might turn her around and force oral sex on her at this point. I might just lay back, or I might be on my knees and have Lois on her stomach. I will have cleaned myself off when I went to get the towel for her, so I don't present a sloppy prick. It's more of a dominance situation now, I'm taking more control of the sex—not that I haven't had control from the beginning, but now I'm more emphasizing the fact that I'm gonna get pleasure. It's also a tease as far as women are concerned. They love to be taken once you get to a certain point. They want you to make them do things. It's delicate, you want it to be pleasurable for them, but once you really get into sex with somebody, they're open to that stuff.

We might do other things—like I love to have tits hanging down on me. I like to get underneath Lois and have her brush my face and my body with her nipples. It changes her focus—a lot of her focus has been down in her clitoris, and I'm trying to get it out into other areas. I might grab her body and have her shake herself. Or she'll rake her tits across me, they get really excited doing that. I'm hairy-chested and she can just brush the hair, so it feels good to me as well as to her. She might slide her tits up around my head, and around—at this point I like to be all around a woman, fold my body in all different ways, slithering like a snake, going all around touching everywhere. That'll lead to a point where she'll lay back and I'll get her knees up and enter her again, or stroke her by fucking her outside the vagina. The cord underneath a penis is pretty strong, and it has those ridges, so it can cause quite a bit of arousal on the clitoris. While I'm doing that I tend to slip in and out, this is a well-lubricated vagina so it's easy. I'll pull her legs up in front and squeeze 'em so she has a tightened aspect, and I can go in her or rub along her from that angle.

Now if I can keep from coming, I tend to focus more explicitly on rear-entry fun. At the very end, when I'm taking the woman, I want her doggie-style. But whether I'm in or out at this point, I'll have Lois in front of me so I can reach around with both hands and use my fingers on her clitoral area. Not right on it, mostly around and at the base of it. As I understand the clitoris, it's a bundle of nerves that come together and they rise like a stalk. There are five or six bundles that come in there from separate areas, and you can stimulate the different ones. I'm not really sure of the physiology, but that's what I'm trying to do, I'm trying to locate them just by fooling around. I may be entering her or I may not, but there's a lot of heaving and up-and-downing going on, her head is coming back, her mouth is open, her eyes are closed, and there's a lot of heavy panting and moaning and groaning and back-arching and good-sounding stuff going on, so I feel like it's successful one way or another.

If we have time I'll probably stand up now, like alongside a bed or a dresser or a cabinet or wherever we happen to be, and I go back to touching and feeling. What I like to do at that stage, I'll just spread her legs, and I mean just completely expose her rear and tilt her over so she's bent down from the waist. At this point she's completely wet and I like to move that wetness down her legs, just schmear it all over. I'm less concerned with messy at this point, I don't care anymore. And I'm letting Lois know what it feels like, that she's excited, that she's running, the faucet is on, and I'm smearing her own juices up and down the insides of her thighs and the backs of her legs. Around that time I generally do hand manipulation into a couple of quick orgasms for her. The clitoris at that point can easily be hurt, so I do it with the palm of my hand because it doesn't have any sharpness and it's a real easy motion, like a sucking motion. She's all exposed and wet, the parts are starting to hang down, the labia and the tender areas are pretty much out, so it doesn't take a lot.

After that I'll take over, I'll get in and thrust. I like to pull her really close and tight and enter as deeply as possible. Usually I'll be on my knees. Sometimes her legs will be well spread and I'll be up and under, sometimes I pull her back so she's more or less on top, but it's all rear entry. I'm done relatively soon at that point, but hopefully she will have been so excited that this is what she's been waiting for, and her response is just as quick as mine is. Once we're done and we've both had orgasms, she really cannot be orgasmed again—I mean, she can be, if you touch her she goes Jell-O, but it's sharp, she would rather not. It's enough. She'd much rather fold up in my arms and mellow out for a while.

When I finally take the sex, it's because I have built it up to a point where the taking of it is going to be the best. It's going to be the consummation for both of us, and I've got a completely willing partner. I want her to be jelly, way beyond that earlier flush of, Okay, I'm ready, you can have me. Beyond where she can talk to me in my ear and tell me the things she wants. I want her where she can't help but be leaking all over. At the early stage, she can be thrusting and you can be thrusting at the same time, and you can get all out of rhythm. She's got her agenda and you've got yours, and things are chaotic. Whereas at the state of complete submission, it's easiest for me to get a focus on doing my business. I don't go at it real hard, I go at it in a smooth, rhythmic way, where I'm trying to feel the whole inside of her along the whole of my penis. I don't want any interference with that. I don't want her herking and jerking around. She's completely receptive, and it feels like the vagina does a number on its own, tightening in different places that I don't think are in her control.

It's funny, I don't think about this very much, but it occurs to me that what I'm looking for is an almost mythic situation, where the state of arousal is so high that there's a rhythmic wave inside the vagina, the way the muscles are contracting, it's like pulling the penis in. And she's not doing it herself. I've experienced it once, or a few times, and I keep trying to get it again. I remember the feeling, and my penis got overenlarged, it was like it went boom, and filled extra. Whoa, I didn't have much choice, it was happening. It takes an extreme level of excitement to get to, past all the barriers a woman has, all the training, all the psychology, I mean everything, every layer that's laid on top by society, all the way down to the base animal. It's a rare experience. Lois has voluntary control over her vagina, she can squeeze as much as she wants, but this is different. It's a pulsating effect that runs up through the cervix and through the limbs. I don't think you could learn it. Well, I don't know, maybe you can. Maybe it's part of a discipline somewhere. [Laughs.] Can you imagine? That would be a wonderful kind of training. But people don't even get turned on to the possibility of this kind of thing going on. They don't understand what their own bodies can do.

6

WORKING

P ROSTITUTES CALL IT "the life." Porn actors refer to "the business." Economists marvel at "the sex industry." Under whatever name, sex generates big money in America: eight billion dollars a year for pornography alone. Tens, perhaps hundreds of thousands of people work in the industry at any given time. The authors of *The Janus Report on Sexual Behavior* estimate that the number of American women who have exchanged sex for money at some point in their lives may be five million—whereas there are four speakers in this chapter.

I point up the disparity in numbers to highlight the danger of drawing sweeping conclusions based on these interviews. The reasons people enter any area of the sex industry, and their experiences in it, vary as greatly as people's reasons for getting married and the quality of their marriages. Yet that is not the public perception. Sex workers—as some prostitutes and others in the industry call themselves—are so marginalized, so stigmatized, that our images of them are constructed largely of stereotypes. The culture also fosters a prurient fascination with people who sell sex. This voyeuristic hunger annoys Claudia Mercurio, who started as a stripper and is now a call girl: "I get tired of explaining myself all the time. I meet people and think they're nice and they probably wouldn't have a problem with me being a prostitute, but I'd have to explain it to them: Yeah, I like my work, blah blah blah. If I said I was a graphic designer, people would go, 'Oh, that's cool,' and shut up."

These speakers, then, are individuals who only have in common that they get paid for having sex. The first is a preoperative transsexual streetwalker, a "chick with a dick"; two act in adult films; the fourth charges two hundred dollars for an hour of her time at home. One way to read their interviews is to measure them against popular images. The most deep-seated stereotypes of sex workers portray them as amoral harlots and/or pathetic victims. Regina, the streetwalker, arguably comes closest: she grew up poor and black in the inner city, her relations with "tricks" seem the most impersonal and exploitive, and she admits to getting a charge out of "knowing I'm doing something bad." But Sandra Marquez, who also grew up poor and was sexually abused as a child, would find hilarious the notion that her stripping and porn acting make her a victim. For her, sex work is part of a general sexual flowering, including an open marriage, group sex, and bisexuality.

This touches on another cliché: that sex workers hate what they do and feel no sexual pleasure in doing it. That is not true for these four. They all say (as does as Fay Canastel, in Chapter 9) that sex work, like other work, is sometimes fun and sometimes awful; and that professional sex, like personal sex, is sometimes rewarding and sometimes disastrous. They also say that starting sex work was a key to unlocking their own sexualities. For John Mulholland, a shy, repressed college student sixteen years ago, one thing porn films offered was a way to have lots of sex with highly sexual women. For Regina, "It's like sexual freedom. . . . You're getting paid to do something, and that gives you the freedom to do it. To be kinky." For Claudia, "Becoming a stripper was the best thing I've ever done. . . . I came out of this environment where I felt so negative about my body, and sex, and relations between men and women. . . . It was like, I can do this, and I can be good at it, and I don't have to have a perfect nose, and be blond, and have big tits."

But even Claudia, who mostly enjoys working as a call girl, plans to stop before long, citing the danger of AIDS and the heavy stigma. The nexus of sex and money is complicated for all these speakers.

When sex for the cameras isn't going well, both John and Sandra have to fake it, which neither enjoys. John regrets that porn directors always demand "violent," "bone-jarring" sex rather than the gentler, subtler style that comes more naturally to him. "I'm looking for what's real in life," he says—and to keep himself going on the set, he often fantasizes that he and his partner are having "real" sex, at home in his bed. Sandra's self-esteem seems closely linked to her newfound ability to turn others on, to be "an animal." Regina muses: "You're going to feel guilty, because you're accepting money for sex. I mean, *whoo*—sex is supposed to come naturally and beautifully, and all that other crap. But you say, I'll get over it."

There is, undeniably, something sad about each of these interviews. The speakers are ambivalent—but then, so is nearly everyone else in this book.

REGINA

She is not yet completely a she—but close enough. At twenty, she has been taking female hormones for ten months, and the effects are dramatic. Six feet tall, black, with high cheekbones and an impressive hair weave, she has curves that draw attention on the street. She is wearing tight bluejeans and a man's white shirt knotted at the waist, exposing the midriff. The sex-change operation will come someday, she figures: "Sooner rather than later, I hope." For now, she earns her living "on the stroll," which also supports her training as a dental hygienist. Like others in her current profession—and in the New York nightclub scene, which she adores—she prefers to be known by a single name. Her given name is Reggie.

She was born in the South and raised in Bedford-Stuyvesant. Her father left the family when she was three or four. "He played a major role in my life until I was fifteen, and then he sort of drifted away. He wanted to get on with his life. I haven't seen him for a while." Regina still lives with her mother—who works in the subway system—and two younger brothers. Her mother's attitude toward Regina's gender flip can be divined from a phone conversation when I call the apartment: "Hello, is Regina there?" "No, he isn't."

Reggie knew at age five that he was attracted to boys, "but my mother kept me so sheltered. When I got to junior high school, the kids knew more than I knew about sex, about everything. And this name-calling business started: faggot, gaylord, sissy. Kids are the cruelest monsters alive, I swear to God." A suicide attempt at fourteen helped straighten him out. "After it happened I said, What the hell am I killing myself for? Who am I satisfying? Fuck it, I want to be myself. I started not paying anyone no mind." In high school he was popular, a good student, openly gay, and sexually active. "It was mostly oral sex and touching. I always played the woman role, the passive role. I became the queen of oral sex." He also became a "club kid," something of a fixture in the disco world, and "Regina" was born as a transvestite go-go dancer. But he never felt comfortable as a gay man: there was something deeper working. "I had this fantasy person. Her name was Clarissa Strong. It started when I was nine. I always used to imagine I was her. She was beautiful. She was in movies, on shows. She was huge. She would win Oscars. That character was a big part of my life until I started becoming her. Move over, Clarissa."

. **. . .** .

Last summer I decided the go-go jobs weren't coming the way I wanted them to. I wanted more money. So I said, What can I do? I knew about Andy's. The girls were talking about making millions at Andy's as drag queens. One day I got up the courage and went there, and sure enough there were a lot of girls. They were beautiful. I was amazed. They carried themselves like women. They looked like women. There was one that just blew me away. Her name was Destiny. She was go-go dancing on the stage. Oh my God, she was incredible-looking, I thought I was going to die just looking at her. It hit me for a moment that she was real. Then I said, Wait a minute, remember where you are. No one here is real. But God, she gives the real women a run for their money.

That night I did make money. [Laughs.] Some black guy. He liked me. I went off with him. I did the deed. I said, I'm going to do this more. And then I started hanging out in the streets around Andy's. Playing the hooker thing. Turning tricks. The main thing was blowjob, blowjob, blowjob. Sucking on latex. You think of it as sucking cock, but no, it's sucking on latex. It became the easiest job in the world. I would go to a club, make an appearance, and head for Andy's at one or two. Hang out till four, five, six, depending on how I was feeling. Make some late money, come home, and be like, Oh, I made money, had fun. Perfect night.

Back then I wasn't thinking about a lot of money. I had a limit—four or five guys a night, sometimes two or three, depending on how much I got from one guy. Some guys, I'd get more, if I work it a certain way, ask them if they want anything extra. Some nights I wouldn't make anywhere near the amount I wanted. I usually wanted to make one hundred dollars, but I might end up with sixty, eighty. Other nights I'd think, Ah, I'm just gonna come out and make sixty dollars and go to a club and party, I'd end up going home with one hundred seventy-five, two hundred dollars, just from the car thing.

When I started out, I was just a drag queen. When you get the boobies, and you start looking more like a woman, that's when the men start flocking to you. In September I started doing hormones, and I took a break for four months or so. Came back out, push-up bra, hair done nicely, and the cars were lined up, honking at me. The girls were like, "You bitch, what the hell are you doing? That outfit, you always wear slutty stuff. Bitch. You're a whore." I go, "I dress like a whore, what's wrong with that?" They go, "You're gonna make money tonight, momma."

Even before the hormones, I started dressing more feminine. As a drag queen, the idea was not to look like a woman at all. The idea was to look like a creature, an accident from somewhere. I wore platinum blond wigs, G-strings. But at Andy's I would go with the real-girl look. Well, not too real. I would make it a little slutty, because I had a nice body even then. A lot of the men are into fashion. When I started learning about the fashion fetish, I went back to my wardrobe, *whoosh!* Got out all the nasty stuff. That nasty stuff made it a very comfortable summer out there. I would make a note of every little thing I found out, and go, Hmmm. Red lipstick always works. You got to wear red lipstick. High heels. Dresses, dresses, always they want dresses. Never have shorts, uch. Never G-strings. They want you to be in a dress, and have the figure for a dress. Always, always show cleavage. Never hide it. Never button your shirt up. Wear your push-up bra. They want to see outrageous boobs, outrageous bodies, and hips. They want to see hair. They want to see lips. They want to see big dangling earrings. They are very picky. They want guys, guys, guys, but they want a guy dressed up as a girl. Why they want all this other bullshit to go with it, the boobies, the makeup, the hair, I never understood. But the better I looked, the more money I made. With the hormones, forget it. I started looking like glamour-queen city.

I always talk before I get in the car. I have to ask questions. Sure, you have your Mace, your razor blade or whatever to defend yourself, but still. Nothing has ever happened to me. If I have someone who's a little crazy, a little drunk, or a little funny-acting, I handle it like a pro. Maybe a guy tells you he's got the amount you want but you don't take the money in the beginning. Then at the end he tells you he only has this much. So you learn: Take the money first. And you have to have condoms. Never say you don't have a condom. Some of the men go, "Do you do it without?" "Sorry, safe sex all the time. Bye."

A guy who doesn't know: that's a tricky situation. That happened to me once. We were driving around till I said, "You do know I'm a guy, right?" He's like, Oh God. I go, "You should avoid this area." He's like, "I didn't know, you girls look so good. But that's not what I'm looking for." Nowadays I tell them before I get in, I say, "You do know I'm a guy, right?" And the faces they make—like, "I know, c'mon. Don't act stupid." One guy told me, "Oh baby, the way you said that just turned me on. Get in the car."

It's a thrill. A big thrill. Right from the start, I got a sexual kick out of it. The money thing, that turned me on. It's like sexual freedom—they put the money in your hand, and you're free. You can do whatever you want. You don't have to go through any talking and easing into it. Like if I was with somebody, let's say, and I just met them, and they wanted to get a little intimate, and maybe I did too, I would go into it very slowly, with all this bullshit, all the talking, a little kissing. . . . On the stroll it's like [snaps fingers], you're getting paid to do something, and that gives you the freedom to do it. To be kinky. I love it. I amaze myself. It's also a control thing. I know I'm in control, because I'm the one turning them on. You get into voices, how you talk to them. And as good as I can turn them on, I can turn them off. I can control whether I'm giving them a bad time or a good time. I started realizing how powerful that is, being sexual, being passionate. That became an art. I was like, Mmmm, I like this art. I'm going to master it.

Usually we have sex in their car. Which I find a turn-on. A lot of guys go, "I want to take you to a hotel." I'm like, "What? Let's have fun here for a while." I love doing it in cars. I don't care what kind of car, just as long as it's spacious, because I'm a tall girl. The minute I get in the car, I get turned on. I would never do a guy on the street.

And I never liked hotels, I don't know why—lying on sheets that somebody else might have been on, that gets to me. Even nice hotels, I've been to the Ramada Inn, the Marriott, and I'm thinking, No no no, I don't like this hotel business. I'll do it, but I leave myself outside the door. Go in, do what you gotta do, and get out. I don't get aroused at all—at least, nowhere near the arousal I get in a car.

Sometimes if the guy is cute, you really get into him. Start thinking about him, go home saying, He was fine, he was fine. Then you say to yourself, But no, got to be a businesswoman at all times. Don't enjoy it. Wake up. He's a trick. The girls always go, Eh, he's a trick, he's a freak. The girls out there have no respect for the men, just like the men have no respect for us. It's perfect, because we both hate each other.

Actually, the scene is so small that I run into all these men again. My life became a weekend of regulars. I would go, Time to meet Dan. I felt better that it wasn't strangers. I would know about their lives, where they lived, their jobs. For some reason they had a thing about talking to me. They would tell me about their sex lives. I didn't want to know if they were married. I lose a lot more respect for a man if he's married and doing this. I start thinking, Whoa, honey, why are you messing around with a drag queen if you've got a wife and kids at home?

I know what they're looking for, that doesn't bother me. I know they're looking for girls like me—chicks with dicks. Sometimes they want to see mine, and sometimes they don't. I get more of the don'ts. But I deal with it when I have to. They'll pay me twenty-five dollars for a blowjob and then they'll want to do me on top of that. I've been known to go, "Well, baby, you only said you wanted me to do you, so if you want to do me, you got to give me a little bit more." In the beginning I was strict like that. Now, sometimes, I just go, "Sure, go ahead." And charge nothing. I don't know why, it's like I don't care anymore. I've gotten nicer. I guess I've gotten more confident about the way I look, so I'm more happy. I just lay back and go, I'm going to enjoy this. Especially if the guy is really good-looking. I just hope they're not trying to get something to happen. Some will try to do it for a long time, I'll be like this [slumps back in chair, looks bored], and they'll be, "Wait a minute, don't you like coming?" I'm like,

"No, I don't. Honey, look at me. I got fuckin' titties. I don't think I like coming too much." They just laugh.

Some of the girls like to get off. They'll come back and say, "Yeah, I came like a beast." Or, "I came so much my panties are dirty," that's a good one. But I've only come once since starting hormones, and that was in the beginning, after two months. The doctors say this isn't true, but I know when you come you get more manly. May stir up those male hormones. Maybe make hair grow on your face, or your balls look bigger. Or you start growing hair here [points to chest]. God forbid, I see one hair there and I get crazy. So when they're doing me, I enjoy it for a while, until it's fully erect. I do like the feeling of getting hard, I'm not going to lie about it. I go with the flow. But I don't want to come. I start thinking about something boring or sad. I had to master that, because I know I could come if I let the person go on and on.

Some men just want to see if I'm bigger than they are. I get a lot of guys with not too much going on down in that area, if you know what I mean. So maybe they feel funny about it, and they just want to see: God, if a queen has it bigger than mine, I'm gonna be really depressed when I go home. They see mine—I'm just average myself, even a little below. Because of hormones, I'm a lot below. And they're like, Oh, thank God. This man thing instantly comes over them again, where they start acting so macho. They'll go, "Do you want to do me?" The voice will get deeper. It's really funny.

It's also a black thing. They think because you're black that you have a big one. Then there are the faggoty types who like big ones. They say, "Are you well endowed?" They always use that word. I mean, this is ridiculous. How dare they? I just go, "Uch, go away. Go find a real guy who'll give you a real dick." I'll use my man voice to scare them. This is mostly white guys. That bugs the hell out of me. I go, "Look, I can tell you personally, not all black people have big dicks, so just drive on."

Then there are the cops. Us girls and cops, that's a book in itself. I've had four cops. The first one I saw twice. The second one I saw four, five times. The other two I just saw once. Never in uniform, they wouldn't risk that. But I had a juicy incident that happened this Saturday. This was cute. I was standing outside—I swear, I wasn't even there to do business. I'm dressed in my club outfit, not even hookerish. But this cute guy wanted me to talk to him. He was parked in a car. I looked at him, and he goes like this [makes come-hither motion]. I was like, "Let me see what this freak wants." We call them all freaks and faggots. Sometimes we tease them. They go, "I'm usually straight. I've got a girlfriend." We go, "Yeah, but does she know you're a faggot?"

I went to this guy's car and he said he wanted a blowjob. I gave him the price, which was twenty-five dollars, and I got it. So I got in. He started driving. He said, "I'm gonna find someplace to park, because I have to get back to work real soon." I was like, "Oh yeah, what do you do?" "I'm a cop." And he pulled out his walkie-talkie. "I arrest queens." I said, "I've never been caught, Jesus, I've never been caught. I've always been really, really careful." Because the cops I've dated have taught me what signs to look out for. I said, "Are you arresting me?" He said, "No. That's not why I'm here. I like the way you look, and you seem nice. I want to do business with you." I said, "You cops, you want me to do you for free, and then you're gonna take me in and make it look like we didn't do anything. Oh, you're good." He was laughing at me the whole time, saying, "I'm not gonna arrest you. I can, though, if you want. Cut it out, I'm serious." He's like, "C'mon, do you want to or not?" I said, "If not, am I gonna be let out of the car?" He said, "No, I'm gonna arrest you if you don't." I said, "Oh, you're good."

Well, this guy was passionate. He rocked my world. I was like, God, I got twenty-five dollars out of it, and he is cute. I mean he had everything. I think maybe it was his first time, because he wasn't really into it at first. Then he started getting comfortable. He played with my boobies, pulled them out of my bra. I was mostly satisfying him. I had to touch him, and then he said, "Do you kiss?" I was like, "On the lips?" He was like, "Yeah." I was like, "Why would you want to kiss me?" He's like, "Because you have really nice lips." I said okay. Cops, they all want to get a kiss, I don't know why. I don't kiss nobody, but I enjoyed kissing this guy, you better believe it. Then I sucked latex. That latex was pretty stretched. [Laughs and squeals.]

Well, when a man is well-endowed, you can't deny it. This guy was there. He was perfect. Body, everything. Hairy chest. He's gonna be on my mind for a while. And he was a cop. So exciting.

Now I mostly see regulars. I go to their house, and they take good care of me. I guess you call them, what—sugar daddies? I got two or three of those. [Laughs.] They want to see you, they'll make it worth your while. One of them is named Fred. He's such a nerd—glasses, practically balding, chubby. Late forties, early fifties, but looks older. The first night, he wanted to pay me one hundred fifty dollars to go to a hotel and kiss him and have him grind on me. I was like, Why not? As long as you can't get a disease kissing. I'll just close my eyes and picture someone else. But Fred is a good kisser. This old guy is one of the best kissers I've had. Honestly, I was shocked. After that, he started getting into me, because I was responding. I didn't just lay there and let him slobber all over me. I mean, I get excited too. He made himself sexy. So he calls me once a month, once every two months, whenever he can break free. I think he lives far away somewhere, Boston maybe.

Then there's Stanley the cocaine dealer. I see Stanley once or twice a week. He's good for one hundred, two hundred dollars a week. At first I left it one-sided, I said, "I'll call you." But I had to give him my number eventually, I've been seeing him about four months now. He's black, he treats me like the ultimate hooker. [Laughs.] He gets mad when I don't call him, like I'm leaving his house, and I say, "I'll call you when I have time." One time he slammed the door, he said, "Bitch, I'll cut your face. I'll make you un-beautiful." At first I was like this [vamping]: "Ooo, I hope you're kidding." He's like, "I'm not playing, you know how I feel about you." I think he was a little drunk. I said, "You better open the door, mister, or there will be two sliced-up faces at this apartment." He let me out. We laughed.

Stanley is usually sweet. Money-wise there's no problem. He always has it for me right there on the table. Even cab fare. When I come dressed too slutty to go out in daytime, he pulls out that extra twenty, like, "Ugh, you look good tonight. That's to get home." He gives me one hundred dollars. That's what I get for an hour, but with him I stay a long time. I sleep there. That's why he likes me. He has a VCR. He has this big huge bed with a canopy. All these African prints, and zebra skins, these little African statues. . . . I love all that shit. He always thinks about me foodwise: "Want something to eat?" Goes out, leaves me in his house alone. He doesn't fuck me over, because I don't fuck him over.

Basically what Stanley wants is someone to kiss on. At first just bodywise. Lips didn't come till later, 'cause I had a boyfriend, and I was like, "Ugh, no, I'm saving it for him." Stanley likes to see me naked. The female top, the somewhat male bottom. He likes the fact that I'm soft. The skin factor, the legs factor, the boobie factor, he likes all that. He's mostly a below-the-waist man. He likes behinds and legs, that's all he looks at. He doesn't like big boobs, so he loves mine.

In the whole four months I have known him, Stanley has never come. I have seen him every week, so we're pretty tight. He will pre-come a lot, but he will never come. I don't know why. I guess something's wrong, but he don't say nothing, and I don't say nothing. I go down on him, he loves that, but he will not come. It's sort of frustrating, but if I get tired, I just stop. All right, time's up. The first time, it was like, Hmmm, doesn't this guy want to come? Then it started occurring to me that it's not all about that. It's strange, I think he needs affection or something. Maybe that's what he's really after, somebody to be in bed with him, someone to sleep with him. I'll stay with him, he'll lie there wrapped around me really tight. He's very affectionate. Sometimes I feel for him.

I wouldn't kiss Stanley for the first couple of weeks, and then I broke up with my boyfriend. After that, one night Stanley just came at me and I didn't turn away. It took me a while to respond, but then I did. Who would have thought, me wanting to kiss Stanley? He doesn't really know how to kiss. He likes the way I kiss him because I put my all into it. I know if he's happy, he'll keep wanting to see me. And if he keeps wanting to see me, I'll keep a nice safe bank account. [Laughs.] But he doesn't know how to kiss. It's too wet. I feel like I'm being licked by a dog. I would never call him a dog, I have too much respect for the man. But there are times when I stop him. I go, "Ugh, Stanley, let me show you how."

Mostly Stanley likes rolling around, all that stuff. He likes being dramatic in bed. It's as if he's acting or something, with the sounds, the moaning. Like we're doing a soap opera scene, rolling all around, falling off the bed, acting like we're madly in love. He'll keep going till he gets tired, and then it's over. Sometimes I feel like I'm going to laugh, but I don't say anything. I'm performing up a storm. That's how it feels when I'm with every trick: showtime, time to go on. I know I'm pretty sexy, but sometimes you just work it a little bit harder. Don't do it too hard, because they'll know, but work it. I do get turned on, but hey, I still keep it in mind what I'm doing there. I can never lose track of that. Sometimes he'll say things, not in a mean way, but in a tactful way, I'll get the picture that we're still—we got to stay at that distance. We can be close, but not too close. Not that kind of close where I'll forget about asking about the money. For some reason he likes giving money to girls. He gets off on that.

At one point I thought, Maybe I should get closer and stop this business thing. Then I said, Why? It's helping me out, it's helping him out, leave it the way it is until he says something. It's not that weird to make out with him. I'm there, but I'm not there. I enjoy it, but not all of me is there. The moral part of me just seems to go somewhere else. [Laughs.] That leaves room for Mr. Devil to go, Okay, fine, give in to temptation.

There's a part of me that says I shouldn't be enjoying this. I go, Look what kind of relationship I have with Stanley. What's so great about it? What's so intimate, what's so fun about it? What's the turn-on? Then I say to myself, Don't be stupid. The turn-on is the money, of course. And just doing it. Because you know damn well you're going to get a high off it. Yeah, you're going to feel guilty, because you're accepting money for sex. I mean, *whoo*—sex is supposed to come naturally and beautifully, and all that other crap. But you say, I'll get over it. I'll have fun. That's what gets me off, knowing I'm doing something bad. *Whoosh,* the blood starts flowing, and I go, Oh, I'm alive. I'm doing something bad.

JOHN MULHOLLAND

After sixteen years of acting in porn films, "I've probably had sex with a thousand women, the majority of those in front of a camera. I've done maybe twelve hundred scenes in films, but I've worked with some women as many as forty times. So it's a guess, but I'd say six hundred or seven hundred in films, and as far as nonprofessional sex, most of my one-time partners came through swing parties. I've also been to prostitutes quite a few times. Otherwise, I haven't had that many lovers. I'm very shy, very quiet, and very slow with women. I'm not any better at getting old-fashioned dates than I was when I was thirteen."

He is thirty-eight, a slim man with a gentle manner and voice, living in a cozy house in Los Angeles. He remains close to his conservative upper-middle-class Catholic family, though he doesn't talk with them about what he does for a living. In college he studied Greek, philosophy, and theater, and since graduating he has pursued a parallel career in "straight" acting and dance—"by 'straight' I mean I don't have sex." But his tastes run to the avant-garde, and he earns little from the straight work. He has never been married. "It's hard to have a relationship when your job is going off and having sex. Some people work it out well, but for most of us it's real hard."

His sexual vocation was evident early: "I was a masturbator from birth, as far back as I remember. I've had orgasms my entire life. When I was eight or nine I started ejaculating. I thought, Oh, boy, I finally broke it. Then it kept happening, so I figured, Well, it hasn't fallen off yet, it must be okay. But I had very little sexual activity with girls. I lost my virginity the week before my twenty-second birthday, and right after that I started doing films. I saw an ad in the Berkeley Barb. *I thought the chance to be in a movie was exciting, but the main reason was to have sex. The first time I ever gave or got oral sex was in that shoot. I came into the room, met the woman, the camera was set up, and the director said, 'Okay, you guys start having sex.' "*

303

• • •

There are many more women than men in this business. For every man I've known over the years, I've known ten women. There's much more turnover among the women. Most don't last even a few months, much less years, whereas I can think of ten men who have been around as long as I have, and some have been working for twenty years. The difference is partly the social pressures on women around sexual stuff. The atmosphere is so negative that it pushes women out really fast, but it's supportive of men. I've had hundreds of guys say to me, "Gee, I wish I had your job." I don't think I've ever heard a woman say that to a porn actress. Plus this is a very, very difficult business for men. You have to function in front of cameras, in front of people, while you're saying lines. Even in a regular Hollywood movie it gets pretty stressful. Now try doing all that while you have an erection. Very few men can do it, so that's why people like me work regularly.

The people in this industry all tend to be highly sexual. A woman who doesn't like sex will not work in films for long, and the men have to be highly tuned, ready to go pretty fast. But everybody in the business has their own hit on how they work with other people. Some keep it pretty distant. I'm more comfortable with a woman when I feel like we're working as a team. I tell myself this woman is now my lover, and in a way I give her real love. I've certainly had the experience of distance, where I'm going to have sex with somebody and I don't even want to know their name, I just want to fuck. That's a strong thing, I like that, but for me it's not the best way. If I meet someone for the first time on the set, hopefully I get a few minutes to say, "Hi, my name is John," and talk a little while. Sometimes I'm comfortable with somebody right away, and sometimes I'm not going to be comfortable at all. If it's someone new in the business, that can be good, because I can say, "I know what's going on here, I'll be your mentor." It's also special the first time you work with someone, even if she's worked a hundred times before. I'll accept less money to work with someone new. It may end up badly but you never know, and that's what's exciting. Although I'd rather get them when they're new to the business, because once they've been around a while, they get into this porn thing. I'm looking for what's real in life. The more real, the better. If twenty different directors have prompted her to go, "Oh! Oh! Oh!" that may override what she's feeling even if she's enjoying the sex. I can't always tell how much is faking and how much is real.

The sex itself varies too, just like in private life—it can be either good or bad. There are many times when the director says, "Okay, we've got enough of that," and I'm unhappy we have to stop. I can protest, but that's not professional. I remember one scene with this woman—we had worked a couple of times before and had really good sex. We were in this bathroom, and she was sitting on the countertop. I'm standing there, they weren't ready for us to do anything yet, they were still tweaking the lights, the director was saying, "A minute or so, we'll be there." It was some kind of fantasy flashback, some dialogue and intercourse. I was very strongly there for her, and she was for me, so I started getting into it before they were ready. We were going at it, really frenzied, and it was a little bathroom, so the lighting guy is about this far away from my back, he's fixing the lights, and the director is over there in the corner hiding his eyes. This director has made a lot of porno movies, but he's not really comfortable with people having sex, and this was real, we weren't doing it for the camera. I thought they were a minute or thirty seconds away, but it turned out they had the wrong light, they had to do a bunch of stuff, so we're going five minutes. I'm completely crazed, I'm worried if I push her back we're gonna break the mirror because we're going at it so hard. The director even says a couple times, "Okay guys, we don't need you to do that yet, save it." But I'm not gonna stop.

So we do the scene. They only need about twenty seconds for this flashback, so I figure they're gonna shoot thirty seconds. I want to come tremendously, because I don't have any other scene that day and I'm having great sex, and the thought that I'm not gonna get to come isn't pleasant at all. I know if I have an orgasm it's going to be tremendous, so I go ahead and come in her, which is unusual. I asked her if it was okay, because when you're coming inside someone, it gets into the whole disease business. But she's pretty new, and she's multiorgasmic, she's in her sixth orgasm in four or five minutes, so she's out of control, she says something like, "Go ahead, I don't care, just keep going." If I had caught her at another moment, she might have said, "No, don't come inside me." I have to admit I took advantage of the situation. She was so crazed with lust that we could have brought in the whole crew to do her and she wouldn't have cared less. I also judged—and this is something I learned from the films. I know exactly how long it will take me to come, I mean to the second. Almost all the other guys in the business can do the same thing, it's a learned response, but it took me years. I knew I had somewhere between ten and fifteen seconds before the director was going to stop us because he wanted to reset the lights for the next shot. I wanted to have as much pleasure as I possibly could, so I went for fourteen seconds and ejaculated just as he was going to walk over and pull me off her.

Other times it's hard—for one reason or another I don't want to be there, my body and my mind are working against each other. It might be something happening on the set, the director is yelling at the woman, or she's not somebody I work with very well. Fortunately it doesn't happen too often. When it does, I get myself into a fantasy place. I have so many different fantasies, everything from violent stuff to sweet, tender "I-love-you-my-princess" stuff. Just yesterday I did this scene with a woman I have strong feelings for—I wish she was my lover, actually, but she's married. Her husband was there watching the scene, very supportive, I like him very much. If I didn't like him so much I'd probably run him over with a truck and steal his wife. The scene was set up in an alley—not a real alley, in a studio. I'm having sex with these two women, and this other couple comes along and starts having sex in the same place. In the first part of the scene, I was kissing this woman and the other woman was down on her knees giving me head. What was arousing was not the woman giving me head, but holding this woman in my arms and kissing her very intensely. That's what got me up. Then later on I was fucking her on a car seat inside this abandoned car. We'd been having sex for ten minutes very powerfully, and she had two orgasms so she was calming down but we were still at it. She was on her knees leaning over this car seat, and I was behind her. I knew we were getting to the part where I was going to have to come fairly soon, but I wasn't quite there with her. I was tiring, I could feel a hint of a not-quite-strong erection. I needed to refocus—that's a word you hear a lot from guys in the business, *focus*. So I put myself in a different place. I fantasized that we were at home in my bed, and she was on her back with her legs spread and I was pounding into her. That's a very strong image for me, and *boom,* I was charging up the hill again. I did the come shot on her ass, although I tried to talk the director into letting me do the missionary position. He didn't need that much footage, he said, "Well, if you really need to do that position to come, I'll let you do it." I said, "No, it's okay, I'll suffer."

Sometimes if I'm having trouble, the only thing that works is a gang-rape fantasy. I've talked to some women about that, but I'm hesitant because there are so many political negatives about the violence. Plus at a personal level it's funny, telling somebody, "Gee, it was really nice raping you." On the other hand, a lot of women have the same fantasy. I've been told, "Well, I couldn't quite come to orgasm, but I pretended you were number six in a long line of guys, and I came like crazy." This woman yesterday joked about it afterward—I said something about the speed and the strength of it, and she said, "Why didn't you fuck me harder?" I mean, it was pretty hard, our pelvises were like this [slaps hands together rapidly]. But her feeling was—More, more, I want it harder.

On the set, I'm constantly being pushed, prodded, groomed, patted on the head for being very powerful and very high-energy, making lots of noise, moving fast, doing unusual positions. Men and women both are expected to be loud and fuck violently and fast and big and broad. The industry presents a very skewed version of sex. The directors, the producers, the distributors, the theater owners, they're all saying, This is what we want. So the actors don't get much chance to go any other direction. Partly it's the people who are drawn to the industry—a lot of them are involved in S/M stuff. I'm not myself, but a huge number are. It's also in the nature of cameras and micro-

phones. A camera is not a human eye. It's a limited device. When two
people make love intensely, totally tuned in, moving slowly and whispering, that may be tremendously exciting but the camera doesn't get
it. The camera makes demands, and because of that the directors
make demands. "I can't hear anything, I can't see any movement, is
anything happening?"

I tend to deal with women in a light and gentle way, that's my
style. I've worked to do that in films, even though I know it doesn't
go over very well. It's been a battle ever since I got into the industry,
all sixteen years. When I first got in and saw a couple of the men, I
thought, This is harsh, this is angry, this is hateful, I don't want to do
what these guys are doing. But I run the risk of doing the sensitive
male thing, and then I hear about it from reviewers, or people make
jokes. Part of it is that I'm shy and quiet and not very outgoing, and
the camera can see that even if I'm not aware of it. But some stuff I
am aware of. For years I had people make fun of me—they still make
fun of me—for smiling during sex, or after an orgasm. These people
think sex should be a nasty, dirty, grungy thing, like, Yeah, fuck the
bitch. These are women as well as men. But I think there's a tremendous range in sex. So I'll smile, because this is making me happy, so
why not show that? Or I might gently kiss up and down a woman's
legs. Some directors say, "I'll let you do that for a couple of minutes,
but only if you tie her up. Or if she's begging you to fuck her." Then
it's teasing, so that's okay.

Most of the time, the expectation is so much for violent sex that
if you're not doing that, you get self-conscious, and you think, Jeez,
maybe this isn't going well. But sometimes it works out and everybody on the set gets real quiet. I did a scene last year that even got
good reviews. I was sure they'd give us horrible reviews, like, Oh,
God, namby-pamby sex again. It was an actress I've worked with a
lot, and this was the best sex we've ever had. We had a good feeling
that day, I hadn't seen her for a year, and we talked a lot before the
scene. When we started it was like two dancers doing a slow dance.
I had an erection for the whole half hour of the shoot, and the cameraman did everything handheld, he moved with us and we moved
with him. It was like three people having sex, really. I don't think I

ever moved fast, but there was moaning and groaning, I was constantly at the point of orgasm, she had several orgasms, it was wonderful sex but it was slow and relaxed and easy, and I never got tired. Whereas at the end of a lot of scenes I can be exhausted, drenched, a pool of sweat at my feet, and my stomach muscles hurt and my back's sore and my arms are aching because I've literally been holding the woman up.

When I started in the business, I'd have what seemed to me powerful sex—it was fast, it was athletic, unusual positions—but it wasn't this pounding, screeching, this-is-the-last-thing-we-do-before-we-die kind of thing. I had to learn to become more high-energy—and that's nice, it's very arousing. Probably the most emotional sex I've ever had has been the intense, violent kind, where I'm pounding in and out with all my strength. I get pretty badly bruised sometimes. I had to find that within me, and it's something I learned from the work. I bring it to my private life, too. The women I have loved most in my life, the ones where I've considered marriage, I had that kind of sex with. I had one girlfriend where we actually played with rape fantasies. She had been raped in real life, so there was a lot of stuff there. Over a couple of years it came out that she wanted to be violently dominated. Sometimes she would even start an argument, and it took me a long time to understand that she was saying, I want a certain kind of sex. She couldn't say it directly. She'd stir up a fight out of nowhere, and it was confusing, because I didn't want to make a mistake and say, Oh, she's being irrational, it means she wants me to rough her up sexually. But I was usually on the mark. I'd grab her roughly and say, "I've had enough of this, I'm going to fuck you now. You need a good fucking. I'm gonna use you." And she'd go, "No, no, stop it, don't do this, don't you dare." Now, this woman was a dancer and a martial arts expert, she was in really good condition and probably could take me out. I don't think I ever bruised her or hurt her, but it was a fine line. It would end in a very powerful orgasm for me, and it was a bit frightening, because here I am raping the woman I love. But greater love came out of it.

I have to be careful with this stuff for lots of reasons—personally, emotionally, even politically. I want to be as clear as I can and not do what I feel a lot of people in the industry do, which is they have this kind of sex with blinders on. It's automatic, and pretty soon you up the ante and you can only find fulfillment in whips and chains. I want to make sure I don't get stuck in one style.

For example, my way of getting turned on during a shoot—a lot of guys like to be given head. I'm fifty-fifty on that. What I like is to nibble at the woman's ear and lick around her neck and kiss her cheek and touch the back of her neck and play with her hair while she's stroking my cock with her hands. I can stroke myself, but I much prefer if she's doing it because I like to have my hands free to fondle and caress her and hold her in my arms. If a woman gets down on her knees and gives me head, it might take her twenty minutes. But I will get an erection quickly if I can kiss her neck and ears. It's a romance thing, like I'm making love to her. I don't know any other man in the business who likes that. I've talked to women who say, "Oh yeah—so-and-so likes to have his nipples tweaked, and you like to kiss my neck." They make fun of me, but for most of them it's nice. If a woman has a choice between somebody who's gonna nibble at her ear and somebody who requires a forty-five minute blowjob, she's probably gonna choose the nibbler. So the women reward me, even if the reviewers and the directors don't. It means a lot to me that women in the business trust me and respect me and know that I'll treat them nicely. They always say, "Thanks, that was really nice." I've never had a woman say, "Jeez, that felt bad," or "You hurt me." Whereas I've heard women talk about certain other guys and say, "That was awful, I felt degraded."

What's hard in my private life sometimes is letting go of control. I make my living by having intense sex with a beautiful woman whose job is to get me off. It's not her job to have an orgasm. Well, it is, but the camera doesn't read it as well, and she can fake it. I can't fake it, and her job is to help me ejaculate. In some sense, having an orgasm at the right time is what I'm known for. So I'll never get back what I had when I was younger, that explosive excitement—gee, look what happened, I came! I can't conceive of coming just because I'm so excited I can't stop it. Psychologically I can let go as well as I ever did, but not physically. I've learned too well to have it under control.

What I don't have any control over is intensity level. I can't control whether it'll be great sex or okay sex—that's in the nature of the relationship and the moment. But I do know how to have an orgasm, and I can control when. Sometimes that feels like too much control, and it's kind of depressing. Like I hold off coming, and when I finally get around to it, I've lost the edge. If I'd just let myself come in the first twenty seconds I would have had a stupendous orgasm, but I thought, Well, gee, I can have intercourse for three hours if I don't come now. Okay, three hours later I've had three hours of good sex, but I never get past good. Even when I come it's just good. Maybe it would have been better to have twenty seconds of awe-inspiring, seeing-God type sex.

I've been asked so many times, Don't you get jaded? Well, I've seen many people drop out of the business, men and women—they can still perform sexually, but it's not what it was. It's like, Ho-hum, sex again. That hardly ever happens with me. Never in private life, and not that often in the films. Like yesterday, that shoot I mentioned—I had this second scene with a woman I've worked with many times. I had known her for a couple of years and never worked with her, and suddenly we're working twice a week for the last month or so. She wasn't the one I was really hot for yesterday, she was the one giving me head while I was kissing the other one. Well, I had to go into a full sex scene with this one right afterward. It was the last scene of the day. I had already come. We're by ourselves, and we've had sex a lot recently, so it's like, Well, yeah, this is good, but it's not what it could be. Certainly not what it was the first couple times we had sex. It took a while for me to come. I had to be happy about the position I was in, and how comfortable I was, all these little things. It was mostly just okay. But it varied within the scene—there were a couple moments of bone-jarring, wild lust. At one point we were in missionary position on this couch, and she was letting me know that it was feeling good now, because it took a few minutes for her to relax into the thing. She gave me a couple of cute little looks, and then we're an inch away from each other and I don't even know where the camera is, maybe behind low, getting crotch shots, or maybe wide-body shots, but we're really close and we're intensely looking into each other's eyes, and I'm kissing her and nibbling at her. I'm thinking, This is full-out sex now, this is sex the way I like it. There was a little fantasy going on as well—like, she and I are having sex for real, not for the cameras, we're not getting paid to do this. So it went from so-so to good and back to so-so, up and down with the level of excitement.

On the other hand, some days I do three scenes, and I'm like, Jeez, can I have a fourth?

SANDRA MARQUEZ

We're in a two-bedroom apartment on the second floor of a house near the beach in Venice, California. In the living room, a boy and girl, perhaps six and eight, take a moment out from watching TV to study the stranger. I greet their mother as "Gloria," her nom de porn, the only name I know her by at this point. Her husband, Andy, a smallish, stocky man with a deep tan, whispers to me that I shouldn't use that name around the house, because the kids have never heard it. Sandra and I repair to the bedroom for the interview, and the kids check in periodically to see what's happening. A surfboard leans in the corner; on the wall is a large black-and-white photo of her nude, face down on a bed, her back arched.

She is twenty-eight, a slim, dark-skinned, animated woman wearing short shorts and a halter top. She was born in Bakersfield—her parents were Colombian immigrants—and she grew up poor after her father left the family when she was ten. Even before that, her childhood was rough: "My father was always mean to us. I hate him. He spanked me, he humiliated me. He'd treat us like we were animals or something." She was also raped by a male baby-sitter when she was about six, and sexually abused by a female baby-sitter when she was seven or eight. "Probably more things happened to me that I don't even remember, because I was a really pretty little girl and I developed quickly. Around seven or eight everybody started trying to do sexual things to me, and some succeeded of course. And then after my father left, my mom had this big house with a lot of rooms and people would stay there. All these lowlifes were living in the house, and they would perform sex out in the open—in the bathroom, the living room, you name it. It was disgusting—first of all I get raped, and then my mom tells me sex is bad, and it isn't right for a lady to have sex with lots of men. I basically thought sex was awful."

She started dating Andy in high school, first had sex with him when she was fifteen, and married him when she graduated. He was two years older and in the army. "He taught me a lot. How to be responsible, be

313

more sociable, travel—I grew up with him." Before they married she
"played around with a few guys" when he was away on duty, but since
then she has been monogamous—until recently.

· · ·

When Andy would go to a field problem in the army I'd be left
maybe a week to a month, sometimes three months. That's when I
started getting into masturbation, because—one thing I must say
about myself, I've never liked to make a fool out of anybody. He's my
husband and he's in the army. A lot of women fool around when their
husbands are gone, bring guys into the house, screw in front of the
kids. I don't think that's cool at all. So I masturbated. Got a dildo and
used that. When he came back we'd have sex, but I'd always have the
lights off. I wasn't too proud of my body. When I was a teenager I
had this great chest, but after my babies my breasts just went *pfoo,*
because I breast-fed. And my stomach's sort of flabby on the bottom
because of the babies. So I preferred to be in the dark. I wasn't open.
He would get sex, but I wouldn't do nothing, I would just be there.
Then Andy would talk to other girls and I'd be jealous.

When he got out of the army, we moved here. He was working as
a trucker and I was a waitress. I started hanging out with this one
waiter guy. I was feeling attracted, and I thought, Oh my God, I can't
feel this way, I'm married, this is horrible. It went on for a long time,
I'd hang out at this guy's place after work, and one time I fell asleep
in his bed and woke up and we started kissing and stuff. About a
week later I drank a whole bottle of wine and I told Andy, "You
know what? I got to tell you something." Then I tell him and I say,
"What'd you think about an open relationship?" He says no and he
walks away. Five minutes later he comes back and says, "Open relationship?" I say, "Yeah, you see other people, I see other people.
That way we can do everything in the open. No one is cheating. But
if you don't want that, no problem, we won't do it." He decided it
was a good idea. I guess he thought, Maybe it'll open Sandra up.
Maybe it'll help our relationship, get that jealousy out.

The rule is, if a person gets too attached, we have to let go of that person. They have to know right in the open that you're married and you just want to have a good time. Like I went out with this one guy, really nice, good sex and everything, but he got attached and I had to say bye. The other rule is, Let me know where you are. If you're going to stay out late, let me know. If you want to go somewhere for two or three days, let me know. At the time, I told him, "I don't really want to know what you do with the girls," because I still had jealousy in me. Now I can ask, "So what did you do?"

Right around that time I did a couple videos, amateur ones. I needed the money, my car broke down and I needed a thousand dollars. This guy said he'd give Andy and me some money, and we decided it would be good for our bills, so okay, we did it. I was terrified. The guy wanted to see me dance and do a masturbation thing and have sex with Andy. To me that was too much, like, This guy is gonna see me do all this? No way. So I drank, I got real tipsy, and we did it and it was fun, and I couldn't believe I got paid for having so much fun. Then the guy said if I wanted to do another video it would be a gangbang. I said okay. It was a story where my husband tells me, "I have a surprise for you," and three guys show up. I had to get real tipsy to do that one, too. It kind of turned me on—I'm always hesitant to do anything before, and afterward I like the feeling. But still I told Andy I didn't want to do it anymore, 'cause I wasn't ready for being with other people. Not the kind of people they chose for me.

Around the same time, I started dancing. I had this waitress friend, she told me she's gonna get big boobs and try dancing because she's gonna be a doctor and she needs to save money. I decided to try it, too. I started off as a go-go dancer, then two days later I started as a topless dancer, four weeks later I started as a nude dancer, and since then I've been dancing at the same club, and that was a year ago.

From that I got more opened, because you're nude, you have to have some sexuality in you. There's no way you can go in there and take your clothes off and not have anything, 'cause you're not gonna make a lot of money. And that's when I started meeting girls who were bisexual. I was like, Oh my God. I met this one girl Zoe, that's her stage name, she always looked at me, made advances on me. I asked her why she liked girls, I said, "Is it because men are assholes or something?" She's like, "No, I just like doing girls." Okay, great.

She'd follow me around, like when I was table-dancing with customers, and she'd stick out her tongue at me, and I didn't want to make her feel like an idiot, so I stuck mine out with my eyes closed, and wow. We played around in front of these guys to blow them away. But I was blown away, too. I was thinking to myself, Oh my God, I'm kissing this girl in front of these men. I was like a little girl growing up.

Finally I had a threesome with Andy and this other girl I met at a gay club, and then we did it with Zoe, and we had some foursomes, and I was like, Wow, I'm bisexual, it's beautiful and I'm not ashamed. So after having all these sexual activities with girls and foursomes and swing clubs, I was ready to do another video. I called up this guy I knew, and that's when I did my first feature. I had a blast. This was about six months ago. Now I've done over a dozen amateurs and four features. That's what I'm aiming for, the feature ones, 'cause you get a screen credit, and you can get box covers, which is great. If you get a box cover, when you go on tour dancing they can say you're a porn star, and your rates go higher, it's beautiful.

In amateur videos you can get any kind of guy, they can be really unattractive. But amateur is easier—go ahead, have sex. In features you have dialogue, you have to act, you have to lie, it's faking everything. Like say a guy is doing anal, he'll stick it in for a minute or two, then he comes out and he's pretending to do it so they can do other shots. And you have to fake it, that it feels good. You're acting the part, and you get paid well. In a feature there's a story—it's like, Here's your script, and professionals are doing your hair, you have to dress the part of the character. And it's "Cut!" "Cut!" "Cut!" until they get it right. You have to stop and go.

My first feature was on this boat, we went to Catalina. I didn't know anybody and I was kind of scared and at the same time excited. The people were good-looking and they turned me on, and I met this guy who really intrigued me. His name is Bram, he's an actor, and since that boat scene we still do each other whenever we can. He lives in San Francisco. He sounded intelligent, like he has things going, and we talked and talked, and eventually I thought, Well, if I'm going to have sex with someone, I might as well do it with someone I like, right? He asked me if I wanted to go downstairs to the room and talk some more. I knew that meant sex, 'cause the cameramen were wandering around trying to get action. So I said okay and we were about to do our scene, but Bram looked like he was about to throw up. I said, "Go throw up, don't throw up on me!" That made us get closer a little, and he started feeling better, so we had sex outside on the boat with the cameraman videotaping us.

Usually I don't think about the cameraman, only when he needs angles, like the shot of the girl's pussy or the dick going inside her, and they want you in a certain position, and you can't move as much because the camera is right there. That turns me off 'cause you're not being yourself, you're being plastic. They want you to—"Okay, this way. Stop. Stay there. Now move." Well, come on. But that's what the viewers want, I suppose. And they prefer the women to be real loud, real vocal, screaming. Now, if the guy's doing me well, yeah, I'll be verbal. But sometimes in features, 'cause it's so stop-start, you get into it and they go "Cut!" It's hard. I'm like, okay, got to be verbal, verbal, verbal. But it's not really me.

Other times—like I did an amateur two weeks ago with a girl and a guy. The girl was really into girls, which is cool. If you get with a girl and you can tell she's just getting paid for it, you don't know what to do with her 'cause she might not like it or freak out. Since this girl likes girls, I could do whatever I wanted. I love pleasing people. So toward the end, she was lying down on the floor and I was on top of her like doggie-style, squatting over her, kissing her, and he was doing me from behind, which was really good. Then after he came, she and I rolled over, and we're still making out, and the cameras are still going, and the cameraman got a lot of footage, and he said okay, and we were still going at it, just attacking each other. It was great, really great. We just kept going. I don't know why he didn't keep shooting.

In that kind of scene I completely forget the camera. I'm like an animal when I make love. I move a lot. I'm very energetic. If I'm into it and you turn me on and this is the first time I've done you, forget it. It's gonna last forever. It's gonna be until next morning. I'm very sexual, I think because in my early age I was so inhibited and I thought sex was so bad. It's coming out now. Even the cameramen, the crew—when they're stopping for something, to set up a light, you start to talk to them and that turns you on, because they're looking at you all naked, and you're like, Cool. They're getting turned on so it's a good feeling. At first they're just strangers, but when you get to know them you start thinking, I like this guy and now he's gonna see me having sex. Then you perform more 'cause they're like, Wow, she's hot. You know they want you.

If the sex isn't good, I'm like, Oh my God, I'm being videotaped and I'm not doing my best here, and I'm not looking sexual, I'm gonna get bad reviews. Then I become a robot. But even when it's good, it's different from having sex at home. You're with this person, he's gonna make love to you, and you have to play the part where you're gonna enjoy it. You're not gonna do what you'd normally do. Like kissing. There's not a lot of kissing on videos. And if the person kisses you and you don't like the way they kiss, that's a turn-off already. In my private life, when the guy turns me on, God, we're gonna make out. I feel that's something sacred, when I kiss someone, I put passion into it. Then when you do each other it's even more exciting. I think foreplay is better than the intercourse itself. But if I'm doing a video, I don't miss the kissing or the foreplay. It's just a video, I'm gonna get paid anyways. I'm doing my best. If the guy doesn't want to play with my tits, no problem. If he isn't making me feel good, if his dick is inside me and I'm not feeling anything, I'll play with my clitoris and make myself get off so I can look good. I've learned to do that in my personal life. You know something funny? I've been masturbating a long time, but I never played with my clitoris. It's weird to say that, but I got off in other ways. Now I realize, God, I know how to turn myself on even more. I learned that from films. I did a feature with two girls and a guy, and the girl kept playing with my clitoris as he was fucking me, and I flew. I was like, "Yes!" They were telling me, "You're an animal," and I'm like, "Thank you."

I've really become—what do they call those people who like to show their bodies? Exhibitionists. I could have sex right there—say if I was turned on with Andy, and you're watching TV with your wife, I'd do it right there in the room. One time I was with Bram at the porn convention in Vegas. We got together with this couple, and we thought we were going to switch off, but it didn't happen. That was okay, 'cause we hadn't seen each other for a while and he'd been wanting to do me all through the day. We were in this hotel room with two beds, so he took his clothes off, and I took my clothes off, and we were just doing each other. The couple, they were doing each other on the other bed, but they stopped, and we kept going like nobody was around. These people were kind of freaked out, but in a nice way, like "Go ahead, it's better than video." First they were watching, and then they played gin rummy, and they started cracking jokes. I'm trying to get into the jokes, but I can't, I'm like, "How about when I finish?" We kept going and it was great, Bram came and came. He came five times in two and a half hours. The first time he just spit it out when he was behind me. We were screwing for about forty-five minutes in different positions so it was time for him to come. He came all over my back, and then he cleaned up. Then he started back on me, except I was on my back this time. No problem, he comes on my stomach. Then back to doggie position, he came once, and then he came again, *boom!* He was hard the whole time. I came a lot of times, couldn't really count. I just kept coming and coming, and he kept coming, and I'm like, Okay!

I'm more sexual now with Andy, too. It's like—say I have a date with a guy, and I'm with him all night, and then I come home the next morning, I attack Andy because I'm turned on even more. I'm more happy and more loving and more playful and I tease him and have even better sex with him. I tell him my stories while we're having sex, what I did, and he gets off on the stories, he's like, "Oh God, really?" I'm like "Yeah, and then he did this and did that." He's like, "Ohhh," and he comes. I'm more intimate with him, especially when I'm with girls. If Andy and I have a threesome with a girl, and then we get together one-on-one, I start touching him like I'd touch a girl, softly and gentle and timid. It makes him feel something different from just doing each other. Like with girls, starting from their toes to their thighs and stomach and their breasts and neck, the way I kiss them and the way they kiss me—it's like we're exchanging our feelings. When you have sex with a guy you don't do a lot of touching, it's basically just getting wild, screwing hard. I like both, I like to be soft and I like to be wild.

I'm not used to people catering to me, even if it's in sex. If a guy's giving me head, I feel I have to do something for him, I have to give

him a blowjob or something. If a girl is giving me oral sex, I feel I
have to eat her out, do something to make her feel good, so she can
be aroused and amazed by me. It's like a power thing where they're
just melting on your feet. You could tell them, Bark like a dog, and
they'd bark. But I'm always thinking, Is this person okay? I can't lie
there and relax and not even care if they're feeling good. When I get
into my animal state, I'm after them, I'm attacking them, I'm like a
lion.

Like just last Friday we were at a swing club, and I took over the
scene. Okay, these are all open-minded people, that's why we're
there. And once you make your little clique at the club, the ones you
feel comfortable with, you get invited to their room and you have a
few couples there. We met this one couple through the phone, 'cause
they wanted to do videos. They said they'd meet us in the club and
we could talk more business. The girl was really good-looking. Her
husband was good-looking. The other couples were young. And I
went off. I did everybody. I started off with her, 'cause she wanted to
do us. She came up between Andy and me in the room, and she laid
her head on my lap and her body on Andy's lap, and I attacked her.
We did everything possible. She came. Everybody was just staring at
us and I was getting turned on by that. She said, "No more, honey,
I'm really tired now." No problem, there are more people to get to.
She fired me up. I attacked this other couple. Gave this guy a
blowjob, played with his girlfriend. Then *boom,* I went to this girl
over here with her husband. Attacked her. We're sixty-nineing each
other, I'm on the bottom with her on top of me, and he starts going
inside his wife, so I'm licking him and licking his balls while he's
doing her. They're like, "Uhh! Uhh!" and I'm having a great time,
buried underneath. The guy gets off, I come up, and Andy comes
over to me and says, "You know what? Why don't you do Julie's husband?" Julie was the girl I started with, she wanted me to do her husband 'cause he's real shy. I was having a good time in my little crowd
there, I'm like, "Not right now." Andy's like, "C'mon, OK?" So I
went up to the guy and started making out with him. I'm stripping off
his clothes, giving him a blowjob. I put him down on the bed and sat
on him, I was pulling his hair, then I turned over and he was doing
me doggie-style, pounding me. He was the only one that did me. And

I'm thinking, Look at these people, they're getting so turned on. I had it all covered, the way I looked, the way I performed, I was witty—and they all wanted me. I knew it. I was making myself available to the people who wanted me, that was my duty for the night. And my husband watching me, he could not believe what he was seeing.

I woke up in the morning dying 'cause I had a hangover. Some of us spent the night in a hotel, all tangled up on the beds. The people were so pleasant, babying me, "You want an aspirin?" We went out for breakfast, and this one guy, all he did was talk about me, "You're incredible, you're wild, you're wicked, such a little girl with so much energy"—they're all tall, so I'm considered a little girl, plus I look really young. They kept telling me it was amazing how I kept going and kept everybody active. They were all impressed. It felt real good.

So I think being sexual has made me stronger mentally. I don't feel guilty anymore. I can do whatever I want, no one is going to make me feel horrible. I'm more sociable. I'm not alone. I get a lot of business in videos or dancing, and I'm invited to parties. All that helps my mentality. When I was growing up, my mom and her stupid friends would say, You're a whore, you're a bitch, you're a loser, you'll never amount to nothing—'cause I was always doing bad in school. But now I'm like in my second life, where everybody's like, She's beautiful, she's wonderful. Sometimes I can't believe it, 'cause it's always been in my mind that I'm a lowlife. That I would be one of the bums in Bakersfield, one of those girls who would have a drunk husband or be an abused wife. Now they see I live in Venice, and I don't need anybody.

And all this has happened in a year and a half. It seems like forever, but it's just a year and a half!

CLAUDIA MERCURIO

She works in Boston, out of a small, sparsely furnished Beacon Hill apartment with a view of the Charles. I sit on a chair, she on the bed. She is twenty-four, dark-haired, big-boned, and friendly, though there is something contained about her: she is not looking to please. A few months before our talk, she dropped out of a PhD program in Chinese literature—"It wasn't the right program for me, which was too bad since I've always loved school. It was an old-boy network committed to producing research profs who'll turn out monographs. That's not a living, breathing profession. So I just left." She has been doing sex work for three years, on and off; at present she earns a decent living doing "in-calls"—seeing clients at her place—for two hundred dollars an hour.

She grew up in the suburbs; her father was a computer engineer, her mother a nurse. "My father is an overbearing, loud, angry, alcoholic man, and my mother has never been happy being in this world. Totally negative about sex. Twice, when I was between the ages of eleven and fourteen, she told me that sex is always damaging or destructive or painful—I don't remember the exact words—for at least one person involved, and that person is almost inevitably the woman. I also hated my body. I got most of that from her, and from my father, too. Ever since I was little he told me I was ugly. He'd tease me about my nose. I remember one time telling him I was interested in being a journalist, and he got real sarcastic: 'Oh, yeah, with a face like yours, you could definitely be on TV.' "

From an early age she has been bisexual; her first great romance was with a girl in high school, but through college she mostly slept with men. After graduating she moved into the city. "What I wanted to do was become a cocktail waitress, a sex worker, and do volunteer work. Within a couple of months I was doing all three, so I was very happy. Becoming a stripper was the best thing I've ever done. I felt like I was home. I came out of this environment where I felt so negative about my body, and sex, and relations between men and women, and after five weeks of stripping

I had more hours than anyone. It was like, I can do this, and I can be good at it, and I don't have to have a perfect nose, and be blond, and have big tits. I was letting all that shit go."

• • •

I knew at the age of eleven that I was going to be a whore. I have diaries from then, I was writing about my mother and saying, "I don't know what she's going to say when she finds out I'm selling my body for money." It was like, I can do anything I want, anything. If I want to be a whore, that's what I'm going to do, and my mother's not going to tell me not to. I found these writings later, when I was actually working as a prostitute. I was surprised.

I did stripping for about eight months, then I went on a four-month trip to South America. Came back, went back to stripping, and started doing out-call domination work with a friend of mine. We did that for about three months and I was asked by another friend if I wanted to do doubles prostitution, and I thought, Well, hell, the time is now. So I started doing doubles with her. I was still stripping. It became clear to me that I needed to live alone, and that prostitution was something I could do to support myself, so I moved into my own apartment. Eventually I stopped stripping, continued doing prostitution, making money. I plan to do it for another year or two until I put some money away, enough to support myself for three or four months while I look for other work, so I can get out of the business.

Why do you want to get out?

Well, there's three things I contend with every day. The first one is disease. I put myself in danger every time I do a call, 'cause I don't know what's going to happen. If it were just venereal disease I wouldn't be anywhere near as nuts about it. But I'm afraid of AIDS, and I don't like the fact that there are boys out there who don't respect my life, who would be willing to put me in danger, for a trick. I think that's really dumb, I hate that. A couple of months ago I had this guy who fucked me from behind and slipped off the condom and came inside of me. That was the most damaging experience I've had.

I stopped working for about three weeks because of the way he fucked with me.

The second thing is the stigma. I get tired of explaining myself all the time. I meet people and think they're nice and they probably wouldn't have a problem with me being a prostitute, but I'd have to explain it to them: Yeah, I like my work, blah blah blah. If I said I was a graphic designer, people would go, "Oh, that's cool," and shut up. But with this I gotta tell what the life is like, and it gets old. Also not being able to tell my parents, I hate that.

The third thing is the feeling that I can't do this forever. These are my years when I'm supposed to be working toward a career. That's ingrained in me. The way I rationalize it is by saving money. I make a lot more money now than I would be able to do otherwise, so I can do this for a while and put aside money and then go work at a career.

For the most part the work itself is fine. I mean, it's a pain in the ass dealing with the public. The hardest thing is answering the phone and setting up appointments with people who don't show up. I present myself as a professional and I act in a professional manner, and men who are soliciting my services are willing to waste my time. But let's say the guy shows up. Then it could go one of two ways. The experienced guys generally strip down, and they undress me, and we either fuck right away or they hang out and ask me about my life. Then there are the guys who don't know how to behave: Do I take my clothes off first? Does she take her clothes off, or do I take her clothes off? Okay, I'll just sit over here by the window. . . . Those are the ones where I'm like, "Nice view, huh? So what do you do?" I'll sit over here at a nonthreatening distance, and finally I say, "Would you like to come sit a little closer? Is there something particular you'd like? Can I give you a massage, or would you like me to undress for you?" However I read it, I go with it.

Everybody needs someplace they can go and be catered to. When the men come in, I try to be genuinely pleasant. Not like a little geisha girl, but at the lowest common denominator—you're a human being, and I'm about to see you naked, and I'm about to see you in a sexual space, which for many people is vulnerable, and I would like it to be a pleasant experience for you, and not just a hot orgasm. The orgasm is part of it, but I try to say, Hey, I'm happy you're here. I can't do that with all my clients. Some come in and I'm like, Wow, I'm going to be really happy when this is over. Either the chemistry's not there, or they're not aware of my feelings or what feels good to me, so they blunder around. Even with them, it's not like, Oh my God, this guy is such an asshole. It's more like, This guy doesn't know how to turn me on and that's too bad, but I don't hate him, I just want him out of here, off my body, I need him to go now.

The fucks are so standard it's not even funny. I mean, not to be totally horrible, but it's the one-night-stand fuck, the trick fuck—a little bit of smooching, or not, a little bit of breast worship, a little bit of groping between the legs, a little oral sex, and then fucking, usually with me on top. Ninety percent of the time I start out on top, I don't know why, guys just like it. Could be for visual reasons, or their partners aren't comfortable with being on top, or they just want to lie back and be fucked. For the most part guys finish either missionary style, or I finish them off orally.

There's a whole other group of guys, I'd say about forty or fifty percent are either impotent or not able to get off in any other way than masturbating. I really enjoy them, they tend to be the most fun. The sex tends to be more creative. They tend to be more sensuous, more into pleasing me. I'm not servicing their rock-hard cock. I may do that some, but I don't have to do it in a way to get them off, because I'm not going to be able to get them off and they know it. I get a warmer sense from it. It's more about having someone there while they pleasure themselves, rather than having a piece of meat to stick their cock into until they come. And these men tend to be older, in their fifties or sixties, so they're not into impressing me. They're looking for somebody sweet and attentive, and I'm happy to do that.

The kind of client I dislike the most, the most difficult energy-wise, is the kind that needs to prove what a great lover he is. He's going to spend fifty minutes of his hour attempting to either eat me or fuck me into the ground. I'm like, You know, dude, I get myself off in ways you probably can't even imagine. To these guys, vibrators are anathema, and the idea of fisting, or being fisted—what's that? They're not interested in expanding their minds. They're like, Well, these are the three standard porn-film ways to fuck, and I'm gonna do that till my hour's up. These clients tend to be younger, thirties and early forties, they want to live out a porno film, and I'm the will-ing, attractive female to do it with. I want to say, Oh, man, you're not really having that much fun with this, I certainly am not having much fun—couldn't we do something else? I would rather deal with men who want to get done. I like being a wet dream, that's really hot. I say, "Lie on your back. I'm gonna talk dirty in your ear. I'm gonna play with your cock, and I'll do it really slow and sensuous. I'm gonna use my mouth. I'm gonna fuck you." It's like, I'm going to be the sexy woman that you wish all women were.

On the other hand, getting done does not feel good to me. I only have one or two clients who even get close. Part of it's just a bound-ary. I don't like having clients make me come. I had this one guy for a while—I couldn't see him anymore, because he could make me come like clockwork. I mean, he was frightening. I felt bad about it for a while, I had some kind of guilt about it, like, Why don't you want to see this guy even though he makes you come? It's okay for you to come. But another part of me was like, No, I don't want it from him. It's fine for me to be aroused, but I don't want to come. After I come I tend to be tired, I'm not as interested in fucking, and professionally I have to keep up the same level of intensity to get this guy off. So that's not a good place to be in. I'm also not thrilled with perfect strangers having the key to the way I tick. My orgasm is not something I want to spread around. It's not for sale. When I do a trick, my job is to pleasure my client. It can turn me on, it helps if it's hot, but shifting the focus from his pleasure to my pleasure makes it a lot more work. And when I orgasm—I come very easily, but after I come I feel very open emotionally. There's a fragility around it, and I don't want blind strangers smashing around.

I will not only fake orgasms, I will hide my orgasms. I've always thought of this work as a kind of aikido. Aikido is a defensive martial art, it's not aggressive. It comes from the stance of taking another per-son's energy when they come at you, and moving it away. Deflecting energy. You can come at me full force, and that's fine, I'm going to put that energy right where I want it. You get what you need, but you're not getting at the center of me.

It's all about being in control. If I were not in control, guys would come in here and do whatever they wanted, and there's nothing like that in what I do. A guy comes in, we take our clothes off, he starts touching my body, and I am in perfect control. I spend a lot of time moving men away from the parts of the body I don't want them to spend too much time on. Basically my breasts and my clit, which are two really good ones, right? Or my ears, I don't like having my ears worked over. But let's say my neck—I love having people touch my neck or kiss my neck. Or my asshole. For some reason, in terms of pain or sensitivity, a man can touch my asshole—I've had men touch my asshole in a way that I think, They're really pushing it. But it doesn't hurt me. I may ask them to go more gently. They can put their fingers in, and if their nails are hurting, I say, "Look, your fingernails are too sharp and you're going to hurt me."

But my clit is extremely sensitive. I'd just as soon they didn't pay any attention to it. And my breasts—many women who work as prostitutes will say this, breasts are like *Bam!* Automatic! That's what turns a woman on, glom glom glom, bite bite bite. Your breasts work harder than any part of you, to the point where I now have very sensitive breasts. Around my nipple, it feels really nice to have that touched and bitten and stuff, but my nipples themselves are terribly sensitive, and unless it's done right, it's grating, it's too much. When a man starts in on my breasts, I'm aware of counting, One, two, three, okay—now I need you to do something else. Move to the other one, move to my neck, move to my mouth, but move. I do it by the way I move my body, the noises I make, or I'll tell them, "I'm sorry, honey, I like having my breasts played with, but I need you to do that more gently." Or I'll say, "I really like having my butt squeezed and grabbed and touched." That's true, if a guy wants to make me happy, just flip me over and squeeze and knead my butt for hours. Some guys hear it, some don't. They think, No, what she really wants is to have her nipples gnawed on.

Probably with every regular client I've had to say at some point, "That doesn't feel good," or "Gently," or "I'm getting sore." But most of the time, I just shift the energy. Like if a guy is going down on me, I fake coming and get him the hell off me. Or I move. It's a small area, so you don't have to move much to refocus sensation. Or I use my sounds. It's kind of like training a dog. If they start sucking on my labia, I make huge amounts of noise. For the most part a wom-

an's labia have no sensation. I'm going, "Oh, that feels good!" If
they're directly on the clit, I either make no noise at all or make a dis-
tress noise and move away. Trying to give them reinforcement to do
what I want, which is basically, Stay the fuck away from my clit.

This guy who could always get me off, he used to do it orally. Jesus Christ, yeah. He's this little Filipino guy, little cock—and he could
also fuck me to orgasm. Unbelievable. But he's deeply into martial
arts, so he's deeply into control. I think he knows a lot about the way
sex works, and he's good. He's one of these guys who make me feel
like there are sex sorcerers, people who understand energy in a way
that most of us bumbling idiots don't. It took me a while to get to
where I could work aikido on him, and I still couldn't always do it.
When he would move on me, when he would touch me, I could feel
the energy he was building around my body. Having him fuck me until I came was okay—it didn't feel as invasive. When he would go
down on me he was directly stimulating my clit, and that gives me a
very powerful orgasm if you do it right. When he would fuck me, he
was stimulating my G-spot, which gives me more like a plateau, little
up-and-down orgasms. It was weird. Certain clients teach me amazing lessons.

I would try to shift his energy away by moving or by breathing.
Breath is very important. You can generate sexual energy just by
breathing. I could sit here and bring myself to orgasm by breathing.
It wouldn't be like a clitoral orgasm, not that powerful, but definitely
an orgasm. When I take a breath in, I'm aware of it creating a line all
the way down to my cunt. I don't have a huge faith in the idea of
chakras, but it's an interesting conception, having energy centers in
your body and breath being the connector. The whole spinal column
of energy and consciousness, through your throat and into your heart
and lungs and belly and gut, and through to your cunt. Having that
all be in line. Sometimes what I do if a guy is coming on too strongly
and it's getting intense, I move sexual energy down into my feet. I deflect it.

Really? How do you do that?

Do you know *anything* about sex? Generally when you're having
sex, your focus is on your genitals. That's where the tension is. Well,
I move it. I start concentrating on my feet, what my feet are feeling,

sending the energy in my cunt to my feet. You can move your sexual energy anywhere, consciously. Another place that's good is right here in my throat, because that's where my breath is. Say someone's going down on you and you don't want to come. One of the quickest ways to come is to think about your dick, right? This is the opposite. I think about another part of my body, and breathe into it, and move my hips so that my clit isn't being stimulated. It's a good exercise—I have excitement and sensation, but not in a way that's directed toward orgasm. It's like bringing my whole body into a state of arousal. I can't always do it, I'm not a Tantric guru, but it's useful. The guy can go to town, spend all this time on my cunt, and I'm thinking about my feet, or my throat, or my chest. Sometimes I clench and unclench my hands, which brings the energy into my hands and arms. And I keep it flowing back and forth. If I lie here and hold my breath like this [demonstrates], everything stays where it is. I'm locked. That's how most people come, over the edge. They hold it very tight, and then *bam!* They come. But you don't have to do that. You can keep it at a lower level of energy and move it through your whole body.

I have to say, even in my private sex life, I don't look for my lovers to get me off in the way I can get myself off. There are things another person can do to me that I can't do to myself, like fist me. But to give me orgasms, I don't look for that in other people. What I want is more the heat, the energy, somebody to snuggle with afterward. Even with lovers I'll masturbate myself to orgasm. I don't look for amazing technique in my lovers anymore. I look for a simpatico, an awareness, and I look for genuineness of energy. I'm not looking for somebody to drive me crazy with passion. Which is not to say that doesn't happen. I'm just not looking for it. I'm not looking for anything right now, but if I were, it'd be either the extended emotional intimacy thing, or somebody who embodies some kind of intense, clear sexual energy that I could go up against in an equal way.

See, you can be in love, and that involves sex, but it involves lots of other things, talking and eating and sleeping together, doing things for the other person. Sex with that kind of intimacy, we call it "making love," and it's very powerful, but it's not necessarily the hottest sex. To me, hot sex is when people tap into archetypal energy and

move outside themselves. You can have it along with love or completely removed from it. I come to this mostly through S/M. The hottest states I've ever been in have been when I no longer feel like my
name is Claudia. I'm someone else, I'm demonic, I'm a goddess, and
the person I'm playing with is on that level. My last steady lover was
a woman who identifies as a man—not that she lives as a man, but as
a very masculine woman. She is extremely wrapped up in her penis—
which is a dildo, or a set of dildos. And she is very definitely a top. I
was submissive, I wore a collar part of the time. I had never done that
before, eroticizing submission to a man and to his cock. But of course
I was dealing with a woman wearing a dildo. I can't even tell you how
hot it was—so much hotter than the real thing, there was so much energy around it, the devotion involved in worshiping an inanimate object. Incredibly hot. And there was age-play stuff, a daddy–little girl
dynamic as well. That was very deep for me.

Some of my most satisfying sessions with clients are when I can
tap into that archetypal energy and play with it. Like yesterday—this
was a very sweet call, it's why I like my work. This guy wanted someone to be a private dancer for him. He wanted an attractive woman
who exudes sexual confidence. I put on a pair of very high heels and
a little miniskirt and stockings, so when he followed me up the stairs
he'd be able to see the tops of my stockings. He came in, he was very
nervous, the poor boy, mid-forties, an accountant—although he was
wearing tennis shoes. Anyway, he was sitting over in the corner, and
I put some music on. I was nervous, too, I'm always nervous when I
have to dance for somebody. But he kept telling me how gorgeous I
was, so it was easy.

I danced for him, he was totally blown away, he's like, "Oh my
God, this is such a fantasy, this is so incredible." He let me know I
was attractive to him, and he was intimidated by me. So I started really getting into it, being the magnanimous sex mother. I let him
know I was powerful, but I wasn't going to hurt him. It was great, I
was able to tease him and turn him on and get him off. And he was
right there, he was being really nice and touching me in a nice way,
and being respectful with the way he was asking me to do stuff. I was
like, Sure, honey, you talk to me that way and I'll be really sweet to
you. Now, if he had been like, "Turn around and spread those cheeks

and let me see your butthole," I'd be like, Um, okay, sure, I'll do that, but I'm not going to be sweet while I do it. And the next thing you ask for, I may say no.

The entire scene took half an hour. I jacked him off and he came almost immediately. I stroked his dick about four times. Then we smoked a cigarette together, and he was still nervous, his hands were shaking. Then he told me he had never been to a prostitute before, so he was terrified. I was like, "Oh, if you had only told me this was your first time!"

7

HOOKED

S EX AS A DRUG. Sex as compulsion. Sex as obsession.
These notions have shaped American discourse on sex ever
since the country woke up woozy following the bacchanal of the seventies. As journalists Steve Chapple and David Talbot write in *Burning Desires,* "Sexual desire became pathology. . . . Suddenly groups
appeared all over the country for people who felt miserable about
their physical and emotional cravings. Their urges were incompatible
with their family life, with social convention, and with the dangerous
new viral reality. And yet they could not seem to control their lust
through willpower alone, so they flocked to a growing number of
self-control fellowships for moral support." Those fellowships were
mostly twelve-step programs, as sex took its place in the constellation
of addictive behaviors addressed by the "recovery movement."

Chapple and Talbot, along with some sexologists, sneer at organi-
zations like Sexaholics Anonymous, which they view as champions of
a reversion to Augustinian loathing of the sins of the flesh. It is certainly true that leaders and members of sexual recovery groups often
go to extremes in denouncing lustful thought and behavior, and that
the measures some of them advocate—no masturbation whatsoever,
no homosexual behavior—would do Saint Augustine proud. But it is
also true, as the interviews in this chapter make clear, that for some

people sexual addiction is real and devastating. To use Chapple and Talbot's snide phrase, they can no more "control their lust through willpower alone" than an alcoholic can control his drinking. They do, in fact, need help—and the twelve-step programs, whatever their drawbacks, are one place to find it.

Two of the speakers here, Danny Wappinger and Archie Hunter, are members of a twelve-step group. They are both gay men, though the programs are crowded with straights, too. Their interviews raise a question: Is sexual addiction a matter of attitude? Could another person demonstrate an equally gargantuan appetite and be perfectly well-adjusted? Probably so. But Danny and Archie's problem is not simply that they are ashamed of themselves. The elements that stand out are compulsiveness and escape. Danny tells the classic addict's story: He was out of control as soon as his sex life started. He could not refrain from behavior he hated, and he would continue long after there was any reasonable prospect of satisfaction. "Sometimes I'd already have had five blowjobs. So here I am in this bookstore, and in my mind I've decided I desperately need one more. The three guys who are there have already done me once, I'm clearly not going to get it from them. But I'd just hang out waiting for something to change."

Danny goes on: "Sex is fun. It feels great. And I wasn't someone who was particularly happy. The home life was miserable and scary, so it was an escape." Andy Bevilaqua's addiction to phone sex was less consuming, but still left him with hundreds of dollars' worth of bills each month until he put a block on his phone. He, too, talks about escape: "It was definitely like a drug. . . . I'm craving that feeling, and I'm avoiding something else—feelings of pain, sadness, frustration, anger, helplessness." For Archie Hunter, anonymous sex was just one addiction: He abused alcohol and drugs, too.

Archie's interview offers another matter to ponder: the raptures that can be reached in "unhealthy" acts. His particular erotic taste will cause revulsion in many readers, and he believes he must now leave it behind. But how many of us can describe our sex in such ecstatic terms: "There were times when I thought, If I'm gonna die, it should be right now, because I'm perfectly at one with everything. I was in my element. This was me in my purest form."

The fourth speaker here, Lucy Michaels, is not a sex addict. But her type of erotic obsession is very common—she is in love with a married man. She says "there's no future in it," and considers the affair temporary: "I can't go on like this." But on the evening that we recorded the second session of our interview, her lover called and wanted to come over, even more so after Lucy told him she had "a friend" visiting. He insisted, she unhappily gave in, and I was struck by how she could not tell him no. She seemed, in a word, hooked.

DANNY WAPPINGER

He got "hooked" the moment he started having sex, at eighteen, with men in adult bookstores, and it took him the better part of twelve years to kick the habit. What drove him seems mysterious even to him, though it certainly included his father's alcoholism, emotional starvation in a middle-class, Scottish–Irish Catholic family, and the effort, from early childhood, to conceal the dark secret of his homosexuality. "Typically, in the literature about alcoholic families, there's one kid who takes on all the symptoms. That was me. As an eight-year-old I was taken to a psychiatrist because I had psychosomatic pains. I made a suicide attempt at fifteen. In my freshman year of college I nearly died of a bleeding ulcer. I'm the only one of the six kids who doesn't get along with my parents. It's interesting—of the six, three are gay, though I'm the only one who's out. By the time I was eleven or twelve I was fully aware that I was homosexual. But I got the message loud and clear that this is not the kind of thing you want anyone to know. I didn't even masturbate. I thought any acknowledgment of my sexuality was going to betray my homosexuality. I didn't play sports. I was sort of smart. I was a sissy. People called me a faggot, because I was a little swishy."

Now he seems anything but: a strapping twenty-nine-year-old, deep-voiced, bearded, muscular. His earring, wire-rimmed glasses, and jet-black hair swept back in a ponytail do nothing to soften the impression of masculinity. He lives in San Francisco, where he works in a doctor's office and writes screenplays. He has been "getting sober," sexually, for two years, with the help of Sexual Compulsives Anonymous.

* * *

I lived at home during college. One night during my freshman year, I was driving home and I took a wrong turn. I ended up on this strip of highway right by the airport, where the adult bookstores were. Something possessed me to go in one. This is the old days, 1981, when there were booths. You put a quarter or a token in a slot, and there's an eight-millimeter projector behind a glass wall. It shows movies on another wall. Some of the movies were straight, and some were gay. And written on the glass wall was something like, "For blowjob, leave door open." They were getting ready to close, so I didn't stay, but I filed it away.

A week or two later I called them on a Saturday afternoon. "Is this the kind of place where men meet men?" "Yes, sometimes." I went back that night. Until this point, I had never masturbated successfully. I had had one blowjob on a camping trip. I left the booth door open, and a guy came in and gave me a blowjob. I closed the door after he left. It couldn't have lasted three minutes. While I was pulling my pants back up, I heard him out there telling the other guys: "He came like that [snaps fingers]!" These were mostly older men. I was eighteen. I was suddenly very, very popular.

You hear people talk about escalation periods in addiction. There was no escalation period. Like that, I was hooked. I was trying to deal with the guilt and shame of getting sex there, but I couldn't stop going. To use the booths, you had to buy two dollars' worth of quarters or tokens. I would go and get all the action I could off those two dollars in each bookstore. Overnight, I went from not having any sex at all to having sex at least three times an episode, at least three episodes a week. Some nights I probably had as many as ten. I mean orgasms. Yeah, I could come twice with the same erection, which I thought was perfectly normal because I could do it. That made me even more popular.

Most of the men grossed me out. The only interesting thing about them was that they were interested in me. And they were only interested in what was between my legs. But it was the first attention I had ever gotten, and I couldn't stop. I would go out into the parking lot and throw away the tokens and go, "Oh, I'll never come back here again!" And be back two nights later.

I knew I didn't want to be doing it, but I knew I couldn't help doing it. I would count the days: How long has it been since I did it? It seemed so wrong, so bad. Let's face it, I was an eighteen-year-old boy having sex in pay-to-enter places with older men all the time. Never knowing their names. Never with my shoes off. Ten times a week. I was being trash. I wasn't raised the kind of boy who would do that. It's easier for me to take now, because I'm almost thirty years old and I did it for ten years. [Laughs.] Do you remember when *Cruising* came out, how disgusted everyone in America was? Imagine stepping into *Cruising* at the tender age of eighteen. And suddenly you're not just watching this movie, you're the star. It was shocking. But there's this bottom-line nerve-endings thing. Sex is fun. It feels great. And again, I wasn't someone who was particularly happy. The home life was miserable and scary, so it was an escape. And there was attention. But it was attention from these men—they were rarely my own age. They reeked of menthol cigarettes, or were drunk. Sometimes my penis would be sticky afterward from whatever was in their mouth before. Or I would try to kiss them, just to make it more than some old man kneeling to give me a blowjob, and it would make me sick. Sometimes I would push them away in the middle of this and say, "I can't do this, I'm horrible."

Ninety-eight percent of the time they blew me. I didn't do them. That started a pattern that's still hard to break—like, I'm the one who is young and virile. In some ways it was an even exchange, except I'm the younger one. They always made it seem like they were getting more than I was getting. Like I was letting them blow me, more than they were letting me have a blowjob. But in my mind, I was getting the better end of the deal. I was cool and distant. I was like, You are the lucky one. I'm young and beautiful, and you're the one who really wants it. I can take this or leave it, but don't touch me. There was a sick game going on. And of course the guys were into that. They love it. The more you do that, the more they want you.

Before too long, I had discovered the T-rooms* on campus. I was having sex in public toilets with guys my own age. It didn't really change anything, but other things got added. It was more of an exchange. But it was still mostly about me getting serviced. I'm not going to say I never sucked anybody's cock in a bathroom or a bookstore, but the overwhelming majority of the time it was about

*Public restrooms where men have sex.

this power thing. Even in my relationships—my three real relation-ships have all been with older men, and much drama was made of that. The last one, Larry, was fifteen years older than me. We met in a porn movie house. I saw him first, I decided that he was the one I was going home with, but I got him to suggest it. I controlled it. And I asked him in the movie house, "Do you like to get fucked?" "No, not usually." That was the big thing. If they said they didn't like to get fucked, that was the best. Because then the big challenge was to fuck them. My track record was very good. I don't think it was ever rape. If they said no, they said no. So I took him home. He said he didn't like to get fucked. I fucked him anyway. A lot. We had sex all night. And we ended up having a relationship. But when we had sex, it was still about my orgasm.

When I was nineteen I took some time off from school and went to New York. I went to my first bathhouse, where you could have sex in a bed. Up to this point, I had left bars with men, and I had left bookstores with men, but not very often. I had actually been fucked in a booth with my pants around my ankles, but not very often. And it wasn't very fun. And I identified wanting to be penetrated as a weakness—like, it's okay to be gay as long as you're the man. But sex in a bed was different. There's a lot more you can do, and it was a lot easier. Getting fucked is something you have to learn how to do. It was something I took to like a pro. This was in 1982, when most peo-ple still hadn't heard of AIDS.

Then I went back to school, and something happened. A friend of mine raped me. This guy had a crush on me, and he got me very drunk. I'm violently ill, puking my guts up. I collapse on his couch. He says, "You don't have to sleep on the couch, you can sleep on the bed." I'm not sure what's going on, because I'm really drunk. I get in the bed, I get undressed, and he rapes me.

After that rape I stopped getting fucked. Well, a few times, but hardly ever after that. And if I hadn't stopped—y'know, I don't be-lieve in the god of Abraham and Moses, and I don't believe that Jesus Christ died for my sins. I have an easier time thinking about titans rolling dice to see what they're going to do with us next. But if I hadn't stopped getting fucked, I'd be dead. This was the summer of 1982. I would be dead, no question about it.

Still, since then, I haven't had much—if any—healthy sex. In ten years, I never had sex with somebody I knew first. I still haven't. Even my relationships—both Leon and Andy, I had sex the second time I saw them, and Larry I picked up in a porn theater. I have a romantic streak four miles wide, and I had this Cinderella idea that I was going to meet Mr. Right, who would take me away. But basically, the bad years were the same thing over and over again. Getting up in the morning with too little sleep. Going to the closet, taking out a pair of pants, not being able to wear them because they had come all down the front of them from the last time I wore them. Going to work. Spending most of the morning mixing hot chocolate and coffee, just to get up to zero, to a functioning level. Occasionally—this is toward the end, when I had my office job—I'd go to a T-room at lunch. Now, I know there's no such thing as going to a T-room for ten minutes. I'd go on the off-chance that there'd be someone to have sex with. But one is never enough. So going to a T-room meant getting back to work late from lunch.

Usually there's more than one T-room in the same building, so you go from the fourth floor to the seventh floor to the sixth floor to the fourth floor, looking for someone. If you're a T-room queen, you have a radar for them. It's weird. If there's one in a building, I'll find it. Seemingly by chance, but I'll find it. You just walk in, and you can smell it. I don't have a well-developed sense of smell, but when I walk into a T-room—and I don't mean the smell of come, I mean the smell of sex. Some of the most fun T-rooms I have ever been in have been accidental. I walk in and suddenly everybody is painfully nonchalant. I'm like, Oh, God, I'm gonna love this. All the urinals are filled, and all the stalls are filled, and everybody is nonchalant? This is gonna be great. [Laughs.] And once it's established that you are looking for fun, people back up from the urinals to reveal that they have full-blown hard-ons and are jerking off. Someone who's standing at one of the urinals will go back to giving a blowjob to the guy standing at the next urinal. There's no etiquette per se. My disposition was always, We're here, we've obviously checked our shame and pride at the door [laughs], let's not pretend. I prefer contact sports to spectator sports, but spectators can become assistants, so I had no problem with letting guys watch. My favorite thing to do, both in bathhouses and T-rooms, was to start a riot. Get as many guys groping, sucking, kissing as possible. There'd be men who look down their noses at that: I am just here to suck a cock of a very hot eighteen-year-old, and you guys are spoiling my fun. Or they'd be disdainful of other stuff that was going on in the same public toilet. I'm like, You're going to look down on the sex someone is having in a public toilet because you think the sex you're having in a public toilet is better? I might be sick, but at least I know when to call a spade a spade.

Now, sometimes there'll be only one person there. And sometimes that one person will be crazy. I've seen him before, and he's just crazy, weird. Or it's someone I had before, so I'm not interested. But after an hour, I'll give in. If I've been going to the three T-rooms in this one building over and over again for an hour, and I'm not getting anywhere, I'll let him give me a blowjob. So there were plenty of blowjobs from trolls. And real sick stuff, too. Guys who would say, "I'm not comfortable here, let's go to one of the other bathrooms." A non–T-room. Then they'd want me to shit on the floor. And I'd do it. They'd want me to step on their dicks, or spit at them while they're sucking me off. Knowing full well that these are disturbed individuals, that I am a party to something very sick that I'm not comfortable with at all, I would do it because I had never done it before.

Through it all I was damn lucky. I am lucky I'm alive. I just tested negative for the third time last week. That's a miracle. I only started practicing safe sex in 1986. I got the clap, and then I got it again six weeks later. That's when I realized that, well, if I could get the clap from fucking somebody in the ass, I could get AIDS from it. From what I understand, the risk of getting HIV from doing the fucking with a rubber is minimal. If you think about it logically—maybe I'm wrong, but it seems to me that when you're fucking, body fluids go one way, so germs and viruses go that way. It's not realistic to think that the HIV virus is going to swim up your urethra. But will you find a self-respecting doctor who will say it's okay to do? Absolutely not. And if your penis is dripping or has sores, it's certainly going to increase the probability. So from '86 on, I was always using rubbers.

The last two years I was out there, I knew I was out of control. It went from addictive to more addictive. It got harder to be fun, and then it got impossible. The need for a fix became so overwhelming. I knew about SCA and was fighting going in. I finally lost.

The weekend I finally got sober, I went home Friday night, had dinner, worked out, went over to my office to write a little bit. Immediately agitated. I decide I'm going to walk around and clear my head. I go out of my way to leave everything at my desk, so I don't go to a bookstore. Well, I get back to the office, still agitated. There's this guy there I can't stand. That's all the excuse I need. I take my bank card, get out ten dollars and wander around inside a bookstore for a good long time. There's no one interesting there. Finally get a blowjob from somebody, 'cause if I say I'm going to leave after the next orgasm and I get my pants zipped up and get out of there, I will leave. It hardly ever happens, because usually it's like, That wasn't so bad, I'll wait for the next one. But I got out. Went back to my office. Got my stuff to go home. Went to the park. It's late March, but it's cold. Didn't have a hat on. This guy comes up, high on coke. I fuck him without a rubber. He's short, he can sit—this is my favorite. He gets his pants down so that he can sit on my lap, and I mount him. Then I can stand up, and he's suspended in midair, with his arms around my neck. Now mind you, we are outside, it's forty degrees [laughs], in an open park, with traffic on two sides. We see someone coming. I'm sure it's a cop. We stop. The someone coming is a crack addict, who sits there watching us while he smokes crack. The other guy gets flipped out and goes away. There is no one else in the park. I haven't had an orgasm yet. The only guy there is the crack addict. He says: "Do you want to fuck me?" I don't, but I know I have to. He puts a rubber on me. He's a crack addict, outside, in the middle of the night, with a T-shirt on, but he has the sense to put a rubber on me. I don't want to fuck him, because God knows what he has. He's probably a junkie, too. So I jerk off into the condom. I know I'm not leaving the park till I have an orgasm, so I jerk off. Take the condom off, tell him to go home, it's too cold. Now, this is a low point in my life. [Laughs.] But I was doing this two, three nights a week. For some reason, this is the one that got me.

I spend the next day sick in bed. I work as a bartender on a catering job that night. Get out at three o'clock. On my way home I go back to the park. No one is there. And that's what finally hit me over the head. I have some friends who say, "You don't have to hit me in the face with a brick more than three times." That was the third brick. It was bad enough that I was there the night before and I was going to fuck this crack addict in a T-shirt. It was bad enough I spent the next day sick in bed. But then I went back for more, twenty-four hours later? The next day I got up and went to my first SCA meeting.

In SCA you define sexual sobriety for yourself. I am now on my third test case as far as "trying to integrate sex into my life as a healthy element." That's part of the verbiage of SCA: "We are not here to repress our God-given sexuality, but to learn how to express it in ways," etc. Or as someone said at the last meeting, "I didn't come here to become a nun." One way you learn to integrate is to make up a sexual recovery plan. It's a written guideline of your personal dos and don'ts. My plan is fairly liberal and fairly straightforward: No sex before three dates. That leaves very little gray area. There's no way I can justify three dates between picking up a guy on Castro Street and my house. Stop here for a Coke, stop here for a coffee. . . . [Laughs.] As far as other don'ts, I don't pick up anyone in the street. I don't go in adult bookstores. The one do on my list is that I want to spend the night with someone, not have sex and then get dressed and go home.

Last summer, after I'd been on my plan for fourteen months, I went back out there. I was doing my laundry, and this guy looked at me, and I looked at him, and before I knew it, I was in his apartment. I didn't have a blackout or anything—I remember in the elevator saying to myself, I can get out of this right now if I want to. This is definitely going to be a slip. Then, he didn't want me to kiss him: "Don't kiss me, kiss my tits." Which is like, I'm sorry, but why bother? It was over in like three minutes. I fucked him, and he came before I did because he was jerking himself off. He let me fuck him after he came. I thought, That was all right, but I know where I can get better. Actually I didn't know where I could get better, but I was certainly willing to find out. I finished my laundry, went out and fucked two more guys. One of them had KS* on his arm. I'm fucking someone who has

*Kaposi's sarcoma, a skin lesion associated with AIDS.

AIDS. What was I thinking? And the condom broke. I felt it break, so I pulled out and started jerking myself off. Now, remember, this is the second time I've had sex the same day. It's also the third time I've had sex in fourteen months. Does the term *projectile ejaculation* mean anything to you? I got it in his eye. He was pissed off.

After that I ran into two guys on their way to an SCA meeting, so I went with them. People came over and hugged me and said, "Make it be over, make it be over." It might have been more helpful if they had been a little more punitive. I'm okay, you're okay? I'm not okay, I'm a fucking mess! I'm going back out there, I'm risking my life, and you're telling me I'm okay, not to worry about it? I was out there about a month. And everything I ever heard about addiction turned out to be true. Within two weeks I was worse than I'd ever been. Within three weeks I was going to the baths every night, having eight, ten tricks a night. You have to pay overtime after four hours, and I was paying overtime every night. Then rustling up enough money in the cab on the way home to go to a bookstore. Or cruise the park. All night, every night. I was waiting for it to be enough. Like, One more time, and this will be a satisfying experience. But guess what?

One day my sponsor called me. He knew I had been out there. He called me at home and said, "What are you doing?" I said, "I went out and got laid." He yelled at me, "When are you going to stop this?" I said, "I don't know. Maybe I'll stop today, but I hate that Wednesday meeting." He said, "Maybe you should do a Ninety-Ninety." That means ninety meetings in ninety days. I said, "I know, but it's so inconvenient." He said, "You're gonna die, that's gonna be inconvenient too! You can find time to have sex with all these sleazy guys, that's convenient?" I knew he was right, so I did a seven-seven. But I didn't want to stop. I wasn't good and ready. It took me a good six weeks.

Now I'm back seven months and I'm not showing any signs of slipping. I haven't had sex in that time. I masturbate on and off, but sometimes I try to stop that, too. I'm dating this guy named Harold. Another friend set me up with him. And I'm realizing that I'm twenty-nine years old and I don't know a thing about dating. But what I'm also finding out is that neither does anybody else.

Harold and I have had two dates. We may or may not go out tomorrow night. That will make the magic three. [Laughs.] After the first one, I walked him to his house, pecked him good night and ran away. I didn't realize I was running, but I did. Then I thought, Fuck, I let him get away without making the next date. I spent the rest of the weekend—Is he gonna call? Is he gonna call? The confidence thing. But he called. After the second date I walked him home again. And again, the good-bye kiss: What do I do? I know that I don't want to just peck and run away. On the other hand, I don't want to be the Whore of Babylon. I also don't want to get beaten up for kissing another guy in the street. So I just winged it. And it happened. It was the nicest, most intimate kiss I probably ever had. We kissed for maybe a minute. It was just nice—the novelty of that. It was so *nice.* The fact that I could kiss someone and find a middle ground between a quick peck and putting my whole head in his mouth. He leaned his head in, and I leaned my head in. I kept my mouth open a little, just enough that it didn't have to get major league, but it could. It got minor league. He had his tongue in my mouth, I had my tongue in his. I slipped my gloved hand around his neck. It was raining, we both had umbrellas up. He seemed as nervous as I was, and I guess it's neat that he's not afraid to seem nervous. So it was just perfect for that night. It didn't hurt the old self-esteem one little bit. I felt like he liked me as much as I liked him.

Something we talk about in SCA—we all tend to confuse sex, love, and intimacy. Just because someone is willing to have sex with you, you think they like you. As we have every reason to know, that's not necessarily the case. [Laughs.] But this did feel like he liked me. Maybe I'm confusing things, but I don't think so. It was a lot easier to be confident that he'd call, walking away after that kiss.

ANDY BEVILAQUA

"I'm a city boy," he begins, *"born and bred in Manhattan."* He is thirty-two, handsome, a stylish dresser, with something magnetic in his soft voice and intense gaze. His apartment is in perfect order and tastefully done: black leather furniture, large posters on the wall from Rauschenberg and de Kooning exhibitions, and two golden retrievers lounging on the carpet. He is recently unemployed, having quit after eight years at a public relations firm, and is pondering new directions for his life.

His father is a manager at a department store, his mother a ticket broker. *"They came from working-class and became middle-class. It was an anxious home, very high stress levels, where people put everything under the rug. One side of me felt, These people care for me and love me. On the other side I felt unsafe and distrusting. I didn't get responded to. That comes into play very strongly in my sex life."*

As a child and an adolescent his sexual impulses battled with his role as his parents' good boy. *"Sex during high school was horrendous. I had this girlfriend, and I still cringe—you could tell she wanted me to do something, but I didn't have the courage to even reach over and kiss her. I was so passive. I never rebelled or did drugs or anything."* But in college he began to change. After losing his virginity at seventeen, *"my sexual relationships just kept going. And I started to discover the two sides of me. I attracted women who really cared for me, because I have a sensitive, gentle, sweet side. But I also have a decadent, adventurous, mischievous side, my dark side."*

Since college he has explored many sexual avenues: affairs, *"little dating things,"* longer relationships, S/M clubs—and phone sex. Next to the telephone in his kitchen is a fortune-cookie fortune that reads: *"An old wish will come true."*

I play. Sexuality for me is a way I can play. The creative side of me comes out, I go to the limits, I push it. And over the years, I've developed the ability to bring out the dark side of women. It's a phenomenon, people have told me. I'm talking thousands of people, people I don't even remember anymore. I can be talking to a woman, and all of a sudden—it happened just the other day. It was this woman from work, the first time I ever talked to her outside of work. We're on the phone, and suddenly she says to me, "I just love giving blowjobs to guys when they're driving. And I love masturbating in the car while the guy is driving. Putting my legs up and playing with myself." Another woman I used to work with told me she really likes kitchen counters—loves to be eaten and fucked on kitchen counters. They tell me because I create that environment where they can. I allow them to get through their fears and judgments. And it turns me on.

It started in college. I just decided to do it one day. I'd go through the phone book and call people and say I was a male stripper. I'd find a name—like, say, Diane. I'd call and say, "Diane, my name is John, and I got your number from a friend who said you're giving a party. I'm a male stripper, and I want to come audition for you." Or I'd call and ask for some other name, and when she says I have the wrong number I'd say, "Oh, my God, I think she wanted to hire me as a male stripper for her party." That's engaging. The pretext lets her know there's something sexual there, and she can grab it or not. Most of the time she'd say, "You have the wrong number," and I'd say okay. But once in a while she might say, "God, I've always thought about doing that." Or, "Oh, describe what you look like." There's the response. It's all response to me. The best piece for me is when their voices changes, that magic moment when you feel the shift and—got it! It's like winning the horse race. And depending on the person, they would go to different degrees of getting turned on. Some would describe their experiences when they saw a stripper. Once in a while, if someone gave me a really good cue, the talk might get more intimate. They'd tell me what they really like, their favorite positions, whatever. Sometimes I'd masturbate while I was doing it. I might not come but I'd be touching myself.

I get a little uptight talking about this, because it's something different—a different way of expressing sexuality, and people might look down on it, like it's a version of the obscene phone call. But if the person said, "No, I'm not interested," I'd hang up. I didn't want to frighten or offend anyone. My goal was to have that connected conversation about sex we're all looking for. If the person didn't want to have it, fine, but it's amazing how many did. It would blow your mind. We're all sexually obsessed on some level. Everybody has that dark and mischievous side they want to play in. If they don't, they're kidding themselves.

Then I got into a phase with pay phones. There's something about a pay phone ringing on the street, it's mysterious. How I got started on that—I answered a pay phone one day and a guy was there. He said, "Hi, how ya doin'?" I said, "Fine." He said, "Are you horny today?" I said, "I'm horny every day, what else is new?" He said, "Well, would you like for me to blow you? I'd really like that." I said, "Well, I'm not really into that, but it's exciting just talking about it." And I was turned on just by the fact of having a sexual conversation with a stranger. I said, "You have a good day," and hung up. But I had karma—I could walk down the street and the phone would ring. There was a period in the late eighties where a lot of gay guys were making those calls. I happen to love gay sexuality, it's so primal, like, Let's fuck, no bullshit, I like what you've got, give it to me. It's genuine, it's great. Well, I apply that mode to women, because women are a little more repressed. It's not that they don't have that, they all have it, if you've heard what I've heard. They're just a little more secretive. If you make a comfort zone where they feel safe and trusting, it comes out.

After that first phone call, I thought, Wow, if I wanted to, I could go get a blowjob right now. Wouldn't it be great if that were a woman on the phone? So I decided to reverse it. I took numbers from pay phones on the street, and I started calling. The pay phones were liberating, because I didn't have that guilt about calling someone's house. It's not so intrusive. In a phone booth, the person is making the decision to pick up the phone. I still use the male stripper routine because that makes the sexual allusion and they can either pick it up or not. With this type of call it's very quick. It's like hit-and-run, spontaneous combustion. Phone booths are also kind of mystical, if you think about that person walking by just at that moment. It's like rolling the dice. They pick up the phone, and they think they're play-ing a joke on you by answering. They say hello and I say, "Joanne, please." Maybe they say, "This is Joanne." I say, "Joanne, how are you, I was returning your call, and I'd really like to dance at your party. What routine would you like me to do—delivery boy, doc-tor . . . ?" And they say, "So you're a stripper?" I say, "Yeah, yeah." Then maybe they tell me I've got the wrong number, and I go, "Oh, no, I have to talk to Joanne. Man, I'm having a really rough night. So how are you?" They go, "Oh, I'm fine, I'm with some friends, just coming from a restaurant," blah blah. Then maybe they say, "So, what do you look like?" Then I can go any direction I want to, de-pending on my mood. There's always a way of bringing it around to sex. If you're smart and you have an agenda, you can get it there.

I'm telling you, I have heard everything under the sun. I had one girl recently, on the younger side, low twenties, and she just said, "Oh, my God, I'm so horny today, I can't believe I'm talking to you, I just don't know what to do . . ." Jackpot! This girl sounded adora-ble. She was with her friends, they're saying, "Come on, what are you talking to him like that for?" But she was right there. I've had girls say, "God, I'd love to have a cock inside me. I'd love to be sucking on a cock." It depends on where they want to go.

Another time, this woman picked up the phone and we got into a conversation. Fifteen minutes later we're talking about our favorite sexual positions. She's telling me she loves it doggie-style, she gets the best penetration that way. I said to her, "You sound absolutely great. I'd love to dance for you." She said, "Okay, I'm gonna come over." My buzzer rings downstairs, and I'm thinking, Nobody will ever be-lieve this. Here comes this woman up the stairs, with a black leather jacket, kind of tall, sexy, leggings. She comes into the house, she's a little tipsy. She goes to the bathroom. She says, "So, put on some mu-sic." I put it on and we're dancing in the middle of my room, where twenty minutes earlier I was lying in bed wanting to jerk off. She takes off her jacket, and she's wearing this undershirt where you can see her nipples. She's coming up behind me and playing with my nipples and touching me all over. Then she turns around and I get behind her. It was like being in a bar and getting turned on by a woman dancing, only a little more forward. Then it got to the point where she lay down on the floor and I wanted to take off her clothes, and she said, "I better not, I might regret this. I've got a boyfriend and I'm gonna feel guilty." I was slightly disappointed, but it was okay. I said, "No problem, we had a lot of fun here, this was great. Thanks for coming over anyway. And you keep picking up those phones!"

Another time, I made a pay-phone call about two in the morning. I had that itch, wanted to have that contact. Woman picks up the phone, we're talking, and she says, "My friend Sheila is here." I said, "Why don't you put Sheila on the phone." Now, Sheila and I hit it off. I actually liked this person. She was talking about spiritual stuff, and I have that side, we're having a great conversation. She's saying, "You know, I can tell by the way you talk, you're incredibly soothing, you'd make a great therapist." I go, "Really? That's very perceptive, because I'm considering it." Sometimes when I'm in that mode, my penis is saying, "Bring up sex, schmuck!" But I was feeling good. To make a long story short, we exchanged phone numbers and to this day I talk to her three or four times a week. I've never met her. And here's what happened. It's spooky. I eventually brought up the subject of sex. And I'm basically sexually dominant. This woman says, "Oh, God, I can't believe that, because I'm a true submissive. I love being dominated by a guy." Now we're having a half-hour talk of her telling me how she likes to be tied up, how she likes to be treated. Just the other day, I felt horny, called her up, and I said, "You know, I sometimes picture you riding me." Her voice changes—she goes, "Really?" I say yeah, and I start to tell her about things I picture—bathing her, washing her, soaping her breasts. She goes, "God, that sounds great." Then I asked her—she loves to talk about this—I go, "When you give a guy a blowjob, what's your favorite way to do it?" She says, "Well, I love being on my knees, 'cause being on my knees with him standing is so submissive." I said, "Do you like looking at his cock in his pants, does that really turn you on?" She says, "I love that." Then I personalize it, I say, "I would love to be standing in front of you." She says, "Oh, that would really turn me on." "Do you like having your breasts played with when you're giving a blowjob?" "Yes, I like it very much. I also like to be fingered." "How many fingers do you like inside of you?" "I love two fingers." "And why do you like blowing a guy so much?" "Because I'm getting him excited and I know I can't wait for him to fuck me." "Do you like to fuck for a long time?" "Yes, I get lost in it, I like to fuck forever, until it's painful." So then I said, "Well, I've really been thinking about you being on top of me, and while you're riding me I'll be spanking you." She said, "Oh, God, I love that." The next few seconds or minutes I was masturbating and I came, it was great. What's bad about that, I ask you?

I don't know whether she masturbates. I don't even ask, because there's a piece of her that doesn't want to, so if she's doing it I don't want her to focus on it, because it gets her conscious of what she's doing and she stops. She has big-time conflicts going on right now, she's afraid to get into a relationship because she's frightened of her own obsessions. She said, "I know you and I would hit it off, so I don't even want to meet you." We did schedule one time to meet— that was so hot, she was going to come over on a Tuesday night, and she said she was going to be dressed in stockings and heels and a short skirt, and she was going to come into my house, open the door, get right down on her knees, and do it. But she didn't show up.

You have to play to each audience. I can be on the phone with another woman—like the one from work that likes sucking guys in cars. She'll say to me, "What are you doing?" I'll say, "I'm touching myself. God, I'd love to be touching you. What are you doing?" She goes, "My pussy is incredibly wet, I'm touching it because I'm getting very turned on, I have this primal reaction to you. I don't know what it is, but you're getting me so excited." I go, "Oh, that makes me happy, because I'm very excited too," and she has this powerful orgasm on the phone. So it's different depending on the person. It's like if you were with the person live—some women you can touch one way and they'll respond to it, another woman if you touch her that way it'll bomb.

From the woman's point of view, she gets to be right there in the moment, and she's anonymous. That's why it works, because of anonymity. It's like a confessional. It's safe, the person can't see you and what you're doing, so you can be talking to them, getting aroused and touching yourself without telling them. It's also safe in that there's no intimacy past a certain point. It creates an illusion of openness, but there's a real openness in there somewhere. And with AIDS, the phone is the way to go. You get to release, it's not costly because you don't have to go out and date, and you go to sleep after you're done.

It's a very powerful drug. I went through a phase for many years—if I said I had a thousand phone conversations, I wouldn't be overstating it. I could have a different partner every night, and I did. I could not wait to get home to the phone. It was a little out of balance, I was aware of that, but it got me through that period. In the late eighties the party lines started to happen. These are lines where everybody can talk at the same time—the 550- and 970- numbers. The bi line, the submissive line, the B&D line, the lust line. When those came in I got more compulsive, because there were people on the line that you knew were in the same place. When they call 970-LUST, you know you have a good shot. There are more men than women that call, like any bar situation. It's hit-or-miss, you can get on the line and there can be one woman and eight men, and you don't connect. Other times you're the only one on the line and there's this woman saying, "Hi, I'm Gina and I'm incredibly horny today, I want a guy who will tie me up and do different things to me."

Sometimes everyone's talking at the same time, competing, it can be very annoying. Then you try to get the woman to call you back. Most everyone on the party line wants somebody to call them back. But it's hard—the woman has to take an interest in calling you. Sometimes she says yes, sometimes "No, I don't call people back," or "I want to stay on the line, I'm not interested." Some women do it on the party line. If a woman has a fantasy about jerking off while six guys are listening—I've heard that many times. "Guys, I'm playing with myself and I'm so horny, I wish all of you were here watching me and jerking off on me." Then everybody gets to do their thing, everybody gets to act it out.

Plus you get to be whoever you want. I play different roles. One is the opposite body type of mine—I say I'm six-four, bulky, muscular, I work out in the gym. And I'll go for the *Vogue* look, say I have really long hair, down to the shoulders, sometimes blond, sometimes dark. I'll say blue eyes, or dark eyes. It's not a body type I'd like to have but it fits what I think they'll find attractive. I used to open my voice a little to make it deeper and lower. Huskier. I might have been compensating for a weakness in my voice, because I've been told that on the phone some of the tones get knocked out and I sound feminine. It's funny, this came up in therapy— the days I feel like I'm not enough, like I'm small and helpless, or invisible, I go to that body type. These days I don't have to go to that body type so much, I don't have to be six-four with a fourteen-inch cock.

They always tell me about their bodies, too. They say, "Do you like a big bust?" I say yeah, and they say, "I'm a thirty-eight D." "Oh, that sounds great." Who knows what's real? I think a lot of the women are honest, I don't know why. Maybe because a lot of them say they're overweight. Since I don't want to make anyone feel bad, I go with it. I make it erotic, being with a heavy woman. In a state of sexual excitement you can make yourself feel anything. I listen to the voice quality, and I listen to the mentality, if the person is getting turned on. It would turn me on in a different way if she looked like Michelle Pfeiffer and I knew that, but what turns me on is starting from point zero and getting the response. Then I want to take it to higher levels and hear them do or say outrageous things. I want to draw out as much of the dark side and the demons as I can. I remember one woman from Syracuse, I said, "Why don't you lie on the floor and get a cucumber and masturbate?" She said, "I'd love to." I heard the fridge open, and I heard down there, too. This was the second or third time I'd spoken to her. It turns me on even more if I get a sense that they live a straight life—a banker by day, and all of a sudden I'm getting this wild response on the phone. But it's like playing a jazz solo—you have to hear where the beat's going.

Other times—to really blow the lid off the box—I go into a much higher voice and play a woman. That came into my mind because I'd be mistaken for a woman, and I thought, Wouldn't this be interesting? Well, if I'm playing a woman to another woman, a lot of times she's less threatened and she lets out even more. The number of women who want to have bisexual experiences—it's gotta be eighty-five percent. One woman was obsessed with calling me, we exchanged numbers and she'd tell me about her bi experiences, but she'd also talk about her experiences with men. She'd tell me how much she loves unzipping a guy's pants and taking out his cock, and this one boyfriend she had, how she loved his cock so much. I remember another call—this woman called from her office, she worked late for some film company, I swear to God, she masturbated on the floor of her office, closed the door and masturbated. It's an amazing world. Her name was Angela. She wanted to be with a woman and she had never done it. When she was masturbating on the floor we were talking about what she was doing: "Oh, I'm touching my pussy, I have three fingers inside me, I wish they were your fingers, I want to be touching your pussy, I'd love for you to be eating me, I wanna eat you, please let me, I wanna play with your breasts and you can play with mine." Then I have to think like a woman and play in those body parts.

One couple liked to call me as a woman, and they would be fucking while they were on the phone. They would get wild and beg me to come over: "Please come over, she wants you, I want you, you can do anything you like." They would both get on the phone, Marty and Maxine. They were from Long Island, he was a trucker and she was like a bookkeeper. Very nice people. We spoke to each other for years. They used to fuck and oh, God, it was hot, she used to scream out his name. She used to beg me to sit on her face while he was fucking her, and she had huge breasts and she wanted to rub them all over me. Sometimes I just spoke to her and she'd masturbate. I introduced a "boyfriend" in this, too. She'd always ask me, "How's Frank?" Sometimes I'd say we were having sex. It's difficult to make the right noises when you're talking, so I'd say, "He's eating me." People believe what they want to believe. Sometimes Maxine would ask to talk to Frank, and she'd get me off on the phone while her husband was fucking her. Or sometimes as a woman I'd have an orgasm and make sounds like a female coming. It was magic.

I could do the phone for hours. At times it became very obsessional. When I want that response, I'll be on the phone for a long time. If I don't get the response, don't get the right person, sometimes it's hard for me to hang up. When I did it for hours I would never come more than once. That's not my style. I like to have it last a long time, and when I come it's like the party's over. I'd just keep myself at a level of arousal, but often I wouldn't hit the right one. I was on the line looking, looking, and then I'd find it and have sex, boom. That would be the end. And I'd go out and have a hamburger, because I'd be starving at that point.

It was definitely like a drug. There's no difference, making fifty phone calls a night and having five hard-liquor drinks. About six months ago I actually put a lock on my phone so I couldn't call those numbers, because I'd have a few hundred dollars' worth of phone bills every month. So I think some of my sexuality is an addiction, in the sense that I'm craving that feeling, and I'm avoiding something else—feelings of pain, sadness, frustration, anger, helplessness. I used to feel so many things so deeply that it was too frightening. At times I wasn't conscious of that, at others I was, and the phone was a vehicle to help me get through it. At least it gave me some barometer of what was going on. If it got out of balance and I was doing it obsessionally, I'd say, okay, I'm in a state.

So now I have mixed feelings about the phone sex. I love it, I celebrate it, I think it's a brilliant survival mechanism. But I'm aware when it tips over and goes too far.

LUCY MICHAELS

"Five million times a day," she says, "I think about sex. Everything reminds me of sex. When I'm at work"—she is a cook in a fancy restaurant—"and I make bread in the morning, like when you make a hard roll, you take a lump of dough and roll it in your hand in a circular motion. And you do two at a time. Well, that's like kneading somebody's breasts. Or when you make baguettes, you roll out the square of dough, then you roll it all up, and you pinch a seam all the way along the edge, flatten it down and roll it into a long roll. When you go to pick it up, it has the weight and feel of a cock. It really does, I'm not exaggerating. You lift it carefully, and you put it in the pan, and line up that seam, and it's just like the vein that runs along the bottom of a cock. You know what they say about men, that if you don't know what a man is thinking, he's thinking about sex? Well, that's me. I feel a little alone with it. The women I know don't feel the way I do. Someone once told me I have the sexual appetite of a gay man. Whereas," she adds, laughing, "my ex-husband had the sexual appetite of a straight woman."

She is forty-two but has the look of a gamine: thin, with close-cropped hair, and big, sad, expressive eyes and mouth. She grew up in a middle-size Pennsylvania city. Her father left when she was three, and her mother "was extremely cruel to me when I was a kid. When I was younger than three, my father was still around, she would leave me alone in the house. I remember standing at the front door saying, 'I want to go with you,' and having her say, 'You can't go with me. I'm going someplace where monkeys bite little girls.' There were no hugs, no kisses, nothing."

She escaped home at eighteen and married at twenty-four to a man named Jimmy, who was a good friend but whose disinterest in sex was as extreme as her interest. Even at the beginning, "I initiated everything. I had all the ideas. He was just a willing dick." For some years they had an open marriage at her insistence, and she had a half dozen affairs. They *separated, then got back together. "I tried everything. I used to say to him, 'What do you want? I'll be anyone you want. I'll do anything you want. Anything.' He'd say, 'I don't know.' About a year ago I started having an affair. And three months ago I left Jimmy."*

• • •

This is the most bizarre situation. This guy I'm seeing is Czech. His name is Pavel. He's thirty-seven, so he's five years younger than me. When I met him, he spoke barely a word of English. I learned Czech so I could speak to him. Now he speaks some English—not perfectly, so sometimes we have to lapse into Czech. He has a wife and a fourteen-year-old daughter in Czechoslovakia. She thinks he's coming back, even though he's been here three years. When he left for America, the woman he was having an affair with followed him here. Now he lives with her and has a baby by her. And he has me. And he's the hottest thing on two feet. It's wonderful. I see him once or twice a week. I keep saying, "Why can't I have you all the time? That's all I want, I want to have you all the time." He says, "If you had me all the time, I wouldn't be this hot." It's probably true. [Laughs.]

When we met, he was a dishwasher and I was a cocktail waitress. He kept making advances. I thought he was just joking around. But I was desperately lonely, and I hadn't had sex in months, and Jimmy was away on a business trip. So in very rough English, with lots of hand signals, I suggested to him that he follow me home one night. The first time, he had trouble getting hard because he was so nervous. I could see he was having trouble breathing. But it was wonderful, because eventually, when he did get an erection and we were fucking, he was all over me. He was stroking my hair, running his hands all along my body. At one point I had my ankles on his shoulders and he was reaching over and kissing the bottoms of my feet. I had been neglected for so long that he could have done a lot less and I would have been happy. But I was ecstatic. He made me feel so loved.

When we first got involved, his—the woman he lives with had

just become pregnant. She wouldn't have sex with him through the entire pregnancy. For a while we had either my house or his apartment, because she cleaned houses during the day. And what changed that? She had the baby. [Laughs.] Then she was home every day. So we were fucking in cars, we were out in the open, anyplace we could find. And we were having sex every single day. Sometimes twice a day. And I never ever got tired of it. I never found him predictable. The whole feeling about him deepened and deepened. When I fall in love, I fall in love with every part of a person's body. I love his eyebrows, his forehead, his cheeks, his ears, his nose, everything. You could start with the head and work right down to the toes, there's something that gives me great pleasure about seeing and touching every part. Just to touch him at all makes me feel good. We started in late January, and by early spring I felt this way about him. The idea of being in love with him brought me to tears. It was like, I feel so tenderly toward him, I feel he's unlike anybody I've ever known. He's the most honest person I've ever met. He's the most compassionate person I've ever met. When I'm upset—sometimes I get upset with him, like, "I don't see you enough, where have you been? How come I have to sit here and wait for you to show up? I have a life too." He always listens, he always hears me. I've never gotten that from anybody in my life, ever.

When he comes over, all I have to do is open the door, and his face lights up. He is delighted to see me. He hugs me really, really hard. He's very happy. And when we're having sex, he just comes at me and at me. He makes me have orgasm after orgasm. He tries seven zillion different positions: How's this feel? How's that feel? I'll say, "Enough, enough, I'm dying already, you already killed me," and he won't stop. He wants to be absolutely sure I'm as happy as I can possibly be. I've never seen anybody try that hard, I swear. To the point of exhaustion. And he doesn't just fuck-fuck-fuck, it's not like that. He'll come at me with his penis, then his hands, then his mouth. Everything. He's constantly thinking. His brain is working the whole time we're making love: What else is going to make her come? What does she like? That time he was kissing my feet, I told him that made me feel wonderful. So sometimes he'll do that, and then he'll slyly look at me and smile, like, I know I'm making you happy.

Here's how our sex usually works: When he first comes over, he kind of lays low. I can't tell if he needs a transition before we have sex, or if he's waiting for me to make the first move. So we sit on the couch. He'll make small talk, like, "What did you do at work today?" And I'm like, Come on, fuck me, what is this? We only have so much time, how much are we going to spend talking? I'm the one who starts the more lingering kisses. I'll kiss him a little, and if he doesn't respond to that, I'll unbutton his shirt, and I'll kiss his chest, and I'll work my way down to his cock. I wish it were the other way around. There are times when I feel like I blow him too much. He knows if he lays back and acts like he's not interested in having sex, that's what I'm gonna do to get him interested. It's silly that I know it and still do it. If I had a goal in our sex life, it would be to do that less often and wait till he made the move. I just don't have the patience. [Laughs.]

Foreplay is usually him playing with my breasts, because that will bring me to orgasm. So it's sex for me, but it's foreplay to him. Sometimes he does it through the clothes I'm wearing, and sometimes he reaches under. I like him to twist the nipples. Sometimes hard, sometimes not. Sometimes to the point of pain. If I don't come soon enough, he presses harder, and then I do. My breasts have always been sensitive, but I never opened up and let go with it the way I do with him, so it becomes an orgasm. I'll come several times that way. He doesn't touch my cunt. By the time we get to genitals, he wants to be involved, too. Sometimes I'll stroke him while he's playing with me. He likes me to press right behind his balls, in front of the anus and behind the balls. If I do that, it escalates, we're moving right into the bedroom.

One thing I'd like—he never undresses me. I think it would exciting for him to say, "So how was your day," and reach over and start unbuttoning my clothes. Talk to me while he was undressing me, but talk about anything other than sex. And if foreplay was slower than it is. A lot of times I'll shrug his hands off and go, "Wait a minute, look what you're doing, slow down a little." And then two seconds later, he's back to the way it was. [Laughs.] He will undress me if I ask, but he doesn't do it provocatively. He doesn't look me in the eye while he's doing it. It's mechanical. He's thinking, Let's get these clothes off. Usually we both just walk in the bedroom and take off

our clothes and get in bed. I'd like more time. You know, at the end
of sex, you come, it's over, and then everything slowly drifts down.
It's like a feather, it doesn't just plummet to the earth. Well, if sex
could only build the same way, I think the whole experience would
be rounder, more complete.

We start out fucking in the missionary position. He doesn't kiss a
lot during sex. When he wants to be a good kisser, he can be. If he's
trying to be charming, he can be excellent. Or if it's a tender moment.
But it doesn't seem to be as important to him as it is to me. When he
first enters me, he looks me right in the eyes. That's a real connection
for me, a great moment. Then eventually he'll want to change position, and he does lots of different things. Sometimes he'll crouch
right in front of me and fuck me. Sometimes he'll put my legs up on
his shoulders. He's concerned about the fact that his penis isn't as big
as he thinks it should be. I had a big discussion with him last week,
that the average penis is six and a half inches long. He's seen too
many sex movies, you know? So he's always trying to get into me really deeply. Sometimes he hurts me. I keep trying to tell him that deep
is not that important. We hardly ever have sex side to side, either
from behind me or facing me, unless I ask for it. And then we always
finish with me on all fours and him standing alongside the bed. That's
his favorite position. It's the most exciting for him, and the easiest for
him to come. We have like a signal. When I'm totally happy—and
that's all he wants, is for me to be totally satisfied—then I'll go like
this, I'll turn my hand over. [Turns hand from palm-up to palm-
down.] Or he'll do the signal, like, Are you happy now, can we move
into the final position? Then I'll get on all fours, and that's it.

I come in all different positions, depending on what's going on.
He always comes doggie-style or with me blowing him. I told him
that the next time we make love, I want to see his face when he
comes, because I never have. He said okay. Ideally, it would be nice
to come with someone face to face, with his arms around me, holding
me close. Something he does do sometimes is push my shoulders into
the bed. If I'm getting more and more excited, that catapults it,
makes it that much easier to come. When he's fucking me from behind I don't usually come. If he's thrusting really hard I can. But
sometimes that's not what he wants in order to come. What he likes

is a certain tilt of my hips. He likes them tilted up and away from him. He'll push them until he gets them right where he wants them, and then he can come. Usually from fucking me slowly. Not slamming his body into my ass, just a normal rhythm. I'm always reaching underneath to massage his balls as I sense he's getting closer to coming. Sometimes he reaches around and plays with my tits at the same time. Then it's like, Don't do that, just do what you want to do, I've already had everything I want. But sometimes I just give in to it, because my coming excites him so much.

I go down on him pretty often. In fact, I do it more than I want to. [Laughs.] When I'm doing that, I want him to come. And if he comes, that's it, it's over. I don't know if this is peculiar to thirty-seven-year-old men or what, but I've never been with a man before who comes once and that's it. He is not interested beyond that point. I can get him hard again, and he'll do anything to me, but he doesn't really want to get hard, and he doesn't want to fuck. And I mean for hours afterward. That's it, he came, and he's happy.

I love the feel of him in my mouth. I love it. I like the fullness. Sometimes I like to thrust him very deeply in my throat. There are times when I'm horny and that's what I'm horny for, that feeling deep back in my throat.

Sometimes, if we do it with me on the bottom and him on top, I like it because he really fucks my throat. It's forceful. It's almost a rape situation. Definitely power on his part, because he's over me, and he could push me into the bed, or the floor, whatever. My neck and head are not going to be as strong as his hips. So I'm powerless, and that's very exciting. At times like that, I'm not doing anything tender, I'm not trying to stroke him or be nice to him. This is a whole different role. The word that comes to mind is *submission,* but I'm not comfortable with the idea of submitting to anybody. [Laughs.] So it doesn't fit me, but it's the word that fits the situation and how I want to feel. I want to feel like he's stronger than I am, and he's deciding what's being done here, and he's doing it, and I have to go along.

Same thing with having my ass fucked. I like that. It's not his favorite thing, but we used to do it a lot. What I like about it is that it's very sensitive there. The walls of the vagina have very few nerve endings, if any. But in my ass I can feel every inch. A guy could be this big [puts fingers two inches apart], and it would be incredibly exciting. You can feel every bit of the length, and the in-and-out motion. Plus it's forbidden, that's exciting. And then there's the idea that every bit, every fiber of my being is tuned in to the erotic. If I could figure out a way to have my nose or my ears fucked, I'd probably try it. Sometimes I wish I had big tits so somebody could fuck me between the tits. I just like being totally available, totally open.

I never touch myself when we're fucking, because he has a thing about masturbation. He doesn't want me to masturbate when he's not around. He doesn't masturbate either. This is important to him. He's an Eastern European man. He wants to be the source of my sexual pleasure. I masturbate anyway, but not when we're together. Sometimes, when he's massaging my clit and he's just a millimeter off the mark, I want to put my finger there, because I know if I do it I'll come. And those are the most—I want to say those are the most intense orgasms, but they're really not. It's just that at the moment it seems like it's going to be. Being that close to a clitoral orgasm, and knowing you could have one in one second, and not having it, that's very, very frustrating. But usually wherever he's touching is so close that if he keeps at it long enough, I'll come anyway. I have moved his finger to the right place, but I try not to do that too much because I don't want to hurt his ego.

There's something men do that really isn't fair. I'm thinking back even to the first time with Pavel. A man cannot even know a woman, and not have the slightest feeling for her, and do all these little tricky things that make her feel so loved. That's not fair. That's pretending. It works, but it's still not fair. When they look deeply into your eyes and stroke your hair. Or when they give you gentle little kisses that seem to have a lot of feeling behind them. I guess what's really behind them is the excitement of the moment, because he may not know you well enough to feel that way about you. But if it causes you to feel that way, then you get carried along with it. And when the whole thing is over, and you think about how nice it was, you realize that a lot of it was imagined, or his intention wasn't what you would have liked to believe it was.

Still, I'll take it. [Laughs.] If somebody can communicate that, I'll take it, even though I know it's not love. It's like I'm stealing the love without ever letting on that I need it. I don't know if that'll ever change. It's my secret: We're having sex, but to me, I'm getting love. That way the other person doesn't have to feel how needy I am.

Pavel constantly tells me I'm a wonderful lover, and he's had a lot of women. He used to be a taxi driver in Prague, and he tells me that he slept with practically everybody who got into his cab. [Laughs.] The men that I've connected best with sexually are men who were very into sex. Men who had lots of women. Men who thought sex was really important. The difference with me is that I'm willing to go deeper and deeper, get more and more involved. The guy may be just getting to the point where he can fuck me, that's what he's after. And I'm going, Hey, this is exciting, let's keep this going, let's keep this alive, let's thrive on it.

So what's the difference between what Pavel is doing to me and what I'm doing to him? He knows he has a commitment elsewhere. He knows he can't put his whole heart into this. I'm his secret lover. I'm his forbidden woman. I'm his recreation. He's trying to make me as happy as he can, so I'll stick around as long as he wants me. It crosses my mind that he might have other girlfriends. Fear of AIDS makes me hope he doesn't. [Laughs.] There are two things I think would stop him. One is that when he gets very, very nervous, he can't get an erection. That didn't stop him from fucking *me,* though. The other is his problem with the English language. It's frustrating for him. So I don't know. When I ask him, he says, "I don't have time for any more women in my life. I work all day. I have the baby at home at night. I have her on weeknights. I've got you on the weekend. That's plenty."

But he used to like to have sex with me every day. I'll say, "We used to be together every day. Now it's once a week. It's driving me crazy." He'll say, "But you know, once a week is a lot more exciting." Well, he seemed pretty excited when it was every day—

At this point in our conversation the phone rang, and it was Pavel. A few minutes later he arrived, clearly unhappy to find me in the living room. As I made my exit, he did his best to explain: "I am sorry. Czech man not like American man." The interview continued a week later.

I can give you a great insight into why I've decided to stay with him a little longer. He was so upset, so shaken to find you here. On some level he had taken me for granted, and the bottom just fell right out. He said to me, "I know that you're looking for love. I've been looking for love my whole life. But I want to tell you that the kind of love you want was only had by two people ever, and that was Romeo and Juliet, because they were willing to die for each other." And I said, "I know, but I'm still gonna look anyway." Then we were sitting on the couch, and he said, "Where is Lucy? Where is the woman who kisses me and holds me and loves me?" We started kissing and his kisses were so tender. You know what it feels like when you've been crying, and then somebody kisses you, and your mouth feels softer? He was showing me how vulnerable he was, and that endeared him to me.

But in between seeing him, I'm thinking about how my life is going to change, because I know I can't go on like this. I plan to keep seeing Pavel until someone else comes along. I think that's fair, I'm not just being selfish, because he's still getting something out of this. But it's going to hurt me a lot to hurt him. We've had long conversations about this maybe three times. I say, "Hey, you've got your girlfriend, you get to go home to her every night. I deserve to have a man in my life that I'm involved with, that I can sleep with, wake up in the morning with. All the things you do." And he says, "Every time we talk about this, it's another mark on my heart. I have three marks on my heart. I remember every one. Please, no more marks."

Even if he left his girlfriend and offered to be with me, there's no future in that. As nice as he is, as wonderful as he is, I have no delusions that I could change him. Look how long he's been this way. Look how many women he's been this way with. And I wouldn't want to be the one at home. God, no. Which is like the ethical problem, right? How come I find it so easy to be the other woman, when I know how miserable it must be to be the one at home? Well, I'm unethical. Basically I'm a straightforward, honest person. But I give in to temptation. I do know I'll never do this again. Unless there were extremely extenuating circumstances, I will never ever become involved with a married man again. It's a waste of time. Why involve my heart when there isn't a future? It's like—it's like being in a full-size maze. There are lots of hallways and lots of doors. What you're looking for is a room that's white. And you open the door, and the room is black. Why keep opening the door to the room that's black? You know it's black, so proceed down the hall. That's what I have to do in my life. Open the next door.

ARCHIE HUNTER

"I'd kill for some good anonymous sex," he says, and looks like he means it. But for the time being, sex with strangers is out of the question: He is trying, for the first time in his life, to make a go of a mono-gamous relationship. A stocky, bullet-headed forty-two-year-old with short sandy hair, wearing jeans and a workshirt, he lives in a new de-velopment in the Connecticut countryside with his lover of three years, Donald. He works as a repairman for the local electric company. Twice a week he travels into New York City for meetings of Sexual Compulsives Anonymous.

He was born poor. His father was an alcoholic who left when Archie was eleven, after which the family survived on welfare and his mother's occasional prostitution. "I have no recollection of my mother before the age of eleven, because I was totally preoccupied by my father. I was terri-fied of him. He was wildly unpredictable, and he was always coming at me. He didn't like the way I did just about everything. Whereas I was ob-sessed with him. I remember how he moved, how he talked. I remember the shape of his cock and his ass. I guess I was very tuned in to the male body at a young age. But I also was aware that I was perceived as a sissy. My father hated that about me. He was always on me to be more of a boy."

Archie started having sex with other boys at fifteen or sixteen. After dropping out of college, getting drafted, and doing a tour in Vietnam, he returned home and lived with a woman for three years. "Cheryl is proba-bly the only person I ever deeply loved. We had a tumultuous, passionate, romantic relationship. But sexually it was a disaster. I had no interest in women. I never should have been sleeping with her, but I kept trying. So early on, I started to equate sex with failure."

Since then he has had a twelve-year affair with a married man; two live-in relationships before the present one; and countless partners in bookstores and highway rest areas, which he calls "the woods." Through-

out, sex was fueled by alcohol and drugs. When we talked, he had been
sober for four years and drug-free for three.

• • •

I'm fascinated with the cock and everything it does. Always have
been. When I was thirteen, I'd go to the drive-in theater and go to
the men's room and stand at a urinal for twenty minutes, a half-hour,
pretending to take a leak, while I looked up and down the line of
people, watching them pee. When I go to the woods, I will pretty
much suck anybody's dick. There is something completely fascinating
and captivating about watching a man take his cock out and getting
on my knees and bringing him to orgasm. But with me it's always
driven, always excessive. It's never casual. It excites me terribly, and
then when it's over, I want to do it again. I walk around and wait for
it to happen. Sometimes it happens six, seven times in a row. Sometimes it doesn't happen at all. You can hang out for hours, and nothing happens. Or sometimes it's two or three or four people at a time,
standing around me. I'm on my knees in the middle, going from one
to another. That thrills me.

I have no interest in being sucked off. I like to play with my own
cock while I'm working on somebody, and if somebody wants to go
down on me, that's fine. It happens occasionally, but few and far between. It's the last thing I really want. Once I come, I lose the impetus to keep going, and basically I want to keep going from person to
person.

When I first got involved with Donald, I was still going out. He
knew about it, he didn't like it, and I eventually cut it off. But then
I kind of replaced it with compulsive masturbation. That's one more
thing I'm trying to get away from. I don't do anything anymore. I'm
boring. Life is empty. Trust me, it is. I go through real periods—I
mean, all the effort I've put into trying to break addictions over the
last few years is a killer. And I still wonder whether my true self isn't
the addictive individual. I didn't mind giving up booze, I didn't mind
giving up drugs, but I do mind giving up sex. There are times when
I don't think I'm being true to myself. I ask myself, Do I really belong

in this relationship? Then I go to a meeting and I realize, yeah, I'm monstrously compulsive. There is nothing healthy about what I do when I'm out there. I go to the woods and spend six, seven hours just hanging around waiting for something to happen. This is not fun, like you have sex and then you can leave.

Probably the peak of my sex life came in the early 1980s. Toward the end of the seventies I discovered that I liked to get pissed on. It took me by surprise, and I was kind of horrified at first, but I let it go and developed a passionate interest for it. I found out about it when I was living with my first lover. I noticed that he could piss with a hard-on. That set off a light [snaps fingers]. I have no idea why, or where it came from, but I became preoccupied with it. I wanted him to piss in my mouth. I didn't know what it meant, I just wanted him to do it. And he did it, reluctantly, at one point. It was really—ugghh, foul, but I wanted him to do it again. At the same time, I was shamed over it. I thought, I don't need to be into this. This isn't normal. This is crazy. How could I be into this? I have some dear friends up in New Haven, and I confided this secret to them. They were merciless. I used to go up there on weekends after I split up with this guy, and they would introduce me as "Splash."

Then I started going into New York to the Mineshaft. The Mineshaft was a disgusting little place, the bowels of the earth. It was a hole. I say that with all reverence. It was wonderful in its own peculiar way. The excesses of the seventies were right there. It's amazing what men will do when they get together. It had various rooms and levels, and down in the basement was what they called the Tub Room. There were a couple of bathtubs, and people would get in the tubs, and people would piss on them. I'd go down there and hang around. I was fascinated. Also positive that I would never be able to do anything like that. I didn't think I had the balls. I was afraid somebody would see me. So I'd go in the club, I'd have a beer upstairs, I'd walk around, I'd go downstairs and check out the scene to see if anything was going on. Or I'd hang around in the Tub Room and watch people get pissed on. Eventually I got closer to the tub. Maybe I'd piss on someone. Or I'd sit fully clothed on the edge of the tub. If you sit on the edge, if you're lucky, somebody will come up to you and maybe put their dick in your mouth. Or you can reach your hand down, somebody's taking a leak on somebody, and you can stick your hand in there. God only knows why.

Then it seems like a quick jump—at one turn I wasn't sitting in the tub, and the next turn I was. I don't remember how I got from one place to another. But pretty soon I was going to the Mineshaft and heading right downstairs. I only had a few hours, and I was going to commandeer the area and make the most of it. It got to be very specific, very fixated. I wasn't there to meet anybody. I wasn't there to chat. It might have been nice to suck a dick or two, but I had a reason for being there. I went right for the oomph, so to speak. If there was a free tub, I would take off my clothes, hop in. I like to kneel, with my ass on my feet, in this position. [Demonstrates.] Facing out. And I'd just sit there for hours and have people come by and piss on me.

At first I had a lot of trouble accepting that this is where my interests lie. I thought it was abnormal. And if we were to do a survey locally, I'm sure we'd find that most people would concur. But I've also realized that to me it's very normal, very comfortable. It's what I like. It took me a while to get over that hump, but I'm perfectly at ease with it now.

Those times at the Mineshaft were some of the purest, most glorious moments I've ever spent. Very drug-induced. Always with speed or cocaine, acid, poppers, whatever. It was a wonderful, marvelous, freeing experience, as close as I've ever come to being in touch with something spiritual, something universal. It sounds ludicrous, but it was a fascinating time. I used to laugh and think, On this given night, I am the guy in the tub at the Mineshaft. Out there, in New York, people whisper about this sort of thing going on, and I am that guy. Loving every fucking minute of it. And dumbfounded that I would ever get to this point.

There were times when people would do more than piss on you. They would spend time with you. They would fuck my face, spit in my mouth, stuff their fingers down my throat. Get sloppy. I love sloppy sex, the sloppier the better. Sloppy, sweaty, bodily fluids, piss, spit, being able to moosh your face in somebody's ass, or their face, the way you become part of it, where there's—it's hard to explain—where kissing goes beyond kissing and becomes like face-eating, in and out of the nose, over the eyes, that ... that ... that meshing. When I suck somebody off, it's wet, it's sloppy, I like it forceful, I like it pounding, I like somebody working my head, working my mouth, holding my head down, fucking my face, taking their cock and beating my head with it, whatever the hell it comes down to. Oh dear, yeah, all that wonderful stuff. It's like I'm always trying to extend the limit. If you're gonna kiss me, let's go for it, let me suck on your chin, let me fuckin' stick my tongue up your nose, let me lick your eyes. If I'm gonna eat your ass, I'm gonna be down there, and my whole face is gonna be in there, I'm gonna be digging my head into your ass, your ass is gonna be soaking wet, and my face is gonna become part of it. Keep pushing the edge a little bit further to see how far it goes, and the further it goes, the more erotic it becomes.

I guess it's funny, but I never looked at this as a humiliating kind of thing. I look at it as intimacy. Somebody spitting in my face, or pissing in my face, it's not that they're humiliating me. They're giving me something I like. And I want to participate. I want to be at the other end of what it is you're giving me, or doing for me. It's never: Humiliate me, put me down, make me feel like shit. It's: Give me pleasure. If you're pissing on me, I'm guiding the scenario. I'm leading you in a particular direction. I'm having a time. I'm not hoping you'll come along and degrade me. There are people who get in the tub and lie totally flat and don't move. They're on their backs, and they let people piss on them. I don't understand that. I don't get any pleasure out of lying inert and having somebody piss on my leg, or my crotch or my groin. That's pure dead weight. So I think those people are looking to be humiliated.

I always felt I wanted to do the tub with a certain amount of dignity. [Laughs.] At first there was a part of me that didn't think it was a very prideful thing to be doing. So I developed a style early on so I could actually get into the tub. It used to be a joke with some friends: I do the tub with class, whereas some of these other queens are totally useless. I'd bring a pair of briefs that were disposable. Sometimes a T-shirt. There was a fascination about having somebody piss on my clothes. I'd kneel in the tub. And when somebody would start pissing, I would moan—no, *moan* is a poor word. It was animal, pure and simple animal. Somebody would be standing there, and I'd do a hit of popper [mimics sharp inhaling], and they would start pissing, and my head would go into it, my face would go into it, and I'd be an animal. *Grroowww!* I'd be shaking my head. I'd bring my head up into it, my face up into it. I'd drink a little, I'd splash around, I'd shake my head, I'd be growling. I guess it was growling, I don't know what else to call it. Whatever it was, it was well-received. It was important to me to feel like I wasn't coming off like one of those other people.

But as time went on, I didn't give a shit. Nothing mattered except being there and doing it. I didn't care if I was seen. I got to be so free there, I experienced so many wonderful moments, that I didn't give a shit about anything. I was there, I was in my essence, and I was having a ball. I opened up to people about it, people in my life. The shame went away. Plus, lots of people do it. Lots and lots of people do it. People love to get pissed on. No big deal.

I wish I could sum up exactly what makes it glorious for me. Physically it feels wonderful, I love it. The piss is mostly beer piss, so there's no taste at all. It's like water. I like to see a cock pissing on me, I like to see the piss coming at me. But it's more an emotional thing: It's somebody's essence, going from his body into my body. There were times when somebody would pop his cock in my mouth and take a piss, and I would think, That piss never saw the light of day. It's a bizarre kind of recycling thing: It went from him into me, and then out of me again. I also think it has a special appeal because it's so outlandish, so off the wall, so forbidden. It's like pushing things one step further: There's the penis, and you suck on it and work on it, and now it's going to piss on you. That's about the ultimate thing the cock does, to piss. When somebody comes, they come, whereas this is completely covering you, and it's pouring out, like one long orgasm.

It's also freeing, in the sense that it leaves me totally uninhibited, totally unaware, totally suspended in the moment. I'm not thinking about having a good time, I'm not worrying about my dick, I'm not thinking about where I am, or what I'm doing, or what the weather is like. To the point where I'd laugh— There I am, sitting in the tub, three people lined up, maybe four, and I'm laughing and crying and having a hell of a good time. When it's over I come back to reality.

But while it's happening, I'm somewhere else. I leave the world for a little while. I have never been able to do that before or since. I mean, if I'm in the woods, I can get lost for a brief period, I can put a dick in my mouth and work on it, but not like this. You gotta realize, I'm sitting there for like three, four hours. I'm doing drugs. I'm doing poppers. It's dark. There's dozens of people coming by. It's sweaty. It's sloppy. It's not like being in the woods and wondering if some cop is standing over there watching me. The Mineshaft was designed for sex. I could do anything there and not worry about anything happening to me, or being interrupted, or bothered.

There were times when I thought, if I'm gonna die, it should be right now, because I'm perfectly at one with everything. I was in my element. This was me in my purest form.

I rarely had an orgasm in the tub. Usually I didn't even have a hard-on. I was so drugged up that my cock wasn't of major importance. The last thing that happens to me when I'm on any kind of drug is getting a hard-on. In a way, being in the tub has nothing to do with sex at all, sex as we know sex. Fucking, sucking, stroking, touching. But it's very, very erotic. I don't think you have to define erotic as having a hard-on or having an orgasm.

I'd do it again in a minute, if I could. I would never have stopped if things hadn't changed. AIDS, the Mineshaft closing, the whole ten yards.

At the same time I was going to the Mineshaft, I was living with this banker. It was a strange kind of relationship. He had no interest—or no ability—to be intimate or physical with me. In the several years we were together, maybe he went down on me once. I don't think we ever kissed. Basically what we did was I worked on him. I'd work on his cock, his balls, whatever. And we did piss scenes. But eventually I wanted more. I needed some attention. I needed somebody to hold me. I needed somebody to want to be near me. I wondered why he wasn't more interested in me, because I was feeling all these flowery things about him. I wanted to get more involved, and he didn't. So I left. And what I took away from it was an alcohol problem.

I got sober in '89. I met Donald a year after that, and I've been with him for three years. And right now, sex is a big issue between us.

There's very little going on between us sexually. Part of that is because I'm into this SCA thing. I think I need some kind of abstinence. I'm just not comfortable with sex. I don't know what to do with it. Half of me wants to go run around outside, and half wants to figure out how to make love to him. In between, there's a lot of confusion, and I'm not having a very good time.

I've been going to SCA meetings for about two months. I go to one meeting a week, but I want to start going to more. Donald is dying to get me to go to more meetings. He's very supportive. He's very easy, the exact opposite of me. He's centered, calm, nonaddictive. I'm a raving loon. I'm out there on any given day trying to drive myself crazy. In fact, you're catching me at an odd moment. I feel like I'm hitting bottom. For the last week and a half I've been on a roll, obsessively. I've been thinking about the woods. I've been beating off constantly. It's a physical feeling. It permeates everything I do. Prior to that, I had a wonderful six or seven weeks. I was going to the meetings, feeling pretty decent, and we had been getting along well. Making love a couple of times. Then, I don't know what happens exactly, but it just slips out from under me.

One big problem is my worry about impotence. I've always been preoccupied with my dick and whether it's going to work. Ever since I lived with Cheryl when I was young, that has been the dominant factor in my life, flat out. To this day I am wildly preoccupied about whether or not I'm going to get it up. That's what sex is about for me: apprehension and fear. The quickest way for me to eliminate that is to go to the woods, drop my drawers, and go down on someone. I fare best in sleazy, anonymous situations. But when I get into bed with someone, I don't work. Because it doesn't make any sense to me. It doesn't turn me on. I don't understand the idea of people stroking and touching. I spent all my life doing anything but that. But even in the woods, impotence is always on my mind. It haunts me.

So in every one of my relationships, it was always understood that I came with a problem. Even so, the first year with Donald was very comfortable. I'd go through periods where I didn't think I could perform, and we'd talk it through. And I'd go through periods where everything was fine. We'd get into bed and make love. But I guess I've been keeping a lot of it inside. I've been kidding myself. We were together, we were having sex, but I was dabbling in compulsive behavior. I've been masturbating constantly the whole time we've been together. Pornography. The whole mental part of it—the taunt, the tease, the obsession, driving and feeding it. Whenever I'm in a sexual situation, or when I'm masturbating, I think about things from the past. I zero in on some number I sucked off in the woods. Only recently am I trying to figure out how to stop that. So every week lately, it's a whole new ballgame. I think I'm going to have to give sex up entirely, because right now it's the enemy. I mean, big-time it's the enemy. Sex and I aren't getting along.

Donald and I had sex last night. Or we attempted to have sex last night. It was going wonderfully. But I just bought a Sony Trinitron thirty-two-inch-screen TV, and of course any faggot with any sense is going to stick a porn tape in. We went into the living room and put the tape in and got into it. But somewhere in the middle I lost it. I became more interested in what was going on in the tape than in what I was doing. My cock went down. I had no interest in Donald. I'm thinking, How come I can't do that? How come I can't be there with those people? How come I can't go suck big dicks? And once I'm into that mode, the moment is lost. Sex is actually annoying. It becomes repulsive. I feel guilty, because part of me is desperate to be out there, and it's like betrayal. I have to walk away—I'm sorry, this is over. Don't touch me.

It's sad, because I'm a very sexual person. I love sex. I wish I were more able to get some joy out of it. But I've been abusing it for so long that it may be time to knock it off, give it a rest. There are times when I get some brilliant flashes of what it could be like. To be captivated by what Donald and I are doing. To be really into giving him pleasure. Or to have him suck my cock, to be comfortable and relaxed with the intimacy. There was a time recently when he came home from work and I was in bed. I had a slight headache. He got into bed with me, and we put our arms around each other. It was a warm, sensuous, sexual feeling. My cock started to get hard. We started to kiss. It was very intimate, and I was very turned on. I was licking his tits, playing with his tits, I got up, he was lying on his back, I was kneeling up over his face, he was sucking on my cock, I was fucking his face. Then I laid back down and he was sucking on my dick. He brought me to orgasm. I was relaxed. Then he sat on my chest and beat off while I ripped on his tits and talked dirty to him. He likes to have his tits really mutilated. And I talk about fucking him, which is something we haven't done. I say, "I've got my cock up your ass, how does a dick feel up your ass, boy? I'm gonna rip these tits off while I fuck your ass and you jerk that dick." That kind of stuff. There have been a number of those moments. I don't know where they come from. They always amaze me.

One thing I found out over the last four, five years is that it gets better. If you keep plodding along, it gets better. Five years ago I was sitting alone drinking. I don't do that anymore. I don't do poppers anymore. I don't do drugs anymore. I'm in a relationship. I have a home. Sex is the last frontier, so to speak. If I can get this under control, I should have it made. The whole experience of being with another person comfortably, that's what I'm going for. That's what this had better be about, because if I get to the end of all this bullshit and that isn't the case, I'm going to be one unhappy camper. I'll have wasted the last five years getting there, when I could have been out sucking all that strange dick.

8

SILENCES

"**B**OY, DO I HAVE AN AWFUL SEX LIFE!" Not everyone in this chapter is as categorical as Holly Franklin, but sex for most of them has gone sour in some way. They range in age from twenty-one to sixty-seven, and their dilemmas differ. What echoes throughout is silence.

Few of us were taught as children to talk about sex, though parents who came of age since the sexual revolution tend to be more open than their parents were. For all but the youngest people I interviewed—such as Sue White in this chapter, whose mother "talked to me about sex all the time"—Eros was the elephant in the living room that everyone pretended not to see. Small wonder that people hit adolescence, and marriage, with little or no ability to express themselves about something so central to their happiness.

The silences here vary in form, duration, and motivation. Holly's upbringing, with a depressed mother and a distant father who never touched each other, seems to have left her with such dismal self-esteem that her entire sexuality was smothered. Finally awakened in her twenties, she had an affair with a man so conflicted about sex with her that she estimates they made love twenty times in five years. "I was always waiting for this guy to come around, and I kept saying to myself, 'That's all I'm going to get. That's all I'm worth.' " The sex, at least, was a pleasure for her when it happened. In contrast, Helen Sharpe was married for many years, had sex every other day with her husband, and has slept with lots of other men—but rarely enjoyed it. "I can't talk about sex to a guy," she says. "Even when there are times that I know exactly what I'd like them to do, I don't say anything. Except for one night, I have never, ever asked any person I've had sex with to do anything to me or for me. I absolutely can't do that."

Why do people keep silent for years, lifetimes? One reason is a sense of inadequacy. In Helen's marriage, "I always felt there was something wrong with me because I never had a vaginal orgasm. Al used to finger-fuck me. And I wanted to come and get it over with, because I didn't think that was the way you should have sex. . . . I thought if you were a normal woman, you had an orgasm the way you were supposed to." Another reason is fear of revealing one's erotic self: appetite, fantasies, specific desires. Equally common is the fear of hurting a partner. Women frequently talk about shielding their mates: Sue White has never had an orgasm, and has never said so to either her husband or her lover. "They must think I always do, so I just don't bring it up. I don't want to hurt their egos." But this is not the province of women alone. Michael Filion, whose desire for his girlfriend is waning because he dislikes their sex, has hardly talked to her about it: "I'm terribly afraid to hurt her feelings and lose her." And often the silences don't even begin in bed. Donna Klein, a housewife with young children, is baffled by her lack of lust. She has few complaints about how her husband makes love—but during our talk it became obvious how angry she is about the division of labor in the household, and about his tendency to come home from work and watch TV for hours.

A clandestine affair, of course, is a type of silence. We assume that people who take lovers want more or different sex, but they may be looking for something else. Sue and her husband, Freddie, make love at least once a day. "Sex is our entertainment, it's what we do when we spend time together." What they don't do is communicate. "The affair I'm having is more for emotional reasons. Freddie is very self-centered. We get along pretty well, but a lot of times he's not a good person to talk to. . . . This other man, he and I have a lot in common and we talk a lot."

One of the classic rationales for maintaining silence is what New York sex therapist Steve Rosenheck calls the Myth of Spontaneity: If sex doesn't work without effort, it won't ever work. Michael Filion is a believer: "I get angry with Beth that it isn't easy for us. . . . I don't want to work on sex. I'm not saying this is right, but I feel like it should be a given." Sex, however, is rarely a given, even between two people in love. As Michael himself learns—and as the speakers in the chapter following this one prove—talk can clear the way for passion.

HOLLY FRANKLIN

She is thirty-two, a WASP, raised in the suburbs; her father was a lawyer, her mother a housewife. She has older brothers. The atmosphere at home was chilly. "My parents never touched, as far as I know. She was depressed, he was distant. I can remember my mother trying to get my dad to hold her, and he just couldn't do it. He was a tall, distinguished-looking man, always wore a Brooks Brothers suit. Sort of like a wise man. Looked up to at the firm. But there was nothing between them. It was kind of sad. I remember once when I was about fourteen, we went up to Niagara Falls. I was an unhappy teenager, didn't want to be traveling with my parents. I was off by myself, and I remember my dad whistling at me. I turned around, and he was holding my mother's hand. He wanted to show me that. I never saw them do that before, and I never saw them do it afterward."

Sex was barely mentioned in the household. Holly started menstruating at almost fifteen and didn't masturbate until she was twenty. "I wasn't aware of my sexual self. It was nonexistent. I remember in fifth grade there was a group of us that played spin the bottle, and I isolated myself and decided I was never going to have a boyfriend." *In fact, while she lost her virginity at twenty,* "I was pretty asexual except for a couple of one-night stands. I still felt I was too tall, I had a big nose, I was ugly. It was just my lot in life. I was pretty miserable about it, but I didn't feel there was anything I could do."

Now she lives in an apartment that seems oddly unfinished—walls torn open, paint stripped—with the work looking as if it has languished for some time. She is unemployed by choice, having quit her secretarial job at an ad agency a year ago because she was having an affair with one of the executives. The relationship ended a few weeks before our talk. She is five foot ten, with long dark hair, pale skin, dark eyes, and, yes, a prominent nose. Beside the couch where she sits as we talk is a child-size rocking chair with a Raggedy Ann doll in it.

• • •

I had been working in the agency for a month when this guy named Jules came in for an interview. He was French. He had his hair back in a ponytail, and he had this great-looking suit on, and these great glasses. He left, and I winked at him and said, "Bye, Jules," and he called me from a pay phone ten minutes later and said he had to see me. I was so manic, I was just flying. And he was so adorable. He took me to lunch and grabbed me at the restaurant, in the middle of the day. I said, "This is too quick," and he said, "We will have dinner tonight."

Jules had this great theory that everybody wants to fuck, so we should fuck, and then we'd get to know each other, or go to the movies, or to dinner. It was sort of liberating for me, who figured I was never going to sleep with anybody and wasn't even attractive to anybody. He said [imitating French accent], "You Americans, you all 'ave zees problem. Ze American man 'ave to take you to ze movies and 'ave to wine you and dine you—forget it. We always want to fuck. We are animals. So let's fuck." And we would. I was so high from it all. He told me that I was beautiful, that my problem was that I was an American and I was uptight. I guess this was my blossoming.

Sex with him was very exciting. He'd take off my clothes in the elevator. He helped me get my first orgasm with a man. He understood that I wasn't having orgasms, and he wanted to help me. So he'd get porn videos for me to watch. I eventually found that I'd have one eye on the video when we were making love, and I did have an orgasm with him after a couple of months. We were having intercourse. I didn't realize that I could touch myself at the same time. I believed in the vaginal orgasm, and that I didn't need to do that. But he suggested I touch myself, and once I did, I had an orgasm. After he suggested it, it was okay.

I saw him on and off for two years, and we didn't sleep together that often. I've never lived with a guy. Never had a guy sleep over for more than two nights. With Jules, it would be twice a week for three weeks, and then I wouldn't see him for three months. There was something about knowing I would never be involved with him that made me loosen up and not feel scared of him. I didn't have to worry about a relationship. I sure wouldn't want to introduce him to my mom. I wasn't even interested in listening to him talk. I'd see him at nine p.m. on a Saturday night, and he'd ask me to leave by one a.m. because he had another girlfriend. I was still thinking that this is all I deserve, this is fine, this is my lot in life. I take what I can get. But eventually, there was makeup in the bedroom, and I realized he was living with another woman. Finally I got the message he had actually married her. I don't have a lot of respect for myself or him at that time, but he helped me get my first orgasm, and he seemed free.

Not long after I met Jules I started seeing someone in the office. It was a small office, about ten of us, we were like a family. I was the only woman. Talk about sexual harassment—we'd talk blowjobs, anything, and I was the focus of it. I loved the attention, I never took offense. This one guy, Alex, he lived with another woman, but he started saying how attractive I was. I think he thought he was saying it to be nice, but I took it as a come-on. We used to go out for a drink every once in a while after work, and he'd rub my hands, he'd massage them. I thought this was so wonderful, this sense of being touched. Then it went to hands under the table. One night we went out for dinner, it was a really cold night, and I said, "Kiss me, get it over with." He wouldn't do it. I finally just grabbed him and said, "Kiss me," and he did. At that point, he was still like, "I can't be doing this, I live with a woman, but you're so attractive, and I'm not really happy with this woman, but I can't do this." And I thought, What a nice guy, he must care about this woman enough to respect the relationship for whatever's left of it. I think it also made me feel a little less like a slut. There was more to us than just sex. We were friends first. It wasn't like Jules.

We kissed in November, and I think in February we eventually had intercourse. He didn't want to. We had a hard time at the office. There was a compulsion to it in the beginning. If nobody was around, we had our hands all over each other. We were a bit out of control. But he was always—"No, I can't do this," and he'd stop and pull himself together. So it was a real struggle. We didn't take our clothes off until the night we made love. And then, for about five years I had an on-and-off relationship with him. We had sex maybe twenty times altogether. While he lived with this woman, we had a very passionate relationship. Then he moved out and got very distant. It was like he didn't want to sleep with me because he was still connected to this other woman, and all we had was sex between us. So it was very frustrating sexually for the last three years. There were periods of six months when we didn't sleep together. He couldn't do it. I think I became too much to contend with. I wanted sex, and I wanted it right away. He needed to be held and talked to before he could have the sex. We reversed the typical roles.

Alex is hard to deal with. He's nine years older than I. He's heady and complicated. He's overweight. He's overbearing, aggressive, obnoxious. Having older brothers, I was used to that. But he was so attractive to me. There was an awkwardness about him. He described himself as the fat little boy in school. Kids making fun of him. He didn't have friends. But very bright. So there was always this wounded quality about him that I saw in myself as well. Two wounded children helping each other.

Sex was great with him. I think in five years, there were maybe two times I didn't have an orgasm. Well, at the beginning I was still seeing Jules, so I didn't have an orgasm with Alex until after I had one with Jules. So intercourse wasn't that satisfying. But he and I were great kissers, so sometimes that was enough. I remember—we'd start kissing, and it was electric. I never had his tongue in my mouth—it was always my tongue in his, which I just loved. I realized that I don't quite know what to do with a tongue in my mouth. I'm a little scared of it. Once I asked him to put his tongue in my mouth, and I just laughed, it felt so awkward. But when I put mine in his, it was like diving into something soft and warm, it was wonderful.

He also was very complimentary. He told me that I looked great. That was a big part of the lovemaking, it was an ego thing. We were together, and he was saying things about me that made me feel good. That I have a great body. That I have a great pussy. That I wear great clothes. And from the moment we kissed until the end, we were always together, even after it. Holding each other. I felt like I became someone else. I finally got to bring out my sexuality, and I liked who I was. I felt somehow powerful. I felt sexy. I felt so alive, so present.

And I remember after I had sex, my hair looked great. It was as if it relaxed. It didn't look stupid. There was always a wave in it.

At the beginning, when he was still living with this other woman, we had some pretty erotic times. Pulling each other into doorways and groping under our shirts. I liked doing it outdoors. I don't think it was the feeling that someone might come up on us, but that sense of me being free. Once we did it in the daytime in a park. We did it several times outside at night. Once we had sex at a rest stop on the highway, once in a car in a parking lot. But I mostly remember the first time we did it outdoors. It was five-thirty in one of those parks that face on the river. This was in our passionate days, when we couldn't keep our hands off each other. We left after work one day and ended up there not quite knowing where to go. I knew he was turned on, and I just said, "Let's do it." I remember how easy it was to come. He was sitting on a bench and I straddled him, chest to chest. I guess I yanked my underpants off to one side, and he pulled out his cock. The intensity was so incredible that I came in two strokes. I touched myself and came. Me who was new to orgasm. I was so amazed. There were cars going by, and it just happened that nobody came by to walk their dog, and nobody shouted at us from a window.

I liked his body because it was big. There was a lot to hold. I also felt safe because he was fat, and I consider myself thin. I thought, for some crazy reason, that no other woman would fall in love with this guy—even though there was another woman in love with him the whole time. I loved his penis—erect or not erect. I just loved it. I thought it was a nice size. It looked nice. But he wasn't really a sensualist. There was never that sense of him being overwhelmed by the moment. Maybe this has more to do with the fact that he never initiated sex. There was always a question whether he was going to turn off. I had voices saying, Are we going to finish? Is he going to leave me? After he leaves, am I going to see him again? Will this be my last orgasm with this guy?

We'd usually have oral sex before intercourse, but I would never have an orgasm while he was going down on me, because I knew I couldn't have another one later. I seem to be a one-orgasm-a-night girl. So I'd ask him to stop, and he'd come inside me. In the beginning, I was still counting how many times I'd had sex so I wanted him to come inside me so I could say, This is one more step away from my virginity. For a long time I called myself the oldest living virgin, although I'd slept with him plenty of times. I felt like it was something that was easily going to be taken away from me. So the penetration was important. I felt, When a guy goes down on me, it's still masturbation, and I do enough of that and should have the real thing.

I always preferred the missionary position. He'd lift himself up on his hands. I sometimes needed him to kiss me while we were fucking so I could get more aroused, and that was hard for him because he's passionless. Sometimes I'd ask him to lick my neck, or I'd bite his arm. I need something in my mouth. Sometimes I'd just rub my lips on his arms. I needed that connection, and if he was up too high I'd miss something. I didn't claw on him. With my right hand I'd be touching myself, and the other one was stretched out rather than touching him. Sometimes I liked it if he'd talk dirty to me, like near the orgasm, when I needed him to encourage me, to be my coach. Not, "Fuck me, you slut from hell," but "Baby, I want you to come." They weren't necessarily soft and gentle words, but they were pleasant words.

It's funny—in order for me to have an orgasm, I have to mentally think the orgasm is coming in the room. Like a person. Definitely a human, but not old or young or male or female. It's like the orgasm is going to come down the hall, and once it gets in the room it's all right for me to let go. I have to picture it coming in, rather than the orgasm coming from inside me. It often makes me think it's my father coming down the hallway, though I don't know why that comes to mind. But it's enough for it to just come in the room. Then it disappears or becomes part of me. I picture it coming in the door, and then I either come soon after that, or right when it comes in the door.

I always come first. Alex waits for me. He doesn't come with pleasure if I haven't come. We hardly ever come together, so there's always that sense of someone watching you. He's pretty verbal—he moans and groans, and he often has tears in his eyes afterward. Sometimes he cries, he snuggles his head into mine. It's just a release for him, he's a little sobby and then it's over. One of the parts I love, usually after we make love he lies full on top of me and squooshes me into the mattress. I love the sense of having his full weight on me and being able to hold him. I feel like he's always there—he doesn't get up to go to the bathroom. He doesn't smoke a cigarette or leave me in any way after we make love.

The problem was starting to make love. There were only two times when he initiated sex—two times in five years. A very passive person. Something about him didn't want to be responsible for making love. We always started because I wanted to. I knew if he kissed me on my ear or he started kissing my nipples, then we would make love. But so often, he would back off. He'd say, "No, it's not a good time." I'd get very upset. I felt so screwed up. But I was a party to it, because I allowed it to happen. Then I'd cry, and he'd get very sad. He'd say, "I know, I'm an awful person. I'm really confused. You can't believe the confusion I'm going through. I feel so awful that I'm hurting you this way, but I don't know what to do." So most of the time, I could never really let go, because he might be gone in twenty minutes. I just had those two signals that let me know it was okay to pursue it.

We once had a fight: I said, "You made love with me four times last year." He said, "Four times? It must have been at least thirty." I said, "I have a box of eight condoms, and four are missing. That means we've made love four times." He said, "At least thirty." "No, count them, four times." So I was always waiting for this guy to come around, and I kept saying to myself, That's all I'm going to get. That's all I'm worth.

Boy, I have an awful sex life!

I used to love it when Alex would kiss my face. I thought it was so loving, that he'd want to kiss this face. I've had so few male relationships that I think I must have some aura that says, "Don't come near me." When he would kiss my face or stroke it or look in my eyes—I was always so touched by that. Because I don't feel attractive, I put a lot of bearing on him making me feel attractive. I spend a lot of time looking in the mirror thinking, This is an imperfect face. This is ugly.

So Alex kissing my face was more than sex for me. It was a validation of my whole being. I was being held by this guy, and my face was being kissed. I felt like, My mother never loved me, but this guy will. It was something I didn't know was missing in my life until I started doing therapy—this sense that I never got held as a baby. They call it mirroring. Mirroring is smiling back and being happy with the baby. It gives the baby a feeling that it exists. I never had that. With my mother, I was often talking to the side of her face, and never having her look at me. I had to learn about someone looking into my eyes. Alex did it naturally, and then I felt comfortable enough to tell him how much I liked it and how much I hadn't had it. Looking at me and touching me. Kissing me. Little kisses.

I never got used to it. It amazed me every time he would do it. I thought it was so special that I couldn't get it from anybody else in the world.

SUE WHITE

She is twenty-one, married two and a half years, a month into an affair, and so matter-of-fact about it all as to be a bit disconcerting. Perhaps, she says, that comes from the way sex was first presented to her. "My parents are very religious, they practically live at their church, but they aren't prudish. My mother talked to me about sex all the time. When I was six and I started going to school, I'd come home saying 'fuck' and 'shit' and all this stuff. My mother asked me, 'Sue, do you know what that means?' She explained it all and said, 'It's just not very good to go around saying these things.' Later on she wanted to be sure I knew what birth control was. She stressed that it was really important to not get pregnant. I started to have sex when I was fifteen, and I think they knew. They just didn't want me to be emotionally damaged by anything.

"Until I was seventeen or so I didn't have boyfriends as such. I had a group—there were about ten of us, and we were all close friends. We'd have these parties every Wednesday and Saturday night, and I think we all had sex with each other at some point. It was interesting. Very casual. So I've had a lot of sex. It's not that I think about it so much, but I always have people who are attracted to me, and maybe I don't have the phobias that other people have—like being worried that if you have sex with someone they won't like you the next day, or they're only going to like you because of sex, or if you perform badly they're going to hate you. I've always been sure of myself sexually. I'm open with it, and I've never been shy to take my clothes off, and if I wanted to kiss someone I'd go up and kiss them."

She is indeed attractive: long, straight, jet-black hair, pale skin, green eyes. She is wearing a low-cut minidress and very high heels. She lives in Washington, where she works in an office and attends college.

• • •

I moved to the city when I was eighteen. After I had been here about a month I went out with this man. His name is Freddie, he's in a band, and he's three years older than I am, so of course I thought he was really romantic. It surprises me now, and I would never do this now, because I didn't even know him. He came home with me, and we had sex, and we kept going out every night, and we got married two months later and that was it.

It was on a whim. We probably got married because we had really good sex and it made us crazy. One night we were sitting around and he said, "Let's go get married." I thought it sounded pretty funny. I'm like, "Oh, okay, let's do it." So the next morning we went and filled out a marriage license. You have to wait twenty-four hours. We almost weren't going to do it because we didn't want to get the blood test. But you don't have to have that anymore. So we went back the next day and got married.

At the time marriage seemed like a logical idea. I hadn't thought about it as a permanent thing. It wasn't that we had fallen in love. We were in a whirlwind. Later on, when we settled down, we fell in love. It was like we had an arranged marriage, because we didn't know anything about each other. I thought I knew him, but I didn't, of course. I think if we hadn't moved in together immediately, we would have parted ways and never seen each other again after six weeks. Moving in sealed everything. It was more of a commitment than being married. And after that we were determined to stay married because everyone we knew had placed bets on how soon we'd get divorced. They were like, "This is ridiculous, you'll only stay married a month." The longest bet was about a year, so we've definitely beat out the longest bet.

Mostly at first it was sex. It was very passionate. It was like we already knew each other sexually. There was no awkwardness at all. He's a very open person, and he's always been active sexually, and I guess he knew what he was doing. So most of it was him, his personality. Now that I've been married to him, I might describe him as overbearing, but then I just thought he was the most charming person. He's not at all wishy-washy. If he has an opinion, he'll say it, and some of them are farfetched. He thinks all criminals should be killed. He'll sit in front of a room of people who have a different opinion, and he'll state his very loudly, and he really doesn't care if someone thinks different. Anything he wants, he'll go after it full force. He kind of overwhelmed me.

He also has a really big sexual appetite. We still have sex once or twice a day, which I guess is unusual. I've cooled off a little bit because I work and go to school full-time, but he hasn't. I'm always hitting him and telling him to go away, but he doesn't. We have sex anytime, all the time. Late at night. After dinner. In the morning. He used to work across the street from me, and we'd have sex at lunch in the men's room in his building. We've had sex all over the place. The men's room at a fancy hotel, which was funny. We were waiting for a movie, and we had about an hour till the show started, and we didn't have anything to do, so we went into the hotel. He went in the men's room and said, "Sue, it's empty, come in here." We had sex in the stall, standing up. It's a clumsy thing, because bathrooms aren't made for sex, so there isn't any way to do it comfortably. You're always straddling a toilet or tripping over it. We have sex in a lot of buildings. Residential hotels work best because they have a doorman, but it's generally kind of low-maintenance so they don't ask you what you're doing. You just walk in looking like you belong there. Then we take the elevator to the top floor, and if there's a roof, we walk up to the top of the stairs and there's usually a little space. No one walks up there. But you can't do it in the winter, because it's cold.

Sometimes we'll have sex several times in a day. He almost killed me one day, he wanted to see how many times he could have sex. He said he thought he could do it twenty-five times. I think he got up to sixteen and then it was midnight and I told him he had to stop because the day was over and it wouldn't count.

We like everything. You name it, I'm sure we've done it. Oral sex, anal sex. He brings home porn films, which I don't like but he does, so I let him watch. I can't let any girlfriends of mine spend the night, because he always wants me to have sex with them while he watches. He's like, "Sue, crawl in bed with her." I say, "Freddie, no." It gets embarrassing. He tries to get us drunk. If it's a close friend of mine, I warn her, so she'll be expecting it and we tease him. One night a girlfriend of mine and I got terribly intoxicated. She and I are very affectionate, we're always kissing each other. We came home and I don't remember what happened. He says we did it, but I don't believe him. I think she and I were more likely to have been throwing up than having sex.

If I'm tired, I've found it's easier to just have sex with him than try to dissuade him. He'll guilt me into it. If I tell him no, he'll say—he means this to be funny—he'll say, "Then I'll just have to satisfy myself." He starts to masturbate, and he'll run his elbow into me while he does it, and he'll make little sighing noises [imitates his deep sigh]. "Oh, my wife doesn't love me, and she won't have sex with me, and I'm all alone, and I might as well get used to this." I get sick of it after a while and have sex with him. I usually end up liking it even if I try not to. I'll try and just stare at the ceiling. A long time ago I told him this joke. It's about how different types of girls have sex. There are supposed to be three types, but I only remember two. The sorority girl lies there and says, "Drunk. I'm so drunk." The wife lies there and says, "Beige. I think I'll paint the ceiling beige." So whenever he has sex with me when I don't want to, I look at the ceiling and intone, "Beige. I think I'll paint the ceiling beige."

Sometimes he wakes me up in the middle of the night. He'll literally roll on top of me and lie there and look at me. He tries to kiss me. If I get woken up I'm very cranky. I'll actually hit him because I'm asleep and I don't want him to bother me. Like Thursday, I remember Thursday. Every Thursday night he goes out to a club. He came home about two A.M. He climbed into bed and I guess he had been sitting there for a long time looking at me while I was asleep. He began to kiss me, and I woke up, and I started yelling at him, and he was being really nice, so I felt guilty for yelling. I started to kiss him back, and I wasn't quite awake yet. This is all cloudy, it's like remembering a dream. I don't think we had oral sex at all, because I was asleep. I don't think it was unusual in any way. The usual middle-of-the-night, Sue's-asleep encounter might last fifteen minutes. It's straight fucking, nothing else. No unusual positions. It's like having sex with one of those dolls. I lie there and he pushes me around. He might grab my leg and pull it up, or roll me over, but I'm not moving much. It takes a while for me to get aroused, but once I wake up completely I am. Usually just about the time I'm awake, he has his orgasm and falls asleep. Then I'm awake, and it takes me a while to fall asleep, so I get up and do stuff around the apartment. But I don't mind. If it was that way every time, it would certainly bother me, but it's not, so it doesn't.

We're always joking around with each other. If he doesn't want to have sex—which never happens, he's usually just pretending—I'll try to persuade him. It's a little joke to see how ridiculous I can be. I start out using his tactic, and I say, "Oh, my husband doesn't love me." That doesn't work, he sits there and watches his TV. I finally found one that works. I crawl up and look at him pitifully and say, "Please, just a few pumps?"

Freddie doesn't like me to suck him to orgasm. Neither of us really likes it. It's messy, it's not really tasty, it's high in calories, and if you aren't going to swallow it, it's sort of disgusting right after someone has an orgasm to go running off in the bathroom to spit. He doesn't go down on me as much as I do on him. He has this phobia about dirty pussy, and I can understand that. If I haven't washed immediately before, he won't do it. I've started enforcing the same rules with him, I make him go and wash. I like oral sex, but not as much as fucking. I like actual sex more than foreplay. But I've never had an orgasm. I read that a lot of women don't until they're older, so I don't worry about it. I figure that trying to have one would make it frustrating, so it will happen when it happens. I never masturbated, I don't really like it. What I like about sex is not just sex. I wouldn't sit around and do it myself. What I like is the other person.

I do get close to orgasm, and I yell really loud when I'm having sex. I yell words and phrases. Some of them don't make sense. I don't notice it, because I assume I'm saying a word. I'll say Freddie's name and it sounds like I'm speaking in tongues. It all depends on the level of enjoyment—the lowest level would be talking dirty, then comes moaning and screaming, and babbling is the high point. He's really proud of himself then. It makes him feel he's made me lose complete control of my faculties, and I've gone insane because he's such a fabulous lover. I guess that's true, but I wouldn't say that to him because his ego's too big already.

I'm definitely not looking for more sex than I already have. The affair I'm having is more for emotional reasons. Freddie is very self-centered. We get along pretty well, but a lot of times he's not a good person to talk to. He's not an emotional support. He's distant. He'll spend a whole day without saying anything to me because he doesn't feel like talking, which drives me up a wall. The only things he'll talk about are concrete things—is the weather warm or cold, what we're going to do. He won't sit and discuss ideas or contemplate a dream. And we have nothing in common. We don't like the same movies. He'll want to watch *Rambo* and I'll want to watch *Last Exit to Brooklyn*. I read a lot, he reads comic books. He watches loads of TV, I don't like to watch any TV. Sex is our entertainment, it's what we do when we spend time together, because we don't like any of the same things.

This other man, his name is Alvin, he and I have a lot in common and we talk a lot. He's thirty-five, so he's a lot older than me. Except for the fact that we're both involved with other people, we have a very normal relationship. We're getting to know each other slowly. It's the opposite of the way I was married. We met in school. We were in two classes together, and there was an hour break in between. We'd go to coffee shops. Then we started spending a lot of time together. After a few months of hanging around, one night we decided we were going to run around to different clubs. Then we started going out every Thursday night, listening to music. On Thursday Freddie and I always go out separately with our friends, so he never asked who I was with.

One night I came to Alvin's apartment right after work. I had a bag with me, because I change clothes at work. I said, "I'm going to leave my bag here and get it later." To me that was a clear signal that I was going to come back to his apartment after going out. He's very innocent, he told me later, "Oh, I thought you'd stay downstairs and I'd go up and get it and call you a cab." I thought that was kind of nice. So I went up to get my bag, and he and I started to kiss, and things went on and we had sex. It was something he'd been thinking about for a while, and we had spoken about it. We said, "How involved are we going to get with each other?" He tells me about his girlfriend and I tell him about Freddie, we bitch to each other about them.

We haven't had sex that many times because we don't have that much time to spend together. Alvin's a very good lover. Of course he's not as oversexed as Freddie, I don't think many people are. And sex is much gentler with him. Freddie is very, very aggressive, and Alvin isn't at all. If Freddie wants me to move over to the other side of the bed he'll pick me up and throw me over there. If Alvin wants me to, he'll say, "Can we move over?" He waits to see what I want. He likes giving oral sex more than getting oral sex. He's interested in pleasing me and making me happy more than anything else. He doesn't know I don't have orgasms. Since I'm so loud, neither of them has ever asked me, and I know if a man thinks a woman hasn't had an orgasm, he asks. They must think I always do, so I just don't bring it up. I don't want to hurt their egos.

I tease Alvin in bed. Freddie likes to be teased sometimes, but not too much. He wants to get down to business. Alvin on the other hand adores being teased. Like if I'm kissing him, I'll come close, but I won't. Or I'll kiss him a little and then stop. And if I'm on top of him, I'll hold my pussy right above him for a long time before I—there's not really a word for it. Before I engulf him. But I don't know him very well sexually so it's hard to say very much about him. It's not intense yet between us. The feelings are, but the actual physical sex. . . . Because in time you get to know what the person likes, the way they like to be touched, and where. What makes them happy and what makes you happy and how the two things come together.

I think about Alvin sexually a lot. Sometimes I think about him when I'm having sex with Freddie. But you always desire someone more when you don't know them as well. It's a different kind of desire. With Alvin, I'll sit and think about him during the day. With Freddie, I've thought about him as much as I'm going to. It's not like I'm going to sit and get all tittery about him at work. I have to actually touch Freddie to get excited about him, but with Alvin I can just think.

Anyway, like I said, the real reason I'm having this affair isn't sexual, it's emotional. Freddie knows I need to talk to people. He knows I need someone to seem like they really care about me. Alvin is more caring. He's more interested in things. If I went to Freddie and said, "Oh, I had a really interesting day at work," he would go, "I have to make a phone call." If I said that to Alvin, he'd say, "Oh, really? What was it? Tell me about it." Alvin is also very complimentary. He thinks I'm a goddess. He really likes pale women with black hair. He says, "I'd like to paint you, I'd like to draw you and take photographs of you."

I don't like the illicit part of the affair. Mostly it's a nuisance, because it's very difficult to find time, and I don't like lying to Freddie and sneaking around. If he wouldn't mind, I'd tell him. I'd be very happy having two men and having them know about each other. I don't think Freddie would go for that, he'd show up with a gun. But I don't really feel guilty. It's strange. Actually, more than feeling bad for Freddie—since I don't think he'll ever find out about it—I feel sort of bad for Alvin, who likes me a lot. He never gets to spend any time with me. He and his girlfriend don't get along that well. He doesn't want to live with her. He recently gave me the keys to his apartment and told me, "If you ever want to move in one day, just bring your stuff over." I think he wants to get married and settle down with someone, and I don't think it'll be me. For one thing, the way we met, if we were in a relationship I don't know if either of us would be able to trust the other one. Actually, I would trust him, but I don't know that he would trust me. He always says women can lie but men can't. The minute a man lies a woman knows it, that's what he says. I don't really agree, but in that frame of mind I don't think he'd ever be able to trust me.

Lately I've been feeling like a woman from a romance novel. They always have the women in exotic locations—I guess Washington can qualify as exotic. And there are always two fabulous men vying for this woman's attention. I think I have two men who most women would be happy to have one of. They're both nice and loving and warm people, and I'm having a really good time. I probably have the most active sex life in the world. One night I came home from having this long sexual encounter with Alvin. Freddie was lying there in bed. He said, "I've been waiting up for you." I thought, Oh, great. He goes, "I'm horny. Come over here." The next day at work, someone said, "Sue, how come you always look so happy? How do you do that?" I said, "I don't know, I just have a positive outlook on life."

MICHAEL FILION

He is thirty-three, a saxophone player who lives in Los Angeles and works as a studio musician when he is not touring with rock 'n' roll acts. He grew up in a conservative, lower-middle-class Southern California town, his father a businessman and his mother a housewife. "It was a pretty good house to grow up in. There was a lot of love, there still is, and my sister and I are very close. But there was a lot of screaming and yelling—my mother wore her heart on her sleeve and said whatever was on her mind. She told me later that things were nip and tuck in the marriage when I was young. They went to therapy together. I guess they were trailblazers, not many people did that in those days.

"I don't know much about their sex life. I have some old pictures of them and they both look extraordinarily sexy. My father had smoldering Eastern European looks, and my mom had that Marilyn Monroe-ish look, a full face with a big, juicy woman's body. They're not terribly physical with each other, they hug and kiss, but there's never innuendo in the air. They've had separate beds for as long as I've been conscious, because they have different sleeping habits. I never talk to them about it, but they aren't rigid people. Sex was unspoken, not a terrible taboo."

He has led an active sex life, though high school was "the acme of my sexual prowess. That's not to say I didn't behave promiscuously in college or when I moved to LA, but there was a time in my youth when my self-esteem from A to Z was about my sexual exploits. I don't think that's unusual for a strapping young man with sperm coming out of his ears. It was all pretty tame—I never slept with a man, never with two women, or with another man and a woman. I'm happiest one on one. And recently, sex has become less important in my life, as other aspects have become more."

He has been with his present girlfriend, Beth, for two years. Judging from the pictures around his apartment, she bears a strong resemblance to

Marilyn Monroe. "Emotionally, this is the best relationship I've ever had. But it's not the greatest sexually."

• • •

I met Beth when we were doing a tour together. I was playing in the band, she was a backup singer and dancer. I was living with someone, she was married to her then-husband. We hit it off and started spending a lot of time together. We talked about our personal lives. I was confused about my relationship with Joan, where that was leading. I knew Beth's marriage wasn't good, and she wanted to get out of it. We started sleeping together, and it was pretty exciting, there was a great deal of passion. And we continued to sleep together before I decided to end the thing with Joan and she separated from her husband.

She had much less sexual experience than me. She wasn't a terribly wild teenager, she was overweight, and she met Peter when she was very young. I always felt with her, even at the beginning, that she was nervous about sex—that she liked it, but she was nervous about it, and she was afraid to be wanton. She felt guilty in some way. That came across in nervous laughter, not being able to talk during sex—although she does say she's pleased after we do it, she says that all the time. In the beginning, I was pretty thrilled with how the sex affected her. I was so happy to be pleasing somebody so much that what I wanted didn't matter. Then I guess over time it started to matter.

I don't want a lot of sex with Beth anymore. I know that frustrates her. I don't talk about it as openly as I should, because I'm terribly afraid to hurt her feelings and lose her. But she just doesn't arouse me much anymore. She's not as connected to the act as she should be, or as I would want her to be. I don't understand frenzied sex, the kind of sex where you're out of control but it's not really felt. In so much of our lovemaking, she seems to be enjoying the hell out of it, and I'm sort of below or on the side or above her saying to myself, What is so good about this? She's making all this noise, and she's moving so fast that I can hardly feel anything. I start to feel even more lonely than if I was alone in the room.

I don't remember that being true in the beginning. I remember it being a brand-new person and a brand-new body and a brand-new feeling. There was a lot of clandestine behavior, we were living in these hotels and everyone in the show was usually on the same floor, and Beth's husband had come to visit, so everyone knew she was married, and everyone knew I had a girlfriend, so we did a lot of sneaking around between rooms and trying not to make too much noise while we were having sex. The first time we made love was one of those fast and furious mind-numbing experiences that even at the time I figured, Well, that was pretty special, but I know I can't keep that up. No way am I gonna want to do that in a year. It was just so frantic. It had a beginning, a middle, and an end, but I don't remember the middle. I remember the first touch and then going to sleep, but everything in the middle was loud and fast and hard. I don't even like to make love that way.

So I think our sexual biography got off on the wrong foot, and a lot of bad habits have resulted from that. I liked her a lot and the first encounters were wonderful, but I felt terribly guilty, and because of the tension we never talked about what started to go wrong. When we began to have our own relationship, the sex took a downturn for all the obvious reasons, because it wasn't illicit anymore but also because we weren't talking about it. Two people who are having illicit sex don't talk about sex. That's what people in a relationship do. So we never learned to deal with it.

One thing about sleeping with Beth is that it's the same every time. It's not soft and flowing sometimes and harder other times. There have been times when I've wanted to try something different— although I never say, "This is what I want to try." We usually have sex at night. Usually in the bed, usually at her house, because she doesn't have a roommate, and it's a nicer place. We usually start—it never feels natural to begin to make love with her. It feels very herky-jerky. I know she really wants to make love, and I know I don't. It's not so much that she does something specific to make my dick go limp; it's more that I'm uninterested, I know what's coming up is going to be very much like the last time.

Usually we get in bed, and usually I'm not wearing anything and she wears my pajamas, and sometimes nothing happens and I'll try to go to sleep and she'll stew, and other times we do make love. Maybe she takes the initiative, maybe I do. Sometimes I do out of guilt. But generally she'll snuggle up or climb on top of me and start to kiss me, and I'll kiss back, and then I'll get an erection. Foreplay can go on for quite a while, half an hour, sometimes we do nothing but foreplay. But she's not creative. She does touch, but there's an awkwardness. A gesture as simple as reaching down to grab me by the cock—well, it's not *specific* somehow. It's like the difference between "She fondled my leg" and "She tickled the crease below my kneecap with her fingernails." Or the difference between "She reached down and grabbed me by the dick" as opposed to "She swirled two fingers around the head of my penis." She does more of a grope. She seems awkward.

Generally I bring her to orgasm before I penetrate her. It's more exciting for me to have not climaxed yet and to give her an orgasm. And she can only have an orgasm by manual or oral stimulation. Generally it's manual. She likes it best when I'm behind her and she's on her knees with her head down on the bed and her butt up in the air. When I'm doing that, her response doesn't feel overdone, it seems authentic. She is very quickly aroused. She gets very damp very quick, almost quicker than I would like. I don't mind the dampness, dampness is good, but whether I'm doing it manually or orally or fucking her, there seems to be a point where I'm left alone. Physically she gets really tense, and she breathes heavily, and her release is very spasmodic. She cries out, and there's a lot of twitching. Sometimes I'll slip the penis in just for a little variety and try to bring her off with my hand while I'm inside her, but that never works. There's something strange that happens when she has a penis inside her, I don't think she can come at all.

Still, foreplay is mostly enjoyable, until I penetrate, and then I usually start to feel like it's just not any good anymore. It seems like she gets excited much quicker than I do, so there's huffing and puffing and speed-fucking so early on that I'm not ready for it. There's no gray area, it's either sit still or buck wildly. We spend a lot of time in one of three positions—her on top, me on top in the missionary, or me behind her. But it's the same whichever position we're in, she's in this frenzied state. I assume she knows she won't achieve an orgasm, yet she behaves as if she's on the brink. And that could go on for three days if you were inhuman. She makes a lot of noise, maybe not actually screaming, but definitely moaning. And she has a tendency to make it as frenetic as possible. I can't do that forever, so I'll slow down and try some different speed or some different motion, but her reaction is to try to go back to the quick piston thing. What happens to me is that eventually, the combination of hearing the same moan or cry, over and over, with a lot of "Oh!"s and "Oh God!"s, and knowing it will never resolve, and the quick in-and-out of my penis, which starts to feel numb—that's where it stops, nothing of interest happens after that. I start thinking, What are we doing here? You're making all this noise, and you're rocking back and forth, and you seem to be enjoying it, but it can go on for three hours and we'll never get anywhere.

Sometimes I get the feeling that she's doing it solely for my benefit, meaning that she's acting. The noises and the bucking seem very self-conscious. But who am I to say or even know how much she's enjoying herself? Maybe enjoying herself is getting as many endorphins as she can in the base of her skull. Endorphins are those things that runners get off on when they break their twentieth mile. The body drugs that make you feel like you're walking on cloud nine even though you're about to drop dead. I think everyone gets endorphins if they fuck long and hard enough. So maybe if I asked, she'd say she's in ecstasy. And she might say, Why aren't you? Which is why I never ask her! All I know is that she's not the only person I've fucked, and I can't believe that two people can be so detached, that one can feel so out to sea and the other can be in the throes of such ecstasy.

I have never asked her about it. I have often thought of asking, but it never seems to be the right time to stop, with all this stuff happening, and go, "Honey, are you really getting off on this?" It's insulting to do that. There must be a loving way to say it, but I don't know what it is, or when it should be said. After we make love she always seems to be very happy and satisfied, and I'd be afraid to bring it up.

When I come—sometimes it happens when she's giving me oral sex, although not often. That's one of the things I have been able to talk to her about, how I like that. And she has gotten pretty good at it. If we're fucking, she generally wants me behind her, and sometimes it takes an inordinate amount of time for me to come, because by that point I'm feeling abandoned. I have been known to fantasize I'm with someone else, and I hate myself for that, too. I don't do it a lot, because even as I'm doing it, I feel guilty. Sometimes I fantasize about an old fave, or a woman I've never slept with. While Beth is turned away from me I feel like now's the time, while she's unaware, bucking back and forth. But I don't think it's fun.

There was a time about a year ago when I couldn't keep an erection, which was weird. It was a result of just not being happy in the act, I don't know how else to explain it except that I felt lonely and it didn't excite me. But eventually that changed, I was able to talk about it a little bit, why it wasn't happening. She wanted to know what I was feeling, and what she could do about it, and we actually talked about some things she could do, and that's how we got out of it. Some manual things she could do with her hands and her mouth, the proper amount of spit. . . . I don't like having to teach about sex. I remember feeling very uncomfortable about having to explain why I needed lubrication while she was pumping me with her hand. It seemed like another instance of, Why don't you know this already, why can't you figure this out? I told her that what feels real nice is a combo of hands and mouth, with the top hand playing with the head of the penis and her mouth coming over the top and making sure the entire shaft is lubricated. And not to be afraid to really work it, if there's enough lubrication you can really grab hold and make it a joystick. She was tentative, I guess she hadn't done much of that.

I don't know why sex is so hard for me to talk about. I'm sure it has something to do with my family. I also have the feeling that if sex isn't innately understood it's never going to be fantastic anyway. I'm much more comfortable with someone who just knows, whose body knows the right thing to do at the right time. I'm always on the fence about talking, depending on who I'm with—if I'm with somebody who's easy talking about sex, I can jump to her side of the fence, but if I'm with somebody who's reticent, I become like that. There have been women I communicate with as naturally as talking right now. I laugh and crack jokes. Beth and I don't crack too many jokes, it's too much work. I get angry with Beth that it isn't easy for us. I get angry with her for not being aware that something else is possible, that bodies communicate in different ways. I don't want to work on sex, I feel like—and I'm not saying this is right—I feel like it should be a given. If it's something you don't know naturally, will talking about it make a difference?

Not long after our first conversation, Michael decided to test the waters, and we met again a couple of weeks later.

Well, we had an encounter late one weekend morning, and it wasn't working out. I was losing my erection, and it was obvious that we had to talk about what was happening. I started out by saying that I feel lonely sometimes when we have sex because she seems to go away. She gets all wrapped up in her "Do me, do me, do me" attitude. I explained to her that when I lose my erection, that's why. If I'm going to have sex with someone, I don't want to feel as if I could just be masturbating. We ended up talking not so much about the nuts and bolts, it turned into a conversation more about our history and our personal histories. I think we learned a lot.

For one thing, I learned that her first sexual experience was a rape. I never knew that, and it surprised me. She also said she kept looking for our sex to be like it was the first few times. For two years, she has been wondering what happened to that passion. My explanation was that our sex got to be boring, it wasn't illicit anymore, it wasn't growing, and we weren't talking about it, and I began to feel lonely. She said, "The reason you were feeling lonely is because I was feeling insecure and inadequate. I didn't know whether you wanted me." Her feeling about my turning off was that she had to try harder. She tried to make it better by going at it harder—this exaggerated, lusty, loud, growling sex thing. That's fine if it's genuine, everyone tries to make sex exciting, but it was like a bad porno act. A lot of what she said wasn't necessarily news, so much as putting things together that I knew all along. I understood what she meant about feeling the need to work hard. I think her sexual self-esteem isn't terribly high. I know she gets very hot when we make love, you can tell by certain things, like wetness and skin color and blushing and nipple erection. But whether she's aware of it or not, she goes out of her way to let me know that she's hot, and I don't need that. It's like gilding the lily.

After we talked, the sex was different for a while. It was fun. It was more spontaneous. We weren't trying to achieve anything in any set amount of time. It just happened. Sometimes it went on for a long time, sometimes it was over in a flash, and we didn't care. That was nice. It was lovely to have her there all the time. She apparently still found it satisfying, she had orgasms—actually, a couple of times she didn't have orgasms, and I knew she didn't care, and I didn't care, which is new for me, too.

So we had quite a few really nice experiences—and then the last couple of times . . . Beth went on the pill recently. She got tired of running off and putting in a diaphragm, and I got tired of condoms. So she went on the pill, and the last couple of times we've been back to frantic. Maybe it's because she doesn't have to worry about birth control anymore, but for me it's like, Ugh, slow down, please. The last time we made love, I started to get that overwhelming feeling, Why am I doing this anyway? My erection went a little soft. I almost stopped in the middle and said, This is not good. But I didn't want to do it like that. I felt it would hurt her feelings. So it needs to be dealt with, and I want to deal with it before it goes too far again.

DONNA KLEIN

The interview is tough to conduct: We talk in the company of her five-year-old daughter and a two-year-old son, so for the first hour the tape recorder must be turned off every five minutes while an orange is peeled or a toy fetched. Finally the girl goes next door to play with a friend, the boy settles down in front of Peter Pan, *and we are interrupted only by periodic cries of "Crocodile! Crocodile!" Another son, eight, is in school. The mother is forty-four, pretty, buxom, with wavy auburn hair to her shoulders. She is wearing a black sweater and white tights with black stars, and she looks fatigued, as befits a housewife with three young kids. Her domain is a large townhouse condo in a town on the New Jersey shore. The living room is done in whites and beiges and floral prints. Everything is astonishingly tidy. Her husband, Mike, is a chemist at a drug company. Before having children, Donna worked in advertising.*

Her parents are devout Methodists. "They were very, very strict. Sex was bad, everything was bad. I had a conversation with them recently, they were talking about oral sex on TV. My father got hysterical: 'Cows do that!' Meaning that cows and other animals lick their private parts. He couldn't believe humans do it. On the other hand, he thinks a lot of old people die off because they don't sleep together anymore. Whenever he and Mom stay here, I can hear them giggling in their bedroom, Mom going, 'Oh, Ted. Oh, Ted.' They follow each other around like puppy-dogs, they tell each other how much they love each other and say, 'I just hope God takes me first.' I think the reason I've been married three times is I keep looking for their relationship. Now that I'm older and wiser, I realize it's not usually like that. There's the passionate period where you can't get enough of each other, and after a few years it wanes, and after kids it really wanes and everything changes."

Her first husband was her high school sweetheart; it lasted a year. In her twenties, after a period of being "very wild," she married an older

man who later became domineering and abusive. Ten years ago she left
him and soon met Mike, "a good ol' boy from Texas."

• • •

Mike and I were very sexually active for about two years. We weren't wild, like with other people or anything, but we were all over the place—on the floor, on the couch, on the bed, in the shower, everywhere. Plus we were trying to have children, so we were doing it with that in mind. Then I had a lot of problems with my pregnancies. I lost two pregnancies before I found a doctor who understood what was wrong. I had to be in bed for the last five months with each kid. If I was pregnant five seconds, we didn't want to disturb the fetus, so we didn't have sex. I mean, I did things to him, but he didn't do anything to me, because I didn't want to have a climax. Then I had C-sections, so I wasn't feeling real good afterward. Then I was nursing, so the parts of my body that used to be erogenous zones were nurturing zones. I used to be real skinny, so I feel fat and unattractive. And I'm just tired. If you've had children pawing on you and hanging on you all day, the last thing you want when you get in bed is to have anyone pawing on you. It's hard for men to understand. I can lie there and feel really bad about it, but at the same time I can't just submit.

Quite frankly, I don't care about sex now. I'm asexual, and it scares me. I've changed a thousand degrees. When I met Mike I was the aggressive one all the time. I was always wanting sex. I would think of ways to cajole him into doing it, like if he was tired, I'd go, "I know you can't do it again. . . ." A couple of his friends once told me, "You're gonna kill this guy." It was a joke, but now he wishes I was like that even a little bit.

I'd say we have sex about once a month on average, but we've gone for months at a time without doing it. He's understanding, but—like the other day before he left, he said, "I've got to get laid one of these days, because I'm looking at everyone—all the women in my office, every woman I pass on the street, every cocktail waitress. . . ." He goes, "I'm horny, you got to help me here." He has said to me on three or four occasions that he doesn't want to have an affair, but if I don't stop doing this—that is, start doing it—he's gonna be forced. Sometimes he gets real angry and says, "Do you know how many people do it this little? Ask your girlfriends if their husbands will go for months without sex. They'll all say no. This is grounds for divorce. You're withholding sex. You're not even fulfilling your conjugal duty." And then I'll do it out of guilt, because it does make me feel bad that I'm not doing what I should.

Once you stop doing it, everything becomes so obvious when you do do it. Every kiss and every caress and every moment gets magnified in my mind because it's been so long, and then it feels real awkward and clumsy. I don't want him to tell me that I better start having sex with him. I just want it to happen. When you're both thinking about it, and you're the one who's not wanting it, when you go to kiss him or put your arms around him, it becomes so calculated. I'm worried about what he's thinking and what he's expecting—like, C'mon, keep going. So it's nothing like when we first got together, we'd start kissing and fall on the floor and screw.

These days he doesn't even push it when we get into bed because he's been rejected so often. If he starts making motions I usually say I'm tired, and he just says okay and rolls over. At first he would continue to kiss me and hold me, but now he doesn't do that, because very rarely would I go from saying I'm too tired and then get into it. So at this point neither one of us is very aggressive, unless he's so horny he can't stand it. He wants me to be the aggressor again, he would really like that, so I'm trying to figure out how to do it. If I have a few drinks I'm less inhibited and a little more aggressive. That's happening more lately—not more than once a month, but it's happening. Sometimes I'll have a few glasses of wine on purpose.

I don't know what's wrong with me. I asked my gynecologist what was happening, and he says, "You've got to change this, because your marriage is not gonna last." He says, "You're tired, make time for yourself. Get a baby-sitter. Go out, have a special time." Well, we do all that, we go out to dinner and the movies, but then we come home and we have three kids all over us because they don't go to bed early, and that wrecks it. I even went on an antidepressant drug when Kelly was about two, I was having a real down period, and lack of desire is a symptom of depression. So I tried antidepressants to see if that would help, but it didn't. Then this year I took a class at my church, and through that I became much more involved with Mike, because it was learning to accept him more unconditionally and forget about the things that bother me. Just focus on the points that I love and that first attracted me to him. It helped, we actually made love once a week for a while there, but it only lasted about a month.

One thing about Mike, he's a boisterous, crazy kind of guy. Sometimes I need him to be different. When he comes in he's real off the wall and loud instead of being more sensitive. He'll go to hug me or grab me, and he'll hurt me. He thinks it's funny, but it's not funny. I told him that the other night. When he said, "I'm looking at everyone with a vagina right now," I said, "Well, you need to be a little different with me, because it's hard for me to switch gears when you're all boisterous and nuts. You've got to be a little more gentle and sensitive to my moods." Our kids are up till nine, nine-thirty, and I've been up with them since six-thirty. I do the house and kids by myself. My husband has never gotten up with the kids at night. His thing is, "I have to go to work, I have to be on my toes, I can't afford to be tired." Well, Kelly has nightmares. Last night I was up with her twice. So sleep is a large part of my problem.

He helps somewhat with the kids, but not to where I think it's enough. If I go away on a Saturday and ask him to watch the kids for two or three hours, when I get home he's had it, so I would think he'd be more sensitive to me needing a break. Like if I want to take a bath by myself, he doesn't understand that I'd really love him to keep the kids down here and let me have twenty minutes. I end up with the kids splashing the water and playing with me in the bath. I don't get any time to myself, so I don't feel pampered at all. He also likes TV. I understand he's tired when he gets home from work and he wants to zone out and relax. At the same time I wonder, Well, if we just turned the TV off and put the kids to bed earlier and sat and had a cup of tea and talked, wouldn't that be just as nice as watching TV? But he thinks of that as work, having to come up with conversation. So usually I put the kids to bed and fall into mine, and he comes to bed hours later.

Well, here I am bitching about my husband. I don't want to do that, but there are a few things I would appreciate. I try really hard to be what he wants me to be, but I think that's why our sex suffers, because there's a little resentment. It's hard for me to feel loving when I'm thinking, Can't you put the damn kids to bed! Can't you carry your plate to the sink! When we got married he told me, "If I marry a woman I want her to pick up after me. I don't want to do domestic chores, I'm not programmed for that." I said, "Oh, honey, no problem, I'm a workhorse, I'll clean and iron and cook and everything will be fine." But now that we have kids it's different. I want to say, Hey, that was okay, but now I need some help once in a while. And he's not willing to renegotiate. I mean, he's a nice person, a lot of this stems from being the good ol' boy from Texas, where you go out and make that money and you get a good ol' woman to take care of everything else.

So when I get into bed, the last thing I want to do is be real loving and giving. I'm kind of nurtured out at that point. I'd like to cuddle and be warm together and have a quiet conversation once in a while, but the second I touch him in any way he's like, It's time! We talk about it, and he says, "I'm so damn horny that as soon as you touch me or kiss me or put your arms around me, I get this big erection, I can't help it." So now I pull away even more, because if I don't want to initiate sex, I can't have a warm, intimate thing.

A Christian counselor once told me that for women, foreplay is everything that happened after the last time you had sex until this time. He said, "Men are like dogs. We just jump on and jump off. But women, they need to have the romance and the loving feeling to go with it." I think that's really true. But the funny thing is, even when I go into sex thinking "Yuck," if I end up doing it anyway I'm usually happy at the end. It's true that there are times when I'm really, really tired and he's really, really aggressive, and I'll put myself somewhere else and just go through the motions to get it over with. But if I do get caught up in it, I enjoy it and wonder why I don't do it more often. And he's so happy afterward, he calls me from work the next day and says, "That was great!" It's kind of sad, I'm thinking, Oh, I'm not a very good wife, it makes him so happy and we have this close feeling, for that reason alone I should make myself do it.

Sometimes I think I should just be more mechanical, like service him. He doesn't want to be serviced, he wants the whole loving thing. He wants me to change back to the way it used to be. But maybe if I forced myself to do it, like a calculated thing to get him off my back, even if it was just oral sex or masturbation, I'd realize it was nice. Maybe it's like smiling—if you smile even when you're feeling bad, pretty soon you start feeling better.

A few weeks ago we went out of town for the weekend. A friend of ours who's in the travel business invited us to this convention at a big hotel. Mike said, "You can drink your little heart out," because he knows I get more amorous. Well, there were big gala dinners every night, and it was really fun. The first night we were drinking and coming on to each other at the party, we walked back to the room together holding hands and hugging and kissing. We both knew what we were in for, and we couldn't wait. It was like the old days. I wasn't bombarded with thoughts of what he expected and what I should be doing next. It flowed just like teenagers. That happens when we go away and leave all the tension about the house and kids. But then we get home and fall into our routine, and a month or two can go by before you know it.

There's nothing I would change about our sex itself. Mike is very giving, he thinks about me a lot. We usually start out kissing. Then a little petting and kissing on the neck and he does a lot of caressing different parts of my body, like my breasts. A lot of times we do oral sex for each other, or he masturbates and I help, just fondling him while he's doing it. Then we end up having regular sex with me on top, and we both climax and go to sleep. I usually climax two or three times before we have intercourse, and then he'll climax once and he'll be tired and won't be able to do it again, and that's fine with me by that point.

I guess I like the middle of sex more than the beginning or the end. I mean the kissing and petting and oral sex part, almost more than I like the intercourse part. Once we get to intercourse I'm thinking more. I'm concentrating on climaxing and not on just the good feeling. I have to be on top, and I have to be bent over at a certain angle for more clitoral stimulation. And I'm concentrating on whether I'm doing it right for him. He doesn't care about the position, he's just happy to have sex, especially at this point. But he has erection problems every once in a while, performance-anxiety type stuff. He loses his erection, so he comes out and masturbates. I lie next to him and kiss him and hug him and touch him, I feel like I'm there in an intimate way, so he's not doing it all by himself. But I still feel a bit like I haven't done my job. I asked him about it and he said, "It's not you, it's me. It's just a function of my body. I'm real turned on and I want this, but something happens."

The other thing about intercourse is that Mike is a big guy. He's like six-three, two hundred sixty pounds. Well, he's down to two hundred forty now. He started working out in the last couple months, and he's gained a lot of stamina and lost some weight. But when he was real big he'd get tired easily and out of breath. And he has this big gut. His stomach hangs down, and—this is really hard to describe without getting embarrassed—it kind of gets in the way. I'm grinding, and I bump into his stomach. I have to move around to a position that works, and it's not always easy. I hate to admit it because it seems so unimportant, but it is kind of unattractive, this big fat belly. I love this person, and I have to see past it, but it's comical sometimes. One night we stopped sex because we were laughing so hard, and I told him, "It's like a bunch of monkeys under a blanket, everything is going in every direction."

That's part of why I like the foreplay better—it's hard to get going in intercourse sometimes. And I climax much better with oral sex than with intercourse. A lot of times I'll climax during oral sex and want to zone out for a few minutes. I'm enjoying the feeling, and I'm real sensitive, every nerve is on end. But he hasn't climaxed, so he's on to the next act. I'm a little less willing at that point, but I never let him know. We have intercourse and maybe I climax again, but it's not as strong or as good as the oral-sex climax.

The middle part feels like the prelude even though I like that part the most. I guess in my little pea-picking brain I'm thinking that intercourse is the act, that's where you're supposed to end up. Mike does tell me it's more satisfying to climax inside me and for me to climax with him. He says it gives him a closer feeling to me, and I kind of agree with that. But when I think about it—I mean, I've never thought about sex as much as I have today—there have been times when he's brought me to oral climax and it was great, it was all I needed, I felt really close to him. We didn't have to go on.

I don't talk easily with him about sex. I feel a tension—I'm less likely to say things like "come" and "masturbate" and those words. I guess it's because of my religious upbringing. He likes to talk about it more, like the next day he'll go, "I really loved that, let's do that again," or "I love it when you give me a blowjob." I always go, "Oh, honey!" He jokes with me because he knows it's hard for me and I get all embarrassed and I'd rather just do it and not talk about it and go along with my little blinders on.

What we do talk about all the time is how little we do it. It's the biggest problem in our marriage, and it mushrooms because sex is the part that makes you feel good about the other person. When that's not working it affects everything else. I'm wondering about reading some books or going to a counselor or a sex therapist, but I don't know if I believe in that. I don't want to delve back into my childhood and my relationship with my father and all that stuff. I just want to figure out why I don't want to have sex and how to change it. I think it might change when the kids get older and we have more freedom—if I'm still married by then. [Laughs.] I don't want to go on to a fourth husband. Enough is enough already.

HELEN SHARPE

A twelfth-floor condominium overlooking the ocean in Southern California. Everything is in place: the chairs around the dining room table, the magazines neatly laid out—even a big bowl of fruit looks arranged. The couch and armchairs are leather, the carpet a thick, off-white plush. The lady in residence is slim, white-haired, lightly tanned, very attractive. She is wearing a white blouse, loose-fitting flowered slacks, and sandals. She is a retired executive who looks younger than her sixty-seven years.

She grew up in St. Louis. Her father was an engineer and her mother a journalist. "My mother pushed me in terms of learning things. I was reading and writing before I was four, and I went to college when I was sixteen. I was very popular, I looked young, but I had developed. I didn't do well scholastically at all. I'd have a date almost every night, and sometimes on weekends I'd have a golf date in the afternoon and go out with somebody else in the evening. I started going steady when I was a junior. But never even did any heavy petting. If a boy went to put his hand on my breast, I'd just move it away and let him know I didn't want that to happen."

After college she moved to Chicago and went to work for a large company. There she fell in love with a man six years her senior. They married when she was twenty-one. He had been married before. She was a virgin.

. . .

Al was very, very good at making love. I've had a lot of experience, and I've never slept with anybody who was so potent. He could make love for a long time. He was well-hung. His orgasms were big. But we were married twenty-five years, and I never particularly enjoyed sex with Al. The main reason was that I felt something was

411

wrong with me because I never had a vaginal orgasm. Al used to
finger-fuck me. And I wanted to come and get it over with, because
I didn't think that was the way you should have sex. This was a long
time ago, when you didn't read all this stuff. I thought if you were a
normal woman, you had an orgasm the way you were supposed to,
and it was a wonderful experience. I had very little feeling inside my
vagina, probably because I was so damn tense, wanting so much for
it to happen. But I always pretended it was wonderful, and I always
thought that Al believed me. I don't know if he did or not. I don't
think I was a great sex partner for him. I was not passionate. I wasn't
dying for it. The whole time we were together, we made love every
other night. Not every night, and not every third night. Every other
night. And on the off nights, I used to feel, Well, I'm glad I don't
have to make love tonight.

I almost always had an orgasm from his masturbating me. I'd
bring it on as fast as I could, but it wouldn't be all that fast, and I'd
be really relieved when I had it, because okay, that was almost the end
of making love. He would wait for me, then he'd have an orgasm.
And we'd make love for quite a while. He wouldn't start touching me
till maybe fifteen minutes or so of actual fucking. You know the joke
about what wives do during sex: I'd look at the ceiling . . . [Laughs.]
Trying to pretend I'm really loving this. And as I say, Al was a very
terrific lover. He did wonderful things and said the right things, and
he was really concerned about my enjoying it. I felt that if I hadn't
been all screwed up, we would have had a wonderful sex life. If I was
the way I am now, I would have enjoyed sex with him and he would
have enjoyed it a lot more. But I was all tied up.

So that was sex in my marriage. Sometimes I'd fake an orgasm. I
don't know if I did it a lot, but I did it. Even when I was doing it, I
wouldn't be sure if Al knew I was faking, but I don't think so. In fact,
I think Al felt our sex together was not bad. Pretty good. He certainly
enjoyed sex with me—and lots of others, too, it turned out. [Laughs.]
After we made love, he'd say things like, "Oh, Jesus, it's a good thing
you can't remember what it feels like when you make love, otherwise
nobody would do anything else."

We never, ever talked about sex. And very rarely—a few times—
had sex in a screwball situation, on the floor, that kind of thing. Or

like in the middle of the afternoon, you say, "Jesus Christ, let's go screw someplace." I don't remember that ever happening.

Al had a lot of affairs. I first found out about it during the war. I felt like somebody had dropped me ten feet. But after that I had affairs, too. Not affairs really, just episodes. Starting in '46, and going from then all the rest of my life, I have casually gone to bed with guys. When I say casually, if a guy really wants to go to bed with me, and it seems really important to him, I think, "Well, why not?" I should say "thought," because I've changed a bit over the last couple of years. But during my marriage, and even more after Al and I split in 1968, I probably had sex with—well, a lot of different men, I couldn't even tell you. [Laughs.] I don't know whether it's closer to twenty or two hundred. And these were not at swinger parties, these were people I know. I worked for a big company, and every one of the top executives was kind of in love with me. I slept with—well, I guess every one, except for the CEO, who was about forty years older than me. [Laughs.] I had real affairs with three of them. Only one while I was married to Al. It wasn't that serious, we just slept together a lot. He was married. And I didn't enjoy it, the sex I didn't enjoy at all, but he just kept bugging me and bugging me. He'd get a hotel room. I'd say, "God damn, Fred, I've got work to do, I don't want to go to a hotel room." He was always overweight, I think he weighed about one hundred ninety pounds, so once I said, "Fred, you're too goddamn fat, when you get down to one hundred seventy pounds I'll sleep with you." About a month later he says, "I'm one hundred seventy pounds!" And he stayed down there, too. [Laughs.] One thing about him was he knew I didn't like the sex. He'd read books and stuff about what you do to excite a woman, he was always horsing around trying to kiss me in the right places. I'd usually have an orgasm, but I've only had three or four orgasms in my life that were really something. That includes when I'm masturbating, too, for that matter. Ordinarily it's not that great. I'll get aroused, so it seems like a good thing to do, but it's usually a disappointment. With Fred, I didn't pretend like I did with Al. I could have an orgasm if he masturbated me, but he knew I didn't want to, and I didn't make a pretense.

Another one of my colleagues—this man is a very prominent executive. Very concerned about his reputation, very proper. I'm sure he has never had sex with anybody except his wife and me. He really can't get a hard-on, and never could. He's much younger than I. We started having sex about ten years ago. What used to happen is that I was half smashed all the time. I didn't go staggering around, but I would drink every night. We always drank, all of us did. And after I'd had four or five bourbons, my inhibitions were down. The first time Ralph and I had sex was after some convention. He had driven me over and was driving me back. We got in the car and he started horsing around. We just masturbated each other. I didn't enjoy it at all, but he did. He sort of got a hard-on, and he had an ejaculation without ever getting very hard. Since then, I've probably met him in a hotel or motel or at my house about fifteen times. I hate to have sex with him, I mean I really hate it. It's so goddamn much work, just to get the penis doing anything at all. He's very passionate himself. When he comes to my house, he'll go to the bathroom to get undressed. I'm lying on the bed naked, and he comes out, and I mean he can hardly stand it to see me naked. I'm sure you've heard about men who have an orgasm, and it's like they're in the death throes? It's like he's dying. Very unpleasant. The whole damn thing is terrible. I hate it! I'm trying to remember the noises he makes, like a death rattle, and *UUUHHH!* [Laughs.] It's not like anything else I've ever heard. Since the first time we had sex I've hated to go to bed with him, but in some strange way I can get more excited thinking about him than about other men. I suppose it's because he gets so excited with me.

Anyway, he kept begging me, kept after me, and I kept saying, "Ralph, no, we can't do that." He was working on this big deal, and it came through. He said, "Helen, there's only one thing that could make me really happy about this." I said, "What's that?" "If you let me fuck you." I said, "Okay, Ralph, okay." This was his reward. So from then on, every time—he has a lot of big projects, and he always closes the deals, he's a very good dealmaker—he calls me and says, "Helen, they're announcing the contract tomorrow, and if we get it ..." I say, "Ralph, I don't think so." "C'mon, now, you promised ..."

Why do you keep going to bed with these guys when you don't really enjoy it?

I don't know how to answer that. I do like to have people like me. It's not to impress them. It's like doing a favor for somebody. If you're a real good cook and you can make a real nice dish, and somebody said, "That's my favorite dish, would you cook it for me," it's like that. And every man is different, I'll tell you. [Laughs.] I've slept with the husbands of good friends of mine, and heard them say in a way I believed that they love me. Not that they don't love their wives or they want to leave their wives. I think that's a hell of a lot more common than people think, that guys sleep with the friends of their wives. But generally I've gone to bed with a guy because he wants to, and have not particularly enjoyed it. I feel like, He wants to, he likes me, I want him to keep on liking me, and I don't care. It never seems that important to me. Part of it is sleeping with a guy and seeing him the next day and acting like, Oh, hi, how are you? No emotional overlay at all. One of these guys who's married to a friend of mine, I've had a close affair with him, and when I see him I don't act any different. I don't know what the hell he thinks. He's told me he loves me, we've slept together—I haven't slept with him for a quite a long time, but I see him and talk to him. "How are you? Did you see the paper today?" I would never think of calling him "darling" or anything like that.

Then there's Curt. He was one of my colleagues. I started going with him when Al and I split. He's cute about sex. I like his attitude, which is very up-front. He hadn't screwed anybody but his wife, and her very seldom. He's a guy who got married to have children. But he always liked to screw me a lot. He could always get a hard-on. In fact, half the time he had a hard-on. But sex wasn't that great with Curt. He could come fast if you want him to, and he's a funny guy, always asking, "What do you want me to do?" He reads a lot, but he's not able to touch you or do things—somehow everything he does, it's like he just read that this is what you should do. There's no feeling, or no awareness of how I'm reacting. He thinks if he agitates the clitoris, that'll do it, but it just gets to be an irritant. And I like to have a man fondle my breasts. Curt does it, but there's something mechanical about it. He's not getting any pleasure out of it. He's so anxious to be doing something he thinks will give me pleasure that he's not feeling it himself.

I had one interesting night with Curt. I did one of these encounter groups. I came out of it feeling wonderful, terrific about myself. And I went out to Tahoe to meet Curt. When I saw him I said, "Oh, Curt, I'm going to do something with you tonight, and it's going to be terrific." He said, "What?" I said, "I am going to do to myself everything that I've always wanted you to do to me." Well, by the end of the day, he was so scared. [Laughs.] So we have a nice dinner and drinks and go to bed, and I do it. I say, "Now, here, I'd like to have you first of all stroke my breasts, and then this, and this is the way I'd like you to kiss me," and I go through the whole goddamn thing for about half an hour. I was doing it to myself, but kissing him, too, and touching him and having him touch me. I felt totally able to express myself. I didn't have any reluctance or embarrassment at all. I had never masturbated with a man before, but I did that night. I was teaching him foreplay. But it didn't take. I think he was probably so shell-shocked that he didn't even hear what I said, because none of it did any good. I mean none of it. But I enjoyed that night a lot. [Laughs.] That was seven years ago, when I was sixty.

About three years ago I met this guy at a spa. His name is George. He got a fix on me and started following me around, really being darling. Making me feel attractive. He's married, and he's much younger than I am, I think about fifty-five. But he loves older women. At the spa they had these beautiful young women, in great shape, and I'd say, "Isn't she cute?" And he'd say, "Oh, I don't like those young things." Nothing happened at the spa, but on the bus back to Phoenix he said, "Would you stay with me tonight?" I said I wasn't sure, because I was supposed to stay with a friend of mine. He said, "Well, you'd have to stay all night, because it takes me a long time. I can't just do it, so you couldn't get up and go home." I said, "Well, okay." So we stayed at his hotel. The sex wasn't very satisfying physically—I don't remember if I had an orgasm or not—but it was satisfying emotionally. Since then I've spent weekends with him maybe half a dozen times, and it's been very nice. I think it would be terrific if he could really get a hard-on. The best he can do is get hard enough to get inside me, and then he can have an orgasm. But for a year and a half, I felt madly in love, in a way I never did with Al or anyone else. I really felt like a kid. George lives a million miles away, but he'd call me at least once a day, and I got letters almost every day, five or six pages handwritten. So I really enjoyed our sex, even though it wasn't terrific sex. In fact, I have had real vaginal orgasms with George, even though he can hardly get his penis hard enough to stay inside me. I just have more feeling for him. I'm excited when we get into bed. That almost never happens to me. I never want to go to bed. I hardly ever get aroused until I'm actually touched. And I don't usually like long, long lovemaking, but if he's doing it, it's just fine. He's pretty special when he goes down on me. He likes to do that. He thinks it makes up for not getting a very good erection. I don't care so much, but it bothers him.

I've had sex with three or four guys in the last couple of years, and not one can really get a hard-on. I suppose it's because they're older, although the fact is I think a lot of guys never could. So usually when I make love now, I'll spend a long time trying to get the guy hard. Sometimes I like that, sometimes I don't. I've got to say, most of the time I don't, but with George it's okay. Otherwise, it's a lot of work. And emotionally it's more work too. They try to be playful about it, they say, "Oh, that little cocksucker, you can't rely on him." As though it doesn't happen all the time. Maybe they get a little upset, or disappointed, like they've let me down. Actually, if a guy doesn't worry about that and just goes ahead and loves a woman, that's enough.

What I long for now isn't a man who would get hard, but to get involved with a guy. I like George, but I wouldn't want to be married to him. What's changed in the last five or ten years is that I'd like to have sex with a guy who I really, really love. If I felt the way I do now when I was married to Al, my sex life would have been totally different. I think it would have been hot, heavy, passionate lovemaking. We might have had sex a lot of the time, not just at night every other day. Part of it is I feel differently about myself. Right from the beginning, I felt there was something wrong about me because I didn't have an orgasm the first time we made love, and I never had an orgasm the way I was supposed to, the way everybody else did. The way I thought everybody else did. Even in a social situation, to be a warm person you've got to feel good about yourself. If you think you're not equal to the situation, you hang back. That's how I was in my sex. I was very passive. I'm much less passive now. [Laughs.] I'm laughing because the last number of times I've gone to bed, I initiated a lot of things. Instead of waiting for a guy to touch me, I might touch him, or go down on him, or get on top. Stuff I never did before. Even with Al, if we went into a different position, it was always him that wanted it. Now I'll suggest it, not even because I would like it, but because I think the guy would.

Still, I can't talk about sex to a guy. In fact, my whole life I've only talked about sex with one woman friend. Some of the men I've been with ask me what I like, and it gives me a chance, but I always say I like what they're doing, even when I don't. Even when there are times that I know exactly what I'd like them to do, I don't say anything. Except for that one night with Curt, I have never, ever asked any person I've had sex with to do anything to me or for me. I just absolutely can't do that. Never ever. Or even take someone's hand and put it where I want. I've never done that with anybody.

I make love to men the way I think they would like me to make love to them. What I'd like . . . I suppose I'd like to have a man make love to me very romantically. Kissing on the eyes and the ears and the neck, being very slow, and enjoying it, so there's a feeling that a guy really wants to be doing what he's doing. That he's getting pleasure out of your body. And there's no hurry. It's more an attitude than anything specific. If I have the feeling that the guy is enjoying it, okay. But it goes the other way, too. It seems to me that it's so easy to do the right thing, just being loving, that even with somebody I like, it annoys me when he doesn't do it. I think, Jesus Christ, if I were he, I'd know what to do. And not because I'm a woman, either. When I'm doing things to a man, I'm not sure that I'm doing the right thing, but at least I care about what I'm doing, and I do what I think he's going to find pleasure in. With a little sensitivity. Not a lot of men do that.

9

TURNING POINTS

THIS CHAPTER FOCUSES on change. Many interviews in the book could fit into such a chapter, of course, since few are about sex in stasis; but for these seven speakers, the defining experience of sex in recent years has been a fundamental shift, whether internal or external, welcome or wrenching.

Sometimes the change springs largely from growing up. Jake Austin and Kathy O'Brien mirror each other: Both are grappling with performance anxiety, his classically male, hers female. Jake, twenty-nine, talks about his "sexual self-image—the sex god who has these screaming orgasms, the best lover ever." Kathy, thirty-eight: "My goal in sex was always to take care of the men and not think about myself. To be sexy, and make them crazy." As a result, lovemaking for both used to be frantic, aggressive. Now they are learning to linger—as Kathy says, to be less "goal-oriented." Jake has a new girlfriend: "The first time we kissed, we didn't use tongues at all. It was just about lips. It was a revelation to have kissing be about lips, as opposed to, I've got to get my tongue in there." Kathy's new lover "talked to me, told me to slow down. . . . It can build up by teasing, and I had never seen it that way."

Ingrid Thorpe, the "nice girl from Annapolis," suffered from the opposite of performance anxiety: She was passive and let her husband set the sexual tone. "Whatever I got, that's what I took, and what he wanted to do, that's what we did." But as time went by, "I started feeling, Well, y'know, I'm here too, maybe I want something more, or different." After a period of rage—"every time he touched me I was angry"—she got his attention, and they worked out some artful compromises. Now that she has become "a player" rather than a victim, she finds herself more willing to cater to his tastes, such as sex at five in the morning: "Somehow I started viewing sex as something nice I could give him, that I wanted to give him because I loved him, as opposed to something he was going to take from me."

Other changes are not so benign. One is aging, as Rachel Silver laments: she hates her "shriveled" skin, she has trouble finding partners, and she has not yet persuaded any of her friends to try lesbianism. And then there are disasters that turn into triumphs. Jim Hollister's wife had a radical mastectomy a few years before our talk, at a time when their erotic life already was shaky. Neither of them is a sensualist, and both are shy. But out of dogged determination not to let sex wither, they kept trying: "We'd force our way through it. That alone would be a minor achievement. It'd pave the way for the next time." To Jim's delight, "by touch and feel, by exploring," he found ways to pleasure Evelyn that let her sexuality blossom. "It was something that was waiting to happen. It was just like unlocking a door. I'm amazed that we didn't discover it before."

Alex Woodleigh unlocked another sort of door when he started an extramarital affair, fell instantly in love, and discovered a kind of sublime, body-and-soul sex. "It sheds a completely different light on what sex can be. It's like our bodies merge. . . . I say to myself, Okay, here's what's happening: There are these two people, and they're an expression of God's love. That's such a new thought to me that I don't even know what I mean by it." Fay Canastel, too, found links between sex and spirituality in a surprising place: her work as a call girl.

Kathy O'Brien sums up this chapter when she says: "It seems strange, I'm thirty-eight years old and just learning." I would only add: There is nothing strange about it.

JAKE AUSTIN

He is twenty-eight, single, an actor on the way up, now playing a small part in a hit Broadway play. He comes from old Rhode Island stock; his father owns a mid-size company, and his mother taught in a prep school. He is on the short side, with a big-boned, soft face, blue eyes, full lips, and brown hair straggling down to his shoulders, a requirement for his part in the play. "A shy WASP," he calls himself: "I tend to be the guy who stands in the corner of the dance floor and doesn't do anything and hopes that some woman will approach him." Yet a sweetness about him makes it easy to imagine plenty of women doing just that.

"I come from an extremely close family. As a kid I thought I was the luckiest guy in the world. I realize now that there was something fucked up about it, but I didn't want to admit it was fucked up. It was a way of dealing with the fact that my father tended to bash me, not physically most of the time, but verbally. My dad was a hard man. Nothing was ever good enough. And my mother never came to my aid, even though she adored me. She didn't love me, she adored me. Which wasn't really what I needed. So instead of saying, 'Fuck you, Daddy, leave me alone,' or 'Fuck you, Mommy, you've gotta take better care of me,' I decided my father was right, that he was perfect and he had every right to treat me the way he did. Until recently, I would have said my childhood was idyllic. But it wasn't. I was pretty scared most of the time about where the next blow was going to come from."

In high school he was afraid of girls to the point of paralysis. Finally, in the spring of his senior year, he "hooked up" with a girlfriend, and lost his virginity on graduation night. But it was not until college that his sexual education began.

• • •

Lately I've been realizing how much sex for me is tied up with my parents. With my father, it's about my right to have a dick, too. And my mother—well, this woman in college almost *was* my mother. She had a strong resemblance to my mother. She was sixteen years older than me. And it was through her that sex really started for me.

Her name was Catherine. She taught me dance all through my freshman year. In the fall of my sophomore year I studied with her again, and we became close. We'd go out to meals together. I never had that kind of relationship with a teacher before. So of course I was having fantasies about her. I thought, No, this is so forbidden, it'll never happen, it's something I would never do. But in October, on my birthday, she gave me a present. She kissed me on the cheek when she gave it to me. I'll never forget that kiss. It was just a kiss on the cheek, but I could feel both her lips pressing, and the way she did it was such a vulnerable gesture. It was so loaded. I could feel the imprint for the whole day.

I was supposed to live with a friend of mine that fall off campus, but he decided at the last minute to go to Europe. So I applied for a dorm room, but it was too late and I had nowhere to live. Catherine said, "Well, I have a studio in my house, you can have that." She lived on the other side of this little town. I said yes. Pretending to everybody, including myself, that we were just going to be great friends, and nothing was going to happen. I moved in, and we lasted about two or three days. Of incredible tension. One afternoon I came home to get something, and I was going back over to campus. We were in the hallway. She said something like, "Well, I'm going over to the store, are you coming home for dinner?" "Uh-huh." End of conversation. We just looked at each other, and it was clear. We started kissing, we went into her bedroom, and it was, "Oh, I've wanted to do this for so long, I've been holding back, I've been so afraid." For me it was totally forbidden territory, because she was older and she was a teacher, and I was taking two of her classes that semester. She had been denied tenure, so she was on the way out, and the stakes weren't quite so high for her. But for me, in terms of my parents, it was this huge act of rebellion.

I really did have to go back to campus, so we were on the bed for a while, and we didn't get our clothes off, we just kissed. The way

Catherine kissed me back, what she did with her tongue in my mouth—I remember feeling weak, and my head spinning around. It's funny, I don't know if we made love that night, but I'm sure we did. And from then on, we spent the whole term together in this house, fucking all the time, and nobody knew. We'd be in the middle of a meal, and we'd look across the table and just fall on the floor and start going at it.

I loved her body. She was thin, but she was a little bit big through the hips. She had small breasts. She had a great mouth, and she was so loving, she gave me a sense of physical, passionate loving. Being with her was my first real experience of what an orgasm could be like. I had these orgasms that would build and build and build and build and build, and I'd think, I'm never gonna get there, I'm never gonna get there, my head's gonna blow off before I come. We got into this whole thing of how loud I would scream. It was like a joke, we'd wonder if the people across the street could hear me, and she loved it.

For me, it was like a whole different world. It was all about walking this tightrope and entering this wild and different world that I had never been connected to. Playing these forbidden games. Catherine was initiating me sexually, she was teaching me to dance, she was changing my life. I was always half-aware that it had something to do with my mother—that there was a clear "Fuck you" going on. In two senses. "Fuck you, Mom," and also [speaks seductively] "Fuck you." And Catherine formed my whole sexual self-image—the sex god who has these screaming orgasms, the best lover ever. She used to say to me, "I can't believe I'm only your second lover, you're so great." It started this whole syndrome with me, feeling a need to be worshipped sexually. She fit it perfectly. I was her golden boy. I was her young sex prince.

But I was pretty naïve about the effect I was having on her. The next term, I was going to France to study. Right before I left, my parents found out about the affair. They were really shocked. Of course they blamed her a lot, but they told me I had violated a trust. I told Catherine, "Listen, they don't understand, it's me and you, I love you, and everything's gonna be fine." But when I got away to France, it was like this thing hit me. I felt completely different. Part of what made me pull away was she started sending me letters full of all this sexual stuff. "Your incredible penis," and "your young electric body on top of me." These homoerotic postcards of guys giving blowjobs, and these nude women. And then taking it to the next level of, "You're the only man I ever loved, I can't imagine life with anyone else but you." In a way I found it flattering, but it made me uncomfortable. It was like, No, now you're taking this too far. Finally I stopped writing. I had an affair with a girl in France. At the end of the term I was going to a ballet school in Germany. Catherine was going to be there. But by the time I got there, the backlash had happened. I think we made love twice, and we kept looking away from each other. It was an awful time. After that, I went back to college, and she went to live in Chicago, and I never saw her again.

In one way, sex with Catherine was the perfect introduction. It wasn't like she was the teacher and I was the student. It was like she said to me, Go ahead and do it, and if it's wrong, I'll tell you. But she never did. There was nothing I couldn't do to her. She would accept anything, and she kept telling me, "I can't believe you haven't been doing this for years." So sex was one of the first places where I ever felt completely free and open and like I didn't have to question anything. I knew what I was doing. There was no fear. I could just fuck, and everything was great. For the first time, I didn't feel like I was getting in my way.

But in another way, being with Catherine backfired on me, because I expected it to be like that with other women. And for a while, it was. I remember a few years out of college, the first time a woman said to me in bed, "What are you doing? Don't do that." I was floored. I didn't think it was something you could say. I played it kind of wounded, like, "How can you say that?" But inside I felt more aggressive, like, What the fuck are you talking about? How can you even question what I do? Because part of my whole thing about fucking is my belief that I'm some kind of god in the bedroom. I have this need to have my cock worshipped. I have to feel like the woman is totally into it. And almost all my relationships have been with women who would do that for me. Of course, the worst thing about it is it keeps me from really having a relationship. It keeps me in a fantasy, and once the fantasy wears off, the romance is over. I've never had a relationship last longer than five months.

One night last year I was out with a friend of mine and this waitress he knew. Sexy woman, exotic, the type I'd never have the nerve to speak to. We went out drinking and got loaded, and Tim ducked out, leaving us alone. I was like, Oh my God, because he had done all the work, he was the smooth one, and then he split. We ended up going dancing, and we started kissing, and after one hot stretch she said to me, "I can't believe the difference between the way you talk and the way you kiss." Because I was sticking my tongue down her throat, doing my voracious number. It's like I *attack* sex. I'm afraid of slowing it down. If I'm gonna be fucking, I'll fuck like crazy, gotta have a huge dick and fuck like crazy to avoid dealing with whatever's making me anxious. Women have always said to me, God, you can't get enough. But I think the reason I can't get enough is that if I slow down, the fears start to crowd in on me: Does this woman really want to be with me? Is she going to leave? Is my cock good enough? It's hard for me not to use sex as a seal of approval.

Now I have this very tentative thing going with a woman named Hilary. I met her doing this play. I've known her for more than a year, and when we first went into rehearsal, I thought she was nice, but she wasn't physically attractive to me. As I got to know her, she became attractive.

The first time we kissed, we didn't use tongues at all. It was just about lips. It was a revelation to have kissing be about lips, as opposed to, I've got to get my tongue in there. There's something incredible just about lips. The second time we kissed, I had this expectation: Now I have to use my tongue, it can't be just about lips this time. So I forced it into this tongue-kissing, and she said to me, "You kiss like you eat." I said, "What do you mean?" She said, "Like you're gobbling me up." I tend to eat really fast, huge mouthfuls, like livestock. It hit me when she said that. Because when I started to French-kiss her, it felt completely wrong. I said to myself, I don't need to do this, why am I doing this? I'm not even enjoying it. And what kicked in instantly was, Oh, she doesn't kiss well, her teeth are too big, her lips aren't sensitive enough. All this negative stuff. Judging her sexually. So I was able to stop and say, Okay, I don't need to do this, plunge in and gobble her up.

The first time we got into bed together was at some friends' house in the Catskills. We spent two nights in our underwear. We did some nice dry-humping, but there wasn't any fucking. Just kissing and touching each other. It was amazing to do that and not feel the need to push it. Honestly, it was new to me. We said to each other that for both of us, it felt in a lot of ways like the first time. Staying completely with what was happening right then and there. And I was *seeing* her, not getting caught up in a fantasy of what it was supposed to be. Just seeing Hilary. She's on top of me, she's in her underwear, I'm in my underwear, she's rubbing herself against my dick, I know she can feel my dick, and I'm starting to have a sense of feeling her pussy through her underwear. And just letting that be, not thinking, What do we do now? Now we're going to have to fuck, because we're this close. Or, How do I get her underwear off? Or, We haven't talked about safe sex. Or, Will our friends hear us?

There was a quality to the pleasure that was different, too. It was in things I would rush past before. It was like having skin orgasms. I've always loved the feel of skin to skin, but I've always associated it with me being on top and my stomach touching her stomach, my chest touching her chest. This was lying side by side, or her just brushing my chest with the back of her hands. It's like I used to see sex in black-and-white. Pleasure: Okay, pleasure has to do with cock, pussy, mouth. My mouth on her pussy, my dick inside her, my mouth to her mouth, a little bit my mouth to her breast. And that was about it. There were zones where the pleasure was. I've always told myself that I don't know what to do with my hands in sex. For me what's active is my mouth. My hands don't really go anywhere, they're secondary. But I've begun to think my hands can do just as much. I'm realizing that pleasure exists in more places.

The first time we made love—the only time, so far—I thought, we're not gonna make love tonight. But it just kept going. We'd stop, take a break, and plunge back in. It kept escalating. Finally it was like, are we gonna stop or are we gonna take off our underwear? I said, "I'll take off my underwear if you take off yours." And she said yes. Then she started holding my dick in a way I've never felt before.

She was running her hand along it, cupping my balls, and then running her finger up to my asshole and back down, and up my dick, and back. . . . I was on all fours, and she was on her back reaching up between my legs. The thing that made it so unbelievable is that usually my experience of women holding my dick, it's like they're holding a doorknob. There's a lack of awareness of what they're holding, and I feel like they're gonna hurt it in some way. Hilary was touching me, and immediately she knew how to handle it. It was exquisite. Friends of mine talk about getting a hand job. I can't imagine getting a hand job from a woman. I've never been with a woman who could handle my dick in a way that I would find anything other than . . . well, alarming. [Laughs.] But this time, I felt I could come if she stayed with it.

Then I started to eat her out. Usually that's something I don't do the first time around. But I really wanted to. This was another new thing for me. The anxiety said, Don't do it, she'll think you're dirty, she's not ready, it's too soon, that's the next step, it's something you reserve for new territory next time. But I just said, No, I want to do this, I'm gonna do it. There was something about her pussy that was really pleasing to me. I couldn't see it, but the way it felt in my mouth. The size of it. The way it moved as I moved my tongue through it and over. It was responsive. There's something amazing about the quality of the skin in a woman's pussy. It's not like the skin anywhere else on the body. It's budding. I guess the nightmare image of a pussy for me is this big wet sloppy loose thing, and hers felt like—the image I have is of this bud, this very small and compact yet alive thing.

Then she stopped me. She started to close her legs, and in her twisting she pushed me away. Which was okay. We started kissing again, and then we started fucking, and that's when I got caught up in, Okay, this is the first time. I really, really like this person, and I want this to go somewhere, so the first time has to be spectacular. That ends up distorting it, or making it into something it isn't. I mean, it was still great, but I was aware of the moment when she started going away from me. It was about the time when I gave myself completely over to the need for it to be incredible, instead of letting it be what it was. It has to do with a fantasy I have, couples I look up to, who say, "Yes, the first time we made love, both of us knew this was it." So I had to make it amazing, because this was the time we were always going to remember. Now, I'll always remember it, but for a different reason. [Laughs.]

After I came and we quieted down, I asked her what had happened. One of the words she used was, there was an abandon to what we were doing that scared her. She says she's always enjoyed sex and had a great time, but there were patterns she had in old relationships that made it safe for her. I think the way we're approaching this one takes away that safeguard. Same thing for me. She also said that she doesn't feel she has the right to stop anything sexually. When things get scary for her, she doesn't have the right to say, I don't want to do this anymore. Which we're going to have to be able to do, if we're going to have sex with each other. But it becomes a double whammy, because when she does say that, it's hard for me to hear it as anything but, You're no good. And that wipes out all the pleasure we give each other.

So that's it. We've slept together once. And then we've backed off—not with the intention of ending it, but having come up against a bunch of fears. In the past, having had sex with a woman, I would not have been able to handle stopping the sex. I would have had to get right back at it to prove that my dick works. Or I would have left her. But now we're trying to work through some stuff. Sometimes it feels like a weird psychodrama we're going through, but I hang in because I feel like there's a real possibility there. And I feel like it's about time, at age twenty-nine, that I tried.

KATHY O'BRIEN

She is thirty-eight, a slim, fast-talking strawberry blonde with her hair cut short, fashionably large glasses, and a pixieish face. She is wearing a silk blouse with a bold geometric print, a short skirt, and black stockings: "Some days I like to get dressed up, even if I'm not going anywhere." She is a copywriter who recently lost her job and is now free-lancing; in one corner of her studio apartment is a desk with her computer and a jumble of papers. The room is sparsely furnished, the walls mostly bare, because she recently moved in.

She grew up in the suburbs. Her father was a city kid, Irish working-class with no college education, who made a successful career as an industrial designer. Her mother is a housewife. "We're a close family. Very, very close. But my parents always argued, always yapping at each other. It was chaotic. And my father is difficult. He's a great guy, and the things I love most about myself, like my joyousness and my enthusiasm, I get from him. But he was very critical. He flies into rages. He's adamant about things, opinionated. He would do things like tell you you were stupid. He made me crazy that way. The perfectionism thing is a curse."

Her parents were prudish about sex but not repressive. "It wasn't one of those straitlaced WASPy situations. When I was twelve or thirteen my mother got out the biology book and explained how it worked. What's really funny is she didn't mention that you move, or how people touch each other, or how emotional it can be. So I had this idea that you just sort of laid there. Then I had sex with my first boyfriend, who talked me into it. He was saying, 'Oh, you don't really love me.' I was sixteen. All I could think of—he was moving up and down inside me and I was thinking, 'God, this is like dogs.' But we were madly in love. And pretty soon we were having incredible sex. We had sex all the time. Everywhere. We screwed our brains out. It was so amazing. A lot of people have terrible experiences when they're teenagers, but this was unbelievable. In some ways, I think it's the best sex I'll ever have."

*She has been married twice, and has been separated from her second
husband for two and a half years. She is also a recent graduate of The Forum (formerly est), which she says has changed her life.*

• • •

I love sex. I love to talk about it. I love to do it. I love it, I love it,
I love it. But I've had a bad history with men. I mean, I've always
done well with friends, and at work. But I've had really bad scenes
with men. I get involved very fast, and it's torrid and conflict-ridden.
Even with my high school boyfriend—I don't remember this, but my
family reminds me. I was always crying. He was always mad at me because I did something to hurt him. There's something about the mix
of intense sexual attraction and conflict. . . .

But that's over. Those days are over. I'm breaking those patterns.

With my second husband, it was classic. I met him at a party. I
wasn't physically attracted to this guy. He's not good-looking. He's
got a big nose. He's got this curly dark hair. He's starting to bald.
He's like forty-two. But he's so charismatic and so charming. And he's
got this great voice. He's very sexy in his own way, he's very confident, and that to me is sexy. A pretty powerful person. He's this big
wheel in the company I was working for. He invites me to his hotel.
We order room service. Out of the blue, he asks me what I look for
in a man. What are the qualities I'd want in a mate? The first one on
my list is passion. Meanwhile, I have on this high-necked blouse, I
look like Suzy Schoolhouse. He goes, "You? You?" He was floored.
Then he comes over and starts unbuttoning my blouse. He just starts
taking my clothes off, I swear to God. I have never had anybody do
anything like that. There had been no contact. No kissing, nothing.
We had just met. It was so aggressive and bold that I thought it was
great. But I stopped him, and he went back to his seat. Then he said
the first quality he'd want in a mate was fidelity. Which I also thought
was great. So he ended up having all my clothes off and in bed.

The next day he went back to Atlanta. I heard from him two
weeks later, and we started this torrid affair. I'd go visit him on weekends. He would come here. In a brief period we fell in love. We were

on the phone ten times a day. But the sex—the first couple of times, he lost his erection. We couldn't really finish. I was starting to wonder. The first time, you chalk it up to excitement, and then the second time. . . . But I fell in love, I was wildly attracted to him, and every once in a while it was really good. He would do oral sex on me, and I would get off, and it would be great. So I said, Oh, okay, maybe losing the erection is an aberration. But it always was a problem.

I started faking orgasms in the courtship period. I had never done that before. It takes me a long time to come, but with my first boyfriend and my first husband it wasn't a problem, and in my one-night-stand period I never came but they didn't seem to care. But with him, I wanted him to think I was this incredible orgasmic person, so I was faking it like crazy. It was to make him feel better about himself, because it was hard to come when he got soft all the time. I would sometimes fake it way before he got soft.

See, my goal in sex was always to take care of the men and not to think about myself. To be sexy, and make them crazy. And if the goal is so centered on them, you're not gonna take care of yourself. It's not just their responsibility to help you get off. You have to take some responsibility for yourself. But I spend so much of my time trying to please the other person that I totally forget about me. It's also taking control, instead of letting them do me. I'm sucking on their nipples, fondling their genitals, stroking them. I'll do this thing where I just take over, like I'm in charge. There are times in sex where that's natural. The woman does a guy, and then it reverses. It goes back and forth. But for years, I just focused on what I could do for them.

So I faked orgasms. I faked multiple orgasms. In the beginning he thought I was this wildly sexual person. But then it was terrible, because I had to keep on doing it, and it was dishonest and stupid. It was so stupid. I felt like it was a big thing for him to have me come. I don't know, maybe I was just reading into it, but I was always worried abut how fragile his ego was, and I felt like to make him feel sexy and desirable I had to have all these orgasms. After we got married I stopped faking the multiple orgasms, but I kept faking. Not every time, just when I couldn't come, or I didn't feel like it. And he doesn't know. I never told him.

After the romantic euphoria wore off, we started fighting right away. There started to be signs that this guy was bad news for me. For one thing, he was an alcoholic. He was very mean, always putting me down. It was just a terrible marriage. At least once a week, I would be, like, Why am I with this guy? He also hit me. He hit me maybe seven, eight times. He didn't beat me up, but he'd slap me. A lot of women would say, "Forget it, I can't put up with this." We did two years of counseling, but that was a disaster. It just prolonged the marriage.

I'd say for the first two or three years, we had a nice sexual relationship even though he couldn't keep an erection. He would take care of me orally. He was pretty good at doing that, and every once in a while, like maybe once a month, we'd have okay sex. He wouldn't lose it. So I would just rationalize that I was content with that. I was in love, and it got to the point where I even made the comment to one of my girlfriends that sex is overrated, which coming from me is ridiculous. It was really weird, 'cause for a long time he wanted to have sex every morning and every night. And it's not very fun to be having sex with somebody who goes soft a lot.

The routine was, we would kiss for a while. He was a terrible kisser. A sloppy, wet kisser. I love kissing. I think kissing is such an expression of how you feel about the person. To me it's the best part of sex, even though I like fucking a lot. Kissing is like magic. But this was too rough. He would stick his tongue in really hard. I like tongue action, but this was thrusts. It wasn't gentle. I always hoped he would get it, but I guess I decided early on that this is the way he kisses, and I accepted it. So we'd kiss. Then he would suck on my nipples. Then I would fondle him. Then he would get inside me and just do it. If that didn't work out, he would roll over, and I'd be on top and try to come. But a lot of times, he'd get soft. Not totally soft, but partially. It was rare that he was very, very hard. So he'd get back on top and stay in me and keep pumping, trying to get his erection back. Sometimes he would, and then it would be this great effort to come. I'd get tired of it, so I'd fake it. He'd keep trying, and it could take forever. By then I'd be dry and sore. Lying there waiting for it to happen. Eventually he would ejaculate. It was horrible, but he would come.

Sometimes I would do oral sex on him, but I really didn't like doing it. I felt totally incompetent. First of all, I had no idea how to do it. And the only way he could come was if he was on top, ramming it down my throat. I would try to suck him off with him on his back, but he would get soft and I felt like a failure. So he would ram it down my throat, and it would take so long. I would be practically gagging. It was excruciating. Tears would come to my eyes. Toward the end of the marriage I stopped giving him blowjobs because I hated it so much. He seemed very hurt that I wouldn't do that anymore. Then he stopped doing oral sex on me. So I wasn't getting off at all. Then it totally fell apart. In the last year we were having sex about once every two months. At the very end, if I made any move toward him, he would move away.

That marriage really deadened me to sex. Completely. It was about ten years, considering that I didn't have sex for a year and a half after I left him. A decade of bad sex. Then, the first two guys I slept with after the breakup were premature ejaculators. Can you imagine? Two in a row! I told this friend of mine, "I'm like a woman in the desert." And then I met Cy when I did The Forum. The seminar lasted a weekend, and he kept following me and smiling. He's a very nice-looking guy. Very tall. He's got this great smile. Just friendly, a nice person. Every time I turned around, he'd be smiling at me.

We went out a couple of times and took it slow. The second date, he came back here and I thought I was going to jump him that night. That's usually my pattern. I had decided I wanted to. But we started kissing and it really wasn't good. I stopped the kiss and said, "I'm really nervous." He said, "I'm nervous too." So we didn't continue. Before the third date, I said to him on the phone, "I want to sleep with you in the worst way." We were supposed to see each other in a week. But once I know what I want, I'm not a patient person. So we got together sooner. He came over. I remember when we finally did end up in bed, I was really aggressive, getting on top. Being really fast. He talked to me, told me to slow down. He said I was grinding into him too much, and that made him lose his erection. I remember him telling me there are a lot of tender parts of the body. The neck. Using the tongue a lot. The ears and earlobes. Weird places. It doesn't have to be this whole . . . I always took it like sex has to be this big bang. Frantic, almost. But he takes his time. It can build up by teasing, and I had never seen it that way. I was always very goal-oriented. A lot of it was about me wanting them to think I was this sex queen. Doing what they want, servicing them. It's not like I'm doing it just to perform, but there is a lot of performance involved. He made me stop doing that. It was a turn-off to him.

He has a very slow way of making love. It reminds me of my high school boyfriend. Back then, the way sex worked was great for me because there would be a lot of foreplay. Often we were at my parents' house. He'd be sucking on my nipples for hours because my parents would be in the other room, and when they would come in, we would cover ourselves up. I would just have my blouse open. Lying by the stereo. So I'd get all this stimulation for hours, and I'd be crazy by the time we ended up doing it. As you get on in life that doesn't happen. Everybody wants to get to it. And it's not just the men, the women too. You just don't give foreplay as much time. You fall into a pattern where in the beginning of the relationship there's a lot of foreplay, and then that ends. It becomes more like getting down to business. But for me, it takes a long time to get stimulated to the point where I can come fairly quickly. And this guy takes his time.

He's really great at oral sex, that's the other thing. I remember the first time, it took me a long time to come, but he just kept doing it. When I came, I started to pull him up, and he kept going. I was like, Okay. . . . I started to pull him up again and he just looked up at me and said, "I like it down here." I thought, Wow, this is so great. He's so sweet. I told that to a girlfriend of mine, and she goes, "Marry him."

He also taught me how to do a blowjob. Getting blown is his favorite thing in the whole world. But the first few times I sucked him, I really didn't know how to do it. He described it to me. I didn't know that you stroke up near the head. That's where it's sensitive, and that's how you can get somebody off. I didn't understand that you can just suck on the tip. I always thought you have to have the whole thing in your mouth the whole time. In and out and in and out, gag city. I didn't realize it didn't have to be so difficult. I really got it when we rented a porno film. The whole thing was oral sex, ten different scenes of oral sex. I didn't know it was going to be a teaching tool when we rented it. I just thought it would be a turn-on, and it was, although it was pretty silly. We were laughing at it, but I finally got it. How you move your hand. Where you put your mouth. Then I really got into it. I'd get wet when I was doing it. I would start out just kissing him. Then suck on his nipples. Then I would go down and suck on the head, and on his balls. What he really likes as fore-play to my giving him a blowjob is for me to use my tongue a lot around his balls and his anus. That drives him crazy. At first I thought, Wow, this is kind of weird. But I did it because he would just go crazy. He would put his legs up, offering it to me practically. So I would do that for a long time, around his anus with my tongue. He'd be in a frenzy. Then I'd start sucking on his dick, using my hand up and down. I wasn't sure how hard to do it, I was always afraid I'd hurt him. But I got better and better at it, and at one point I sort of figured it out. Although I never got to the point where I could get him off by moving my hands without him moving at all. So I would hold him, and he would move. I was also afraid of biting him with my teeth. I remember in the very beginning, I would stretch my lips over my teeth to try and protect him. I would end up with these sores in-side my lips, because he told me, "Kathy, no teeth."

It's exciting to have a penis in your mouth. Using your mouth on the genitals. There's almost something nasty about it, like, Oooohhh, how could you do that? Plain old intercourse is normal and accepted. I'm not saying oral sex is taboo, because it's not. But there is an ele-ment of, Isn't this nasty? It's something I realized, I said to Cy, "I'm too much of a good girl. I think what I need to do is be like those nasty girls." He goes, "Yeeaaaaah."

I don't know, for me the penis is . . . sex. It's power. That's the whole thing about sex, isn't it? Everything revolves around the penis. For me it does. To play with it, to suck on it. . . . Now that I'm learn-ing how to work with it, it's pretty neat because it makes me feel pow-erful. I can make it react, or thrill someone with it. Besides the pleasure I can get from it. Plus, I don't know what it is, but men just love blowjobs *so much*. Women joke about it all the time, that if you can give a good blowjob you can have whatever you want. I went out with some friends one night and we met some guys in a bar. We had dinner with them. They were nice, and they had these two women with them. My girlfriend went into the ladies' room with this other woman, who was dating this one guy. The woman goes, "I just met

him. I've been dating him for three weeks. He'll do anything for me."
My girlfriend goes, "Oh, you must give a really good blowjob." And
the woman goes, "Yup."

Oral sex is fine, I like it, but I really like to fuck. I like the good
ol' in-and-out, up-and-down. It doesn't have to be fancy. You don't
have to be standing on your head. I like plain old missionary sex. It's
hard to find these days. [Laughs.] To have a hard cock in me—it just
makes me crazy. When the man first pushes in—it feels so good because you're pretty contracted, so you really feel the sensation, really
really feel it. Your outer lips are more sensitive than inside, so when
the head goes through the lips you can feel it. Sometimes your clit
also gets rubbed while it's happening, and that feels good. I love that
part. I love to prolong it. Like I won't let him in for a while, I keep
teasing him. My legs are strong, and I usually keep people out. Then
there's the sensation of being filled. I love feeling a man in me. I need
someone who's good-sized because I'm pretty stretched out. I'm a big
girl. I think it has to do with my first boyfriend. Having a lot of sex
early on with this guy who was big stretched me out, and a little penis
just doesn't do it.

Cy's pretty big, but we had problems with intercourse. The thing
is, it's hard for me to come. And the pattern that has emerged over
the years is that I have to be on top. Maybe it's the way my abdominal
muscles work or something, because I have to be pushing down. And
I think my clitoris is really high from my opening. So there has to be
friction. His penis has to be all the way in, and I have to be bearing
down to get any friction going. I like the man to be still, so I can control the movement. It gets in my way when they start moving, it gets
me off the rhythm. I'm not sure why, but it always worked that way
for me. It's very rare that I have come with someone on top of me.
But Cy would get soft when I was on top. Usually we'd start out with
him on top, and then we'd roll over, but he couldn't keep an erection
that way. We were just starting to work on that when we stopped seeing each other. So I don't think I ever came with him inside me,
which is what I really like.

There was one time when it was pretty thrilling. I was on all fours,
and he came in from behind. But it was everything that led up to it.
A lot of kissing on my neck and back, which drives me crazy. Then he

came in from behind and pumped really hard, and it was great. I
didn't come, but I don't always have to come, and I still love it.

I also have this thing about my nipples. What makes me come fast
is if you suck on my nipples while we're screwing. It sends a shock
way through my system. Cy didn't do that until I finally told him
about it. He would do it a little while, but never long enough, and I
was embarrassed to tell him. That's another thing—I've never ever
said to anyone what to do, until recently. Never. Never. I've never
been able to. But with this relationship, we told each other what we
want. It was an education. It seems strange, I'm thirty-eight years old
and just learning.

Cy and I broke up because he's in the middle of a divorce and I
fell in love with him. He's starting a business, and he has the idea that
he doesn't want to get involved. That's been painful. So now I'm
struggling with being single again. A lot of my friends are married.
My best girlfriend has a new boyfriend. It's lonely. [Suddenly, she is
crying.] I don't know why I'm so emotional today. It was okay for a
long time, because I was getting over my divorce. But Cy opened up
this whole well for me. The possibility of being in a relationship
again. So now I'm looking. I'm open. And I'm meeting nice, healthy
men. It's weird—I've always been suspicious of men. I'd say to people, "I don't like men." And when you think men aren't nice, that's
who you meet. Now I think there's a whole world of other men out
there, really nice people. I'm not attracted to many of them. The
chemistry thing is rare. But I have a sense it's not going to take very
long. I know it's going to happen.

JIM HOLLISTER

He is a classic sixties survivor: fifty-one years old, tall, thin, graying, a former bohemian and New Left radical, now part-owner of a cooperatively run recycling business in a Midwestern city. He has been married to his second wife, Evelyn, for eight years; they have a six-year-old son. But the road to this stable life has been arduous—he took drugs and drank heavily for years, hitting bottom with a suicide attempt in 1978—and today he seems to live carefully, within well-marked boundaries, for fear of lurking chaos. He describes himself as a workaholic, and is a serious amateur photographer. "I'm not a pleasure-bound person. I don't go out to eat. I don't drive fast cars. Everything I do is goal-oriented. The closest I come to leisure is watching basketball games on TV."

He was born into an upper-middle-class WASP family in New England, to parents who are "incredibly closed off. No display of emotion at all. Very businesslike. Nobody ever missed a beat, but you never saw anybody hug or kiss." Any mention of sex, of course, was taboo, and an early sign of what he calls his "subversive nature" was the drawings of naked women he began producing at age eight or nine. But his actual sexual experience has been limited. He lost his virginity at nineteen, married at twenty-three, was divorced at thirty-six, and has slept with "six or seven" women in his life.

• • •

The first thing I told Evelyn when I met her was, "Be careful, because I'm an alcoholic." Fortunately, that didn't stop her. For the first six months or so of our relationship, I was still an alcoholic, but I knew I couldn't continue. It was just a matter of when I was going to make the leap. She quickly made it clear that first of all, there wasn't going to be any relationship unless I did it. And second, she was go-

438

ing to help me. I was about forty. She was thirty.

In the beginning we were pretty sexually active, I guess like most couples. I was coming off my one and only truly carnal relationship, with my previous girlfriend Alya. There was a lot of chemistry with her. There was no chemistry with Evelyn. I came to her out of need for help. She was divorced and lonely like me, and she wanted to embark on a family, something solid in her life. It was a project for her. But our sexual life was pretty good. It wasn't like the way I had felt with my first wife, where it was a chore. It just wasn't wildly exciting, either.

We'd make love every two or three days. That went on for two years, let's say. For me, part of it was a carryover from Alya, made me feel that I was a lover, that I could perform. On Evelyn's part, coming from a failed marriage, and very few prior relationships, and quite possibly never having had an orgasm, she probably felt that sex was something you had to do to ensure a relationship. I don't think it was ever noxious to her, but it probably wasn't the first thing on her mind. But that didn't bother me. Being a recovering alcoholic, for the first three or four years my overwhelming need was to stay straight. Sex just wasn't up there on my big list at all. It never has been.

I'm trying to remember how it was. We used a lot of baby talk. We still do. It isn't so much the words, it's more like being ridiculous, letting that evolve into toilet humor, or adolescent jokes, so that you're reduced to giggles. Then start tickling or something like that. We'd get silly, it would be eleven o'clock at night, and we'd go from there into kissing. Then a foreplay period. Foreplay would be me stroking her, and she would stroke me. My penis. I would just touch her all over. Then I would come into her, either while she was on her back, or with me on my back, or me behind her. Those are the three positions we'd use. I'm not very long-lasting, I probably have an orgasm—it's hard to estimate, but it's fairly quick. Probably two minutes, a really short period of time. Then we'd cuddle, say nice things to each other, and go to sleep.

One problem was that she doesn't like to be touched in front. If she's lying on her back, she doesn't want to be touched anywhere on her front. She gets ticklish. She doesn't like it. That was a real problem, of course. But once we were involved, once I was inside of her, in the heat of it, I guess, then I could touch her. It was only in the foreplay that I couldn't do that. But it was hard to achieve that point where she was excited enough to open up to receive me.

Since that time, the first two years, I'd say it's been [moves his hand in a declining arc]—*Ooooooo,* like that. After two years we decided to have a child. There was some sexual activity there. Once Evelyn became pregnant, it began to fall off a lot. Sammie was born in '85. After that, sex became virtually nonexistent. Evelyn was the first one to admit she had no desires whatsoever. Eventually we made love again, maybe six or nine months later. It was pretty drab. Forced. I was discovering that I couldn't do it by myself. I needed to have a partner who was fully engaged, who wanted to have sex. If you took a slice through late '85, early '86, that would have been the picture. We were struggling to find intimacy without any real pleasure.

Then Evelyn turned up with breast cancer. She had a radical mastectomy, and it took her maybe six months to recover enough from that to have our first sexual experience. But since then, we've been able to achieve a sort of decent sexuality by talking about it and working at it. It's almost like opening a door—you have to crank the door open. Once you get the door open, a certain amount of spontaneity and feeling can come through.

It's hard, of course. Now, not only can I not touch her in the front, but it's a real problem area. A mastectomy is a disfiguring thing. She feels ugly, like she's half a woman. She had an implant, but those things aren't—she had it taken out. They're ugly, they don't work at all. This one didn't, anyway. It didn't look anything like a breast, it just looked like a lump. It had the scar right through the middle of it, so it was very Frankensteinlike. It's been traumatic for her. She's under psychiatric care. But after a while we both recognized that we couldn't not have sex. I wasn't looking for a sexual charge, like wild excitement. It was more the act of coming together. Having this touching, goofing around, sweet talk, softness, on some sort of regular basis, to remind us that one is male and one is female, and we're here for a reason, we're not just managing the house.

I find it difficult to discuss sex. I never did with my ex-wife. I never did with Alya. I never did at first with Evelyn. Partly because

of my need to repress things about sex as being bad. And partly because, in the sixties, my feelings and attitudes were magical. You
don't explain things, they just happen. If you talk about them, they'll
go away. So that was on one side. On the other side was the fact that
nothing was happening, and I had to find a way to make it happen.
I had to swallow a lot of feelings of not wanting to do this because of
the mastectomy, and my own need not to talk about sexual issues. I
had to overcome all that. But I was willing. And it wasn't painful,
once I started doing it. I started realizing that I could touch her in a
certain place, down here, and say, "How does that feel? Do you like
that?" Then she could also find the courage to say, "That's okay,"
or "That's not okay." After that it was relatively easy to find the
route home.

We did it by trial and error. We'd say, Okay, let's give it a shot, we
know it's gonna be a problem. [Laughs.] We'd usually carry it
through, have sex in one way or another. Sometimes it would be very
gray and unappealing, and we'd hardly get through. Sometimes we'd
find something good about it, and we'd say, That was all right, and
we'd try to incorporate it. At first it was pretty dismal. We'd say,
Gotta try it. We'd go upstairs and try. Sometimes I couldn't get an
erection, because it was too cold-feeling. Or she'd just say, "I can't do
it." The atmosphere was heavy with, This isn't going to work. We got
past that by saying, All right, maybe it doesn't feel right, but let's keep
on going anyway. I'd try to get an erection, and sooner or later I
would. I'd masturbate next to her—thinking of someone else, of
course. I'd whip myself up [laughs], and then we'd force our way
through it. That alone would be a minor achievement. It'd pave the
way for the next time. You'd at least know you could get through it.
That was the fear: You were going to feel worse afterward than you
did before. If you don't feel worse afterward, that gives you enough
incentive for the next time.

At that point we didn't know about her lying on her stomach and
my touching her only on her back. We had to do a lot of trial and error, of caressing, to discover that. I don't know how many times, but
a lot. We had to refine it. How it started out, she would just come in
and lie on her stomach because she'd get really uptight to lie on her
back. Okay, well, here's her back, at least I can touch that. I'd start

there, and I would stroke her on her butt, down her legs, and then it makes sense to start to probe, maybe something will happen that way—Eureka! All of a sudden I would notice: She's moving, she's stirring! It was like waking the dead. Well, how does this happen after all this time? I must be doing something, what am I doing? And we would talk—she would tell me what felt good.

I think there are two reasons why it took so long for us to figure this out. One was that in the beginning, before Sammie was born, Evelyn's main goal was to get through the whole process of making love. She would be active, and her activity was to masturbate me until I got hot enough, and then she would put me in her. She really controlled the operation. There wasn't any real foreplay. But now, she doesn't have the desire to do that. There are too many other bad feelings—about her breasts, about her whole baggage of psychological things. She's more or less going along for the ride. And not too thrilled about it. So it's up to me to find a route.

At some point, after many dismal failures—not failures, just dismal experiences—I could tell she was beginning to respond. I was putting my finger down, touching the underside of her vagina from the rear, and it became obvious this was pleasurable to her instead of obnoxious. Because she started to move, the way you do when you— side to side a little bit, up and down. Like masturbating. I would move my fingers and she would move her body. She'd start to get wet. Then she would also push herself up on her arms and allow me to touch her breasts and her stomach and her shoulders. It was almost like an animal, the way animals indicate when they're at a certain point in their mating movements. Then she would begin to move rapidly, in a circular way. My fingers are inside her at this point.

That was a big move, for her to lift herself up, and it didn't happen just like that. What happened at first was that I'd begin to manipulate, and she'd get excited enough that it would be like before the operation, just slightly excited, and then I'd come into her. But at some point she began to understand, and I began to understand, that this was *her* experience. She wasn't merely going through the paces. She was doing it. She was breathing deeply, she was moving in a sexual way. Her muscle tone—when you're in a sexually excited state, it seems to me it's a little bit like working out, where the blood is flowing to the outer muscles. You start feeling everything—like on your arms, or your legs, you feel it everywhere. You become eroticized. And there's a kind of muscle tone—I mean, this was a real eye-opener for me. I had never, ever observed this before. With anybody.

I divide sex into two categories. One is masturbatory sex, and the other is communal, shared-experience sex, which is very deep and very wide. My experience with Alya was the carnal masturbatory type. We both got a kick out of it, we liked it, but it didn't have anything to do with anything spiritual or deep. I know there are people who are very erotic, who can become quivering nerves in sex. And you don't have to be in love, or have a deep spirit to do that. But in the average person, when you reach that point, there is something happening to you. You're transcending. You're getting into another realm. And I noticed that happening to Evelyn. The muscle tone, the rhythmic breathing, the pelvic thrusts. It was classic. What had been a no-trespassing zone suddenly became on fire. Her breasts, her sides, down here—anyplace in the front. I would touch her and there'd be something in response—either in her voice, her sound, or she'd push forward, toward me. It didn't take her long to get to that point, either. A couple of months, maybe not even that long. It was something that was waiting to happen. It was just like unlocking a door. I'm amazed that we didn't discover it before. It's shocking, in retrospect.

I learned mostly by touch and feel, by exploring. It wasn't so much a verbal thing. She was reticent to say "No," or "I don't like that." If it was something I already knew she didn't like and I did it anyway, she'd say, "Cut it out." But if I didn't know, then she'd just try to give me an indication. It was like a puzzle, trying to find out where everything fit. For example, I can't touch her behind the knees. It drives her nuts, she starts kicking her legs. She doesn't like the back of her neck to be touched. I remember that one. That's a very unusual place not to be able to touch. But she would go like this [shakes head], trying to get my hand away. I said, "What, I can't touch your neck? How did you get through necking?" I always make jokes, because that was the way we would keep from going after each other. I'd try to slide it off, make it look silly and go on to the next thing. Because it's a painful job, trying to reconstruct sex after a traumatic experience. You can be resentful. I could get angry at her for denying me for so long. She could get angry at me for pushing it. In fact, there was some resentment on my part, but I found my own crazy ways to deal with it. Pornography, masturbation, workaholism. Sure, I wanted it to happen, but I wasn't going to lash out. I was just going to try and make it work.

There were times when I'd be touching her, and something would go wrong, and I'd feel angry. It'd come to me like a coldness, a withdrawal. I wouldn't be able to get an erection. I'd get ticklish. When that happens I know I have to readjust my mindset to get back in the right groove. If you do it right, you can get your body and mind going in the same direction. First I'd try to make a joke out of the situation. Be silly. Then stop and just lie there. Try to breathe deeply, which changes the blood flow a little bit. It's like meditation, where you change the picture in your mind from the one that's happening to the one you want. And slowly your body starts to come around. I would think about really making love with her, where it was pleasurable, where it was stimulating. Every once in a while it wouldn't work, usually when I was very tired or in a bad mood or something. But most of the time it worked.

I had to learn how to touch her vagina. I did ask her about that— but mostly before or after sex, rather than during. I had to learn the right clitoral manipulation. There was a certain part that was better to touch, lower down toward the rectum, as a way of getting in, let's say, and then once in, once she was wet and open, to go just so far, and then keep the motion restricted, not get too heavy-handed. Not make too big a motion or too strong a motion. She told me at one point that she preferred in general to have me be stationary and her move. That's a little too clinical, because what happens of course is that I'm getting aroused, too, I'm sort of using the bed, both of my hands are engaged, her hands are by her side or pushing herself up, so the only way I can get stimulated is by rubbing against the bed. So I'm getting excited, and I'm beginning to focus also on the rest of her body. And I forget, I'm not thinking about all the things I'm supposed to be doing. [Laughs.] So she has to tell me, "You're in too far," or something like that.

I don't remember her first orgasm, but I do remember when she told me, "Guess what? I had an orgasm!" That first orgasm was really—it produced some good feelings for us. We had been struggling for so long, and she had been in such misery. She had a nice bright smile on her face. For a while, I couldn't tell when she reached climax. I knew she was very excited, which was new—all of this was new. Quite honestly, I'm so inexperienced with women who have orgasms—Alya did, but I was always so drunk with her that I can't remember what it was like for her. My first wife never did. So with Evelyn, I wasn't sure. Now I think I can tell. She keeps moving, she's grinding herself into the bed, still up on her arms, with her head thrown back. Her voice level doesn't rise much, she breathes very heavily, and it comes faster and deeper. She makes some noise, but it's not loud, not like a big shriek or anything.

We stop when we both get exhausted. It goes on for a while, probably ten or fifteen minutes, and then my hands get tired. [Laughs.] Or she'll just roll over, and then she'll get on me and I come into her while she's on top of me. That's her preference. Actually it's mine too. She's very small, I'm too big for her when I'm on top. She has complained about that. If she's on me it's no problem at all. And I prefer it because she's more accessible for touching. If I'm on her, she gets kind of swallowed up. If she's on top, she's all there, right in front of me, and if she's open to my touching her, which she is at that stage, it's a lot easier. I like to hold her rear end and her waist. Touch her shoulders and her breasts. I stroke her breasts very gently, stroking across the nipple. Or cupping from underneath. She prefers a very soft touch. And even at that stage, her stomach is tricky.

These days our sex gets to be a little bit ritualized, I must say, because there are only certain motions I can do. She might start out on her back, but I know I can't be touching her that way, so if we're going to go anywhere, she has to get on her stomach. [Laughs]. She flips right over, she knows exactly what she has to do. And I know exactly what I have to do. We go through all the parts, the foreplay—I can't dive right into her vagina. I do a caressing, circular motion on her back, down in the small of the back, through the waist, down her side, up over her buttocks, down to her thighs. Not behind the knees, and careful of the neck. [Laughs.] It's almost like a massage, you feel the tension draining out. I know by feel when it's time to start moving into the erogenous zone. It's like a seduction in some ways. I don't do anything rough, because that will kill it.

I can't say there's any heat in our marriage. It's not about heat or desire. We have an understanding that sex is a magical act. It produces something—well, it produces children, but it also produces a kind of feeling for the other person that goes beyond any other kind of expression. It increases the depth and width of the relationship. I think Evelyn is a more sexual person than she thinks she is. The urge is there, the impulse is there, the sexuality is there, if you push the right buttons. And we stumbled on the right buttons at a time when—it was a saving thing, overcoming what seemed to me insurmountable odds. If it had just been dismal, constantly, endlessly, we would have given up. And who knows what happens then? So this—it was more than rejuvenating. It created a new sexuality, because I liked it too. This is the first time I felt it was within my power to excite a woman. Alya used to get excited, but she was a sexy person anyway, and if it wasn't me it would have been someone else. But when you can elicit sexual feeling in someone where it's very tough, where it's hidden—that means you're creative, you have some ability. Plus, I can talk about it with her. We can think about it together. We can almost shake hands afterward—like, This is great, let's do it again!

INGRID THORPE

She is a WASP, forty-seven years old, a lapsed Lutheran of Southern descent, a "nice girl from Annapolis married to a Jew from Brooklyn." We talk at their house on Long Island's South Shore. Mel seems her opposite: swarthy and tousled to her pale, kempt blondness, voluble and earthy to her more cerebral reserve. But she is no stranger to her feelings: She cries more than once in remembering unhappy loves from the past. She holds an important job at a foundation; he owns a mid-sized business.

Her father was a businessman, her mother a housewife. The marriage was unhappy. "They had nothing in common, led very separate lives. Mom had a character like an alcoholic. You never knew what was going to be there when you walked in the door, whether she was going to be angry or lovey-dovey. She was crazed about us ruining our reputations. Which meant having sex. And heaven forbid, getting pregnant.

"Aside from some childhood play, I didn't feel a physical sexual feeling until I was in college. I mean, I even had a boyfriend in high school, and we did some heavy petting, hands on breasts, hands on crotch, and I never felt anything. Nothing. Then in college I had a hopeless crush on a girl. We did a little bit of kissing, never any clothes off. But it was a big, big turn-on for me. And I started masturbating. I wanted some outlet for these feelings. I also felt like everybody else knew about something I didn't know anything about, and what was it? I remember the first time I had an orgasm, and I was by myself. I just cried and cried because it seemed like there ought to be somebody else there, and why wasn't I good enough to have somebody else involved in having an orgasm? Why did I have to do it alone?"

Through her twenties and thirties she had a sequence of affairs with men who, for one reason or another, were unavailable for anything lasting. She met Mel in 1975.

• • •

I don't have sexual feelings that run away with me. I'm just too in-control a person. My sister is much more uninhibited. She talks about losing herself in sex. She had some guy she was having an affair with, and three hours would go by and it was like being on drugs. I'd have to take a truckload of LSD to have that happen. I mean, I can have an orgasm and be thinking about how to rearrange the furni-ture. [Laughs.] Too bad, but that's how it is. Actually, I think it's re-markable I can have orgasms at all, considering my bringing up.

I remember very clearly meeting Mel, standing in the lobby of a Ramada Inn. We were both doing a workshop, kind of an encounter group. He seemed really friendly and easy to be with and natural. We had to pick partners to go through the whole four days with. We picked each other. Some of the exercises were physical, you were supposed to caress each other's face or something, and he would move his hand down to my breast. It wasn't that I minded, but it wasn't in the rules. Hold on, let's do it by the rules!

But we started dating afterward. We met in August, and we dated all that fall. We slept together pretty soon, he could probably tell you the exact date. He remembers the first time. I don't at all. My sex life at the time was mostly just masturbating. He had left his wife about five years before. He got married very young so he didn't have much sexual experience. When the marriage ended, he went on an absolute sexual rampage. He told me once he made love to five different women in a day. He had incredible sexual energy, maybe neurotic sexual energy. When I met him, he had been living with a woman for a year or two and had just moved out.

I was very undemanding sexually for a while. Whatever I got, that's what I took, and what he wanted to do, that's what we did. I guess as it came to be more like real life, I started feeling, Well, y'know, I'm here too, maybe I want something more, or different. I remember at first our sex was rough. I don't mean slap-around rough, but a lot of *uh-uh-uh-uh-uh* [moans frantically]. Him being on top of me or behind me and going in and out really hard. Him rub-bing himself inside me really hard to get off. I felt like I had to keep up. I had to have orgasms all the time. That meant he would do it, or I would touch myself and help it along, or whatever, but it was a lot of effort. It wasn't bad, I liked it, it was fine, but after a while it was too much. It was no good as a way of life. It was too athletic. Too much jumping around, changing positions, and rough instead of gentle physical activity. Instead of sliding in and out slowly, he'd go *brr-rr-rr-rr-rr.* [Laughs.] Sometimes still, when he holds me, his grip is too hard. I tell him, "When I get osteoporosis, my bones are gonna snap! Can't you hold on to the bedpost or something?" He loses himself much more than I do. I doubt he thinks about redecorating or even about business when he's coming.

Then there was a period when I was furious at him all the time. Every time he touched me I was angry. I didn't tell him about it, because I thought it was something I had to deal with. But I felt very intruded upon by his wanting sex. Waking me up at five in the morning to fuck. I felt used and invaded, and that he wasn't considering me. I didn't feel any of his love coming for me. See, that's something—he expresses love sexually, and I just wasn't brought up to think that sex was a joyful expression of love. I was brought up to think that sex was this thing that men wanted of women, and women were supposed to withhold. So it took me a long time to get used to the idea that when he wanted to make love to me, he wasn't just this horny guy who could stick it in a cow and it'd be just as good. That it had something to do with me. An appreciation of me, and a response to me. It took me so long to get that. So long. At first, I was grateful to have somebody in my life who wanted to make love to me. It made me normal, somehow. Then, when it became something I had in my life, all my feelings about it began to surface. I started to stick up for myself. I realized that if I was going to have sex in my life, I had a right to have it be nice for me.

Sometimes I had to really get angry with him and let him know how angry I was to get him to pay attention. To make some of the changes I wanted. I let him have it a couple times. And even then, he just took it, he didn't get all funny. There were times when I said, "I must have told you a hundred times—" For example, I can't stand to have my clitoris touched. With his mouth or hand or anything. It hurts. So I said, "I've told you a hundred times not to touch me there, why do you keep doing it?" Oh. It was like he said to himself, Oh, I guess she really means it. [Laughs.] Part of the anger was that I felt like I wasn't getting through. I wanted to suggest it a few times and have him pick right up on it, and that would be the end of that. But it wasn't happening. I was pissed that I had to do more than that, and I felt inhibited about doing more. But I realize now, that's just what it takes. I felt like I was dealing with a child. You tell it seventeen times to close the door, and the last time you hand the kid his head on a platter, and from then on he closes the door.

Sometimes even now he'll do the same thing. Like he loves to do oral sex. He'd move his tongue the same way for five minutes if you'd let him. Well, after a while it begins to hurt, like anything you do repetitively. He once told me this joke about a man who traced out the letters of the alphabet with his tongue, and it made him a great success with women. I said, "That guy had something. Remember that. Don't forget it." But every once in a while, I'll have to say, "Um, could we move on to another letter of the alphabet here?"

In general, he's very playful in bed. He has a wonderful attitude about sex, which is that it's just mechanics. It's just something you learn how to do. For him it's not all tied up with emotional fantasies. The one place where we still have a bit of a problem is I would like him to move in and out more slowly, and he tends to lose his erection. He says, "Well, I'd like to, I'll do that a couple of times, but I can't do it three or four times because I won't have any erection left." I have a feeling I could have an orgasm with him inside me doing practically nothing, but he can't do nothing. So a lot of what he does to have an orgasm is too much for me. I get numbed out.

But he has become much more gentle. He says how pleased he is that he learned that. He even says, "You have no idea how incredibly responsive you are, how wonderful it is to make love to you." Of course, I have no idea about that. While I'm feeling like an inadequate weirdo, he's finding me this natural, desirable hot cookie.

Our lovemaking doesn't have much variety to it. Every once in a while we'll get out the porn movies and the vibrators. It's fun, but it isn't a big part of our sex life. Usually we're just lying there reading at night, and one of us cuddles up to the other one, spoonlike, and drapes one arm over and grabs the other's crotch. The other one turns over. There's a little kissing and rubbing around, and then I get on top of him, or more typically he gets on top of me. He gets inside me and we do our foreplay just like that. He can just lie on top of me, inside me, and I can just slightly move against him, and I get really turned on by it. What sometimes happens is, I get turned on and then he does something that's too hard, and it numbs me. So he has to be careful. If he needs to rub himself back and forth to keep his hard-on, then he has to do something soft for me. He's perfectly happy to do that. He rubs back and forth and up and down, and then he bounces on me a little, just a little, bumping my mons. Pretty soon I start to come. I like to squeeze his buns and press him into me. I'll have a couple of orgasms, and sometimes he'll want to make me have more, and I'll say, "No, go ahead, you have one now." So he rubs himself in and out real hard, and as he's coming I press myself into him and grab his buns and I'll come, too.

It feels weird if we go as long as a week without making love. We do most of our lovemaking on weekends, it's more relaxed. We fall in the national average of two or three times a week. And now that I don't feel so intruded upon by making love in the morning before we get up, we do that sometimes on weekdays. Somehow I started viewing sex as something nice I could give him, that I wanted to give him because I loved him, as opposed to something he was going to take from me. Sex wasn't something in which I got done to, sex was something I could be a player in.

So in the morning, I don't feel so desperate: "What do you mean, waking me up at five o'clock?" He always wakes up then, and we've been together so long that I tend to wake up then, too. Might as well fuck as anything else. [Laughs.] I don't usually come, but I don't let myself get so worked up that I feel left in the lurch. In the beginning, I felt that sex was a tension reliever for Mel. I felt like, Let him relieve his tension somewhere else. Now, when we make love, it always feels like it's connected to me. Or I make the agreement that he can use my body. Which is okay, too. It's sort of a joke—he says, "Do you mind if I use your body for the next two minutes?" I say, "Yeah, sure, go ahead." He'll get inside me and come very quickly and say, "Thanks, I can go to work now." And I say, "You're welcome, have a good day."

Mel professes to be totally happy with our sex, and I can only believe him, because he doesn't show any signs it's not true. And when
he is unhappy, like sometimes if I'm too passive, or if he feels— For
example, he likes to look at porn movies. I'm not that turned on by
them, because most of them put women in such shitty positions.
Also, part of me thinks they're disgusting and you shouldn't watch
them, it's not okay, nice girls from Annapolis don't watch porn movies. They do turn me on. But if Mel thinks that what he calls recreational sex is unavailable to him, he gets really upset. If I'm resisting,
like he wants to watch a porn movie and I say, "Oh, no. . . ." If I do
that too much, he gets upset. But he tells me right away. So I take a
look and think, This is stupid. It's really a part of him, he wants that
and needs that. And if I don't give it to him, it's stupid of me. So I do.
I take the initiative and say, "Let's rent a movie." Or, "Let's pull out
the vibrators." Somehow it's very threatening to me, I think it's going
to cost me something terrible. But of course it doesn't cost me anything.

When we were first courting, this friend of Mel's told him it was
really great to make love if you cover your bodies with coconut oil
and roll around on a plastic sheet. We did that once and I loved it.
But things I love that much scare me, so I pull back. We did it a second time, and it didn't work at all. Same way with anal sex. The first
time anybody did that to me, it was fantastic. Before I really knew it
existed, and I didn't know what was happening, it was incredible. If
you could separate my head from it, I love anal sex. But ever since
then, I've had a much different time with it. I think it's because I like
it so much. It puts me over that threshold of control I have to maintain. It scares the shit out of me. So now when I do that, my sphincter
tightens up, it's really painful. Every once in a while Mel will take out
the vibrators, and it takes a while but it lets loose and it's okay. It's a
production number [laughs], but as long as he doesn't feel I'm denying him that, he doesn't have any other bones to grind—no, not
bones to grind. . . .

I think both Mel and I are controlling in sex. He can't just let me
do it to him. We both like it a certain way. I can't come from being
on top of him. And when we make love, there's always part of me
that's outside, watching. I would love to be free of that. It takes a lot

of energy to be yourself and watch yourself at the same time. I'd love to be able to experience total abandon. I'd like to be able to come in more positions. I feel inadequate because I can't. But Mel says, "What are you complaining about? You have three orgasms a time! Do you need to do it in ten positions, too?"

ALEX WOODLEIGH

He is forty-two, head of computer services at a large company in Ohio, and father of two boys, ten and five. His marriage is unconventional: He and Anita, a psychologist with a private practice, have been together fifteen years, but for the last three they have "opened" their relationship, with the understanding that both will disclose their other ties. She has had one serious love affair, which ended when she refused to leave Alex; he has had less consuming liaisons—until now.

He is a handsome, energetic, optimistic man, full of plans and projects. After working as a hippie housebuilder in the late sixties and early seventies, he became fascinated with computers around the same time he met Anita. Both he and Anita had considerable sexual experience. "We courted for a long time before we slept together. I thought she was totally beautiful and strong. She's smart, independent, unconventional, stands up for herself. When we had sex for the first time, it was fireworks for both of us. And we've had a really good sex life over all these years, even when it was hard, when we had the kids, when she wanted less sex than I did. I marvel at how it can be always different."

However, he struggles with a tendency to "lie and hide things"—a tendency he traces to his childhood. His father was an insurance agent who led a double life, having two children with a lover while married to Alex's mother, who herself spent years secretly addicted to barbiturates. The marriage broke up when Alex was fourteen. "I became kind of strong and silent as a result of all that. I didn't see it as a painful childhood, but there was a lot of tension in the house, and I was always trying to figure out where it came from." His own secrets have included two short affairs in the years before opening the marriage. "When I told her about them, Anita was furious. She said she could never trust me, and I said that was probably true. All I could do was live day by day, maybe she'd end up trusting me again."

Six weeks before our talk, Alex fell in love with another woman.

• • •

It happened at a conference in Miami. This woman Diane was there. I've known her for a long time but not well. She's married. She's also a good friend of another friend of mine, and I said I'd say hi to her. So I did. Thursday night there was this big reception. I started talking with her, we had a couple shots of tequila, and we were attracted. We walked on the beach, sat and talked, and—well, one thing led to another. How do these things happen? It was pretty clear that we were either going to bed together, or we would walk away and never be able to see each other because we wouldn't be able to stand it. The attraction was instantaneous, physical and emotional. I don't know why it would happen after years of associating, but it did.

We went back to her room. I still wasn't absolutely sure I was going to stay the night, or what we were going to do. But I stayed, of course, and it was magical. It was magical from that moment, and it's been magical every time I've been with her. We had two nights in Miami. We spent a day together here where we didn't make love, because by then I had told Anita and she wasn't giving her permission at that point. Then we made a business trip together and spent three nights. And we spent last night together because Anita and the kids are out of town.

Anita knows all about it, though right now she's pretty angry. I didn't think it would be a big issue, given what we've been doing for a while. But it was. First of all, because I did it without telling her first. But that wasn't the big problem. What really set her off was that I talked to her while I was in Miami and didn't tell her anything was going on. But Anita and I worked through that, it seemed to be okay. She actually had a meeting with Diane and that went pretty well. But during that time—it was about four weeks from the time we were in Miami to when we went on the trip together—I talked with Diane at least once a day. It was obvious to Anita this was no ordinary affair.

It got scarier and scarier until I finally said, "Well, if you really don't want me to do it, I won't." That was fine for about a week, as long as she knew she had that power, it was okay. Then suddenly it wasn't. I was getting ready to go on the business trip with Diane, and it got very upsetting for Anita when she came face to face with that. And of course I was completely scared to tell Anita what was happening for me, for fear it would drive her away. She asked me if I was in love with Diane. I said yeah, but I didn't say it was this complete obsession. I felt taken over. "Possessed" is more accurate than "obsessed."

Right now, Anita is not sleeping with me. She says she can't bear to be with me. Meanwhile, Diane told her husband about us. They had an understanding before that if either of them ever had an affair, they just didn't want to know. So she wasn't going to tell him. But eventually she realized she had to say something. She put it in the context of opening up the relationship and allowing him some freedom, too. So far he's been fine about that. I think she was probably more discreet and a little smarter than I am, she didn't make it obvious just how involved we are. But he's giving her complete freedom, and she has told him she's not going anywhere, she's not leaving him. I've been clear with Anita about that, too.

My sex with Diane—it feels spiritual. I would never have said anything like that before, but it's different from any experience I've ever had. It sheds a completely different light on what sex can be. It's like our bodies merge. If there were such a thing as an aura, or a spiritual body—it's a connection at that level, instead of one that feels just physical. When we make love, it's like I disappear. Athletes talk about being in the zone—this is like being in the zone for hours. It's not like I'm doing anything or making anything happen. In some religions they say, It's the dance, not the dancer. This is like I'm being danced.

If you were looking from the outside, just looking at these two people in bed, it would be like, God, aren't they ever gonna stop? We made love for two hours straight last night, I had an erection the whole time, and I felt something like orgasm many, many times, although I didn't ejaculate until near the end. We started out—we rented a room in a fancy hotel. I took her out to play tennis. We got all sweaty, and she had a top on with no bra, and her nipples were out—she was just beautiful. She's about five-five, five-six, dark hair, dark eyes, very dark skin—she's Italian. She's forty-two, same age as me. So we went back to the hotel. Had a drink at the bar. Drank about half of it and went upstairs, taking our drinks with us. And just took our clothes off. I lit two candles. We started holding each other and kissing. And we—disappeared. From then on it's hard for me to remember, because I wasn't thinking.

I remember after we were kissing for a while, I made her put her arms back, so she wasn't doing anything, and just licked her nipples. Used my hands to feel all her body. One thing that happens for each of us sometimes is just shuddering. Her body shudders, like the energy is too much. Later on I remember touching her clitoris with my penis for a long time. Very slow, very sensual, having my penis in her pubic area, inserting just a little bit, not a lot of penetration. I don't know how long that lasted, but I'm pretty sure it ended up in fast and furious, energetic huffing and puffing and pumping.

Somewhere in there I spent a lot of time licking her body and sucking her breasts and using my fingers on her clitoris and around there and in her anus. She was mostly on her back, though it happened other ways, too. One time [laughs], she ended up on her back with her head down between the two beds, like in a back bend with her legs in the air. I was holding her by her thighs. Then—let's see, at one point she got on top of me, and we did slow and fast, uncontrollably shuddering. Then she turned over, or I turned her over, and I came in from behind. Slow at first, and then I pushed hard and got almost violent. Then I told her to suck me. She spent a long time doing that, also slow and fast. She does this thing—it's the best. When she starts sucking me, I try to grab her and touch her, but she'll take my hands and put them back on the bed. So I'm lying completely open, and she's sucking. Hard and soft. She sucks my balls. Then I think she got on top of me again. There's a point for both of us where slapping is the right thing to do. She'll slap me right on my balls, or my anus. It's slightly painful, and it drives me nuts. Or I'll slap her on the butt, harder than I've ever slapped anybody making love. I'll bring her down so she's on my chest and I can reach all the way behind her.

Then last night, for the first time, I used some oil and softened her anal area and came in there very, very slowly. Used my hand to touch her clitoris and inside her. I did that for a long time. Then, I don't know, I think she sucked me again, and finally she turned over on her stomach again and I came in behind and finally ejaculated. I don't know how to describe that, it's like an explosion of explosions. It feels almost like I can't separate from her after that. I couldn't tell you how many times she came, but it was a lot. And there are times when I come—well, I don't come, but I get a wave of sensation like an orgasm, and I'm satisfied—you know how you sort of hit a peak and slow down? I get satisfied but I stay hard and I don't ejaculate. Usually at the culmination of the fast and furious there's a release, and it feels like, Okay, that's what that was about. Now we can go slower again. So from the time we got back to the hotel room, there wasn't one moment when we were resting, but it felt like we weren't *doing* anything. There's no planning to it—now I'll do this, and then I'll do that. It's like watching it happen—wow, this is interesting, I'm along for the ride. The roller coaster gets up to the top and goes back down. Whether you want to or not, you're on that ride, and the experience of your stomach rising up, you don't have any choice about that. You just let go.

I don't think at all. I don't have any fantasies. Almost every other time I've had sex I think, Should I come or shouldn't I? Is this the right time? Or I get to a point where—Uh-oh, it's too late. With Diane I just don't think about it. It'll happen when it happens. Last night I came at the end, but other times I've come after an hour or so and we've gone on and on, I'm still hard enough to be in her, or if not she'll be on top of me rubbing my penis with her clitoris for a long time. Without any sort of, Wait a minute, this has gone on long enough, I've already come, I don't need this. And eventually I get hard again.

We don't talk much, although words sometimes come out of my mouth [laughs]—"Oh God, oh God, oh God, I can't believe this is happening." We're in the fourth hour of fucking, and I've already come twice, and there doesn't seem to be any end. It runs all the way from tender to fierce, like an animal. I might even grunt. Or she'll say, "I don't know where this is coming from, it's unbelievable." There are also times when I'll burst into tears, or she will. I'll look up at her and see tears in her eyes. One night in Miami I found myself saying, "How could we have ever been separated?" I was overcome with something like sadness, and I burst into tears. She was on top of me and we were fucking away. It just came out of my mouth and I started crying. I have no idea what I meant, it had no connection with anything logical. I could make up something, like we're soulmates, or we've been connected in a past life, but I don't believe in any of that. It just felt like somebody I had been away from for a long time, and we were coming back together. Or if you had someplace you went for vacations as a child, a wonderful, wonderful place, and as you get older you forget about it. And then if you go back there, it's not just a return to that place, but to that time when everything was wonderful, and you were a kid, and you didn't have to worry about anything, and it was summer.

Off and on during the whole thing, I go into this dreamy state. It's like—I was going to say my head explodes, but that sounds painful. More like my consciousness explodes. It goes from being something internal and focused to something infinite—like, *boom!* It happens sometimes when the sex is fast and sometimes when it's slow. At first it's like I'm inside space and time, I know what's going on, I could tell you that the different parts of my body are this way and that way, and yes, it feels good. Then the explosion, and I couldn't tell you. I couldn't tell you what my body is doing. I don't feel one part of me against one part of her. When I touch her, the contact goes beyond those physical points. I don't know why I call that spiritual, but it's more than physical, and it ain't emotional, so what is it? When this explosion thing happens and I close my eyes, there's more light than dark. So what have we got here, angels or what? [Laughs.] I say to myself, Okay, here's what's happening: There are these two people, and they're an expression of God's love. That's such a new thought to me that I don't even know what I mean by it. So where is this coming from? I don't know where the hell it's coming from. [Laughs.] It's coming from God, or grace, or somewhere. I can't even believe I'm saying this. I used to be a Marxist!

Look at me, I'm shaking all over, just talking about it. Diane says the same thing, it's never been like this before, the sex or the relationship. Because we talk the same way we have sex. If you listened to our conversation, it would be stupid. She tells me what she did, and I tell her what I did. And we laugh. There's nothing extraordinary, but I feel extraordinary and so does she. I walk away with this silly grin. And if we're apart, the way I described it to her the other day, I feel like there's a hole in my heart. Not a bad hole, not like I'm bleeding or a part of me is gone, but wherever she is, a part of me is there.

In one way it scares the shit out of me. Whatever is happening, it's got my marriage at risk—a fifteen-year, very solid, stable marriage. I mean, we've gone through all sorts of things, and I think most anybody who knows us would say we have one of the most successful marriages they've ever seen. Yet I'm willing to let it be at risk. That's frightening. I'm in a quandary: Can I have it all? My marriage has been wonderful, and our sex has been great. I don't want to lose that. Yet there's this other thing that I don't even understand.

FAY CANASTEL

Her San Francisco apartment is decorated in what she calls "faux harem"—lots of hanging fabric, big pillows, mirrors, Oriental prints. The only incongruous detail is the riot of books; they are piled everywhere, overflowing the bookshelves. I notice Coleridge, Graves, Paglia, Lessing, many volumes of psychology, and Archaeology magazine. Fay is in her mid-forties, with straight blond hair, green eyes, and lined features—"the life I've lived is in my face." Her outfit matches the decor: tight red jeans, sheepskin boots, and a low-cut red blouse with a fuzzy black cardigan. She is a prostitute, doing in-calls for two hundred dollars an hour. She is also studying mythology and women's history, and is often asked to write or lecture on her ideas.

The life she has lived began in Africa, where her father worked for an American multinational. "Puberty in the tropics. I had my first orgasm with an English boy. We were sitting in a restaurant, almost on the Equator, in the rainy season, and the restaurant was built over a river—a totally fecund atmosphere. We were just kissing and I had an orgasm. So I go bouncing home to Mommy and Daddy: 'I've just had the most wonderful feeling, I was kissing Nigel, and it was so great!' I remember them looking at each other. They were quite liberal for the times—this was the early sixties. But the next thing I know, I'm on a plane for boarding school in Massachusetts."

She was bright, rebellious, bored—and it was the sixties. After high school she shunned college and embarked on twenty years of sex, drugs, booze, marriage, travel, and various jobs that finally landed her in California. In 1984 she joined AA and dried out. "I was depressed, suicidal. In the late eighties I found myself competing with other women for eleven-dollar-an-hour temp jobs. That's when I decided to try being a sex worker. In AA, there were girls standing up and saying, 'My self-esteem was so low that I was a whore.' I'd sit there thinking, Boy, you're doing better than me, my self-esteem is so low that it never occurred to me I could get paid for sex. I asked around and met this woman who did out-calls. She took me under her wing, and I gave her a third of what I earned so it was profitable for her to teach me. When I started to get the hang of it, I developed a style of my own."

• • •

A guy calls. He leaves a name and number on a voice-mail service, and I either call or do not call him back. If I think he's drunk or rude I don't call. If I talk to him, I ask what he does for a living. I'm looking to hear respect. Intelligence and humor also help. I don't want him showing up expecting some twenty-year-old bimbo. I usually say I think there's a lot more to sex than mechanics—atmosphere, conversation, dress. Some guys go, "Oh, great, that's just what I'm looking for." Then I usually say my model is like we're boyfriend and girlfriend, and we haven't seen each other for a long time. I often mention that I only give one appointment a day. I tell him I like to enjoy myself, and if I work too much I don't. A lot of guys have had bad experiences in massage parlors, where the girls can't wait for you to get out. I make it obvious he has the whole hour to play with. One client a day is about my average, but I will do three. So I lie about that, but it's for a higher truth.

People ask me, "Who are your clients?" I say, "Well, who is your boyfriend?" That surprises them. They think, Maybe a husband who's been married a long time, and his wife is pregnant. . . . But I get a lot of young men who have young girlfriends. A lot of guys say their wives or girlfriends don't like them to eat their pussy, or don't like other things. Or just don't like sex a lot of the time. Good whores have an uncanny intuition, we can find the heart of the person very quickly. I have a rapport with certain types—I'm good with Vietnam vets, ex-Jesuits, guys with a philosophical streak. But I also accept whatever a man presents when he comes in. I'm not trying to figure out if he's telling the truth. That's part of his freedom. If he wants to be dashing and debonair for an hour, he can be. If he wants to be a groveling slave, that's fine. I address that as if it's the real thing. There's a suspension of disbelief on both sides, because I also represent something more than I am. At night, with the candles and the fireplace, and my hair down and my makeup on, I have a glamorous image. I think my age might even be comforting. I'm not threatening, whereas a perfect twenty-five-year-old might be.

When he arrives I sit him in this chair. I always wear the same thing, it's a uniform. Black lace-top stockings, high heels, a short tight black skirt, and a black angora sweater. A push-up bra, I have to wear that to have the appearance of anything at all. And always pearls, because I'm a lady. And I light incense and candles, partly in worship, partly as a reminder to myself of the larger principles. It helps establish my moral turf rather than the world's moral turf. And it welcomes him into my space.

That's my altar over there in the corner. Ever since I joined AA I've been looking for spiritual inspiration, some sense of the divine. So I tried the only way I know to find something: I went to the library. This was a couple of years after becoming a sex worker. I started reading the feminist histories of pre-Christian, pre-Judaic religions. Of course, the picture of sexuality is quite different. The central figure on my altar, I made that, it's an icon based on a carving of the goddess Ishtar. She's the Babylonian goddess of love and fertility. The sacred prostitutes were her priestesses. When you went to the temple, you had sex with a priestess. The body hadn't been separated from the spirit back then, sex was seen as a way toward the divine instead of an obstruction. On the far right is a West African figure, a menstrual figure. The other things on the altar have ritual meanings—there's a Lilith figure, and an old clay pot, and a marble apple, and candleholders I made myself, and a picture of the planet Venus, which was called "Harlot of the Evening" because she came out as the men came home from work in the fields. I think of my apartment as a temple, with me as the priestess. I don't push my beliefs on the clients, but I might introduce them to Ishtar. I might say, "It used to be when you went to the temple, you got to make love to a priestess. That's a lot more fun than a dry wafer on your tongue, right?"

I always hug the client when he arrives. That establishes body contact, friendliness, that I want to lay my hands on his body as much as he wants to lay his on mine. I'll usually find something nice to say about his body, something genuine. Then I do some walking around, chatting, lowering the blinds, getting him something to drink, changing the music, so he can get his bearings and find out if he wants to be here or not. Then I'll move in and sit on his lap so he can smell my perfume. I flirt, do some sensual play. Partly that's good for weeding out cops. A cop wants to talk money. He's probably wearing a wire. So I like to get the sensual energy going. Then I tell him, "You can put your offering on the altar," and he leaves the money. I never touch it.

I always say my specialty is passion, rather than any specific tricks. I don't fake it. I'm too lazy to fake it. I can do some light role-playing, but one reason I don't work so much is that what I bring is genuine. The idea is to get real desire going, build up some tension, make it obvious we're going to spend time getting to the fucking. I tell him, "I love to be stroked, I'm like a big pussycat, make me purr."

I have a test that I do when we're fooling around, I call it the finger test. Some of us can be given an orgasm by a stroke behind the knee, or on the foot. Others, especially the older guys, it's their genitals and that's it. So I'm sitting on a chair facing the guy, I'm in my stockings and heels, we're fooling around, and I'll suck his fingers. That should be an erotic experience. If it isn't—and I can tell, I'm looking at his face—if he's like, What is she doing? Is she some kind of weirdo? I want her to suck my cock! If that's written across his face, then I know, Okay, this is how it's gonna be. In fact, if a guy is a total log, meaning the only visible sign of life is an erection, I'll give him back half his money and ask him to leave. If he's lying there with a hard-on, but not a moan, not even a breath, and I've gone half an hour cavorting around but there's nothing coming back, I just stop. He may be quite happy, all he's expecting is a hard-on, but I'll say, "I can't do this, it's demeaning to both of us." Some are puzzled, and some agree. It doesn't happen that often, but it's important to know you have the choice.

Or maybe I'm finding I can't get started. A guy comes in and I realize I have nothing to draw on. My body's dead. I can be smiling and laughing, but it's unbearably hard work even to do that. Then I'll say a prayer, usually with a glance toward the altar. I call on the—I don't want to say spirits, because on some level I don't believe any of this stuff. I call on the temple harlots over the millennia, in all the temples, in all their power. I say, Do it for me, I don't have it, come into me, girls. And it works—there's a switch that goes on, and suddenly I'm laughing and joyous and excited. It has to do with a sense of one's own sexuality and power as a voluntary thing. For most of my life, whether a fuck was good or not depended more on the man than on me. Sex hinged on relationships and emotions and cultural pressure. Now, my sexuality is separate from other things. It has a form and a shape of its own. I can switch it on and off.

Another trick I use to get things going—I take off his shoes, like the dance-hall girl and the cowboy. As if he was wearing cowboy boots. I turn around and bend over so he's looking at my ass, and make a big show of wiggling around while I'm undoing the laces. He gets to relax and focus on the business at hand. Plus it looks great, it's all the images in erotic magazines come to life. I always take his socks off at that point, and I usually joke, "There's nothing more undignified than a naked man with his socks on." I want a lot of laughter going. Then I'll do a certain amount of undressing. I'll take off my sweater. I'll have him pull my skirt down while I'm standing with my back to him. All this time I'm looking for clues to his sexuality. How does he move? How does he respond to me? Does he want to bend over me, does he want me to bend over him? Does he want to surrender, or has he come in with a program? I used to ask clients about fantasies, but I stopped because I got so little back. Most of them either don't have any, or they're not telling.

I take off his shirt so we can rub skin. I want to get him all sensitized. Then at some point I'll take his pants off and usually kiss him all the way down. When it comes to oral sex, I don't go over the head of a cock until the condom's on. But I'll lick under his balls, up the back of the shaft, the underside of his thighs, so I've got all the skin around there working. And I'm kissing around his neck and fingers. I get his pants off, and then usually we'll lie down. There are always variations on this, of course. Even though I say I want to act like boyfriend and girlfriend, I don't really want to, because I don't want him to take the initiative. I've got a routine, and I find it bothers me, say, if he starts to take his own shoes off. Jesus Christ, now what am I gonna do for that five minutes? I have to laugh at myself, because if the routine is broken, it's harder work for me.

After we're on the bed, I often caress his body with my nipples. Again, the idea is to get everything tweaky, until he can't stand it anymore. By this time I'm usually naked except for my black stockings. And then I'll say something like, "I think it's time to wake up my pussy, it's still asleep." It may or may not be, but this never does any harm. I sit down with my cunt facing in his direction. I might get some lube, get out the vibrator, and start playing with myself, and he can join in or not. Playing with my own pussy is a great turn-on to men. The greatest gift that I bring, and all good whores bring, is the absence of shame. This gives the guy an opportunity to be as fascinated as most of them are, to go ahead and look and touch and stare and stare some more. And even be given a guided tour: No, not there, here. I might say, "Don't worry about the clit so much. That's about as meaningful as the head of your cock." They might want to play with the vibrator themselves. It's sex education. And they find it such a turn-on that I'm turned on. You've got to think, What are their wives and girlfriends like?

I realized early that a big part of my job is response. I'd say eighty percent of my clients want my pleasure to be part of their pleasure. Now, it can get into the macho thing where they want you to have an orgasm. It's like a trophy. But that's still a genuine part of their stimulation. If it's not genuine, if there's no passion in it, I don't like it. I'll say, "You don't have to play with me, this is not about any sort of obligation." But if I'm playing with my pussy, and he joins in or not, I'll start to get very turned on. At that point I'll often be playing with his cock, too. What I want to establish is the similarity between our bodies. We look different, but in fact we're not. I run my tongue up between his balls and the back of his shaft, and I show him how to run his hands up my pussy between vagina and clit. That's the area men tend not to know about. I tell him, "This on you is like this on me." Ohhh.

Very often they'll want to eat my pussy. I don't say no to that. A lot of girls do. I keep notes on all my clients, and *PW* means "pussy worshiper." It's a real phenomenon. Guys just love pussy. They don't know why they love pussy. They're ambivalent about loving pussy, about burying their face in it and losing themselves. One of the myths about prostitution is that the clients of whores are the old, the weird, and the dangerous, and that our anonymity gives them freedom to be aggressive; the beast in man comes forth, the dark side. On the contrary—what I've found is that my anonymity allows most men to be vulnerable rather than aggressive. I'm amazed how many men pay me two hundred dollars an hour essentially to eat my pussy. Now, I know when guys get together in a locker room, none of them is saying, "Oh, I just ate my girlfriend's pussy out for three hours, I can't get enough of that stuff." I think it's more like, "Well, I gave it to her for three hours." The big secret among men is this tender neediness. The wonder of the female body, this great unmet curiosity.

I usually try to delay intercourse as long as I can reasonably get away with it. Long enough that he gets full value for the hour. I don't want him coming in half an hour, that's not my riff, but I don't want to work more than an hour. Occasionally you get a nickle-and-dimer, often an attorney, who's very aware of time, and dammit, he's not gonna come until the fifty-ninth minute. That gets to be a battle of wills, which can be fun. I usually win. But I'm constantly reading cues. Just because I'm getting bored with something doesn't mean the guy is. He can play with my pussy as long as he wants. At some point if he's eating my pussy and I'm enjoying it, I'll just let go. I'll stop doing anything to him. My job at that point is to keep my body moving, always responding, and to tell him how good he's making me feel. I do a lot of dirty talking in my work. At first that was hard, but it's gotten easier as the years have gone by, and it helps turn me on sometimes.

I might have an orgasm at that point, though not as often as I used to. If he's very focused on me having an orgasm, sometimes I fake one just so he'll get his mind back on himself. He's still trying to please his wife or something, and it's sweet, I don't want to deflect it, so the nicest thing to do is fake an orgasm and get on with it. I have to say, though, that my pure animal passion seems to be slipping away. When you start doing this work, if you really like sex, it's like living a fantasy for a while. Your passion is so natural. I'd be having so much fun that I'd run longer than an hour all the time. It was like opening up Pandora's box—and Pandora's box originally meant good things, not bad things. I'd walk down the street smiling, like I was having the biggest joke. I never had so much good sex in my life, and I had all this cash, and I felt wonderful. I knew it couldn't last, I was warned by professionals to conserve energy or I'd burn out. But I was saying, Damn, if every girl knew about this, there'd be no secretaries or bank clerks in the country. It's no wonder they make it illegal.

I've had a lot of casual sex in my life, and a lot of sex with love. In sex with love, you surrender more, boundaries blur. But in this work I found that happening with strangers. And not just with strangers, with insurance executives. Five-foot-nine, white insurance guys in suits, guys I would never have given a second glance to. I can't tell you how many times I've been in a bad mood, and some guy will start to touch me and hold me and kiss me, and others have been doing the same thing, but for some reason with this guy I get very passionate. There's always a split second where I resent it, because then I'm not quite so much in control. It's like, Oh, this ain't kiddin', this is real. Then I'll let go and enjoy it and be grateful. But it forced me to reexamine my ideas about sex and love and the religion of the thing. When you have sex and love, you maybe have a transcendent experience. Well, I can have that kind of profound sex with a total stranger, so I look at it like I'm communicating directly with the divine. It's no longer about this person you love. It's no longer about a personal agenda. All women have fucked to get the garbage taken out, or to be loved, or whatever. We've separated the body from the soul. I think anonymous sex is a place to rediscover that connection because it's so pure. You can go straight for the biggie, rather than stopping off for all the diversions.

But I haven't had that experience in the past year. The clients are still getting great pleasure, but it's not the same sort of pleasure. They don't know what they're missing, so that's all right, I'm not worried about whether I'm doing good work. I just don't come to it with raw passion anymore. It may be the difference between having lots of sex and not having much. A lot of what we call passion is in fact relief. I think very few people get enough sex. It's trite but true. So when I started doing this work, the sex itself was exciting because I had as little as everybody else. It's like working in a candy factory—at first you eat a lot of candy. After a while, you don't.

You end up replacing passion with skill and professionalism. It becomes more a matter of discipline and dedication and less a matter of personal satisfaction. But sometimes I do worry that I've lost interest in sex. I find now that my body is on a fifty-minute clock. It rises up to an orgasmic peak, dit, dit, dit, plateau level, orgasm, come down, and that's it. I went to bed with an old lover for a night a couple weeks ago. It was the first time in a year I'd slept with someone other than a client. And I found there was more pleasure than I'd been finding in my work. That was a comfort—Oh, good, it's still there.

When it's finally time to fuck the client, I always stand astride him and lower myself slowly on his cock and make him watch—"Look at it, doesn't that look nice?" Again, working against shame. I'm squatting over him, and I have thighs of steel, so I can bounce up and down for a while. Then I'll shift down—same position, but on my knees rather than my haunches. Then we'll probably go through the three standard positions: me on top, missionary, doggie-style. I'll do a lot of talking. Sometimes I'll say I want to fuck him, because a lot of men want to be fucked. I don't mean playing with the asshole, though that might happen. I mean they want to surrender control. They want to be sex objects. So a lot of them like to hear that I want to fuck *them,* usually when I'm on top. I'm also amazed to find how thrilling doggie-style is to guys. They seem to think it's outrageous. Dear oh dear—I guess there's too much missionary in their lives. What's nice about finishing doggie-style, which I often do, is that up till then I've been in charge. With doggie-style, we get to briefly and safely play the other way. They get to focus on my ass, which is one of my stronger points. I'll put my head on the pillow and spread my arms out. I'm very conscious of what the view is from where they are. Then they come into their strength and I play weak. I make all the helpless noises. I'm not talking dirty anymore, it's just good animal passion.

It's my experience that to surrender in sex is hard. It uses the same skills as surrender to God, and the same voice comes in to mess up the process. My faith in the divine comes and goes, because this voice keeps saying, "What if there isn't anything there?" Same thing in sex. The voice says, "Your hair looks terrible. Your tits are too small. Your ass is too fat. And he doesn't really mean it. And you forgot to put on your earrings." When I work, I'm trying to override that voice. If I can surrender to my sexuality, then I can give it to the guy. People think of the whore as the wicked serpent, the vamp. In fact, those of us who are good at it, what makes us good is we're playful. I don't mean cute, I couldn't be cute in a month of Sundays. I mean there's this toy called pleasure, and there's a lightness and an innocence to it. If you can release guys from their worries about performance, if you can pull them back from that full-scale tilt toward orgasm, then you've done some good work.

The great gift I get from the work has to do with creativity. I have known since adolescence that my sexual self is my truest self, but it was murky, it was unclear, I only got to it through other people. Women have such a fragile sense of our own identities, we rely so much on what others think of us. But I always felt my sexual self was entire unto itself. It came from the inside rather than the outside. I could never get any validation for that idea. In therapy, sexuality tends to be treated as pathology. If you're fucking a lot of guys, you're compensating. What you really want is love. Now I can finally turn around and say, No, what I wanted to do was make love to a lot of guys. Period. That's what I do well.

A sexual self without ambivalence or shame is very potent. I've mostly banished shame with a mixture of sex work and spiritual work. Now I feel untouchable in some ways. I still worry about the IRS and the law and my bills and everything else, but I'm at ease. As a recovering alcoholic and a prostitute, I say to people, "I'm a drunk and a whore. Now what are you going to do to me? You can make life uncomfortable, but you can't touch my core." And that core now has shape, and reason, and reward. Being paid for sex did something for my sense of self-worth. We're always told that the cheapest thing you could do is get paid for sex. Well, I'm sorry, this is the essence of capitalism. I'm going to market with who I am.

And that sense of self opened up my other senses. There's a myth about Lilith, who was banished from paradise. According to Jewish tradition, Eve was not the first woman created. The first was called Lilith, and she was Adam's equal. Everything was fine until it came to sex. Then Lilith refused to lie beneath Adam in the missionary position, which was the correct position in both Jewish and Christian thought. For her act of sexual defiance, God's response was: Out! She was exiled from paradise and went to live in the caves by the Red Sea, where she coupled with demons—presumably in any position she wished. Well, what Lilith represents is women's creativity and sexuality. The Jungians call her "the banished feminine." Sex as a creative source. And anthropologists talk about sexuality as an intellectual stimulation, how it's the key to creative thinking and culture. Since I've been doing this work, I started my studies, I write essays and poetry, I've been making art. I have more awareness of the world around me. I trust my aesthetic sense more. I've claimed my vocation, and everything else has flowered.

In ancient Greece, *horasis* was the type of transcendence achieved through sex with a sacred prostitute. Her work was transformation. Men were civilized through the sexual act, put in touch with something more than themselves. I'm always surprised when my theories actually play out in my own life, but I think sex work has done that for me. This has been like a four-year initiation. I can't see the future. I may move on to something else soon. But the transformation I've been giving to others has also been working on me.

RACHEL SILVER

She was born in 1921 and raised in Brooklyn, the oldest daughter of middle-class Jewish parents. She first slept with a man when she was eighteen. She was married and separated twice by 1955. At sixty-nine, she looks back with some amazement. "I've been single since 1955. That's like a lifetime. We're talking thirty-five years." They were years filled with incident: She raised two children by herself, pursued three different careers, and had many lovers. A few of her relationships spanned two decades. "I would say sex played a central role in my life. It was always on my mind. And I found that I was even more sexy in my forties and fifties than I was in my twenties and thirties. I was more creative about it. I wanted to make more of it. I felt the fullness of it more." She has also, since the early 1970s, built a successful consulting business. We talk in her apartment in a high-rise, with a striking view of Central Park. One wall is crowded with photos of her family, among them a formal portrait of her as a fifteen-year-old bombshell in a Hollywood-style glamour pose, with flowing dark hair and pouting lips. Today her hair is shorter and dyed a reddish tint; she is about five-six, trim, and wears a straw-colored pantsuit. She looks considerably younger than she is, and as she talks and relaxes, the beauty she so enjoyed in her youth is suddenly there again.

• • •

About five years ago, I decided I wanted to have a steady man in my life. I've spent the last eighteen years building my career, and I've had a good time doing that. I never thought about getting married again. It's just not important to me. But I decided I really wanted a man in my life. So I advertised in *New York* magazine. And I met about twenty-five men. Most of them were pretty dreadful. A failed, drunken vaudeville hoofer. An eighty-two-year-old man who first told me he was sixty, and behaved badly when he took me out. Then I met Andy. He was nice, clean-cut, from Long Island, a blue-collar man with a degree in electrical engineering. Two years younger than I. Retired. A wholesome fellow, likes to garden, grow vegetables. As it turned out, he's also stubborn, pigheaded, and a very limited person, not sophisticated. But we found out we had things in common. We both like sports. I like to bike and skate and cross-country ski. He likes that too. And he would put up with the other things I like to do, like go to plays and films. He did that just to be company to me. And we stayed together, off and on, for about four and a half years.

After eight or nine dates I finally got Andy into bed. He was very shy, very backward. A typical gentile [laughs]—they're not very sexy as a rule. He probably has the biggest cock I've ever seen. He's a big man, huge hands, huge feet, and a huge organ. But no ability to use it properly at all. He didn't consider he had any sexual problems. [Mimics deep voice:] "I have no sexual problems." But he suffered from premature ejaculation. I tried to make it work with him, but sex was very painful. And sex has never been painful for me. It was a combination of his ineptitude, the size of him, and the fact that I could never relax and enjoy it. Also, I had to teach him different things to do. He was strictly missionary position—on top, come, and then go to sleep. I said to myself, My whole life has come down to this? I'd rather not have any man at all! But it was nice to go out. Suddenly you're a couple and you're invited all over the place. A single woman, an older woman, in New York, is a pariah. Nobody wants her around.

We tried to work out a sexual relationship, and to some extent we did. We'd always say, "We have to practice this more often. When you practice, you get better at it." Then we'd say, "But we never have time." He would only come into the city on weekends, so we only had two nights a week. And we'd always be tired. Older people get tired. If you're up at six in the morning and running around all day, by ten o'clock at night, the last thing in the world you want to do is have sex. We found that the mornings were nice. It's just your natural self in the morning, it's an activity that's not drink-laden or food-laden. And he was very nice to me. I taught him to give me massages, wonderful back massages, leg massages. I'd put the oils out and ask him to do it, and he'd do it. That was a good turn-on for me.

But I remember, with other men, having intercourse that could go on and on and be wonderfully exciting and under control. This was something Andy just couldn't do. With him, we're talking about a minute. I could be brought to orgasm manually afterward, but it just wasn't the same. He wasn't a sensual person. He didn't recognize what I enjoyed. He didn't know how to touch me so that it felt good in his own fingers. I don't think his fingers had that sense. I think he'd say to himself, Oh, this is what she wants, I'll give her a few minutes of this and see how it works. He'd do oral sex on me, and I liked that very much. Although I always felt he was working at it, I didn't feel he liked it very much. He was doing it as a favor to me. I've had men who love doing that, and their loving it communicates great joy. I like to do it to men, too. Love to do it. A lot of men don't want to come that way. They don't feel right about it, like it's wrong. [Laughs.] They like the sucking part, but they stop you before coming. Andy was like that. I said, "Please do, I'd love it." But no. He wasn't interested in masturbating, either. He said he never masturbated, didn't want to talk about it. I'd say, "Oh, you must have. It's such a big, beautiful cock, you must have enjoyed it very much." But he'd never admit anything about it. I used to like to masturbate him and look at myself doing it. But he was too embarrassed.

I bought Andy a book on how to relax. How to control your thoughts when you're making love. It was a different approach to this premature ejaculation problem. It said instead of putting your mind on something else, which is what they always tell people, you should leave your mind on exactly what you're doing, and imagine a flow, and so on. But it backfired totally. He was insulted that I got him the book, and I don't think he ever read it. It made things worse.

The funny thing is, it wasn't sex that broke us up. I could put up with that. It was nice to have a man around. But he would constantly get angry with me and walk out. He wouldn't talk to me. We'd see each other for eight or ten weeks, and for no reason I could determine, he'd start an argument and walk out the door. Then he'd call back a few weeks later, "Let's get together again." Stupid, childish behavior. Finally I said, "There's nothing to come back for."

Now, I don't have any men because I don't meet any. I see men in my career, but they're all much younger than I am. I can't find anybody I'd like to have sex with, someone with whom it would be a reasonable thing to do. I'm talking about somebody at least fifty, fifty-five years old. Men that old who are attractive always have somebody. Whenever I meet someone my age who's vibrant and successful and looks like he'd be a terrific guy, he's either got a wife who's twenty-five years younger, or he's got young girlfriends. Or I might see a younger man, but that's totally ridiculous. I would find it most unfortunate to go after anybody like that. I'd be too old, too uninteresting, or not attractive enough sexually. It's like a memory that I have—young, handsome, sexy guys. I can remember what it was like, but I can't do anything about it. [Laughs.]

No man looks at me today with any kind of sexual interest. And if they don't look at me with any sexual interest, they're not going to get any from me. It's kind of an animosity I have with men now. I mean, I don't even get the time of day from any man. I'm an older woman. And I say, Fuck the bastards. That's my attitude. I used to hear this from women who were much younger, when I was forty. They'd say, "I'm a nonperson. I'm at a party, and no man wants to talk to me." I'm talking about nice-looking ladies. Well, that's how men are to me now, twenty-five years later. Maybe I was always more open and more responsive, and they caught that interest from me. Now that I have less, they're not picking up anything from me, and they're not being aggressive. I want men to be aggressive now. I'm not going to approach a man, because I'm afraid to be rejected. So I've just given up.

Still, I don't want to spend the rest of my life without close physical and emotional relationships. I think about being with women a lot. Not because I want to be with a woman, but because there are so few men around, and I have so many women friends. I think it's a subject worthy of discussion, but I can't get my friends to talk about it. That women are left without men and without sex. Who are the men who are available to us? Where are they? I don't know. I think they died. Women live longer, some of the men become gay, some of them are still with their wives, which is fine, and lots of them are with younger women. There are a few men in their sixties who are around and not married, but, how can I tell you?—they're just not appealing. So many women are so terrific, they have so much going for them, and then we have these broken-down old men. Who have 1940s attitudes toward women.

Would you believe I went to Roseland last night? With some of my women friends. They have swing dancing there. I tried to talk about all this, and I was absolutely stymied. I said, "Look at all these lovely women all over the place. There aren't even any men to dance with them. Why are we so dependent on men? Why can't women care about each other and set up relationships?" "Oh," they said, "you mean lesbians?" I said, "That's so silly, none of us are lesbians. We've been with men all our lives. But there aren't any around anymore. Are we supposed to stop all sexuality? Why can't women even give each other massages, just touching? Why can't we do that for each other?" "Oh, well—" They stop right there. They are scared to death.

I have to tell you about one time when I did have a bit of an experience. It was seven or eight years ago. There was a very striking woman whom I'd met through some friends. I had a house out in Easthampton that was given to me for the weekend. She came out with me, along with another woman friend. She was very sexy, and I don't know how it happened, but there got to be a little sexy thing going on between her and me. She walked around naked quite a lot, showing off her body. Like she expected me to come to her and touch her. Which I did. We were lying in beach chairs sunbathing naked, and I kissed her. She responded. We went inside and masturbated each other. It was exciting. Afterward I went out to a little bar with her, and we were carrying on a little, kissing and holding each other. But nothing ever happened after that. I called her a couple of times, but she would never call or talk to me. I got so turned off by that rejection that I didn't consider it again for a long time.

Now I really would like to be a lesbian, but I don't know how. I'm basically not a lesbian, I'm not bisexual, but there are so many more women around. I had a wonderful day today with four women. Not one of them is a lesbian, not one of them would consider having a lesbian relationship. They're all looking for men. It's really *tragic.* So maybe I should go to a place where lesbians hang out, and see what goes on. I might find an older woman like myself, who would be a good companion. It might be wonderful. Because I know what a woman likes, and so would another woman. We wouldn't have a penis [laughs]—but there are substitutes.

I have to admit, too, sex isn't as important to me now as it was before. Since my early sixties I've noticed a decline in my interest. Before, there was a great urgency for sex. To this day I don't understand why I can go week after week, month after month, and not desire sex. Maybe a lot of that has to do with hormones. Also, I feel I need the right person more than I used to when I was young and sexy. I know more what I like in a man. I know what I like sexually. So I'm more selective. I can't be swept away the way I once was.

Another thing that stops me is how I feel about my body. I had a gorgeous body at one time. Broad shoulders. Fairly good-size breasts, high. Not terribly small waist. A flat stomach, small hips. Long, slender legs, and long, slender arms. I had a body like a man with breasts. I enjoyed displaying it and using it, and I got a great deal of pleasure for myself. I always left the lights on, I never hid under the covers. I liked to see myself being made love to. I used mirrors, all of that. Now that I'm older and my body is declining, it's very hurtful to me. I don't want to expose myself to anybody. I'm self-conscious. I'd prefer to make love with my clothes on.

Summers are always wonderful for me. Beaches, bathing suits, getting tan. I found the sun very sexual. Well, now I have skin cancer. I can't stay out in the sun. That's a terrible blow to me. I break out in rashes, and I look terrible. My eyes get all swollen. I'm always covered with hats and clothes. That was never the case until a few years ago. And my skin is shriveling up. I never knew that skin shriveled up. It does. You look in the mirror, and you say, What's *that?* The skin is just shriveled up and hanging, you want to kill yourself. I happen to have beautiful breasts, still do, and a good figure, and I exercise and play tennis and all that. My body's very good for a person my age. But skin shriveling up and brown spots all over are unattractive. And if it's unattractive to me, I wouldn't like it in someone else. Maybe it was a narcissistic sexuality I had. I used to like myself so much, I used to like my juiciness so much, that I turned myself on. I used to watch myself masturbate in a mirror in my late twenties because it turned me on. And now that my body doesn't turn me on anymore, I've stopped being sexy.

I haven't had any sex to speak of since last July. I actually have to force myself to masturbate now. Well, I'm half-joking, but I'll say to myself, It's been a week, maybe I'll try it tonight. I have no desire to do it, but maybe I need sexual release and don't know it. I also worry about becoming dry. About a year ago I got a call from a young man I had a long affair with. I hadn't seen him in a long time. He's twenty-five years younger than me, which makes him about forty-five now. I've known him since he was twenty-five. He still looks like a kid, great body, very sexy. We went out to dinner, and he came over, and we had sex. I had a wonderful, wonderful time. I had an orgasm from intercourse, everything. It was like a little bonus in life. [Laughs.] And I noticed that I wasn't dry, which was nice to see. Oooo, my juices are still flowing. But he never called me again, and I won't call him.

Then, a few weeks ago, I ran into another old boyfriend. He's married, a very repressed person, but totally unrepressed with me. Fabulous in bed. You'd never know it to look at him, he's like the stiffest uptight Englishman. I hadn't seen him for six or seven years. He came over for coffee. When he went out the door, he grabbed me and kissed me. I didn't even want to kiss him, I was angry at him, he hadn't called me for years, and we were so close for so long. But I let him kiss me, and the way he kissed me and the way he held me and the way he ran his hands through my hair and over my face, I was melting down to the floor. It was like, I don't believe what I'm feeling, it's incredible, I feel like I'm fourteen and being kissed for the first time and discovering the wonderment of it all. Now he wants to start things up again, but he's up in the country for a month. I'm hoping I'll see him when he comes back. I want to know I'm still in the game.

10

BEING THERE

SIX PEOPLE HAPPY with their sex lives: a baby-boomer couple with children; a lesbian S/M expert; a married woman nearing forty; a minister married forty years; and a young gay man whose lover just died of AIDS. Their sex isn't perfect; by and large, it's not earth-shaking. It's just good. Why are they happy?

First, there is a sense of calm, especially among the four married speakers. They seem neither driven nor anxious; sex is neither a Grail, nor a test, nor an albatross. This is related to something else they mention: an acceptance of reality. Barbara Brandt and Joe Hoffman, like most couples with twin jobs and young children, have trouble finding time, as Barb says: "I think he'd like to make love more than we do, and I'd like to make love more than we do. But we don't because this is our reality. It doesn't feel like an issue." Eli Gregory, at sixty, rarely gets aroused as fast as he once did, and that upset him at first. So he and his wife talked about it, read about it, and made peace with it, adjusting expectations. And Sam Kaulahuana has a new, down-to-earth attitude: "I used to equate sex with love—like, God, I gave this person so much, and they didn't love me. . . . Now I see, Well, I gave them an hour or two in bed. I didn't give them my best, I gave them a good time. So I can go to bed with somebody and see it for what it is. It doesn't mean I'm going to be married to him for the rest of my life."

The sense of calm extends to sex itself. Except for Lori Eschilman, none of the people in this chapter go in for elaborate experiments, acting out fantasies, or even violent passion. Barb remarks that while sex with old boyfriends had jagged ups and downs, with Joe "it feels more like the ocean, all these layers and depths. I can get lost in it and feel safe. . . . Maybe safety sounds dull, but it doesn't feel dull. Our sex isn't boring. It's certainly more than pleasant. But it's not ecstatic." Joe agrees, saying that while their sex "isn't nearly as heated" as before, "it's never the same, never ever the same way twice. What more could two people ask for?"

Another quality notable here is alertness. The speakers seem profoundly conscious of their partners—of their quirks, moods, likes and dislikes, of their existence as separate people. Such alertness often does not come easy, as Eli makes clear in recalling the early years of his marriage. But once evolved, it makes all the difference: These people *listen*. Lori, in her S/M play, seems able to sense just what her "bottoms" want or need at a particular moment. Joe is aware, and is not offended, that often Barb would rather be tickled than have sex, and he has developed skill in tickling her just the way she likes.

This points up one more element of good sex: generosity. Not only does Joe know what Barb likes, but he is eager to do it, at least most of the time. Larrice Freeman's husband often wants more sex than she does, so she obliges him with quickies. "And even then, it's not a normal quickie. With Eddie, it's forever. But y'know, I don't complain."

And how do these giving people know what to give? Intuition, sometimes—but more often, talk. They talk to their partners—not right away, perhaps, and not without embarrassment, as Eli says: "I have to admit that we still find it difficult to talk about sex. Yet when we have, it's been so rewarding. I remember saying one time, 'Why did we wait to talk about this?' We learn slow, I don't know what's so dumb about us." Slow or not, the point is that we can learn. Lori and her playmates talk before a scene to build trust, and after it to examine what happened. Joe and Barb tell each other just what they like—though curiously, they seem to disagree as to how much they talk. She says, "We do it subtly, through action and reaction, rather than words. . . . Not a lot of conversation." He says they talk frequently, both in bed and out—and at her instigation. "These conversations happen because of her, definitely. She is very comfortable talking about sex. It took me a while to learn." He also makes a point worth stressing here: Because of Barb, he can now talk to his children as well. And not simply about the facts of life, but "the fact that you don't have to settle for bad sex, or rushed sex, or shallow sex."

Sam Kaulahuana has lived through enough to put anyone off sex forever: incest, growing up Catholic and gay, finding out he is HIV-positive, losing his companion Max to AIDS. Yet somehow, the experience of loving Max, listening to his grim tales of compulsive sex, and nursing him has opened Sam up. "The weird thing is, I've had a lot of sex since Max died," he muses. "And there's a different quality to my sex. I express myself more. I'm a lot more adventurous. And it's more pleasurable. It actually feels almost spiritual." Maybe that's because he is making love in the shadow of death. But whatever the reason, it has led to the simple insight that ends this book.

BARBARA BRANDT

She lives in an old clapboard house on the leafy main street of a Midwestern town, with her husband of four years, their two-year-old daughter, and older children from previous marriages who live there part-time. They have an excitable mongrel dog and a beat-up Saab with save-the-environment bumper stickers. The house is pleasantly messy, with toys scattered far and wide. Barbara manages home and kids when Joe is away on sales trips, and works part-time at the local elementary school. She is thirty-five, ten years younger than her spouse (whose interview follows this one). There is a nature-girl quality about her—when I arrive, she has just finished a six-mile walk, her pale skin is flushed from the cold, and her wavy red hair spills over a down parka. Once the interview starts, she often covers her face with her hands and pleads jokingly, "Can we stop now?"

She was raised in a wealthy New England suburb, her father a doctor who died when she was in her teens. "He was sick the whole time I was growing up, so I definitely have abandonment issues. I was a rebellious kid, a wild kid. I was a lot stronger, more willful, more confident than my mom. When I look at it now, I was doing the classic looking for limits— which I never would have admitted then—and I never got any from her." Barbara lost her virginity in eighth grade, had boyfriends steadily through high school and college, and married the year she graduated. The marriage lasted seven years. After a brief lesbian phase, "I saw some other guys, no big deal, and then I met my honey."

· · ·

One night I was out walking my dogs. I had just gotten done telling this man that I wasn't going to see him anymore, and I was expecting to feel sad, because I wanted to have a relationship. I was walking around going, When am I going to feel sad? Probably pretty soon, maybe when I go around the next block, I'll feel sad. But I felt wonderful. And I ran into Joe. I knew him slightly, we had always had the smallest of small talk. This time we walked around for a couple of hours, we opened our mouths, and all these heavy things came out. It was pretty clear that he was my guy. But it took a bit longer than that. He was slow. He didn't kiss me for a while. I kept going, Maybe he doesn't like me. Me, who was used to: If you're not in bed with somebody thirty seconds after you meet them, they're probably not attracted to you. He was living in a new house, and I said, "Can I come over and see your house?" I went over and we sat and talked, and all his kids ran around. That was okay, I think we held hands. Then we went to a movie—and we talked. Then we took a walk by the river, and he still didn't kiss me. I was getting worried. I mean, the river, nighttime? Then the next time he kissed me, and we slept together. So I felt better. [Laughs.]

I'm not sure what was going on with him. He was just getting out of a relationship. And he was unsure if I liked him. Boys tend to be a little dense about that kind of stuff. So he was waiting until he knew. I don't know what more I could have done to the guy [laughs], I was sending pretty strong signals. It's funny—it wasn't like I was attracted to him, I wasn't removed enough to be attracted to him. *Attracted* indicates to me more of a yearning, and I wasn't yearning. All of a sudden it was there. We were having these heavy discussions about clarity and purpose and emotions and dysfunction and recovery—because Joe's a recovering alcoholic, he's been sober six years, and my mom's an alcoholic. It just clicked and clicked and clicked. And I had done a lot of work on myself emotionally since I split up with Ethan. I was in therapy—I love to be in therapy, I'll do it at the drop of a hat. I'm not now because we can't afford it. But Joe was like a reward for working on myself and clearing myself up.

Our sex has gone through phases. It's all related to what kids are in the house. For a while we had every other weekend free because his kids would be with their mom and my son would be with his dad. That's a big deal to me—I find with the older kids, they're up and around after we've gone to bed, and they do walk in. I used to say to Jeb, that's Joe's oldest, "You know what? Either we're having sex, or we could be having sex right now." I'd be blunt and try to embarrass him, because I figured that might get through his thick little skull. So there's a pattern—if the kids weren't around, we'd have sex in the living room, we'd have it whenever we wanted. Now with the baby, she sleeps right off our room, and that makes a difference. She just started sleeping through the night, and a lot of times, if I'm tired and I get horizontal, I want to go the big night-night. We still have weekends without the big kids, when there's only the baby, and there's naptime. But it's still naptime—you can either clean house, or have sex. Plus, Joe travels, and I don't ever want to have sex by obligation, I think that's the quickest way to ruin something. Sometimes I think, Okay, this is the last night before he goes away, you should do it. Then I go, Hmf. And we talk about it. Either I decide, Oh, I want to, and he wants to, or we don't. I'd rather not have it than have it because I feel I should.

Once Jeb walked in when I was giving Joe head, this was early in the relationship, and it was awful. It was dark, we were on the couch, and I just pretended I was napping down there. But it was embarrassing to be caught that way. So for the last couple of years, the living room doesn't feel safe to me. Spontaneity is limited, in terms of where I feel safe enough to lose myself.

The other day I thought of—this was cool, I told Joe about it last night. I heard some Van Morrison cut. His newer stuff is not so clear-cut, like "Moondance," it's more out there and dreamy. Well, sex with Joe is like that. As opposed to in my younger days, sex was more like Pink Floyd. There's not that do-or-die, I've-got-to-win-this-person feeling. I had this boyfriend in college, Sal, I called him Stupid Sal. He was probably the most dysfunctional person I've ever met in my life, and we had great sex. Great, great, great sex. Across the board, forever. We went out for a long time, longer than I like to admit. He was an older guy, a Vietnam vet, he was in college on the G.I. Bill, and he was just wild. Charming and wild. He always fucked around on me, from day one. He'd fuck all my friends. One time when we had broken up, he tried to rape me. Sex with him was all about pressure—would I be good enough, would I be alluring enough, would I be sexy enough, that he would stay with me for that thirty seconds. If we were at home, we had to have great sex or he'd say, "I'm going out to the bar." The stakes were so high that the sex was charged pretty big. That was my pattern for a long time—if somebody was a real jerk, it was hot, because of all those things that make for high, passionate sex.

With Joe there's not that intensity. Instead of being jaggy like this [makes violent up-and-down motions with her hand], it feels more like the ocean, all these layers and depths. I can get lost in it and feel safe. It's not the reason for anything. When I was younger, if I really wanted to have sex with somebody and it didn't happen, it was crushing. Now, if I feel like having sex and Joe wants to sleep, it's not life-and-death. Maybe safety sounds dull, but it doesn't feel dull. Our sex isn't boring. It's certainly more than pleasant. But it's not ecstatic.

We don't have sex a whole lot, either—maybe once a week, not even that much sometimes. I think he'd like to make love more than we do, and I'd like to make love more than we do. But we don't because this is our reality. It doesn't feel like an issue. When the opportunity presents itself, it's always fun. If he's gone and I feel sexual, then I'll masturbate. But if I'm not very interested, it doesn't feel like this unfulfilled burning thing.

Another thing that affects our sex life is the seasons. Our house is really cold and drafty, and I'm a lot less inventive in the winter because I don't want to be cold. A couple weeks ago Joe's mom took the kids and we went away. We just turned up the heat in this stupid motel room and had sex a bunch of times. The first few times were pretty quick—you have your priorities. It might not last, they might call and say the kids are sick. Then you believe the time is really there, so it gets longer and more drawn-out.

I like his hands a lot—especially when I'm on top, I like his hands on my hips, guiding my hips. I like his shoulders a lot, they're exciting because they're so manly. I like kissing him. Sometimes I'm particular about kissing—if he kisses me too long in one position it makes me cuckoo. If a lip stays too long, I think it died or something, and I don't like dead lips. The only thing he doesn't like and I wish he did like, because I like it a lot, is kissing him on the neck. And I'm not talking hickey material here. I think he was permanently warped in junior high school. Sometimes if I'm feeling stupid, I'll dive for his neck. He doesn't want me to, he pushes me away. Someday he's gonna shoot me.

Now, my favorite thing in life is to be tickled lightly. My father used to tickle me every morning for half an hour. My little alarm would go off and I'd get in bed with my dad, and he'd tickle me lightly and talk to my mom about their day. It was really sweet, and that's my favorite thing, it's better than sex, because you don't have to ever do anything back. You can just lie there and drool. I love that. Different places—legs, back, butt, neck. My dad used to do it with a broom straw. Now we have a tickle-stick that Joe does it with, a shish-kebaby thing, a little wooden skewer. It has a cover so it doesn't get broken. It has a very important place in our lives. [Laughs.] Joe drags it over me—it has a little point, which is better than a dead old fingertip. He has to do it real light. Sometimes it's sexually exciting, if that's what I want it to be. But if not, it can be just pure physical pleasure. I drool and say thanks and go to sleep. It's completely one way, I never touch him while he's doing it. Usually I'm lying on my stomach. If I'm thinking it's a preliminary to sex, I'll have him tickle me more on my butt, or my breasts. And probably the other areas, but with sex in mind it's different. Generally it just feels blissful. Dreamy. I'm not thinking. I have to think all the time to coordinate all these kids, their schedules, my job, and I'm good at that. So it's wonderful to just not. Pure sensation.

I don't think he's tickling me all the time with a hard-on, but he's pretty up for sex anytime, it doesn't take a whole lot of suggestion to have it turn that way. If he has enough energy to be tickling me, he's gonna have enough energy to make love. Sometimes I start to want him inside me, maybe quicker than he wants to be inside me. He'll say, "Well, I'm probably gonna come pretty quick, because I'm pretty excited." And I'll say that's what I want.

I find it really exciting to excite him. I like to hear his breathing get harder. I like the ol' dick [laughs], and I like the changes it goes through as it gets more excited. Sometimes we'll play with each other, and that's exciting, as long as I can hear him breathe. I go, "I'd like you to breathe louder," or "I like it when you breathe louder." Sometimes he'll go down on me, and sometimes I will, but not very often.

That has definitely changed—I give head less. I like giving head, but I think it's an acceptance-winning thing. I also don't think of giving head as a bedroom activity, it's something you do in the car or in the TV room. Traditionally it's what you do when you don't want to fuck, or you can't, the whole adolescent thing. He can go down on me in the bedroom, but I very rarely do him. It's interesting, I never thought of this before. I'll have to add it to the repertoire. [Laughs.]

When he's going down on me, it's only exciting if I can feel him being hard. Otherwise I start worrying that I'm taking too much time. So he gets in a position where I can play with him with my feet, or he curls around so I can do it with my hand. One thing—if we're mutually masturbating each other, and I start going faster, I like to push it to the breaking point. Then he'll start moving faster on me, and that's not exciting. It needs to be slow. If it gets too frantic, it's too much for me. I'll have to say, "You need to slow down." And he goes, "Well, you're pumping away there, too." I say, "Yeah, but that's different." [Laughs.]

Oral sex is pretty great, but what I like best is feeling that first thrust inside. Wanting, wanting, wanting, and then getting it. I like the old in-and-out. I don't often come that way. A lot of times Joe will come, and then he'll play with me more. It's calmer for him once he's come, so I don't feel as much pressure. His needs are taken care of, and I can focus on my needs. I can even decide if I don't want to, and that's okay. In general I like doing better than being done to. If he's just playing with me, and I'm not playing with him, then he's doing it for an outcome, and I feel too much like I have to have that outcome or else he'll be disappointed that he invested all this work. So it's not fun. He gets maybe a couple of minutes of free time until he has invested too much, and then it's obligatory that I do something to make him feel good. I start thinking I should come, or I shouldn't come, or he's getting bored, or what is he getting out of this? And then my mind is so in it, I can shoot that one.

It's like the thing men always say to women, "Oh, it's okay that you have little tits, it doesn't matter, your body is fine." Well, in this society it's not okay if you have little tits. We're all raised on "big tits are wonderful." Or women tell men, "Oh, it's okay if your dick is small, honey." Well, it's not okay, it's just what you have to deal with.

I was only with one man who had a really little dick, and it makes a huge difference. But how can you break somebody's heart and say, "You know what? You have a teeny dick." How can you be honest about something like that, when it's not their fault? So I feel that way in reverse. I have no tits, and Joe is like, "I love your body." I'm thinking, He has to say that. And he's probably a better human being than I am. Like he always tells me that he'd love me if I got really fat, and he'd still sleep with me. But I don't think I'd sleep with him if he got fat. I'd still love him, because he'd be the same person, but I wouldn't want to touch him, because it'd be gross. So when he's playing with me and I'm just lying there, I don't believe him when he says he likes it. And it seems like there's still the desired outcome—to give me pleasure, which reads orgasm, so there's pressure.

I've never really talked to him about it. When it comes to sex, this thing about open and honest communication—I think we still want the person to *know*. We want it to be that romantic, I-don't-have-to-tell-him, he-reads-my-every-thought type of thing. With Joe, I enjoy sex more because we do it subtly, through action and reaction, rather than words. Although to know me, you wouldn't think I'm one to mince words. Now, kissing—kissing is a big enough point that I speak up. [Laughs.] But touch, speed—all those little things you just know from knowing the person better. It doesn't make it dull, it makes it better, to know him more. For example, he likes having his balls played with. Well, I'll do that and bite his nipple at the same time, knowing he likes both. Or with me, if something doesn't feel good, I'll move his hand, show him what feels good. Not a lot of conversation. Like my breasts are so variable—sometimes it feels good if he touches them hard, sometimes it feels good soft. If he's trying the hard method, and it's a soft day, I'll touch his hands, or I'll say, "Softer, easier."

And Joe is so cool—if I say something, he doesn't take offense and get all weird. He just does what I want. He's amazing. I did a good job in hooking up with him. There have just been a couple of times—and they haven't been sexual. I think it was about tickling. This was a while ago. Especially with tickling, where he isn't getting a whole lot out of it, I feel like if he's investing his time, he might as well be doing something I want. So I did say I wanted him to do something differently, and he acted a little huffy about it. But he has never done that sexually.

On the other hand, if I tell him I like something, he increases it. Like putting his hands on my butt—when he's on top of me, he reaches under and gets my butt. That feels good, I like the image of him controlling me. Or if I'm on top and he's guiding my hips, that takes some of the work off me. It gets hard to do all that leg stuff, it's nice to have a little help. [Laughs.] The take-charge stuff is nice. I don't like passivity in a man.

Other things we've added—nuancy things, like building energy. I pay more attention to where the energy is going, building it, crafting it. Sometimes I like to imagine pulling it up from his legs and down from his trunk, focusing it. That's fun, I feel like I have a purpose, I've got a plan here. [Laughs.] To be in touch with that energy—that's what being a good lover is, not whether you stroke at the right place or the right speed. It's a feeling of being receptive enough to feel it, yet in control enough to craft it and mold it. Maybe it's what surfing is like, when they talk about riding those waves, and you feel like you're really there. It's like light in his body, I get a sense of light, a soft, diffused light. I coax it and guide it. I set a pattern for it, show it there's a channel. You can do little kisses in a line, kiss kiss kiss, or you can stroke, or push, or pull. The same thing is also true with darkness. When he comes into me, sometimes with that first push, it's like there's a vast darkness. It's not a scary darkness, it's not a hollow darkness, it's a warm darkness. Not an absence, not a void—just a nice little warm fuzzy darkness. [Laughs.] It's like—it's everything. I'm talking heaven-and-earth type everything. It's huge. It's the purpose. It's the point. And the two of us are creating it, tapping into it, being a part of it.

I think of floating in the ocean. I feel connected to something that's been happening for a long time, and it taps into something greater than we are. The tides, all that. Sometimes he moves inside me and I think, This is really ancient. It's part of the rocking, the old in and out. I flash on the energy flow, God, whatever it is that's right, that's in sync, that's as it should be.

I was thinking about this the other day: Sex has had so many roles in my life. As a rebellion, as a creation, as a partnership. When I was young it was a rebellion. When we were trying to get pregnant, it was a creation. With Stupid Sal, it was sex as conquest, and sex as esteem, which came from the conquest. It was monumental sex, but I don't miss it at all. God, no, I don't miss it. I still like to flirt a lot, I'm a big flirt. And Joe is so cool about it—like there's this cute little boy at the bookstore, and when I come home, Joe goes, "Oh, how's Alan?" When you flirt, you make that connection—it's the same thing as fucking somebody, and it's a lot safer and a lot easier. You can play it out, or you can know it's there. I'd just as soon know it's there. It's about making the connection, and that's what sex is about. I don't have any huge desire to follow that connection with anybody. A fuck is a fuck is a fuck. A great fuck is a great fuck, but it's still a fuck, that's what I think. And if I've got somebody I like, and I like having sex with, and we have this great life together—I can't imagine there would be some fuck that would be worth hurting Joe's feelings.

JOE HOFFMAN

He seems younger than his forty-five years—sandy blond hair falling over his forehead, lively blue eyes, a round, open face, a ready laugh. Jeans and a sweatshirt complete the look; only a modest paunch suggests middle age. The boyish air, he says, reflects an extended boyhood. "I grew up finally, but I was thirty-five, thirty-seven years old before it happened. It took me that long to start accepting responsibility for a few things. I married Barbara—it'll be four years in June. We were together for about a year before that. And it's been wonderful, it really has. Just great. Life is good. I mean, no free lunch, but life is good."

His parents' marriage didn't offer much of a model: "They didn't talk about anything. They both kept their anger until it just boiled over. I can remember my mother slamming around the kitchen. My father beat me occasionally—he didn't throw things, but he'd slam around, too. I think if two people had a relationship like that today, and they didn't go to counseling, they'd get divorced. But in those days you didn't do that. So I had a lot of stuff to work through. I was pretty old before I figured out I didn't have to do it that way."

He married fresh out of college, kicked around from job to job, and drank too much. Six years ago he went to AA and sobered up. His sex life has been more orderly, a series of monogamous relationships. "Barbara was wilder than I was by a long shot. Sometimes she starts to tell me things, and I say, 'You know, I don't really think I want to hear about that.' Even when I was drinking, I only had a couple one-night stands. I hung out in bars, but I didn't go to pick somebody up. Let's get our priorities straight here—I went to get drunk. Barbara and I have talked about me being on the road so much these days, it would be easy to have affairs. But I can't handle that emotionally. I'm old enough to know I don't want that kind of doubt and grief. I wouldn't want her doing it to me, so I certainly wouldn't do it to her."

• • •

I suppose Barbara told you the story of how we met. I was on a walk, I crossed the street, ran into Barbara, and the rest is history. We started talking to each other, and we haven't quit.

I had been with another woman before Barbara, we almost got married, and I couldn't figure out why it was so difficult. I knew it could be easier. It had to be. I had reached the point a couple of times where I seriously considered killing myself out of anger, just to get back at this woman—like, I'll fix your ass, I'm going to kill myself and leave a note and tell you why I did it. So it took me a long time to get shut of that. In the meantime I started with Barbara. I was a little reluctant, because Barb—she was amazing. She had already figured out what she wanted. And the interesting thing about Barb is that once she figures out what she wants, it happens. It took me a while to see that this one could work. I could talk to her. We got along. She got along with my kids. My kids got along with her. It doesn't mean it wasn't difficult at times, but we worked through things instead of butting heads all the time.

Barb and I had good sex right from the beginning. It's enjoyable, it's fun, it's inventive, and we talk about it a lot. With the pressures of family and all, it's not as frequent as I might want sometimes—or Barb might want. But we don't have any difficulty in telling each other that, and it's real easy to do something about it. If someone says, "Let's figure out a way we can be alone together for a couple of hours," you can do something. We established that early—if that's what I want, I have to say it, not expect her to read my mind. And vice-versa. There are times she'll say to me, "I'd really like to screw tonight," or "It's been so long since we screwed, I've forgotten how." "Oh, yeah? I bet I can show you."

Like this evening, if I wasn't doing this interview, we would probably take the time to have sex because Robin is asleep and we don't have any other kids here. Before we had Robin, we had two weekends a month when the kids were all with their other parents. Two full weekends a month. It was wonderful—we might sit around naked and talk to each other, maybe have sex, go to bed and have some more. We work out our schedules so we can have free time with each other. Not necessarily to have sex, but just to have time together. We might spend an entire evening sitting on the couch here reading and not say ten words to each other, but it's time being close to each other with no distractions, no telephone. The TV isn't on. The kids don't need anything. It's great.

I find her real exciting, as much as I ever did. I don't think my desire for her has diminished. It might have changed a bit—things I didn't find as exciting before, I find more so now. I enjoy watching Barb dress—dress or undress. Lying in bed watching her take her clothes off, that's a turn-on for me every day. When she comes into the bedroom after a shower or a bath, that's exciting. To see her naked—her legs, her butt, she has a very nice body—or in the summertime, maybe just in a swimsuit. She looks really good to me.

Our sex isn't nearly as heated as before. It used to be the get-out-of-your-clothes-in-three-seconds kind of thing. A lot more wrestling around, pushing yourself off the wall or the headboard. We still do that occasionally, but usually we take a lot more time. We spend more time talking before sex and after. It's not as— I don't want to say it lacks passion, that certainly isn't the case. And I don't want to say it's not as spontaneous. It's not as driven, as anxious. But still, it's never the same, never ever the same way twice. What more could two people ask for?

Probably the biggest change I've made is to be more conscious of what I'm doing. I try and be conscious of what her wants are, what feels good to her, what she'd like to try or do. Prior to this—well, more times than not, I was just concerned with what I wanted. For example, Barb likes to be tickled. Early on, she indoctrinated me to the importance of the tickle stick. It's a little bamboo skewer. We keep it next to the bed—oh yeah, I can find it in the dark. [Laughs.] Some guys have the dildo, I've got the tickle stick. A pencil doesn't make it, no no. I've tried all sorts of things—I've tried feathers, I've tried different types of watercolor brushes, I thought that would feel real good. Nope: tickle stick. The brushes don't feel right. Not enough pressure, not sharp enough. Sometimes she says, "This is better than sex, I'd rather do this than sex." Okay, if that's what will make you feel good, hey, I'll sit here and tickle you with the tickle stick. Sometimes I'll tickle her for an hour—well, not for an hour, only on her birthday—and she'll just fall asleep. But it can be very nice foreplay as well, depending on what the mood is. Maybe she wants her shoulders tickled, her neck tickled, or her arms tickled or her butt tickled. If she wants a certain area, she'll say so, most definitely. And you don't quit till you do it behind her ears and through her hair. [Laughs.] Sometimes I might put my other hand somewhere else, like I might rub her leg while I'm tickling her back, but she might tell me that's distracting. Or we'll be watching TV, and she'll put her leg up or lay her arm over me or just fall over in my lap and say, "Tickle my neck, will you?" That's not a signal she wants to have sex. She wants me to tickle her. Sometimes that becomes sex, but not that often. If she wants to have sex, she'll say, "I want to go to bed tonight, I want you to tickle me for ten minutes, and then we'll screw." Okay, sounds great to me.

Other things she likes: More than anything, she likes me to play with her clit. Just rub it with my fingers. She also likes kisses on her neck, on her ears. Maybe playing with her nipples, maybe not. That's a joke between us, because sometimes it drives her nuts. She'll swat my hand away: "Stop that! Quit!" Other times it feels great, and I never know—like, Okay, I'm going to try it until she hits me. [Laughs.] But playing with her clit, that seems to be always arousing. Sometimes I'll sit there and rub her clit until she comes. Then maybe we'll screw, or maybe we won't. A lot of times we do. But there's never any routine. That's what I found boring about my first wife, there was a set routine, real predictable. With Barb, if I feel like she's not responding to what I'm doing, I'll ask her. If she's just lying there, or her breathing doesn't change—"Does that feel good? Is that the right spot? What can I do?" Sometimes we'll screw and I'll come and she won't. I'll say, "Do you want me to play with you some more?" She'll say, "Yeah, I do." Or, "No, that's okay, I don't feel like it." Sometimes I might play with her after I've come, and get hard again, and come again. So it's never the same.

I had to learn how to touch her clit. First of all, it requires some kind of lubrication. I might spit on my fingers, or we keep some oil by the bed. I can remember being clumsy about it early on. She'd have to stop me—I was going too fast, going too hard. I can remember her saying, "You're in the wrong place." Well, show me where. I mean physically, show me. Where is it? "It's dark, you can't see it." Turn on the light, now it's not dark. Rub so I can see it. Okay, now I understand. Over time, I've learned where the places are. I can find them in the dark now. But early on I couldn't. I'd say—and this was good foreplay, too, watching her play with herself—"Okay, show me. Are you sure?" Other times she would take my hand, or my finger, and she would put it right exactly where it was supposed to be, and she'd move it the way she wanted me to move it, and she would apply pressure to the back of my fingers, the amount of pressure she wanted, until I got the hang of it, and then she would take her hand away. If I got out of sync or something, she'd put her hand back and show me until I got it right. A few weeks later I might need some re-education, so she'd show me again. [Laughs.] Now I'll ask before I get told it's not right—like, "Does that feel good? Am I rubbing too hard? Too fast?"

She likes me to rub around her clit, gently, with one finger, barely touching it. Just float on there. Sometimes she'll say, "A little harder." Mostly it's real lightly around it. Circular motions. Sometimes her clit will get harder than other times, and I'll rub it up and down. Sometimes I'll rub it with two fingers, depending on what I'm perceiving through my fingers. I don't usually put my fingers inside her, because that's not what she's interested in. Sometimes I'll just get started playing with her clit and she'll tell me she wants me to mount her and come inside rather than messing with her. Or she'll get on top of me. I'll come, we'll lie there a while, and then I'll ask, "Do you want me to play with you some more?" She doesn't come that often from me being inside her, I don't think. But what I'll do a lot of times is play with her until she almost comes and then take my fingers away and go inside, and we come together. That's pretty neat. That's the most fun for me. I mean, it's all fun, but that's the most fun.

She also really likes to see me play with myself. Early on in the relationship she asked me if I would masturbate for her. It was one day when I was at home by myself, housecleaning, and she came over. There's a big bedroom upstairs with a big carpet. We were playing on the floor, kissing and stuff, and she asked me if I would do that. I said yeah. She said, "Okay, do it." So I did. I stood up, and she was sitting on the floor watching me. I had never done that in front of somebody. It blew her mind, because she said other guys wouldn't do that. I said, "Why not? That's what you wanted to see, wasn't it?" Later on, not that day, she told me, "That really excites me, I like to watch that." A couple of times I've used it as leverage. If I want to have sex and she's not interested, I start to play with myself in bed and she'll get excited enough to go ahead and have sex. But I don't do that much, because I don't think it's fair. [Laughs.]

There are times when we're having sex and she's not into it, she can't come. "I can't focus," that's the word she uses. So we'll stop. Maybe we'll talk about it a little bit. She'll say, "I'm too tired, I've got too many things going on in my head, I'd just as soon not do it. Let's go to sleep, maybe try later. Wake me up in the middle of the night." I might do that, but not very often. Sometimes I'll say, "Well, I'm going in the bathroom to jerk off, I've got this hard-on a cat couldn't scratch." Or I might lie there next to her and start to jerk off. That's when she says, "Okay, you're not playing fair." Well, no, I'm not, I told you what I wanted, and I want it. [Laughs.] But she's right, it isn't fair. If she says no, and she's serious, I'm not going to push it if it's going to drive her nuts. I'm not gonna be a pain in the ass, I'm not gonna play the power thing. Once in a while, if I'm really, really horny, I will go ahead to the bathroom and jerk off, and then go to bed. And there are many times when she'll say, "I don't feel like screwing, but I'll jerk you off if you want. Or give you a blowjob." Sometimes that's fine, sometimes it's not what I want. Usually we're pretty in tune with each other. "I'd like to screw." "Yeah, I would too. Maybe we can do that tonight." We get into bed and talk about it, or I start fooling around with her, and she says, "I guess I don't want to do that." Okay, I'm not that in need of coming that I have to jerk off. I'll wait till tomorrow.

On my side, let's see, what do I like? I like her playing with my balls. I like going down on her a lot. I like it when she jerks me off sometimes—not always. It's funny, talking about pressure and motion—when she's playing with me I'm just as particular about how fast, how hard, and all that. Like if I'm playing with her, and she's jerking me off, she gets going a mile a minute, and I have to reach out and grab her by the wrist—slow down, slow down. I let go of her wrist, and in her excitement she starts right back in. I go, "You're gonna wear that thing out, y'know, slow down! Too fast, too hard!" At the same time she's telling me, "Slower, slower, lighter, lighter." I'm going slower and lighter, and she's just flailing away. But we've managed to work it out pretty well. We listen to each other.

Maybe that's the best thing—we have the ability to talk about it. We spend a lot of time talking to each other. Work, family, kids, what's going on in the world, ideas, what makes us feel good, what makes us not feel good. And in there we talk about sex. It's not something that comes up once a day, but I'd say once a week. We might talk about it two or three minutes, or we might spend quite a while. I'm trying to think how it comes up—it might be that we had some really good sex the night before. Or we didn't have good sex, maybe we were interrupted, or it wasn't as good as we both know it can be. So we'll talk about it. If one of us had a really vivid dream, we'll share that—like, "I dreamed I was screwing you, and you were standing on your head in a wheelbarrow." She'll say, "Were you inside the wheelbarrow or outside?" Or we might talk about things we like. She talks about the color of my dick when it's hard, and how exciting that is to her. How good it feels for me to be inside her. The way it feels good when I hold her. I'll say, "Yeah, I really like doing that, I didn't realize it was pleasurable enough that you'd bring it up in conversation. What other things can I do?" For instance, how much it excites her to see me play with myself—I didn't realize that until it came up two or three times. Then I figured, Okay, this is a point to remember.

We talk about sexual fantasies: What would you like to do? Being restrained and tickled is one of hers. Nothing else sticks in my mind. One of the things I suggested was to have her sit with her back to me and a mirror in front of her, and I would play with her, and she could watch. She thought that was a good idea. We've never done it, but we might sometime. Another one I had was foot-fucking. I said, "You're on your back and you've got your feet oiled and I'm screwing your feet. You're playing with yourself and we're both getting real hot." Usually we just joke about it. It's been said that the American male has a sexual fantasy every thirty seconds. I don't know if it's that often, but I think about sex a lot. I'll say to Barb, "You know what I thought of? You won't believe this one." I'll tell her, and she'll say, "You're a sick puppy," or "Oh, that sounds interesting." But we haven't ever done anything planned, like, You do this and I'm gonna do this. Whatever we end up doing is spontaneous. I've suggested tying her up and tickling her, and she says, "Maybe we'll try that some other time."

These conversations happen because of her, definitely. She is very comfortable talking about sex. It took me a while to learn, I haven't always been that open. She drew me out. But it's gotten to the point now where I'll bring up the subject. And there's something else I think is important—as a result of being able to talk with Barb, I've learned to talk openly with my children. I mean, she had to push me into having a good, objective discussion about sex with my oldest son. And by the time my daughter got into her teens, it was dinnertable conversation. We're like, "This is stuff you need to know. Your brothers aren't here, it's just the three of us, this is a good opportunity to talk about it, so we're gonna do that." She might say, "Aw, I don't want to." "Well, we really need to tell you these things, and we need to know you understand." Everything from birth control to safe sex to the fact that you don't have to settle for bad sex, or rushed sex, or shallow sex. I'd just as soon my daughter didn't have sex now. I know she has in the past, I don't know whether she is now or not. But one time Barb asked her, "How was it? Was it good? Did you enjoy it?" My daughter said it wasn't all it was cracked up to be, and Barb said, "You know, you don't have to settle for bad sex just for the sake of having sex. It can be fun. It can be great." To be able to talk to my daughter like that is pretty unique, I think. So I really thank Barb, because I know I couldn't have done it on my own.

Sex is a never-ending subject, you can talk about it forever. And it ties into lots of other things in our lives. It's a close, intimate connection I make with Barb. It's all about centering and grounding. I'm gone for a week at a time, and she's here managing the household, taking care of the kids, doing her job. When we come together, we're running at two different speeds, and our heads are in different places.

Sometimes it takes a little while, a day or two of conversation and being around each other. Then having sex brings it all together. It comes to where we're moving at the same rate, the same rhythm. Getting in touch with each other, beyond conversation. It's how we get back in tune.

LORI ESCHILMAN

"I am a sadist," she says proudly. "I get off on taking somebody really far physically." For nearly ten years, since her early twenties, she has been exploring the erotics of dominance, submission, and pain. She began with experiments in college—"I would tie a girl up and then not know what to do"—and is now an accomplished "top" who sometimes leads sex workshops in San Francisco. We talk in her North Beach apartment, which has a youthful, hippie-ish feel, and which she shares with a gay man. She has dark curly hair, pale blue eyes, a round face, and a plump body clad in black pants and shirt. She works for a graphic design company.

Her father is a doctor, her mother a ceramist. "I had a normal childhood, no big traumas. My parents seem pretty happily married. But ever since I was a tot I always challenged them. I came out as a lesbian when I was seventeen, and that created a lot of family difficulty. Then when I came out as an S/M person, it was another big thing, they were very worried about my well-being. Part of the process with my mother included my learning about her sexuality, that she had sex a lot and enjoyed it. There's a masturbation story which is pretty funny. My mother has a vibrator that my father gave her one year. When I used to come home from college, I knew where she kept the vibrator, and I knew they never used it, so I would put it in my room and use it for the vacation. One summer I came home and it wasn't there. I was going crazy, I'm really a vibrator addict. Finally I was just so horny I said, "OK, Mom, sit down. Where's the vibrator?" She's like, "What!" I said, "Look, here's the deal. I've been stealing your vibrator for three years, and I need it now." She was blown away, but she goes into her room, comes back with the vibrator, and says, "By the way, have you ever used the jet in the hot tub?" I go, "Oh, yeah, sure." I had never done it, of course. I should give her credit for turning me on to that. Later on that day I went down to the hot tub, and she was right, it was great."

• • •

When I was in college, I lost my virginity in a rape. After that I really shut down—I didn't tell anybody about it, I didn't get any support. For years afterward my sexuality was pretty limited. I was very into conquest, I went after a lot of straight women. Since then I've had a lot of healing, but the most important experience was this weeklong event put on by the S/M contingent of the Radical Faeries. It was up in the country, they do it every year, but this was the first time women were invited. There were six or seven women and about fifty men. It was a very powerful queer situation. When I say "queer" I don't mean odd, or just homosexual, but more like adventurous. There are people whose main orientation is heterosexual who are very queer. It's a devotion to exploring who you are sexually, and usually when people do that it includes crossing the boundaries of who they think they are. It's the pursuit of the unknown or the frightening.

So I was up at this place, eighty acres with a beautiful meadow filled with wildflowers, and this enormous oak tree. The Faeries called it the sacred oak tree. I was avoiding the tree, but one day I decided to walk around the meadow, and finally I found myself coming down this road toward the tree, and I started to cry. There was a hammock underneath, and I got in, it was the kind that wraps around you, and I lay inside and just wept and wept. It felt like my body had opened and my spine was weeping, and my tears felt like blood. I was mourning the part of me that had been stolen by a stranger, that I could never get back.

That night we had a campfire where we evoked Kali, who's the goddess of destruction and change. And later two important things happened to me. The first was that I brought a man to orgasm. I jerked him off, and it was wonderful. I told him it was the first time I had ever done that, and he said, "Wow, you do it just like a fag." I loved that. Then another man brought me to orgasm that night, using his hand and his leg. It wasn't like being fucked, it wasn't about penis-vagina, but it was animal, it was energy and rough-and-tumble. And it was about trusting a man, allowing him to bring me pleasure.

Since then I've done a lot of play with a lot of different partners, both men and woman. I do have one primary partner, my lover, Angelica. We've been together two and a half years now. But we have—well, we call ourselves "omnigamous." We play together with other people, as well as separately. That kind of relationship is a lot of work, because jealousy is a real emotion. But you don't have to succumb to it. You just have to have clear definitions and communication. I would never go to Angelica and say, "Oh, by the way, I've been seeing this other person for the past three months." I let her know what I'm planning. I might say, "I have a boner for this girl, I'm gonna see about getting a playdate with her." Or, "I have a boner for this girl, shall we make a playdate together?" Because Angelica might have a boner for her, too.

There's a little bit of imbalance, I play with other people more than Angelica does, because that's how we're wired. I get off on meeting somebody and talking with them and acting on the attraction, like a spontaneous eruption. Angelica gets off on knowing somebody for years, having this vast knowledge of them, and then maybe connecting and playing. My energy has a maleness to it. I have a real fag sexuality. Even in our relationship, I'm the butch one and she's the femme. I just wish there were more opportunities to have anonymous connections. I mean, lesbian sex clubs are a joke. I go, but it's like, Who are all these women and why are they talking so much? I have these fantasies of going up to women and saying, "Excuse me, what are you talking about? Are you talking about the office? Are you talking about movies? Listen—do you want to fuck her? And do *you* want to fuck *her?* Well, go in one of the cubbyholes in the back and do it! And shut up!"

I have regular play partners, and I play with new people sometimes, and I play with gay men, mostly at parties. I enjoy fisting men and fucking them with a dildo, I've had incredible experiences with that, as well as fisting gay women both vaginally and anally. I very rarely play with straight men, and the ones I have played with are pretty queer. They don't get freaked out if a man touches their body, and they don't come on to me in an oppressive way. There's a kind of eroticism that most straight men have about lesbians, a lecherousness that has a high yuck factor for me. It doesn't affect me as much as it affects Angelica, she's a very pretty girl who gets a lot of attention from straight men. If a straight man comes on to me, he's exceptional. I don't have the look that society presents as the ideal. It's not stopping me from getting laid, thank God, but my attractiveness is about something else, and most straight men don't see it. They don't walk into a room and go, "Oh, she's hot." Whereas I might be the hottest woman in the room as far as what I like to do and I'm willing to do.

With queer men there's a kind of safety I don't even feel with lesbians. I can approach them with no baggage. With another lesbian there's always a possibility, the nesting-instinct stuff. When I play with fags there's a purity of energy that comes from it being just an event. It can be passionate and moving and powerful and heartfelt and loving, but it's an event, separate from my issues about relationships. I have a friend who calls it the screen-door effect: You can get fresh air but not have any bugs.

I love fucking a man up the ass and giving it to him good. I get into this fag spirit, by which I mean knowing what you want sexually and going for it, not being afraid of rejection, being okay with your desires. I spent a lot of time, especially in my twenties, being afraid of my desires. I've always hung around with gay men, but in the last three or four years I started thinking, Okay, I love this person, why do I have to stop at my skin because I'm a lesbian? We can give each other enormous pleasure. It's not evil or dangerous. When I fuck a man, I'm still a dyke.

I did a great scene a couple months ago with my gay friend Freddie. He and I had a playdate to fuck him up the ass at this party. It was me and another woman and him. We suspended him from the ceiling with a winch. His legs were held up with ankle restraints that were attached by a rope to a bar above him. And he was in a suspension harness around his thighs and waist and shoulders, so it was like he was sitting up with his legs straight out in front of him. I lay down on the ground and we'd raise him up and then lower him down on my cock—which is a dildo on a harness. We'd raise him and lower him, and I could take his legs and spin him around on the cock, back and forth. We were all laughing and having a fabulous time.

I also do some regular vanilla sex, mostly with Angelica. But even there—I can't imagine a sexual experience that doesn't involve a transference of power. Like if we're having vanilla sex, I love to talk dirty, and it's almost like I'm channeling. A lot of talking dirty is about—I hesitate to say degradation, but that's really what it is. Or doing daddy scenes, I take on the persona of Daddy with her being a little girl. Or if I'm with a guy, making him be a little boy to my dyke daddy, which can be a blast.

Mostly I like to play with people so it's like going on a journey, and nobody knows where it's going. I'm not so much interested in dominance and submission. I'm interested in somebody giving me their trust rather than their will—saying, Okay, I trust you to take me somewhere. I've found that playing with the boundaries of what your body will accept can get you really deep really fast. I haven't found any other way that's as effective. And it has to do with a certain skill and intuition that a top needs in order to take someone there.

This New Year's Eve I played with a girl who had never bottomed before. I brought her to a Black Leather Wings party. I knew that her mother has been slowly dying for like five years. I started out by restraining her on a massage table. No big bondage thing, I just made it so she couldn't fall off or run away or hit me if she got pissed off. I gave her some safe words, the standard ones, *yellow* and *red,* meaning, "This is getting intense," and "This is too intense." I also gave her a word that meant, "The end, I'm outa here, untie me." That was *hematite,* because I had given her this hematite egg to hold in her hand. It's a grinding stone, and it's also a good stone to put inside someone's cunt when you're fucking them.

She was naked. I was wearing my standard play outfit, which is boxer shorts rigged so I can put suspenders on them, and some blue Doc Marten boots, and a petticoat kind of thing. A gender-fuck outfit. Also I was wearing my cock—I had a dildo harness on with the cock coming through the boxer shorts.

I started just rubbing her skin with my hands, patting, some light spanking, getting the blood flowing. Then I did some harder spanking. I played the S/M game—spanking somebody till it gets a little intense, then pulling back and playing in a more safe zone, and then pushing again. Invariably you get further because their endorphins are kicking in, so you keep pushing that envelope of what somebody can receive pleasurably. It's like their body gives you permission—either they go, "Oww!" and pull away, or they go with it.

Then I used a flogger on her for quite a while. It's a leather whip, pieces of leather maybe half an inch wide coming out of a handle. I flogged her in the places that are safe—you don't want to do the lower back or around the kidneys or the coccyx. I did the fleshy parts of her ass and her thighs and her back between the shoulder blades. She started to cry, and I said, "You know I'm not going to stop if you cry, that's a sign we're doing the right thing. So go ahead and cry." I kept pushing and coming back and pushing and stopping and doing sweet things, like caressing her with a piece of rabbit fur or the palm of my hand. Then she said "red" to the flogging. I said, "Okay, fine." I was thinking what I really needed was something to give more specific pain. So I went and found a candle and started to drop hot wax on her. It was effective because she got incredibly angry with me, and I started to pursue her anger. She was going, "Oh, you bitch, you bitch, it hurts! Ow, you're so mean!" I'm like, "Yeah, I'm mean. I'm a sadist, you got that right." [Laughs.]

Up till then I had been real quiet. But with the wax she got into this anger place and I said, "Look, you're not angry at me, who are you really pissed at?" She started to cry again and get enraged at her mother. It was obvious what was up, I knew from the information she had given me. What happened was the flogging had opened the doors, and then the wax got very specific so she could have this catharsis. I think S/M often does that, it opens channels for pain to be released. She started feeling all the things she's not allowed to feel—like, her mother's been dying for five years, how can she possibly be angry, the poor woman's in pain all the time. I was encouraging her to have the anger, but then telling her she's a bad girl for having it. That put her through all the emotions, the anger and the guilt about the anger. I was working those demons from both sides. She was saying, "Sometimes I just want to kill her and put her out of her misery."

During the scene I was mean to her, calling her an ungrateful daughter. But afterward I was real nurturing, holding her and letting her cry some more for those feelings, and letting her know she's not a bad person for having them. Letting her have those dark places that are scary, especially around death and dying. She came out of it with a smile on her face. I untied her and we sat and cuddled for a while and watched some other stuff going on in the room and ate some nuts and hung out. It was a simple scene, no bondage, no suspension, just flogging and hot wax did the job. There was no sex per se. There was no orgasm. Sometimes the culmination of a scene is orgasm, and sometimes it's not.

A few days later I called her back to see how she was doing, whether she was left too open, whether she needed to get together for some closure. We did get together a week or so later for dinner. It was nice for her to talk about it, because it was the first time she had done a scene, and stuff was coming up about the whole nature of it, like was this okay, was it healthy or was it crazy? To me that kind of follow-up is important. Even in the vanilla world, or the het world, even if you have no intention of sleeping with the person again— you've had this intense thing, maybe it was disastrous and maybe it was fantastic, but you should always check in and see how somebody is doing.

When I'm doing a scene like that, I feel energized and strong and skilled. Those feelings are erotic to me. I feel them in my chest and my hips and my guts and my cunt. Yeah, it makes my cunt wet, but it also makes me smile all over, like all my pores are smiling. I feel like such a stud. [Laughs.] And it's not just the act of inflicting pain, it's the exchange of power. Sometimes I'll get out feelings of my own. I went to a sex club a couple of months ago with this girl who had told me she didn't want to play. Okay, so I'm playing with other people. She came up later and said, "Oh, maybe I do want to." I said okay, tied her up, and started giving her a whipping. She started saying, "Stop, stop, stop!" I was like, "Fuck you, you're the one who didn't want to play. You're always changing your mind. Who the fuck do you think I am? I'll whip you until I'm good and done." Granted, she had a safe word. I even checked in with her and said, "You know what to say if you really want me to stop, right?" She said yes. I said okay, and I brutalized her. I got out my aggressions, because she completely pissed me off.

Often what makes a scene good is resistance. She's screaming, "Stop, stop!" and I have to decide whether to stop. When somebody's screaming like that, they don't necessarily mean, More, more! They may mean, This is getting intense. But I know the intensity is what they want, and they may want help to get beyond that. I can either encourage them, like, "Feel the pain and go with it," or I can go the other way, like, "Fuck you, deal with it, bitch! You wanted to be here, fuckin' deal with it!" Being the evil mommy instead of the nice mommy. I can say, "You're a worthless piece of shit and I'm gonna piss all over you." Now, I don't really think this person is worthless. It's like acting—if you're playing a mass murderer, there's a part of you that could be a mass murderer. Every character that has ever been written exists within all of us. It's an exploration of part of my psyche. It's a safe place to explore my dyke—I mean, my dark side. [Laughs.] But I stay conscious that it's a safe and consensual interaction, so it never gets out of control.

Tops have to have limits, too. Emotional pain is a dangerous thing to play with. A bruise will go away, but sometimes things come up that I don't feel I can handle. It's important for me to feel like I can stop the scene and say, "This is going too far." It might be issues of child abuse, where the person really goes off, and then I might bring the scene to a close or do something else, maybe do a fisting or talk about what's coming up. Even with physical pain, there are things I'm not interested in doing. I don't want to cause permanent marks or make people bleed. In my playing with Angelica—she's an intense masochist, there are things I can't do for her. There's a level of whipping she needs a man's strength for. I can't hit her that hard, and I can't bring myself to do it, either. When I'm at my physical limits with a whip, I'll probably go to using the stick. It's a long piece of willow, maybe half an inch thick. I might make her choose a number of strokes between fifty and one hundred, that's a really mean thing to do. Or I'll make her choose a number between twenty and one hundred, and she'll choose twenty, and I'll go, "Nope! Wrong! It was fifty." Or she'll pick thirty, and I'll say, "I forgot to tell you, it's three times whatever number you pick." That's intense for her and for me, but she can take more than that.

Playing as a top, the journey is about driving the boat, or navigating. Scoping out the seas. Feeling inspiration. Playing the ebb and

flow of somebody's energy, or their emotional state. You get an impulse and act on it and it works, and all that happens in a split second. It can be a slap out of the blue—you're doing something sweet
to somebody, and all of a sudden, Wham! And they go, "Uhh!"
There's a release, you can see it, so you keep going. You can tell
whether someone is writhing because they're enjoying something, or
because they're not.

As a top I might get off or I might not. I did a scene with Angelica
recently and afterward she said, "What do you want? Do you want
me to eat your cunt? Do you want to use the vibrator?" I was like, "I
feel so good I don't want anything. An orgasm would be anticlimac-
tic." That's not always the case. Sometimes I have an orgasm during
a scene, I'll play with the vibrator or get fucked. I'm not an easy orgasm. Angelica, you can look at her the right way and she'll come.
Lucky her. For me it requires a lot of stimulation and a lot of concentration. I get all kinds of little surges, what I call mini-orgasms, I can
have those while I'm topping, but as far as an actual boom!, I have to
have a vibrator. Often right after the scene I'll take out the vibrator
and do myself, or somebody else will hold the vibrator or play with
my nipples while I'm vibrating.

It's only recently that I've enjoyed being fucked. Last summer at
a gathering of the Black Leather Wings I had a realization that a lot
of my sexual growth has been with hard-dick energy. I felt like my
hard-dick spirit was there, and I was leaving my cunt behind. I
wanted to find some balance. I put that out to the group at large. The
next day I was lying on the lawn, just resting and feeling the cool
grass, and all of a sudden these people descended on me and started
playing with me. It wasn't like they had planned it. One of them was
a gay man who had never touched a cunt before, he was touching me
and having his own thing about dealing with a woman sexually. Then
this woman came up and started to play with my cunt. I didn't know
what she was doing, I felt the sensation but I didn't know what she
was using inside me. And I started having this catharsis, I felt like
I was crying and having intense orgasms at the same time, like my
cunt was crying. Afterward she took this hematite egg out of my cunt.
It kind of plopped out and she put it on my belly, and I looked at it

and started to laugh and cry, like kids do, laughing and crying and laughing and crying. It was incredible, it was so healing. It was about having the courage to say what you want and being in a wonderful enough community that they'll provide it. I treasure my community for that. I can say, I'm afraid, I'm curious, I need something, and people come back and say, I'm willing to take you there—or try, anyway.

ELI GREGORY

He is the pastor at a Protestant church in a small city—a silver-haired, slightly built man wearing a white shirt, blue blazer, dark slacks, and loafers. "You'll find our church very eclectic—there's Democrats, Republicans, and both of them are very strong in what they stand for. I think our theology would border more toward conservative than liberal. My role is mostly teacher-counselor and doing a lot of pastoral care. I visit people who are sick, and I've established a ministry for people to be related on a one-to-one basis with people who are having a crisis. I do some counseling, as far as receiving people and hearing their story, and if it's at a level where I can say, 'I'd like to walk along with you,' I might meet with them a few times." *He speaks carefully, formally, so his outbursts of spontaneity or slang come as a surprise.*

He was raised in northern Michigan in a fundamentalist family. "My mother never worked. My dad ran a hardware store. Both of them were very active church people. I think he lived in the shadow of my mother. She was gregarious and warm and engaging, and we would wonder what he was thinking. But he was the decision-maker. He wouldn't ask, he would tell. He was not abusive, there was never an angry word spoken in my home, but it's distant from what I would call an inclusive relationship. My mother was the submissive, pleasing one.

"Sex was always a hidden thing. We didn't speak about it. I didn't have a date until I was a senior in high school. Then I went off to bible school, and in the first year I met my future wife." *They married at twenty and have been together forty years. She is the only woman he has ever made love with.*

• • •

One thing I have always struggled with in my own sexuality is being slow to develop in my genitals. That was very apparent as I went through junior high school, and went to the shower, and here are these kids my same age fully developed and hanging with goodness. And here I was still trying to spurt out a little bit of growth. It was very embarrassing. I also remember one time camping out on the edge of Lake Michigan with a couple of friends my age when we were in the seventh grade, and these two guys were available to share their penises, and I couldn't do that. We were in sleeping bags, and they had their flashlights, and they were, "See? Look," they were getting erections big and tall and I wasn't ready to do that. I lived with that through those years of growing up—the comparison, which is always so deadly. In my fifties I was still thinking about it, that I was slow to develop and not hung like other guys. In other words, in an erection I'm tall and strong, but when that subsides I'm small and strong.

Before we got married, Peggy and I had very limited touch, except to do some necking. And that was not extensive or often. I never explored her body. Very puritanical. We had an unspoken agreement, you might say, that we knew our limits. We were both very called, very sincere, very desirous of doing God's will, which is the place I am even now. It hasn't been a struggle to feel that's important in my life.

And compared to how it is now—right now, I'm preparing three couples who are about to be married. Back then, nobody said a word to me about anything—what it was to communicate, what it was to prepare financially, what it was to be a sexual partner. So I know those beginning weeks and months were very disappointing to my wife. I didn't know what she needed or what would be helpful. I had no desire to investigate her body, touch her carefully and tenderly. I think there was a small measure of preparing my wife, and then for me, after entering and . . . humping, soon after that there would be an ejaculation. It's hard to go back and remember those times. It was routine, mechanical—you did it and it was over with. My attitude was, That's what we're here for, isn't it? What more do you want? And Peggy never said she wanted more, because she came to marriage as a virgin. We were innocent. I think also, she was given to feel guilty, always saying, "How can I find out what's wrong, so I can confess it and get it cleared out?" Her goal not only was to fulfill some religious call, but to be a homemaker and mother and a wife. So we didn't demand much of each other, and the pleasure we had was very limited.

We had our first child the year after we married. Two years later we had our second. Two years later we had our third. Three years later we had our fourth. Peggy did diapers for almost nine years straight. She was very focused on children, very busy, and very tired at night. Still, we were having sex four or five times a week. She fulfilled the role I saw in my mother, the submissive, obedient, happy, cooperative female. I don't think she knew what would make sex better, except she had a sense that this wasn't all there was. I had no idea whether she had orgasms or not. We didn't talk about it until the tenth or eleventh year of our marriage. When we did, she said, "Do you know I'm still waiting?"

I have to say, I feel very sad about those years. I was very, very selfish. Very uncaring. Very . . . simple. It's discouraging to have to admit that.

After our last child was born we began to talk about it. There was the feeling that we needed to look at who we were, how we were behaving sexually. We made a decision that we would have no more children, and we needed to work at that. At the same time, we didn't want to not have sex. So what would make it better? There was talk about foreplay, so that Peggy could indeed have an orgasm, how I could contribute to that. And how could she contribute toward her own fulfillment, what was it that was especially arousing. Those were the kinds of questions we were asking each other.

We also began to be involved in teaching and organizing young married groups, and we began to read some stuff we'd never read before, on sexuality or the sexual behavior of a married couple. We had not delved into the call this made on our lives, to be speaking about these things to young people. I mean, if we were gonna be the experts, we ought to get with it. So I'd say that was the key to opening a door. There was a book entitled *The Intimate Marriage,* and there's a very good book that's Christian-oriented called *The Gift of Sex*. And a lot of other books—I have a list of twelve or thirteen I give to couples when I counsel them. With these books, it was like the horizons lifting: Look what we can be.

I should say: Another dimension of our marriage is that there's no consideration of divorce. That would be absolutely unacceptable to think about. It affects our sexuality because of the permanence—we will be there for each other, there's not going to be anybody else. I promised you I will not be unfaithful, so if we can't do it, who's gonna do it? There's a high level of promise and commitment as well as a growing desire. I guess another thing that would be right to say is that Peggy had a hysterectomy when she was thirty-six, so there hasn't been this concern about children, and there's a great deal of freedom. I have never used a condom. She used gel in the beginning, and then the pill came into existence, but some of that stuff wasn't successful, I'm here to tell you.

Sex was hard to talk about at first, because it had been such a closed topic. But I think the woman in her felt the need, because she had a growing awareness from her reading. She'd say, "See?" One of the things we talked about was that for me, there was more ease in arriving at a climax, and she needed more response and touch and encouragement. She needs to be prepared for the act. You have an erection, and you penetrate, and then good-bye? No! That was hard for me to hear. I don't think any of us as males like to be corrected, especially by a female. So there was a bit of a struggle, but also a deep desire to be connected and make Peggy happy.

She told me she needed more fondling. She told me how tender her nipples are—I mean in a good way. I realized that just to exercise and touch those—well, now I find great pleasure in having her nipples in my mouth, moving them through my tongue and all. That still delights me, arouses me in a way that's higher than anything else. I had never done that before, not with my mouth. She has very small breasts and she's always been embarrassed about that. Sometimes she doesn't feel open enough to be naked in front of me in the daylight. I've told her that big breasts are not important to me—I remember one author said you can only have one spoonful at a time. [Laughs.]

Those were comforting words. I have said to her, "The inner person is more valuable to me than anything," but I certainly enjoy her physical body. My wife is very trim. Women always admire her body and can't imagine she's had four children. She looks like she's forty years old, but she's sixty. Now we're both getting wrinkles, her hair is getting gray, but she's naturally blond so it doesn't show up as much. She has a very beautiful hourglass figure. But in the old days we always made love in the dark, and if we were naked by daylight we'd turn our backs to each other.

So we discovered that her arousal was a slow-growing process, compared to a man. And all the foreplay was leading up to this, and there was not only for her a potential and hopeful orgasm but there was also a follow-up of that, which I didn't realize was needed or appreciated. So the whole flow of what goes on when you have a sexual experience—it can be ten minutes, or it can be two hours. Two hours! That was a brainstorm to me. And then be awake three hours later and start all over again? Those were new ideas.

I don't remember when she had her first orgasm, but now she has them quite often. Not knowing how to compare my behavior with other men, I have wondered if I don't come earlier than maybe I could or should. As a result there's a lot of fingering of her clitoris after I've come, if she's available to it. That often doesn't result in an orgasm, 'cause her energies have been—I don't know if there's been a disappointment, or whether my fingering doesn't produce a continuation of that higher level. But at times she's so high that it's a real enjoyment to pleasure her.

We just love to hold each other, when we begin sleeping and before we get out of bed. Being close to each other—that sense of, I love you, I want you, I care for you, and you're special to me. Even though sometimes it's not verbalized, we know it and it's so appreciated, especially by my wife. But I have come to see that I need that cuddling, too. I have my head on Peggy's shoulder just as much as she has her head on my shoulder. And the thing that has been so amazing to me in this time of my life is to find the continuous—I don't want to say increasing, because that wouldn't be true—but awakening with this erection that says, I've got to do something. That's wonderful.

I woke up that way this morning, and it was satisfaction enough to be close to Peggy. At other times when I'm wired and bushy-tailed I enjoy going for it. So there's variety from simplicity to full expression. But knowing that wherever we are along that spectrum, there's satisfaction. And we don't need to expect the same thing every time.

It's initiated mostly by me. I think early in our marriage I didn't respond to her initiations, and she was very disappointed. For a long time she didn't try it anymore. Through these later years, five or six years, there has been more commonality of initiating. But it's still mostly me. As far as timing, it's either as we're going to bed or as we're waking up. We also have naps during the afternoon, but traditionally it's going to bed. Or I'll wake up at three-thirty, and whoa! Look at Peter down here! I gently wake up Peggy and identify for her what's going on, and she says, "Whoa!" Sometimes she'll say, "Oh, I'm so sleepy," and I have to understand that. I can't put pressure, I realize that mine is not hers, we have to give and take at those moments.

But when the desire rises in me and Peggy is available, I'll reach out for her, and I'm usually very gentle, I find myself reaching for her face or shoulders or coming close to her and wrapping her in my arms, and after we've kissed each other I'll find myself going down. I love to involve myself with her breasts and hold onto her buttocks, that evokes her response and goes up her vagina and into the lower parts of her body. It's usually up to me to decide the position, and usually I'm on top or she's on top. I might have massaged her clitoris and made it harder if that would be helpful. If I were to put her on her back, she often takes my penis and rubs it up and down her vagina for her own pleasure. Even in and out briefly. She'll play with me until there's a full desire, a "Let's go with it" kind of thing. At the same time I'll be up so I'm still massaging her with my mouth and tonguing her nipples.

If she's on top of me and I'm underneath, I find it very pleasurable to be fully penetrated, deep, and being able to go back and forth to these nipples that are standing over me. That also delights her very much. I won't even move inside her at first. It's a sensation that I'm in her as fully as I can be, an awareness that I am *in her,* and she is mine, this is *the one* I do this with. I can't find anything more pleasurable than this, we are as close as we ever will be. I am in my wife as deeply as I'm gonna—I guess I probably have six and a half, seven inches, I think that's pretty normal. So wow, let's make this moment special. Sometimes I say, "Can I be quiet, can I just stay here?" There might be a slight movement by me to let her know I'm there—not that she doesn't know, but just to add to it. It's not an up-and-down bang bang bang. It's a continuation for me of knowing we're still in foreplay, and I'm helping her to be aroused. She's still with her knees forward and up above me, with my gyrations and movements on her nipples. I hear her sounds, I hear her pleasure, and I want to do that for her.

Then when it seems time I'll start moving, and when I feel desirous and she's ready I put my knees down and she comes down on me by putting her legs down, so we're flat on top of each other. Then she does the action, or we both move, but as I realize it's coming I can't move anymore, and I just let her move, and I have a climax at that point. Mmm—the waterfall. [Laughs.] And sometimes she'll have a climax at that same time. But more than likely it's followed by her lying on her back and me massaging her nipples and her clitoris, so she keeps active and comes to a climax. Often when she has an orgasm she will burst into tears. What a joy—I love her. She'll sigh and gasp and the tears will come. Then she'll let me know when it's enough and it's beginning to hurt a little bit or something, and she'll take me in her arms and thank me, and we're just there together with the awareness of our pleasure. It's full, we've come to the ultimate of why we've done what we've done.

We have also been available—in the last twelve years, compared to the other twenty-eight—to have oral sex. That's been so pleasurable, a delightful development in these years of our lives. Something that might have been abhorred in our former life—it was outside the pale, for religious reasons. As if only those who are carried away and are deviants would do this. Can you imagine thinking that? The religious perspective—if you take it to its fullest extent of conservatism, sex is something you do, but don't expect to be pleasured. It's for procreation. You certainly don't have sex when your wife is pregnant. Well, I gave that idea up a long time ago, I can remember having sex when my wife was in her ninth month. As for oral sex, the idea is, Christian people don't do that. I can remember being in a workshop with an author of a number of books, some of them on marriage, and him speaking of the possibility that oral sex is just fine, and if it's not okay with you, that's fine too, and having people in the audience afterward saying how terrible he was. But after reading some of the nonreligious books, we realized that oral sex was something we had never tried. Wow, look what we're reading here! We can try that. It doesn't say, "Not to be tried by religious persons."

I do have to say that oral sex has diminished compared to what it was when we first decided to do it. It's occasional, rather than regular. For a while it was exciting. Now it's something we could do but don't need to do. And she never brings me to orgasm that way. I enjoy more being inside her. I think also there might be a sense that I don't want her to do that to me. I guess I associate it with the end result of two gay guys.

I also have to admit that we still find it difficult to talk about sex. Yet when we have, it's been so rewarding. I remember saying one time, "Why did we wait to talk about this?" We learn slow, I don't know what's so dumb about us, but to break that ice and say "We need to talk about this" is really challenging. For example, these days my arousal is sometimes slow in coming—after fifty-five it's less than in former years. The frustration was quite deep. Finally, Peggy would say, "We've got to talk about this," we would, and wow! Here we go! Another time—initiated by Peggy again—we read some author, a well-respected author on the sexuality of human beings. We read about the age flow and not to expect much, and that it's okay, orgasm is not the end-all. It's more an appreciation of our bodies, the touching and the aggressive—I might say, "I need to hold you *tight,* I want you," or "I want you *near me,* I want you to *touch* me and *hold* me." I would say that, and so would she. And more than likely we would come to a climax, simply because we knew that we wanted and needed each other.

A little while ago we had a relaxed week, and we went away to a bed-and-breakfast. We made love twelve times that week. I'm kind of

proud of that. The inn was lovely, and we had time off, but also leading up to it was my sense that I really want this woman. And she was
responding. We'd wake up in the night, and there was only one time
when she said, "I'm too tired." Twelve times in one week. I said to
myself, "Yeah, Eli! You're all right!"

LARRICE FREEMAN

She is a forty-two-year-old black woman whose warm, sassy, slangy style seems a cover for a more fundamental shyness. She is dressed for our talk in loose black slacks and a bright red sweater. "I grew up on a farm," she begins. "Lived out there on the farm, went to school in town. I was the oldest in my family—four brothers and two sisters. And I was a tomboy. Always into sports and doing everything out of doors. What really got Dad was that I wanted to go into farming, and none of the boys did. But Mom's always been a priss-priss. I don't think I was what she wanted me to be." Her parents split up when she was young and she divided her time between them. "We were never explained anything about sex, by either one. What we learned, we learned on our own. My mother never even explained to us about getting our periods. I had no idea about sex. When all of us girls were starting to smell the boys and hang out in mixed company, some girls had slumber parties out in the backyard. The guys would sneak over. This is really gross, this is so embarrassing, but in ninth or tenth grade, this boy got in my sleeping bag and put his finger up my crotch and scared the mortal shit out of me. I had kissed him before, but when he did that I just took off running. Left the slumber party, left all my shit, had no shoes on, and went home. This old car was sitting there and I got in, locked the doors, and prayed to God that I wouldn't get pregnant. That's how stupid I was. By eleventh grade I think most of my girlfriends were doing the do, but—I don't know what it was about me. I was always the last one to know anything. I was scared to death of sex."

Now she lives with her second husband Sam, working endless hours to make a go of a small farm. They have been together "ten or eleven years, married five or six, I'm not sure."

. . .

My first marriage lasted four years. It was no big deal. I still haven't figured out what got me into that relationship. I started dating Raymond my senior year in high school. He was a few years older, and I was like, This guy is crazy about me. I couldn't believe that, so I was taken in. We lived together a few years before we got married. The first time we were supposed to get married, it was two weeks before and I hadn't made no plans. He was getting all on my case, so I rode that through, and the next year I was like, Okay, make those plans and get him off my back. I was too stupid to realize I didn't make the plans because I didn't love him in the first place.

When we were dating he knew I was a virgin. He knew I was backward. And he never, ever touched me sexually. We'd go riding, we'd do a lot of fun things, we did a lot of kissing. That's what really turned me on to this man. I fell in love because he never touched me. It was like, God, this is great. The kissing was very innocent and the petting was very light, and I loved it. Probably if he'd touched me the first time, I'd have hated him forever and that would have been it. But he didn't. I think he was turned on by the fact that I was so naïve. He was used to girls saying, "Sure, go ahead," legs open. Here he had this dummy, didn't know nothin'. I think that gave him a thrill.

I used to smoke pot, and we were quite high the first time we ever made love. It was cool, but I could only do it if I was high. If I wasn't high I'd lay there like a board. Pot relaxed me enough that I could go through it. But it was never what sex is supposed to be. I never had an orgasm the entire time. I never had an orgasm until Sam. It seems so unreal, to go all those years. But everything has to be just right for me. And he didn't really give a shit about me. I could be really turned on, I could really want sex, but he didn't do anything for me. He just got on and did what he needed, and that was it. About the time I'm ready to start poppin', boyfriend was done. Roll off and go to sleep. I'd fake orgasms. I don't think he cared whether I had 'em or not, but if I wanted him to get off me real quick, I'd fake them big time. I knew how quick he was anyway, and he'd just be that much quicker. [Laughs.]

It was terrible. Well, I didn't know what to think because I didn't know what it was supposed to be like. So I just played it off. I hardly ever got upset about it. I couldn't talk to him about it. We never had any real personal conversations. And I'd lie to my friends. I'd get in groups and people would start talkin' about sex, and oh, yeah, our sex life was great. I was ashamed. At one point I thought there was something wrong with me. But now I know it wasn't me. It was the way I was brought up—well, not really the way I was brought up, I think the way I was brought up saved me from being worse. Dad always told me I didn't have to take any shit off anybody, that I could do what I wanted. At least he built a little confidence in me. But the fact that nobody told me anything about sex—I don't resent it because back then people just didn't say anything. At least my parents didn't, I guess because of the way they were raised.

After a while I couldn't stand for him to touch me or even be near me. This was after I first had an inkling he was running around. I didn't know for sure, but it was something I felt. Finally I caught him at it, and not too long after that I left him.

Then I dated this other guy for a while, Josh. Real nice guy. I enjoyed his company but I wasn't in love with him. Sex was better, though. Josh was more considerate, I could come close to an orgasm, but I never did have one. I still faked. I don't know, with Raymond I never got a chance to know anything, and then with Josh, I was afraid I wouldn't do right, or please him, or know what the hell was what. When I felt he was getting close to an orgasm, I'd fake one just so he wouldn't think—I thought if it took me too long, he'd think I was a nympho. I was so dumb, I thought this was supposed to happen to me quick, or when it happened to him, and nothing was happening. So, y'know, I thought a nympho was when you have to have it all the time, keep going, keep going forever and ever and never stop. And when you have an orgasm, you have to go again and again and again. So if I thought I was getting close, I'd go [mimics panting]—"Oh, yeah, oh yeah, hallelujah!"

With Sam now, I just say, "Don't you dare stop, oh, don't you dare stop!" And he knows. [Laughs.] He can do it.

I also didn't want to get into a thing with Josh based on sex. He was a neat guy, but he was getting too serious. Which might be why I didn't have an orgasm with him, because I was holding back. Anyway, I met Sam at a party. He was very funny. We danced and we talked, and he wouldn't leave me alone. Every time I looked around he'd want to talk or dance. He's so crazy, that boy—he could strike up a friendship with a rock. And we just clicked. I told him, "You can't keep bugging me like this, I'm here with someone else." He said, "Oh, I don't care," and he kept on. He told me he wanted to take me to see some farm the next day, and I agreed. Josh wanted to take me home that night, and I said, "I'm tired, I just want to go to sleep." It didn't dawn on me that I was attracted to Sam, but that's what it was.

Before we knew it we were constantly dating. We had sex after maybe five or six dates. I can remember it. Yep, it was wonderful. It was probably as close to what I had ever dreamed of as I could get, without it being an actual dream. He did all the right things. He took his time. Lots of foreplay. He was very gentle. And he talked to me. He wanted to know what I wanted. That was hard for me. But I cringed a little bit and eased my way into it. The first thing I remember saying was, "Whatever you want." And I remember thinking, That was stupid. That was really stupid. He said something like, "Well, I want what makes you happy." I never actually told him what I wanted. He was getting so close anyway that I didn't want to blow what was going on. This was the first time ever, having sex and talking it through, and I was a little flabbergasted by the whole thing.

He didn't get me off right at first. I came real close, but I was too uptight. I was still not together yet. My head was back with the old shit. I had to have all the lights out. I didn't want to be undressed in front of him with the lights on. But he just kept on going—like he came, and he would still do things to please me. He'd be right back where he left off. He'd caress me and kiss me, he'd kiss my breasts, and the way he held me—he'd just keep on. I didn't actually fake an orgasm, but I let him know I enjoyed it. He probably didn't know whether I had one or not. He probably thought I did. For one thing, I was used to faking them, but also I wasn't used to feeling what I felt. That excited me enough to where I would squeal a little, and there was a little more motion than what I ever did before. And he just kept on and kept on and kept on until he knew I was satisfied. [Laughs.] It was absolutely fantastic. It was the first time I ever realized what sex was about. I actually had a part and a say as to what was going on. I could enjoy it and not feel weird about it, not feel like I was wild or "ho"-ish or dirty.

I vaguely remember when I had my first orgasm, it wasn't too long after that. Like the third or fourth night. I never did tell him I hadn't had one before. Nah, the boy would get the big head. And there's a part of me that still feels like I'm not totally normal. I'm kinda different from most people I know. I hide my insecurities, and that comes out as Billie Jean Badass. Like there's nothing you could do or say that would ever hurt me. Which is a total lie, my feelings can be hurt so easy. And sexually—well, I'm not—a lot of the girls I know, they go out of their way to do things to entice their husbands. I don't. I never put on sexy nightgowns or try to make myself sexual. I wear makeup, and the basic reason I do that is because I've always felt that when you have a flaw, you have to do something else to make up for that flaw. I have this big body, so I'll try to wear some makeup to make up for the fact that I'm overweight. Which is ridiculous, ain't nothin' gonna hide all this shit hangin' out here. But as far as sexy nighties, openin' up the door for your husband with nothing but his shirt on—I don't do stuff like that. These days I wear blue jeans and sweaters, anything but sexy. That's what I work in, that what I'm comfortable in, anything that's baggy and loose. He happens to think my sweatshirts are sexy. But some things them girls do—wow. They'll put on just a shirt, or something just down to here, and they parade around with nothing else on. Or they get sexy negligees or those things with the garter belts and all that crap. Most of 'em wear that stuff every single night. I'm like, "You do what? Honey, give me a granny gown and leave me the hell alone." It's probably a turn-on once in a while, but I can't see doing it all the damn time.

I think they do it for themselves. It makes them feel sexy. Most of them are running around seeing other guys, other than their mates. That's all they want to talk about, is sex. That's all they give a damn about. Well, I like sex, but sex is not that important to me. If Sam wasn't home, I could go forever until he got back, and it wouldn't bother me, the sex part. Maybe it's because we work together day in and day out. When we're apart, we miss each other like crazy, but I don't feel like we have to have sex every time we turn around. I don't like to go very long without, though. If we go three or four days without any sex because we're too tired and we don't have the time, well, somewhere along the line we have to make time. If we're not working so hard, like in the winter, we have sex once every two or three nights. When the work is heavy, we might go three weeks. And that's me, not Sam. He could go all the time. It don't bother him, how tired he is. He's ready *right now.* But when we get in and get cleaned up and make that dinner and I hit that pillow, that's it. Lights out, I'm done, stick a fork in me.

Once in a while there's tension about it, we've talked about it, we've even argued about it, but it's never amounted to anything. He might get a little huffy for ten or fifteen minutes. He's pretty good about it. We both know how strenuous our life is, we can't put in the hours we put in and have sex every night. Not some Sam Williams sex anyway. Because he likes to go for a long time. When he says quickie, it's not a normal quickie. For Sam, it's forever. [Laughs.] I don't complain, I figure this is what I always wanted, but still I end up screaming at him, "Will you stop! Will you hurry up!" But no, he's not about to. Sometimes I try to make him come and *cannot* do it. Certain ways that I move, he can get beside himself, and it don't make any difference. Sam loves you to roll them hips. You can roll them hips real good, and boyfriend is beside himself. But it seems like it just makes him stronger. Or I talk to him real low and real smooth and sexy. Not dirty, just sexy. Things like, "You feel really good inside me, I like the way you move." Usually that eggs him on a little bit, gives him the swelled head. [Laughs.] But come? No. I don't care what you do, he's not gonna come until he's good and ready.

I very seldom initiate anything. I might be horny as hell, but I won't say, "Let's get it on." I always let him do it, even if I feel, This is what I want, and I want it now. Let it be his idea. I don't know if I'm too embarrassed or ashamed, I don't know what it is. I want to do it, but then I don't. The only time I did: I went somewhere to get some equipment fixed, and my girlfriend came along. Then I said, "Let's stop in and have dinner and a beer before we go home." There were some guys there I knew, they kept buying us beers, and hell, we was about shit-faced. I went home, and Sam was already in bed, and I threw the covers back, and I just raped his ass. I didn't even think about what I was doing, I just went in and did it. He loved it, too, boy. He said, "I hope every time you go to town you have a couple beers before you come home."

Sam is a lot more sexual than I am. Well, aggressive, maybe. I guess I'm sexual but in a different way. I'm not as up-front. He's like, Hey this is it, this is where I'm at. I'll throw a hint rather than just say, Hey, let's do it, dude. Like there's a radio station that plays real nice romantic music. I'll put the radio on and set it for an hour, so you don't have to get up and turn the damn thing off. He pretty much knows if I do that, I'm in the mood. But that's probably the only first move I ever made. Once in a while I might say, "Are you coming to bed?" That's a good hint, too, because if I'm tired, I just go to bed and that's it.

Of course, after all the years we've been together, sex is totally different. Every year we're together, things get better and better. We learn more about each other, even though we're pretty open, I don't hide too much of anything. But it seems like there's always something new to learn, something a little different or a little better. I don't have the hangups I used to have. I can be pretty much free with myself, other than the fact that I don't initiate anything. When we first got together, I wasn't real active. And I would never have said, "No, I don't feel like it, take your ass to sleep because you ain't gettin' shit tonight." Now I feel comfortable to do that. Even if he gets mad it's only gonna be for a little while. So it's better. I'm forty-two years old. I know a hell of a lot more now than I did then. And I like a hell of a lot more, too. It just feels better, every little thing. It feels more right, more normal, more . . . good.

I never used to move. I just lay there and took it. Now I move, and I let him know where I want him and what I want him to do and when I want him to do it. A little more shallow penetration, a little more boob action—but it has to be at the right time. Timing is the key for me. Once we're into things, I like both the penetration and the boob stuff, but it all has to be timed. If you go to the boobs too soon, it's a turn-off. Has to be gentle, too, I don't like it rough. Gentle to medium. Not too rough, not too light. Real light is kind of aggravating. Did you ever have somebody rub your skin and it feels like a burn? Well, if it's real light on my boobs, it feels like a burn. Same way with the skin on my back. If you apply a little pressure, it feels real good, but I can't stand that real light stuff.

It seems like he does more to me than I do to him. I don't know why, unless it's just because it takes me longer than him. I do spend a lot of time playing with his penis. I like doing that, I think that's neat. [Giggles.] And if we have time, I like to kiss his body and really take time. I like to lick between his legs and then go up his balls, that really fries his mind. I never would have done that in the beginning, it took me years to get relaxed enough. I like to tease him for a while and then maybe a little oral sex. Of course, when I go down on him I can't get that whole thing in my mouth. But I go so far, and I do the bottom half with my hand. I get him close to coming, but I ain't no swallower. [Laughs.] He can get as close as he wants to, but girlfriend ain't swallowin' shit.

When we're having sex I either like him on top of me or sideways, when we're lying side by side, my back in his belly. That's harder for him but it's easier for me. I have a bad back, so I can't get into kinky positions or I'll die, I can't walk the next day.

If I want to go for a while, I know what not to do with him. What's going to make him last longer. I will not roll my hips much. Just real gentle rolling, side to side and up and down. I don't want to play with his ears or even just massage him around his neck, or around his ears. His little boobies get sensitive, too, he can't stand a certain touch on them either. It can't be too aggressive and it can't be too light, and he doesn't like a lot, just a little bit. But if I want it to go on, I don't do that, I don't grab his butt, 'cause that turns him on, and I don't squeeze him on the back too much—I have to be pretty much passive until the time is right. Then we get past a point and I can do all those things, it's cool, it turns him on but it just builds him up until the magic moment. You have to read the timing. I try to make us come together. I know when I'm getting close, and then I know what to do so we can come together. It's not going to be right at the same time, but we're both gonna get off before everything is over. I'll rub his ears a little bit, then go down and rub his neck and his back, and I might even come between us and rub in the crotch area. If he's getting ahead of me we might just stop and do foreplay to where I'm gonna get closer and he's gonna be more relaxed. I rub his penis and he sucks my breasts and does a little finger action. I don't like deep finger action, just shallow. Not so much clit, that tickles me. I can't take that, it makes me want to tighten up, and my body starts shaking.

When I have an orgasm, it's usually from fucking. See, we have a lot of foreplay. Once we've had enough foreplay, then it's fairly easy for me to have an orgasm. He's pretty good, he can slow himself down, like he can be ready to explode and know I'm not ready, and then he'll change and do a little something else to wait on me. I still feel like it's harder for me than what I imagine for other women. I don't always have to have an orgasm to feel satisfied, either. It depends on how tired I am, on how we start out, if it's something we both want. If I'm just obliging him, I don't normally have an orgasm. But there have been times when I don't want to and he does, and I don't want him to keep bugging me, so we do it anyway, and we don't go through any foreplay, we just do it, and then there's something about it that's just—the next thing you know I'm having an orgasm. Wheew, cool, that was all right!

I don't think I would change anything about our sex. I just wish we had more time. But when we do have time we make up for it. The romance and the sex and the love get all mixed in together, it feels great, and he shows it and he says it. Even the next day, he'll say, "Wasn't that great?" I love that. When it's special, it's so wonderful and uplifting and so—I don't know, something that good can't happen all the damn time anyway.

SAM KAULAHUANA

He is a soft-spoken thirty-one-year-old with dark skin and long, straight black hair framing handsome Asian features. He was born in Hawaii but his father was in the army, "so we hopped around a lot, mostly in the South. I never had a lot of friends, I didn't feel like I fit in. I wanted to be a jock, like all the other guys, but I never was. I had long hair, and I always thought I talked like a girl. I had a very high voice. Usually I was the only Asian. Plus my family was very Catholic, always going to church. So I was a loner for a long time.

"My dad is very passive, but my mom is very strong-willed. After he retired he had like a nervous breakdown, and since then he hasn't done much of anything. My mom takes care of him. She—let's see, how do I say this? I have some incest issues with her. I have always been shut down when the subject of sex came up, and I never knew why until it hit me one day. I remembered that my mother used to come into my room when my dad was away. It started when I was twelve, in the seventh grade. I had just reached puberty. She would sleep in the same bed with me. She'd rub up against me, weird things. I would stay awake at night and try to get as far away from her as possible. After it had gone on for a few months, I told her, 'You can't come into my room anymore. I don't want you here. It's not right.' After that she stayed out. But until then I felt very threatened. It just felt—even as I'm talking about it now, I remember how it felt—like being violated. Part of me wanted to have sex with her, so I guess the only way I could squelch that desire was to take myself in the opposite direction. One morning I woke up and looked at her and said to myself, 'I'm gay.'

"Up to that point I was attracted to boys and girls. After the seventh grade, the thing with my mom, it was mostly boys. I always thought, Well, this is just a phase I'm going through. Even when I started sleeping with guys, I kept saying, As soon as I'm out of high school, this is going to stop. It just never did."

At the time we talk, he has recently finished nursing his lover Max through the final stages of AIDS. He lives in a large city, works as an AIDS counselor and educator, and practices various New Age healing methods.

• • •

I can remember exactly when I was infected. I met this guy in the fall of '87. His name was Rick. We started dating. At that point in my life, my dates were few and far between. In the beginning the sex was safe, basically just holding and stuff. Hugging and sucking, without him coming in my mouth. I never liked people coming in my mouth. A lot of body rubbing, mutual masturbation. Very simple. But after a while he started to want to go further. It was always without a condom, and I would always say no. Then one night I got pretty drunk, to the point where I was an easy mark. [Laughs.] And he entered me. It was strange, because he entered me and came very quickly. I'll always remember that moment. I went from being drunk and out of it to being very alert. There was a burst of adrenaline or something, and I thought, Oh my God, what have I done? And then, Oh well, what can I do now, it's already done. I think I went to the bathroom and tried to wipe myself. It had been so long since I had done it that the next day there was blood.

We continued to have unsafe sex after that. I used the rationalization, Well, he hasn't been with anyone for three years. And I haven't been with anybody, so it's okay. I knew he was monogamous with me, so I just kept doing it. I hadn't lost anybody to AIDS up to that point. I realize now that I was in complete denial. There was an epidemic going on, but it hadn't touched my circle of friends.

After a while we broke up. I felt like the only thing we ever did was get drunk and have sex. And the sex wasn't even that good. The thing that attracts me in sex is more the nurturing part of it, as opposed to the physical act. And my experience has been that most guys are clods. I was talking about this with a friend, like, "Why do guys think they have to do it so quickly?" For some reason they think it's better if they're slamming you with no awareness of what they're doing. It's like they're cleaning a toilet. I wonder about some of these people. Like, Could you slow down? Do you want to get it over with that quickly? I said to this friend, "Why is it that we sleep with these guys? Why do we put ourselves through this? Why does it seem so important that we have someone in our lives that we can do it with?" My friend was laughing, he said, "The way you talk, it sounds like you don't enjoy it. And if you don't enjoy it, why do it?" I said, "Well, I don't do it that much." [Laughs.]

A lot of people in the gay community have their hang-ups about being tops or bottoms. They think of themselves as tops, and that's all they want to do. Maybe because of the way I look, people tend to assume that I'm a bottom. I guess I'm comfortable with that position, but there are times when I wouldn't mind being a top. [Laughs.] These guys, they'll do it to you, but God forbid you ask to do it to them. "Oh no, I don't do that." Then I think, Well, this is a one-sided relationship, you can do it to me but I can't do it to you?

I guess it's my personality. I haven't had anybody tell me I'm effeminate lately, but with my hair being long, the clothes I wear, I tend to be more girlish than mannish. That's what people tell me. So they figure I'm a bottom. Like Angel, the guy I'm dating now, he goes, "I assume you're a bottom." Just right out. Then I say, "Yeah, for the most part, I guess I am." For a long time, I would be very passive and let people do whatever they wanted. Or I would ask them, "What's your pleasure? What can I do?" I'd please them, and then I'd masturbate. Also, some guys, when they suck—you'd think they'd know what to do, because they have one, too, you'd think they'd know that teeth can hurt. I don't like being on the receiving end of that. So I would just please them. And if I kept them busy, I could avoid anal intercourse. A lot of guys like to do that, but I usually don't. And even though I'm considered the passive one, if I'm the one who's doing all the pleasuring, they usually don't think about it. I keep them distracted by sucking them, using my tongue, using massage techniques. Actually, what it is, I like to be in control. And the one who's giving all the pleasure is more in control.

Another thing I have to contend with, there are a lot of—we call them Rice Queens. White guys who like Asians. People who are attracted to me because of the way I look. That's another reason I didn't sleep with a lot of people earlier. I felt: You don't even know what I look like. You don't see a person here, you see two eyes that go like this.

So between one thing and another, I was not that sexually active. I tested positive three years ago. There was one whole year when I didn't sleep with anybody. That's why I have a hard time when I hear about these gay guys who have had sex with thousands of people. I'm thinking, God! I may have had sex with a hundred, maybe not even that many. I would go to bathhouses with my friends, and I would be the only one who would sit there and watch what was going on. I didn't like the idea of these people who I didn't know touching me. And when I did have sex with someone in those places, I never enjoyed it. At one point I had a couple of friends who were like sex buddies. We'd sleep together. But I was the kind of person that when I'd sleep with someone, I would be sure I was in love with them. And those relationships never lasted.

Then I met Max. I first met him about four years ago. I would run into him off and on for the next couple of years, and I'd always make it a point to talk to him, but nothing ever happened. Then a girlfriend of mine asked me if I'd be interested in going out on a date with someone I knew, and I said, "It's been so long, I'd go out with any-one." She said, "It's Max." So that's when he came into the picture. I went out with him and we had the best time. Our status came out immediately. I told him mine, and then he said, "Sam, I have AIDS. Is that a problem?" I said, "Not unless we make it one."

The sex I had with Max was wonderful. It was simple. But the amount of communication, and intimacy, and feelings that we had. . . . When I was with Max I never looked at another person. It was the first time I felt that I was actually *with* someone. I didn't need anything else. I would get so excited with Max, just being next to him. And when I came, it was like shifting consciousness, because it felt so powerful. Even though we didn't—because of his illness, we didn't explore different positions and stuff. But we took baths to-gether, and we touched each other in such reaffirming ways. Max would ask for what he wanted, and I learned to ask for what I wanted. He would take my hand and show me where he wanted me to touch him. Take my head and lead me where he wanted me to go.

I'd suck him. I learned how to give a massage with my chin. Usually on his back, but also around the lining of his stomach or his legs. There was a way I could do it—he'd be lying there on his stomach, and I would go up his back with my chin, and our bodies would meet, and then I'd come back down, like teasing him. Or I would take his hand and show him where to touch me. I used to love to kiss him. I would love for him to nibble my ear. He used to take his tongue and explore my body, just run it all over. And I would do the same for him. In fact, I did it to him first, and he liked it so much, I said, "Well, can't you do it to me?"

I never entered Max, but he fucked me more than a few times. That was always really pleasurable, too. He was very gentle. I would always come quickly with him, because by the time he would enter me I would be ready. Sometimes I'd come without even touching myself. I would just give myself to him. But toward the end of the relationship we didn't do that, because he wasn't strong enough.

I remember the last time we made love. It was a Saturday morning. He reached over to touch me, and I was kind of tired. I wasn't in the mood. He was a little more persistent than usual. First he was touching my cock, and I wasn't excited. Then he touched my chest. Then he started grinding his hips into me. Then he started nibbling on my neck and on my ear. Then he had an erection and he was putting it between my legs. It started off low-key, and it ended up aggressive. We never had sex like that. I had never moved around so much. Like at first I was on my back, and then I was on top of him, and then I was here, and then I was over there, and then I was standing up over the bed, and he sat up, and he was sucking me off that way. Then I was sitting on him, and he was bucking his hips so hard that I was going up in the air. He wasn't inside me, but at one point he lifted me up and I hit my head on the wall. I said to myself, Boy, there's something going on here, this is not our usual morning roll. That's when it struck me that this was the last time. I didn't know whether to make it last really long, or whether to just go with it. I was wondering what I could do, what new twist I could do to make it really something for him. So I just surrendered and let him do whatever he wanted. I was almost totally passive. I had to try real hard to keep from crying. It was wonderful, very intimate, and very sad at the same time. When we finished, he was glowing. He said, "Boy, I was really into it this morning, wasn't I?" I said, "Yes, you were." He said, "At first you seemed a little more reserved than you normally are, but you got into it, too." I said, "Yes, I did." I remember putting on this happy face and glossing it over and trying to get on with the morning. I said, "Did you take some kind of vitamin last night? Did you do some kind of drug you want to tell me about?" He talked about it after that, like, "Oh, that morning, I was really good, wasn't I?"

This was the end of September. He started to get really sick in October. We had a wedding ceremony in November. But even afterward, on the honeymoon, we didn't have sex. He was too sick. His medication made him impotent. We held each other, and we kissed. I would masturbate. I even told him at one point, I said, "Max, you know, if we don't ever make love again, it's okay with me." Because he felt like he needed to do that, to give me that before. . . . But I said, "You don't need to, you've given me other things."

He didn't die right away. His KS had started to multiply on his face, but he was still functional. He was going to work, taking yoga classes. But then he started calling in sick. He just couldn't. He had trouble getting up the stairs. He was always tired. I had to cook for him. But our relationship got even better. It kept growing and growing. He taught me a lot. [He is crying.] He finally died last March.

Then something really strange happened. Not long after Max's funeral, I was going down the street and I saw Rick and his current partner Simon. Things went on, and a couple of weeks ago I got a phone call one Sunday morning, and it was Simon saying that Rick was sick. It was the same hospital that Max passed away in, and as it turned out he was in the same room. Which was fairly intense. I always knew I had something to complete with Rick, because when we stopped seeing each other it was very abrupt. But I didn't know what it was. For three days, every chance I got I would talk to him. I'd tell him, "I'm sorry about such-and-such," whatever came to mind, trying to see what it was. I apologized for leaving. But nothing seemed to go. About the third day, I thought, Not only is he not responding, but I'm sure he can't enjoy this, because he's in bed with all these IVs and stuff. He's trapped, and here's this person standing over him giving him this overload of information. So I let it go. The next day I told him I'd give him a massage. At the end there was this feeling of camaraderie. I just told him, "Did you ever think that we were going to go through this, when we were dating four years ago?" And he said no. He was pretty weak. Then I told him there was a great possibility that one of us had infected the other, because at the point when I tested, he was the only person I'd had unsafe sex with in five years. And when I tested, I had told him immediately. He said, "Yeah, I know." I told him, "I just want you to know that if I infected you, I'm sorry. And if you infected me, I forgive you." He looked at me and smiled. And that was it. That was what I had to settle with him. But not being one to leave that alone, I went further. I said, "Did you know you were HIV-positive when you were dating me?" He said, "Yes, I've known since college."

I remember I was holding his hand. And I just looked at him. And I thought, You fucking bastard. That was three years before you knew me. And you still insisted. So you knew. I was standing there holding his hand. I kind of went into shock, because it was like, I just forgave you, but I didn't have all the pieces. The rage I felt at that moment, I have never felt anything like that. I said to God, God, you gotta give me some insight into this, because if you don't, I'm going to take this horrible situation and make it worse. I envisioned ripping out his IVs and killing him. So I went back to that moment when it happened, that first time we had unsafe sex. I remembered how I completely sobered up, and what came to my mind: Oh God, what have I done? I said I. I had a choice in it.

Over the next few days I came to the conclusion that I had to take responsibility. I thought, I do forgive you, but more than anything, I forgive myself. I'm still pretty angry about it. Sometimes my life seems unmanageable, I'm so angry about it. I wonder why I got this knowledge. But before Rick died, I came to love him again. I felt like, Gosh, we've been through all this, and yes, you did infect me, and you knew about it. But now you're suffering for it.

The other weird thing is, I've had a lot of sex since Max died. He told me he wanted me to go on with my life and not wait six months or a year. He died in March. I started dating in April. I've slept with four or five guys in six months, and that's more than I slept with in the two years before I met Max. But there's a different quality about the sex. I express myself more openly. I'm a lot more adventurous. And it's more pleasurable. It actually feels almost spiritual. I'm discovering all these sexual feelings that I suppressed for years. It feels like new life coming through.

I used to have a lot of people cruising me, like if I went to the gym, and I would run away. Now, if they're attractive, I say, Well, why not? Let's see what happens. I don't have unsafe sex, but I'm willing to explore. I have these sexual feelings, and the worst that can happen to me has already happened. You know, the Moral Majority says that AIDS is a thing you get because of your promiscuity and your deviant lifestyle. I don't feel like I had a deviant lifestyle. I had a life, and I did what I did. But I always used to tell myself, when guys would cruise me, It's wrong. Now I don't. And I have a lot more offers than ever before. So I've had some anonymous encounters. Mostly just masturbation. I look at it like playing. I figure, kids do this when they're young, they explore. So why don't we? It's not complicated. I don't have to explain my status. Whatever happens, happens, and then we're up about our way with a smile.

Even my body has changed in the last few months. I've always had a gut. For some reason I'm getting really toned. I guess it's a reflection of how I'm feeling about myself. I feel more attractive after having loved Max. I came out of it with a sense of my own beauty. Loving him, and him loving me back, finally being able to have a relationship with someone where it went both ways. I'm not afraid anymore to express what I want to happen in bed. I say, Yeah, gee, it would be nice if we could do this. Or, How do you feel about this? Before, I would give myself to pleasure someone, but not give people the chance to pleasure me. Now I'm learning to do it both ways. And I'm more spontaneous. I used to plan what I would do before I got in bed: This is how I'll make him groan. And he'll love me for it. Now I just let it unfold. I haven't had anal intercourse with Angel yet. He keeps telling me that he's a top. But I'm feeling like I don't want to assume either role. I'd like us to be more flexible. And I think I'll be able to speak up.

Sometimes I used to dread sex, because I would always want more and never get it. I realize that I would never get it because I would never ask for it. And I used to equate sex with love—like, God, I gave this person so much, and they didn't love me. I gave them my best. Now I see, Well, I gave them an hour or two in bed. I didn't give them my best, I gave them a good time. So I can go to bed with somebody and see it for what it is. It doesn't mean I'm going to be married to him for the rest of my life. But it's a way I can communicate with someone on levels other than speaking.

I got a different slant on sex from Max because he was a compulsive sex addict. When he was with me he had been sober for a little bit over a year. He would talk about his experiences, and he felt very badly about them. He would tell me about going into rest rooms and meeting these guys and having them just stick it up his ass. Getting it over with in five minutes. And seeing toilet paper on the floor. He could never be sure whether these people were healthy. They would smell. And he would do this three times a night, or more. He said he could never get satisfied. I was fascinated by these stories. I would ask questions, like, How long did it take? Did you carry lubricant around? Didn't the smell in the bathrooms bother you? I had all these questions because I never allowed myself to experience that. But I realized I had a lot of the same fantasies. I remember one time I heard about a rest room on campus, where you could go and guys would be there, and you could fool around and it was safe. So I went one Saturday morning. And God forbid, I met this guy I worked with. He said, "Oh, Sam, cruising the john." I was so ashamed of myself, so humiliated and embarrassed. It never occurred to me that he was there to do the same thing. I immediately assumed the role of the bad person.

Sometimes I got the feeling that Max was telling me these stories because I would find him unlovable if he told me enough—like, he would tell me something that would totally disgust me, and he'd be able to chase me away. He was always afraid of being left, so he'd try to get me to leave him. He would say, "What do you think?" He would expect me to judge him. But I never once felt that Max was a bad person. I know it was a very dark thing for him, but I also know he wouldn't be the person that he was if he hadn't gone through that. I got the sense that he felt he got AIDS as a punishment. But I had a completely different take. It made me feel like, God, it's so human. All these people are just so human, whatever they're doing, whatever way they get through.

For some reason, hearing his story made me feel liberated. I figured, if Max can do it and turn out as well as he did, I can do it, too. I've always thought about sex, I've always been curious, and now I think if I want to act on it, there's nothing wrong with that. Since Max died, I have even been to bed with a woman. I never entered her, but we did a lot of—I guess you call it heavy petting. It was so pleasurable, I was really excited. I told her at the end, "This is amazing." She goes, "Why?" I said, "I haven't been with a woman in ten years." She said she could never have told. She actually told me I was very masculine, which to me was a compliment. So it was nice, but first I had to be open to it. I knew I was attracted to her the moment I met her. She was in town for a meeting and someone had arranged for her to stay with me. At first she was going to stay in the front room. Then I said, "You can sleep in my room if you feel comfortable." It wasn't really a matter of her feeling comfortable, it was a matter of me feeling comfortable. Part of me wanted to sleep with her, but I was scared. I thought, God, what if something does happen and I can't get it up? What if I start remembering my mother? But when we started, it was wonderful. She touched me, I would guide her hand, and it was wonderful. I found that I was able to touch her with my entire body—hands, mouth. I was wondering, Is this what straight people do? Then I came to the conclusion, No, this is what *people* do. It's not whether you're straight or gay or whatever. This is what people do.

ACKNOWLEDGMENTS

MY FIRST AND DEEPEST THANKS go to the nearly 120 people I interviewed for this book. They were trusting enough to talk about a touchy subject with someone they had never met before—or, in a few cases, someone they knew very well, which made it even touchier. To those who do not appear in these pages, I offer particular thanks for their time and effort—and an apology.

Before interviewing even began, however, I had to find a publisher, and various people were instrumental in that effort. George Hagman, psychologist and *amigo* extraordinaire, single-handedly kept the idea alive when I was ready to chuck it. Dr. Margaret Nichols offered her expertise, her enthusiasm, and numerous leads. Patricia Sexton lent me an office and put up with me for more than a year. Prudence Crowther, Jonathan Nossiter, and Lynn Schnurnberger read the proposal and made invaluable suggestions. Others who read the proposal or parts of the book and who helped me talk out ideas include Patricia Cobey, Denise Demong, Mark Epstein, Dalia Kandiyoti, Arno Karlen, Millie Klingman, Nancy Milford, and Amy Stein.

Throughout, the book's preeminent champion has been Suzanne Gluck, my agent at ICM. She believed in the idea, put me through rewrites of the proposal, transmitted her excitement to publishers, and, most important, kept a deal alive by force of will when negotiations threatened to blow up. Since then she has shepherded the book in the manner an author dreams of. I am grateful.

An equally important ally has been Lori Lipsky, my editor at Viking, who is as expert at soothing a frazzled writer as she is at wielding a red pencil. Her comments and ideas were crucial in making the book what it is. Also at Viking, Nan Graham and Cathy Hemming have been boosters from the start, making me feel welcome and supported.

This book could not have been written had I not been granted a lengthy leave of absence from *Business Week* magazine. For that I am deeply indebted to Ciro Scotti, Barbara Boynton, and Steve Shepard. The magazine's generous policy of granting leaves has been a boon to many a writer. Tom Reed of *Business Week* coached me through my rookie weeks on a new computer. And in the boon-to-writers department, no one ranks higher than Renata Miller, executive director of the Writers Room, which has been my home away from home for three books stretching over thirteen years. Renata's no-nonsense style helps keep it a perfect place to work.

Since most of the speakers in the book came to me through word of mouth, I would like to thank the many people who asked their friends the nutty question, "Would you like to be interviewed about your sex life?" Some of my best leads, of course, came from interviewees who appear in the book, and I cannot name them for reasons of privacy. But among the scouts who do not figure in these pages, I offer thanks to Esther Allen, Tracy Bernstein, Paul Bresnick, Sally Brown, Michele Capozzi, Moira Denham, Dierdre Depke, Jack Franklin, Helen Gavzer, Nina Hartley, Allyn Kahoe, Aleta Kaufman, Paula Kimbro, Judith Levine, Bob and Mary Peterson, Candida Royalle, Lee Sachs, Eva Stettner, Christine Stortroen, Randy Stortroen, Donna Sturman, Patty Waters, Peggy Webb, Lauren Wechsler, and Terry Williams. I owe special thanks to Keith Hennessy, who was tireless in finding subjects for me in the San Francisco sex-radical community.

Other good samaritans who housed me on the road, hunted for housing, or labored in various ways to smooth my path include Marty Jerome; Teri Katz; my sister Charlo Maurer and her significant other,

Paul Gregory; Ellen Webb and Sandy Walker; Sara Webb, Jon Love, and Tracy Howard; and Scott Smith.

The hundreds of hours of tape recordings that went into the making of this book were transcribed by an intrepid and humorous team: Veronica Austin, Matthew Caws, Elka Deitsch, Lena Jones, Kate Cunningham, Kathleen Madden, Laura Rabhan, Andrea Slattery, Amy Stein, Raven Tyler, and Valerie Tyler. Thanks to all.

And finally, Heather Brown, my wife, helped me in countless ways, reading every bit of the book as it came off the computer, asking questions, suggesting changes, arguing, listening, putting up with my absences, and generally smoothing the ups and downs. It is an honor and a joy to have her in my life.

BIBLIOGRAPHY

Barbach, L., and L. Levine. *Shared Intimacies: Women's Sexual Experiences.* New York: Doubleday, 1980.

Benjamin, J. *The Bonds of Love: Psychoanalysis, Feminism, and the Problem of Domination.* New York: Pantheon, 1988.

Blumstein, P., and P. Schwartz. *American Couples.* New York: William Morrow, 1983.

Brame, G., W. Brame, and J. Jacobs. *Different Loving: An Exploration of the World of Sexual Dominance and Submission.* New York: Villard, 1993.

Chapple, S., and D. Talbot. *Burning Desires.* New York: Doubleday, 1989.

Delacoste, F., and P. Alexander, eds. *Sex Work: Writings by Women in the Sex Industry.* Pittsburgh: Cleis Press, 1987.

D'Emilio, J., and E. Freedman. *Intimate Matters: A History of Sexuality in America.* New York: Harper & Row, 1988.

Ehrenreich, B., E. Hess, and G. Jacobs. *Re-Making Love: The Feminization of Sex.* New York: Anchor Press, 1986.

Fisher, H. *Anatomy of Love: The Natural History of Monogamy, Adultery, and Divorce.* New York: W.W. Norton, 1992.

Heyn, D. *The Erotic Silence of the American Wife.* New York: Turtle Bay Books, 1992.

Hite, S. *The Hite Report.* New York: Macmillan, 1976.

———. *The Hite Report on Male Sexuality.* New York: Knopf, 1981.

Janus, S., and C. Janus. *The Janus Report on Sexual Behavior.* New York: John Wiley & Sons, 1993.

Kaplan, L. *Female Perversions: The Temptations of Emma Bovary.* New York: Doubleday, 1991.

Lawson, A. *Adultery: An Analysis of Love and Betrayal.* New York: Basic Books, 1988.

Levine, L., and L. Barbacyh. *The Intimate Male.* New York: Anchor Press/ Doubleday, 1983.

Margulis, A., and D. Sagan. *Mystery Dance: On the Evolution of Human Sexuality.* New York: Summit Books, 1991.

Masters, W., J. Johnson, and R. Kolodny. *On Sex and Human Loving.* New York: Little, Brown, 1985.

Money, J. *Gay, Straight, and In-Between.* New York: Oxford University Press, 1988.

Person, E. *Dreams of Love and Fateful Encounters.* New York: W. W Norton, 1988.

Samois. *Coming to Power: Writings and Graphics on Lesbian S/M.* Boston: Alyson Publications, 1987.

Sontag, S. *AIDS and Its Metaphors.* New York: Farrar, Straus and Giroux, 1989.

Stoller, R. *Observing the Erotic Imagination.* New Haven: Yale University Press, 1985.

———. *Pain & Passion.* New York: Plenum Press, 1991.

———. *Porn: Myths for the Twentieth Century.* New Haven: Yale University Press, 1991.

———. *Sexual Excitement: Dynamics of Erotic Life.* New York: Pantheon, 1979.

Talese, G. *Thy Neighbor's Wife.* New York: Doubleday, 1980.

Thompson, M., ed. *Leatherfolk: Radical Sex, People, Politics, and Practice.* Boston: Alyson Publications, 1991.

Tripp, C. A. *The Homosexual Matrix.* New York: McGraw-Hill, 1975.

Vance, C., ed. *Pleasure and Danger: Exploring Female Sexuality.* Boston: Routledge & Kegan Paul, 1984.

FOR THE BEST IN PAPERBACKS, LOOK FOR THE

In every corner of the world, on every subject under the sun, Penguin represents quality and variety—the very best in publishing today.

For complete information about books available from Penguin—including Pelicans, Puffins, Peregrines, and Penguin Classics—and how to order them, write to us at the appropriate address below. Please note that for copyright reasons the selection of books varies from country to country.

In the United Kingdom: For a complete list of books available from Penguin in the U.K., please write to *Dept E.P., Penguin Books Ltd, Harmondsworth, Middlesex, UB7 0DA.*

In the United States: For a complete list of books available from Penguin in the U.S., please write to *Consumer Sales, Penguin USA, P.O. Box 999— Dept. 17109, Bergenfield, New Jersey 07621-0120.* Visa and MasterCard holders call 1-800-253-6476 to order all Penguin titles.

In Canada: For a complete list of books available from Penguin in Canada, please write to *Penguin Books Canada Ltd, 10 Alcorn Avenue, Suite 300, Toronto, Ontario, Canada M4V 3B2.*

In Australia: For a complete list of books available from Penguin in Australia, please write to the *Marketing Department, Penguin Books Ltd, P.O. Box 257, Ringwood, Victoria 3134.*

In New Zealand: For a complete list of books available from Penguin in New Zealand, please write to the *Marketing Department, Penguin Books (NZ) Ltd, Private Bag, Takapuna, Auckland 9.*

In India: For a complete list of books available from Penguin, please write to *Penguin Overseas Ltd, 706 Eros Apartments, 56 Nehru Place, New Delhi, 110019.*

In Holland: For a complete list of books available from Penguin in Holland, please write to *Penguin Books Nederland B.V., Postbus 195, NL-1380AD Weesp, Netherlands.*

In Germany: For a complete list of books available from Penguin, please write to *Penguin Books Ltd, Friedrichstrasse 10-12, D-6000 Frankfurt Main I, Federal Republic of Germany.*

In Spain: For a complete list of books available from Penguin in Spain, please write to *Longman, Penguin España, Calle San Nicolas 15, E-28013 Madrid, Spain.*

In Japan: For a complete list of books available from Penguin in Japan, please write to *Longman Penguin Japan Co Ltd, Yamaguchi Building, 2-12-9 Kanda Jimbocho, Chiyoda-Ku, Tokyo 101, Japan.*